The Political Writings of George Washington

The Political Writings of George Washington, in two volumes, includes Washington's enduring writings on politics, prudence, and statesmanship. It is the only complete collection, for his political thought has received less attention than the writings of other leading founders such as Thomas Jefferson, James Madison, John Adams, and Alexander Hamilton. Covering his life of public service – from his young manhood, when he fought in the French and Indian Wars, through his time as commander-in-chief of the revolutionary army; his two terms as America's first president, and his brief periods of retirement, during which he followed and commented on American politics astutely – the volumes also include firsthand accounts of Washington's death and reflections on his legacy by those who knew him or reflected deeply on his significance. The result is a more thorough understanding of Washington's political thought and America's Founding.

CARSON HOLLOWAY is Professor of Political Science at the University of Nebraska at Omaha. He is co-editor, with Bradford P. Wilson, of *The Political Writings of Alexander Hamilton* and the author of *Hamilton versus Jefferson in the Washington Administration: Completing the Founding or Betraying the Founding?*

BRADFORD P. WILSON is Executive Director of the James Madison Program in American Ideals and Institutions at Princeton University. He is co-editor, with Carson Holloway, of *The Political Writings of Alexander Hamilton*, published by Cambridge University Press.

The Political Writings of American Statesmen

Co-edited by Bradford P. Wilson (Princeton University) and Carson Holloway (University of Nebraska at Omaha), the Political Writings of American Statesmen publishes volumes collecting key documents by leading American political figures throughout the nation's history. The volumes aim to offer – through the documents – an understanding of the vital issues of the time and of the enduring questions of justice, prudence, law, and constitutional government that characterize the development of American republicanism. Wilson and Holloway are the co-editors of the first two works in the series: *The Political Writings of Alexander Hamilton* (2017) and *The Political Writings of George Washington*. Works on John Jay and James Madison are in progress.

George Washington bust. Photograph from Mount Vernon website © Jean-Antoine Houdon : public domain

The Political Writings of George Washington

Volume I: 1754–1788

Edited by

Carson Holloway
University of Nebraska, Omaha

Bradford P. Wilson
Princeton University, New Jersey

CAMBRIDGE
UNIVERSITY PRESS

Shaftesbury Road, Cambridge CB2 8EA, United Kingdom

One Liberty Plaza, 20th Floor, New York, NY 10006, USA

477 Williamstown Road, Port Melbourne, VIC 3207, Australia

314–321, 3rd Floor, Plot 3, Splendor Forum, Jasola District Centre, New Delhi – 110025, India

103 Penang Road, #05–06/07, Visioncrest Commercial, Singapore 238467

Cambridge University Press is part of Cambridge University Press & Assessment, a department of the University of Cambridge.

We share the University's mission to contribute to society through the pursuit of education, learning and research at the highest international levels of excellence.

www.cambridge.org
Information on this title: www.cambridge.org/9781009343886

DOI: 10.1017/9781009343916

© Cambridge University Press & Assessment 2023

This publication is in copyright. Subject to statutory exception and to the provisions of relevant collective licensing agreements, no reproduction of any part may take place without the written permission of Cambridge University Press & Assessment.

First published 2023

A catalogue record for this publication is available from the British Library

ISBN – 2 Volume Set   978-1-009-34729-7   Hardback
ISBN – Volume I   978-1-009-34388-6   Hardback
ISBN – Volume II   978-1-009-34404-3   Hardback

Cambridge University Press & Assessment has no responsibility for the persistence or accuracy of URLs for external or third-party internet websites referred to in this publication and does not guarantee that any content on such websites is, or will remain, accurate or appropriate.

This book is dedicated to the memory of George Washington, the Father of our Country.

Contents

List of Figures	*page* xxvii
Acknowledgments	xxviii
Introduction	1

Part I From Colonist to Patriot: 1754–1775

To Richard Corbin, February–March 1754	9
To Horatio Sharpe, Governor of Maryland, April 24, 1754 (Excerpts)	10
To Mary Ball Washington, August 14, 1755	11
To Andrew Montour, October 10, 1755	12
To Robert Dinwiddie, Lieutenant Governor of Virginia, October 11, 1755 (Excerpt)	13
To Denis McCarty, November 22, 1755	14
Address to the Officers, January 8, 1756	15
To Robert Hunter Morris, Deputy Governor of Pennsylvania, April 9, 1756 (Excerpt)	17
To John Robinson, Speaker of the Virginia House of Burgesses, April 18, 1756	18
To Robert Dinwiddie, Lieutenant Governor of Virginia, April 22, 1756 (Excerpt)	20
To Lieutenant Colonel Adam Stephen, May 18, 1756 (Excerpt)	21
Proclamation of War Against the French, August 15, 1756	22
To Robert Dinwiddie, Lieutenant Governor of Virginia, March 10, 1757	23
To Colonel John Stanwix, July 15, 1757 (Excerpt)	26

To Robert Dinwiddie, Lieutenant Governor of Virginia, September 17, 1757	27
To James Wood, July 28, 1758	29
To Robert Cary and Company, September 20, 1765 (Excerpt)	30
To Robert Cary and Company, July 21, 1766 (Excerpt)	31
To Capel and Osgood Hanbury, July 25, 1767 (Excerpt)	32
To George Mason, April 5, 1769 (Excerpt)	33
To Robert Cary and Company, July 25, 1769 (Excerpt)	35
To Burwell Bassett, April 20, 1773 (Excerpt)	36
To Burwell Bassett, June 20, 1773	37
To George William Fairfax, June 10, 1774 (Excerpt)	38
To Bryan Fairfax, July 4, 1774 (Excerpt)	40
To Bryan Fairfax, July 20, 1774 (Excerpt)	41
To Bryan Fairfax, August 24, 1774 (Excerpt)	43
To Robert McKenzie, October 9, 1774 (Excerpt)	45
To John Connolly, February 25, 1775	47
To George William Fairfax, May 31, 1775 (Excerpt)	48

Part II Commander-in-Chief: 1775–1778

Address to the Continental Congress, June 16, 1775	53
To Martha Washington, June 18, 1775 (Excerpt)	54
To Burwell Bassett, June 19, 1775 (Excerpt)	56
To John Parke Custis, June 19, 1775 (Excerpt)	57
To the Officers of the Five Virginia Independent Companies, June 20, 1775 (Excerpt)	58
To John Augustine Washington, June 20, 1775 (Excerpt)	59
To Martha Washington, June 23, 1775	60
To the New York Provincial Congress, June 26, 1775	61
General Orders, July 4, 1775 (Excerpt)	62
To the Massachusetts Provincial Congress, c. July 4, 1775	63
General Orders, July 5, 1775 (Excerpt)	64

General Orders, July 7, 1775 (Excerpt)	65
General Orders, July 16, 1775 (Excerpt)	66
To Jonathan Trumbull, Sr., Governor of Connecticut, July 18, 1775	67
To Brigadier General John Thomas, July 23, 1775	68
General Orders, August 10, 1775	70
To Lieutenant General Thomas Gage, August 11, 1775	71
To Lieutenant General Thomas Gage, August 19, 1775	72
To the Inhabitants of Bermuda, September 6, 1775	74
To the Inhabitants of Canada, c. September 14, 1775	75
To John Hancock, President of the Continental Congress, September 21, 1775 (Excerpt)	77
General Orders, October 26, 1775 (Excerpt)	78
General Orders, October 31, 1775 (Excerpt)	79
General Orders, November 5, 1775 (Excerpt)	80
To Lieutenant Colonel Joseph Reed, December 15, 1775 (Excerpts)	81
To Major General William Howe, December 18, 1775	82
General Orders, January 1, 1776 (Excerpts)	83
To Lieutenant Colonel Joseph Reed, January 14, 1776 (Excerpts)	85
To Lieutenant Colonel Joseph Reed, February 10, 1776 (Excerpts)	87
To Joseph Johnson, February 20, 1776	89
General Orders, February 27, 1776 (Excerpt)	90
Proclamation on the Occupation of Boston, March 21, 1776 (Excerpt)	91
To the Boston Selectmen and Citizens, March 1776	92
To the Massachusetts General Court, April 1, 1776	93
To Lieutenant Colonel Joseph Reed, April 1, 1776 (Excerpts)	95
To John Hancock, President of the Continental Congress, April 18, 1776	97
General Orders, May 15, 1776 (Excerpt)	98
To John Augustine Washington, May 31, 1776 (Excerpt)	99

General Orders, July 2, 1776 (Excerpt)	100
General Orders, July 9, 1776 (Excerpt)	101
General Orders, July 23, 1776 (Excerpt)	102
General Orders, August 1, 1776	103
To Lund Washington, August 26, 1776 (Excerpt)	104
General Orders, September 6, 1776 (Excerpt)	105
To John Hancock, President of the Continental Congress, September 6, 1776 (Excerpt)	106
General Orders, September 19, 1776 (Excerpt)	107
To John Hancock, President of the Continental Congress, September 22, 1776	108
To John Augustine Washington, September 22, 1776 (Excerpt)	109
To Lund Washington, September 30, 1776 (Excerpt)	110
To Lord Richard Howe, January 13, 1777 (Excerpt)	112
To General William Howe, January 13, 1777	113
General Orders, January 21, 1777 (Excerpt)	115
To William Livingston, Governor of New Jersey, January 24, 1777	116
Proclamation Concerning Persons Swearing British Allegiance, January 25, 1777	117
Circular to Eleven States, January 31–February 1, 1777	118
To John Hancock, President of the Continental Congress, January 31, 1777 (Excerpt)	119
To John Hancock, President of the Continental Congress, February 5, 1777 (Excerpts)	120
General Orders, February 6, 1777 (Excerpt)	122
To Walter Rutherford, February 14, 1777	123
To John Hancock, President of the Continental Congress, March 1, 1777 (Excerpt)	124
To Robert Morris, March 2, 1777 (Excerpt)	126
To Major General Joseph Spencer, April 3, 1777 (Excerpt)	128
Proclamation of Pardon to Deserters, April 6, 1777	129
To Richard Henry Lee, April 24–26, 1777 (Excerpt)	130

To Brigadier General John Glover, April 26, 1777	131
To Major General Stirling, May 6, 1777	132
To Colonel François Lellorquis de Malmedy, May 16, 1777	133
To Richard Henry Lee, May 17, 1777 (Excerpt)	135
To Colonel George Baylor, May 23, 1777 (Excerpt)	137
To Major General William Heath, May 23, 1777 (Excerpt)	138
Circular Instructions to the Brigade Commanders, May 26, 1777 (Excerpt)	139
General Orders, May 31, 1777 (Excerpt)	140
To John Hancock, President of the Continental Congress, June 3, 1777	141
General Orders, June 4, 1777 (Excerpt)	143
General Orders, June 7, 1777 (Excerpt)	144
To John Hancock, President of the Continental Congress, June 8, 1777 (Excerpt)	145
To Charles-François-Adrien Le Paulmier Annemours, June 19, 1777 (Excerpt)	146
General Orders, July 25, 1777 (Excerpt)	147
To Major General John Sullivan, July 25, 1777	148
To Philippe-Hubert Preudhomme de Borre, August 3, 1777 (Excerpt)	149
General Orders, September 4, 1777 (Excerpt)	150
General Orders, September 5, 1777 (Excerpt)	151
General Orders, September 6, 1777 (Excerpt)	153
To Bryan Fairfax, September 24, 1777 (Excerpt)	154
To Bryan Fairfax, September 25, 1777 (Excerpt)	155
General Orders, October 3, 1777 (Excerpt)	156
To John Hancock, President of the Continental Congress, October 13, 1777 (Excerpts)	157
General Orders, October 15, 1777 (Excerpt)	159
To Henry Laurens, November 1, 1777 (Excerpt)	160
To Brigadier General Thomas Conway, November 5, 1777	161

To Henry Laurens, November 23, 1777 (Excerpt)	162
To Henry Laurens, November 26, 1777 (Excerpt)	163
General Orders, December 17, 1777 (Excerpt)	164
To Henry Laurens, December 22, 1777 (Excerpt)	166
To Henry Laurens, December 23, 1777	168
Circular to the States, December 29, 1777 (Excerpt)	172
To Major General Marie-Joseph-Paul-Yves-Roch-Gilbert du Motier, Marquis de Lafayette, December 31, 1777	174
To Henry Laurens, January 2, 1778 (Excerpt)	176
To Major General Horatio Gates, January 4, 1778	177
To Henry Laurens, January 13, 1778	179
To William Gordon, January 23, 1778	180
To a Continental Congress Camp Committee, January 29, 1778 (Excerpts)	181
To Henry Laurens, President of the Continental Congress, January 31, 1778	187
To William Livingston, Governor of New Jersey, February 2, 1778 (Excerpt)	188
To William Buchanan, February 7, 1778	189
To Major General Horatio Gates, February 9, 1778	190
To Richard Henry Lee, February 15, 1778 (Excerpt)	193
General Orders, March 1, 1778 (Excerpt)	194
To Bryan Fairfax, March 1, 1778	196
To Henry Laurens, President of the Continental Congress, March 7, 1778 (Excerpt)	198
To Lieutenant General John Burgoyne, March 11, 1778 (Excerpt)	202
To Patrick Henry, Governor of Virginia, March 27, 1778	203
To Patrick Henry, Governor of Virginia, March 28, 1788 (Excerpt)	204
General Orders, April 6, 1778 (Excerpt)	205
General Orders, April 12, 1778 (Excerpt)	206
To John Banister, April 21, 1778	207
General Orders, May 2, 1778 (Excerpt)	212

Part III The Road to Victory: 1778–1783

To Major General Alexander McDougall, May 5, 1778 (Excerpt)	217
To Major General Lafayette, May 17, 1778	218
To Brigadier General William Smallwood, May 19, 1778 (Excerpt)	219
To Richard Henry Lee, May 25, 1778 (Excerpt)	220
To Gouverneur Morris, May 29, 1778 (Excerpt)	221
To Landon Carter, May 30, 1778 (Excerpt)	222
To John Augustine Washington, May 1778	223
To Brigadier General Thomas Nelson, Jr., August 20, 1778 (Excerpt)	225
General Orders, August 21, 1778 (Excerpt)	226
To Vice Admiral Charles-Hector Théodat Estaing, September 11, 1778 (Excerpt)	227
To Major General Lafayette, October 4, 1778 (Excerpt)	228
General Orders, October 21, 1778 (Excerpt)	229
To Henry Laurens, President of the Continental Congress, November 11, 1778 (Excerpt)	230
To Henry Laurens, President of the Continental Congress, November 14, 1778	231
To Joseph Reed, President of the Supreme Executive Council of Pennsylvania, December 12, 1778 (Excerpt)	234
To Benjamin Harrison, Speaker of the Virginia House of Delegates, December 18–30, 1778 (Excerpts)	236
To Major General Israel Putnam, January 18, 1779 (Excerpt)	239
To the Continental Congress Committee of Conference, January 20, 1779	240
To John Jay, President of the Continental Congress, March 15, 1779 (Excerpt)	244
To Brigadier General Thomas Nelson, Jr., March 15, 1779 (Excerpt)	246
To Henry Laurens, March 20, 1779 (Excerpt)	247
To George Mason, March 27, 1779 (Excerpt)	248
To James Warren, March 31, 1779 (Excerpt)	250

To John Jay, President of the Continental Congress, April 14, 1779 (Excerpt)	252
To Brigadier General William Maxwell, May 7, 1779	257
To Gouverneur Morris, May 8, 1779 (Excerpt)	259
To John Jay, President of the Continental Congress, May 10, 1779 (Excerpt)	260
To the Delaware Nation, May 12, 1779	261
To John Armstrong, May 18, 1779 (Excerpt)	263
To Colonel Daniel Brodhead, May 21, 1779 (Excerpts)	265
Circular to the States, May 22, 1779 (Excerpt)	266
To Bryan Fairfax, June 30, 1779 (Excerpt)	268
To Major Henry Lee, July 9, 1779 (Excerpt)	269
To Joseph Reed, President of the Supreme Executive Council of Pennsylvania, July 29, 1779 (Excerpt)	270
To John Jay, President of the Continental Congress, September 7, 1779 (Excerpt)	272
To Edmund Pendleton, November 1, 1779 (Excerpt)	274
To Major General Robert Howe, November 20, 1779 (Excerpt)	276
General Orders, January 28, 1780 (Excerpt)	278
To Joseph Reed, President of the Supreme Executive Council of Pennsylvania, February 15, 1780	279
To Samuel Huntington, President of the Continental Congress, April 3, 1780 (Excerpt)	280
To Joseph Jones, May 14, 1780 (Excerpt)	282
To Samuel Huntington, President of the Continental Congress, May 27–28, 1780 (Excerpt)	284
To Joseph Reed, President of the Supreme Executive Council of Pennsylvania, May 28, 1780	285
To Joseph Jones, May 31, 1780 (Excerpt)	289
To Anne-César, Chevalier de La Luzerne, June 5, 1780 (Excerpt)	290
To John Augustine Washington, June 6–July 6, 1780 (Excerpt)	291
To Jonathan Trumbull, Governor of Connecticut, June 27, 1780 (Excerpt)	293

To Joseph Reed, President of the Supreme Executive Council of Pennsylvania, July 4, 1780	294
To Fielding Lewis, July 6, 1780 (Excerpt)	296
To Mrs. Esther de Berdt Reed, July 14, 1780	298
General Orders, July 20, 1780 (Excerpt)	299
To Joseph Jones, August 13, 1780	300
To Samuel Huntington, President of the Continental Congress, August 20, 1780 (Excerpt)	302
Circular to the States, August 27, 1780	308
To Samuel Huntington, President of the Continental Congress, September 15, 1780 (Excerpt)	310
General Orders, September 26, 1780 (Excerpt)	311
To James Duane, October 4, 1780 (Excerpt)	312
To Brigadier General John Cadwalader, October 5, 1780 (Excerpt)	313
To Lieutenant Colonel John Laurens, October 13, 1780 (Excerpt)	315
Circular to the States, October 18, 1780 (Excerpt)	316
To George Mason, October 22, 1780 (Excerpt)	321
To James Duane, December 26, 1780 (Excerpt)	322
To John Hancock, Governor of Massachusetts, January 5, 1781	323
To Lieutenant Colonel John Laurens, January 15, 1781	325
General Orders, January 30, 1781 (Excerpt)	329
To Robert R. Livingston, January 31, 1781	331
To Samuel Huntington, President of the Continental Congress, February 3, 1781 (Excerpt)	333
To John Sullivan, February 4, 1781	335
General Orders, February 18, 1781 (Excerpt)	337
To Philip Schuyler, February 20, 1781 (Excerpt)	338
To John Parke Custis, February 28, 1781 (Excerpt)	339
To Reverend Joseph Willard, March 22, 1781	341
To Major General John Armstrong, March 26, 1781 (Excerpt)	342
To John Mathews, June 7, 1781 (Excerpt)	343

To the Magistrates of the City of Philadelphia, December 17, 1781	344
To Thomas Chittenden, January 1, 1782 (Excerpt)	345
Circular to the States, January 31, 1782 (Excerpt)	347
To Philip Schuyler, February 6, 1782 (Excerpt)	349
To Major General Alexander McDougall, March 2, 1782	350
To Benjamin Harrison, Governor of Virginia, March 10, 1782 (Excerpt)	351
To James McHenry, March 12, 1782 (Excerpt)	352
To Colonel Lewis Nicola, May 22, 1782	354
To Archibald Cary, June 15, 1782 (Excerpt)	355
To John Laurens, July 10, 1782 (Excerpt)	356
To Elkanah Watson, August 10, 1782	357
To James McHenry, September 12, 1782 (Excerpt)	358
To Thomas Paine, September 18, 1782 (Excerpt)	359
To Major General Nathanael Greene, September 23, 1782 (Excerpt)	360
To Benjamin Lincoln, Secretary at War, October 2, 1782	361
To James McHenry, October 17, 1782 (Excerpt)	363
To Reverend William Gordon, October 23, 1782	364
To Jonathan Trumbull, Governor of Connecticut, November 13, 1782	365
To Major Benjamin Tallmadge, December 10, 1782 (Excerpt)	366
To Major General Nathanael Greene, February 6, 1783 (Excerpt)	367
General Orders, February 15, 1783 (Excerpt)	368
To Benjamin Harrison, Governor of Virginia, March 4, 1783 (Excerpt)	369
To Alexander Hamilton, March 4, 1783	370
To Robert Morris, Superintendent of Finance, March 8, 1783	372
To Alexander Hamilton, March 12, 1783 (Excerpt)	373
To the Officers of the Army, March 15, 1783	375

To Elias Boudinot, President of the Confederation Congress, March 18, 1783	379
To Joseph Jones, March 18, 1783	381
To Benjamin Harrison, Governor of Virginia, March 19, 1783	383
To Lund Washington, March 19, 1783	385
To Arthur Lee, March 29, 1783 (Excerpt)	387
To Robert R. Livingston, Secretary of Foreign Affairs, March 29, 1783 (Excerpt)	388
To Major General Nathanael Greene, March 31, 1783 (Excerpt)	389
To Alexander Hamilton, March 31, 1783 (Excerpt)	390
To Theodorick Bland, April 4, 1783	391
To Alexander Hamilton, April 4, 1783	393
To Theodorick Bland, April 4, 1783	395
To Marquis de Lafayette, April 5, 1783 (Excerpts)	399
To Alexander Hamilton, April 16, 1783	401
General Orders, April 18, 1783 (Excerpt)	403
To Alexander Hamilton, April 22, 1783 (Excerpt)	405
To Lieutenant Colonel Tench Tilghman, April 24, 1783	407
To Jean de Neufville, April 25, 1783	408
To Benjamin Harrison, Governor of Virginia, April 30, 1783	409
To Elisha Boudinot, President of the Confederation Congress, May 10, 1783 (Excerpt)	410
Circular to the States, June 8, 1783	411
To John Augustine Washington, June 15, 1783 (Excerpt)	419
To Elias Boudinot, President of the Confederation Congress, June 17, 1783	420
To Reverend William Gordon, July 8, 1783 (Excerpt)	422
To Major John Joiner Ellis, July 10, 1783	425
To George William Fairfax, July 10, 1783 (Excerpts)	426
To Robert Stewart, August 10, 1783 (Excerpt)	427
To George Martin, August 10, 1783	428

Address to the Confederation Congress, August 26, 1783	429
To James Duane, September 7, 1783	430
To Jean-Baptiste Donatien de Vimeur, Comte de Rochambeau, October 15, 1783 (Excerpt)	435
To Armand-Louis de Gontaut Biron, Duc de Lauzun, October 15, 1783 (Excerpt)	436
Farewell Orders to the Army of the United States, November 2, 1783	437
To the Ministers, Elders, Deacons of the Reformed German Congregation of New York, November 27, 1783	440
To the Marine Society of the City of New York, November 29, 1783	441
To the Members of the Volunteer Association and Other Inhabitants of the Kingdom of Ireland Who Have Lately Arrived in the City of New York, December 2, 1783	442
To the General Assembly of Pennsylvania, December 9, 1783	443
To the Merchants of Philadelphia, December 9, 1783	444
To the Militia Officers of the City and Liberties of Philadelphia, December 12, 1783	445
To the Trustees and Faculty of the University of the State of Pennsylvania, December 13, 1783	446
To the Learned Professions of Philadelphia, December 13, 1783	447
To the American Philosophical Society, December 13, 1783	448
Address to the Confederation Congress on Resigning His Commission, December 23, 1783	449

Part IV From Soldier to Statesman: 1783–1788

To the Mayor and Commonalty of Alexandria, December 31, 1783	455
To Jonathan Trumbull, Jr., Governor of Connecticut, January 5, 1784 (Excerpt)	456
To Jean de Neufville, January 6, 1784 (Excerpt)	457
To Benjamin Harrison, Governor of Virginia, January 18, 1784 (Excerpt)	458
To Chevalier Jean de Heintz, January 21, 1784	460

To Philip Schuyler, January 21, 1784	461
To Marquis de Lafayette, February 1, 1784 (Excerpt)	462
To Comte de Rochambeau, February 1, 1784 (Excerpt)	463
To the Citizens of Fredericksburg, February 14, 1784	464
To Henry Knox, February 20, 1784 (Excerpt)	465
To Friedrich Wilhelm August Heinrich Ferdinand von Steuben, March 15, 1784 (Excerpt)	466
To James Craik, March 25, 1784	467
To Thomas Jefferson, March 29, 1784 (Excerpts)	469
To Antoine-Jean-Louis Le Bègue de Presle Duportail, April 4, 1784 (Excerpt)	471
To William Gordon, May 8, 1784	472
To the State Societies of the Cincinnati, May 15, 1784	473
To Jonathan Trumbull, Sr., Governor of Connecticut, May 15, 1784 (Excerpt)	477
To Henry Knox, June 2, 1784 (Excerpt)	478
To Edward Newenham, June 10, 1784 (Excerpt)	479
To James Madison, June 12, 1784	480
To the Virginia Legislature, July 15, 1784	481
To Jacob Read, August 11, 1784 (Excerpt)	482
Diary Entry, October 4, 1784 (Excerpt)	483
To Benjamin Harrison, Governor of Virginia, October 10, 1784	485
To Jacob Read, November 3, 1784 (Excerpt)	491
To Officials of the City of Richmond, November 15, 1784	493
To George Clinton, Governor of New York, November 25, 1784 (Excerpt)	494
To Henry Knox, December 5, 1784 (Excerpt)	495
To George Chapman, December 15, 1784	496
To Samuel Chase, January 5, 1785 (Excerpt)	497
To Benjamin Harrison, January 22, 1785	498
To Richard Henry Lee, President of the Confederation Congress, February 8, 1785 (Excerpt)	500

To Patrick Henry, Governor of Virginia, February 27, 1785	502
To Hugh Williamson, March 15, 1785 (Excerpt)	503
To James Duane, April 10, 1785 (Excerpt)	504
To William Carmichael, June 10, 1785 (Excerpt)	505
To William Goddard, June 11, 1785	506
To George William Fairfax, June 30, 1785 (Excerpt)	507
To David Humphreys, July 25, 1785 (Excerpt)	508
To Marquis de Lafayette, July 25, 1785 (Excerpts)	510
To Edmund Randolph, July 30, 1785 (Excerpt)	512
To William Grayson, August 22, 1785 (Excerpt)	513
To Richard Henry Lee, President of the Confederation Congress, August 22, 1785 (Excerpt)	514
To James McHenry, August 22, 1785 (Excerpt)	515
To François-Jean de Beauvoir Chastellux, September 5, 1785 (Excerpt)	517
To Richard Varick, September 26, 1785 (Excerpt)	518
To George Mason, October 3, 1785	519
To James Warren, October 7, 1785 (Excerpt)	520
To Patrick Henry, Governor of Virginia, October 29, 1785	522
To David Humphreys, October 30, 1785 (Excerpt)	523
To Edward Newenham, November 25, 1785 (Excerpt)	524
To James Madison, November 30, 1785 (Excerpt)	525
To David Stuart, November 30, 1785 (Excerpt)	526
To Henry Lee, Jr., April 5, 1786 (Excerpt)	527
To Robert Morris, April 12, 1786	528
To Marquis de Lafayette, May 10, 1786 (Excerpt)	530
To John Jay, Secretary of Foreign Affairs, May 18, 1786 (Excerpt)	532
To William Grayson, July 26, 1786 (Excerpts)	533
To Comte de Rochambeau, July 31, 1786 (Excerpt)	534
To Thomas Jefferson, August 1, 1786 (Excerpt)	535

To Anne-César, Chevalier de La Luzerne, August 1, 1786 (Excerpt)	536
To John Jay, Secretary of Foreign Affairs, August 15, 1786	538
To Marquis de Lafayette, August 15, 1786 (Excerpt)	540
To John Francis Mercer, September 9, 1786 (Excerpt)	543
To Bushrod Washington, September 30, 1786 (Excerpt)	544
To Henry Lee, Jr., October 31, 1786 (Excerpt)	545
To James Madison, November 5, 1786	546
To Bushrod Washington, November 15, 1786	548
To Edmund Randolph, November 19, 1786	550
To David Stuart, November 19, 1786 (Excerpt)	551
To James Madison, December 16, 1786 (Excerpt)	552
To Edmund Randolph, Governor of Virginia, December 21, 1786	554
To David Humphreys, December 26, 1786 (Excerpt)	555
To Henry Knox, December 26, 1786 (Excerpt)	557
To Thomas Johnson, December 28, 1786 (Excerpt)	559
To Jabez Bowen, January 9, 1787 (Excerpt)	560
To Henry Knox, February 3, 1787	561
To Thomas Stone, February 16, 1787	563
To Benjamin Lincoln, Jr., February 24, 1787 (Excerpt)	565
To Henry Knox, February 25, 1787 (Excerpt)	566
To Henry Knox, March 8, 1787 (Excerpt)	567
To John Jay, March 10, 1787 (Excerpt)	568
To Benjamin Lincoln, March 23, 1787 (Excerpt)	569
To Edmund Randolph, Governor of Virginia, March 28, 1787 (Excerpt)	570
To James Madison, March 31, 1787 (Excerpt)	572
To Henry Knox, April 2, 1787	575
To Edmund Randolph, Governor of Virginia, April 9, 1787 (Excerpt)	577

To Thomas Jefferson, Minister to France, May 30, 1787 (Excerpt)	578
To David Stuart, July 1, 1787 (Excerpt)	579
To Alexander Hamilton, July 10, 1787	581
To Marquis de Lafayette, August 15, 1787 (Excerpt)	582
To Henry Knox, August 19, 1787 (Excerpt)	583
Diary Entry, September 17, 1787	584
To the President of Congress, September 17, 1787	585
To Marquis de Lafayette, September 18, 1787	586
To Benjamin Harrison, September 24, 1787	587
To David Humphreys, October 10, 1787 (Excerpt)	588
To James Madison, October 10, 1787 (Excerpt)	589
To Henry Knox, October 15, 1787 (Excerpt)	590
To David Stuart, November 5, 1787 (Excerpt)	591
To Bushrod Washington, November 9, 1787	592
To Alexander Hamilton, November 10, 1787 (Excerpt)	595
To Catherine Sawbridge Macaulay Graham, November 16, 1787 (Excerpt)	596
To David Stuart, November 30, 1787 (Excerpt)	597
To James Madison, December 7, 1787 (Excerpt)	598
To Edward Newenham, December 25, 1787 (Excerpt)	599
To Thomas Jefferson, Minister to France, January 1, 1788 (Excerpt)	600
To Edmund Randolph, Governor of Virginia, January 8, 1788 (Excerpt)	602
To Comte de Rochambeau, January 8, 1788 (Excerpt)	603
To Nicholas Simon van Winter and Lucretia Wilhelmina van Winter, January 8, 1788	604
To Richard Butler, January 10, 1788 (Excerpt)	605
To Marquis de Lafayette, January 10, 1788 (Excerpt)	606
To Marquis de Lafayette, February 7, 1788 (Excerpt)	608
To Eléanor-François-Elie Moustier, February 7, 1788 (Excerpt)	610

To Benjamin Lincoln, February 11, 1788 (Excerpt)	611
To James Madison, March 2, 1788	612
To Eléanor-François-Elie Moustier, March 26, 1788 (Excerpt)	613
To Henry Knox, March 30, 1788 (Excerpt)	615
To John Armstrong, April 25, 1788 (Excerpt)	616
To François-Jean de Beauvoir Chastellux, April 25, 1788 (Excerpt)	619
To Marquis de Lafayette, April 28, 1788 (Excerpt)	621
To Samuel Griffin, April 30, 1788 (Excerpt)	624
To Marquis de Lafayette, May 28, 1788 (Excerpt)	625
To Francis van der Kemp, May 28, 1788 (Excerpt)	627
To James Madison, June 8, 1788 (Excerpt)	628
To David Stuart, June 8, 1788 (Excerpt)	629
To Marquis de Lafayette, June 18, 1788 (Excerpt)	630
To Richard Henderson, June 19, 1788	632
To John Lathrop, June 22, 1788	634
To Mathew Carey, June 25, 1788	635
To Charles Cotesworth Pinckney, June 28, 1788	636
To Benjamin Lincoln, June 29, 1788	638
To John Jay, Secretary of Foreign Affairs, July 18, 1788 (Excerpt)	640
To John Langdon, President of New Hampshire, July 20, 1788	642
To Jonathan Trumbull, Jr., July 20, 1788	643
To James McHenry, July 31, 1788	645
To James Madison, August 3, 1788 (Excerpt)	647
To Thomas Nelson, Jr., August 3, 1788 (Excerpt)	648
To Charles Pettit, August 16, 1788	649
To William Tudor, August 18, 1788 (Excerpt)	651
To Alexander Hamilton, August 28, 1788	652
To Benjamin Lincoln, August 28, 1788	654
To George Richards Minot, August 28, 1788	656
To Joseph Mandrillon, August 29, 1788	657

To Edward Newenham, August 29, 1788 (Excerpt)	658
To Thomas Jefferson, Minister to France, August 31, 1788 (Excerpt)	661
To Annis Boudinot Stockton, August 31, 1788	664
To William Barton, September 7, 1788 (Excerpt)	666
To Henry Lee, Jr., September 22, 1788 (Excerpt)	668
To James Madison, September 23, 1788 (Excerpt)	671
Index	673

Figures

1 Part I: From Colonist to Patriot	*page* 6
2 Part II: Commander-in-Chief: 1775–1778	50
3 Part III: The Road to Victory: 1778–1783	214
4 Part IV: From Soldier to Statesman: 1783–1788	452

Acknowledgments

We wish to express our gratitude to Cambridge University Press for publishing this work. We must particularly thank our Cambridge editor, Robert Dreesen, for encouraging us to pursue this project and for guiding us through the process of preparing these volumes for publication. Our thanks are also due to those scholars who acted as reviewers for the project and who offered their support and helpful suggestions for improvement. In addition, we wish to thank Washington scholars William B. Allen, William Hay, and Kevin Weddle for their advice at critical junctures in our research. Finally, we gratefully acknowledge the efforts of earlier editors and compilers of Washington's writings, whose work has inspired and helped to guide our own.

Carson Holloway would like to thank the Claremont Institute's Center for the American Way of Life for its support for his work. He also thanks the Center's director, Arthur Milikh, for his friendship. In addition, he wishes to express his gratitude to his colleagues at the University of Nebraska at Omaha for their friendship and encouragement, and to the College of Arts and Sciences for a faculty development fellowship that materially assisted the completion of this project. Finally, he is grateful to his wife, Shari, and his daughters – Maria, Anna, Elizabeth, Catherine, Jane, and Emily – for their love and support, and for listening patiently to his frequent dinner table observations on the greatness of George Washington.

Bradford Wilson wishes to thank the James Madison Program in American Ideals and Institutions at Princeton University and its director, Robert P. George, for providing a uniquely hospitable home for scholarly work on the political thought of American statesmen. He thanks Antonin Scalia and Princeton University librarian Jeremy Darrington for their research assistance, and Grace Snell for her assistance with the preparation of the manuscript. To classicist Solveig Gold we owe the translations in the text of Latin passages well known to the Founders' generation. Finally, he wishes to express his gratitude to his wife Elle, his children, and his grandchildren for the love, support, and pleasant distractions they have offered during his work on the great George Washington.

Introduction

He changed mankind's ideas of political greatness.

Attributed to Fisher Ames

George Washington is the single most important figure among the American Founders and perhaps the single most important statesman in all of America's history. As such, his career has been studied extensively by scholars and is well known to a wide audience. Most educated Americans can recite Washington's most famous contributions to the establishment of the nation's independent constitutional republic, for which the people of his generation dubbed him the "father of his country": his role as commander-in-chief of the revolutionary army, his celebrated decision to shun power and return to private life after independence was won, his re-emergence from retirement to preside over the drafting of the Constitution in the summer of 1787, and his service as president during the critical first two terms, during which the new government was put into operation and placed on a stable footing.

Washington has been somewhat neglected, however, as a political thinker. Multitudes of books and articles have been published on the political thought of men such as Thomas Jefferson, James Madison, Alexander Hamilton, John Adams, and Benjamin Franklin. There is no comparable body of work on Washington's political thought. This is certainly understandable in a way. Unlike many of his great contemporaries, Washington was not a trained lawyer and was not the beneficiary of the liberal education offered by the various colonial colleges that existed in his day. Nor was he a prodigy of wide-ranging and profound self-education like Franklin. In general, Washington had a much less theoretical cast of mind than any of these figures. He was much more thoroughly a man of action.

Nevertheless, taking the more theoretical Founders seriously as political thinkers points us back in the direction of the careful study of Washington's political thought. For the most theoretically accomplished of the Founders joined with the ordinary people of their generation in regarding Washington as the greatest man of their time – indeed, as one of the greatest men of all time. If we accept the well-established consensus that men like Jefferson, Madison, Hamilton, Adams, and Franklin made contributions to political reflection that are of enduring consequence, then it must follow that the political man to whom *they* looked up with admiration as their superior is worthy of our serious attention. For those of us who could not know him at first hand, however, his greatness can only be experienced fully through a consideration of his political writings.

We encounter in Washington's political writings not the theoretical greatness we find in the other leading Founders, but something that is nevertheless a genuine greatness of mind. Indeed, Washington is probably the clearest American example of something like Aristotle's *megalopsuchos*, the magnanimous or great-souled man, who claims the highest honors and responsibilities and is in fact worthy of them. This greatness of mind or soul is not only morally edifying but also intellectually instructive because of its subtlety and complexity. In comparison to the more philosophically inclined Founders, Washington was a simpler man – but he was never simple-minded. On the contrary, his political writings reveal a remarkable and beautiful wholeness and balance of soul, a mind capable of accommodating and giving due credit to the various competing goods that are essential to a just political order – and to a just life of political action. We encounter in Washington's political writings an unwavering patriotism (of course), but also a willingness to confront the country's defects candidly, to acknowledge the just claims of other countries, and even (occasionally) to entertain cosmopolitan dreams of universal brotherhood. We find a man who objected to the abuses of British power not only as a threat to individual rights but also as an insult to American honor – a man who combined modern Lockean individualism with a kind of traditional nationalism. We find an absolute commitment to maintaining high standards of personal and political conduct, while still recognizing and sympathizing with the numerous moral frailties to which human beings are subject. And throughout we find an astute and even cunning judge of political situations and political actors, always assessing them on the basis of a sober and realistic appreciation of human nature.

We have selected and edited this two-volume collection of Washington's political writings in order to encourage greater interest in and study of his political thought and statesmanship. The work is, indeed, part of a much larger project. It is the second title in Cambridge University Press's the Political Writings of American Statesmen (Bradford P. Wilson and Carson Holloway, series editors), which was inaugurated in 2017 with the publication of *The Political Writings of Alexander Hamilton*.

We certainly recognize and are grateful for the earlier collections of Washington's writings. We nevertheless think that the present work makes a unique contribution by being more comprehensive than some of the earlier works and more focused than others. In the last part of the previous century, William B. Allen published *George Washington: A Collection* (Liberty Fund) and John Rhodehamel published *George Washington: Writings* (Library of America). Although they are excellent introductions to Washington's mind, their status as one-volume works necessarily limits their range of coverage. Moreover, Rhodehamel's Library of America volume includes a great deal of Washington's personal correspondence and therefore necessarily omits much that is of primarily political interest. In contrast to these limited collections stand the various past efforts to bring out a complete collection of Washington's papers, most notably John C. Fitzpatrick's *The Writings of George Washington* (published by the George Washington Bicentennial Commission) and the University Press of Virginia's massive and comprehensive *The Papers of George Washington*. These latter works will remain essential tools for scholarly specialists, but they are so sprawling that they cannot offer the convenience of the present work. Moreover, by compiling everything that Washington wrote, they necessarily include a vast number of documents that are of little interest to the student of politics. In contrast to these earlier works, we have tried to include all of Washington's writings that are of enduring political interest but, at the same time, *only* what is of enduring political interest. We aim, by collecting these materials together in a single two-volume work, to encourage more students of political theory and statecraft to turn their attention to Washington's thought.

In trying to include everything that is of *enduring* political interest, we have necessarily chosen to exclude writings that, while political, are so mundane as to be of no interest to the student of statecraft or political thought. Washington wrote so many political documents that it would be impossible to include all of them while keeping the compilation to a manageable size (to say nothing of keeping it thoroughly interesting to contemporary readers). Our primary rule of selection has been to include whatever touches on matters of principle and its application to practice, as well as whatever gives an account and Washington's evaluation of the pivotal moments in the Founding of the nation. Put another way, we have tried to include all political writings that truly reveal Washington's mind and character. Accordingly, we have excluded the multitude of Washington's writings that were merely necessary to the execution of his administrative duties as commander-in-chief and as president.

The Political Writings of George Washington is arranged chronologically into two volumes, and each volume is further divided into parts that correspond to the main periods of Washington's public life. Volume I, the present volume, is divided into four parts that trace the first half of Washington's public career. Part I: From Colonist to Patriot: 1754–1775 collects writings from Washington's young manhood and early middle age, up to the time he became commander-in-chief of the American army. These materials reveal the public-spiritedness that was a constant throughout Washington's life, but they also illustrate the most important change in its orientation. As an ambitious young man, Washington sought distinction in the service of the Crown, while in his maturity that ambition was turned toward defending the rights of the rising American nation from the injustices that arose from British imperial rule.

Part II: Commander-in-Chief: 1775–1778 presents writings connected to the first part of Washington's service as the leader of American military forces during the War for Independence. Here the reader encounters Washington's remarkable combination of diffidence and self-confidence: a diffidence in his abilities accompanied by absolute confidence in his rectitude and dedication to duty. These materials also trace Washington's efforts to build the army into an effective fighting force while tirelessly impressing upon the minds of the soldiers the nobility of the aims for which they were fighting. They further reveal

Washington for the first time in his life dealing with the delicate problems of justice and prudence that attend supreme military command: learning how to deal wisely with the enemy, the citizenry, his military subordinates, and his political superiors.

Part III: The Road to Victory: 1778–1783 compiles Washington's political writings from the alliance with France – a key turning point in the war – to the concluding of peace with Great Britain and Washington's subsequent retirement from public life. Here we find the ardent patriot coming to the realization that patriotism alone was not enough to carry the war to a successful end. Enthusiasm, he observed, had done what it could in the beginning of the contest, which could now only be won by realistic appeals to the self-interest of those on whose exertions the outcome depended. Here, too, we find Washington confronting the problems that arose from the lack of effective governing power in the Articles of Confederation – experiences that, for the rest of his life, influenced his political thinking and convinced him of the need for a stronger central government.

Finally, Part IV: From Soldier to Statesman: 1783–1788 presents materials from Washington's first period of retirement and the early stages of his return to public life. After eight years of near-constant exertion in pursuit of the nation's independence, Washington was now free to embrace the repose for which he so ardently yearned – but not for long. His writings from these years chronicle his growing alarm at the disorders that seemed to flow from the weakness of the nation's government, and his fear that America, having honorably won its independence from Great Britain, would now disgrace itself by proving incapable of effective self-government. This growing sense of crisis led him to reconsider his resolution to retire and finally convinced him to return to public service – first by agreeing to chair the Constitutional Convention, and then by taking upon himself the responsibilities of the presidency.

Throughout the work we have made light modifications to Washington's original texts in order to make them more accessible to contemporary readers. Probably our greatest intervention has been to modernize Washington's punctuation. In general, his punctuation is often difficult to follow, partly because the conventions of his day were different from those of our own, but also partly because his command of those conventions was less certain than that of his more formally educated peers. Our aim in modernizing the punctuation has always been to preserve Washington's meaning while at the same time rendering it more immediately evident to the modern reader. Put another way, we have tried to save readers the mental effort of "translating" Washington's punctuation, so that their minds may instead be occupied wholly with following the train of Washington's thought and appreciating the vigor, clarity, and dignity of his expression.

We have also modernized Washington's spelling and capitalization, although we have left the latter undisturbed when he capitalized a whole word with the intention of emphasizing it. Likewise, italics are retained for words that Washington chose to emphasize. We have also preserved Washington's capitalizations in his references to God and Providence. We have generally filled in words that Washington abbreviated and ones (usually names) left partly incomplete (such as Mr. H—— for Mr. Hamilton or C—— for Congress). In addition, we have modernized Washington's uses of "a" and "an" and have corrected errors in subject–verb agreements. Otherwise, where we have changed or added words – either as a correction of Washington himself, to reflect his obvious intention, or as a correction of a transcription error – we have indicated as much in an endnote.

We consulted John C. Fitzpatrick's *The Writings of George Washington* and the University of Virginia's *The Papers of George Washington* in supplying missing letters from obviously incomplete words and in supplying missing or illegible words. Occasional blank spaces in the text are Washington's own.

Fig. 1 Part I: From Colonist to Patriot: (Public Domain)
www.mountvernon.org/george-washington/artwork/life-portraits-of-george-washington/#g-1081_m-1-washington-1772-charles-willson-peale

PART I

From Colonist to Patriot: 1754–1775

To Richard Corbin, February–March 1754

Dear Sir:

In a conversation at Green Spring you gave me some room to hope for a commission above that of a major, and to be ranked among the chief officers of this expedition. The command of the whole forces is what I neither look for, expect, nor desire; for, I must be impartial enough to confess, it is a charge too great for my youth and inexperience to be entrusted with. Knowing this, I have too sincere a love for my country to undertake that which may tend to the prejudice of it. But if I could entertain hopes that you thought me worthy of the post of lieutenant colonel, and would favor me so far as to mention it at the appointment of officers, I could not but entertain a true sense of the kindness.

I flatter myself that under a skillful commander, or man of sense (which I most sincerely wish to serve under), with my own application and diligent study of my duty, I shall be able to conduct my steps without censure, and in time render myself worthy of the promotion that I shall be favored with now.

To Horatio Sharpe, Governor of Maryland, April 24, 1754 (Excerpts)

May it please Your Excellency,

It is with the greatest concern I acquaint you that Mr. Ward, ensign in Captain Trent's company, was obliged to surrender his small fortress in the forks of Monongahela, at the summons of Captain Contrecoeur, commander of the French forces, who fell down from Venango with a fleet of 360 canoes and bateaus, conveying upwards of one thousand men, eighteen pieces of artillery, and large stores of provisions and other necessaries. Mr. Ward, having but an inconsiderable number of men (not exceeding 30), and no cannon to make a proper defense, was forced to deliver up the fort on the 17th instant. They suffered him to draw out his men, arms, and working tools, and gave leave that he might retreat to the inhabitants with them. I have heard of Your Excellency's great zeal for His Majesty's service, and for all our interests on the present occasion; therefore I am persuaded you will take proper notice of the Indians' moving speech, and think their unshaken fidelity worthy your consideration ....

I ought first to have begged pardon of Your Excellency for this liberty of writing, as I am not happy enough to be ranked among those of your acquaintance. It was the glowing zeal I owe my country that influenced me to import these advices, and my inclination prompted me to do it to you as I know you are solicitous for the public weal and warm in this interesting cause—that should rouse from the lethargy we have fallen into the heroic spirit of every freeborn Englishman, to assert the rights and privileges of our king (if we don't consult the benefit of ourselves), and rescue from the invasions of a usurping enemy Our Majesty's property, his dignity, and lands.

To Mary Ball Washington, August 14, 1755

Honored Madam,

If it is in my power to avoid going to the Ohio again, I shall; but if the command is pressed upon me by the general voice of the country, and offered upon such terms as can't be objected against, it would reflect dishonor upon me to refuse it. And that, I am sure, must or ought to give you greater cause of uneasiness than my going in an honorable command; for upon no other terms I will accept of it. At present I have no proposals made to me, nor have any advice of such an intention, except from private hands. I am Dr. Mm &c.

To Andrew Montour, October 10, 1755

Dear Montour,

I wrote some time ago a letter of invitation from Fort Cumberland, desiring yourself, your family, and friendly Indians to come and reside among us. But that letter not coming to hand, I am induced to send a second express with the same invitation, being pleased that I have it in my power to do something for you on a better footing than ever it has been done. I was greatly enraptured when I heard you were at the head of 300 Indians on a march towards Venango, being satisfied that your hearty attachment to our glorious cause, your courage, of which I have had very great proofs, and your presence among the Indians would animate their just indignation to do something noble, something worthy of themselves, and honorable to you. I hope you will use your interest (as I know you have much) in bringing our brothers once more to our service. Assure them, as you truly may, that nothing which I can do shall be wanting to make them happy. Assure them also that, as I have the chief command, I am invested with power to treat them as brethren and allies, which I am sorry to say they have not been of late. Recommend me kindly to our good friend Monocatootha and others. Tell them how happy it would make Conotocaurious[1] to have an opportunity of taking them by the hand at Fort Cumberland, and how glad he would be to treat them as brothers of our great king beyond the waters. Flattering myself that you will come, I doubt not but you will bring as many of them with you as possible, as that will afford me what alone I want: that is, an opportunity of doing something equal to your wishes. I am, Dear Montour, Your real Friend & Assured Hble Servt

Go: Washington

N.B. I doubt not but you have heard of the ravages committed on our frontiers by the French Indians, and I suppose the French themselves. I am now on my march against them, and hope to give them cause of repenting their rashness.

To Robert Dinwiddie, Lieutenant Governor of Virginia, October 11, 1755 (Excerpt)

I would again hint the necessity of putting the militia under better regulation, had I not mentioned it twice before, and a third time may seem impertinent. But I must once more beg leave to declare (for here I am more immediately concerned) that unless the assembly will enact a law to enforce the military law in all its parts, I must with great regret decline the honor that has been so generously intended me. And for this only reason I do it: The foreknowledge I have of failing in every point that might justly be expected from a person invested with full power to exert his authority. I see the growing insolence of the soldiers, the indolence and inactivity of the officers, who are all sensible how confined their punishments are, in regard to what they ought to be. In fine, I can plainly see that under our present establishment we shall become a nuisance, an insupportable charge to our country, and never answer any one[2] expectation of the assembly. And here I must assume the freedom to express some surprise that we alone should be so tenacious of liberty as not to invest a power where interest and politics so unanswerably demand it, and from whence so much good must consequently ensue. Do we not see that every nation under the sun find their accord therein? And without it no order, no regularity can be observed. Why then should it be expected from us (who are all young and inexperienced) to govern, and keep up a proper spirit of discipline, without laws, when the best and most experienced can scarcely do it with? Then, if we consult our interest, I am sure it is loudly called for. For I can confidently assert that the money expended in recruiting, clothing, arming, maintaining, and subsisting soldiers who have deserted has cost the country an immense sum, which might have been prevented were we under restraints that would terrify the soldiers from such practices. One thing more on this head I will recommend, and then quit the subject, and that is to have the inhabitants liable to certain heavy fines or corporal punishments for entertaining of deserters, and a reward for taking them up. If this was done, it would be next to an impossibility for a soldier to escape. But, on the contrary, as things now stand, they are not only seduced to run away, but are also harbored and assisted with every necessary means to make their escape.

To Denis McCarty, November 22, 1755

I am very sorry you have given me occasion to complain of your conduct in recruiting, and to tell you that the methods and unjustifiable means you have practiced are very unacceptable and have been of infinite prejudice to the service. Of this I am informed by many gentlemen, as well as by all the officers who were ordered to recruit in these parts—and am further assured that it is next to an impossibility to get a man where you have been, such terror have you occasioned by forcibly taking, confining, and torturing those who would not voluntarily enlist. These proceedings not only cast a slur upon your own character, but reflect dishonor upon mine, as giving room to conjecture that they have my concurrence for their source. I must therefore acquaint you that such behavior in an officer would shake his commission! Let it then be a warning to you, who I still hope erred more through inadvertence than design, for which reason I shall forget the past, in sanguine hopes of what is to come. I am &c.

G:W.

Address to the Officers, January 8, 1756

Lieutenant Colonel Stephens has orders to read the following suspension and admonition to all the officers.

"Whereas the court of inquiry that was held yesterday in behalf of our sovereign lord the king, for examining into a complaint against Lehaynsius Dekeyser, ensign in the Virginia Regiment, for a breach of the twenty-third article, fifteenth section of War, were unanimous in opinion that he was not only guilty of the crime for which he was arrested, but had acted inconsistently with the character of a gentleman, and scandalously for an officer, whose character should be preserved by the nicest rules of honor.

For these and other reasons, unnecessary to enumerate, I think it for the honor of His Majesty's service, and the good of the regiment, that the said Lehaynsius Dekeyser be suspended; and he is hereby suspended and debarred from holding any post or having any connection with the said regiment, until the governor's pleasure be known, or until he is acquitted by a general court martial, if he thinks proper to appeal for a further hearing.

This timely warning of the effects of misbehavior will, I hope, be instrumental in animating the younger officers to a laudable emulation in the service of their country. Not that I apprehend any of them can be guilty of offenses of this nature. But there are many other misdemeanors that will, without due circumspection, gain upon inactive minds, and produce consequences equally disgraceful.

I would therefore earnestly recommend, in every point of duty, willingness to undertake and intrepid resolution to execute.

Remember that it is the actions, and not the commission, that make the officer, and that there is more expected from him than the title. Do not forget that there ought to be a time appropriated to attain this knowledge, as well as to indulge pleasure. And, as we now have no opportunities to improve from example, let us read for this desirable end. There is Bland's and other treatises which will give the wished-for information.

I think it my duty, gentlemen, as I have the honor to preside over you, to give this friendly admonition, especially as I am determined—as far as my small experience in service, my abilities, and interest of the service dictate—to observe the strictest discipline through the whole economy of my behavior. On the other hand, you may as certainly depend upon having the strictest justice administered to all, and that I shall make it the most agreeable part of my duty to study merit and reward the brave and deserving. I assure you, gentlemen, that partiality shall never bias my conduct; nor shall prejudice injure any. But throughout the whole tenor of my proceedings I shall endeavor, as far as I am able, to reward and punish without the least diminution."

G:W.

To Robert Hunter Morris, Deputy Governor of Pennsylvania, April 9, 1756 (Excerpt)

Dear Sir,

I had scarce reached Williamsburg before an express was after me with news of the French and Indians advancing within our settlements and doing incredible mischief to the inhabitants, which obliged me to postpone my business there and hurry to their assistance with all expedition. When I came to this place, I found everything in deep confusion, and the poor distressed inhabitants under a general consternation. I therefore collected such force as I could immediately raise, and sent them in such parties, and to such places, as 'twas judged most likely to meet with the enemy—one of which, under the command of Mr. Paris, luckily fell in with a small body of them as they were surrounding a small fort on the North River of Cacapon, whom they engaged and (after half an hour's close firing) put to flight with the loss of their commander, Monsieur Donville (killed), and three or four more mortally wounded. The accident that has determined the fate of Monsieur has, I believe, dispersed his party, for I don't hear of any mischief done in this colony since, though we are not without numbers who are making hourly discoveries.

I have sent you a copy of the instructions that were found about this officer, that you may see how bold and enterprising the enemy have grown, how unconfined are these ambitious designs of the French, and how much it will be in their power (if the colonies continue in their fatal lethargy) to give a final stab to liberty and property.

Nothing I more sincerely wish than a union to the colonies in this time of eminent danger, and that you may find your assembly in a temper of mind to act consistently with their preservation. What Maryland has, or will do, I know not. But this I am certain of: that Virginia will do everything that can be expected to promote the public good.

To John Robinson, Speaker of the Virginia House of Burgesses, April 18, 1756

Dear Sir,

It gave me infinite concern to hear by several letters that the assembly are incensed against the Virginia Regiment and think they have cause to accuse the officers of all inordinate vices, but more especially of drunkenness and profanity! How far any one individual may have subjected himself to such reflections I will not pretend to determine. But this I am certain of, and can with the highest safety call my conscience, my God! and (what I suppose will still be a more demonstrable proof, at least in the eye of the world) the orders and instructions which I have given, to evince the purity of my own intentions, and to show, on the one hand, that my incessant endeavors have been directed to discountenance gaming, drinking, swearing, and other vices, with which all camps too much abound; while, on the other, I have used every expedient to inspire a laudable emulation in the officers, and an unerring exercise of duty in the soldiers. How far I may have mistaken the means to attain so salutary an end behooves not me to determine. But this I presume to say, that a man's intentions should be allowed in some respects to plead for his actions. I have been more explicit, sir, on this head than I otherwise should, because I find that my own character must of necessity be involved in the general censure; for which reason I cannot help observing that if the country think they have cause to condemn my conduct, and have a person in view that will act, that he may do. But who will endeavor to act more for her interests than I have done? It will give me the greatest pleasure to resign a command which I solemnly declare I accepted against my will.

I know, sir, that my inexperience may have led me into innumerable errors; for which reason I should think myself an unworthy member of the community and greatly deficient in the love I owe my country, which has ever been the first principle of my actions, were I to require more than a distant hint of its dissatisfaction to resign a commission which I confess to you I am no ways fond of keeping.

These sentiments I communicate to you, sir, not only as to a gentleman for whom I entertain the highest respect and greatest friendship, but also as a member of the assembly—that the contents, if you think proper, may be communicated to the whole. For, be assured, I shall never wish to hold a commission when it ceases to be by unanimous consent.

The unhappy differences which subsisted so long about command did, I own, prevent me from going to Fort Cumberland to enforce those orders which I never failed to send there, and caused, I dare say, many gross irregularities to creep into that garrison (which you know is in another colony). But whose fault was that? Ought it not to have been attributed to the officer commanding there (Captain Dagworthy), whose business it was to suppress vice in every shape? Surely it was. However, I am far from attempting to vindicate the characters of all the officers, for that I am sensible would be a task too arduous. There are some who have the seeds of idleness too strongly instilled into their constitution, either to be serviceable to themselves or beneficial to the country. Yet even those have not missed my best advice, nor have my unwearied endeavors ever been wanting to serve my country with the highest integrity. For which reasons I should ever be content in retirement and reflect with no little pleasure that no sordid views have influenced my conduct, nor have the hopes of unlawful gain swerved me in any measure from the strictest dictates of honor! I have diligently sought the public welfare and have endeavored to inculcate the same principles on all that are under me. These reflections will be a cordial to my mind so long as I am able to distinguish between good and evil. I am &c.

G:W.

To Robert Dinwiddie, Lieutenant Governor of Virginia, April 22, 1756 (Excerpt)

Honorable Sir,

This encloses several letters and the minutes of a council of war, which was held upon the receipt of them. Your Honor may see to what unhappy straits the distressed inhabitants, as well as I, am reduced. I am too little acquainted, sir, with pathetic language, to attempt a description of the people's distresses, though I have a generous soul, sensible of wrongs, and swelling for redress. But what can I do? If bleeding, dying! would glut their insatiate revenge, I would be a willing offering to savage fury and die by inches to save a people! I see their situation, know their danger, and participate in[3] their sufferings, without having it in my power to give them further relief than uncertain promises. In short, I see inevitable destruction in so clear a light that, unless vigorous measures are taken by the assembly, and speedy assistance sent from below, the poor inhabitants that are now in forts must unavoidably fall, while the remainder of the county are flying before the barbarous foe. In fine, the melancholy situation of the people; the little prospect of assistance; the gross and scandalous abuses cast upon the officers in general—which is reflecting upon me in particular, for suffering misconducts of such extraordinary kinds—and the distant prospects, if any, that I can see, of gaining honor and reputation in the service are motives which cause me to lament the hour that gave me a commission, and would induce me at any other time than this, of imminent danger, to resign, without one hesitating moment, a command which I never expect to reap either honor or benefit from—but, on the contrary, have almost an absolute certainty of incurring displeasure below, while the murder of poor innocent babes and helpless families may be laid to my account here!

The supplicating tears of the women, and moving petitions from the men, melt me into such deadly sorrow that I solemnly declare, if I know my own mind, I could offer myself a willing sacrifice to the butchering enemy, provided that would contribute to the people's ease.

Lord Fairfax has ordered men from the adjacent counties; but when they will come, or in what numbers, I cannot pretend to determine. If I may judge from the success we have met with here, I have but little hopes, as three days incessant endeavors have produced but twenty men.

To Lieutenant Colonel Adam Stephen, May 18, 1756 (Excerpt)

Mr. Boyd will receive by this conveyance three thousand pounds for payment of the troops—has orders to pay no officers who, upon settlement, fall indebted to the country—and even those that are clear, if they can do without their pay, are desired not to draw for all, if he has not money to pay the soldiers fully.

I want much to pay them off, to appease murmurs and silence complaints. I received a remonstrance of theirs in justification of their behavior. Tell them that I hope their conduct will ever be stimulated by a just sense of their duty—that heroic bravery and sobriety, influenced by a hearty zeal to serve their country, will always be the standard of their actions, and is the certain means of meriting my regard and esteem, as well as obtaining the love and applause of the country, while a contrary behavior, you may strongly assure them, shall never fail to meet with adequate punishments. Instances of this are now before them of Nathan Lewis, Corporal James Thomas, and Henry Campbell—all under sentence of death: the first for his cowardice at the action at Edwards's, the others for desertion. I have a warrant from the governor for shooting of Lewis, and shall delay the execution until the arrival of the new recruits. The others were tried but today, and the proceedings of the court will be sent to the governor. If he approves the sentence, I shall make it my particular care to see them executed, as I shall every individual that offends in the like cases.

Proclamation of War Against the French, August 15, 1756

You see, gentlemen soldiers, that it hath pleased our most gracious sovereign to declare war in form against the *French* king and (for divers good causes, but more particularly for their ambitious usurpations and encroachments on his *American* dominions) to pronounce all the said French king's subjects and vassals to be enemies to his crown and dignity, and hath willed and required all his subjects and people, and in a more especial manner commanded his captain general of his forces, his governors, and all other his commanders and officers, to do and execute all acts of hostility in the prosecution of this just and honorable war. And though our utmost endeavors can contribute but little to the advancement of His Majesty's honor, and the interest of his governments, yet, let us show our willing obedience to the best of kings, and by a strict attachment to his royal commands, demonstrate the love and loyalty we bear to his sacred person. Let us by rules of unerring bravery strive to merit his royal favor, and a better establishment as a reward for our services.

To Robert Dinwiddie, Lieutenant Governor of Virginia, March 10, 1757

Honorable Sir:

We may, I think, with great propriety and justice represent:

That the Virginia Regiment was the first in arms of any troops upon the continent in the present war.—That the three years which they have served has been one continued scene of action.—That whilst other troops have an agreeable recess in winter quarters, the nature of the service in which we are engaged, and the smallness of our numbers, so unequal to the task, keep us constantly in motion.—That, nevertheless, all these services have hitherto been performed with great spirit and cheerfulness, but that continuing in a service precarious and uncertain, hazarding life, fortune, and health to the chances of war, for the present and a bare subsistence, is matter for serious and melancholy reflection. It tends to promote languor and indifference. It sickens that laudable and generous emulation so necessary among troops. It is nipping in the bud our rising hopes—hopes that we have been led to cherish. It is discouraging to merit, and, I can't help repeating, that it is in the highest degree dispiriting to the officers, more especially those who, having thrown themselves out of other employments, are now to look forward and see that they are wasting the prime of their lives and constitutions in a service the most uncertain and precarious, in which they can expect to be continued no longer than hard blows and continual dangers require their aid—and when those causes cease, are then dismissed, perhaps in a state of disability and indigence from wounds, etc.

These are reflections that must have due weight in every breast but the idiot's and madman's, and have made our officers anxiously solicitous to know their fate—at once—and the full extent of their dependences, that they may regulate their conduct accordingly.

We can't conceive that being Americans should deprive us of the benefits of British subjects, nor lessen our claim to preferment. And we are very certain that no body of regular troops ever before served bloody campaigns without attracting royal notice.

As to those idle arguments which are oftentimes used—namely, you are defending your own properties—I look upon to be whimsical and absurd. We are defending the king's dominions. And although the inhabitants of Great Britain are removed from (this) danger, they are yet, equally with us, concerned and interested in the fate of the country; and there can be no sufficient reason given why we, who spend our blood and treasure in defense of the country, are not entitled to equal preferment.

Some boast of long service as a claim to promotion—meaning, I suppose, the length of time they have pocketed a commission. I apprehend it is the service done, not the service engaged in, that merits reward—and that there is as equitable a right to expect something for three years hard and bloody service as for ten spent at St. James's, etc., where real service or a field of battle never was seen.

If it should be said, the troops of Virginia are irregulars, and cannot expect more notice than other provincials, I must beg leave to differ and observe in turn that we want nothing but commissions from His Majesty to make us as regular a corps as any upon the continent—because we were regularly enlisted, attested, and bound during the king's or colony's pleasure. We have been regularly regimented and trained, and have done as regular duty for upwards of three years as any regiment in His Majesty's service. We are regularly and uniformly clothed, officers and soldiers. We have been at all the expense that regulars are in providing equipage for the camp. And in few words I may say, we labor under every disadvantage, and enjoy not one benefit, which regulars do.

How different from us the establishment of all other provincials is may easily be discerned by considering that they are raised for a season: assembled in the spring and are dismissed in the fall—consequently are totally ignorant of regular service. They know their dependence and had nothing to expect—therefore could not be disappointed. They are never clothed and are at little expense, as they act as irregulars and paid exorbitantly. There remains one reason more, which of itself is fully sufficient to obviate scruples, and that is: we have been in constant pay and on constant duty since the commencement of these broils, which none others have.

And we flatter ourselves it will evidently appear that the advantages gained by the enemy, and the ravages committed on our frontiers, are not owing to the inactivity of the Virginia Regiment—in proof of which we appeal to the many bloody skirmishes with the enemy last campaign, to our behavior at Monongahela and services in the campaign of 1754, to the number of officers and men killed in battle, etc., etc.

Recounting these services is highly disagreeable to us, as it is repugnant to the modesty becoming the brave; but we are compelled thereto by the little notice taken of us, it being the general opinion that our services are slighted or have not been properly represented to His Majesty. Otherwise the best of kings would have graciously taken notice of us in turn, while there are now six battalions raised in America, and not an officer of the Virginia Regiment provided for, notwithstanding many of them had distinguished themselves in the service before orders were issued for raising one of the battalions above mentioned. Whereas, the disregarding the faithful services of any body of His Majesty's subjects tends to discourage merit and lessen that generous emulation, spirit, and laudable ambition so necessary to prevail in an army, and which contributes so much to the success of enterprise.

I, in behalf of the officers of the Virginia Regiment, beg that Your Honor will be pleased to take their case into particular consideration, and, as they think themselves particularly entitled to Your Honor's patronage, give them reason by your earnest endeavors with His Lordship to hope for a soldier's reward, and redress their grievances in whatever manner shall seem to Your Honor most conducive to their interest and His Majesty's service. We are all sensible that nothing but earnest application can obtain promotion, while there are so many dependents. And we now hope, as justice and equity are clear on our side, and as this seems to be the crisis of our fate, that no stone will be unturned to bring this about. I am Honble Sir Yr most Obedt Hble Servt

Go: Washington

To Colonel John Stanwix, July 15, 1757 (Excerpt)

Militia, you will find, sir, will never answer your expectation. No dependence is to be placed upon them. They are obstinate and perverse. They are often egged on by the officers, who lead them to acts of disobedience. And, when they are ordered to certain posts for the security of stores, or the protection of the inhabitants, will, on a sudden, resolve to leave them, and the united vigilance of their officers cannot prevent them. Instances of the above nature I have now before me, which put me to some difficulty.

No man, I conceive, was ever worse plagued than I have been with the draughts that were sent from the several counties in this government to complete its regiment. Out of 400 that were received at Fredericksburg, and at this place, 114 have deserted, notwithstanding every precaution, except absolute confinement, has been used to prevent this infamous practice. I have used the most vigorous measures to apprehend those fellows who escaped from hence (which amounted to about thirty) and have succeeded so well that they are taken, with the loss of one of their men, and a soldier wounded. I have a gallows near forty feet high erected (which has terrified the rest exceedingly); and I am determined, if I can be justified in the proceeding, to hang two or three on it, as an example to others.

To Robert Dinwiddie, Lieutenant Governor of Virginia, September 17, 1757

Honorable Sir,

A letter of the 22nd ultimo from Captain Peachy came to my hands the other day—contents as follows (here was inserted the letter). I should take it infinitely kind if Your Honor would please to inform me whether a report of this nature was ever made to you, and, in that case, who was the author of it?

It is evident from a variety of circumstances, and especially from the change in Your Honor's conduct towards me, that some person as well inclined to detract, but better skilled in the art of detraction than the author of the above stupid scandal, has made free with my character. For I cannot suppose that malice so absurd, so bare faced, so diametrically opposite to truth, to common policy, and in short, to everything but villainy as the above is, *could* impress you with so ill an opinion of my honor and honesty!

If it be possible that Colonel Corbin (for my belief is staggered, not being conscious of having given the least cause to anyone, much less to that gentleman, to reflect so grossly)—I say, if it be possible that Colonel Corbin could descend so low as to be the propagator of this story, he must either be vastly ignorant in the state of affairs in this county at *that time*, or else he must suppose that the whole body of inhabitants had combined with me in executing the deceitful fraud. Or why did they almost to a man forsake their dwellings in the greatest terror and confusion? And, while one half of them sought shelter in paltry forts (of their own building), the other should flee to the adjacent counties for refuge, numbers of them even to Carolina, from whence they have never returned.

These are facts well known, but not better known than that these wretched people, while they lay pent up in forts, destitute of the common supports of life (having in their precipitate flight forgotten, or were unable, rather, to secure any kind of necessaries) did dispatch messengers of their own (thinking I had not represented their miseries in the piteous manner they deserved) with addresses to Your Honor and the assembly, praying relief. And did I ever send any alarming account, without also sending the original papers (or the copies) which gave rise to it?

That I have foibles, and perhaps many of them, I shall not deny. I should esteem myself, as the world also would, vain and empty, were I to arrogate perfection. Knowledge in military matters is to be acquired by practice and experience only. And if I have erred, great allowance should be made for my errors for want of it—unless those errors should appear to be willful, and then I conceive it would be more generous to charge me with my faults and let me stand or fall according to evidence, than to stigmatize me behind my back.

It is uncertain in what light my services may have appeared to Your Honor. But this I know, and it is the highest consolation I am capable of feeling: that no man that ever was employed in a public capacity has endeavored to discharge the trust reposed in him with greater honesty, and more zeal for the country's interest, than I have done. And if there is any person living who can say with justice that I have offered any intentional wrong to the public, I will cheerfully submit to the most ignominious punishment that an injured people ought to inflict! On the other hand, it is hard to have my character arraigned and my actions condemned without a hearing.

I must therefore again beg, in more plain and in very earnest terms, to know if Colonel Corbin has taken the liberty of representing my character to Your Honor with such ungentlemanly freedom as the letter implies? Your condescension herein will be acknowledged a singular favor done. Your Honor's most obedt Hble Servant,

G:W.

To James Wood, July 28, 1758

My Dear Colonel,

If thanks flowing from a heart replete with joy and gratitude can in any measure compensate for the fatigue, anxiety, and pain you had at my election, be assured you have them. 'Tis a poor but, I am convinced, welcome tribute to a generous mind. Such I believe yours to be.

How I shall thank Mrs. Wood for her favorable wishes, and how acknowledge my sense of obligations to the people in general for their choice of me, I am at a loss to resolve on. But why—can I do it more effectually than by making their interest (as it really is) my own, and doing everything that lies in my little power for the honor and welfare of the county? I think not, and my best endeavors they may always command. I promise this now, when promises may be regarded, before they might pass as words of course.

I am extreme thankly to you and my other friends for entertaining the freeholders in my name. I hope no exception were taken to any that voted against me but that all were alike treated and all had enough. It is what I much desired. My only fear is that you spent with too sparing a hand.

I don't like to touch upon our public affairs. The prospect is overspread by too many ills to give a favorable account. I will therefore say little, but yet say this: that backwardness appears in all things but the approach of winter. That jogs on apace.

To Robert Cary and Company, September 20, 1765 (Excerpt)

The Stamp Act, imposed on the colonies by the Parliament of Great Britain, engrosses the conversation of the speculative part of the colonists, who look upon this unconstitutional method of taxation as a direful attack upon their liberties, and loudly exclaim against the violation. What may be the result of this (I think I may add) ill-judged measure, and the late restrictions of our trade and other acts to burden us, I will not undertake to determine. But this I think may be said: that the advantages accruing to the mother country will fall far short of the expectations of the ministry. For certain it is that the whole produce of our labor hitherto has centered in Great Britain—what more can they desire?—and that all taxes which contribute to lessen our importation of British goods must be hurtful to the manufacturers of them, and to the common weal. The eyes of our people (already beginning to open) will perceive that many of the luxuries which we have heretofore lavished our substance to Great Britain for can well be dispensed with, whilst the necessaries of life are to be procured (for the most part) within ourselves. This consequently will introduce frugality and be a necessary stimulation to industry. Great Britain may then load her exports with as heavy taxes as she pleases, but where will the consumption be? I am apt to think no law or usage can compel us to barter our money or staple commodities for their manufacturies, if we can be supplied within ourselves upon the better terms. Nor will her traders dispose of them without a valuable consideration and surety of pay. Where then lies the utility of these measures?

As to the Stamp Act taken in a single and distinct view, one, and the first, bad consequence attending of it I take to be this: our courts of judicature will be shut up, it being morally impossible under our present circumstances that the act of Parliament can be complied with, were we ever so willing to enforce the execution; for not to say, which alone would be sufficient, that there is not money to pay the stamps, there are many other cogent reasons to prevent it. And if a stop be put to our judicial proceedings, it may be left to yourselves, who have such large demands upon the colonies, to determine, who is to suffer most in this event: the merchant or the planter.

To Robert Cary and Company, July 21, 1766 (Excerpt)

The repeal of the Stamp Act, to whatsoever causes owing, ought much to be rejoiced at; for, had the Parliament of Great Britain resolved upon enforcing it, the consequences, I conceive, would have been more direful than is generally apprehended, both to the mother country and her colonies. All, therefore, who were instrumental in procuring the repeal are entitled to the thanks of every British subject and have mine cordially. I am Gentn Yr Most Obedt Hble Servt

                                                            Go: Washington

To Capel and Osgood Hanbury, July 25, 1767 (Excerpt)

Unseasonable as it may be to take any notice of the repeal of the Stamp Act at this time, yet I cannot help observing that a contrary measure would have introduced very unhappy consequences. Those, therefore, who wisely foresaw this, and were instrumental in procuring the repeal of it, are, in my opinion, deservedly entitled to the thanks of the well-wishers to Britain and her colonies, and must reflect with pleasure that, through their means, many scenes of confusion and distress have been avoided. Mine they accordingly have, and always shall have, for their opposition to any act of oppression; for that act could be looked upon in no other light by every person who would view it in its proper colors. I could wish it was in my power to congratulate you with success in having the commercial system of these colonies put upon a more enlarged and extensive footing than it is, because I am well satisfied that it would, ultimately, redound to the advantages of the mother country, so long as the colonies pursue trade and agriculture, and would be an effectual let to manufacturing among themselves. The money, therefore, which they raise would center in Great Britain, as certain as the needle will settle to the poles. I am Gentn Yr Most Obedt Hble Servt

Go: Washington

To George Mason, April 5, 1769 (Excerpt)

At a time when our lordly masters in Great Britain will be satisfied with nothing less than the deprivation of American freedom, it seems highly necessary that something should be done to avert the stroke and maintain the liberty which we have derived from our ancestors. But the manner of doing it to answer the purpose effectually is the point in question.

That no man should scruple, or hesitate a moment, to use arms in defense of so valuable a blessing, on which all the good and evil of life depends, is clearly my opinion. Yet arms, I would beg leave to add, should be the last resource, the dernier resort. Addresses to the throne, and remonstrances to Parliament, we have already, it is said, proved the inefficacy of. How far, then, their attention to our rights and privileges is to be awakened or alarmed by starving their trade and manufactures remains to be tried.

The northern colonies, it appears, are endeavoring to adopt this scheme. In my opinion it is a good one, and must be attended with salutary effects, provided it can be carried pretty generally into execution. But how far it is practicable to do so I will not take upon me to determine. That there will be difficulties attending the execution of it everywhere, from clashing interests and selfish, designing men (ever attentive to their own gain, and watchful of every turn that can assist their lucrative views, in preference to any other consideration) cannot be denied. But in the tobacco colonies, where the trade is so diffused, and in a manner wholly conducted by factors for their principals at home, these difficulties are certainly enhanced, but I think not insurmountably increased, if the gentlemen in their several counties would be at some pains to explain matters to the people, and stimulate them to a cordial agreement to purchase none but certain enumerated articles out of any of the stores after such a period, nor import nor purchase any themselves. This, if it did not effectually withdraw the factors from their importations, would at least make them extremely cautious in doing it, as the prohibited goods could be vended to none but the non-associater, or those who would pay no regard to their association, both of whom ought to be stigmatized, and made the objects of public reproach.

The more I consider a scheme of this sort, the more ardently I wish success to it, because I think there are private as well as public advantages to result from it—the former certain, however precarious the other may prove. For, in respect to the latter, I have always thought that by virtue of the same power (for here alone the authority derives) which assumes the right of taxation, they may attempt at least[4] to restrain our manufactories, especially those of a public nature—the same equity and justice prevailing in the one case as the other, it being no greater hardship to forbid my manufacturing than it is to order me to buy goods of them loaded with duties, for the express purpose of raising a revenue. But as a measure of this sort will be an additional exertion of arbitrary power, we cannot be worsted, I think, in putting it to the test. On the other hand, that the colonies are considerably indebted to Great Britain is a truth universally acknowledged. That many families are reduced—almost, if not quite—to penury and want, from the low ebb of their fortunes, and estates daily selling for the discharge of debts, the public papers furnish but too many melancholy proofs of. And that a scheme of this sort will contribute more effectually than any other I can devise to emerge the country from the distress it at present labors under, I do most firmly believe, if it can be generally adopted. And I can see but one set of people (the merchants excepted) who will not, or ought not, to wish well to the scheme, and that is those who live genteelly and hospitably on clear estates. Such as these were they—not to consider the valuable object in view, and the good of others—might think it hard to be curtailed in their living and enjoyments. For as to the penurious man, he saves his money, and he saves his credit, having the best plea for doing that, which before perhaps he had the most violent struggles to refrain from doing. The extravagant and expensive man has the same good plea to retrench his expenses. He is thereby furnished with a pretext to live within bounds, and embraces it. Prudence dictated economy to him before, but his resolution was too weak to put it in practice; for how can I, says he, who have lived in such and such a manner change my method? I am ashamed to do it. And besides, such an alteration in the system of my living will create suspicions of a decay in my fortune, and such a thought the world must not harbor. I will even continue my course, till at last the course discontinues the estate, a sale of it being the consequence of his perseverance in error. This, I am satisfied, is the way that many who have set out in the wrong track have reasoned, till ruin stares them in the face. And in respect to the poor and needy man, he is only left in the same situation he was found—better I might say, because as he judges from comparison, his condition is amended in proportion as it approaches nearer to those above him.

Upon the whole, therefore, I think the scheme a good one, and that it ought to be tried here, with such alterations as the exigency of our circumstances render absolutely necessary; but how, and in what manner to begin the work, is a matter worthy of consideration. And whether it can be attempted with propriety, or efficacy (further than a communication of sentiments to one another) before May, when the Court and Assembly will meet together in Williamsburg, and a uniform plan can be concerted, and sent into the different counties to operate at the same time, and in the same manner everywhere, is a thing I am somewhat in doubt upon, and should be glad to know your opinion of. I am Dr Sir Your most Obt humble Servant

G: Washington

To Robert Cary and Company, July 25, 1769 (Excerpt)

Gentlemen,

Enclosed you will receive invoices of goods wanted for myself and Master Custis for this place and our plantations on York River, as also for Miss Custis, which I beg may be sent by Captain Johnstoun if the orders get to hand in time—if not, by any other vessel bound to this river. But if there are any articles contained in either of the respective invoices (paper only excepted) which are taxed by act of Parliament for the purpose of raising a revenue in America, it is my express desire and request that they may not be sent, as I have very heartily entered into an association (copies of which I make no doubt you have seen, otherwise I should have enclosed one) not to import any article which now is, or hereafter shall be, taxed for this purpose, until the said act or acts are repealed. I am therefore particular in mentioning this matter, as I am fully determined to adhere religiously to it, and may perhaps have written[5] for some things unwittingly which may be under these circumstances.

To Burwell Bassett, April 20, 1773 (Excerpt)

Dear Sir,

The interruption of the post for several weeks prevented our receiving the melancholy account of your loss till within these few days. That we sympathize in the misfortune and lament the decree which has deprived you of so dutiful a child, and the world of so promising a young lady, stands in no need, I hope, of argument to prove. But the ways of Providence being inscrutable, and the justice of it not to be scanned by the shallow eye of humanity, nor to be counteracted by the utmost efforts of human power or wisdom, resignation, and, as far as the strength of our reason and religion can carry us, a cheerful acquiescence to the divine will is what we are to aim at. And I am persuaded that your own good sense will arm you with fortitude to withstand the stroke, great as it is, and enable you to console Mrs. Bassett, whose loss, and feelings upon the occasion, are much to be pitied.

To Burwell Bassett, June 20, 1773

Dear Sir,

It is an easier matter to conceive than to describe the distress of this family, especially that of the unhappy parent of our dear Patcy Custis, when I inform you that yesterday removed the sweet, innocent girl into a more happy and peaceful abode than any she has met with in the afflicted path she hitherto has trod.

She rose from dinner about four o'clock, in better health and spirits than she appeared to have been in for some time, soon after which she was seized with one of her usual fits, and expired in it in less than two minutes, without uttering a word, a groan, or scarce a sigh. This sudden and unexpected blow, I scarce need add, has almost reduced my poor wife to the lowest ebb of misery, which is increased by the absence of her son (whom I have just fixed at the college in New York, from whence I returned the 8th instant) and want of the balmy consolation of her relations—which leads me more than ever to wish she could see them, and that I was master of arguments powerful enough to prevail upon Mrs. Dandridge to make this place her entire and absolute home. I should think, as she lives a lonesome life (Betcy being married), it might suit her well, and be agreeable both to herself and my wife. To me most assuredly it would.

I do not purpose to add more at present, the end of my writing being only to inform you of this unhappy change. Our sincere affections are offered to Mrs. Bassett, Mrs. Dandridge, and all other friends, and I am very sincerely Yr Obedt & Affecte Hble St

Go: Washington

To George William Fairfax, June 10, 1774 (Excerpt)

Our assembly met at this place the 4th ultimo, according to prorogation, and was dissolved the 26th for entering into a resolve, of which the enclosed is a copy, and which the governor thought reflected too much upon His Majesty and the British Parliament to pass over unnoticed. This dissolution was as sudden as unexpected, for there were other resolves of a much more spirited nature ready to be offered to the house, which would have been adopted respecting the Boston Port Bill, as it is called, but were withheld till the important business of the country could be gone through. As the case stands the assembly sat the 22 days for nothing—not a bill being passed, the Council being adjourned from the rising of the Court to the day of the dissolution and came either to advise or in opposition to the measure. The day after this event the members convened themselves at the Raleigh Tavern and entered into the enclosed association, which, being followed two days after by an express from Boston, accompanied by the sentiments of some meetings in our sister colonies to the northward, the proceedings mentioned in the enclosed papers were had thereupon and a general meeting requested of all the late representatives in this city on the first of August, when it is hoped and expected that some vigorous measures will be effectually adopted to obtain that justice which is denied to our petitions and remonstrances. In short, the ministry may rely on it that Americans will never be taxed without their own consent, that the cause of Boston (the despotic measures in respect to it I mean) now is and ever will be considered as the cause of America (not that we approve their conduct in destroying the tea), and that we shall not suffer ourselves to be sacrificed by piecemeal—though God only knows what is to become of us, threatened as we are with so many hovering evils as hang over us at present, having a cruel and bloodthirsty enemy upon our backs, the Indians, between whom and our frontier inhabitants many skirmishes have happened, and with whom a general war is inevitable, whilst those from whom we have a right to seek protection are endeavoring by every piece of art and despotism to fix the shackles of slavery upon us. This dissolution, which it is said and believed will not be followed by an election till instructions are received from the ministry, has left us without the means of defense, except under the old militia and invasion laws, which are by no means adequate to the exigencies of the country; for, from the best accounts we have been able to get, there is a confederacy of the western and southern Indians formed against us and our settlement over the Allegheny Mountains. Indeed, Hampshire, Augusta, etc. are in the utmost consternation and distress. In short, since the first settlement of this colony, the minds of people in it never were more disturbed or our situation so critical as at present—arising, as I have said before, from an invasion of our rights and privileges by the mother country, and our lives and properties by the savages, whilst a cruel frost, succeeded by as cruel a drought, hath contributed not a little to our unhappy situation, though it is now thought the injury done to wheat by the frost is not so great as was at first apprehended—the present opinion being that take the country through half crops will be made. To these may be added—and a matter of no small moment they are—that a total stop is now put to our courts of justice (for want of a fee bill, which expired the 12th of April last, and the want of circulating cash amongst us); for shameful it is that the meeting of merchants, which ought to have been at this place the 25th of April, never happened till about ten days ago; and I believe will break up in a manner very dissatisfactory to everyone, if not injurious to their characters.

To Bryan Fairfax, July 4, 1774 (Excerpt)

As to your political sentiments, I would heartily join you in them, so far as relates to a humble and dutiful petition to the throne, provided there was the most distant hope of success. But have we not tried this already? Have we not addressed the Lords and remonstrated to the Commons? And to what end? Did they deign to look at our petitions? Does it not appear, as clear as the sun in its meridian brightness, that there is a regular, systematic plan formed to fix the right and practice of taxation upon us? Does not the uniform conduct of Parliament for some years past confirm this? Do not all the debates, especially those just brought to us, in the House of Commons, on the side of government, expressly declare that America must be taxed in aid of the British funds, and that she has no longer resources within herself? Is there anything to be expected from petitioning after this? Is not the attack upon the liberty and property of the people of Boston, before restitution of the loss to the India Company was demanded, a plain and self-evident proof of what they are aiming at? Do not the subsequent bills (now, I dare say, acts) for depriving the Massachusetts Bay of its charter, and for transporting offenders into other colonies or to Great Britain for trial, where it is impossible from the nature of the thing that justice can be obtained, convince us that the administration is determined to stick at nothing to carry its point? Ought we not, then, to put our virtue and fortitude to the severest test?

With you I think it a folly to attempt more than we can execute, as that will not only bring disgrace upon us, but weaken our cause; yet I think we may do more than is generally believed, in respect to the non-importation scheme. As to the withholding of our remittances, that is another point, in which I own I have my doubts on several accounts, but principally on that of justice; for I think, whilst we are accusing others of injustice, we should be just ourselves. And how this can be whilst we owe a considerable debt, and refuse payment of it to Great Britain, is to me inconceivable. Nothing but the last extremity, I think, can justify it. Whether this is now come is the question.

To Bryan Fairfax, July 20, 1774 (Excerpt)

That I differ very widely from you in respect to the mode of obtaining a repeal of the acts so much and so justly complained of, I shall not hesitate to acknowledge. And that this difference in opinion may probably proceed from the different constructions we put upon the conduct and intention of the ministry may also be true. But as I see nothing, on the one hand, to induce a belief that the Parliament would embrace a favorable opportunity of repealing acts which they go on with great rapidity to pass, in order to enforce their tyrannical system, and, on the other, observe, or think I observe, that government is pursuing a regular plan, at the expense of law and justice, to overthrow our constitutional rights and liberties, how can I expect any redress from a measure which hath been ineffectually tried already? For sir, what is it we are contending against? Is it against paying the duty of 3d. per lb. on tea because burdensome? No, it is the right only we have all along disputed, and to this end we have already petitioned His Majesty in as humble and dutiful a manner as subjects could do. Nay more, we applied to the House of Lords and House of Commons in their different legislative capacities, setting forth that, as Englishmen, we could not be deprived of this essential and valuable part of our constitution. If, then (as the fact really is), it is against the right of taxation we now do and (as I before said) all along have contended, why should they suppose an exertion of this power would be less obnoxious now than formerly? And what reasons have we to believe that they would make a second attempt whilst the same sentiments filled the breast of every American, if they did not intend to enforce it if possible? The conduct of the Boston people could not justify the rigor of their measures, unless there had been a requisition of payment and refusal of it. Nor did that measure require an act to deprive the Government of Massachusetts Bay of their charter, or to exempt offenders from trial in the place where offenses were committed, as there was not, nor could not be, a single instance produced to manifest the necessity of it. Are not all these things self-evident proofs of a fixed and uniform plan to tax us? If we want further proofs, do not all the debates in the House of Commons serve to confirm this? And hath not General Gage's conduct since his arrival (in stopping the address of his council, and publishing a proclamation more becoming a Turkish bashaw than an English governor, and declaring it treason to associate in any manner by which the commerce of Great Britain is to be affected) exhibited unexampled testimony of the most despotic system of tyranny that ever was practiced in a free government? In short, what further proofs are wanting to satisfy one of the designs of the ministry than their own acts, which are uniform and plainly tending to the same point: nay, if I mistake not, avowedly to fix the right of taxation. What hope, then, from petitioning, when they tell us that now or never is the time to fix the matter? Shall we after this whine and cry for relief, when we have already tried it in vain? Or shall we supinely sit and see one province after another fall a sacrifice to despotism? If I was in any doubt as to the right which the Parliament of Great Britain had to tax us without our consents, I should most heartily coincide with you in opinion that to petition, and petition only, is the proper method to apply for relief, because we should then be asking a favor, and not claiming a right, which by the law of nature and our constitution we are, in my opinion, indubitably entitled to. I should even think it criminal to go further than this, under such an idea; but none such I have. I think the Parliament of Great Britain hath no more right to put their hands into my pocket, without my consent, than I have to put my hands into yours for money. And this being already urged to them in a firm but decent manner by all the colonies, what reason is there to expect anything from their justice?

As to the resolution for addressing the throne, I own to you, sir, I think the whole might as well have been expunged. I expect nothing from the measure. Nor should my voice have accompanied it, if the non-importation scheme was intended to be retarded by it; for I am convinced, as much as I am of my existence, that there is no relief for us but in their distress. And I think, at least I hope, that there is public virtue enough left among us to deny ourselves everything but the bare necessaries of life to accomplish this end. This we have a right to do, and no power upon earth can compel us to do otherwise, till they have first reduced us to the most abject state of slavery that ever was designed for mankind. The stopping our exports would, no doubt, be a shorter cut than the other to effect this purpose; but if we owe money to Great Britain, nothing but the last necessity can justify the non-payment of it. And therefore I have great doubts upon this head, and wish to see the other method, which is legal, and will facilitate these payments, first tried.

I cannot conclude without expressing some concern that I should differ so widely in sentiments from you in a matter of such great moment and general import, and should much distrust my own judgment upon the occasion, if my nature did not recoil at the thought of submitting to measures which I think subversive of everything that I ought to hold dear and valuable—and did I not find, at the same time, that the voice of mankind is with me. I must apologize for sending you so rough a sketch of my thoughts upon your letter. When I looked back and saw the length of my own, I could not, as I am also a good deal hurried at this time, bear the thoughts of making off a fair copy. I am Dr Sir Yr Most Obedt Humble Servt

Go: Washington

To Bryan Fairfax, August 24, 1774 (Excerpt)

In truth, persuaded as I am that you have read all the political pieces which compose a large share of the gazettes at this time, I should think it, but for your request, a piece of inexcusable arrogance in me to make the least essay towards a change in your political opinions. For I am sure I have no new lights to throw upon the subject, or any arguments to offer in support of my own doctrine, than what you have seen, and could only in general add that an innate spirit of freedom first told me that the measures which administration hath for some time been, and now are, most violently pursuing, are repugnant to every principle of natural justice, whilst much abler heads than my own hath fully convinced me that it is not only repugnant to natural right, but subversive of the laws and constitution of Great Britain itself, in the establishment of which some of the best blood in the kingdom hath been spilt. Satisfied, then, that the acts of a British Parliament are no longer governed by the principles of justice, that it is trampling upon the valuable rights of Americans, confirmed to them by charter and the constitution they themselves boast of, and convinced beyond the smallest doubt that these measures are the result of deliberation, and attempted to be carried into execution by the hand of power, is it a time to trifle, or risk our cause upon petitions which with difficulty obtain access, and afterwards are thrown by with the utmost contempt? Or should we, because heretofore unsuspicious of design and then unwilling to enter into disputes with the mother country, go on to bear more, and forbear to enumerate our just causes of complaint? For my own part, I shall not undertake to say where the line between Great Britain and the colonies should be drawn, but I am clearly of opinion that one ought to be drawn and our rights clearly ascertained. I could wish, I own, that the dispute had been left to posterity to determine, but the crisis is arrived when we must assert our rights or submit to every imposition that can be heaped upon us, till custom and use will make us as tame and abject slaves as the blacks we rule over with such arbitrary sway.

I intended to have written[6] no more than an apology for not writing, but find I am insensibly running into a length I did not expect, and therefore shall conclude with remarking that if you disavow the right of Parliament to tax us (unrepresented as we are) we only differ in respect to the mode of opposition. And this difference principally arises from your belief that they (the Parliament, I mean) want a decent opportunity to repeal the acts, whilst

I am as fully convinced as I am of my existence that there has been a regular, systematic plan formed to enforce them, and that nothing but unanimity in the colonies (a stroke they did not expect) and firmness can prevent it. It seems, from the best advices from Boston, that General Gage is exceedingly disconcerted at the quiet and steady conduct of the people of the Massachusetts Bay, and at the measures pursued by the other governments, as I dare say he expected to have forced those oppressed people into compliance, or irritated them to acts of violence before this, for a more colorable pretense of ruling that and the other colonies with a high hand.

To Robert McKenzie, October 9, 1774 (Excerpt)

Dear Sir,

Your letter of the 13th ultimo from Boston gave me pleasure, as I learnt thereby that you were well and might be expected at Mount Vernon in your way to or from James River, in the course of the winter.

When I have said this, permit me with the freedom of a friend (for you know I always esteemed you) to express my sorrow at fortune's placing you in a service that must fix curses to latest posterity upon the diabolical contrivers; and if success (which by the by is impossible) accompanies it, execrations upon all those who have been instrumental in the execution.

I do not mean by this to insinuate that an officer is not to discharge his duty, even when chance, not choice, has placed him in a disagreeable situation. But I conceive when you condemn the conduct of the Massachusetts people, you reason from effects, not causes. Otherwise you would not wonder at a people who are every day receiving fresh proofs of a systematic assertion of an arbitrary power, deeply planned to overturn the laws and constitution of their country, and to violate the most essential and valuable rights of mankind, being irritated and with difficulty restrained from acts of the greatest violence and intemperance. For my own part I confess to you candidly that I view things in a very different point of light to the one in which you seem to consider them, and though you are led to believe by venal men (for such I must take the liberty of calling those new-fangled counsellors which fly to and surround you, and all others who for honorary or pecuniary gratifications will lend their aid to overturn the constitution and introduce a system of arbitrary government)—although you are taught, I say, by discoursing with such men, to believe that the people of Massachusetts are rebellious, setting up for independency, and what not, give me leave, my good friend, to tell you that you are abused, grossly abused. And this I advance with a degree of confidence and boldness which may claim your belief, having better opportunities of knowing the real sentiments of the people you are among, from the leaders of them in opposition to the present measures of administration, than you have from those whose business it is not to disclose truths but to misrepresent facts in order to justify as much as possible to the world their own conduct. For give me leave to add, and I think I can announce it as a fact, that it is not the wish or the interest of the government, or any other upon this continent, separately or collectively, to set up for independence. But this you may at the same time rely on, that none of them will ever submit to the loss of those valuable rights and privileges which are essential to the happiness of every free state, and without which life, liberty, and property are rendered totally insecure.

These, sir, being certain consequences which must naturally result from the late acts of Parliament relative to America in general, and the Government of Massachusetts Bay in particular, is it to be wondered at, I repeat, that men who wish to avert the impending blow should attempt to oppose it in its progress, or perhaps for their defense, if it cannot be diverted? Surely I may be allowed to answer in the negative. And give me leave to add, as my opinion, that more blood will be spilt on this occasion (if the ministry are determined to push matters to extremity) than history has ever yet furnished instances of in the annals of North America, and such a vital wound given to the peace of this great country as time itself cannot cure or eradicate the remembrance of. But I have done. I was involuntarily led into a short discussion of this subject by your remarks on the conduct of the Boston people, and your opinion of their wishes to set up for independency. I am well satisfied, as I can be of my existence, that no such thing is desired by any thinking man in all North America—on the contrary, that it is the ardent wish of the warmest advocates for liberty, that peace and tranquility, upon constitutional grounds, may be restored, and the horrors of civil discord prevented.

To John Connolly, February 25, 1775

Dear Sir,

Your servant, on his return from Williamsburg, affords me occasion to answer your polite letter. I confess the state of affairs is sufficiently alarming, which our critical situation with regard to the Indians does not diminish. But as you have written[7] to Lord Dunmore relative to the prisoners under your charge, there can be no doubt of His Lordship's having now transmitted you the necessary directions on that subject. I have only to express my most ardent wishes that every measure, consistent with reason and sound policy, may be adopted to keep those people, at this time, in good humor; for another rupture would not only ruin the external but internal parts of this government. If the journal of your proceedings in the Indian war is to be published, I shall have an opportunity of seeing what I have long coveted. With us here, things wear a disagreeable aspect; and the minds of men are exceedingly disturbed at the measures of the British government. The King's Speech and Address of both houses prognosticate nothing favorable to us; but by some subsequent proceedings thereto, *as well as by private letters from London*, there is reason to believe the ministry would willingly change their ground, from a conviction that forcible measures will be inadequate to the end designed. A little time must now unfold the mystery, as matters are drawing to a point. I am, dear sir, your friend, and most obedient humble servant,

G. Washington

To George William Fairfax, May 31, 1775 (Excerpt)

Before this letter can reach you, you must undoubtedly have received an account of the engagement in the Massachusetts Bay between the ministerial troops (for we do not, nor cannot yet, prevail upon ourselves to call them the king's troops) and the provincials of that government. But as you may not have heard how that affair began, I enclose you the several affidavits that were taken after the action.

General Gage acknowledges that the detachment under Lieutenant Colonel Smith was sent out to destroy private property, or, in other words, to destroy a magazine which self-preservation obliged the inhabitants to establish. And he also confesses, in effect at least, that his men made a very precipitate retreat from Concord, notwithstanding the reinforcement under Lord Piercy, the last of which may serve to convince Lord Sandwich (and others of the same sentiment) that the Americans will fight for their liberties and property, however pusillanimous, in His Lordship's eye, they may appear in other respects.

From the best accounts I have been able to collect of that affair—indeed, from everyone—I believe the fact, stripped of all coloring, to be plainly this: that if the retreat had not been as precipitate as it was (and God knows it could not well have been more so) the ministerial troops must have surrendered or been totally cut off. For they had not arrived in Charlestown (under cover of their ships) half an hour before a powerful body of men from Marblehead and Salem were at their heels, and must, if they had happened to have been up one hour sooner, inevitably intercepted their retreat to Charlestown. Unhappy it is, though, to reflect that a brother's sword has been sheathed in a brother's breast, and that the once happy and peaceful plains of America are either to be drenched with blood or inhabited by slaves. Sad alternative! But can a virtuous man hesitate in his choice? I am, with sincere regard and affectionate compliments to Mrs. Fairfax, Dear Sir, Your Most obt servant,

G. Washington

Explanatory Notes

1 The Indian name Conotocarious, meaning "town taker" or "devourer of villages," had been bestowed on George Washington by the Half-King in 1753.

2 It is possible that Washington here intended "anyone's." Since this alternate reading is uncertain, however, we have left the text as it is.
3 We have added this word, which Washington had omitted.
4 Washington may have intended "at last" here. In other words, he is expressing the concern that *in the end* the British will use the asserted power of taxation as a means of restraining American manufacturing. It is, however, difficult to be certain of this alternate reading.
5 Corrected from Washington's "wrote."
6 Corrected from Washington's "wrote."
7 Corrected from Washington's "wrote."

Fig. 2 Part II: Commander-in-Chief: 1775–1778
www.gettyimages.com/detail/illustration/painting-of-general-george-washington-at-the-royalty-free-illustration/594381295?adppopup=true

PART II

Commander-in-Chief: 1775–1778

Address to the Continental Congress, June 16, 1775

The president informed Colonel Washington that the Congress had yesterday unanimously made choice of him to be general and commander-in-chief of the American forces, and requested he would accept of that appointment; whereupon Colonel Washington, standing in his place, spake as follows:

"Mr. President, though I am truly sensible of the high honor done me in this appointment, yet I feel great distress, from a consciousness that my abilities and military experience may not be equal to the extensive and important trust. However, as the Congress desire it, I will enter upon the momentous duty and exert every power I possess in their service and for the support of the glorious cause. I beg they will accept my most cordial thanks for this distinguished testimony of their approbation.

"But lest some unlucky event should happen unfavorable to my reputation, I beg it may be remembered by every gentleman in the room that I this day declare, with the utmost sincerity, I do not think myself equal to the command I am honored with.

"As to pay, sir, I beg leave to assure the Congress that, as no pecuniary consideration could have tempted me to have accepted this arduous employment at the expense of my domestic ease and happiness, I do not wish to make any profit from it. I will keep an exact account of my expenses. Those I doubt not they will discharge, and that is all I desire."

To Martha Washington, June 18, 1775 (Excerpt)

My Dearest,

I am now set down to write to you on a subject which fills me with inexpressible concern—and this concern is greatly aggravated and increased when I reflect on the uneasiness I know it will give you. It has been determined in Congress that the whole army raised for the defense of the American cause shall be put under my care, and that it is necessary for me to proceed immediately to Boston to take upon me the command of it. You may believe me, my dear Patcy, when I assure you in the most solemn manner that, so far from seeking this appointment I have used every endeavor in my power to avoid it, not only from my unwillingness to part with you and the family, but from a consciousness of its being a trust too great for my capacity, and that I should enjoy more real happiness and felicity in one month with you, at home, than I have the most distant prospect of reaping abroad, if my stay was to be seven times seven years. But, as it has been a kind of destiny that has thrown me upon this service, I shall hope that my undertaking of it is designed to answer some good purpose. You might, and I suppose did, perceive from the tenor of my letters that I was apprehensive I could not avoid this appointment, as I did not even pretend to intimate when I should return. That was the case. It was utterly out of my power to refuse this appointment without exposing my character to such censures as would have reflected dishonor upon myself and given pain to my friends. This I am sure could not and ought not to be pleasing to you, and must have lessened me considerably in my own esteem. I shall rely, therefore, confidently on that Providence which has heretofore preserved and been bountiful to me, not doubting but that I shall return safe to you in the fall. I shall feel no pain from the toil or the danger of the campaign. My unhappiness will flow from the uneasiness I know you will feel at being left alone. I therefore beg of you to summon your whole fortitude and resolution, and pass your time as agreeably as possible. Nothing will give me so much sincere satisfaction as to hear this, and to hear it from your own pen.

If it should be your desire to remove into Alexandria (as you once mentioned upon an occasion of this sort), I am quite pleased that you should put it in practice; and Lund Washington may be directed by you to build a kitchen and other houses there proper for your reception. If, on the other hand, you should rather incline to spend a good part of your time among your friends below, I wish you to do so. In short, my earnest and ardent desire is that you would pursue any plan that is most likely to produce content and a tolerable degree of tranquility, as it must add greatly to my uneasy feelings to hear that you are dissatisfied and complaining at what I really could not avoid.

As life is always uncertain, and common prudence dictates to every man the necessity of settling his temporal concerns whilst it is in his power, and whilst the mind is calm and undisturbed, I have, since I came to this place (for I had not time to do it before I left home) got Colonel Pendleton to draft a will for me by the directions which I gave him, which will I now enclose. The provision made for you, in case of my death, will, I hope, be agreeable. I have included the money for which I sold my own land (to Doctor Mercer) in the sum given you, as also all other debts. What I owe myself is very trifling, Cary's debt excepted, and that would not have been much if the bank stock had been applied without such difficulties as he made in the transference.

I shall add nothing more at present, as I have several letters to write, but to desire you will remember me to Milly and all friends, and to assure you that I am with most unfeigned regard, My dear Patcy, Yr Affecte

Go: Washington

To Burwell Bassett, June 19, 1775 (Excerpt)

Dear Sir,

I am now embarked on a tempestuous ocean from whence, perhaps, no friendly harbor is to be found. I have been called upon by the unanimous voice of the colonies to the command of the Continental Army. It is an honor I by no means aspired to. It is an honor I wished to avoid, as well from an unwillingness to quit the peaceful enjoyment of my family as from a thorough conviction of my own incapacity and want of experience in the conduct of so momentous a concern. But the partiality of the Congress, added to some political motives, left me without a choice. May God grant therefore that my acceptance of it may be attended with some good to the common cause, and without injury (from want of knowledge) to my own reputation. I can answer but for three things: a firm belief of the justice of our cause, close attention in the prosecution of it, and the strictest integrity. If these cannot supply the places of ability and experience, the cause will suffer, and more than probable my character along with it, as reputation derives its principal support from success. But it will be remembered, I hope, that no desire or insinuation of mine placed me in this situation. I shall not be deprived therefore of a comfort in the worst event if I retain a consciousness of having acted to the best of my judgment.

To John Parke Custis, June 19, 1775 (Excerpt)

Dear Jack,

I have been called upon by the unanimous voice of the colonies to take the command of the Continental Army. It is an honor I neither sought after, or was by any means fond of accepting, from a consciousness of my own inexperience and inability to discharge the duties of so important a trust. However, as the partiality of the Congress have placed me in this distinguished point of view, I can make them no other return but what will flow from close attention and an upright intention. For the rest I can say nothing. My great concern upon this occasion is the thoughts of leaving your mother under the uneasiness which I know this affair will throw her into. I therefore hope, expect, and indeed have no doubt of your using every means in your power to keep up her spirits by doing everything in your power to promote her quiet. I have, I must confess, very uneasy feelings on her account; but as it has been a kind of unavoidable necessity which has led me into this appointment, I shall more readily hope that success will attend it and crown our meetings with happiness.

At any time, I hope it is unnecessary for me to say, that I am always pleased with yours and Nelly's abidance at Mount Vernon, much less upon this occasion, when I think it absolutely necessary for the peace and satisfaction of your mother, consideration which I have no doubt will have due weight with you both and require no arguments to enforce.

To the Officers of the Five Virginia Independent Companies, June 20, 1775 (Excerpt)

Gentlemen,

I am now about to bid adieu to the companies under your respective commands, at least for a while. I have launched into a wide and extensive field, too boundless for my abilities, and far, very far, beyond my experience. I am called by the unanimous voice of the colonies to the command of the Continental Army: an honor I did not aspire to, an honor I was solicitous to avoid upon full conviction of my inadequacy to the importance of the service. The partiality of the Congress, however, assisted by a political motive, rendered my reasons unavailing; and I shall tomorrow set out for the camp near Boston. I have only to beg of you therefore (before I go—especially as you did me the honor to place your companies under my directions, and know not how soon you may be called upon in Virginia) for an exertion of your military skill, by no means to relax in the discipline of your respective companies.

To John Augustine Washington, June 20, 1775 (Excerpt)

Dear Brother,

I am now to bid adieu to you, and to every kind of domestic ease, for a while. I am embarked on a wide ocean, boundless in its prospect, and from whence, perhaps, no safe harbor is to be found. I have been called upon by the unanimous voice of the colonies to take the command of the Continental Army—an honor I neither sought after nor desired, as I am thoroughly convinced that it requires greater abilities, and much more experience, than I am master of to conduct a business so extensive in its nature, and arduous in the execution. But the partiality of the Congress, joined to a political motive, really left me without a choice; and I am now commissioned a general and commander-in-chief of all the forces now raised, or to be raised, for the defense of the United Colonies. That I may discharge the trust to the satisfaction of my employers is my first wish. That I shall aim to do it there remains as little doubt of. How far I may succeed is another point. But this I am sure of: that in the worse event I shall have the consolation of knowing (if I act to the best of my judgment) that the blame ought to lodge upon the appointers, not the appointed, as it was by no means a thing of my own seeking, or proceeding from any hint of my friends.

To Martha Washington, June 23, 1775

My Dearest,

As I am within a few minutes of leaving this city, I could not think of departing from it without dropping you a line, especially as I do not know whether it may be in my power to write again till I get to the camp at Boston. I go fully trusting in that Providence which has been more bountiful to me than I deserve, and in full confidence of a happy meeting with you sometime in the fall. I have not time to add more, as I am surrounded with company to take leave of me. I retain an unalterable affection for you, which neither time or distance can change. My best love to Jack and Nelly, and regard for the rest of the family concludes me with the utmost truth and sincerity. Yr entire

Go: Washington

To the New York Provincial Congress, June 26, 1775

Gentlemen,

At the same time that with you I deplore the unhappy necessity of such an appointment as that with which I am now honored, I cannot but feel sentiments of the highest gratitude for this affecting instance of distinction and regard.

May your warmest wish be realized in the success of America at this important and interesting period; and be assured that every exertion of my worthy colleagues and myself will be equally extended to the re-establishment of peace and harmony between the mother country and the colonies. As to the fatal but necessary operations of war: when we assumed the soldier, we did not lay aside the citizen, and we shall most sincerely rejoice with you in that happy hour, when the establishment of American liberty, on the most firm and solid foundations, shall enable us to return to our private stations in the bosom of a free, peaceful, and happy country.

Go: Washington

General Orders, July 4, 1775 (Excerpt)

The Continental Congress, having now taken all the troops of the several colonies which have been raised, or which may be hereafter raised, for the support and defense of the liberties of America, into their pay and service, they are now the troops of the United Provinces of North America. And it is hoped that all distinctions of colonies will be laid aside, so that one and the same spirit may animate the whole, and the only contest be who shall render, on this great and trying occasion, the most essential service to the great and common cause in which we are all engaged.

It is required and expected that exact discipline be observed and due subordination prevail through the whole army, as a failure in these most essential points must necessarily produce extreme hazard, disorder, and confusion, and end in shameful disappointment and disgrace.

The general most earnestly requires and expects a due observance of those articles of war established for the government of the army, which forbid profane cursing, swearing, and drunkenness; and in like manner requires and expects of all officers and soldiers not engaged on actual duty a punctual attendance on divine service, to implore the blessings of Heaven upon the means used for our safety and defense.

All officers are required and expected to pay diligent attention, to keep their men neat and clean, to visit them often at their quarters, and inculcate upon them the necessity of cleanliness, as essential to their health and service. They are particularly to see that they have straw to lay on, if to be had, and to make it known if they are destitute of this article. They are also to take care that necessaries be provided in the camps and frequently filled up to prevent their being offensive and unhealthy. Proper notice will be taken of such officers and men as distinguish themselves by their attention to these necessary duties.

To the Massachusetts Provincial Congress, c. July 4, 1775

Gentlemen,

Your kind congratulations on my appointment and arrival demand my warmest acknowledgments and will ever be retained in grateful remembrance.

In exchanging the enjoyments of domestic life for the duties of my present honorable but arduous station, I only emulate the virtue and public spirit of the whole Province of Massachusetts Bay, which, with a firmness and patriotism without example in modern history, has sacrificed all the comforts of social and political life in support of the rights of mankind and the welfare of our common country. My highest ambition is to be the happy instrument of vindicating those rights and to see this devoted province again restored to peace, liberty, and safety.

The short space of time which has elapsed since my arrival does not permit me to decide upon the state of the army. The course of human affairs forbids an expectation that troops formed under such circumstances should at once possess the order, regularity, and discipline of veterans. Whatever deficiencies there may be will, I doubt not, soon be made up by the activity and zeal of the officers, and the docility and obedience of the men. These qualities, united with their native bravery and spirit, will afford a happy presage of success, and put a final period to those distresses which now overwhelm this once happy country.

I most sincerely thank you, gentlemen, for your declarations of readiness at all times to assist me in the discharge of the duties of my station. They are so complicated and extended that I shall need the assistance of every good man and lover of his country. I therefore repose the utmost confidence in your aids. In return for your affectionate wishes to myself, permit me to say that I earnestly implore that Divine Being, in whose hands are all human events, to make you and your constituents as distinguished in private and public happiness, as you have been by ministerial oppression, by private and public distress.

General Orders, July 5, 1775 (Excerpt)

The general most earnestly recommends and requires of all the officers that they be exceeding diligent and strict in preventing all invasions and abuse of private property, in their quarters or elsewhere. He hopes, and indeed flatters himself, that every private soldier will detest and abhor such practices, when he considers that it is for the preservation of his own rights, liberty, and property, and those of his fellow countrymen, that he is now called into service; that it is unmanly, and sullies the dignity of the great cause in which we are all engaged, to violate that property he is called to protect; and especially that it is most cruel and inconsistent thus to add to the distresses of those of their countrymen who are suffering under the iron hand of oppression.

General Orders, July 7, 1775 (Excerpt)

It is with inexpressible concern that the general, upon his first arrival in the army, should find an officer sentenced by a general court martial to be cashiered for cowardice—a crime, of all others, the most infamous in a soldier, the most injurious to an army, and the last to be forgiven, inasmuch as it may, and often does, happen that the cowardice of a single officer may prove the destruction of the whole army. The general therefore (though with great concern, and more especially as the transaction happened before he had the command of the troops) thinks himself obliged for the good of the service to approve the judgment of the court martial with respect to Captain John Callender, who is hereby sentenced to be cashiered. Captain John Callender is accordingly cashiered and dismissed from all farther service in the Continental Army as an officer.

The general, having made all due inquiries and maturely considered this matter, is led to the above determination not only from the particular guilt of Captain Callender, but the fatal consequences of such conduct to the army and to the cause of America.

He now therefore most earnestly exhorts officers of all ranks to show an example of bravery and courage to their men, assuring them that such as do their duty in the day of battle, as brave and good officers, shall be honored with every mark of distinction and regard, their names and merits made known to the General Congress and all America; while, on the other hand, he positively declares that every officer, be his rank what it may, who shall betray his country, dishonor the army and his general, by basely keeping back and shrinking from his duty in any engagement, shall be held up as an infamous coward, and punished as such with the utmost martial severity; and no connections, interest, or intercessions in his behalf will avail to prevent the strict execution of justice.

General Orders, July 16, 1775 (Excerpt)

The Continental Congress having earnestly recommended that "Thursday next, the 20th instant, be observed by the inhabitants of all the English colonies upon this continent as a day of public humiliation, fasting, and prayer, that they may with united hearts and voice unfeignedly confess their sins before God, and supplicate the all-wise and merciful disposer of events to avert the desolation and calamities of an unnatural war": The general orders that day to be religiously observed by the forces under his command, exactly in manner directed by the proclamation of the Continental Congress. It is therefore strictly enjoined on all officers and soldiers (not upon duty) to attend divine service at the accustomed places of worship, as well in the lines as the encampments and quarters. And it is expected that all those who go to worship do take their arms, ammunition, and accoutrements, and are prepared for immediate action if called upon. If, in the judgment of the officers, the works should appear to be in such forwardness as the utmost security of the camp requires, they will command their men to abstain from all labor upon that solemn day.

To Jonathan Trumbull, Sr., Governor of Connecticut, July 18, 1775

Sir,

Allow me to return you my sincerest thanks for the kind wishes and favorable sentiments expressed in yours of the 13th instant. It's the cause of our common country calls us both to an active and dangerous duty. I trust that Divine Providence, which wisely orders the affairs of men, will enable us to discharge it with fidelity and success. The uncorrupted choice of a brave and free people has raised you to deserved eminence. That the blessing of health, and the still greater blessing of long continuing to govern *such* a people, may be yours is the sincere wish of, Sir, Your Most Obedient very humble Servant

Go. Washington

To Brigadier General John Thomas, July 23, 1775

Sir,

The retirement of a general officer, possessing the confidence of his country and the army, at so critical a period, appears to me to be big with fatal consequences, both to the public cause and his own reputation. While it is unexecuted, I think it my duty to make this last effort to prevent it; and after suggesting those reasons which occur to me against your resignation, your own virtue and good sense must decide upon it. In the usual contests of empire and ambition the conscience of a soldier has so little share that he may very properly insist upon his claims of rank and extend his pretensions even to punctilio; but in such a cause as this, where the object is neither glory nor extent of territory, but a defense of all that is dear and valuable in life, surely every post ought to be deemed honorable in which a man can serve his country. What matter of triumph will it afford our enemies that in less than one month a spirit of discord should show itself in the highest ranks of the army, not to be extinguished by anything less than a total desertion of duty? How little reason shall we have to boast of American union and patriotism if at such a time, and in such a cause, smaller and partial considerations cannot give way to the great and general interest? These remarks can only affect you as a member of the great American body. But as an inhabitant of Massachusetts Bay, your own province and the other colonies have a peculiar and unquestionable claim to your services; and in my opinion you cannot refuse them without relinquishing in some degree that character for public virtue and honor which you have hitherto supported. If our cause is just, it ought to be supported; but where shall it find support if gentlemen of merit and experience, unable to conquer the prejudices of a competition, withdraw themselves in an hour of danger? I admit, sir, that your claim and services have not had due respect. It is by no means a singular case. Worthy men of all nations and countries have had reason to make the same complaint; but they did not for this abandon the public cause. They nobly stifled the dictates of resentment and made their enemies ashamed of their injustice. And can America show no such instances of magnanimity? For the sake of your bleeding country, your devoted province, your charter rights, and by the memory of those brave men who have already fallen[1] in this great cause, I conjure you to banish from your mind every suggestion of anger and disappointment.

Your country will do ample justice to your merits. They already do it, by the sorrow and regret expressed on the occasion; and the sacrifice you are called to make will, in the judgment of every good man and lover of his country, do you more real honor than the most distinguished victory.

You possess the confidence and affection of the troops of this province particularly. Many of them are not capable of judging the propriety and reasons of your conduct. Should they esteem themselves authorized by your example to leave the service, the consequences may be fatal and irretrievable. There is reason to fear it, from the personal attachments of the men to their officers, and the obligations that are supposed to arise from those attachments. But, sir, the other colonies have also their claims upon you, not only as a native of America, but an inhabitant of this province. They have made common cause with it. They have sacrificed their trade, loaded themselves with taxes, and are ready to spill their blood in vindication of the rights of Massachusetts Bay, while all the security and profit of a neutrality has been offered them. But no arts or temptations could seduce them from your side and leave you a prey to a cruel and perfidious ministry. Sure these reflections must have some weight with a mind as generous and considerate as yours.

How will you be able to answer it to your country and your own conscience, if the step you are about to take should lead to a division of the army, or the loss and ruin of America be ascribed to measures which your counsels and conduct could have prevented? Before it is too late I entreat, sir, you would weigh well the greatness of the stake, and upon how much smaller circumstances the fate of empires has depended. Of your own honor and reputation you are the best and only judge; but allow me to say that a people contending for life and liberty are seldom disposed to look with a favorable eye upon either men or measures whose passions, interests, or consequences will clash with those inestimable objects. As to myself, sir, be assured that I shall with pleasure do all in my power to make your situation both easy and honorable, and that the sentiments here expressed flow from a clear opinion that your duty to your country, your posterity, and yourself most explicitly require your continuance in the service. The order and rank of the commissions is under the consideration of the Continental Congress, whose determination will be received in a few days. It may argue a want of respect to that august body not to wait the decision. But at all events I shall flatter myself that these reasons, with others which your own good judgment will suggest, will strengthen your mind against those impressions which are incident to humanity and laudable to a certain degree, and that the result will be your resolution to assist your country in this day of distress. That you may reap the full reward of honor and public esteem, which such a conduct deserves, is the sincere wish of, Sir, Your very Obed: & most Hmble Servt

Go: Washington

General Orders, August 10, 1775

It is a matter of exceeding great concern to the general to find that, at a time when the united efforts of America are exerting in defense of the common rights and liberties of mankind, there should be in an army constituted for so noble a purpose, such repeated instances of officers who, lost to every sense of honor and virtue, are seeking by dirty and base means the promotion of their own dishonest gain, to the eternal disgrace of themselves and dishonor of their country. Practices of this sort will never be overlooked whenever an accusation is lodged, but the authors brought to the most exemplary punishment. It is therefore much to be wished that the example of Jesse Saunders, late Captain in Colonel Sergeant's regiment, will prove the last shameful instance of such a groveling disposition, and that for the future every officer, for his own honor and the sake of an injured public, will make a point of detecting every iniquitous practice of this kind, using their utmost endeavors in their several capacities to lessen the expense of the war as much as possible, that the great cause in which we are struggling may receive no injury from the enormity of the expense.

The several pay masters are immediately to ascertain what pay was due to the different regiments and corps on the first day of this instant, that each man may receive his respective due, as soon as the money arrives to pay them. It is earnestly recommended that great exactness be used in these settlements, first, that no man goes without his pay, and next, that not one farthing more be drawn than what is justly due. After this the pay may be drawn once a month, or otherwise, as shall be found most convenient. In the meanwhile, the soldiers need be under no apprehension of getting every farthing that is justly their due. It is therefore expected that they do their duty with that cheerfulness and alacrity becoming men who are contending for their liberty, property, and everything that is valuable to freemen and their posterity.

To Lieutenant General Thomas Gage, August 11, 1775

Sir,

I understand that the officers engaged in the cause of liberty and their country, who by the fortune of war have fallen into your hands, have been thrown indiscriminately into a common gaol appropriated for felons, that no consideration has been had for those of the most respectable rank, when languishing with wounds and sickness, that some have been even amputated in this unworthy situation.

Let your opinion, sir, of the principle which actuates them be what it may, they suppose they act from the noblest of all principles, a love of freedom and their country. But political opinions, I conceive, are foreign to this point: the obligations arising from the rights of humanity and claims of rank are universally binding and extensive, except in case of retaliation. These, I should have hoped, would have dictated a more tender treatment of those individuals whom chance or war had put in your power. Nor can I forbear suggesting its fatal tendency to widen that unhappy breach which you, and those ministers under whom you act, have repeatedly declared you wished to see forever closed.

My duty now makes it necessary to apprise you that for the future I shall regulate my conduct towards those gentlemen who are or may be in our possession exactly by the rule which you shall observe towards those of ours who may be in your custody. If severity and hardship mark the line of your conduct, (painful as it may be to me) your prisoners will feel its effects. But if kindness and humanity are shown to ours, I shall with pleasure consider those in our hands only as unfortunate, and they shall receive the treatment to which the unfortunate are ever entitled.

I beg to be favored with an answer as soon as possible. And am, Sir, Your most Obedt & very Hmble Servt

Go: Washington

To Lieutenant General Thomas Gage, August 19, 1775

Sir,

I addressed you on the 11th instant in terms which gave the fairest scope for the exercise of that humanity and politeness which were supposed to form a part of your character. I remonstrated with you on the unworthy treatment shown to the officers and citizens of America whom the fortune of war, chance, or a mistaken confidence had thrown into your hands. Whether British, or American, mercy, fortitude, and patience are most pre-eminent; whether our virtuous citizens, whom the hand of tyranny has forced into arms to defend their wives, their children, and their property, or the mercenary instruments of lawless domination, avarice, and revenge best deserve the appellation of rebels, and the punishment of that cord, which your affected clemency has forborne to inflict; whether the authority under which I act is usurped, or founded on the genuine principles of liberty; were altogether foreign to my subject. I purposely avoided all political disquisition; nor shall I now avail myself of those advantages which the sacred cause of my country, of liberty and human nature, give me over you. Much less shall I stoop to retort and invective. But the intelligence you say you have received from our army requires a reply. I have taken time, sir, to make a strict inquiry, and find it has not the least foundation in truth. Not only your officers and soldiers have been treated with a tenderness due to fellow citizens and brethren, but even those execrable parricides, whose counsels and aid have deluged their country with blood, have been protected from the fury of a justly enraged people. Far from compelling, or even permitting their assistance, I am embarrassed with the numbers who crowd to our camp, animated with the purest principles of virtue and love of their country.

You advise me to give free operation to truth, to punish misrepresentation and falsehood. If experience stamps value upon counsel, yours must have a weight which few can claim. You best can tell how far the convulsion, which has brought such ruin on both countries and shaken the mighty empire of Britain to its foundation, may be traced to those malignant causes.

You affect, sir, to despise all rank not derived from the same source with your own. I cannot conceive any more honorable than that which flows from the uncorrupted choice of a brave and free people—the purest source and original fountain of all power. Far from making it a plea for cruelty, a mind of true magnanimity and enlarged ideas would comprehend and respect it.

What may have been the ministerial views which precipitated the present crisis, Lexington, Concord, and Charlestown can best declare. May that God to whom you then appealed judge between America and you! Under his Providence, those who influence the councils of America, and all the other inhabitants of these united colonies, at the hazard of their lives, are resolved to hand down to posterity those just and invaluable privileges which they received from their ancestors.

I shall now, sir, close my correspondence with you, perhaps forever. If your officers who are our prisoners receive a treatment from me different from what I wished to show them, they, and you, will remember the occasion of it. I am Sir, Your very Hmble Servant.

Go: Washington

To the Inhabitants of Bermuda, September 6, 1775

Gentlemen,

In the great conflict which agitates this continent I cannot doubt but the assertors of freedom and the rights of the constitution are possessed of your most favorable regards and wishes for success. As the descendants of freemen and heirs with us of the same glorious inheritance, we flatter ourselves that, though divided by our situation, we are firmly united in sentiment. The cause of virtue and liberty is confined to no continent or climate; it comprehends within its capacious limits the wise and the good, however dispersed and separated in space or distance. You need not be informed that the violence and rapacity of a tyrannic ministry have forced the citizens of America, your brother colonists, into arms. We equally detest and lament the prevalence of those councils which have led to the effusion of so much human blood and left us no alternative but a civil war or a base submission. The wise Disposer of all Events has hitherto smiled upon our virtuous efforts. Those mercenary troops, a few of whom lately boasted of subjugating this vast continent, have been checked in their earliest ravages and are now actually encircled in a small space, their arms disgraced and suffering all the calamities of a siege. The virtue and spirit and union of the provinces leave them nothing to fear but the want of ammunition. The applications of our enemies to foreign states, and their vigilance upon our coasts, are the only efforts they have made against us with success. Under these circumstances, and with these sentiments, we have turned our eyes to you gentlemen for relief. We are informed that there is a large magazine in your island under a very feeble guard. We would not wish to involve you in an opposition in which from your situation we should be unable to support you; we know not therefore to what extent to solicit your assistance in availing ourselves of this supply. But, if your favor and friendship to North America and its liberties have not been misrepresented, I persuade myself you may, consistent with your own safety, promote and favor this scheme so as to give it the fairest prospect of success. Be assured that in this case the whole power and exertion of my influence will be made with the honorable Continental Congress that your island may not only be supplied with provisions but experience every other mark of affection and friendship which the grateful citizens of a free country can bestow on its brethren and benefactors.

To the Inhabitants of Canada, c. September 14, 1775

Friends and Brethren,

The unnatural contest between the English colonies and Great Britain has now risen to such a height that arms alone must decide it. The colonies, confiding in the justice of their cause and the purity of their intentions, have reluctantly appealed to that Being in whose hands are all human events. He has hitherto smiled upon their virtuous efforts. The hand of tyranny has been arrested in its ravages, and the British arms, which have shone with so much splendor in every part of the globe, are now tarnished with disgrace and disappointment. Generals of approved experience, who boasted of subduing this great continent, find themselves circumscribed within the limits of a single city and its suburbs, suffering all the shame and distress of a siege. While the trueborn sons of America, animated by the genuine principles of liberty and love of their country, with increasing union, firmness, and discipline repel every attack and despise every danger.

Above all, we rejoice that our enemies have been deceived with regard to you. They have persuaded themselves, they have even dared to say, that the Canadians were not capable of distinguishing between the blessings of liberty and the wretchedness of slavery, that gratifying the vanity of a little circle of nobility would blind the eyes of the people of Canada. By such artifices they hoped to bend you to their views; but they have been deceived. Instead of finding in you that poverty of soul and baseness of spirit, they see with a chagrin equal to our joy that you are enlightened, generous, and virtuous—that you will not renounce your own rights, or serve as instruments to deprive your fellow subjects of theirs. Come then, my brethren, unite with us in an indissoluble union. Let us run together to the same goal. We have taken up arms in defense of our liberty, our property, our wives, and our children. We are determined to preserve them or die. We look forward with pleasure to that day, not far remote (we hope), when the inhabitants of America shall have one sentiment, and the full enjoyment of the blessings of a free government.

Incited by these motives and encouraged by the advice of many friends of liberty among you, the grand American Congress have sent an army into your province, under the command of General Schuyler—not to plunder but to protect you, to animate and bring forth into action those sentiments of freedom you have disclosed, and which the tools of despotism would extinguish through the whole creation. To cooperate with this design, and to frustrate those cruel and perfidious schemes which would deluge our frontiers with the blood of women and children, I have detached Colonel Arnold into your country, with a part of the army under my command. I have enjoined upon him, and I am certain that he will consider himself and act as in the country of his patrons and best friends. Necessaries and accommodations of every kind which you may furnish he will thankfully receive, and render the full value. I invite you therefore as friends and brethren to provide him with such supplies as your country affords; and I pledge myself not only for your safety and security, but for ample compensation. Let no man desert his habitation. Let no one flee as before an enemy. The cause of America and of liberty is the cause of every virtuous American citizen, whatever may be his religion or his descent. The United Colonies know no distinction but such as slavery, corruption, and arbitrary domination may create. Come then, ye generous citizens, range yourselves under the standard of general liberty, against which all the force and artifice of tyranny will never be able to prevail.

G. Washington

To John Hancock, President of the Continental Congress, September 21, 1775 (Excerpt)

It gives me great pain to be obliged to solicit the attention of the honorable Congress to the state of this army, in terms which imply the slightest apprehension of being neglected; but my situation is inexpressibly distressing: to see the winter fast approaching upon a naked army, the time of their service within a few weeks of expiring, and no provision yet made for such important events. Added to these, the military chest is totally exhausted. The paymaster has not a single dollar in hand. The commissary general assures me he has strained his credit for the subsistence of the army to the utmost. The quartermaster general is precisely in the same situation. And the greater part of the troops are in a state not far from mutiny, upon the deduction from their stated allowance. I know not to whom I am to impute this failure, but I am of opinion, if the evil is not immediately remedied and more punctuality observed in future, the army must absolutely break up. I hoped I had expressed myself so fully on this subject, both by letter and to those members of the Congress who honored the camp with a visit, that no disappointment could possibly happen. I therefore hourly expected advice from the paymaster that he had received a fresh supply, in addition to the 172,000 dollars delivered him in August, and thought myself warranted to assure the public creditors that in a few days they should be satisfied. But the delay has brought matters to such a crisis as admits of no farther uncertain expectation. I have therefore sent off this express, with orders to make all possible dispatch. It is my most earnest request that he may be returned with all possible expedition, unless the honorable Congress have already forwarded what is so indispensably necessary.

I have the honor to be, with the most sincere respect and regard, Sir, Your most Obed. & very Hmble Servt

Go: Washington

General Orders, October 26, 1775 (Excerpt)

As several of the officers have not yet signified their intentions respecting the requisitions contained in the orders of the 22nd instant, and as the nature of the case will admit of no delay, the general directs that every officer in the army do forthwith declare to his colonel or commanding officer of the regiment to which he belongs, whether he will, or will not, continue in the service until the last day of December 1776 (if the Continental Congress shall think it expedient to retain him so long). This declaration must be made in explicit terms, and not conditional, as the Congress are to be advised thereof immediately, in order that proper steps may be taken to provide other officers and other men, if necessary. The times and the importance of the great cause we are engaged in allow no room for hesitation and delay. When life, liberty, and property are at stake, when our country is in danger of being a melancholy scene of bloodshed and desolation, when our towns are laid in ashes, and innocent women and children driven from their peaceful habitations, exposed to the rigor of an inclement season, and to the hands of charity, perhaps, for a support—when calamities like these are staring us in the face, and a brutal, savage enemy (more so than was ever yet found in a civilized nation) are threatening us and everything we hold dear with destruction from foreign troops, it little becomes the character of a soldier to shrink from danger and condition for new terms.

General Orders, October 31, 1775 (Excerpt)

As many officers and others have begun to enlist men for the Continental Army without orders from headquarters, the general desires that an immediate stop be put thereto, that the enlistments be returned, and that no person for the future presume to interfere in this matter, till there is a proper establishment of officers, and those officers authorized and instructed in what manner to proceed. Commissions in the new army are not intended merely for those who can enlist the most men, but for such gentlemen as are most likely to deserve them. The general would therefore not have it even supposed, nor our enemies encouraged to believe, that there is a man in this army (except a few under particular circumstances) who will require to be twice asked to do what his honor, his personal liberty, the welfare of his country, and the safety of his family so loudly demand of him. When motives powerful as these conspire to call men into service, and when that service is rewarded with higher pay than private soldiers ever yet met with in any former war, the general cannot, nor will not (until he is convinced to the contrary), harbor so despicable an opinion of their understanding and zeal for the cause as to believe they will desert it.

General Orders, November 5, 1775 (Excerpt)

As the commander-in-chief has been apprised of a design formed for the observance of that ridiculous and childish custom of burning the effigy of the pope, he cannot help expressing his surprise that there should be officers and soldiers in this army so void of common sense as not to see the impropriety of such a step at this juncture—at a time when we are soliciting, and have really obtained, the friendship and alliance of the people of Canada, whom we ought to consider as brethren embarked in the same cause: the defense of the general liberty of America. At such a juncture, and in such circumstances, to be insulting their religion is so monstrous as not to be suffered or excused. Indeed, instead of offering the most remote insult, it is our duty to address public thanks to these our brethren, as to them we are so much indebted for every late happy success over the common enemy in Canada.

To Lieutenant Colonel Joseph Reed, December 15, 1775 (Excerpts)

The account which you have given of the sentiments of people respecting my conduct is extremely flattering. Pray God I may continue to deserve them in the perplexed and intricate situation I stand in. Our enlistment goes on slow. By the returns last Monday only 5,917 men are engaged for the ensuing campaign, and yet we are told that we shall get the number wanted, as they are only playing off to see what advantages are to be made, and whether a bounty cannot be extorted either from the public at large, or individuals, in case of a draft. Time only can discover this. I doubt the measure exceedingly ....

If the Virginians are wise, that arch traitor to the rights of humanity, Lord Dunmore, should be instantly crushed, if it takes the force of the whole colony to do it. Otherwise, like a snowball in rolling, his army will get size—some through fear, some through promises, and some from inclination joining his standard. But that which renders the measure indispensably necessary is the negros; for if he gets formidable, numbers of them will be tempted to join who will be afraid to do it without.

To Major General William Howe, December 18, 1775

Sir,

We have just been informed of a circumstance which, were it not so well authenticated, I should scarcely think credible. It is that Colonel Allen, who, with his small party was defeated and taken prisoner near Montreal, has been treated without regard to decency, humanity, or the rules of war—that he has been thrown into irons and suffers all the hardships inflicted upon common felons.

I think it my duty, sir, to demand, and do expect from you, an éclaircissement on this subject. At the same time, I flatter myself from the character which Mr. Howe bears, as a man of honor, gentleman, and soldier, that my demand will meet with his approbation. I must take the liberty also of informing you that I shall consider your silence as a confirmation of the truth of the report, and further assuring you that whatever treatment Colonel Allen receives—whatever fate he undergoes—such exactly shall be the treatment and fate of Brigadier Prescot, now in our hands.

The law of retaliation is not only justifiable in the eyes of God and man, but absolutely a duty which in our present circumstances we owe to our relations, friends, and fellow citizens.

Permit me to add, sir, that we have all here the highest regard and reverence for your great personal qualities and attainments, and that the Americans in general esteem it not as the least of their misfortunes that the name of Howe—a name so dear to them—should appear at the head of the catalogue of the instruments employed by a wicked ministry for their destruction. With due respect, I have the honor to be Sir Yr Most Obedt & Hble sert

G.W.

P.S. If an exchange of prisoners taken on each side in this unnatural contest is agreeable to General Howe, he will please to signify as much to his Most Obedt

G.W.

General Orders, January 1, 1776 (Excerpts)

This day giving commencement to the new army, which in every point of view is entirely continental, the general flatters himself that a laudable spirit of emulation will now take place and pervade the whole of it. Without such a spirit, few officers have ever arrived to any degree of reputation, nor did any army ever become formidable. His Excellency hopes that the importance of the great cause we are engaged in will be deeply impressed upon every man's mind, and wishes it to be considered that an army without order, regularity, and discipline is no better than a commissioned mob. Let us, therefore, when everything dear and valuable to freemen is at stake, when our unnatural parent is threatening of us with destruction from every quarter, endeavor by all the skill and discipline in our power to acquire that knowledge and conduct which is necessary in war. Our men are brave and good—men who with pleasure it is observed are addicted to fewer vices than are commonly found in armies. But it is subordination and discipline (the life and soul of an army) which, next under Providence, is to make us formidable to our enemies, honorable in ourselves, and respected in the world; and herein is to be shown the goodness of the officer.

In vain is it for a general to issue orders if orders are not attended to; equally vain is it for a few officers to exert themselves if the same spirit does not animate the whole. It is therefore expected (it is not insisted upon) that each brigadier will be attentive to the discipline of his brigade, to the exercise of and the conduct observed in it, calling the colonels and field officers of every regiment to severe account for neglect or disobedience of orders. The same attention is to be paid by the field officers to the respective companies of their regiments, by the captains to their subalterns, and so on. And that the plea of ignorance, which is no excuse for the neglect of orders (but rather an aggravation), may not be offered, it is ordered and directed that not only every regiment, but every company, do keep an orderly book, to which frequent recourse is to be had, it being expected that all standing orders be rigidly obeyed, until altered or countermanded. It is also expected that all orders which are necessary to be communicated to the men be regularly read and carefully explained to them. As it is the first wish of the general to have the business of the army conducted without punishment, to accomplish which, he assures every officer and soldier that, as far as it is in his power, he will reward such as particularly distinguish themselves. At the same time, he declares that he will punish every kind of neglect or misbehavior in an exemplary manner.

As the great variety of occurrences, and the multiplicity of business, in which the general is necessarily engaged, may withdraw his attention from many objects and things which might be improved to advantage, he takes this opportunity of declaring that he will thank any officer, of whatsoever rank, for any useful hints or profitable informations, but to avoid trivial matters. As his time is very much engrossed, he requires that it may be introduced through the channel of a general officer, who is to weigh the importance before he communicates it ....

This being the day of the commencement of the new establishment, the general pardons all the offenses of the old, and commands all prisoners (except prisoners of war) to be immediately released.

To Lieutenant Colonel Joseph Reed, January 14, 1776 (Excerpts)

The hints you have communicated from time to time not only deserve, but do most sincerely and cordially meet with, my thanks. You cannot render a more acceptable service, nor in my estimation give me a more convincing proof of your friendship, than by a free, open, and undisguised account of every matter relative to myself or conduct. I can bear to hear of imputed or real errors. The man who wishes to stand well in the opinion of others must do this, because he is thereby enabled to correct his faults, or remove the prejudices which are imbibed against him. For this reason I shall thank you for giving me the opinions of the world upon such points as you know me to be interested in; for as I have but one capital object in view, I could wish to make my conduct coincide with the wishes of mankind as far as I can consistently—I mean without departing from that great line of duty which, though hid under a cloud for some time, from a peculiarity of circumstances, may nevertheless bear a scrutiny ....

I am exceeding sorry to hear that your little fleet has been shut in by the frost. I hope it has sailed ere this and given you some proof of the utility of it, and enabled the Congress to bestow a little more attention to the affairs of this army, which suffers exceedingly by their over much business—or too little attention to it. We are now without any money in our treasury, powder in our magazines, arms in our stores. We are without a brigadier (the want of which has been twenty times urged), engineers, expresses (though a committee has been appointed these two months to establish them)—and by and by, when we shall be called upon to take the field, shall not have a tent to lay in—a propos, what is doing with mine?

These are evils, but small in comparison of those which disturb my present repose. Our enlistments are at a stand. The fears I ever entertained are realized—that is, the discontented officers (for I do not know how else to account for it) have thrown such difficulties or stumbling blocks in the way of recruiting that I no longer entertain a hope of completing the army by voluntary enlistments, and I see no move, or likelihood of one, to do it by other means ....

Thus am I situated with respect to men. With regard to arms I am yet worse off .... How to get furnished I know not. I have applied to this and the neighboring colonies, but with what success time only can tell. The reflection upon my situation, and that of this army, produces many an uneasy hour when all around me are wrapped in sleep. Few people know the predicament we are in, on a thousand accounts. Fewer still will believe, if any disaster happens to these lines, from what causes it flows. I have often thought how much happier I should have been, if, instead of accepting of a command under such circumstances, I had taken my musket upon my shoulder and entered the ranks, or, if I could have justified the measure to posterity, and my own conscience, had retired to the back country and lived in a wigwam. If I shall be able to rise superior to these, and many other difficulties which might be enumerated, I shall most religiously believe that the finger of Providence is in it, to blind the eyes of our enemies; for surely if we get well through this month, it must be for want of their knowing the disadvantages we labor under.

To Lieutenant Colonel Joseph Reed, February 10, 1776 (Excerpts)

If, my dear sir, you conceive that I took anything wrong or amiss that was conveyed in any of your former letters, you are really mistaken. I only meant to convince you that nothing would give me more real satisfaction than to know the sentiments which are entertained of me by the public, whether they be favorable or otherwise—and urged as a reason that the man who wished to steer clear of shelves and rocks must know where they lay. I know—but to declare it, unless to a friend, may be an argument of vanity—the integrity of my own heart. I know the unhappy predicament I stand in. I know that much is expected of me. I know that without men, without arms, without ammunition, without anything fit for the accommodation of a soldier, that little is to be done—and, which is mortifying, I know that I cannot stand justified to the world without exposing my own weakness and injuring the cause by declaring my wants, which I am determined not to do further than unavoidable necessity brings every man acquainted with them. If under these disadvantages I am able to keep above water (as it were) in the esteem of mankind, I shall feel myself happy; but if from the unknown peculiarity of my circumstances I suffer in the opinion of the world, I shall not think you take the freedom of a friend if you conceal the reflections that may be cast upon my conduct. My own situation feels so irksome to me at times that, if I did not consult the public good more than my own tranquility, I should long ere this have put everything to the cast of a die. So far from my having an army of 20,000 men well-armed, etc., I have been here with less than one half of it, including sick, furloughed, and on command, and those neither armed or clothed as they should be. In short my situation has been such that I have been obliged to use art to conceal it from my own officers ....

With respect to myself, I have never entertained an idea of an accommodation since I heard of the measures which were adopted in consequence of the Bunker Hill fight. The king's speech has confirmed the sentiments I entertained upon the news of that affair—and if every man was of my mind the ministers of G.B. should know, in a few words, upon what issue the cause should be put. I would not be deceived by artful declarations or specious pretenses, nor would I be amused by unmeaning propositions—but in open, undisguised, and manly terms proclaim our wrongs and our resolutions to be redressed. I would tell them that we had borne much—that we had long and ardently sought for reconciliation upon honorable terms—that it had been denied us—that all our attempts after peace had proved abortive and had been grossly misrepresented—that we had done everything that could be expected from the best of subjects—that the spirit of freedom beat too high in us to submit to slavery—and that, if nothing else would satisfy a tyrant and his diabolical ministry, we were determined to shake off all connections with a state so unjust and unnatural. This I would tell them, not under covert, but in words as clear as the sun in its meridian brightness.

To Joseph Johnson, February 20, 1776

Sir,

I am very much pleased to find, by the strong recommendations you produce, that we have amongst our brothers of the Six Nations a person who can explain to them the sense of their brothers on the dispute between us and the ministers of Great Britain. You have seen a part of our strength and can inform our brothers that we can withstand all the force which those who want to rob us of our lands and our houses can send against us.

You can tell our friends that they may always look upon me, whom the whole United Colonies have chosen to be their chief warrior, as their brother. Whilst they continue in friendship with us, they may depend upon mine and the protection of those under my command.

Tell them that we don't want them to take up the hatchet for us, except they choose it. We only desire that they will not fight against us. We want that the chain of friendship should always remain bright between our friends of the Six Nations and us. Their attention to you will be a proof to us that they wish the same. We recommend you to them, and hope, by your spreading the truths of the Holy Gospel amongst them, it will contribute to keep the chain so bright that the malicious insinuations or practices of our enemies will never be able to break this union, so much for the benefit of our brothers of the Six Nations and of us. And to prove to them that this is my desire, and of the warriors under me, I hereto subscribe my name at Cambridge this 20th day of February 1776.

Go: Washington

General Orders, February 27, 1776 (Excerpt)

As the season is now fast approaching when every man must expect to be drawn into the field of action, it is highly necessary that he should prepare his mind, as well as everything necessary for it. It is a noble cause we are engaged in. It is the cause of virtue and mankind. Every temporal advantage and comfort to us and our posterity depends upon the vigor of our exertions. In short, freedom or slavery must be the result of our conduct. There can therefore be no greater inducement to men to behave well. But it may not be amiss for the troops to know that if any man in action shall presume to skulk, hide himself, or retreat from the enemy without the orders of his commanding officer, he will be *instantly shot down* as an example of cowardice—cowards having too frequently disconcerted the best formed troops by their dastardly behavior.

Next to the favor of Divine Providence, nothing is more essentially necessary to give this army the victory of all its enemies than exactness of discipline, alertness when on duty, and cleanliness in their arms and persons. Unless the arms are kept clean, and in good firing order, it is impossible to vanquish the enemy. And cleanliness of the person gives health and soldier-like appearance.

Proclamation on the Occupation of Boston, March 21, 1776 (Excerpt)

Whereas the ministerial army have abandoned the Town of Boston, and the forces of the United Colonies, under my command, are in possession of the same:

I have therefore thought it necessary for the preservation of peace, good order, and discipline to publish the following orders, that no person offending therein may plead ignorance as an excuse for their misconduct.

All officers and soldiers are hereby ordered to live in the strictest peace and amity with the inhabitants; and no inhabitant, or other person employed in his lawful business in the town, is to be molested in his person or property on any pretense whatever. If any officer or soldier shall presume to strike, imprison, or otherwise ill-treat any of the inhabitants, they may depend on being punished with the utmost severity. And if any officer or soldier shall receive any insult from any of the inhabitants, he is to seek redress, in a legal way, and no other.

Any non-commissioned officer, soldier, or others under my command who shall be guilty of robbing or plundering in the town are to be immediately confined and will be most rigidly punished. All officers are therefore ordered to be very vigilant in the discovery of such offenders and report their names and crime to the commanding officer in the town as soon as may be.

To the Boston Selectmen and Citizens, March 1776

Gentlemen,

Your congratulations on the success of the American arms gives me the greatest pleasure.

I most sincerely rejoice with you on your being once more in the quiet possession of your former habitations, and, what greatly adds to my happiness, that this desirable event has been effected with so little effusion of human blood.

I am exceedingly obliged by the good opinion you are pleased to entertain of my conduct. Your virtuous efforts in the cause of freedom, and the unparalleled fortitude with which you have sustained the greatest of all human calamities, justly entitle you to the grateful remembrance of your American brethren; and I heartily pray that the hand of tyranny may never more disturb your repose, and that every blessing of a kind Providence may give happiness and prosperity to the Town of Boston.

Go: Washington

To the Massachusetts General Court, April 1, 1776

Gentlemen,

I return you my most sincere and hearty thanks for your polite address, and feel myself called upon by every principle of gratitude to acknowledge the honor you have done me in this testimonial of your approbation of my appointment to the exalted station I now fill, and, what is more pleasing, of my conduct in discharging its important duties.

When the councils of the British nation had formed a plan for enslaving America and depriving her sons of their most sacred and invaluable privileges, against the clearest remonstrances of the constitution, of justice, and of truth, and to execute their schemes had appealed to the sword, I esteemed it my duty to take a part in the contest, and more especially when called thereto by the unsolicited suffrages of the representatives of a free people, wishing for no other reward than that arising from a conscientious discharge of the important trust, and that my services might contribute to the establishment of freedom and peace upon a permanent foundation, and merit the applause of my countrymen and every virtuous citizen.

Your professions of my attention to the civil constitution of this colony, whilst acting in the line of my department, also demand my grateful thanks. A regard to every provincial institution, where not incompatible with the common interest, I hold a principle of duty and of policy and shall ever form a part of my conduct. Had I not learned this before, the happy experience of the advantages resulting from a friendly intercourse with your honorable body, their ready and willing concurrence to aid and to counsel, whenever called upon in cases of difficulty and emergency, would have taught me the useful lesson.

That the metropolis of your colony is now relieved from the cruel and oppressive invasion of those who were sent to erect the standard of lawless domination, and to trample on the rights of humanity, and is again open and free for its rightful possessors, must give pleasure to every virtuous and sympathetic heart—and being effected without the blood of our soldiers and fellow citizens must be ascribed to the interposition of that Providence which has manifestly appeared in our behalf through the whole of this important struggle, as well as to the measures pursued for bringing about the happy event.

May that Being who is powerful to save, and in whose hands is the fate of nations, look down with an eye of tender pity and compassion upon the whole of the United Colonies. May he continue to smile upon their councils and arms, and crown them with success, whilst employed in the cause of virtue and of mankind. May this distressed colony and its capital, and every part of this wide, extended continent, through his divine favor, be restored to more than their former luster and once happy state, and have peace, liberty, and safety secured upon a solid, permanent, and lasting foundation.

Go: Washington

To Lieutenant Colonel Joseph Reed, April 1, 1776 (Excerpts)

The accounts brought by Mr. Temple of the favorable disposition in the ministry to accommodate matters does not correspond with their speeches in Parliament. How then does he account for their inconsistency? If the commissioners do not come over with full and ample powers to treat with Congress, I sincerely wish they may never put their feet on American ground, as it must be self-evident (in the other case) that they come over with invidious intentions—to distract, divide, and create as much confusion as possible. How then can any man, let his passion for reconciliation be never so strong, be so blinded and misled as to embrace a measure evidently designed for his destruction? No man does—no man can—wish the restoration of peace more fervently than I do; but I hope, whenever made, it will be upon such terms as will reflect honor upon the councils and wisdom of America. With you, I think a change in the American representation necessary. Frequent appeals to the people can be attended with no bad, but may have very salutary, effects. My countrymen I know, from their form of government and steady attachment heretofore to royalty, will come reluctantly into the idea of independency. But time, and persecution, bring many wonderful things to pass; and by private letters, which I have lately received from Virginia, I find *Common Sense* is working a powerful change there in the minds of many men ....

I believe I mentioned in my last to you that all those who took upon themselves the style and title (in Boston) of government's men have shipped themselves off in the same hurry, but under greater disadvantages than the king's (I think it idle to keep up the distinction of ministerial) troops have done, being obliged, in a manner, to man their own vessels, seamen not being to be had for the king's transports, and submit to all the hardships that can be conceived. One or two of them have committed—what it would have been happy for mankind if more of them had done long ago—the act of suicide. By all accounts a more miserable set of beings does not exist than these. Taught to believe that the power of G. Britain was almost omnipotent, and if it was not that foreign aid was at hand, they were higher and more insulting in their opposition than the regulars themselves. When the order issued, therefore, for embarking the troops in Boston, no electric shock—no sudden flash of lightning—in a word, not even the last trump, could have struck them with greater consternation. They were at their wits' end, and, conscious of their black ingratitude, chose to commit themselves in the manner before described to the mercy of the winds and waves, in a tempestuous season, rather than meet their offended countrymen. And with this declaration I am told they have done it—that if they could have thought that the most abject submission would have procured peace for them, they would have humbled themselves in the dust and kissed the rod that should be held out for chastisement. Unhappy wretches! Deluded mortals! Would it not be good policy to grant a general amnesty and conquer these people by a generous forgiveness?

To John Hancock, President of the Continental Congress, April 18, 1776

Sir,

Permit me, through you, to convey to the honorable Congress the sentiments of gratitude I feel for the high honor they have done me in the public mark of approbation contained in your favor of the 2nd instant, which came to hand last night. I beg you to assure them that it will ever be my highest ambition to approve myself a faithful servant of the public, and that to be in any degree instrumental in procuring to my American brethren a restitution of their just rights and privileges will constitute my chief happiness.

Agreeable to your request, I have communicated in general orders to the officers and soldiers under my command the thanks of Congress for their good behavior in the service, and am happy in having such an opportunity of doing justice to their merit. They were indeed at first "a band of undisciplined husbandmen," but it is (under God) to their bravery and attention to their duty that I am indebted for that success which has procured me the only reward I wish to receive—the affection and esteem of my countrymen.

The medal, intended to be presented to me by your honorable body, I shall carefully preserve as a memorial of their regard. I beg leave to return you, sir, my warmest thanks for the polite manner in which you have been pleased to express their sentiments of my conduct, and am with sincere esteem and respect—Sir Yours and their most Obedt & most Hble Servt

Go: Washington

General Orders, May 15, 1776 (Excerpt)

The Continental Congress having ordered Friday the 17th instant to be observed as a day of "fasting, humiliation and prayer, humbly to supplicate the mercy of Almighty God, that it would please him to pardon all our manifold sins and transgressions, and to prosper the arms of the United Colonies, and finally, establish the peace and freedom of America upon a solid and lasting foundation"—the general commands all officers and soldiers to pay strict obedience to the orders of the Continental Congress, and by their unfeigned and pious observance of their religious duties, incline the Lord and Giver of Victory to prosper our arms.

To John Augustine Washington, May 31, 1776 (Excerpt)

I am very glad to find that the Virginia Convention have passed so noble a vote with so much unanimity. Things have come to that pass now as to convince us that we have nothing more to expect from the justice of G. Britain—also, that she is capable of the most delusive arts. For I am satisfied that no commissioners ever were designed, except Hessians and other foreigners, and that the idea was only to deceive and throw us off our guard. The first it has too effectually accomplished, as many members of Congress, in short, the representation of whole provinces, are still feeding themselves upon the dainty food of reconciliation. And though they will not allow that the expectation of it has any influence upon their judgments (with respect to their preparations for defense), it is but too obvious that it has an operation upon every part of their conduct and is a clog to their proceedings. It is not in the nature of things to be otherwise, for no man that entertains a hope of seeing this dispute speedily and equitably adjusted by commissioners will go to the same expense and run the same hazards to prepare for the worst event as he who believes that he must conquer or submit to unconditional terms and its concomitants, such as confiscation, hanging, etc., etc.

To form a new government requires infinite care and unbounded attention; for if the foundation is badly laid, the superstructure must be bad. Too much time, therefore, cannot be bestowed in weighing and digesting matters well. We have, no doubt, some good parts in our present constitution. Many bad ones we know we have, wherefore no time can be misspent that is employed in separating the wheat from the tares. My fear is that you will all get tired and homesick, the consequence of which will be that you will patch up some kind of constitution as defective as the present. This should be avoided. Every man should consider that he is lending his aid to frame a constitution which is to render millions happy or miserable, and that a matter of such moment cannot be the work of a day.

General Orders, July 2, 1776 (Excerpt)

The time is now near at hand which must probably determine whether Americans are to be freemen or slaves, whether they are to have any property they can call their own, whether their houses and farms are to be pillaged and destroyed, and they consigned to a state of wretchedness from which no human efforts will probably deliver them. The fate of unborn millions will now depend, under God, on the courage and conduct of this army. Our cruel and unrelenting enemy leaves us no choice but a brave resistance or the most abject submission. This is all we can expect. We have therefore to resolve to conquer or die. Our own country's honor, all call upon us for a vigorous and manly exertion; and if we now shamefully fail, we shall become infamous to the whole world. Let us therefore rely upon the goodness of the cause and the aid of the supreme Being, in whose hands victory is, to animate and encourage us to great and noble actions. The eyes of all our countrymen are now upon us, and we shall have their blessings and praises if happily we are the instruments of saving them from the tyranny meditated against them. Let us therefore animate and encourage each other, and show the whole world that a freeman contending for liberty on his own ground is superior to any slavish mercenary on earth.

The general recommends to the officers great coolness in time of action, and to the soldiers a strict attention and obedience, with a becoming firmness and spirit.

Any officer or soldier, or any particular corps, distinguishing themselves by any acts of bravery and courage will assuredly meet with notice and rewards; and, on the other hand, those who behave ill will as certainly be exposed and punished—the general being resolved, as well for the honor and safety of the country as army, to show no favor to such as refuse or neglect their duty at so important a crisis.

General Orders, July 9, 1776 (Excerpt)

The honorable Continental Congress having been pleased to allow a chaplain to each regiment, with the pay of thirty-three dollars and one third per month—the colonels or commanding officers of each regiment are directed to procure chaplains accordingly, persons of good characters and exemplary lives, to see that all inferior officers and soldiers pay them a suitable respect and attend carefully upon religious exercises. The blessing and protection of Heaven are at all times necessary, but especially so in times of public distress and danger. The general hopes and trusts that every officer and man will endeavor so to live and act as becomes a Christian soldier defending the dearest rights and liberties of his country.

The honorable Continental Congress, impelled by the dictates of duty, policy and necessity, having been pleased to dissolve the connection which subsisted between this country and Great Britain, and to declare the United Colonies of North America free and independent STATES: The several brigades are to be drawn up this evening on their respective parades at six o'clock, when the declaration of Congress, showing the grounds and reasons of this measure, is to be read with an audible voice.

The general hopes this important event will serve as a fresh incentive to every officer and soldier to act with fidelity and courage, as knowing that now the peace and safety of his country depends (under God) solely on the success of our arms, and that he is now in the service of a state possessed of sufficient power to reward his merit and advance him to the highest honors of a free country.

General Orders, July 23, 1776 (Excerpt)

It is with great astonishment and surprise the general hears that soldiers enlist from one corps to another, and frequently receive a bounty, and that some officers have knowingly received such men. So glaring a fraud upon the public, and injury to the service, will be punished in the most exemplary manner. And the general most earnestly requests and expects of every good officer, who loves his country, not only to oppose such practices, but to make the offenders known, that they may be brought to justice.

General Orders, August 1, 1776

It is with great concern the general understands that jealousies etc. are arisen among the troops from the different provinces, of reflections frequently thrown out which can only tend to irritate each other and injure the noble cause in which we are engaged, and which we ought to support with one hand and one heart. The general most earnestly entreats the officers and soldiers to consider the consequences: that they can no way assist our cruel enemies more effectually than making division among ourselves; that the honor and success of the army, and the safety of our bleeding country, depends upon harmony and good agreement with each other; that the provinces are all united to oppose the common enemy, and all distinctions sunk in the name of an American. To make this honorable, and preserve the liberty of our country, ought to be our only emulation; and he will be the best soldier, and the best patriot, who contributes most to this glorious work, whatever his station, or from whatever part of the continent, he may come. Let all distinctions of nations, countries, and provinces therefore be lost in the generous contest, who shall behave with the most courage against the enemy, and the most kindness and good humor to each other. If there are any officers or soldiers so lost to virtue and a love of their country as to continue in such practices after this order, the general assures them, and is directed by Congress to declare to the whole army, that such persons shall be severely punished and dismissed from the service with disgrace.

To Lund Washington, August 26, 1776 (Excerpt)

I, in behalf of the noble cause we are engaged in, and myself, thank with a grateful heart all those who supplicate the throne of grace for success to the one and preservation of the other. That Being from whom nothing can be hid will, I doubt not, listen to our prayers, and protect our cause and the supporters of it, as far as we merit his favor and assistance. If I did not think our struggle just, I am sure it would meet with no assistance from me. And sure I am that no pecuniary satisfaction upon earth can compensate the loss of all my domestic happiness and requite me for the load of business which constantly presses upon and deprives me of every enjoyment.

General Orders, September 6, 1776 (Excerpt)

The general is resolved to put a stop to plundering and converting either public or private property to their own use when taken off or found by any soldiers. He therefore calls upon all the officers to exert themselves against it. And if the colonels or other officers of regiments see or know of any horses, furniture, merchandise, or such other property in the hands of any officer or soldier and do not immediately take hold of it, giving immediate notice of it to the brigadier general, such officer will be deemed a party, brought to a court martial, and broke with infamy. For let it ever be remembered that no plundering army was ever a successful one.

To John Hancock, President of the Continental Congress, September 6, 1776 (Excerpt)

Before I conclude I must take the liberty of mentioning to Congress the great distress we are in for want of money. Two months' pay, and more to some battalions, is now due the troops here without anything in the military chest to satisfy it. This occasions much dissatisfaction and almost a general uneasiness. Not a day passes without complaints and the most importunate and urgent demands on this head. As it may injure the service greatly, and the want of a regular supply of cash produce consequences of the most fatal tendency, I entreat the attention of Congress to this subject, and that we may be provided as soon as can be with a sum equal to every present claim.

General Orders, September 19, 1776 (Excerpt)

We are now arrived at an important crisis, which calls loudly for the zeal and activity of the best of officers. We see, we know that the enemy are exerting every nerve, not only by force of arms, but the practices of every art, to accomplish their purposes, and that among other pieces of policy, which is also founded on justice, we find them exceeding careful to restrain every kind of abuse of private property, whilst the abandoned and profligate part of our own army, countenanced by a few officers who are lost to every sense of honor and virtue, as well as their country's good, are, by rapine and plunder, spreading ruin and terror wherever they go, thereby making themselves infinitely more to be dreaded than the common enemy they are come to oppose, at the same time that it exposes men who are strolling about after plunder to be surprised and taken. The general therefore hopes it will be unnecessary on any future occasion for him to repeat the orders of yesterday with respect to this matter, as he is determined to show no favor to officer or soldier who shall offend herein, but punish without exception every person who shall be found guilty of this most abominable practice, which, if continued, must prove the destruction of any army on earth.

To John Hancock, President of the Continental Congress, September 22, 1776

Sir,

I had flattered myself that the Congress would before this time have forwarded the amended articles for the government of the army. But as they have not, I think it my indispensable duty to lay before them the necessity, the absolute necessity, of forming an article against plundering, marauding, and burning of houses. Such a spirit has gone forth in our army that neither public or private property is secure. Every hour brings the most distressing complaints of the ravages of our own troops, who are become infinitely more formidable to the poor farmers and inhabitants than the common enemy. Horses are taken out of the continental teams. The baggage of officers and the hospital stores, even the quarters of general officers, are not exempt from rapine.

Some severe and exemplary punishment to be inflicted in a summary way must be immediately administered, or the army will be totally ruined. I must beg the immediate attention of Congress to this matter as of the utmost importance to our existence as an army. I am Sir, with due Respect Your most Obed. & very Hble Servt

Go: Washington

To John Augustine Washington, September 22, 1776 (Excerpt)

The dependence which the Congress has placed upon the militia has already greatly injured—and I fear will totally ruin—our cause. Being subject to no control themselves, they introduce disorder among the troops you have attempted to discipline while the change in their living brings on sickness. This makes them impatient to get home, which spreads universally and introduces abominable desertions. In short, it is not in the power of words to describe the task I have to act. £50,000 should not induce me again to undergo what I have done. Our number by sickness, desertion, etc. is greatly reduced. I have been trying these four or five days to get a return but have not yet succeeded. I am sure, however, we have not more than 12 or 14,000 men fit for duty, whilst the enemy (who it is said are very healthy) cannot have less than near 25,000. My sincere love to my sister and the family and compliments to any enquiring friends concludes me Dr Sir Yr most Affecte Brother

Go: Washington

To Lund Washington, September 30, 1776 (Excerpt)

Dear Lund,

Your letter of the 18th, which is the only one received and unanswered, now lies before me. The amazement which you seem to be in at the unaccountable measures which have been adopted by Congress would be a good deal increased if I had time to unfold the whole system of their management since this time twelve months. I do not know how to account for the unfortunate steps which have been taken, but from that fatal idea of conciliation which prevailed so long—fatal I call it, because from my soul I wish it may prove so, though my fears lead me to think there is too much danger of it. This time last year I pointed out the evil consequences of short enlistments, the expenses of militia, and the little dependence that was placed in them. I assured Congress that the longer they delayed raising a standing army, the more difficult and chargeable would they find it to get one, and that, at the same time that the militia would answer no valuable purpose, the frequent calling them in would be attended with an expense that they could have no conception of. Whether, as I have said before, the unfortunate hope of reconciliation was the cause, or the fear of a standing army prevailed, I will not undertake to say; but the policy was to engage men for twelve months only. The consequence of which, you have had great bodies of militia in pay that never were in camp; you have had immense quantities of provisions drawn by men that never rendered you one hour's service (at least usefully), and this in the most profuse and wasteful way. Your stores have been expended, and every kind of military discipline destroyed by them; your numbers fluctuating, uncertain, and forever far short of report—at no one time, I believe, equal to twenty thousand men fit for duty. At present our numbers fit for duty (by this day's report) amount to 14,759, besides 3,427 on command, and the enemy within stone's throw of us. It is true a body of militia are again ordered out, but they come without any conveniences and soon return. I discharged a regiment the other day that had in it fourteen rank and file fit for duty only, and several that had less than fifty. In short, such is my situation that if I were to wish the bitterest curse to an enemy on this side of the grave, I should put him in my stead with my feelings; and yet I do not know what plan of conduct to pursue. I see the impossibility of serving with reputation, or doing any essential service to the cause by continuing in command; and yet I am told that if

I quit the command inevitable ruin will follow from the distraction that will ensue. In confidence I tell you that I never was in such an unhappy, divided state since I was born. To lose all comfort and happiness on the one hand, whilst I am fully persuaded that under such a system of management as has been adopted I cannot have the least chance for reputation, nor those allowances made which the nature of the case requires; and to be told, on the other, that if I leave the service all will be lost, is, at the same time that I am bereft of every peaceful moment, distressing to a degree. But I will be done with the subject, with the precaution to you that it is not a fit one to be publicly known or discussed. If I fall, it may not be amiss that these circumstances be known, and declaration made in credit to the justice of my character. And if the men will stand by me (which by the by I despair of), I am resolved not to be forced from this ground while I have life. And a few days will determine the point, if the enemy should not change their plan of operations; for they certainly will not—I am sure they ought not—to waste the season that is now fast advancing and must be precious to them. I thought to have given you a more explicit account of my situation, expectation, and feelings, but I have not time. I am wearied to death all day with a variety of perplexing circumstances—disturbed at the conduct of the militia, whose behavior and want of discipline have done great injury to the other troops, who never had officers, except in a few instances, worth the bread they eat. My time, in short, is so much engrossed that I have not leisure for corresponding, unless it is on mere matters of public business.

To Lord Richard Howe, January 13, 1777 (Excerpt)

My Lord,

I am sorry that I am under the disagreeable necessity of troubling Your Lordship with a letter almost wholly on the subject of the cruel treatment which our officers and men in the naval department, who are unhappy enough to fall into your hands, receive on board the prison ships in the harbor of New York. Without descending to particulars, I shall ground my complaint upon the matter contained in the enclosed paper, which is an exact copy of an account of the usage of the prisoners delivered to Congress by a Captain Gamble, lately a prisoner himself in New York.

If this account be true, of which I have no reason to doubt, as Captain Gamble is said to be a man of veracity, I call upon Your Lordship to say whether any treatment of your officers and seamen has merited so severe a retaliation. I am bold to say it has not. So far from it that the officers and seamen taken on board armed ships have been treated with the greatest humanity and not forced to enter on board any of our public or private vessels at war, and those taken in the merchant service have been immediately set at liberty.

From the opinion I have ever been taught to entertain of Your Lordship's humanity, I will not suppose that you are privy to proceedings of so cruel and unjustifiable a nature; and I hope that upon making the proper inquiry you will have the matter so regulated that the unhappy creatures whose lot is captivity may not in future have the miseries of cold, disease, and famine added to their other misfortunes. You may call us rebels and say that we deserve no better treatment. But remember, my Lord, that, supposing us rebels, we still have feelings equally as keen and sensible as loyalists and will, if forced to it, most assuredly retaliate upon those upon whom we look as the unjust invaders of our rights, liberties, and properties. I should not have said thus much, but my injured countrymen have long called upon me to endeavor to obtain a redress of their grievances; and I should think myself as culpable as those who inflict such severities upon them were I to continue silent.

To General William Howe, January 13, 1777

Sir,

I am directed by Congress to propose an exchange of five of the Hessian field officers taken at Trenton for Major General Lee, or, if this proposal should not be acceded to, to demand his liberty upon parole, within certain bounds, as has ever been granted to your officers in our custody. I am informed from good authority that your reason for keeping him hitherto in stricter confinement than usual is that you do not look upon him in the light of a common prisoner of war, but as a deserter from the British service, as his resignation was never accepted of, and that you intend to try him by a court martial as such. I will not undertake to determine how far this doctrine may be justifiable among yourselves, but I must give you warning that Major General Lee is looked upon as an officer belonging to and under the protection of the united, independent states of America, and that any violence which you may commit upon his life or liberty will be severely retaliated upon the lives or liberties of the British officers, or those of their foreign allies, at present in our hands.

I am sorry that I am again under the necessity of remonstrating to you upon the treatment which our prisoners continue to receive in New York. Those who have lately been sent out give the most shocking accounts of their barbarous usage, which their miserable emaciated countenances confirm. How very different was their appearance from that of your soldiers, who have lately been returned to you after a captivity of twelve months. And whether this difference in appearance was owing to a difference of treatment I leave it to you or any impartial person to determine. I would beg that some certain rule of conduct towards prisoners may be settled. If you are determined to make captivity as distressing as possible to those whose lot it is to fall into it, let me know it that we may be upon equal terms. For your conduct must and shall mark mine.

If a real scarcity of the articles of provision and fuel at this inclement season is the cause that our prisoners are debarred them, common humanity points out a mode, which is of suffering them to go home under parole not to serve during the war or until an equal number are released by us for them.

Most of the prisoners who have returned home have informed me that they were offered better treatment provided they would enlist into your service.

This, I believe, is unprecedented, and what, if true, makes it still more unnecessary for me to apologize for the freedom of expression which I have used throughout this letter. But it would be criminal of me to be silent were such abuses, when made known to me, left unrepresented by me. I am with due Respect Sir yr very hble Servt.

General Orders, January 21, 1777 (Excerpt)

The general is very sorry to find that the late general orders, allowing the plunder taken from the enemy to be divided for the benefit of the party that took it, has been so mistaken by some and abused by others. This indulgence was granted to scouting parties only, as a reward for the extraordinary fatigues, hardship, and danger they were exposed to upon those parties. The general never meant, nor had any idea, that any of our own or enemy's stores, found at any evacuated post, were to be considered as the property of those that first marched in. Neither did he mean that any of the public stores, discovered by any of the scouting parties, should be appropriated to their use, unless they found the enemy in actual possession and dispossessed them. Plunder taken under such circumstances, either by militia or continental troops, is[2] to be reported by the commanding officer of the party to some of the continental or provincial generals, who are directed to have all the provisions and military stores so taken appraised by the commissary and quartermaster generals or their deputies, and the party paid the value thereof. Such articles as are taken, not necessary for the use of the army, are[3] to be sold at public vendue, under the direction of the quartermaster general or some of his deputies, for the benefit of the party also. The general prohibits, both in militia and continental troops, in the most positive terms, the infamous practice of plundering the inhabitants under the specious pretense of their being Tories. Let the persons who are known to be enemies to their country be seized and confined, and their property disposed of as the law of the state directs. It is our business to give protection and support to the poor, distressed inhabitants, not to multiply and increase their calamities. After the publication of this order, any officer, either militia or continental, found attempting to conceal the public stores, plundering the inhabitants under the notion of their being Tories, or venduing of plunder taken from the enemy, in any other manner than these orders direct, may expect to be punished in the severest manner, and be obliged to account for everything taken or sold.

To William Livingston, Governor of New Jersey, January 24, 1777

Sir,

The irregular and disjointed state of the militia of this province makes it necessary for me to inform you that, unless a law is passed by your legislature to reduce them to some order and oblige them to turn out in a different manner from what they have hitherto done, we shall bring very few into the field, and even those few will render little or no service.

Their officers are generally of the lowest class of people, and instead of setting a good example to their men are leading them into every kind of mischief, one species of which is plundering the inhabitants under pretense of their being Tories. A law should in my opinion be passed to put a stop to this kind of lawless rapine; for unless there is something done to prevent it, the people will throw themselves of choice into the hands of the British troops.

But your first object should be a well-regulated militia law. The people, put under good officers, would behave in quite another manner, and not only render real service as soldiers, but would protect instead of distressing the inhabitants.

What I would wish to have particularly insisted upon in the new law should be that every man capable of bearing arms should be obliged to turn out and not buy off their service by a trifling sum. We want men and not money. I have the Honor to be with the greatest Respect Sir Your most obt Servt

Go: Washington

Proclamation Concerning Persons Swearing British Allegiance, January 25, 1777

By His Excellency *GEORGE WASHINGTON*, Esq., General and Commander-in-Chief of all the forces of the United States of America.

Proclamation

Whereas several persons, inhabitants of the United States of America, influenced by inimical motives, intimidated by the threats of the enemy, or deluded by a proclamation issued the 30th of November last, by Lord and General Howe, styled the King's Commissioners for granting pardons, etc. (now at open war and invading these states) have been so lost to the interest and welfare of their country as to repair to the enemy, sign a declaration of fidelity, and, in some instances, have been compelled to take oaths of allegiance, and to engage not to take up arms, or encourage others so to do, against the king of Great Britain. And whereas it has become necessary to distinguish between the friends of America and those of Great Britain, inhabitants of these states, and that every man who receives a protection from and is a subject of any state (not being conscientiously scrupulous against bearing arms) should stand ready to defend the same against every hostile invasion, I do therefore, in behalf of the United States, by virtue of the powers committed to me by Congress, hereby strictly command and require every person, having subscribed such declaration, taken such oaths, and accepted protection and certificates from Lord or General Howe, or any person acting under their authority, forthwith to repair to headquarters, or to the quarters of the nearest general officer of the Continental Army or Militia (until farther provision can be made by the civil authority) and there deliver up such protections, certificates, and passports, and take the oath of allegiance to the United States of America. Nevertheless, hereby granting full liberty to all such as prefer the interest and protection of Great Britain to the freedom and happiness of their country, forthwith to withdraw themselves and families within the enemy's lines. And I do hereby declare that all and every person, who may neglect or refuse to comply with this order, within thirty days from the date hereof, will be deemed adherents to the king of Great Britain, and treated as common enemies of the American states.

Circular to Eleven States, January 31–February 1, 1777

Gentlemen,

The great countenance and protection shown and given to deserters, by persons in the different neighborhoods from whence they originally came, has made that vice so prevalent in the army that, unless some very effectual means are fallen upon to prevent it, our new army will scarcely be raised before it will again dwindle and waste away from that cause alone.

I know of no remedy so effectual as for the different states immediately to pass laws laying a very severe penalty upon those who harbor or fail to give information against deserters, knowing them to be such, and strictly enjoining all justices of the peace and officers of the militia to keep a watchful eye over and apprehend all such persons as shall return from the army without a discharge.

In order that this most salutary measure may be carried speedily into execution, I have not only desired Congress to recommend it to the different states, but have myself written[4] circular letters to them all, pressing their compliance with my request. Desertion must cease of course when the deserters find they have no shelter. I am Gentn Yr mo: Obedt Servt

Go: Washington

To John Hancock, President of the Continental Congress, January 31, 1777 (Excerpt)

I must beg you will write to the assemblies of the different states and insist upon their passing a law to inflict a severe and heavy penalty upon those who harbor deserters, knowing them to be such. Our army is shamefully reduced by desertion, and except the people in the country can be forced to give information when deserters return to their old neighborhoods, we shall be obliged to detach one half of the army to bring back the other.

To John Hancock, President of the Continental Congress, February 5, 1777 (Excerpts)

I received a letter from Mr. Chase desiring I would appoint proper persons to make inquiry into and take depositions concerning the behavior of the British and foreign troops in Jersey. This would be an endless task, as their line of march is marked with devastation, and is a thing of such public notoriety that it demands no further proof. I remonstrated with General Howe upon the treatment of our wounded at Princetown; you will see by the enclosed letter from him that he disavows and detests the proceeding. But I fear that too much encouragement is given to such barbarous behavior by the British officers. For in a late skirmish in which Sir William Erskine commanded, Lieutenant Kelly of the 5th Virginia Regiment was slightly wounded in the thigh, but before he could get off the field he was overtaken and murdered in a most cruel manner. General Stephen informed me that he would write to Sir William and inform him that unless such practices were put a stop to, our soldiers would not be restrained from making retaliation ....

From the first institution of civil government, it has been the national policy of every precedent state to endeavor to engage its members to the discharge of their public duty by the obligation of some oath. Its force and happy influence have[5] been felt in too many instances to need any arguments to support the policy or prove its utility. I have often thought the states have been too negligent in this particular and am more fully convinced of it from the effect General Howe's excursion has produced in New Jersey. An oath is the only substitute that can be adopted to supply the defect of principle. By our inattention to this article, we lose a considerable cement to our own force, and give the enemy an opportunity to make the first tender of the oath of allegiance to the king. Its baneful influence is but too severely felt at this time. The people generally confess they were compelled to take protection and subscribe the declaration, yet it furnishes many with arguments to refuse taking any active part; and further they allege themselves bound to a neutrality at least. Many conscientious people who were well-wishers to the cause, had they been bound to the states by an oath, would have suffered any punishment rather than have taken the oath of allegiance to the king, and are now lost to our interest, for want of this necessary tie. Notwithstanding the obligation of the association, they do not conceive it to have the same effect of an oath. The more united the inhabitants appear, the greater difficulty

Howe will have in reconciling them to regal government, and consequently the less hope of conquering them. For these reasons, and many more that might be urged, I should strongly recommend every state to fix upon some oath or affirmation of allegiance to be tendered to all the inhabitants without exception, and to outlaw those that refuse it. I have the Honor to be with the greatest Respect Sir Your most obt Servt

Go: Washington

General Orders, February 6, 1777 (Excerpt)

The general is informed that many frauds and abuses have been committed of late by sundry soldiers who, after enlisting in one regiment, and receiving the bounty allowed by Congress, have deserted, enlisted in others, and received new bounties. For prevention of such unjust and infamous practices, he[6] commands and strictly enjoins all officers of the Continental Army to use their utmost endeavors to detect those who shall be guilty of such offenses and them having apprehended, the[7] cause to be forthwith tried by a general court martial, that they may be dealt with according to their crimes.

The general thinks proper to declare that this offense is of the most enormous and flagrant nature, and not admitting of the least palliation or excuse. Whosoever are convicted thereof, and sentenced to die, may consider their execution certain and inevitable.

To Walter Rutherford, February 14, 1777

Sir,

I have received your letter of yesterday. In answer to it I beg leave to observe that it is not within the scan of human wisdom to devise a perfect plan. In all human institutions—in the accomplishment of all great events—in the adoption of any measure for general operation, individuals may and will suffer. But in the case complained of, the matter may, I think, be answered by propounding a few questions.

Is it not a duty incumbent upon the members of every state to defend the rights and liberties of that state? If so, is an oath extorted from them, to observe a contrary conduct, obligatory? If such oath was not extorted but the effect of a voluntary act, can the person taking offense be considered in any other light than as an enemy to his country? In either case then, where is the injustice of calling upon them to a declaration of their sentiments? Is a neutral character in one of the United States, which has by her representatives solemnly engaged to support the cause, a justifiable one? If it is, may it not be extended to corporate bodies—to the state at large—and to the inevitable destruction of the opposition which, under Providence, depends upon a firm union of the whole and the spirited exertions of all its constituent parts?

Upon the whole, it appears to me that but two kinds of people will complain much of the proclamation: namely, those that are really disaffected and such as want to lay by and wait the issue of the dispute. The first class cannot be pleased; the next are endeavoring to play a double game, in which their present protections may, eventually, become a sure card.

To John Hancock, President of the Continental Congress, March 1, 1777 (Excerpt)

Sir,

I was this evening honored with your favor of the 23rd ultimo, accompanied by sundry proceedings of Congress. Those respecting General Lee, and which prescribe the treatment of Lieutenant Colonel Campbell and the five Hessian field officers, are the cause of this letter.

Though I sincerely commiserate the misfortunes of General Lee, and feel much for his present unhappy situation, yet, with all possible deference to the opinion of Congress, I fear that these resolutions would not have the desired effect, are founded in impolicy, and will, if adhered to, produce consequences of an extensive and melancholy nature.

Retaliation is certainly just and sometimes necessary, even where attended with the severest penalties. But when the evils which may and must result from it exceed those intended to be redressed, prudence and policy require that it should be avoided.

Having premised thus much, I beg leave to examine the justice and expediency of it in the instances now before us.

From the best information I have been able to obtain, General Lee's usage has not been so disgraceful and dishonorable as to authorize the treatment decreed to those gentlemen, was it not prohibited by many other important considerations. His confinement, I believe, has been more rigorous than has been generally experienced by the rest of our officers, or those of the enemy who have been in our possession; but if the reports be true received on that head, he has been provided with a decent apartment and with most things necessary to render him comfortable. This is not the case with one of the officers comprehended in the resolves, if his letter, of which a copy is transmitted, deserves your credit. Here retaliation seems to have been prematurely begun; or, to speak with more propriety, severities have been and are exercising towards Colonel Campbell not justified by any that General Lee has yet received.

In point of policy, under the present situation of our affairs, this doctrine cannot be supported. The balance of prisoners is greatly against us, and a general regard to the happiness of the whole should mark our conduct. Can we imagine that our enemies will not mete the same punishments, the same indignities, the same cruelties to those belonging to us in their possession that we impose on theirs in our power? Why should we suppose them to possess more humanity than we have ourselves? Or why should an ineffectual attempt to relieve the distresses of one brave, unfortunate man involve many more in the same calamities? However disagreeable the fact may be, the enemy at this time have in their power and subject to their call near three hundred officers belonging to the Army of the United States. In this number there are some of high rank, and the most of them are men of bravery and of merit. The quota of theirs in our hands bears no proportion, being not more than fifty at most. Under these circumstances we should certainly do no act to draw upon the gentlemen belonging to us, and who have already suffered a long captivity, greater punishments than they have and now experience. If we should, what will their feelings be and those of their numerous and extensive connections? Suppose the treatment prescribed for the Hessians should be pursued; will it not establish what the enemy have been aiming to effect by every artifice and the grossest misrepresentations? I mean an opinion of our enmity towards them, and of the cruel conduct they experience when they fall into our hands—a prejudice which we on our part have heretofore thought it politic to suppress and to root out by every act of lenity and of kindness. It certainly will. The Hessians would hear of the punishment with all the circumstances of heightened exaggeration—would feel the injury without investigating the cause, or reasoning upon the justice or necessity of it. The mischiefs which may and must inevitably flow from the execution of the resolves appear to be endless and innumerable. On my own part I have been much embarrassed on the subject of exchanges already. Applications are daily made by both friends and enemies to complete them as far as circumstances of number and rank will apply. Some of the former have complained that a discrimination is about to be adopted perhaps injurious to their reputation, and certainly depriving them of their right of exchange in due course, as established upon the principles of equality proposed last year—acceded to by both parties and now subsisting. The latter charge me with a breach of faith and call upon me to perform the agreement. Many more objections might be subjoined, were they material. I shall only observe that the present state of our army, if it deserves that name, will not authorize the language of retaliation or the style of menace. This will be conceded by all who know that the whole of our force is weak and trifling and composed of militia (a very few regular troops excepted) whose service is on the eve of expiring.

To Robert Morris, March 2, 1777 (Excerpt)

The resolve to put into close confinement Lieutenant Colonel Campbell and the Hessian field officers in order to retaliate General Lee's punishment upon them is, in my opinion, injudicious in every point of view and must, I conceive, have been entered into without due attention to circumstances and consequences. Does Congress know how much the balance of prisoners is against us?—that the enemy have near, if not quite, 300 officers of ours in their possession, and we scarce fifty of theirs?—that Generals Thompson and Waterbury are subject to a recall? Do they imagine that these officers will not share the fate of Campbell etc.?—or, possibly by receiving very different treatment, mixed with artful insinuations, have their resentments roused to acts highly injurious to our cause? And that it is much easier to raise than allay resentments, I believe no one will deny. To this may be added that every artifice is now practicing to instill into the Hessians (in Howe's army) an idea of our cruelty to their brethren with us, that we are actually selling of[8] them as slaves. Will not the close confinement, therefore, of their principal officers be adduced as strong evidence of this? The confinement will be proved to them; the cause will be concealed. In a word, Congress should be cautious in adopting measures that cannot be carried into execution without drawing after them a train of consequences that may be destructive in their effects.

To sum up the whole, common prudence dictates the necessity of duly attending to the circumstances of both armies before the style of a conqueror is assumed by either. And sorry I am to add that this does not appear to be the case with us. Nor is it in my power to make Congress fully sensible of the real situation of our affairs, and that it is with difficulty (if I may use the expression) that I can by every means in my power keep the life and soul of this army together. In short, when they are at a distance, they think it is but to say "presto begone" and everything is done—or in other words to resolve without considering, or seeming to have any conception, of the difficulties and perplexities attending those who are to carry those resolves into effect. Indeed, sir, your observations on our want of many principal characters in that respectable senate are but too well founded in truth. However, our cause is just, and I hope Providence will aid us in the support of it.

If the resolves of Congress respecting General Lee strike you in the same light it has done me, I could wish you would signify as much to them, as I really think they are fraught with much evil. We know that the meeting of a committee of Congress and Lord Howe stopped the mouths of many disaffected people. I believe the same would happen in the present instance, for there will be enough to say, if the application is known and not complied with, that the Congress were determined to listen to nothing. But the other matter relative to the confinement of the officers is what I am particularly concerned about, as I think it will involve much more than Congress has an idea of and will bring on repentance when it is too late if carried into execution.

To Major General Joseph Spencer, April 3, 1777 (Excerpt)

Sir,

I am favored with yours of the 26th ultimo, enclosing proceedings of a court martial upon Nagel, Key, and Querry, who are sentenced to suffer death for desertion. The plea of ignorance of our law is frivolous, and if admitted we should never convict a criminal. Examples must be made to put a stop to that prevailing crime, or we may as well disband the army at once. I therefore desire that the most atrocious of the three may be executed and the others pardoned.

Proclamation of Pardon to Deserters, April 6, 1777

By His Excellency George Washington, Esquire
General and Commander-in-Chief of the Forces of the United States of America.
Proclamation
Whereas many soldiers, lately enlisted in the Continental Army, not content with the generous bounties and encouragements granted to them by Congress, but influenced by a base regard to their interest, have re-enlisted with, received bounties from, other officers and then deserted; and whereas it is presumed that many, fully sensible of the enormity of their crimes, would return to their duty were they not deterred by an apprehension of suffering the severe punishment lately inflicted on those found guilty of desertion.

I have thought proper to issue this my proclamation offering free pardon to all those above described, as well as to those who have deserted from other motives, who shall voluntarily surrender themselves to any officer in the Continental Army or join their respective corps before the fifteenth day of May next. And I do strictly enjoin all officers in the army under my command, and entreat the good people of these states, to use their utmost endeavors to apprehend and secure such deserters as shall not avail themselves of this indulgence offered by this proclamation. Given under my hand at headquarters at Morristown this sixth day of April 1777.

Go: W.

To Richard Henry Lee, April 24–26, 1777 (Excerpt)

That Great Britain will exert every nerve to carry her tyrannical designs into execution, I have not the smallest doubt of. Her very existence as a nation depends now upon her success. For should America rise triumphant in her struggle for independency, she must fall. It is not to be wondered at therefore, after she had departed from that line of justice which ought to characterize a virtuous people, that she should descend to such low arts and dirty tricks as will forever remain a reproach to them. None of which have they practiced with more success, and I fear with more dangerous consequences to our cause, than their endeavors to depreciate the continental bills of credit. Nothing therefore has a greater claim to the close attention of Congress than the counteraction of this part of their diabolical scheme. Everything depends upon it.

The complexion of affairs in Europe seems to indicate an approaching storm, but where, when, or on whom it may break is not quite so clear—and ought not, in my judgment, to occasion the smallest relaxation in our preparations. For I profess myself to be of that class who never built sanguinely upon the assistance of France, further than her winking at our supplies from thence for the benefits derived from our trade. And how far the meanness and offers of Great Britain may contravene this, time only can discover and is somewhat to be feared.

To Brigadier General John Glover, April 26, 1777

Sir,

After the conversations I had with you, before you left the army last winter, I was not a little surprised at the contents of yours of the first instant. As I had not the least doubt but you would accept of the commission of brigadier, if conferred upon you by Congress, I put your name down in the list of those whom I thought proper for the command, and whom I wished to see preferred.

Diffidence in an officer is a good mark, because he will always endeavor to bring himself up to what he conceives to be the full line of his duty; but I think, I may tell you without flattery, that I know of no man better qualified than you to conduct a brigade. You have activity and industry, and as you very well know the duty of a colonel, you know how to exact that duty from others.

I have with great concern observed the almost universal listlessness that prevails throughout the continent; and I believe that nothing has contributed to it more than the resignation of officers who stepped early forward and led the people into the great cause, in which we are too deeply embarked to look back or to hope for any other terms than those we can gain by the sword. Can any resistance be expected from the people when deserted by their leaders? Our enemies count upon the resignation of every officer of rank at this time as a distrust of and desertion from the cause, and rejoice accordingly. When you consider these matters, I hope you will think no more of private inconveniences, but that you will, with all expedition, come forward and take that command which has been assigned you. As I fully depend upon seeing you, I shall not mention anything that has passed between us upon this subject to the Congress. I am Sir Your most humble servant

Go: Washington

To Major General Stirling, May 6, 1777

My Lord,

It is with pain I inform you that a complaint has been made to me of your having treated Mrs. Livingston with a degree of roughness and indelicacy which I am convinced your cooler reflection must condemn. Conscious that you have too much regard for your character as a gentleman, and too nice a sensibility of the impulses of humanity, deliberately to commit an indiscretion of the kind, I can only impute what has happened to a sudden transport of passion. And I am persuaded I need only beg you to consider your conduct in this affair to make you feel the impropriety of it and do everything proper to obviate the disagreeable consequences it tends to produce.

I pretend not to interfere in this matter in any other light than as a friend. The respect I have for your reputation will not allow me to be silent, when I cannot but fear you have acted in a manner that will be prejudicial to it. May I not add that the enemies of our cause will take advantage of such a circumstance, from the military rank you hold, to make comments of a very injurious nature.

The present situation of public affairs affords abundant causes of distress. We should be very careful how we aggravate or multiply them by private bickerings. It is not for me to enter into the merits of the dispute that gave rise to the ill treatment complained of; but I must take the liberty to give my opinion that prudence and compassion equally dictate all little differences and animosities calculated to increase the unavoidable evils of the times should be forgotten, or at least postponed—and that Mrs. Livingston's character, connections, sex, and situation entitle her to a degree of respect and consideration incompatible with that kind of deportment which I am informed you have, in this instance, observed towards her. Her son has signified to me that it is his mother's intention to change her habitation as soon as she can find a commodious place for the purpose. Surely you can have no objection to allowing her the time necessary for accomplishing it, and will never think of expelling her by violence and exposing her to all the inconveniences she would naturally experience.

I hope Your Lordship will entertain a just idea of the friendly motives that occasion this letter, and will believe me to be with great regard, Your Lordship's Most Obedt Servant

G. Washington

To Colonel François Lellorquis de Malmedy, May 16, 1777

Sir,

In answer to your letter of the 14th, I must freely confess I do not fully comprehend your meaning, nor can I forbear expressing my surprise that you still hold out the idea of difficulties in your situation, notwithstanding the mark of attention you mention, which has lately been conferred upon you by Congress. It astonishes me that a gentleman of your discernment should find it impossible to make a right distinction between continental and colonial appointments after all the pains that have been taken to explain it. Certainly there is nothing easier to conceive than that an appointment made by the legislature of a particular state, unauthorized by Congress, can have no effect out of that state. The reason is plain: such legislature has only a local jurisdiction and can do no act binding on any other state, much less on the whole continent. Your rank of brigadier in Rhode Island, on a continental scale, is and always has been entirely nugatory. You might request a ratification of it from Congress as a matter of favor, but you could not demand it as a matter of right. And you must be sensible that many substantial reasons, independent of any personal objections to you, oppose your wish.

A perseverance in your mistaken pretensions, after you had seen they could not be complied with, is what I did not expect.

To request to be employed in a manner not derogatory to the rank you held in Rhode Island, according to your ideas of that rank, is to request not to be employed at all. I must repeat what I have before told you, that I cannot consider you in any other light than that in which Congress has placed you; and whatever employment I may at any time have it in my power to give you must be in conformity to that precise rank you actually possess in the Continental Army. If you expect any other, you deceive yourself. Such an employment, though it may appear to you a degradation, would not in fact be so, because your appointment of brigadier is a perfect non-entity in a continental view.

If you formed erroneous notions of your colonial appointment, and in consequence of them made representations to your friends in Europe, which now involve you in perplexities, you ought to consider it as your misfortune and should not build any claims upon it that cannot be admitted. But though the distinctions existing among us may not be well understood in France, as you have hinted in a former letter, is it impossible to give a satisfactory explanation of them to your friends? Or will it be any indelible disgrace to you to confess to them that you have been in an error in your first conceptions, arising from your being a stranger and unacquainted with the nature of our different military establishments? We ought not to convert trifling difficulties into insuperable obstacles.

Let me propose a few more questions. Appeal to your own understanding and conscience and then answer: is not the continental rank you now hold fully adequate to any expectations you can reasonably deduce from the rank you held in the French army, and from the short term of seven month's service in ours? Would not the American officers, who have been in the service from the beginning of the war, have a just cause to complain of your too rapid promotion, were your wishes indulged? And would it not justify those who have been your superior officers in your own country in raising their hopes to a height which it would be impossible to gratify? In short, sir, I cannot bring myself to think that the extraordinary mark of distinction bestowed upon you by the state of Rhode Island is any sufficient foundation for expecting the continent to wave every consideration of policy or propriety in your behalf.

Though I wish not to offend or wound, justice both to you and myself requires that I should plainly inform you that your scruples and difficulties, so often reiterated and under a variety of shapes, are exceedingly perplexing to me, and that I wish them to cease. I am Sir &ca.

G. Washington

To Richard Henry Lee, May 17, 1777 (Excerpt)

Dear Sir,

Under the privilege of friendship, I take the liberty to ask you what Congress expects I am to do with the many foreigners they have, at different times, promoted to the rank of field officers—and, by the last resolve, two to that of colonels.

In making these appointments, it is much to be feared that all the circumstances attending are not taken into consideration. To oblige the adventurers of a nation whom we want to interest in our cause may be one inducement, and to get rid of their importunity another. But this is viewing the matter by halves, or on one side only. These men have no attachment or ties to the country further than interest binds them. They have no influence and are ignorant of the language they are to receive and give orders in; consequently, great trouble or much confusion must follow. But this is not the worst. They have not the smallest chance to recruit others, and our officers think it exceedingly hard, after they have toiled in this service, and probably sustained many losses, to have strangers put over them whose merit perhaps is not equal to their own, but whose effrontery will take no denial.

The management of this matter—give me leave to add, sir—is a delicate point. For although no one will dispute the right of Congress to make appointments, every person will assume the privilege of judging of the propriety of them; and good policy, in my opinion, forbids the disgusting a whole corps to gratify the pride of an individual. For it is by the zeal and activity of our own people that the cause must be supported, and not by a few hungry adventurers. Besides, the error of these appointments is now clear and manifest, and the views of Congress evidently defeated. For by giving high rank to people of no reputation or service you have disgusted their own countrymen—or, in other words, raised their expectations to an insatiable pitch. For the man who was a captain in France, finding another who was only a subaltern there, or perhaps nothing, appointed to a majority with us, extends his views instantly to a regiment. In like manner the field officer can accept of nothing less than a brigade, and so on, by which means the man of real rank and merit must be excluded, or perhaps your whole military system disordered. In the meanwhile, I am haunted and teased to death by the importunity of some and dissatisfaction of others.

My ideas in this representation do not extend to artillery officers and engineers. The first of these will be useful if they do not break in upon the arrangement of that corps already established by order of Congress. The second are absolutely necessary and not to be had here. But proper precaution should be observed in the choice of them, for we have at present in pay and high rank two (Frenchmen) who, in my judgment, know nothing of the duty of engineers. Gentlemen of this profession ought to produce sufficient and authentic testimonials of their skill and knowledge, and not expect that a pompous narrative of their services and loss of papers (the usual excuse) can be a proper introduction into our army.

The freedom with which I have delivered my sentiments on this subject will, I am persuaded, meet your excuse when I assure you that I have nothing else in view than the good of the service.

To Colonel George Baylor, May 23, 1777 (Excerpt)

A chaplain is part of the establishment of a corps of cavalry, and I see no objection to your having one, unless you suppose yours will be too virtuous and moral to require instruction. Let him be a man of character and good conversation, and who will influence the manners of the corps both by precept and example.

To Major General William Heath, May 23, 1777 (Excerpt)

The conduct of those who desert and receive double bounties deserves severe punishment. The practice has prevailed to a great and scandalous degree, and the desertions, after they have come into the field, have been truly vexatious. However, I have heard nothing of such malignity or of so fatal a tendency as the conduct of Lieutenant Colonel Farrington. You say you hope the army will get rid of him. Will not the world, too? I hope the state has provided laws against such offenders, for I cannot conceive that any crime should be punished with more severity or more certain death than what this man has been guilty of. Money is the sinews of war. That in which we are engaged is a just one, and we have no means of carrying it on but by the continental or state notes. Whoever attempts to destroy their credit, particularly that of those emitted by the United States, is a flagitious offender and should forfeit his life to satisfy the demands of public justice. In the case before us, the enormity of the crime is aggravated in a peculiar manner by the post Farrington held.

Circular Instructions to the Brigade Commanders, May 26, 1777 (Excerpt)

Let vice and immorality of every kind be discouraged as much as possible in your brigade; and, as a chaplain is allowed to each regiment, see that the men regularly attend divine worship. Gaming of every kind is expressly forbid as the foundation of evil and the cause of many gallant and brave officers' ruin. Games of exercise for amusement may not only be permitted but encouraged.

General Orders, May 31, 1777 (Excerpt)

It is much to be lamented that the foolish and scandalous practice of *profane swearing* is exceedingly prevalent in the American army. Officers of every rank are bound to discourage it, first by their example and then by punishing offenders. As a mean to abolish this, and every other species of immorality, brigadiers are enjoined to take effectual care to have divine service duly performed in their respective brigades.

To John Hancock, President of the Continental Congress, June 3, 1777

Sir,

I would take the liberty of addressing a few lines to Congress on a matter which appears to me of importance, and which is considered in the same light by many of our officers and others not in the military line.

The subject I allude to is the condition of many persons, now with the enemy, who, deluded by their arts and a misguided attachment to their measures, fled from the protection of the states to find security with them—and who in many instances are in arms against us.

It has been suggested through various channels—and the suggestion seems to be credited, especially as some have already escaped—that many of these unhappy people, convinced of their error and the wicked part they have taken, would embrace the earliest opportunity of leaving the enemy and returning among us, were they sure of being received into our friendship again and of enjoying their property and the rights of citizens.

This subject, in the consideration of it, strikes me as important—interesting and delicate, involving many consequences worthy of mature deliberation and attention. As such, and deeming myself incompetent to it, I think it my duty to submit it to Congress for their discussion, to take such measures therein as they shall esteem necessary and right.

If these people, particularly those in arms, are ingenuous in what has been hinted, and it is their wish, or that of any considerable part of them, to return, I should suppose that it would be expedient and founded in sound policy to give every suitable assurance to induce them to come. Such an event would be attended with salutary effects—would weaken the enemy, distress them greatly, and would probably have a most happy influence in preventing others from joining their arms. On the other hand, the indulgence may be liable to great abuse, supposing it not to be duly regarded—or, if the effects produced by it should be partial, they will not be adequate to the ends in view. Yet, as the enemy on their part are using every device they are capable of to seduce both soldiers and citizens from our service into theirs, and have succeeded but too well, it is generally thought, in the military line, that something should be attempted to counteract them. Whether Congress will be of the same sentiment, and, if they should, what and how extensive the mode and indulgence ought to be, is entirely with them.

There is one difficulty that occurs to me, supposing the measure to be adopted. What line of discrimination can be drawn upon such an occasion, though circumstances should differ and seem to require it? While the poor, deluded, ignorant, duped by artifices and a thousand causes to lead them wrong, have a claim to their country's pardon and indulgence, there are many of well-informed understanding who, from their early avowed, hostile dispositions and inveterate disregard of her rights, and those who have taken a double and treble part, cannot have the same pretensions, whose only view in returning may be to serve their own sordid purposes and the better to promote those plans they have steadily pursued.

One thing more I would observe, which is that if Congress judge an adoption of measures eligible on the subject of my letter, the sooner it is come into the better, for the most obvious reasons. And the time allowed for those to return, who wish the indulgence, should be fixed at a short period—not longer in my opinion than till the _____ day of _____ next. Otherwise, they may avail themselves of the circumstance and wait events to decide their choice. If any good consequences are produced, the means can be renewed and further extended.

Congress will be pleased to excuse me for thus freely communicating my sentiments, especially when I assure them that they are dictated by what I esteem my duty. I have the Honor to be with great respect Sir Your & their Most Obedt Servt

Go: Washington

P.S. The more I consider the subject of my letter, the more important and interesting it appears. I am inclined to think, if the measure proposed should be deemed expedient, that it will be better that the indulgencies and assurances for their return should be communicated through the medium of some second, secret hand, qualified to offer them and negotiate the business, rather than by an act of public authority. Opportunities, I should suppose, may be found by which they may obtain due information in that way, and which will not hold out to the enemy the same cause of suspicion and of vigilance to prevent their escaping. Whatever mode shall be considered most advisable should be immediately adopted. What time should be allowed in the first instance I am at a loss to determine. If the continuance is too short, there may be danger of their not being apprised so as to get off. If 'tis too long, they'll defer matters to the last and act then as circumstances of interest dictate. To err in the former will be least injurious.

General Orders, June 4, 1777 (Excerpt)

The music of the army being in general very bad, it is expected that the drum and fife majors exert themselves to improve it, or they will be reduced and their extraordinary pay taken from them. Stated hours to be assigned for all the drums and fifes of each regiment to attend them and practice. Nothing is more agreeable and ornamental than good music. Every officer, for the credit of his corps, should take care to provide it.

General Orders, June 7, 1777 (Excerpt)

As the army is now on a permanent and honorable footing, and as the general has the credit of it very much at heart, he expects that every officer, on whom the importance of the contest and a regard to his own honor or duty are sufficiently impressed, will lend their aid to support the character of it. To this end, nothing can be more effectual than a close attention to discipline and subordination, and particularly in an exact obedience to all general orders, which is the life of an army. Officers should consider that a repetition of orders is the highest reflection upon those who are the cause of it. An orderly book is a record in the hands of thousands of the transactions of an army, and consequently of the disgrace of those whose insensibility to the obligations they are under, and whose want of a manly emulation of temper, OBLIGE the commander-in-chief to publish their misconduct by repeating his calls upon them to discharge their duty.

    The general appeals to the understanding of every officer and earnestly recommends a serious consideration of these matters. Their engagements with the public, their own honor, and the salvation of their country demand it. The general wishes it on these accounts, and for his own ease and satisfaction; for as nothing is more easy than to conduct an army where a cheerful and ready obedience is paid to every order, so nothing is more difficult and embarrassing, where a careless, licentious, and disorderly spirit prevails. Thus, much is said to lead gentlemen into a proper train of thinking on the subject, and to engage their judgment and feelings on the side of their duty; but it is at the same time necessary to subjoin that a punishment and disgrace will attend those who will not be influenced by more honorable means.

To John Hancock, President of the Continental Congress, June 8, 1777 (Excerpt)

I shall order a return to be made of the chaplains in service, which shall be transmitted as soon as it is obtained. At present, as the regiments are greatly dispersed, part in one place and part in another, and accurate states of them have not been made, it will not be in my power to forward it immediately. I shall here take occasion to mention that I communicated the resolution appointing a brigade chaplain in the place of all others to the several brigadiers. They are all of opinion that it will be impossible for 'em to discharge the duty, that many inconveniences and much dissatisfaction will be the result, and that no establishment appears so good in this instance as the old one. Among many other weighty objections to the measure, it has been suggested that it has a tendency to introduce religious disputes into the army, which above all things should be avoided, and in many instances would compel men to a mode of worship which they do not profess. The old establishment gives every regiment an opportunity of having a chaplain of their own religious sentiments, is founded on a plan of a more generous toleration, and the choice of chaplains to officiate has been generally in the regiments. Supposing one chaplain could do the duties of a brigade (which supposition, however, is inadmissible, when we view things in practice), that being composed of four or five—perhaps in some instances six regiments—there might be so many different modes of worship. I have mentioned the opinion of the officers and these hints to Congress upon this subject from a principle of duty, and because, I am well assured, it is most foreign to their wishes or intention to excite by any act the smallest uneasiness and jealousy among the troops.

To Charles-François-Adrien Le Paulmier Annemours, June 19, 1777 (Excerpt)

Sir,

I have received your favor of the 6th instant, transmitting me your observations on the state of American affairs and the part that France is interested, by the motives of good policy, to act in consequence of it. Your reflections appear to me extremely judicious and well founded, and prove that you have made a good use of your time in collecting the information necessary to regulate your judgment in a matter that so intimately concerns all Europe as well as America. It were to be wished that sentiments similar to yours were impressed upon the French court, and that they could be induced not to delay an event so desirable both to them and to us as the one you are anxious should take place. An immediate declaration of war against Britain, in all probability, could not fail to extricate us from all our difficulties and to cement the bond of friendship so firmly between France and America as to produce the most permanent advantages to both. Certainly nothing can be more the true interest of France than to have a weight of such magnitude as America taken out of the scale of British power and opulence and thrown into that of her own. And, if so, it cannot be advisable to trust anything to contingencies when, by a conduct decisively in our favor, the object in view might be put upon a sure footing.

General Orders, July 25, 1777 (Excerpt)

How disgraceful to the army is it that the peaceable inhabitants, our countrymen and fellow citizens, dread our halting among them, even for a night, and are happy when they get rid of us? This can proceed only from their distress at the plundering and wanton destruction of their property. To prevent these evils is the manifest duty of the officers; and were they closely attentive to that discipline and order which should ever be established in a camp they, for the most part, certainly might prevent them. The commander-in-chief therefore expects that officers of every rank will exert themselves and put a stop to such practices in future. And if no other means are sufficient, that they post sentries round their encampments, who shall take prisoner every man who is guilty of them. And the guilty will most assuredly meet the punishment due to their crimes. Two soldiers in General Sullivan's division found guilty of plundering the inhabitants have lately been condemned to die, and one of them executed. At all events such practices must be prevented, for 'tis our duty to protect the property of our fellow citizens.

To Major General John Sullivan, July 25, 1777

Dear Sir,

It is with no small concern I am constrained to inform you that I am constantly receiving complaints from the people living contiguous to the road of great abuses committed by the division under your command in their march through the country. From their accounts, they have experienced the most wanton and insufferable injuries: fences destroyed without the least apparent necessity, and a great number of horses seized and taken away. In a word, according to them, they have suffered the most flagrant violation of their property. Perhaps their representations may be rather exaggerated beyond the bounds of strict truth. But I cannot but observe that the officers in the quartermaster general's department have informed me that more accounts have been presented to them for injuries done by your division, and of greater amounts, than by the whole army besides, and those carrying too a degree of authenticity with them, being certified in many instances under the officers' hands. At the same time that you are sensible how distressing such a conduct is to the inhabitants, you well know it is highly disgraceful and unworthy of the cause in which we are engaged. Add to this that it has a fatal and obvious tendency to prejudice their minds and to disaffect 'em. I must request, in the most earnest manner, your attention to this matter and to prevent in future, by every exertion in your power, the like proceedings. Point out the scandal and impropriety of it to your officers and urge them, as they regard their honor and reputation, to use their endeavors to restrain such unwarrantable practices. I am Dr Sir Yr Most Obedt Servant.

To Philippe-Hubert Preudhomme de Borre, August 3, 1777 (Excerpt)

With respect to the Tory who was tried and executed by your order, though his crime was heinous enough to deserve the fate he met with, and though I am convinced you acted in the affair with a good intention, yet I cannot but wish it had not happened. In the first place, it was a matter that did not come within the jurisdiction of martial law, and therefore the whole proceeding was irregular and illegal and will have a tendency to excite discontent, jealousy, and murmurs among the people. In the second, if the trial could properly have been made by a court martial, as the division you command is only a detachment from the army, and you cannot have been considered as in a separate department, there is none of our articles of war that will justify your inflicting a capital punishment, even on a soldier, much less on a citizen. I mention these things for your future government, as what is past cannot be recalled. The temper of the Americans and the principles on which the present contest turns will not countenance proceedings of this nature.

I am sorry there is such a difference between Major Mullen and you, but I cannot with propriety consent to your dismissing him without his having had a fair trial and any charges alleged against him being properly proved. As he is now under arrest, you may order a general court martial to be held for his trial and report the proceedings to me, on which I shall determine what appears to be just. I am &c.

General Orders, September 4, 1777 (Excerpt)

Notwithstanding all the cautions, the earnest requests, and the positive orders of the commander-in-chief to prevent our own army from plundering our own friends and fellow citizens, yet to his astonishment and grief fresh complaints are made to him that so wicked, infamous, and cruel a practice is still continued—and that, too, in circumstances most distressing, where the wretched inhabitants, dreading the enemy's vengeance for their adherence to our cause, have left all and fled to us for refuge! We complain of the cruelty and barbarity of our enemies, but does it equal ours? They sometimes spare the property of their friends. But some amongst us, beyond expression barbarous, rob even them! Why did we assemble in arms? Was it not, in one capital point, to protect the property of our countrymen? And shall we to our eternal reproach be the first to pillage and destroy? Will no motives of humanity, of zeal, interest, and of honor restrain the violence of the soldiers or induce officers to keep so strict a watch over the ill-disposed as effectually to prevent the execution of their evil designs and the gratification of their savage inclinations? Or, if these powerful motives are too weak, will they pay no regard to their own safety? How many noble designs have miscarried—how many victories been lost—how many armies ruined—by an indulgence of soldiers in plundering? If officers in the least connive at such practices, the licentiousness of some soldiers will soon be without bounds. In the most critical moments, instead of attending to their duty, they will be scattered abroad, indiscriminately plundering friends and foes; and, if no worse consequences ensue, many of them must infallibly fall a prey to the enemy. For these reasons the commander-in-chief requires that these orders be distinctly read to all the troops, and that officers of every rank take particular pains to convince the men of the baseness and fatal tendency of the practices complained of, and that their own safety depends on a contrary conduct and an exact observance of order and discipline. At the same time the commander-in-chief most solemnly assures all that he will have no mercy on offenders against these orders. Their lives shall pay the forfeit of their crimes. Pity, under such circumstances, would be the height of cruelty.

General Orders, September 5, 1777 (Excerpt)

From every information of the enemy's designs, and from their movements, it is manifest their aim is, if possible, to possess themselves of Philadelphia. This is their capital object. 'Tis what they last year strove to effect, but were happily disappointed. They made a second attempt at the opening of this campaign, but after vast preparations and expense for the purpose they abandoned their design and totally evacuated the Jerseys. They are now making their last effort. To come up the Delaware, it seems, was their first intention; but, from the measures taken to annoy them in the river, they judged the enterprise, that way, too hazardous. At length they have landed on the eastern shore of Maryland and advanced some little way into the country. But the general trusts they will be again disappointed in their views. Should they push their design against Philadelphia on this route, their all is at stake. They will put the contest on the event of a single battle. If they are overthrown, they are utterly undone—the war is at an end. Now, then, is the time for our most strenuous exertions. One bold stroke will free the land from rapine, devastations, and burnings, and female innocence from brutal lust and violence. In every other quarter the American arms have, of late, been rapidly successful, and still greater numbers have been made prisoners. The militia at the northward have fought with a resolution that would have done honor to old soldiers. They bravely fought and conquered, and glory attends them. Who can forbear to emulate their noble spirit? Who is there without ambition to share with them the applauses of their countrymen, and of all posterity, as the defenders of liberty, and the procurers of peace and happiness to millions in the present and future generations? Two years we have maintained the war and struggled with difficulties innumerable. But the prospect has since brightened, and our affairs put on a better face. Now is the time to reap the fruits of all our toils and dangers! If we behave like men, this third campaign will be our last. Ours is the main army; to us our country looks for protection. The eyes of all America and of Europe are turned upon us as on those by whom the event of the war is to be determined. And the general assures his countrymen and fellow soldiers that he believes the critical, the important moment is at hand, which demands their most spirited exertions in the field. There, glory waits to crown the brave—and peace, freedom, and happiness will be the rewards of victory. Animated by motives like these, soldiers fighting in the cause of innocence, humanity, and justice, will never give way, but, with undaunted resolution, press on to conquest. And this, the general assures himself, is the part the American forces now in arms will act—and, thus acting, he will ensure them success.

General Orders, September 6, 1777 (Excerpt)

The general has no doubt but that every man who has a due sense of the importance of the cause he has undertaken to defend, and who has any regard to his own honor and the reputation of a soldier, will, if called to action, behave like one contending for everything valuable. But, if contrary to his expectation there shall be found any officers or soldiers so far lost to all shame as basely to quit their post without orders, or shall skulk from danger, or offer to retreat before order is given for so doing from proper authority of a superior officer, they are to be instantly shot down, as a just punishment to themselves and for examples to others. This order those in the rear, and the corps of reserve, are to see duly executed, to prevent the cowardly from making a sacrifice of the brave, and by their ill example and groundless tales (calculated to cover their own shameful conduct) spreading terror as they go.

That this order may be well known, and strongly impressed upon the army, the general positively orders the commanding officer of every regiment to assemble his men and have it read to them, to prevent the plea of ignorance.

To Bryan Fairfax, September 24, 1777 (Excerpt)

The difference in our political sentiments never made any change in my friendship for you; and the favorable sentiments I ever entertained of your honor leave me without a doubt that you would not[9] say anything or do anything injurious to the cause we are engaged in, after having pledged your word to the contrary. I therefore give my consent, readily, to the prosecution of your inclination of going to England, and for this purpose enclose a certificate or passport to come forward to this army whenever you please.

To Bryan Fairfax, September 25, 1777 (Excerpt)

In my letter of yesterday I assured you, and assured you with truth, that the difference in our political sentiments had made no change in my friendship for you. I esteem and revere every man who acts from principle, as I am persuaded you do, and shall ever contribute my aid to facilitate any inclination you may wish to indulge, as I am satisfied that that honor which I have ever found you scrupulously observant of will never be departed from. I shall add no more, because in the first place I have very little leisure, and in the next because I conceive it unnecessary to multiply words to prove that with sincere regard I am Dr Sir Yr Most Obedt & Affe

Go: Washington

General Orders, October 3, 1777 (Excerpt)

The commander-in-chief has the satisfaction to inform the army that at the southward the continental frigate *Randolph* lately fell in with a fleet of five sail of the enemy's ships and took four of them, one of them mounting 20 guns and another 8—all richly laden. At the northward everything wears the most favorable aspect. Every enterprise has been successful. And, in a capital action, the left wing only of General Gates's army maintained its ground against the main body of the enemy, commanded by General Burgoyne in person, our troops behaving with the highest spirit and bravery during the whole engagement, which lasted from one o'clock till dark. In short, every circumstance promises success in that quarter equal to our most sanguine wishes. This surely must animate every man under the general's immediate command. This army—the main American army—will certainly not suffer itself to be outdone by their northern brethren. They will never endure such disgrace, but with an ambition becoming freemen, contending in the most righteous cause, rival the heroic spirit which swelled their bosoms, and which so nobly exerted has procured them deathless renown. Covet, my countrymen and fellow soldiers, covet a share of the glory due to heroic deeds! Let it never be said that in a day of action you turned your backs on the foe. Let the enemy no longer triumph. They brand you with ignominious epithets. Will you patiently endure that reproach? Will you suffer the wounds given to your country to go unrevenged? Will you resign your parents, wives, children, and friends to be the wretched vassals of a proud, insulting foe—and your own necks to the halter? General Howe promised protection to such as submitted to his power, and a few dastard souls accepted the disgraceful boon. But his promises were deceitful: the submitting and resisting had their property alike plundered and destroyed. But even these empty promises have come to an end; the term of mercy is expired. General Howe has within a few days proclaimed all who had not then submitted to be beyond the reach of it and has left us no choice but conquest or death. Nothing then remains but nobly to contend for all that is dear to us. Every motive that can touch the human breast calls us to the most vigorous exertions. Our dearest rights, our dearest friends, our own lives, honor, glory, and even shame urge us to the fight. And, my fellow soldiers, when an opportunity presents, be firm, be brave, show yourselves men, and victory is yours!

To John Hancock, President of the Continental Congress, October 13, 1777 (Excerpts)

It gives me pain to repeat so often the wants of the army, and nothing would induce me to it but the most urgent necessity. Every mode hitherto adopted for supplying them has proved inadequate, notwithstanding my best endeavors to make the most of the means which have been in my power. The enclosed return will show how great our deficiency in the most essential articles. What new expedient Congress can devise for more effectually answering these demands I know not, persuaded as I am that their closest attention has not been wanting to a matter of so great importance. But circumstanced as we are, I am under an absolute necessity of troubling them that if any new source can be opened for alleviating our distresses, it may be embraced as speedily as possible. For it is impossible that any army so unprovided can long subsist, or act with that vigor which is requisite to ensure success. The return now enclosed is for troops present in camp, besides which there are numbers in the several hospitals totally destitute of the necessaries they require to fit them for the field, and on this account alone are prevented from joining their corps. The recruits coming in are also in the same melancholy predicament. I cannot ascertain with precision what quantity of clothing is at this time in Mr. Mease's hands, but from every account what he has can administer but a very partial relief. I know he is entirely bare of some of the most capital articles we want ….

There is one thing more which I cannot omit mentioning to Congress, and which, in my opinion, has a claim to their most serious attention. I mean the general defective state of the regiments which compose our armies. Congress will find from a view of the returns transmitted from time to time that they do not amount to near half of their just complement. What can be done to remedy this I know not. But it is certain every idea of voluntary enlistments seems to be at end. And it is equally certain that the mode of drafting has been carried on with such want of energy in some states, and so much disregarded in others, that but a small accession of force has been derived from it. These facts are sufficiently interesting of themselves, but there are others to be added. I am told that Virginia, in her regulations for drafting, extended her plan only to nine regiments that were first raised. In what policy this was founded I cannot determine, but the other six are to receive no reinforcements from that source. Nor do matters stop here. The engagements of the first nine regiments, I am informed, were temporary; and, according to the officers' accounts, the longest period to which any of the men are bound to serve is next April. Many are not obliged so long, and there are some who claim a discharge at this time. I do not mention these things through choice, but from a principle of duty, to the end that Congress may devise some timely, effectual provision for the whole, if such shall be in their power. It is unnecessary to enlarge upon the subject, and I will only observe that the consequences of calling the militia into the field in the course of the war have been so severely and ruinously felt that I trust our views will never be turned to them but in cases of the greatest extremity.

General Orders, October 15, 1777 (Excerpt)

The general has the repeated pleasure of informing the army of the success of the troops under the command of General Gates over General Burgoyne's army. On the 7th instant the action commenced, about three o'clock in the afternoon, between the pickets of the two armies, which were reinforced on both sides. The contest was warm and continued with obstinacy till evening, when our troops gained the advanced line of the enemy and encamped on that ground all night. The enemy fled and left behind them 330 tents, with kettles boiling with corn, 8 brass cannon, two twelve- and six six-pounders, upwards of two hundred of their dead, and the baggage of their flying camp. General Frazier is among their slain. Our troops took 550 non-commissioned officers and soldiers prisoners, besides Sir Francis Carr Clark, aide-de-camp to General Burgoyne, a quartermaster general, the commanding officers of artillery, of a foreign brigade and of the British grenadiers, and a number of inferior rank. Two of our generals, Lincoln and Arnold, were wounded in the leg. Besides these our troops suffered very little. They behaved with great bravery and intrepidity and have thus a second time triumphed over the valor of veteran troops. When the last accounts came away, General Burgoyne's army was retreating and ours pursuing.

The general congratulates the troops upon this signal victory, the third capital advantage which, under Divine Providence, we have gained in that quarter, and hopes it will prove a powerful stimulus to the army under his immediate command at least to equal their northern brethren in brave and intrepid exertions when called thereto. The general wishes them to consider that this is the grand American army, and that of course great things are expected from it. 'Tis the army of whose superior prowess some have boasted. What shame, then, and dishonor will attend us if we suffer ourselves in every instance to be outdone? We have a force sufficient, by the favor of Heaven, to crush our foes; and nothing is wanting but a spirited, persevering exertion of it, to which, besides the motives before mentioned, duty and the love of our country irresistibly impel us. The effect of such powerful motives no man who possesses the spirit of a soldier can withstand, and spurred on by them, the general assures himself, that on the next occasion his troops will be completely successful.

In honor of the northern army, and to celebrate their victory, thirteen pieces of cannon are to be discharged at the artillery park at five o'clock this afternoon, previous to which the brigades and corps are to be drawn out on their respective parades, and these orders distinctly read to them by their officers.

To Henry Laurens, November 1, 1777 (Excerpt)

I would take the liberty to mention that I feel myself in a delicate situation with respect to the Marquis Lafayette. He is extremely solicitous of having a command equal to his rank and professes very different ideas as to the purposes of his appointment from those Congress have mentioned to me. He certainly did not understand them. I do not know in what light they will view the matter, but it appears to me, from a consideration of his illustrious and important connections, the attachment which he has manifested to our cause, and the consequences which his return in disgust might produce, that it will be advisable to gratify him in his wishes—and the more so as several gentlemen from France, who came over under some assurances, have gone back disappointed in their expectations. His conduct with respect to them stands in a favorable point of view, having interested himself to remove their uneasiness and urged the impropriety of their making any unfavorable representations upon their arrival at home, and in all his letters has placed our affairs in the best situation he could. Besides, he is sensible, discreet in his manners, has made great proficiency in our language, and from the disposition he discovered at the Battle of Brandywine, possesses a large share of bravery and military ardor.

To Brigadier General Thomas Conway, November 5, 1777

Sir,

A letter which I received last night contained the following paragraph:

In a letter from General Conway to General Gates he says—"Heaven has been determined to save your country, or a weak general and bad counselors would have ruined it." I am Sir Yr Hble Servt.

To Henry Laurens, November 23, 1777 (Excerpt)

I have been endeavoring to effect an exchange of prisoners from principles of justice and from motives of humanity, but at present I have no prospect of it. Yet General Howe has assured our officers it was his wish, and if it could not be done that he should readily agree to their release on parole. The enclosed copies of my letters and his answer will show Congress what has passed between us upon that subject, and at the same time that I had remonstrated against the severe and cruel treatment of the prisoners and proposed the plan of sending in a suitable person to inquire into the facts before the receipt of their resolution. Their sufferings, I am persuaded, have been great and shocking to humanity. I have called upon General Howe for redress and an explicit answer to my letter of the 14th. If I do not receive one by tomorrow night with the most positive and satisfactory assurances that a proper conduct shall be observed towards them in future, we must retaliate, however much we wish to avoid severity and measures that bear the smallest appearance of rigor or inhumanity.

To Henry Laurens, November 26, 1777 (Excerpt)

I was much obliged by the foreign intelligence you were pleased to transmit me. It is agreeable and interesting, and I heartily wish there may be an early declaration of hostilities between France and Britain. From these advices, things seem to be getting in a proper train for it, and it is not easily to be conceived that it can be much longer delayed. However, our expectations have not been answered in this instance, and they may yet be held in suspense. The political reasons that lead to delay on the part of France I do not perfectly understand. As to Britain, her honor is lost in the contest with us, and the most indignant insults will scarcely be able to draw her attention from her present pursuits. The account of Mr. Lee having effected the purposes of his embassy at the Court of Berlin is of great importance, if it be true. In such case administration, however desirous they may be, will probably be disappointed in their schemes of further mercenary aids against us.

General Orders, December 17, 1777 (Excerpt)

The commander-in-chief with the highest satisfaction expresses his thanks to the officers and soldiers for the fortitude and patience with which they have sustained the fatigues of the campaign. Although in some instances we unfortunately failed, yet upon the whole, Heaven hath smiled on our arms and crowned them with signal success. And we may upon the best grounds conclude that by a spirited continuance of the measures necessary for our defense we shall finally obtain the end of our warfare: independence, liberty, and peace. These are blessings worth contending for at every hazard. But we hazard nothing. The power of America alone, duly exerted, would have nothing to dread from the force of Britain. Yet we stand not wholly upon our ground. France yields us every aid we ask, and there are reasons to believe the period is not very distant when she will take a more active part by declaring war against the British Crown. Every motive, therefore, irresistibly urges us—nay, commands us—to a firm and manly perseverance in our opposition to our cruel oppressors—to slight difficulties, endure hardships, and contemn every danger. The general ardently wishes it were now in his power to conduct the troops into the best winter quarters. But where are these to be found? Should we retire to the interior parts of the state, we should find them crowded with virtuous citizens who, sacrificing their all, have left Philadelphia and fled thither for protection. To their distresses humanity forbids us to add. This is not all: we should leave a vast extent of fertile country to be despoiled and ravaged by the enemy, from which they would draw vast supplies and where many of our firm friends would be exposed to all the miseries of the most insulting and wanton depredation. A train of evils might be enumerated, but these will suffice. These considerations make it indispensably necessary for the army to take such a position as will enable it most effectually to prevent distress and to give the most extensive security, and in that position we must make ourselves the best shelter in our power. With activity and diligence huts may be erected that will be warm and dry. In these the troops will be compact, more secure against surprises than if in a divided state, and at hand to protect the country. These cogent reasons have determined the general to take post in the neighborhood of this camp; and, influenced by them, he persuades himself that the officers and soldiers, with one heart and one mind, will resolve to surmount every difficulty with a fortitude and patience becoming their profession and the sacred cause in which they are engaged. He himself will share in the hardship and partake of every inconvenience.

Tomorrow being the day set apart by the honorable Congress for public thanksgiving and praise, and duty calling us devoutly to express our grateful acknowledgments to God for the manifold blessings he has granted us, the general directs that the army remain in its present quarters and that the chaplains perform divine service with their several corps and brigades, and earnestly exhorts all officers and soldiers, whose absence is not indispensably necessary, to attend with reverence the solemnities of the day.

To Henry Laurens, December 22, 1777 (Excerpt)

It would give me infinite pleasure to afford protection to every individual and to every spot of ground in the whole of the United States. Nothing is more my wish. But this is not possible with our present force. In all wars, from the nature of things, individuals and particular places must be exposed. It has ever been and ever will be the case, and we have only to pity and to regret the misfortunes of those who from their situation are subject to ravage and depredation. These facts are evident and obvious to all; and if that system of conduct is pursued by an army which is most likely to give the most general and extensive security, it is all that can be done or expected from it. I assure you, sir, no circumstance in the course of the present contest, or in my whole life, has employed more of my reflection or consideration than in what manner to effect this, and to dispose of the army during the winter. Viewing the subject in any point of light, there was a choice of difficulties. If keeping the field was thought of, the naked condition of the troops and the feelings of humanity opposed the measures. If retiring to the towns in the interior parts of the state which, consistently with the preservation of the troops from their necessitous circumstances might have been justifiable, the measure was found inexpedient because it would have exposed and left uncovered a large extent of country. If cantoning the troops in several places, divided and distant from each other, then there was a probability of their being cut off and but little prospect of their giving security to any part. Under these embarrassments I determined to take post near this place, as the best calculated in my judgment to secure the army, to protect our stores and cover the country. And for this purpose we are beginning to hut, and shall endeavor to accomplish it as expeditiously as possible. I have also, from a desire of preventing the enemy from an intercourse with the Delaware state and from making incursions there, detached General Smallwood with the Maryland forces to take post at Wilmington, which I had reasons to believe the enemy intended. This, however, I cannot but consider as hazardous, and shall be happy if it does not turn out so. I have it also in contemplation to throw a bridge over Schuylkill near this place as soon as it is practicable, by means of which I hope we shall be able in a great measure, with the aid of the militia, to check the excursions of the enemy's parties on the other side.

As to Jersey, I am sensible of her sufferings and exertions in the present contest; and there is no state to which I would more willingly extend protection.

But, as I have observed, it is not in my power to give it in that degree in which it seems to be wished and expected. I cannot divide the army—not superior, from sickness and other causes equally painful, when collected to the enemy's force—into detachments, contrary to every military principle and to our own experience of the dangers that would attend it. If this is done, I cannot be answerable for the consequences. My feelings lead strongly to universal relief, but I have not the power to afford it. Nevertheless, it has been and is still my intention, as soon as I have formed and secured this camp, to detach a small force to aid and countenance their militia. This is all, it appears to me, that can be done; and I hope their apprehensions for the greater part will prove rather imaginary than well grounded—though I confess there are strong reasons to conclude the enemy will not be remiss in their acts of violence and injury there or anywhere else.

To Henry Laurens, December 23, 1777

Sir,

Full as I was in my representation of matters in the commissary's department yesterday, fresh and more powerful reasons oblige me to add that I am now convinced beyond a doubt that unless some great and capital change suddenly takes place in that line, this army must inevitably be reduced to one or other of these three things: starve, dissolve, or disperse, in order to obtain subsistence in the best manner they can. Rest assured, sir, this is not an exaggerated picture, and that I have abundant reason to support what I say.

Yesterday afternoon, receiving information that the enemy, in force, had left the city and were advancing towards Derby, with apparent design to forage and draw subsistence from that part of the country, I ordered the troops to be in readiness, that I might give every opposition in my power; when behold! to my great mortification I was not only informed but convinced that the men were unable to stir on account of provision, and that a dangerous mutiny, begun the night before and which with difficulty was suppressed by the spirited exertions of some officers, was still much to be apprehended for want of this article.

This brought forth the only commissary in the purchasing line in this camp, and with him this melancholy and alarming truth, that he had not a single hoof of any kind to slaughter, and not more than 25 barrels of flour! From hence form an opinion of our situation when I add that he could not tell when to expect any.

All I could do under these circumstances was to send out a few light parties to watch and harass the enemy, whilst other parties were instantly detached different ways to collect, if possible, as much provision as would satisfy the present pressing wants of the soldiery. But will this answer? No, sir: three or four days' bad weather would prove our destruction. What, then, is to become of the army this winter? And if we are as often without provisions now as with them, what is to become of us in the spring, when our force will be collected, with the aid perhaps of militia, to take advantage of an early campaign before the enemy can be reinforced? These are considerations of great magnitude, meriting the closest attention, and will, when my own reputation is so intimately connected and to be affected by the event, justify my saying that the present commissaries are by no means equal to the execution of the office, or that the disaffection of the people is past belief. The misfortune, however, does in my opinion proceed from both causes. And though I have been tender heretofore of giving any opinion or lodging complaints, as the change in that department took place contrary to my judgment, and the consequences thereof were predicted, yet finding that the inactivity of the army—whether for want of provisions, clothes, or other essentials—is charged to my account, not only by the common vulgar but those in power, it is time to speak plain in exculpation of myself. With truth, then, I can declare that no man in my opinion ever had his measures more impeded than I have by every department. Since the month of July, we have had no assistance from the quartermaster general, and to want of assistance from this department, the commissary general charges great part of his deficiency. To this I am to add that, notwithstanding it is a standing order and often repeated that the troops shall always have two days' provisions by them, that they might be ready at any sudden call, yet no opportunity has scarcely ever offered of taking advantage of the enemy that has not been either totally obstructed or greatly impeded on this account. And this the great and crying evil is not all. Soap, vinegar, and other articles allowed by Congress we see none of, nor have we seen them, I believe, since the Battle of Brandywine. The first indeed we have now little occasion for, few men having more than one shirt, many only the moiety of one, and some none at all. In addition to which, as a proof of the little benefit received from a clothier general, and at the same time as a farther proof of the inability of an army under the circumstances of this to perform the common duties of soldiers, besides a number of men confined to hospitals for want of shoes, and others in farmers' houses on the same account, we have by a field return this day made no less than 2,898 men now in camp unfit for duty, because they are barefoot and otherwise naked. And by the same return it appears that our strength in continental troops, including the Eastern Brigades which have joined since the surrender of General Burgoyne, exclusive of the Maryland troops sent to Wilmington, amount to no more than 8,200 in camp fit for duty. Notwithstanding which, and that since the 4th instant, our numbers fit for duty from the hardships and exposures they have undergone—particularly on account of blankets (numbers having been obliged, and still are, to set up all night by fires, instead of taking comfortable rest in a natural and common way)—have decreased near 2,000 men, we find gentlemen, without knowing whether the army was really going into winter quarters or not (for I am sure no resolution of mine would warrant the remonstrance), reprobating the measure as much as if they thought the soldiery were made of stocks or stones and equally insensible of frost and snow. And moreover, as if they conceived it easily practicable for an inferior army, under the disadvantages I have described ours to be, which is by no means exaggerated, to confine a superior one, in all respects well appointed and provided for a winter's campaign, within the City of Philadelphia, and to cover from depredation and waste the states of Pennsylvania, Jersey, etc. But what makes this matter still more extraordinary in my eye is that these very gentlemen, who were well apprised of the nakedness of the troops from ocular demonstration, who thought their own soldiers worse clad than others and advised me near a month ago to postpone the execution of a plan I was about to adopt in consequence of a resolve of Congress for seizing clothes, under strong assurances that an ample supply would be collected in ten days agreeable to a decree of the state (not one article of which, by the by, is yet come to hand), should think a winter's campaign, and the covering these states from the invasion of an enemy, so easy and practicable a business. I can assure those gentlemen that it is a much easier and less distressing thing to draw remonstrances in a comfortable room by a good fireside than to occupy a cold, bleak hill and sleep under frost and snow without clothes or blankets. However, although they seem to have little feeling for the naked and distressed soldier, I feel superabundantly for them and from my soul pity those miseries which it is neither in my power to relieve or prevent. It is for these reasons, therefore, I have dwelt upon the subject, and it adds not a little to my other difficulties and distress to find that much more is expected of me than is possible to be performed, and that, upon the ground of safety and policy, I am obliged to conceal the true state of the army from public view and thereby expose myself to detraction and calumny.

The honorable committee of Congress went from camp fully possessed of my sentiments respecting the establishment of this army—the necessity of auditors of accounts—appointment of officers—new arrangements etc. I have no need therefore to be prolix on these subjects, but shall refer to them, after adding a word or two to show, first, the necessity of some better provision for binding the officers by the tie of interest to the service (as no day, nor scarcely an hour, passes without an offer of a resigned commission). Otherwise, I much doubt the practicability of holding the army together much longer. In this, I shall probably be thought more sincere when I freely declare that I do not myself expect to derive the smallest benefit from any establishment that Congress may adopt, otherwise than as a member of the community at large in the good which I am persuaded will result from the measure by making better officers and better troops. And, secondly, to point out the necessity of making the appointments, arrangements, etc., without loss of time. We have not more than three months to prepare a great deal of business in. If we let these slip or waste, we shall be laboring under the same difficulties all next campaign, as we have done this, to rectify mistakes and bring things to order—for military arrangements and movements, in consequence like the mechanism of a clock, will be imperfect and disordered by the want of a part. In a very sensible degree have I experienced this in the course of the last summer—several brigades having no brigadiers appointed to them till late, and some not at all, by which means it follows that an additional weight is thrown upon the shoulders of the commander-in-chief to withdraw his attention from the great line of his duty. The gentlemen of the committee, when they were at camp, talked of an expedient for adjusting these matters, which I highly approved and wish to see adopted: namely that two or three members of the

Board of War or a committee of Congress should repair immediately to camp where the best aid can be had, and with the commanding officer, or a committee of his appointment, prepare and digest the most perfect plan that can be devised for correcting all abuses, making new arrangements, considering what is to be done with the weak and debilitated regiments (if the states to which they belong will not draft men to fill them, for as to enlisting soldiers it seems to me to be totally out of the question), together with many other things that would occur in the course of such a conference—and after digesting matters in the best manner they can, to submit the whole to the ultimate determination of Congress. If this measure is approved of, I would earnestly advise the immediate execution of it. And that the commissary general of purchases, whom I rarely see, may be directed to form magazines without a moment's delay in the neighborhood of this camp in order to secure provision for us in case of bad weather. The quartermaster general ought also to be busy in his department. In short, there is as much to be done in preparing for a campaign as in the active part of it. In fine, everything depends upon the preparation that is made in the several departments in the course of this winter, and the success or misfortunes of next campaign will more than probably originate with our activity or supineness this winter. I have the Honor to be Sir Your Most Obedt Servant

Go: Washington

Circular to the States, December 29, 1777 (Excerpt)

Sir,

I take the liberty of transmitting you the enclosed return, which contains a state of such of the New York Regiments as are in the army immediately under my command. By this you will discover how deficient, how exceedingly short they are of the complement of men which of right according to the establishment they ought to have. This information I have thought it my duty to lay before you, that it may have that attention which its importance demands, and in full hope the most early and vigorous measures will be adopted not only to make the regiments more respectable but complete. The expediency and necessity of this procedure are too obvious to need arguments. Should we have a respectable force to commence an early campaign with, before the enemy are reinforced, I trust we shall have an opportunity of striking a favorable and a happy stroke. But if we should be obliged to defer it, it will not be easy to describe with any degree of precision what disagreeable consequences may result from it. We may rest assured that Britain will strain every nerve to send from home and abroad, as early as possible, all the troops it shall be in her power to raise or procure. Her views and schemes for subjugating these states and bringing 'em under her despotic rule will be unceasing and unremitted. Nor should we, in my opinion, turn our expectations to, or have the least dependence on, the intervention of a foreign war. Our wishes on this head have been disappointed hitherto, and I do not know that we have a right to promise ourselves from any intelligence that has been received, bearing the marks of authority, that there is any certain prospect of one. However, be this as it may, our reliance should be wholly on our own strength and exertions. If, in addition to these, there should be aid derived from a war between the enemy and any of the European powers, our situation will be so much the better. If not, our efforts and exertions will have been the more necessary and indispensable. For my own part I should be happy if the idea of a foreign rupture should be thrown entirely out of our scale of politics, and that it may have not the least weight in our public measures. No bad effects could flow from it, but on the contrary many of a salutary nature. At the same time, I do not mean that such an idea ought to be discouraged among the people at large, because the event is probable.

There is one thing more to which I would take the liberty of soliciting your most serious and constant attention, to wit, the clothing of your troops and the procuring of every possible supply in your power for that end. If the several states exert themselves in future in this instance, and I trust they will, I hope that the supplies they will be able to furnish in aid of those which Congress may immediately import themselves will be equal and competent to every demand. If they do not, I fear—I am satisfied—the troops will never be in a situation to answer the public expectation and perform the duties required of them. No pains, no efforts on the part of the states, can be too great for this purpose. It is not easy to give you a just and accurate idea of the sufferings of the army at large—of the loss of men on this account. Were they to be minutely detailed, your feelings would be wounded, and the relation would probably be not received without a degree of doubt and discredit. We had in camp on the 23rd instant, by a field return then taken, not less than 2,898 men unfit for duty by reason of their being barefoot and otherwise naked. Besides this number, sufficiently distressing of itself, there are many others detained in hospitals and crowded in farmers' houses for the same causes. In a most particular manner, I flatter myself the care and attention of the states will be directed to the supply of shoes, stockings, and blankets, as their expenditure from the common operations and accidents of war is far greater than that of any other articles. In a word, the united and respective exertions of the states cannot be too great, too vigorous in this interesting work; and we shall never have a fair and just prospect for success till our troops (officers and men) are better provided than they are or have been.

To Major General Marie-Joseph-Paul-Yves-Roch-Gilbert du Motier, Marquis de Lafayette, December 31, 1777

My Dear Marquis,

Your favor of yesterday conveyed to me fresh proof of that friendship and attachment which I have happily experienced since the first of our acquaintance, and for which I entertain sentiments of the purest affection. It will ever constitute part of my happiness to know that I stand well in your opinion, because I am satisfied that you can have no views to answer by throwing out false colors, and that you possess a mind too exalted to condescend to dirty arts and low intrigues to acquire a reputation. Happy, thrice happy, would it have been for this army and the cause we are embarked in if the same generous spirit had pervaded all the actors in it. But one gentleman whose name you have mentioned had, I am confident, far different views. His ambition and great desire of being puffed off as one of the first officers of the age could only be equaled by the means which he used to obtain them; but, finding that I was determined not to go beyond the line of my duty to indulge him in the first, nor to exceed the strictest rules of propriety to gratify him in the second, he became my inveterate enemy and has, I am persuaded, practiced every art to do me an injury, even at the expense of reprobating a measure, which did not succeed, that he himself advised to. How far he may have accomplished his ends I know not, and, but for considerations of a public nature, I care not. For it is well known that neither ambitious nor lucrative motives led me to accept my present appointments, in the discharge of which I have endeavored to observe one steady and uniform conduct, which I shall invariably pursue while I have the honor to command, regardless of the tongue of slander or the powers of detraction.

The fatal tendency of disunion is so obvious that I have, in earnest terms, exhorted such officers as have expressed their dissatisfaction at General Conway's promotion to be cool and dispassionate in their decision upon the matter. And I have hopes that they will not suffer any hasty determination to injure the service. At the same time, it must be acknowledged that officers' feelings upon these occasions are not to be restrained, although you may control their actions.

The other observations contained in your letter have too much truth in them, and it is much to be lamented that things are not now as they formerly were. But we must not in so great a contest expect to meet with nothing but sunshine. I have no doubt but that everything happens so for the best, that we shall triumph over all our misfortunes, and shall, in the end, be ultimately happy. When, my dear Marquis, if you will give me your company in Virginia, we will laugh at our past difficulties and the folly of others, where I will endeavor, by every civility in my power, to show you how much and how sincerely I am, Your Affectionate and Obedient servant,

G. Washington

To Henry Laurens, January 2, 1778 (Excerpt)

Sir,

I take the liberty of transmitting to you the enclosed copies of a letter from me to General Conway since his return from York to camp, and of two letters from him to me, which you will be pleased to lay before Congress. I shall not in this letter animadvert upon them, but after making a single observation submit the whole to Congress.

If General Conway means by cool receptions mentioned in the last paragraph of his letter of the 31st ultimo that I did not receive him in the language of a warm and cordial friend, I readily confess the charge. I did not, nor shall I ever, till I am capable of the arts of dissimulation. These I despise, and my feelings will not permit me to make professions of friendship to the man I deem my enemy, and whose system of conduct forbids it. At the same time, truth authorizes me to say that he was received and treated with proper respect to his official character, and that he has had no cause to justify the assertion that he could not expect any support for fulfilling the duties of his appointment. I have the honor to be with great respect Sir Your Most Obedt Servt

Go: Washington

To Major General Horatio Gates, January 4, 1778

Sir,

Your letter of the 8th ultimo came to my hands a few days ago and to my great surprise informed me that a copy of it had been sent to Congress—for what reason, I find myself unable to account. But, as some end doubtless was intended to be answered by it, I am laid under the disagreeable necessity of returning my answer through the same channel, lest any member of that honorable body should harbor an unfavorable suspicion of my having practiced some indirect means to come at the contents of the confidential letters between you and General Conway.

I am to inform you, then, that Colonel Wilkinson, in his way to Congress in the month of October last, fell in with Lord Stirling at Reading and, not in confidence that I ever understood, informed his aide-de-camp, Major McWilliams, that General Conway had written thus to you: "Heaven has been determined to save your country, or a weak general and bad counselors would have ruined it." Lord Stirling, from motives of friendship, transmitted the account with this remark: "The enclosed was communicated by Colonel Wilkinson to Major McWilliams. Such wicked duplicity of conduct I shall always think it my duty to detect."

In consequence of this information, and without having anything more in view than merely to show that gentleman that I was not unapprised of his intriguing disposition, I wrote him a letter in these words: "Sir—A letter which I received last night contained the following paragraph:

In a letter from General Conway to General Gates he says: 'Heaven has been determined to save your country, or a weak general and bad counselors would have ruined it—I am Sir & ca.'"

Neither this letter, nor the information which occasioned it, was ever, directly or indirectly, communicated by me to a single officer in this army (out of my own family), excepting the Marquis de Lafayette, who, having been spoken to on the subject by General Conway, applied for and saw, under injunctions of secrecy, the letter which contained Wilkinson's information—so desirous was I of concealing every matter that could in its consequences give the smallest interruption to the tranquility of this army, or afford a gleam of hope to the enemy by dissensions therein.

Thus sir, with an openness and candor which I hope will ever characterize and mark my conduct, have I complied with your request. The only concern I feel upon the occasion (finding how matters stand) is that in doing this I have necessarily been obliged to name a gentleman who I am persuaded (although I never exchanged a word with him upon the subject) thought he was rather doing an act of justice than committing an act of infidelity. And sure I am that till Lord Stirling's letter came to my hands I never knew that General Conway (who I viewed in the light of a stranger to you) was a correspondent of yours, much less did I suspect that I was the subject of your confidential letters. Pardon me then for adding that so far from conceiving that the safety of the states can be affected, or in the smallest degree injured, by a discovery of this kind, or that I should be called upon in such solemn terms to point out the author, that I considered the information as coming from yourself and given with a friendly view to forewarn, and consequently forearm, me against a secret enemy—or, in other words, a dangerous incendiary, in which character, sooner or later, this country will know General Conway. But in this, as in other matters of late, I have found myself mistaken. I am Sir yr Most Obedt Servt

Go: Washington

To Henry Laurens, January 13, 1778

Sir,

This will be delivered to you by the Chevalier de Mauduit du Plessis, who was among the first French officers that joined the army of the United States. The gallant conduct of this young gentleman at Brandywine, Germantown, and his distinguished services at Fort Mercer, where he united the offices of engineer and commandant of artillery, entitle him to the particular notice of Congress. He made several judicious alterations in the works at Redbank, showed great good conduct during the action in which the Hessians were repulsed, and was spoken of in consequence in terms of the highest applause by the commanding officer of the post. After the evacuation was determined upon, he became the means of saving some valuable artillery and stores, and cheerfully undertook as volunteer the hazardous operation of blowing up the magazine, etc., without the apparatus usually provided upon such occasions. I must farther add in Mr. Duplessis's favor that he possesses a degree of modesty not always found in men who have performed brilliant actions. It is with pleasure, therefore, that I recommend it to Congress to grant him a brevet of Lieutenant Colonel, a reward due to his merit and which will not have the inconvenience of occasioning any dissatisfaction in the corps to which he belongs. As some particular circumstances have prevented Mr. Duplessis waiting upon Congress sooner, I hope there will be no difficulty in antedating the brevet, so that the recompense may more immediately follow the services which he has done. At the same time, that there may not be any uneasiness on the part of Mr. Fleury, whom Congress has been pleased to reward in the same way, and as their times of service are nearly equal in France, I would propose that Mr. Duplessis's brevet should bear the same date, viz. the 26th November. I have the honor to be with great respect Sir Your most obedt Servt

Go: Washington

To William Gordon, January 23, 1778

I have attended to your information and remark on the supposed intention of placing General Lee at the head of the army: whether a serious design of that kind had ever entered into the head of a member of Congress or not, I never was at the trouble of enquiring. I am told a scheme of that kind is now on foot by some in behalf of another gentleman. But whether true or false, whether serious or merely to try the pulse, I neither know nor care. Neither interested nor ambitious views led me into the service. I did not solicit the command but accepted it after much entreaty, with all that diffidence which a conscious want of ability and experience equal to the discharge of so important a trust must naturally create in a mind not quite devoid of thought—and after I did engage, pursued the great line of my duty and the object in view (as far as my judgment could direct), as pointedly as the needle to the pole. So soon, then, as the public gets dissatisfied with my services, or a person is found better qualified to answer her expectation, I shall quit the helm with as much satisfaction, and retire to a private station with as much content, as ever the wearied pilgrim felt upon his safe arrival in the Holy Land or haven of hope, and shall wish most devoutly that those who come after may meet with more prosperous gales than I have done, and less difficulty. If the expectation of the public has not been answered by my endeavors, I have more reasons than one to regret it, but at present shall only add that a day may come when the public cause is no longer to be benefited by a concealment of our circumstances, and till that period arrives I shall not be among the first to disclose such truths as may injure it.

To a Continental Congress Camp Committee, January 29, 1778 (Excerpts)

Gentlemen,

The numerous defects in our present military establishment, rendering many reformations and many new arrangements absolutely necessary, and Congress having been pleased to appoint you a committee, in concert with me, to make and recommend such as shall appear eligible in pursuance of the various objects expressed in their resolution for that purpose, I have in the following sheets briefly delivered my sentiments upon such of them as seemed to me most essential, so far as observation has suggested and leisure permitted. These are submitted to consideration, and I shall be happy if they are found conducive to remedying the evils and inconveniences we are now subject to, and putting the army upon a more respectable footing. Something must be done; important alterations must be made. Necessity requires that our resources should be enlarged and our system improved; for without it, if the dissolution of the army should not be the consequence, at least its operations must infallibly be feeble, languid, and ineffectual.

As I consider a proper and satisfactory provision for officers in a manner as the basis of every other regulation and arrangement necessary to be made (since without officers no army can exist, and unless some measures be devised to place those of ours in a more desirable situation, few of them would be able, if willing, to continue in it) I shall begin with a few reflections tending to prove the necessity.

Of a Half-Pay and Pensionary Establishment

A small knowledge of human nature will convince us that with far the greatest part of mankind, interest is the governing principle, and that almost every man is more or less under its influence. Motives of public virtue may for a time, or in particular instances, actuate men to the observance of a conduct purely disinterested; but they are not of themselves sufficient to produce a persevering conformity to the refined dictates and obligations of social duty. Few men are capable of making a continual sacrifice of all views of private interest or advantage to the common good. It is in vain to exclaim against the depravity of human nature on this account: the fact is so, the experience of every age and nation has proved it, and we must, in a great measure, change the constitution of man before we can make it otherwise. No institution not built on the presumptive truth of these maxims can succeed.

We find them exemplified in the American officers as well as in all other men. At the commencement of the dispute—in the first effusions of their zeal and looking upon the service to be only temporary—they entered into it without paying any regard to pecuniary or selfish considerations. But finding its duration to be much longer than they at first suspected, and that, instead of deriving any advantage from the hardships and dangers to which they were exposed, they on the contrary were losers by their patriotism, and fell far short even of a competency to supply their wants, they have gradually abated in their ardor. And with many, an entire disinclination to the service under its present circumstances has taken place. To this, in an eminent degree, must be ascribed the frequent resignations, daily happening, and the more frequent importunities for permission to resign, and from some officers of the greatest merit. To this also may we ascribe the apathy, inattention, and neglect of duty which pervade all ranks, and which will necessarily continue and increase while an officer, instead of gaining anything, is impoverished by his commission and conceives he is conferring, not receiving, a favor in holding it. There can be no sufficient tie upon men possessing such sentiments. Nor can any method be adopted to oblige those to a punctual discharge of duty who are indifferent about their continuance in the service and are often seeking a pretext to disengage themselves from it. Punishment, in this case, will be unavailing. But when an officer's commission is made valuable to him, and he fears to lose it, you may then exact obedience from him.

It is not, indeed, consistent with reason or justice to expect that one set of men should make a sacrifice of property, domestic ease, and happiness, encounter the rigors of the field, the perils and vicissitudes of war, to obtain those blessings which every citizen will enjoy in common with them without some adequate compensation. It must also be a comfortless reflection to any man that after he may have contributed to securing the rights of his country, at the risk of his life and the ruin of his fortune, there would be no provision made to prevent himself and family from sinking into indigence and wretchedness. Besides adopting some methods to make the provision for officers equal to their present exigences, a due regard should be paid to futurity. Nothing, in my opinion, would serve more powerfully to reanimate their languishing zeal and interest them thoroughly in the service than a half-pay and pensionary establishment. This would not only dispel the apprehension of personal distress at the termination of the war from having thrown themselves out of professions and employments they might not have it in their power to resume, but would in a great degree relieve the painful anticipation of leaving their widows and orphans a burden on the charity of their country, should it be their lot to fall in its defense.

I am earnest in recommending this measure because I know it is the general wish and expectation, and that many officers, whom upon every principle we should wish to retain in the service, are only waiting to see whether something of the kind will or will not take place, to be determined in their resolutions either of staying in or quitting it immediately. And I urge my sentiments with the greater freedom because I cannot and shall not receive the smallest benefit from the establishment and can have no other inducement for proposing it than a full conviction of its utility and propriety.

I am sensible the expense will be a capital objection to it, but to this I oppose the necessity. The officers are now discontented with their situation. If some generous expedient is not embraced to remove their discontent, so extensive a desertion of the service will ensue, and so much discouragement be cast upon those who remain, as must wound it in a very essential manner. Everything that has this effect has a tendency at least to protract the war, and, though dictated by a well-intended frugality, will, I fear, in the end, prove erroneous economy.

Of Completing the Regiments and Altering Their Establishment

The necessity of the first, in the most expeditious manner possible, is too self-evident to need illustration or proof; and I shall, therefore, only beg leave to offer some reflections on the mode. Voluntary enlistments seem to be totally out of the question. All the allurements of the most exorbitant bounties, and every other inducement that could be thought of, have been tried in vain and seem to have had little other effect than to increase the rapacity and raise the demands of those to whom they were held out. We may fairly infer that the country has been already pretty well drained of that class of men whose tempers, attachments, and circumstances disposed them to enter permanently, or for a length of time, into the army, and that the residue of such men, who from different motives have kept out of the army, if collected would not augment our general strength in any proportion to what we require. If experience has demonstrated that little more can be done by voluntary enlistments, some other mode must be concerted, and no other presents itself than that of filling the regiments by drafts from the militia. This is a disagreeable alternative, but it is an unavoidable one.

As drafting for the war, or for a term of years, would probably be disgusting and dangerous, perhaps impracticable, I would propose an annual draft of men, without officers, to serve till the first day of January in each year—that on or before the first day of October preceding, these drafted men should be called upon to re-enlist for the succeeding year, and, as an incitement to doing it, those being much better and less expensive than raw recruits, a bounty of twenty-five dollars should be offered—that, upon ascertaining at this period the number of men willing to re-engage, exact returns should be made to Congress of the deficiency in each regiment, and transmitted by them to the respective states, in order that they may have their several quotas immediately furnished and sent on to camp for the service of the ensuing year, so as to arrive by or before the first day of January.

This method, though not so good as that of obtaining men for the war, is perhaps the best our circumstances will allow, and, as we shall always have an established corps of experienced officers, may answer tolerably well. It is the only mode I can think of for completing our battalions in time that promises the least prospect of success, the accomplishment of which is an object of the last importance. And it has this advantage: that the minds of the people being once reconciled to the experiment, it would prove a source of continual supplies hereafter.

Men drafted in this manner should not, in the first instance, receive any bounty from the public—which being solemnly enjoined upon each state, and a stop put to the militia substitution laws, would probably be attended with very happy consequences. A number of idle, mercenary fellows would be thrown out of employment, precluded from their excessive wages as substitutes for a few weeks or months, and constrained to enlist in the Continental Army. In speaking of abolishing the militia substitution laws, it is not meant to hinder a person who might be drafted in the annual allotments from procuring a substitute in his stead, himself in consequence being excused. This indulgence would be admissible, and, considering all things, necessary, as there are many individuals whose dispositions and private affairs would make them irreconcilably averse to giving their personal services for so long a duration, and with whom it would be impolitic to use compulsion. The allowance of substitution upon a smaller scale—in the occasional coming out of the militia, for a few weeks, a month, or two—is the thing meant to be reprobated. It is highly productive of the double disadvantage of preventing the growth of the army and depreciating our currency ....

The quartermaster general and adjutant general, as they fill places of the highest trust and importance and ought to be gentlemen of the first military characters, should, if not of the line, have rank conferred upon them, and not less than that of colonel.

In speaking of rank as a spur to enterprise, I am led, by the way, to hint an idea which may be improved and turned to no small advantage. This is the institution of honorary rewards, differing in degree, to be conferred on those who signalize themselves by any meritorious actions, in proportion to the magnitude and brilliancy of the achievement. These should be sacred to the purpose of their institution, and unattainable by loose recommendations or vague though arrogating pretensions—given only upon authentic vouchers of real desert, from some proper board. Congress have already adopted the idea in particular instances, but it were to be wished it could be extended to something more general and systematic. I have not sufficiently employed my thoughts upon the subject to digest them into a proposition as to the nature, variety, and extent of these rewards; but I would in general observe that they may consist in things of very little cost or real value, and that the more diversified they are the better. If judiciously and impartially administered they would be well calculated to kindle that emulous love of glory and distinction to which may be imputed far the greater part of the most illustrious exploits performed among mankind, and which is peculiarly necessary to be cherished and cultivated in a military life.

Of Promotion

Irregular promotions have also been a pregnant source of uneasiness, discord, and perplexity in this army. They have been the cause of numerous bickerings and resignations among the officers, and have occasioned infinite trouble and vexation to the commander-in-chief. To rectify mistakes—introduced by accident, inadvertency, the interference of state-appointments, or other means—employed much of the time of the general officers in the course of last campaign, and to less purpose than could be wished. We find that, however injuriously to the rights of others an officer obtains irregular promotion, he is not the less tenacious of it, but it is with the utmost difficulty, if at all, he can be convinced of the propriety of doing an act of justice by abandoning his claim, though he will confess there was no just cause in the first instance for giving him the preference. But as it did happen, he pretends his honor would be wounded by suffering another who is, in fact, his inferior, to come over him, not considering how much that other was injured by the act which gave him the superiority.

This, however, shows how indispensably necessary it is to have some settled rule of promotion, universally known and understood and not to be deviated from but for obvious and incontestable reasons. Extraordinary promotions founded upon acknowledged worth on the one hand, and acknowledged demerit on the other, would rather excite emulation than murmurs. The prospect of not being shackled to the tedious gradations of ordinary succession would teach the good officer to aspire to an excellence that should entitle him to more rapid preferment, and the fear of being superseded, with dishonor, would teach indifferent ones to exert more activity, diligence, and attention than they otherwise would were they left in a listless security, certain of enjoying the honors and emoluments of progressive rank, let their conduct be ever so undeserving. But this is a matter that ought to be handled with the utmost caution and delicacy. Nothing is more alarming and prejudicial than an injudicious infraction of rank. It discourages merit and foments discontent and disorder. No departure from the established maxims of preferment is warrantable which is not founded upon the most apparent and unequivocal reasons ....

Several new regulations will, I imagine, be found useful in the articles of war, which the judge advocate, from his official experience of the deficiency, can more accurately indicate. One thing we have suffered much from is the want of a proper gradation of punishments: the interval between a hundred lashes and death is too great and requires to be filled by some intermediate stages. Capital crimes in the army are frequent, particularly in the instance of desertion. Actually to inflict capital punishment upon every deserter or other heinous offender would incur the imputation of cruelty and, by the familiarity of the example, destroy its efficacy. On the other hand, to give only a hundred lashes to such criminals is a burlesque on their crimes rather than a serious correction and affords encouragement to obstinacy and imitation. The courts are often in a manner compelled by the enormity of the facts to pass sentences of death, which I am as often obliged to remit on account of the number in the same circumstances, and let the offenders pass wholly unpunished. This would be avoided if there were other punishments, short of the destruction of life, in some degree adequate to the crime, and which might be with propriety substituted. Crimes too are so various in their complexions and degrees that to preserve the just rule of proportion there ought to be a gradual scale of punishments, in order to which whipping should be extended to any number at discretion, or by no means limited lower than five hundred lashes.

Upon the whole, gentlemen, I doubt not you are fully impressed with the defects of our present military system and the necessity of speedy and decisive measures to put it upon a satisfactory footing. The disagreeable picture I have given you of the wants and sufferings of the army, and the discontents reigning among the officers, is a just representation of evils equally melancholy and important; and unless effectual remedies be applied without loss of time the most alarming and ruinous consequences are to be apprehended. I have the honor to be with very great respect Gentlemen Your most obedient servant

Go: Washington

To Henry Laurens, President of the Continental Congress, January 31, 1778

Sir,

I this morning received your favor of the 27th ultimo.

I cannot sufficiently express the obligation I feel to you for your friendship and politeness upon an occasion in which I am so deeply interested. I was not unapprised that a malignant faction had been for some time forming to my prejudice, which, conscious as I am of having ever done all in my power to answer the important purposes of the trust reposed in me, could not but give me some pain on a personal account. But my chief concern arises from an apprehension of the dangerous consequences which intestine dissensions may produce to the common cause.

As I have no other view than to promote the public good and am unambitious of honors not founded in the approbation of my country, I would not desire in the least degree to suppress a free spirit of inquiry into any part of my conduct that even faction itself may deem reprehensible.

The anonymous paper handed you exhibits many serious charges, and it is my wish that it should be submitted to Congress. This I am the more inclined to as the suppression or concealment may possibly involve you in embarrassments hereafter, since it is uncertain how many or who may be privy to the contents.

My enemies take an ungenerous advantage of me. They know the delicacy of my situation and that motives of policy deprive me of the defense I might otherwise make against their insidious attacks. They know I cannot combat their insinuations, however injurious, without disclosing secrets it is of the utmost moment to conceal. But why should I expect to be exempt from censure, the unfailing lot of an elevated station? Merits and talents, with which I can have no pretensions of rivalship, have ever been subject to it. My heart tells me it has been my unremitted aim to do the best circumstances would permit; yet I may have been very often mistaken in my judgment of the means, and may in many instances deserve the imputation of error.

I cannot forbear repeating that I have a grateful sense of the favorable disposition you have manifested to me in this affair, and beg you will believe me to be with sentiments of real esteem and regard. Sir Yr much obliged & Obedt Sert

Go: Washington

To William Livingston, Governor of New Jersey, February 2, 1778 (Excerpt)

Sir,

I have the honor to acknowledge the receipt of your favor of the 26th ultimo.

The recent detection of the wicked design you mention gives me the most sensible pleasure, and I earnestly hope you may be alike successful in discovering and disappointing every attempt that may be projected against you, either by your open or concealed enemies. It is a tax, however severe, which all those must pay who are called to eminent stations of trust, not only to be held up as conspicuous marks to the enmity of the public adversaries to their country, but to the malice of secret traitors and the envious intrigues of false friends and factions.

To William Buchanan, February 7, 1778

Sir,

The occasional deficiencies in the article of provisions, which we have often severely felt, seem now on the point of resolving themselves into this fatal crisis—total want and a dissolution of the army. Mr. Blaine informs me, in the most decisive terms, that he has not the least prospect of answering the demands of the army within his district more than a month longer, at the extremity. The expectations he has from other quarters appear to be altogether vague and precarious, and from anything I can see we have every reason to apprehend the most ruinous consequences.

The spirit of desertion among the soldiery never before rose to such a threatening height as at the present time. The murmurs on account of provisions are become universal; and what may ensue, if a better prospect does not speedily open, I dread to conjecture. I pretend not to assign the causes of the distress we experience in this particular, nor do I wish to throw out the least imputation of blame upon any person. I only mean to represent our affairs as they are, that necessity may be properly felt of exerting the utmost care and activity to prevent the mischiefs which I cannot forbear anticipating with inexpressible concern. I am Sir Your most obedt servant

Go: Washington

To Major General Horatio Gates, February 9, 1778

Sir,

I was duly favored with your letter of the 23rd of last month, to which I should have replied sooner, had I not been delayed by business that required my more immediate attention.

It is my wish to give implicit credit to the assurances of every gentleman; but in the subject of our present correspondence, I am sorry to confess, there happen to be some unlucky circumstances which involuntarily compel me to consider the discovery you mention not so satisfactory and conclusive as you seem to think it.

I am so unhappy as to find no small difficulty in reconciling the spirit and import of your different letters, and sometimes of the different parts of the same letter, with each other. It is not unreasonable to presume that your first information of my having notice of General Conway's letter came from himself. There were very few in the secret, and it is natural to suppose that he, being immediately concerned, would be most interested to convey the intelligence to you. It is also far from improbable that he acquainted you with the substance of the passage communicated to me. One would expect this, if he believed it to be spurious, in order to ascertain the imposition and evince his innocence—especially as he seemed to be under some uncertainty as to the precise contents of what he had written when I signified my knowledge of the matter to him. If he neglected doing it, the omission cannot easily be interpreted into anything else than a consciousness of the reality of the extract, if not literally at least substantially. If he did not neglect it, it must appear somewhat strange that the forgery remained so long undetected, and that your first letter to me from Albany of the 8th of December should tacitly recognize the genuineness of the paragraph in question, while your only concern at that time seemed to be "the tracing out the author of the infidelity, which put extracts from General Conway's letters into my hands."

Throughout the whole of that letter the reality of the extracts is by the fairest implication allowed, and your only solicitude was to find out the person that brought them to light. After making the most earnest pursuit of the author of the supposed treachery, without saying a word about the truth or falsehood of the passage, your letter of the 23rd ultimo, to my great surprise, proclaims it "in words as well as in substance a wicked forgery."

It is not my intention to contradict this assertion but only to intimate some considerations which tend to induce a supposition that, though none of General Conway's letters to you contained the offensive passage mentioned, there might have been something in them too nearly related to it that could give such an extraordinary alarm. It may be said, if this were not the case, how easy in the first instance to have declared there was nothing exceptionable in them and to have produced the letters themselves in support of it? This may be thought the most proper and effectual way of refuting misrepresentation and removing all suspicion. The propriety of the objections suggested against submitting them to inspection may very well be questioned: "The various reports circulated concerning their contents" were perhaps so many arguments for making them speak for themselves, to place the matter upon the footing of certainty. Concealment in an affair which had made so much noise, though not by my means, will naturally lead men to conjecture the worst. And it will be a subject of speculation, even to candor itself. The anxiety and jealousy you apprehended from revealing the letter will be very apt to be increased by suppressing it.

It may be asked, why not submit to inspection a performance perfectly harmless and of course conceived in terms of proper caution and delicacy? Why suppose that "anxiety and jealousy would have arisen in the breasts of very respectable officers, or that they would have been unnecessarily disgusted at being made sensible of their faults when related with judgment and impartiality by a candid observer"? Surely they could not have been unreasonable enough to take offense at a performance so perfectly inoffensive, "blaming actions rather than persons," which have evidently no connection with one another, and indulgently "recording the errors of inexperience."

You are pleased to consider General Conway's letters as of a confidential nature, observing that "time and circumstances must point out the propriety or impropriety of communicating such letters." Permit me to inquire whether, when there is an impropriety in communicating, it is only applicable with respect to the parties who are the subjects of them. One might be led to imagine this to be the case from your having admitted others into the secret of your confidential correspondence at the same time that you thought it ineligible it should be trusted to those "officers whose actions underwent its scrutiny." Your not knowing whether the letter under consideration "came to me from a member of Congress or from an officer" plainly indicates that you originally communicated it to at least one of that honorable body. And I learn from General Conway that before his late arrival at Yorktown it had been committed to the perusal of several of its members and was afterwards shown by himself to three more. It is somewhat difficult to conceive a reason, founded in generosity, for imparting the free and confidential strictures of that ingenious censor on the operations of the army under my command to a member of Congress; but perhaps "time and circumstances pointed it out." It must indeed be acknowledged that the faults of very respectable officers, not less injurious for being the result of inexperience, were not improper topics to engage the attention of members of Congress.

It is, however, greatly to be lamented that this adept in military science did not employ his abilities in the progress of the campaign in pointing out those wise measures, which were calculated to give us "that degree of success we might reasonably expect." The United States have lost much from that unseasonable diffidence which prevented his embracing the numerous opportunities he had in council of displaying those rich treasures of knowledge and experience he has since so freely laid open to you. I will not do him the injustice to impute the penurious reserve which ever appeared in him upon such occasions to any other cause than an excess of modesty. Neither will I suppose he possesses no other merit than of that after kind of sagacity, which qualifies a man better for profound discoveries of errors that have been committed, and advantages that have been lost, than for the exercise of that foresight and provident discernment which enable him to avoid the one and anticipate the other. But willing as I am to subscribe to all his pretensions, and to believe that his remarks on the operations of the campaign were very judicious, and that he has sagaciously descanted on many things that might have been done, I cannot help being a little skeptical as to his ability to have found out the means of accomplishing them, or to prove the sufficiency of those in our possession. These minutiae, I suspect, he did not think worth his attention, particularly as they might not be within the compass of his views.

Notwithstanding the hopeful presages you are pleased to figure to yourself of General Conway's firm and constant friendship to America, I cannot persuade myself to retract the prediction concerning him which you so emphatically wish had not been inserted in my last. A better acquaintance with him than I have reason to think you have had, from what you say, and a concurrence of circumstances oblige me to give him but little credit for the qualifications of his heart, of which, at least, I beg leave to assume the privilege of being a tolerable judge. Were it necessary, more instances than one might be adduced, from his behavior and conversation, to manifest that he is capable of all the malignity of detraction, and all the meannesses of intrigue, to gratify the absurd resentment of disappointed vanity or to answer the purposes of personal aggrandizement and promote the interests of faction. I am with respect—Sir Yr most Obedt Servt

Go: Washington

To Richard Henry Lee, February 15, 1778 (Excerpt)

The enemy are governed by no principles that ought to actuate honest men. No wonder, then, that forgery should be amongst their other crimes. I have seen a letter published in a handbill at New York, and extracts of it republished in the Philadelphia paper, said to be from me to Mrs. Washington, not one word of which did I ever write. Those contained in the pamphlet you speak of are, I presume, equally genuine, and perhaps written,[10] by the same author. I should be glad, however, to see and examine the texture of them if a favorable opportunity to send them should present.

General Orders, March 1, 1778 (Excerpt)

The commander-in-chief again takes occasion to return his warmest thanks to the virtuous officers and soldiery of this army for that persevering fidelity and zeal which they have uniformly manifested in all their conduct. Their fortitude not only under the common hardships incident to a military life, but also under the additional sufferings to which the peculiar situation of these states has exposed them, clearly proves them worthy the enviable privilege of contending for the rights of human nature, the freedom and independence of their country. The recent instance of uncomplaining patience during the scarcity of provisions in camp is a fresh proof that they possess in an eminent degree the spirit of soldiers and the magnanimity of patriots. The few refractory individuals who disgrace themselves by murmurs it is to be hoped have repented such unmanly behavior, and resolved to emulate the noble example of their associates upon every trial which the customary casualties of war may hereafter throw in their way. Occasional distress for want of provisions and other necessaries is a spectacle that frequently occurs in every army, and perhaps there never was one which has been in general so plentifully supplied in respect to the former as ours. Surely we who are free citizens in arms, engaged in a struggle for everything valuable in society and partaking in the glorious task of laying the foundation of an empire, should scorn effeminately to shrink under those accidents and rigors of war which mercenary hirelings fighting in the cause of lawless ambition, rapine, and devastation encounter with cheerfulness and alacrity. We should not be merely equal, we should be superior to them in every qualification that dignifies the man or the soldier in proportion as the motive from which we act and the final hopes of our toils are superior to theirs. Thank Heaven our country abounds with provision and with prudent management! We need not apprehend want for any length of time. Defects in the commissary's department, contingencies of weather, and other temporary impediments have subjected and may again subject us to a deficiency for a few days, but soldiers, American soldiers, will despise the meanness of repining at such trifling strokes of adversity!—trifling indeed when compared to the transcendent prize which will undoubtedly crown their patience and perseverance: glory and freedom, peace and plenty to themselves and the community, the admiration of the world, the love of their country, and the gratitude of posterity! Your general unceasingly employs his thoughts on the means of relieving your distresses, supplying your wants, and bringing your labors to a speedy and prosperous issue. Our parent country he hopes will second his endeavors by the most vigorous exertions, and he is convinced the faithful officers and soldiers associated with him in the great work of rescuing our country from bondage and misery will continue in the display of that patriotic zeal which is capable of smoothing every difficulty and vanquishing every obstacle.

To Bryan Fairfax, March 1, 1778

Dear Sir,

Your favor of the 8th of December came safe to my hands, after considerable delay in its passage.

The sentiments you have expressed of me in this letter are highly flattering—meriting my warmest acknowledgments, as I have too good an opinion of your sincerity and candor to believe that you are capable of unmeaning professions, and speaking a language foreign from your heart. The friendship I ever professed and felt for you met with no diminution from the difference in our political sentiments. I knew the rectitude of my own intentions and, believing in the sincerity of yours, lamented, though I did not condemn, your renunciation of the creed I had adopted. Nor do I think any person or power ought to do it whilst your conduct is not opposed to the general interest of the people and the measures they are pursuing. The latter, that is, our actions, depending on ourselves may be controlled, while the powers of thinking, originating from higher causes, cannot always be molded to our wishes.

The determinations of Providence are always wise, often inscrutable, and, though its decrees appear to bear hard upon us at times, is nevertheless meant for gracious purposes. In this light I cannot help viewing your late disappointment; for if you had been permitted to have gone to England, unrestrained even by the rigid oaths which are administered upon those occasions, your feelings as a husband, parent, etc. must have been considerably wounded in the prospect of a long—perhaps lasting—separation from your nearest relatives. What then must they have been if the obligation of an oath had left you without a will?

Your hope of being instrumental in restoring peace would prove as unsubstantial as mist before a noonday sun, and would as soon dispel. For believe me sir, G. Britain understood herself perfectly well in this dispute, but did not comprehend America. She meant, as Lord Cambden in his late speech in Parliament clearly and explicitly declares, to drive America into rebellion, that her own purposes might be more fully answered by it. But take this along with it, that this plan, originating in a firm belief founded on misinformation, that no effectual opposition would or could be made, they little dreamt of what has happened and are disappointed in their views.

Does not every act of administration from the Tea Act to the present sessions of Parliament declare this in plain and self-evident characters? Had the commissioners any powers to treat with America? If they meant peace, would Lord Howe have been detained in England five months after passing the act? Would the powers of these commissioners have been confined to mere acts of grace upon condition of absolute submission? No—surely no! They meant to drive us into what they termed rebellion that they might be furnished with a pretext to disarm and then strip us of the rights and privileges of Englishmen. If they were actuated by principles of justice, why did they refuse indignantly to accede to the terms which were humbly supplicated before hostilities commenced and this country deluged in blood, and now make their principal officers, and even the commissioners themselves, say that these terms are just and reasonable—nay, that more will be granted than we have yet asked, if we will relinquish our claim to independency? What name does such conduct as this deserve? And what punishment is there in store for the men who have distressed millions, involved thousands in ruin, and plunged numberless families in inextricable woe! Could that which is just and reasonable now have been unjust four years ago? If not, upon what principles, I repeat, does administration act? They must either be wantonly wicked and cruel or (which is only another mode of expressing the same thing) under false colors are now endeavoring to deceive the great body of the people by industriously propagating an idea that G. Britain is willing to offer any and that we will accept of no terms—thereby hoping to poison and disaffect the minds of those who wish for peace and create feuds and dissensions in consequence. In a word, having less dependence now on their arms than their arts, they are practicing such low and dirty tricks that men of sentiment and honor must blush for their fall. Among other maneuvers in this way, they are forging letters and publishing them as intercepted ones of mine, to prove that I am an enemy to the present measures of this continent, having been deceived and led on by Congress in hopes that at length they would recede from their claims and withdraw their opposition to G. Britain.

I am sorry to hear of the indisposition of Miss Fairfax. I should have been pleased could I have congratulated you on a marriage which I heard was in agitation between her and a relation of mine, Mr. Whiting. My best respects to Mrs. Fairfax and your family, and believe me to be Dr Sr Yr Most Obed. & Affe.

Go: Washington

To Henry Laurens, President of the Continental Congress, March 7, 1778 (Excerpt)

By the direction of Congress, I, in the first instance, stipulated with General Howe an exchange of prisoners, officer for officer of equal rank, soldier for soldier, and citizen for citizen. This agreement they have ever approved and repeatedly declared their willingness to carry into execution. Their resolution of the 24th March last empowered me, on condition of General Lee being declared exchangeable, not only "to proceed" to the exchange of prisoners, according to the principles and regulations of the cartel before agreed on, but also to enter into such further principles and regulations as should appear to me most proper and advantageous. A subsequent resolution of the 6th of June holds forth the same language, sanctions my conduct and reasonings in the negotiations about that time on the subject, and directs an adherence to them. No event has occurred since that period by which I could conclude there was any alteration in the views of Congress. So far from it that all my late letters—breathing the same spirit with the former, and pointedly signifying my wish to bring about a general exchange—if not with an express, at least met with a tacit approbation. General Howe at length, by profession if not in reality, is willing to perform the agreement on the conditions required by me and confirmed by them.

It may be said that with whatever powers I was originally vested to negotiate an exchange, the resolution of the 19th December last was an abridgement of them, so far as to annex a new condition: the settlement and payment of accounts previous to its taking place. I had no conception of this being the case in the present instance; however, the letter may warrant the construction. Besides the common principle of preventing the inconveniences necessarily resulting from allowing the enemy to make their payments in paper currency, I had reason to imagine that General Burgoyne's army was more particularly the object of the concluding clause. This interpretation I the more readily adopted, for, exclusive of the affairs of that army, I verily believed that, from the confused, defective state of our accounts relating to prisoners, there would be a considerable balance in favor of Mr. Howe. Nor was the situation of our accounts the only reason for this belief. The prisoners in our hands, especially those westward of the Delaware, as I am informed, have been in a great measure supported by their own labor and at the expense of the enemy, who have had agents constantly among us. If this is the case, the reason of the resolve not applying, the effect ought not, of course.

But perhaps it may be thought contrary to our interest to go into an exchange, as the enemy would derive more immediate advantage from it than we should. This I shall not deny. But it appeared to me that on principles of genuine, extensive policy, independent of the considerations of compassion and justice, we were under an obligation not to elude it. I have the best evidence that an event of this kind is the general wish of the country. I know it to be the wish of the army. And no one can doubt that it is the ardent wish of the unhappy sufferers themselves. We need only consult the tide of humanity and the sympathies natural to those connected by the cements of blood, interest, and a common dread of evil to be convinced that the prevailing current of sentiment demands an exchange. If the country, the army, and even the prisoners themselves had a precise idea of our circumstances, and could be fully sensible of the disadvantages that might attend the giving our enemy a considerable reinforcement without having an equivalent, they might perhaps be willing to make a sacrifice of their feelings to the motives of policy. But they have not this knowledge and cannot be entrusted with it; and their reasonings of necessity will be governed by what they feel.

Were an opinion once to be established—and the enemy and their emissaries know very well how to inculcate it, if they are furnished with a plausible pretext—that we designedly avoided an exchange, it would be a cause of dissatisfaction and disgust to the country and to the army, of resentment and desperation to our captive officers and soldiers. To say nothing of the importance of not hazarding our national character but upon the most solid grounds, especially in our embryo state, from the influence it may have on our affairs abroad, it may not be a little dangerous to beget in the minds of our own countrymen a suspicion that we do not pay the strictest observance to the maxims of honor and good faith. It is prudent to use the greatest caution not to shock the notions of general justice and humanity universal among mankind, as well in a public as a private view. In a business on the side of which the passions are so much concerned as in the present, men would be readily disposed to believe the worst and cherish the most unfavorable conclusions. Were the letters that have passed between General Howe and myself from first to last, and the proceedings of Congress on the same subject, to be published with proper comments, it is much to be feared if the exchange should be deferred till the terms of the last resolve were fulfilled— that it would be difficult to prevent our being generally accused with a breach of good faith. Perhaps, it might be said, that while the enemy refused us justice we fondly embraced the opportunity to be loud, persevering, incessant in our claims, but the moment they were willing to render it we receded from ourselves and started new difficulties. This, I say, might be the reasoning of speculative minds; and they might consider all our professions as mere professions, or at best that interest and policy were to be the only arbiters of their validity.

Imputations of this nature would have a tendency to unnerve our operations by diminishing that respect and confidence which are essential to be placed in those who are at the head of affairs, either in the civil or military line. This, added to the prospect of hopeless captivity, would be a great discouragement to the service. The ill consequences of both would be immense—by increasing the causes of discontent in the army, which are already too numerous, and many of which are in a great measure unavoidable—by fortifying that unwillingness, which already appears too great, towards entering into the service, and, of course, impeding the progress both of drafting and recruiting—by dejecting the courage of the soldiery, from an apprehension of the horrors of captivity—and, finally, by reducing those whose lot it is to drink the bitter cup to a despair which can only find relief by renouncing their attachments and engaging with their captors. These effects have already been experienced in part from the obstacles that have lain in the way of exchanges, but if these obstacles were once to seem the result of system, they would become tenfold. Nothing has operated more disagreeably upon the minds of the militia than the fear of captivity on the footing it has hitherto stood. What would be their reasonings if it should be thought to stand upon a worse?

If a present temporary interest is to be a ruling principle, it is easy to prove that an exchange can never take place. The constitution of our army, in respect to the term of service for which our men engage, and the dependence we are obliged to place on the militia, must for ever operate against us in exchanges and forbid an equality of advantages. Should it be said there are times when it might be more peculiarly unequal and injurious—and that the present is such, on account of the weak condition of our army—I answer that the delay necessarily involved in the previous negotiation on the subject, in delivering the prisoners from time to time in small numbers, and receiving others in their stead, and the mode of delivery at different places, will nearly bring the matter to the point we could wish, and give us leisure to reinforce this army, if it is to be done at all, so as to obviate in a great measure the ill consequences apprehended. But if the argument of interest, on a partial scale, be pursued as far as it will go, not only the general consideration thrown out above, but special ones apposite to every situation, will present themselves that we ought not to exchange. Now we ought not, because our army is weak. When the season is more advanced and it is time for the campaign to open, we ought not, because our army may be strong, and it will be our business to avail ourselves of our own strength and the enemy's weakness to strike some decisive blow. If they, by the protection of their shipping and impregnable works, should be able to baffle our attempts till the period of reinforcements from Europe arrive, it will surely then not be our interest to add numbers and strength to an enemy already sufficiently numerous and strong. Thus, by a parity of reasoning, the golden era will never come which is to relieve the miseries of captivity. Our service must become odious, those who are out of it will endeavor to keep so, and those who are in it will wish to get out of it. Every prisoner the enemy makes will be his soldier, rather than submit to a rigorous and despairing confinement.

If we do not seize the present propitious moment, when the necessities of the enemy press them to reasonable terms, to form and establish a liberal cartel, it is not impossible, in the vicissitudes and reverses of war, that a time may come when we should wish we had embraced it, and interest may strongly impel the enemy to decline it, except on the most unequal conditions. True policy, as well as good faith, in my opinion, binds us to improve the occasion.

There are, however, some ambiguities in General Howe's conduct which require explanation and ought to put us upon our guard. I determined to make the affair of citizens—viz. to procure an exemption from captivity for them if possible, or, if not, since it cannot now be demanded as a matter of right, to fix their exchangeability upon the easiest and most unequivocal foundation—an indispensable preliminary to any further procedure, and, at the same time, to secure the exchange of General Lee and all other officers who have been the particular objects of exception.

The interview intended between General Howe's commissioners and those on our part on the 10th instant is now postponed. I cannot doubt that Congress, in preservation of the public faith and my personal honor, will remove all impediments that now oppose themselves to my engagements, and that they will authorize me, through commissioners appointed for the purpose, to negotiate a more extensive and competent cartel, upon such principles as may appear advantageous and founded in necessity, any resolutions heretofore to the contrary notwithstanding. And I must request that they will favor me with their answer by the earliest opportunity.

The work from its nature will be difficult. Two parties are concerned whose interests are more than opposite in a common view. We shall endeavor to act for the best, and to promote the public service as far as possible though we may not be able to answer the expectations of all. But it should be remembered that, although General Howe's want of men affords a prospect of favorable terms, yet he will not be disposed to sacrifice to it all considerations of general advantage in a contract of such a nature. And it is not even to be hoped that it can take place, except on principles of mutual benefit.

I persuade myself that the freedom I have taken in delivering my sentiments so fully upon this occasion will readily be excused, as it proceeded from a desire to place the motives of my conduct in a just point of view, and from an opinion of duty that led me to a free discussion of a subject which, considered in all its lights, will appear to comprehend consequences of the first delicacy and magnitude. I have the honor to be with great respect Sir Your most Obedt servant

Go: Washington

To Lieutenant General John Burgoyne, March 11, 1778 (Excerpt)

Sir,

I was only two days since honored with your very obliging letter of the 11th of February.

Your indulgent opinion of my character, and the polite terms in which you are pleased to express it, are peculiarly flattering. And I take pleasure in the opportunity you have afforded me of assuring you that, far from suffering the views of national opposition to be embittered and debased by personal animosity, I am ever ready to do justice to the merit of the gentleman and soldier—and to esteem, where esteem is due, however the idea of a public enemy may interpose. You will not think it the language of unmeaning ceremony if I add that sentiments of personal respect, in the present instance, are reciprocal.

Viewing you in the light of an officer contending against what I conceive to be the rights of my country, the reverses of fortune you experienced in the field cannot be unacceptable to me. But, abstracted from considerations of national advantage, I can sincerely sympathize with your feelings as a soldier—the unavoidable difficulties of whose situation forbid his success—and as a man—whose lot combines the calamity of ill health, the anxieties of captivity, and the painful sensibility for a reputation exposed where he most values it to the assaults of malice and detraction.

To Patrick Henry, Governor of Virginia, March 27, 1778

Dear Sir,

About eight days ago I was honored with your favor of the 20th ultimo.

Your friendship, sir, in transmitting me the anonymous letter you had received lays me under the most grateful obligations; and if my acknowledgments can be due for anything more, it is for the very polite and delicate terms in which you have been pleased to communicate the matter.

I have ever been happy in supposing that I had a place in your esteem, and the proof you have afforded upon this occasion makes me peculiarly so. The favorable light in which you hold me is truly flattering, but I should feel much regret if I thought the happiness of America so intimately connected with my personal welfare as you so obligingly seem to consider it. All I can say is that she has ever had, and I trust she ever will have, my honest exertions to promote her interest. I cannot hope that my services have been the best. But my heart tells me they have been the best that I could render.

That I may have erred in using all the means in my power for accomplishing the objects of the arduous exalted station with which I am honored, I cannot doubt. Nor do I wish my conduct to be exempted from reprehension farther than it may deserve. Error is the portion of humanity, and to censure it, whether committed by this or that public character, is the prerogative of freemen. However, being intimately acquainted with the man I conceive the author of the letter transmitted, and having always received from him the strongest professions of attachment and regard, I am constrained to consider him as not possessing at least a great degree of candor and honest sincerity, though his views in addressing you should have been the result of conviction and founded in motives of public good. This is not the only secret, insidious attempt that has been made to wound my reputation. There have been others equally base, cruel, and ungenerous, because conducted with as little frankness, and proceeding from views perhaps as personally interesting. I am Dr Sir with great esteem & regard Yr Much obliged friend & Servant

Go: Washington

To Patrick Henry, Governor of Virginia, March 28, 1788 (Excerpt)

I can only thank you again, in the language of the most undissembled gratitude, for your friendship, and assure you the indulgent disposition which Virginia in particular, and the states in general, entertain towards me gives me the most sensible pleasure. The approbation of my country is what I wish, and as far as my abilities and opportunity will permit, I hope I shall endeavor to deserve it. It is the highest reward to a feeling mind, and happy are they who so conduct themselves, as to merit it.

The anonymous letter with which you were pleased to favor me was written by Doctor Rush, so far as I can judge from a similitude of hands. This man has been elaborate and studied in his professions of regard for me, and long since the letter to you.

My caution to avoid anything that could injure the service prevented me from communicating, but to very few of my friends, the intrigues of a faction which I know was formed against me, since it might serve to publish our internal dissensions. But their own restless zeal to advance their views has too clearly betrayed them and made concealment on my part fruitless. I cannot precisely mark the extent of their views, but it appeared in general that General Gates was to be exalted on the ruin of my reputation and influence. This I am authorized to say from undeniable facts in my own possession, from publications the evident scope of which could not be mistaken, and from private detractions industriously circulated. General Mifflin, it is commonly supposed, bore the second part in the cabal; and General Conway, I know, was a very active and malignant partisan. But I have good reasons to believe that their machinations have recoiled most sensibly upon themselves.

General Orders, April 6, 1778 (Excerpt)

At a general court martial, whereof Colonel Vose is president, March 31st, 1778, Lieutenant Dunn of Colonel Patton's regiment was[11] tried for striking, and ungentlemanlike behavior to, Lieutenant Street and acquitted.

The commander-in-chief confirms the sentence and orders Lieutenant Dunn to be discharged from his arrest, at the same time observing that the frequent proceedings of courts martial presented to him, which seem to originate more from personal prejudice and private animosities than real intention to promote the good of the service, gives him very sensible pain. He wishes the officers of his army to consider themselves as a band of brothers cemented by the justice of the common cause, that a perfect harmony might subsist among them, and that they would settle all personal disputes among themselves in an amicable manner, ever being cautious not to trouble courts martial or the general with private dissensions, or add papers to the public files which may hereafter reflect disgrace upon themselves and the army.

General Orders, April 12, 1778 (Excerpt)

The honorable Congress having thought proper to recommend to The United States of America to set apart Wednesday the 22nd instant to be observed as a day of fasting, humiliation, and prayer, that at one time and with one voice the righteous dispensations of Providence may be acknowledged and His goodness and mercy towards us and our arms supplicated and implored—the general directs that this day also shall be religiously observed in the army, that no work be done thereon, and that the chaplains prepare discourses suitable to the occasion.

To John Banister, April 21, 1778

Dear Sir,

On Saturday evening I had the pleasure to receive your favor of the 16th instant.

I thank you very much for your obliging tender of a friendly intercourse between us; and you may rest assured that I embrace it with cheerfulness and shall write you freely, as often as leisure will permit, of such points as appear to me material and interesting.

I am pleased to find that you expect the proposed establishment of the army will succeed, though it is a painful consideration that matters of such pressing importance and obvious necessity meet with so much difficulty and delay. Be assured the success of the measure is a matter of the most serious moment, and that it ought to be brought to a conclusion as speedily as possible. The spirit of resigning commissions has been long at an alarming height and increases daily. Applications from officers on furlough are hourly arriving—and Generals Heath of Boston, McDougall on the North River, and Mason of Virginia are asking what they are to do with the applicants to them. The Virginia line has sustained a violent shock in this instance: not less than ninety have resigned already to me. The same conduct has prevailed among the officers from the other states, though not yet to so considerable a degree; and there are but too just grounds to fear that it will shake the very existence of the army, unless a remedy is soon, very soon applied. There is none, in my opinion, so effectual as the one pointed out.[12] This, I trust, will satisfy the officers and, at the same time, it will produce no present additional emission of money. They will not be persuaded to sacrifice all views of present interest and encounter the numerous vicissitudes of war in the defense of their country, unless she will be generous enough on her part to make a decent provision for their future support. I do not pronounce absolutely that we shall have no army if the establishment fails. But the army we may have will be without discipline, without energy, incapable of acting with vigor, and destitute of those cements necessary to promise success on the one hand, or to withstand the shocks of adversity on the other. It is indeed hard to say how extensive the evil may be if the measure should be rejected or much longer delayed. I find it a very arduous task to keep the officers in tolerable humor and to protract such a combination in quitting the service as might possibly undo us forever. The difference between our service and that of the enemy is very striking. With us, from the peculiar, unhappy situation of things, the officer, a few instances excepted, must break in upon his private fortune for present support, without a prospect of future relief. With them, even companies are esteemed so honorable and so valuable that they have sold of late from 15 to 2,200£ sterling, and I am credibly informed that 4,000 guineas have been given for a troop of dragoons. You will readily determine how this difference will operate, what effects it must produce. Men may speculate as they will—they may talk of patriotism—they may draw a few examples from ancient story of great achievements performed by its influence. But whoever builds upon it as a sufficient basis for conducting a long and bloody war will find themselves deceived in the end. We must take the passions of men as nature has given them, and those principles as a guide which are generally the rule of action. I do not mean to exclude altogether the idea of patriotism. I know it exists, and I know it has done much in the present contest. But I will venture to assert that a great and lasting war can never be supported on this principle alone. It must be aided by a prospect of interest or some reward. For a time, it may of itself push men to action, to bear much, to encounter difficulties; but it will not endure unassisted by interest.

The necessity of putting the army upon a respectable footing, both as to numbers and constitution, is now become more essential than ever. The enemy are beginning to play a game more dangerous than their efforts by arms, though these will not be remitted in the smallest degree, and which threatens a fatal blow to American independence, and to her liberties of course. They are endeavoring to ensnare the people by specious allurements of peace. It is not improbable they have had such abundant cause to be tired of the war that they may be sincere in the terms they offer, which, though far short of our pretensions, will be extremely flattering to minds that do not penetrate far into political consequences. But whether they are sincere or not they may be equally destructive, for to discerning men nothing can be more evident than that a peace on the principles of dependence, however limited, after what has happened, would be to the last degree dishonorable and ruinous. It is, however, much to be apprehended that the idea of such an event will have a very powerful effect upon the country, and, if not combated with the greatest address, will serve at least to produce supineness and disunion. Men are naturally fond of peace; and there are symptoms which may authorize an opinion that the people of America are pretty generally weary of the present war. It is doubtful whether many of our friends might not incline to an accommodation of the grounds held out, or which may be, rather than persevere in a contest for independence. If this is the case, it must surely be the truest policy to strengthen the army and place it upon a substantial footing. This will conduce to inspire the country with confidence, enable those at the head of affairs to consult the public honor and interest, notwithstanding the defection of some and temporary inconsistency and irresolution of others who may desire to compromise the dispute—and, if a treaty should be deemed expedient, will put it in their power to insist upon better terms than they could otherwise expect.

Besides the most vigorous exertions at home to increase and establish our military force upon a good basis, it appears to me advisable that we should immediately try the full extent of our interest abroad and bring our European negotiations to an issue. I think France must have ratified our independence and will declare war immediately on finding that serious proposals of accommodation are made. But lest from a mistaken policy, or too exalted an opinion of our powers from the representations she has had, she should still remain indecisive, it were to be wished proper persons were instantly dispatched, or our envoys already there instructed, to insist pointedly on her coming to a final determination. It cannot be fairly supposed that she will hesitate a moment to declare war if she is given to understand in a proper manner that a reunion of the two countries may be the consequence of procrastination. A European war and a European alliance would effectually answer our purposes. If the step I now mention should be eligible, dispatches ought to be sent at once by different conveyances, for fear of accidents. I confess it appears to me a measure of this kind could not but be productive of the most salutary consequences. If possible, I should also suppose it absolutely necessary to obtain good intelligence from England—pointing out the true springs of this maneuver of ministry, the preparations of force they are making, the prospects there are of raising it, the amount, and when it may be expected.

It really seems to me, from a comprehensive view of things, that a period is fast approaching big with events of the most interesting importance—when the councils we pursue and the part we act may lead decisively to liberty or to slavery. Under this idea, I cannot but regret that inactivity, that inattention, that want of something which, unhappily, I have but too often experienced in our public affairs. I wish that our representation in Congress was complete and full from every state, and that it was formed of the first abilities among us. Whether we continue to war or proceed to negotiate, the wisdom of America in council cannot be too great. Our situation will be truly delicate. To enter into a negotiation too hastily, or to reject it altogether, may be attended with consequences equally fatal. The wishes of the people, seldom founded in deep disquisitions or resulting from other reasonings than their present feeling, may not entirely accord with our true policy and interest. If they do not, to observe a proper line of conduct—for promoting the one and avoiding offense to the other—will be a work of great difficulty. Nothing short of independence, it appears to me, can possibly do. A peace on other terms would, if I may be allowed the expression, be a peace of war. The injuries we have received from the British nation were so unprovoked, have been so great and so many, that they can never be forgotten. Besides the feuds, the jealousies, the animosities that would ever attend a union with them—besides the importance, the advantages we should derive from an unrestricted commerce—our fidelity as a people, our gratitude, our character as men are opposed to a coalition with them as subjects, but in case of the last extremity.

Were we easily to accede to terms of dependence, no nation upon future occasions, let the oppressions of Britain be never so flagrant and unjust, would interpose for our relief; or at least they would do it with a cautious reluctance and upon conditions most probably that would be hard if not dishonorable to us. France by her supplies has saved us from the yoke thus far, and a wise and virtuous perseverance would, and I trust will, free us entirely.

I have sent Congress Lord North's speech and two bills offered by him to Parliament. They are spreading fast through the country and will soon become a subject of general notoriety. I therefore think they had best be published in our papers, and persons of leisure and ability set to work to counteract the impressions they may make on the minds of the people.

Before I conclude, there are one or two points more upon which I will add an observation or two. The first is the indecision of Congress and the delay used in coming to determinations in matters referred to 'em. This is productive of a variety of inconveniences, and an early decision in many cases, though it should be against the measure submitted, would be attended with less pernicious effects. Some new plan might then be tried; but while the matter is held in suspense nothing can be attempted. The other point is the jealousy which Congress unhappily entertain of the army, and which, if reports are right, some members labor to establish. You may be assured there is nothing more injurious or more unjustly founded. This jealousy stands upon the common, received opinion, which under proper limitations is certainly true, that standing armies are dangerous to a state—and from forming the same conclusion of the component parts of all, though they are totally dissimilar in their nature. The prejudice in other countries has only gone to 'em in time of peace, and then from their not having in general cases any of the ties, the concerns, or interests of citizens, or any other dependence than what flowed from their military employ—in short from their being mercenaries, hirelings. It is our policy to be prejudiced against them in time of war—and though they are citizens, having all the ties and interests of citizens, and in most cases property totally unconnected with the military line. If we would pursue a right system of policy, in my opinion, there should be none of these distinctions. We should all be considered—Congress, army, etc.—as one people, embarked in one cause, in one interest, acting on the same principle, and to the same end. The distinction, the jealousies set up, or perhaps only incautiously let out, can answer not a single good purpose. They are impolitic in the extreme. Among individuals, the most certain way to make a man your enemy is to tell him you esteem him such. So with public bodies; and the very jealousy which the narrow politics of some may affect to entertain of the army—in order to a due subordination to the supreme, civil authority—is a likely mean to produce a contrary effect, to incline it to the pursuit of those measures that many[13] wish it to avoid. It is unjust, because no order of men in the thirteen states have paid a more sanctimonious regard to their proceedings than the army; and, indeed, it may be questioned whether there has been that scrupulous adherence had to them by any other. For without arrogance or the smallest deviation from truth it may be said that no history, now extant, can furnish an instance of an army's suffering such uncommon hardships as ours have done, and bearing them with the same patience and fortitude. To see men without clothes to cover their nakedness—without blankets to lay on—without shoes, by which their marches might be traced by the blood from their feet—and almost as often without provisions as with—marching through frost and snow, and at Christmas taking up their winter quarters within a day's march of the enemy—without a house or hut to cover them till they could be built—and submitting to it without a murmur—is a mark of patience and obedience which in my opinion can scarce be paralleled. There may have been some remonstrances or applications to Congress in the style of complaint from the army—and slaves indeed should we be if this privilege was denied—on account of their proceedings in particular instances. But these will not authorize nor even excuse a jealousy that they are therefore aiming at unreasonable powers or making strides dangerous or subversive of civil authority. Things should not be viewed in that light, more especially as Congress in some cases have relieved the injuries complained of, and which had flowed from their own acts.

I refer you to my letter to yourself and Colonel Lee, which accompanies this, upon the subject of money for such of the old Virginia troops as have or may re-enlist.

In respect to the volunteer plan, I scarce know what opinion to give at this time. The propriety of a requisition on this head will depend altogether on our operations. Such kind of troops should not be called for but upon the spur of the occasion, and at the moment of executing an enterprise. They will not endure a long service, and of all men in the military line they are the most impatient of restraint and necessary government.

As the propositions and the speech of Lord North must be founded in the despair of the nation of succeeding against us—or from a rupture in Europe that has actually happened, or that certainly will—or from some deep political maneuver—or from what I think still more likely, a composition of the whole—would it not be good policy, in this day of uncertainty and distress to the Tories, to avail ourselves of the occasion and for the several states to hold out pardon etc. to all delinquents returning by a certain day? They are frightened, and that is the time to operate upon them. Upon a short consideration of the matter, it appears to me that such a measure would detach the Tories from the enemy and bring things to a much speedier conclusion, and of course be a mean of saving much public treasure.

I will now be done, and I trust that you will excuse not only the length of my letter but the freedom with which I have delivered my sentiments in the course of it upon several occasions. The subjects struck me as important and interesting, and I have only to wish that they may appear to you in the same light. I am Dr sir with great regard Your Most Obedt sert.

General Orders, May 2, 1778 (Excerpt)

The commander-in-chief directs that divine service be performed every Sunday at 11 o'clock in those brigades to which there are chaplains—those which have none to attend the places of worship nearest to them. It is expected that officers of all ranks will by their attendance set an example to their men.

While we are zealously performing the duties of good citizens and soldiers, we certainly ought not to be inattentive to the higher duties of religion. To the distinguished character of patriot, it should be our highest glory to add the more distinguished character of Christian. The signal instances of providential goodness which we have experienced, and which have now almost crowned our labors with complete success, demand from us in a peculiar manner the warmest returns of gratitude and piety to the Supreme Author of all good.

Explanatory Notes

1. A correction from Washington's "fell."
2. We have added the word "is" here.
3. We have added the word "are" here.
4. A correction from Washington's "wrote."
5. A correction from Washington's "has."
6. We have supplied this word, which is missing in the original document.
7. Here we have changed Washington's "they" to "the," which is surely what he intended.
8. Here Washington may have intended "off."
9. We have added this word, which seems to be required by Washington's meaning.
10. Corrected from Washington's "wrote."
11. We have supplied this word.
12. Washington is here referring to the proposal for half-pay for officers' and widows' pensions.
13. We have corrected this from Washington's "may." The change seems necessary to render the passage intelligible.

Fig. 3 Part III: The Road to Victory: 1778–1783
www.gettyimages.com/detail/illustration/digitally-restored-vector-painting-of-royalty-free-illustration/158653348?adppopup=true

PART III

The Road to Victory: 1778–1783

To Major General Alexander McDougall, May 5, 1778 (Excerpt)

I very much fear that we, taking it for granted that we have nothing more to do because France has acknowledged our independency and formed an alliance with us, shall relapse into a state of supineness and perfect security. I think it more than probable, from the situation of affairs in Europe, that the enemy will receive no considerable if any reinforcements. But suppose they should not: their remaining force, if well directed, is far from being contemptible. In the desperate state of British affairs, it is worth a desperate attempt to extricate themselves; and a blow at our main army, if successful, would have a wonderful effect upon the minds of a number of people still willing to embrace the present terms, or indeed any terms, offered by Great Britain. It behooves us therefore to make ourselves as respectable as possible that, if the enemy continue in their present detached state, we may endeavor to destroy them by piece meal, and if, on the contrary, they collect, they may fall heavily upon us in some quarter.

To Major General Lafayette, May 17, 1778

Dear Sir,

I received yesterday your favor of the 15th instant, enclosing a paper, subscribed by sundry officers of General Woodford's brigade, setting forth their reasons for not taking the oath of abjuration, allegiance, and office, and thank you much for the cautious delicacy used in communicating the matter to me.

As every oath should be a free act of the mind, founded on the conviction of the party of its propriety, I would not wish in any instance that there should be the least degree of compulsion exercised, or to interpose my opinion in order to induce any to make it of whom it is required. The gentlemen, therefore, who signed the paper will use their own discretion in the matter and swear or not swear as their conscience and feelings dictate.

At the same time, I cannot but consider it as a circumstance of some singularity that the scruples against the oath should be peculiar to the officers of one brigade, and so very extensive.

The oath in itself is not new. It is substantially the same with that required in all governments, and therefore does not imply any indignity. And it is perfectly consistent with the professions, actions, and implied engagements of every officer.

The objection founded on the supposed unsettled rank of the officers is of no validity (rank being only mentioned as a further designation of the party swearing). Nor can it be seriously thought that the oath is either intended or can prevent their being promoted or their resignations.

The fourth objection stated by the gentlemen serves as a *key* to their scruples, and I would willingly persuade myself that their own reflections will point out to them the impropriety of the whole proceeding and not suffer 'em to be betrayed in future into a similar conduct. I regard them all and cannot but regret that they were ever engaged in the measure. I am certain they will regret it themselves. Sure I am they ought. I am My Dr Marquis Yr Affect frd & servt.

To Brigadier General William Smallwood, May 19, 1778 (Excerpt)

Sir,

I have received your favor of the 17th instant, enclosing the proceedings of a general court martial held by your order. The character you give of Jetson makes him so atrocious that I regret his trial and sentence are not more clear and regular. There could be no more proper object for an example, if it could be made with propriety, than the circumstances you mention designate this man to be. But the proceeding in this affair has not all that precision, authority, and evidence which are essential to affect life. The charge is laid in too general terms to be admitted either at a civil or military tribunal. The only part in which it is specific and definite is the firing on the continental troops, which in itself is no crime but depends upon the manner and circumstances of the fact to make it so, of which there ought to be something descriptive in the charge. In those cases where it is a crime, if the criminal is an inhabitant, we have no law subjecting him to the jurisdiction of a court martial, but he must be referred to the civil power to be tried for treason. There is a resolve of Congress empowering courts martial to take cognizance of inhabitants who have any communication of trade or intelligence with the enemy, or who serve them in the capacity of guides or pilots; but the operation of this law is limited to persons taken within thirty miles of headquarters, which prevents its application to the present case. There is another resolve, a[1] copy of which I enclose, for the trial and punishment of kidnappers. You mention the practice of kidnapping as one of Jetson's offenses. If proper evidence can be adduced in support of it, and the commission has been since the date of the law, you may have him tried on that charge, which will effectually procure him his deserts. Otherwise, he must of necessity be turned over to the civil power of the state to which he belongs, which it is to be hoped will at least take proper precautions to prevent his doing further mischief.

To Richard Henry Lee, May 25, 1778 (Excerpt)

The favorable issue of our negotiations with France is matter for heartfelt joy, big with important events, and must, I should think, chalk out a plain and easy road to independence—from which, I hope, we shall not depart from a mistaken opinion, on the one hand, that the great work is already finished, or, to finish it, adopt measures of precipitation. That G. Britain would have submitted to any indignity from France in order to wreak her vengeance upon America, I have not the smallest doubt; but since the declaration of the king of France through the Marquis de Noailles, they have no choice but war. But how, under their present circumstances, they will conduct it is a matter not so easily understood, as all their ways have been ways of darkness. That they will be under a necessity of giving up the continent, or their islands, seems obvious to me, if the accounts we have received of the French force in the West Indies be true. Halifax and Canada will, I presume, be strengthened. And if they can afford a garrison sufficient, they may attempt to hold New York, unless every idea of subjugating America is given up. In that case, their whole resentment will be leveled at France.

To Gouverneur Morris, May 29, 1778 (Excerpt)

Dear Sir,

I thank you for your favors of the 21st and 23rd instant, both of which have come to hand since my last to you. Had such a chapter as you speak of been written to the rulers of mankind, it would, I am persuaded, have been as unavailing as many others upon subjects of equal importance. We may lament that things are not consonant to our wishes, but cannot change the nature of man. And yet, those who are distressed by the folly and perverseness of it cannot help complaining, as I would do on the old score of regulation and arrangement, if I thought any good would come of it.

It appears to me that British politics are aground, and that administration is reduced to the alternative (if war is declared, which I cannot doubt) of relinquishing all pretensions to conquest in America or must give up her islands. Which she *will* choose, I cannot say. Which she *ought* to do is evident. But how far obstinacy, revenge, and villainy may induce them to persevere, I shall not undertake to determine.

To Landon Carter, May 30, 1778 (Excerpt)

My Dear Sir,

Your favors of the 10th of March (ended the 20th) and 7th instant came safe to hand after a good deal of delay. I thank you much for your kind and affectionate remembrance and mention of me, and for that solicitude for my welfare which breathes through the whole of your letters. Were I not warm in my acknowledgments for your distinguished regards, I should feel that sense of ingratitude which I hope will never constitute a part of my character, nor find a place in my bosom. My friends therefore may believe me sincere in my professions of attachment to them, whilst Providence has a just claim to my humble and grateful thanks for its protection and direction of me through the many difficult and intricate scenes which this contest hath produced, and for its constant interposition in our behalf when the clouds were heaviest and seemed ready to burst upon us. To paint the distresses and perilous situation of this army in the course of last winter, for want of clothes, provisions, and almost every other necessary essential to the well-being (I may say existence) of an army, would require more time and an abler pen than mine. Nor, since our prospects have so miraculously brightened, shall I attempt it, or even bear it in remembrance, further than as a memento of what is due to the Great Author of all the care and good that has been extended in relieving us in difficulties and distress.

To John Augustine Washington, May 1778

Dear Brother,

Your letter of the 27th of March from Bushfield came safe to hand and gave me the pleasure of hearing, or rather inferring (for you are not explicit), that my sister and the rest of your family were well. I thank you for your intelligence respecting the pamphlet of forged letters which Colonel Lee has, and said to be written by me—not one sentence of which, you may rely on it, did I ever write, although so many little family circumstances are interspersed through the whole performance to give it the air of authenticity. The arts of the enemy, and the low dirty tricks which they are daily practicing, are an evincing proof that they are lost to all sense of virtue and honor, and that they will stick at nothing, however incompatible with truth and manliness, to carry their points. They have lately forged and industriously circulated a resolve for Congress, purporting (after reciting with great propriety and plausibility the inconveniencies of short enlistments) that all soldiers who have been drafted for periods short of the war shall nevertheless continue in service during it, and by their emissaries have endeavored and effected the injury of the service by this means—alarming the fears of the soldiery and country.

I am mistaken if we are not verging fast to one of the most important periods that ever America saw. Doubtless before this reaches you, you will have seen the drafts of two bills intended to be enacted into laws and Lord North's speech upon the occasion. These our accounts from Philadelphia say will be immediately followed by the commissioners, and Lord Amherst, Admiral Keppel, and General Murray are said to be the commissioners. These gentlemen, I presume, are to move in a civil and military line, as General Howe is certainly recalled, and, report adds, Lord Howe also. Be this as it may, it will require all the skill, the wisdom, and policy of the first abilities of these states to manage the helm and steer with judgment to the haven of our wishes through so many shelves and rocks as will be thrown in our way. This, more than ever, is the time for Congress to be replete with the first characters in every state, instead of having a thin assembly and many states totally unrepresented, as is the case at present. I have often regretted the pernicious (and what appears to me fatal) policy of having our ablest men engaged in the formation of the more local governments and filling offices in their respective states, leaving the great national concern, on which the superstructure of all and every of them does absolutely depend, and without which none can exist, to be managed by men of more contracted abilities. Indeed, those at a distance from the seat of war live in such perfect tranquility that they conceive the dispute to be at an end in a manner, and those near hand it are so disaffected that they only serve as embarrassments. Between the two, therefore, time slips away without the necessary means for opening the campaign in time or with propriety.

Your accounts of the high prices of fresh provisions in Philadelphia are true, but it affects the inhabitants more than the soldiery, who have plenty of salt meat, peas, etc.

Since I began this letter authentic accounts have come to my hands of France having declared the United States free and independent and guaranteeing to them all the territory formerly ceded by them to Great Britain. My account (from the gentleman who was going on to Congress with the treaty) adds that France have done this in the most generous manner and to our utmost wish. This is great, 'tis glorious news and must put the independency of America out of all manner of dispute, and accounts for the gentle gales which have succeeded rude Boreas of late. A publication of this important intelligence will no doubt be directed by Congress and diffused through the continent as speedily as possible. I shall add nothing further therefore on the subject.

It would have been a happy circumstance if the several states had been industrious in pushing their recruits into the field early, but I see little prospect of it at present, if ever. My love and best wishes, in which Mrs. Washington joins me, attend my sister and the rest of your family, and with great truth I subscribe myself Yr Most Affecte Brothr

Go: Washington

To Brigadier General Thomas Nelson, Jr., August 20, 1778 (Excerpt)

It is not a little pleasing, nor less wonderful to contemplate, that after two years maneuvering and undergoing the strangest vicissitudes that perhaps ever attended any one contest since the creation, both armies are brought back to the very point they set out from, and that that which was the offending party in the beginning is now reduced to the use of the spade and pickaxe for defense. The hand of Providence has been so conspicuous in all this that he must be worse than an infidel that lacks faith, and more than wicked that has not gratitude enough to acknowledge his obligations. But it will be time enough for me to turn preacher when my present appointment ceases. And therefore I shall add no more on the doctrine of Providence, but make a tender of my best respects to your good lady, the secretary, and other friends and assure you that with the most perfect regard I am Dr Sir Yr Most Affecte & Obliged Hble Ser.

Go: Washington

General Orders, August 21, 1778 (Excerpt)

The commander-in-chief has thought proper to pardon the following criminals who were under sentence of death and to have been executed this day: Solomon Lynes, John Craige, Zechariah Ward, Richard Burk, Michael Carmen, William McLaughlin, John Jenkins, Nicholas Fitzgerald, David Potter, and Neil Megonigle.

Notwithstanding the general good character of the criminal as a soldier, the wounds he has received in fighting for his country, the warm solicitation of several respectable officers, and even the special intercession of Captain Scott himself, to whom the injury was offered, it was with extreme difficulty the commander-in-chief could prevail with himself to pardon an offense so atrocious as that committed by Megonigle. The least disrespect from a soldier to an officer is criminal in a high degree and deserves severe punishment. When it proceeds to any kind of personal violence the offender justly merits death, but when it extends to an attempt upon the officer's life, as was the case in the present instance, it assumes a complexion so enormous and aggravated that it wants a name and puts the criminal almost beyond the reach of mercy itself. The general is happy to reflect that this is the first time an instance of this nature has come before him. He thinks it necessary to warn every soldier that a similar one will never hereafter be forgiven, whatever may be the character of the offender or the intercessions of the officers.

Several deserters from the army to the enemy who have since returned, having been permitted with impunity to join their regiments—the general, to prevent an abuse of his lenity by its being drawn into precedent and made an encouragement to others to commit the same crime, takes occasion to declare in explicit terms that no man who shall desert to the enemy after the publication of this order will ever be allowed to enjoy the like indulgence, but whether he return voluntarily himself or fall into our hands by any other means will infallibly suffer the punishment decreed to his crime.

To Vice Admiral Charles-Hector Théodat Estaing, September 11, 1778 (Excerpt)

Sir,

I have had the honor of receiving Your Excellency's letter of the 5th instant, accompanied by a copy of two letters to Congress and General Sullivan. The confidence which you have been pleased to show me in communicating these papers engages my sincere thanks. If the deepest regret that the best concerted enterprises and bravest exertions should have been rendered fruitless by a disaster which human prudence is incapable of foreseeing or preventing can alleviate disappointment, you may be assured that the whole continent sympathizes with you. It will be a consolation to you to reflect that the thinking part of mankind do not form their judgment from events, and that their equity will ever attach equal glory to those actions which deserve success as to those which have been crowned with it. It is in the trying circumstances to which Your Excellency has been exposed that the virtues of a great mind are displayed in their brightest luster—and that the general's character is better known than in the moment of victory. It was yours by every title which can give it, and the adverse element which robbed you of your prize can never deprive you of the glory due to you. And though your success has not been equal to your expectations, yet you have the satisfaction to reflect that you have done essential service to the common cause.

To Major General Lafayette, October 4, 1778 (Excerpt)

The generous spirit of chivalry, exploded by the rest of the world, finds a refuge, my dear friend, in the sensibility of your nation only. But it is in vain to cherish it unless you can find antagonists to support it; and however well adapted it might have been to the times in which it existed, in our days it is to be feared that your opponent, sheltering himself behind modern opinion, and under his present public character of commissioner, would turn a virtue of such ancient date into ridicule. Besides, supposing His Lordship accepted your terms, experience has proved that chance is as often as much concerned in deciding these matters as bravery—and always more than the justice of the cause. I would not therefore have your life, by the remotest possibility, exposed, when it may be reserved for so many greater occasions. His Excellency the admiral I flatter myself will be in sentiment with me and, as soon as he can spare you, send you to headquarters, where I anticipate the pleasure of seeing you.

General Orders, October 21, 1778 (Excerpt)

Purity of morals being the only sure foundation of public happiness in any country, and highly conducive to order, subordination, and success in an army, it will be well worthy of the emulation of officers of every rank and class to encourage it both by the influence of example and the penalties of authority. It is painful to see many shameful instances of riot and licentiousness among us. The wanton practice of swearing has risen to a most disgusting height. A regard to decency should conspire with a sense of morality to banish a vice productive of neither advantage or pleasure. The frequent robberies which have lately prevailed in the vicinity of camp are truly alarming and demand the most vigilant exertions to detect the perpetrators and bring them to the severest punishment.

To Henry Laurens, President of the Continental Congress, November 11, 1778 (Excerpt)

It seems to me impolitic to enter into engagements with the Court of France for carrying on a combined operation of any kind without a moral certainty of being able to fulfill our part, particularly if the first proposal came from us. If we should not be able to perform them it would argue either a want of consideration, a defective knowledge of our resources, or something worse than either, which could not fail to produce a degree of distrust and discontent that might be very injurious to the Union. In the present instance, should the scheme proposed be adopted, a failure on our part would certainly occasion in them a misapplication of a considerable land and naval force which might be usefully employed elsewhere, and probably their total loss. It is true if we were at this time to enter into the engagement we shall be every day better able to judge whether it will be in our power to accomplish what would be expected from us; and, if we should find hereafter that our resources will be unequal to the undertaking, we may give notice to the Court of France in season, to prevent the sailing of the troops and the ill effects which might attend it. But besides that, a project of this kind could not be embraced by France without its having an influence on the whole system of operations for the next campaign, which of course would receive some derangement from its being abandoned. A renunciation of this could not fail to give a very unfavorable impression of our foresight and providence and would serve to weaken the confidence of that court in our public councils.

To Henry Laurens, President of the Continental Congress, November 14, 1778

Dear Sir,

This will be accompanied by an official letter on the subject of the proposed expedition against Canada. You will perceive I have only considered it in a military light. Indeed, I was not authorized to consider it in any other, and I am not without apprehensions that I may be thought in what I have done to have exceeded the limits intended by Congress. But my solicitude for the public welfare, which I think deeply interested in this affair, will I hope justify me in the eyes of all those who view things through that just medium.

    I do not know, sir, what may be your sentiments in the present case; but whatever they are, I am sure I can confide in your honor and friendship, and shall not hesitate to unbosom myself to you on a point of the most delicate and important nature. The question of the Canadian expedition in the form it now stands appears to me one of the most interesting that has hitherto agitated our national deliberations. I have one objection to it untouched in my public letter, which is in my estimation insurmountable—and alarms all my feelings for the true and permanent interests of my country. This is the introduction of a large body of French troops into Canada and putting them in possession of the capital of that province—attached to them by all the ties of blood, habits, manners, religion, and former connection of government. I fear this would be too great a temptation to be resisted by any power actuated by the common maxims of national policy.

    Let us realize for a moment the striking advantages France would derive from the possession of Canada: the acquisition of an extensive territory abounding in supplies for the use of her islands; the opening a vast source of the most beneficial commerce with the Indian nations, which she might then monopolize, she having ports of her own on the continent, independent on the precarious good will of an ally; the engrossing the whole trade of Newfoundland whenever she pleased (the finest nursery of seamen in the world); the security afforded to her islands; and finally of awing and controlling these states, the natural and most formidable rival of every maritime power in Europe. Canada would be a solid acquisition to France on all these accounts, and because of the numerous inhabitants, subjects to her by inclination, who would aid in preserving it under her power against the attempt of every other.

France—acknowledged for some time past the most powerful monarchy in Europe by land, able now to dispute the empire of the sea with Britain, and if joined with Spain, I may say certainly superior—in possession of Canada on our left, and the extensive territory anciently comprehended within its limits, while the other branch of the House of Bourbon possesses New Orleans, the key of the Mississippi, on our right, seconded by the numerous tribes of Indians on our rear from one extremity to the other, a people so generally friendly to her, and whom she knows so well to conciliate, would, it is much to be apprehended, have it in her power to give law to these states.

Let us suppose that, when the five thousand French troops (and under the idea of that number twice as many may be sent) were entered the City of Quebec, they should declare an intention to hold Canada as a pledge and security for the debt due to France from the United States—or under other specious pretenses hold the place till they can find a bond for contention—and, in the meanwhile, should excite the Canadians to engage in supporting their pretenses and claims, what should we be able to say with only four or five thousand men to carry on the dispute? It may be supposed that France would not choose to renounce our friendship by a step of this kind, as the consequence would probably be a reunion with England on some terms or other, and the loss of what she had acquired in so violent and unjustifiable a manner, with all the advantages of an alliance with us. This, in my opinion, is too slender a security against the measure to be relied on. The truth of the position will entirely depend on naval events. If France and Spain should unite and obtain a decided superiority by sea, a reunion with England would avail very little, and might be set at defiance. France with a numerous army at command might throw in what number of land forces she thought proper to support her pretensions; and England—without men, without money, and inferior on her favorite element—could give no effectual aid to oppose them. Resentment, reproaches, and submission seem to be all that would be left us. Men are very apt to run into extremes. Hatred to England may carry some into an excess of confidence in France, especially when motives of gratitude are thrown into the scale. Men of this description would be unwilling to suppose France capable of acting so ungenerous a part. I am heartily disposed to entertain the most favorable sentiments of our new ally, and to cherish them in others, to a reasonable degree. But it is a maxim founded on the universal experience of mankind that no nation is to be trusted farther than it is bound by its interest, and no prudent statesman or politician will venture to depart from it. In our circumstances we ought to be particularly cautious, for we have not yet attained sufficient vigor and maturity to recover from the shock of any false step into which we may unwarily fall.

If France should even engage in the scheme in the first instance with the purest intentions, there is the greatest danger that in the progress of the business, invited to it by circumstances, perhaps urged on by the solicitations and wishes of the Canadians, she would alter her views. As the Marquis clothed his proposition when he spoke of it to me, it would seem to originate wholly with himself; but it is far from impossible that it had its birth in the cabinet of France, and was put into this artful dress to give it the readier currency. I fancy I read in the countenances of some people on this occasion more than the disinterested zeal of allies. I hope I am mistaken, and my fears of mischief make me refine too much and awaken jealousies that have no sufficient foundation.

But upon the whole, sir, to waive every other consideration, I do not like to add to the number of national obligations. I would wish as much as possible to avoid giving a foreign power new claims of merit for services performed to the United States, and would ask no assistance that is not indispensable. I am with the truest attachment, and most perfect Confidence, Dr Sir Yr Most Obed. & Obliged

Go: Washington

To Joseph Reed, President of the Supreme Executive Council of Pennsylvania, December 12, 1778 (Excerpt)

It gives me very sincere pleasure to find that there is likely to be a coalition of the Whigs in your state (a few only excepted) and that the assembly of it are so well disposed to second your endeavors in bringing those murderers of our cause—the monopolizers, forestallers, and engrossers—to condign punishment. It is much to be lamented that each state, long 'ere this, has not hunted them down as the pests of society and the greatest enemies we have to the happiness of America. I would to God that one of the most atrocious in each state was hung in gibbets up on a gallows five times as high as the one prepared by Haman. No punishment, in my opinion, is too great for the man, who can build "his greatness upon his country's ruin."

General Lee's[2] publication in *Dunlap's Gazette* of the 3rd instant (and I have seen no other) puts me in a disagreeable situation. I have neither leisure nor inclination to enter the list with him in a newspaper. And so far as his production points to personality I can and do, from my inmost soul, despise. But when he has most barefacedly misrepresented facts in some places, and thrown out insinuations in others that have not the smallest foundation in truth, not to attempt a refutation is a tacit acknowledgment of the justice of his assertions. For though there are thousands who know how unsupported his piece is, there are yet tens of thousands that know nothing of the matter and will be led naturally to conclude that bold and confident assertions, uncontradicted, must be founded in truth.

It became a part of General Lee's plan from the moment of his arrest (though it was an event solicited by himself) to have the world believe that he was a persecuted man, and that party was at the bottom of it. But however convenient it may have been for his purposes to establish this doctrine, I defy him or his most zealous partisans to adduce a single instance in proof of it, unless bringing him to trial at his own request is considered in this light. I can do more. I will defy any person out of my own family to say that I have ever mentioned his name after his trial commenced, if it was to be avoided, and, when it was not, that I have not studiously declined expressing any sentiment of him or his behavior. How far this conduct accords with his let his own breast decide. If he conceives that I was opposed to him because he found himself disposed to enter into a party against me—if he thought I stood in his road to preferment, and therefore that it was convenient to lessen me in the esteem of my countrymen in order to pave the way for his own advancement—I have only to observe that as I never entertained any jealousy of or apprehension from him, so neither did I ever do more than common civility and a proper respect to his rank required to conciliate his good opinion. His temper and plans were too versatile and violent to attract my admiration. And that I have escaped the venom of his tongue and pen so long is more to be wondered at than applauded, as it is a favor that no officer under whose immediate command he ever served has the happiness (if happiness can be thus denominated) of boasting.

To Benjamin Harrison, Speaker of the Virginia House of Delegates, December 18–30, 1778 (Excerpts)

I can assign but two causes for the enemy's continuance among us, and these balance so equally in my mind that I scarce know which of the two preponderates. The one is that they are waiting the ultimate determination of Parliament—the other that of our distresses, by which I know the commissioners went home not a little buoyed up, and sorry I am to add, not without cause. What may be the effect of such large and frequent emissions—of the dissensions, parties, extravagance, and a general lax of public virtue—Heaven alone can tell! I am afraid even to think of it; but it appears as clear to me as ever the sun did in its meridian brightness that America never stood in more eminent need of the wise, patriotic, and spirited exertions of her sons than at this period. And if it is not a sufficient cause for general lamentation, my misconception of the matter impresses it too strongly upon me that the states separately are too much engaged in their local concerns and have too many of their ablest men withdrawn from the general council for the good of the common weal. In a word, I think our political system may be compared to the mechanism of a clock, and that our conduct should derive a lesson from it; for it answers no good purpose to keep the smaller wheels in order if the greater one, which is the support and prime mover of the whole, is neglected. How far the latter is the case does not become me to pronounce, but as there can be no harm in a pious wish for the good of one's country, I shall offer it as mine that each state would not only choose but absolutely compel their ablest men to attend Congress, that they would instruct them to go into a thorough investigation of the causes that have produced so many disagreeable effects in the army and country, in a word that public abuses should be corrected and an entire reformation worked. Without these it does not, in my judgment, require the spirit of divination to foretell the consequences of the present administration, nor to how little purpose the states, individually, are framing constitutions, providing laws, and filling offices with the abilities of their ablest men. These, if the great whole is mismanaged, must sink in the general wreck and will carry with it the remorse of thinking that we are lost by our own folly and negligence—or the desire perhaps of living in ease and tranquility during the expected accomplishment of so great a revolution, in the effecting of which the greatest abilities and the honestest men our (i.e. the American) world affords ought to be employed. It is much to be feared, my dear sir, that the states in their separate capacities have very inadequate ideas of the present danger. Removed (some of them) far distant from the scene of action, and seeing and hearing such publications only as flatter their wishes, they conceive that the contest is at an end and that to regulate the government and police of their own state is all that remains to be done. But it is devoutly to be wished that a sad reverse of this may not fall upon them like a thunderclap that is little expected. I do not mean to designate particular states. I wish to cast no reflections upon anyone. The public believes (and if they do believe it, the fact might almost as well be so) that the states at this time are badly represented, and that the great and important concerns of the nation are horribly conducted for want either of abilities or application in the members, or through discord and party views of some individuals. That they should be so is to be lamented more at this time than formerly, as we are far advanced in the dispute, and in the opinion of many, drawing to a happy period, have the eyes of Europe upon us, and, I am persuaded, many political spies to watch, discover our situation, and give information of our weaknesses and wants ....

I have seen nothing since I came here (on the 22nd instant) to change my opinion of men or measures, but abundant reason to be convinced that our affairs are in a more distressed, ruinous, and deplorable condition than they have been in since the commencement of the war. By a faithful laborer then in the cause—by a man who is daily injuring his private estate without even the smallest earthly advantage not common to all, in case of a favorable issue to the dispute—by one who wishes the prosperity of America most devoutly and sees or thinks he sees it on the brink of ruin—you are beseeched most earnestly, my dear Colonel Harrison, to exert yourself in endeavoring to rescue your country by (let me add) sending your ablest and best men to Congress. These characters must not slumber, nor sleep at home, in such times of pressing danger. They must not content themselves in the enjoyment of places of honor or profit in their own country while the common interests of America are moldering and sinking into irretrievable (if a remedy is not soon applied) ruin, in which theirs also must ultimately be involved. If I was to be called upon to draw a picture of the times and of men, from what I have seen, heard, and in part know, I should in one word say that idleness, dissipation, and extravagance seem to have laid fast hold of most of them; that speculation, peculation, and an insatiable thirst for riches[3] seem to have got the better of every other consideration and almost of every order of men; that party disputes and personal quarrels are the great business of the day, whilst the momentous concerns of an empire—a great and accumulated debt, ruined finances, depreciated money, and want of credit (which in their consequences is the want of everything)—are but secondary considerations and postponed from day to day, from week to week, as if our affairs wore the most promising aspect. After drawing this picture, which from my soul I believe to be a true one, I need not repeat to you that I am alarmed and wish to see my countrymen roused. I have no resentments, nor do I mean to point at any particular characters. This I can declare upon my honor, for I have every attention paid me by Congress that I can possibly expect and have reason to think that I stand well in their estimation. But in the present situation of things I cannot help asking: Where is Mason, Wythe, Jefferson, Nicholas, Pendleton, Nelson, and another I could name? And why, if you are sufficiently impressed with your danger, do you not (as New York has done in the case of Mr. Jay) send an extra member or two for at least a certain limited time till the great business of the nation is put upon a more respectable and happy establishment? Your money is now sinking 5 percent a day in this city, and I shall not be surprised if in the course of a few months a total stop is put to the currency of it. And yet an assembly, a concert, a dinner or supper (that will cost three or four hundred pounds) will not only take men off from acting in but even from thinking of this business, while a great part of the officers of your army from absolute necessity are quitting the service, and the more virtuous few, rather than do this, are sinking by sure degrees into beggary and want. I again repeat to you that this is not an exaggerated account. That it is an alarming one I do not deny, and confess to you that I feel more real distress on account of the present appearances of things than I have done at any one time since the commencement of the dispute. But it is time to bid you once more adieu. Providence has heretofore taken us up when all other means and hope seemed to be departing from us. In this I will confide. Yrs &ca

G. W——n

To Major General Israel Putnam, January 18, 1779 (Excerpt)

The mutiny of the soldiers in Huntington's brigade was on its first appearance of a very alarming nature; but I am in hopes, from the success with which your spirited exertions were attended in dispersing them, that there is no danger of farther commotion.

The conduct which a commanding officer is to observe in cases of this kind in general is to use every means for discovering the authors of the mischief, to inflict instant punishment on them, and reclaim the rest by clemency. The impression made on the minds of the multitude by the terror of the example, and their inability to take any resolution when deprived of their ringleaders, are a sufficient security against farther attempts. Humanity and policy unite in prescribing such limits to capital punishments when the crime has been so general.

With respect to the application in the present instance, and the doubt which arises from the foundation of complaint which the men have, it is to be observed that their mode of pursuing redress is of so dangerous a tendency as to call for the exercise of wholesome severity; and though the circumstances may require it to be tempered with more lenity than in ordinary cases, such a subversion of discipline and subordination cannot be passed unpunished. You will be best able to judge from the degree of culpability of those in confinement what measures ought to be taken respecting them, if there are any proper subjects for execution among them. It is to be regretted that the matter has suffered any delay.

If the same causes should unluckily give birth to any future mutiny, the conduct above mentioned must be pursued. The severest and most summary example must be made of the leaders, while a representation is made to the rest, in firm and at the same time conciliating language, that no measure compatible with our present circumstances is omitted for providing them, that mutiny will not only be ineffectual in procuring a remedy but involve consequences infinitely worse than the evil complained of.

To the Continental Congress Committee of Conference, January 20, 1779

Gentlemen,

That the officers of the army are in a very disagreeable situation, that the most unhappy consequences are to be apprehended if they are not speedily placed in a better, and that therefore some provision more adequate than has yet been made is absolutely necessary, are truths so obvious and so generally acknowledged that it would almost seem superfluous to say anything to enforce them. But it is a point in which, in my opinion, the public safety is so essentially concerned that I cannot let slip any opportunity of urging its importance and pressing it upon the public attention. I have more than once intimated that even a dissolution of the army is not an improbable event, if some effectual measures were not taken to render the situation of the officers more comfortable. If this event has not yet happened, we ought not to infer from thence that it will not happen. Many favorable circumstances have intervened to protract it, but the causes that lead to it are daily increasing. Had it not been for the happy change which took place in our political affairs last winter—and the new prospects it opened, which for a time diverted the minds of the officers from an attention to their distresses, and encouraged a hope of their having a speedy termination—it is much to be doubted, from the discontents which then prevailed, whether we should now have had more than the shadow of an army. The temporary consolation derived from this has subsided. Their passions have returned into the former channel. The difficulty of supplying their wants has greatly increased. The expectation of the war being near its end has vanished or at least lost a great part of its force. The large fortunes acquired by numbers out of the army afford a contrast that gives poignancy to every inconveniency from remaining in it. The officers have begun again to realize their condition, and I fear few of them can or will remain in the service on the present establishment. It is unnecessary to add that an army cannot exist without officers.

The patience of the officers has been a long time nourished by the hope that some adequate provision was in contemplation. Though nothing satisfactory has hitherto been done, their hopes have been still kept alive. But this cannot be much longer the case, and when they come once to fix an opinion that they have nothing to expect, they will no longer combat the necessity that drives them from the service. It is worthy of observation that the state of inactivity to which we may probably be compelled the next campaign will give leisure for cherishing their discontents and dwelling upon all the hardships of their situation. When men are employed and have the incitements of military honor to engage their ambition and pride, they will cheerfully submit to inconveniencies which in a state of tranquility would appear insupportable.

Indeed, not to multiply arguments upon a subject so evident, it is a fact not to be controverted that the officers cannot support themselves with their present pay, that necessity will oblige them to leave the service unless better provided for, that by remaining in it those who have no fortunes will want the common necessaries of life, and those that have fortunes must ruin them.

The object that ought to be aimed at is not a partial expedient, so far to satisfy the officers as merely to keep them from leaving the service. They ought, if possible, to be interested in it in a manner that will call forth the full exertion of their zeal. It is not enough that we keep an army together; we should endeavor to have one with all those cements that are necessary to give it consistency and energy. The principal one is to make the officers take pleasure in their situation. If they are only made to endure it, the army will be an insipid, spiritless mass, incapable of acting with vigor, and ready to tumble to pieces at every reverse of fortune.

But the great and difficult question is: what provision can be made to answer the purpose in view? I confess I am at a loss even to satisfy my own judgment. Men are in most cases governed first by what they feel and next by what they hope. Present support and the relief of present necessity is therefore the first object to which we should attend. But after revolving the subject in every point of light, I can think of no practicable plan for this purpose that promises to be entirely effectual. An expedient long thought of, but never really carried into execution, will perhaps go furthest towards it and be the least exceptionable of any that can be adopted. I mean the providing them with clothing by public authority at prices proportioned to their pay, at the value of the currency when it was settled. This expedient, if undertaken, ought to be prosecuted in earnest. It should not prove a nominal but a real relief; and, in order to this, not only every exertion should be made to provide supplies on continental account, but each state should be seriously engaged to provide for its own officers till the end is accomplished. If it should be found in some instances that clothing cannot be procured, a complete equivalent in money is the next resource. With this the officers may endeavor to provide themselves; but this substitute would be subject to many inconveniencies that render it infinitely preferable they should be supplied with clothing. An officer may often not be able to supply himself with the money, and in order to do it may be obliged to leave camp and exhaust a considerable part of it in expenses of traveling and subsistence.

It would be necessary to ascertain the quantity of clothing to be allowed in this way and the prices, and to have a pecuniary equivalent fixed in lieu of each article when they cannot be furnished, according to the actual difference between the estimated prices and the real present cost of the articles. This would place the provision upon a certain footing and be more satisfactory than if it should be left to the discretion of the clothier to make what charges and allowances he pleased.

The measure here recommended alone would be far from sufficient. Something must be done in addition to enable the officers to subsist themselves more comfortably in camp. Their present ration and the subsistence money allowed are very inadequate. The manner of living of those who have no other dependence is not only unsuited to the station of an officer, but even indigent and miserable. It would serve in some measure to remedy this if instead of the subsistence money now granted, the commissary general was, every month or every two or three months, to regulate the value of the extra rations they formerly received according to the real cost, at the time, of the articles which compose it, and the commander-in-chief or commanding officer in a department empowered to order payment agreeable to that estimate.

But these expedients, though I should hope they would go a great way towards satisfying the officers, would not give such perfect satisfaction as were to be desired. The most that could be expected from them, if so much, is that they would make their present situation tolerable. They would not compensate in their minds for the sacrifices of private interest and ease which they think they are making to the public good, and for the disagreeable prospect of future indigence which their continuance in the service exhibits after they are no longer wanted in the field. To attach them heartily to the service, their expectations of futurity must be interested. After the steps which have been already taken in the affair of a half-pay and pensionary establishment, it is not without great reluctance I venture to revive it. But I am so thoroughly convinced of its utility that, notwithstanding some disadvantages which may attend it, I am firmly persuaded it would in the main be advancive of the public good. I therefore take the liberty to bring it a moment under review.

I beg leave to repeat what I have said upon some former occasions: that no step could, in my opinion, be taken which would be so pleasing to the officers and which would bind them so forcibly to the service. Our military system would certainly derive infinite benefit from it, and it appears to me that it ought to be a primary object of government to put that upon the best footing our circumstances will permit. On principles of economy, I think there can be no solid objections to the plan. No mode can I believe be devised to give satisfaction which will be more convenient and less expensive. The difference indeed in point of expense between the present form of the half-pay establishment and one for life would be inconsiderable. Seven years will probably be the period of the lives of the greatest part of the incumbents, and few of the survivors will much exceed it. But the difference in the provision in the estimation of the officer's own mind is very great. In one case he has a provision for life, whether it be long or short, in the other for a limited period which he can look beyond, and naturally flatters himself he will outlive. The resolve directing the half-pay for seven years contains some provisos and restrictions which, though perhaps unimportant in themselves, were interpreted in a manner that gave an unfavorable aspect to the measure and more than disappointed its intended effect.

With respect to a pensionary establishment for officers' widows, nothing can be a more encouraging reflection to a married man than that in case of accident to himself his family is left with some dependence to preserve them from want; and nothing can be a more painful and discouraging one than the reverse.

The chief objection I have heard to this plan is that the principle of pensioning is incompatible with the maxims of our government. The truth of this objection I shall not controvert, but I think it applies equally to an establishment for seven years as to one for life. It is alike a pension in both cases—in one for a fixed and determinate, in the other for a contingent, period. All that can be said is we submit to one inconvenience to avoid a greater; and if it operates as a bad precedent, we must endeavor to correct it when we have it in our power.

One thing, however, I think it necessary to observe—that unless the committee should be fully convinced of the necessity of the establishment proposed and should be clearly of opinion that it will meet the concurrence of Congress, the best way will be not to put it to the experiment of a debate. If it be once known that such a question is in agitation, it will again raise the hopes and solicitudes of the officers, and if it fails renew all their former discontents on the same subject and, under their present circumstances, with redoubled violence. It is a point in which their feelings are much engaged, and they ought not to be awakened if they are not to be gratified.

I have just received a letter of the 9th instant from His Excellency the governor of the state of Virginia, accompanied by several late acts of the legislature, both for recruiting their troops and more comfortably providing the officers and men. The general spirit of these acts corresponds with the measures I have taken the liberty to recommend. I have the honor to be with very great respect and esteem, gentlemen, Your most obt Servant

Go: Washington

To John Jay, President of the Continental Congress, March 15, 1779 (Excerpt)

The superior information which Congress may have of the political state of affairs in Europe, and of combining circumstances, may induce them to believe that there will soon be a termination of the war and therefore that the expense of vigorous measures to reinforce the army may be avoided. If this should be the case, I dare say the reasons will be well considered before a plan is adopted which, whatever advantages of economy it may promise, in an eventual disappointment may be productive of ruinous consequences. For my own part I confess I should be cautious of admitting the supposition that the war will terminate without another desperate effort on the part of the enemy.

The speech of the prince and the debates of his ministers have very little the aspect of peace; and, if we reflect that they are subsequent (as I apprehend they must have been) to the events on which our hopes appear to be founded, they must seem no bad arguments of a determination in the British cabinet to continue the war. 'Tis true, whether this be the determination or not, 'tis a very natural policy that every exertion should be made by them to be in the best condition to oppose their enemies, and that there should be every appearance of vigor and preparation. But if the ministry had serious thoughts of making peace, they would hardly insist so much as they do on the particular point of prosecuting the American war. They would not like to raise and inflame the expectations of the people on this subject while it was secretly their intention to disappoint them.

In America everything has the complexion of a continuance of the war. The operations of the enemy in the southern states do not resemble a transient incursion, but a serious conquest. At their posts in this quarter everything is in a state of tranquility and indicates a design, at least, to hold possession. These considerations joined to the preceding—the infinite pains that are taken to keep up the spirits of the disaffected and to assure them of support and protection, and several other circumstances, trifling in themselves but powerful when combined—amount to no contemptible evidence that the contest is not so near an end as we could wish.

I am fully sensible of many weighty reasons on the opposite side; but I do not think them sufficiently conclusive to destroy the force of what has been suggested, or to justify the sanguine inferences many seem inclined to draw.

Should the Court of Britain be able to send any reinforcements to America the next campaign and carry on offensive operations, and should we not take some effectual means to recruit our battalions—when we shall have detached the force necessary to act decisively against the Indians, and the remaining drafts shall have returned home—the force which remains for our defense will be very inconsiderable indeed. We must then on every exigency have recourse to the militia, the consequence of which, besides weakness and defeat in the field, will be double or treble the necessary expense to the public. To say nothing of the injury to agriculture which attends calling out the militia on particular emergencies and at some critical seasons, they are commonly twice as long coming to where they are wanted and returning home as they are in the field, and must of course for every day's real service receive two or three days' pay, and consume the same proportion of provisions.

To Brigadier General Thomas Nelson, Jr., March 15, 1779 (Excerpt)

It gives me very singular pleasure to find that you have again taken a seat in Congress. I think there never was a time when cool and dispassionate reasoning, strict attention and application, great integrity, and (if it was in the nature of things, unerring) wisdom were more to be wished for than the present. Our affairs, according to my judgment, are now come to a crisis, and require no small degree of political skill to steer clear of those shelves and rocks which, though deeply buried, may wreck our hopes and throw us upon some inhospitable shore. Unanimity in our councils, disinterestedness in our pursuits, and steady perseverance in our national duty are the only means to avoid misfortunes. If they come upon us after these, we shall have the consolation of knowing that we have done our best. The rest is with the Gods.[4]

To Henry Laurens, March 20, 1779 (Excerpt)

The policy of our arming slaves is in my opinion a moot point, unless the enemy set the example; for should we begin to form battalions of them I have not the smallest doubt (if the war is to be prosecuted) of their following us in it and justifying the measure upon our own ground. The upshot then must be who can arm fastest and where are our arms? Besides, I am not clear that a discrimination will not render slavery more irksome to those who remain in it. Most of the good and evil things of this life are judged of by comparison, and I fear comparison in this case will be productive of much discontent in those who are held in servitude. But as this is a subject that has never employed much of my thoughts, these are no more than the first crude ideas that have struck me upon the occasion.

To George Mason, March 27, 1779 (Excerpt)

Though it is not in my power to devote much time to private correspondences, owing to the multiplicity of public letters (and other business) I have to read, write, and transact, yet I can with great truth assure you that it would afford me very singular pleasure to be favored at all times with your sentiments in a leisure hour upon public matters of general concernment, as well as those which more immediately respect your own state (if proper conveyances would render prudent a free communication). I am particularly desirous of it at this time, because I view things very differently, I fear, from what people in general do who seem to think the contest is at an end, and to make money and get places the only things now remaining to do. I have seen without despondency (even for a moment) the hours which America has styled her gloomy ones, but I have beheld no day since the commencement of hostilities that I have thought her liberties in such eminent danger as at present. Friends and foes seem now to combine to pull down the goodly fabric we have hitherto been raising at the expense of so much time, blood, and treasure; and unless the bodies politic will exert themselves to bring things back to first principles, correct abuses, and punish our internal foes, inevitable ruin must follow. Indeed, we seem to be verging so fast to destruction that I am filled with sensations to which I have been a stranger till within these three months. Our enemies behold with exultation and joy how effectually we labor for their benefit—and from being in a state of absolute despair, and on the point of evacuating America, are now on tiptoe. Nothing therefore in my judgment can save us but a total reformation in our own conduct, or some decisive turn to affairs in Europe. The former, alas!—to our shame be it spoken!—is less likely to happen than the latter, as it is now consistent with the views of the speculators, variant tribes of money makers, and stock jobbers of all denominations to continue the war for their own private emolument, without considering that their avarice and thirst for gain must plunge everything (including themselves) in one common ruin.

Were I to indulge my present feelings and give a loose to that freedom of expression which my unreserved friendship for you would prompt me to, I should say a great deal on this subject. But letters are liable to so many accidents, and the sentiments of men in office sought after by the enemy with so much avidity—and besides conveying useful knowledge (if they get into their hands) for the superstructure of their plans, is often perverted to the worst of purposes—that I shall be somewhat reserved, notwithstanding this letter goes by a private hand to Mount Vernon. I cannot refrain lamenting, however, in the most poignant terms, the fatal policy too prevalent in most of the states of employing their ablest men at home in posts of honor or profit, till the great national interests are fixed upon a solid basis. To me it appears no unjust simile to compare the affairs of this great continent to the mechanism of a clock, each state representing some one or other of the smaller parts of it, which they are endeavoring to put in fine order without considering how useless and unavailing the labor unless the great wheel or spring which is to set the whole in motion is also well attended to and kept in good order. I allude to no particular state, nor do I mean to cast reflections upon any one of them. Nor ought I, it may be said, to do so upon their representatives. But as it is a fact too notorious to be concealed that Congress is rent by party, that much business of a trifling nature and personal concernment withdraws their attention from matters of great national moment at this critical period—when it is also known that idleness and dissipation take place of close attention and application—no man who wishes well to the liberties of his country and desires to see its rights established can avoid crying out: Where are our men of abilities? Why do they not come forth to save their country? Let this voice, my dear sir, call upon you, Jefferson, and others. Do not, from a mistaken opinion that we are about to set down under our own vine and our own fig tree, let our hitherto noble struggle end in ignominy. Believe me when I tell you there is danger of it. I have pretty good reasons for thinking that administration a little while ago had resolved to give the matter up and negotiate a peace with us upon almost any terms; but I shall be much mistaken if they do not now—from the present state of our currency, dissensions, and other circumstances—push matters to the utmost extremity. Nothing I am sure will prevent it but the interposition of Spain and their disappointed hopes from Russia.

To James Warren, March 31, 1779 (Excerpt)

Our conflict is not likely to cease so soon as every good man would wish. The measure of inequity is not yet filled; and unless we can return a little more to first principles, and act a little more upon patriotic ground, I do not know when it will, or what may be the issue of the contest. Speculation, peculation, engrossing, forestalling, with all their concomitants, afford too many melancholy proofs of the decay of public virtue and too glaring instances of its being the interest and desire of too many, who would wish to be thought friends, to continue the war.

Nothing, I am convinced, but the depreciation of our currency, proceeding in a great measure from the foregoing causes, aided by stock jobbing and party dissensions, has fed the hopes of the enemy and kept the arms of Britain in America until now. They do not scruple to declare this themselves and add that we shall be our own conquerors. Cannot our common country (America) possess virtue enough to disappoint them? Is the consideration of a little dirty pelf to individuals to be placed in competition with the essential rights and liberties of the present generation and of millions yet unborn? Shall a few designing men, for their own aggrandizement and to gratify their own avarice, overset the goodly fabric we have been rearing at the expense of so much time, blood, and treasure? And shall we at last become the victims of our own abominable lust of gain? Forbid it, Heaven; forbid it all!—and every state in the Union! by enacting and enforcing efficacious laws for checking the growth of these monstrous evils and restoring matters in some degree to the pristine state they were in at the commencement of the war. Our cause is noble—it is the cause of mankind!—and the danger to it springs from ourselves. Shall we slumber and sleep, then, while we should be punishing those miscreants who have brought these troubles upon us and who are aiming to continue us in them, while we should be striving to fill our battalions and devising ways and means to appreciate the currency, on the credit of which everything depends? I hope not. Let vigorous measures be adopted—not to limit the price of articles, for this I conceive is inconsistent with the very nature of things and impracticable in itself—but to punish speculators, forestallers, and extortioners, and above all to sink the money by heavy taxes, to promote public and private economy, encourage manufactures, etc. Measures of this sort gone heartily into by the several states will strike at once at the root of all our misfortunes and give the coup-de-grace to British hope of subjugating this great continent, either by their arms or their arts. The first, as I have before observed, they acknowledge is unequal to the task. The latter, I am sure, will be so if we are not lost to everything that is good and virtuous.

To John Jay, President of the Continental Congress, April 14, 1779 (Excerpt)

Conscious that it is the aim of my actions to promote the public good, and that no part of my conduct is influenced by personal enmity to individuals, I cannot be insensible to the artifice employed by some men to prejudice me in the public esteem. The circumstance of which you have obliged me with the communication is among a number of other instances of the unfriendly views which have governed a certain gentleman from a very early period. Some of these have been too notorious not to have come to your knowledge. Others, from the manner in which they have been conveyed to me, will probably never be known, except to a very few. But you have perhaps heard enough and observed enough yourself to make any further explanation from me unnecessary.

The desire, however, which it is natural I should feel to preserve the good opinion of men of sense and virtue, conspiring with my wish to cultivate your friendship in particular, induces me to trouble you with a statement of some facts which will serve to place the present attack in its proper light. In doing this I shall recapitulate and bring into one view a series of transactions, many of which have been known to you, but some of which may possibly have escaped your memory.

An opinion prevailing that the enemy were like shortly to evacuate these states, I was naturally led to turn my thoughts to a plan of operations against Canada, *in case that event should take place.* A winter campaign, before the enemy could have an opportunity of reinforcing and putting themselves in a more perfect state of defense, appeared to promise the most certain and speedy success; and the route by Co'os[5] offered itself as most direct and practicable. In this I fully agreed with General Gates and some other gentlemen whom I consulted on the occasion; and on the 12th of September last I wrote to Congress *accordingly,* submitting it to them whether it would not be advisable to be laying up magazines, opening a road, and making other preparations for the undertaking. They approved the project and authorized me to carry it into execution. I the more readily entered into it from a consideration that, if circumstances should not permit us to carry on the enterprise, the preparations towards it could easily be converted into another channel and made serviceable to our operations elsewhere, *without any material addition of expense to the continent* because provisions, which would compose the principal part of the expense, were at all events to be purchased on Connecticut

River—the only doubt being whether it should be used in an expedition against Canada or transported to Boston, circumstances to determine this. With truth it may be added that, excepting the articles of provisions and forage which, as before observed, would have been bought if no expedition by the way of Co'os had been in contemplation, the *"incredible* expense" mentioned by General Gates in his letter of March 4th amounted to the purchase of a few pairs of snowshoes and some leather for moccasin *only*. If any other expense has been incurred it is unknown to me, must have been by his order, and he alone answerable for it.

In October following Congress entered into arrangements with the Marquis de Lafayette for cooperating with the Court of France in an expedition against that country. In this scheme, one body of troops was to proceed from Co'os and penetrate by way of the River Saint Francis. Others, forming a junction at Niagara, were to enter Canada by that route; and while these were operating in this manner a French fleet and a body of French troops were to go up the River Saint Lawrence and take possession of Quebec.

You are well acquainted with the opposition I gave to this plan and my reasons at large for it. From what has since happened they seem to have met the full approbation of Congress. The ideas I held up were principally these: that we ought not to enter into any contract with a foreign power, unless we were sure we should be able to fulfill our engagements; that it was uncertain whether the enemy would quit the states or not, and in case they did not it would be impracticable to furnish the aids which we had stipulated; that even if they should leave us, it was doubtful whether our resources would be equal to the supplies required; that therefore it would be impolitic to hazard a contract of the kind, and better to remain at liberty to act as future conjunctures should point out. I recommended nevertheless, as there were powerful reasons to hope the enemy might go away, that eventual preparations should be made to take advantage of it, to possess ourselves of Niagara and other posts in that quarter for the security of our frontiers, and to carry our views still further with respect to a conquest of Canada, if we should find ourselves able to prosecute such an enterprise.

This Congress in a subsequent resolve approved and directed to be done. It was not the *least motive* with me for recommending it that operations of this nature seemed to be a very favorite object with that honorable body. The preparations on Hudson's River were undertaken in consequence.

Upon a nearer view of our finances and resources—and when it came to be decided that the enemy would continue for some time longer to hold the posts they were in possession of—in the course of the conferences with which I was honored by the committee of Congress in Philadelphia, I suggested my doubts of the propriety of continuing our northern preparations upon so extensive a plan as was first determined. The committee were of opinion with me that the state of our currency and supplies in general would oblige us to act on the defensive next campaign, except so far as related to an expedition into the Indian country for chastising the savages and preventing their depredations on our back settlements, and that, though it would be extremely desirable to be prepared for pushing our operations further, yet our necessities exacting a system of economy forbade our launching into much extra expense for objects which were remote and contingent. This determination having taken place, all the northern preparations were discontinued except such as were necessary towards the intended Indian expedition.

Things were in this situation when I received a letter from General Bailey (living at Co'os) expressing some fears for the safety of the magazine at Co'os, in consequence of which I directed the stores to be removed lower down the country. This I did to prevent a possibility of accident, though I did not apprehend they were in much danger. Sometime afterwards I received the letter No. 1 from General Gates expressing similar fears, to which I returned him the answer of the 14th of February transmitted by him to Congress (No. 2). Knowing that preparations had been making at Albany, and unacquainted with their true design, he, from a vague expression in that letter that the intention of attacking Canada was still adhered to but that I had changed the plan and was going by way of Lake Champlain or Ontario, either of these routes he pronounces impracticable and represents that by Co'os as the only practicable one. He goes further and declares that "in the present state of our army and the actual situation of our magazines to attempt a serious invasion of Canada by whatever route would prove unsuccessful, unless the fleet of our allies should at the same time cooperate with us by sailing up the River Saint Lawrence." Though I differ with him as to the impracticability of *both* the other routes, I venture to go a step beyond him respecting our ability to invade Canada, and am convinced that in our present circumstances, and with the enemy in front, we cannot undertake a serious invasion of that country at all, even *with the aid of an allied fleet*.

You will perceive, sir, that I have uniformly made the departure of the enemy from these states *an essential condition* to the invasion of Canada, and that General Gates has entirely mistaken my intentions. Hoping that I had embarked in a scheme which our situation would not justify, he eagerly seizes the opportunity of exposing my supposed errors to Congress and, in the excess of his intemperate zeal to injure me, exhibits himself in a point of view from which I imagine he will derive little credit. The decency of the terms in which he undertakes to arraign my conduct both to myself and to Congress, and the propriety of the hasty appeal he has made, will I believe appear at least questionable to every man of sense and delicacy.

The last paragraph of the extract with which you favor me is a pretty remarkable one. I shall make no comments further than as it implies a charge of neglect on my part in not writing to him but once since December. From the beginning of last campaign to the middle of December, about seven months, I have copies of near fifty letters to him and about forty originals from him. I think it will be acknowledged the correspondence was frequent enough during that period. And if it has not continued in the same proportion since, the only reason was that the season of the year, the troops being in winter quarters, and General Gates's situation unfruitful of events and unproductive of any military arrangements between us, afforded very little matter for epistolary intercourse. And I flatter myself it will be readily believed that I am sufficiently occupied with the necessary business of my station and have no need of increasing it by multiplying letters without an object. If you were to peruse, my dear sir, the letters which have passed between General Gates and myself for a long time back, you would be sensible that I have no great temptation to court his correspondence when the transacting of business does not require it. An air of design, a want of candor in many instances, and even of politeness, give no very inviting complexion to the correspondence on his part. As a specimen of this I send you a few letters and extracts, which at your leisure I shall be glad you will cast your eye upon.

Last fall it was for some time strongly suspected that the enemy would transport the whole or the greatest part of their force eastward and combine one great land and sea operation against the French fleet in Boston harbor. On this supposition, as I should go in person to Boston, the command next in importance was the posts on the North River. This properly would devolve on General Gates; but from motives of peculiar scrupulousness, as there had been a difference between us, I thought it best to know whether it was agreeable to him before I directed his continuance. By way of compliment, I wrote him a letter containing the extract No. 3, expecting a cordial answer and cheerful acceptance. I received the evasive and unsatisfactory reply No. 4. A few days after this, upon another occasion, I wrote him the letter No. 5, to which I received the extraordinary answer No. 6 which was passed over in silence.

The plan of operations for the campaign being determined, a commanding officer was to be appointed for the Indian expedition. This command, according to all present appearance, will probably be of the second, if not of the first, importance for the campaign. The officer conducting it has a flattering prospect of acquiring more credit than can be expected by any other this year, and he has the best reason to hope for success. General Lee from his situation was out of the question. General Schuyler, who, by the way, would have been most agreeable to me, was so uncertain of continuing in the army that I could not appoint him. General Putnam I need not mention. I therefore made the offer of it (for the appointment could no longer be delayed) to General Gates, who was next in seniority, though perhaps I might have avoided it, if I had been so disposed, from his being in a command by the special appointment of Congress. My letter to him on the occasion you will find in No. 7. I believe you will think it was conceived in very candid and polite terms and merited a different answer from the one given to it in No. 8.

I discovered very early in the war symptoms of coldness and constraint in General Gates's behavior to me. These increased as he rose into greater consequence, but we did not come to a direct breach till the beginning of last year. This was occasioned by a correspondence which I thought rather made free with me between him and General Conway, which accidentally came to my knowledge. The particulars of this affair you will find delineated in the packet herewith, endorsed "Papers respecting General Conway." Besides the evidence contained in them of the genuineness of the offensive correspondence, I have other proofs still more convincing, which, having been given me in a confidential way, I am not at liberty to impart.

After this affair subsided, I made a point of treating General Gates with all the attention and cordiality in my power, as well from a sincere desire of harmony as from an unwillingness to give any cause of triumph to our enemies from an appearance of dissension among ourselves. I can appeal to the world, and to the whole army, whether I have not cautiously avoided every word or hint that could tend to disparage General Gates in any way. I am sorry his conduct to me has not been equally generous, and that he is continually giving me fresh proofs of malevolence and opposition. It will not be doing him injustice to say that, besides the little underhand intrigues which he is frequently practicing, there has hardly been any great military question in which his advice has been asked that it has not been given in an equivocal and designing manner, apparently calculated to afford him an opportunity of censuring me on the failure of whatever measures might be adopted.

When I find that this gentleman does not scruple to take the most unfair advantages of me, I am under a necessity of explaining his conduct to justify my own. This, and the perfect confidence I have in you, have occasioned me to trouble you with so free a communication of the state of things between us. I shall still be as passive as a regard to my own character will permit. I am, however, uneasy, as General Gates has endeavored to impress Congress with an unfavorable idea of me, and as I only know this in a private confidential way—that I cannot take any step to remove the impression, if it should be made.

I am aware, sir, of the delicacy of your situation; and I mean this letter only for your own private information. You will therefore not allow yourself to be embarrassed by its contents, but, with respect to me, pass it over in silence. With the truest esteem, and personal regard, I am, Dr Sir Yr Obliged & Obedt Ser:

Go: Washington

To Brigadier General William Maxwell, May 7, 1779

Sir,

I have received your two favors of yesterday's date, one of them with infinite concern. There is nothing which has happened in the course of the war that has given me so much pain as the remonstrance you mention from the officers of the 1st Jersey Regiment. I cannot but consider it as a hasty and imprudent step, which on more cool consideration they will themselves condemn. I am very sensible of the inconveniences under which the officers of the army labor, and I hope they do me the justice to believe that my endeavors to procure them relief are incessant. There is, however, more difficulty in satisfying their wishes than perhaps they are aware. Our resources have been hitherto very limited. The situation of our money is no small embarrassment, for which, though there are remedies, they cannot be the work of a moment. Government is not insensible of the merits and sacrifices of the officers, nor, I am persuaded, unwilling to make a compensation; but it is a truth of which a little observation must convince us that it is very much straightened in the means. Great allowances ought to be made on this account for any delay and seeming backwardness which may appear. Some of the states, indeed, have done as generously as it is at this juncture in their power; and if others have been less expeditious it ought to be ascribed to some peculiar cause which a little time aided by example will remove. The patience and perseverance of the army have been under every disadvantage such as to do them the highest honor both at home and abroad, and have inspired me with an unlimited confidence in their virtue, which has consoled me amidst every perplexity and reverse of fortune to which our affairs in a struggle of this nature were necessarily exposed. Now that we have made so great a progress to the attainment of the end we have in view—so that we cannot fail without a most shameful desertion of our own interests—anything like a change of conduct would imply a very unhappy change of principles and a forgetfulness as well of what we owe to ourselves as to our country. Did I suppose it possible this could be the case, even in a single regiment of the army, I should be mortified and chagrined beyond expression. I should feel it as a wound given to my own honor, which I consider as embarked with that of the army at large. But this I believe to be impossible. Any corps that was about to set an example of the kind would weigh well the consequences, and no officer of common discernment and sensibility would hazard them. If they should stand alone in it, independent of other consequences, what would be their feelings on reflecting that they had held themselves out to the world in a point of light inferior to the rest of the army? Or, if their example should be followed and become general, how would they console themselves for having been the foremost in bringing ruin and disgrace upon their country? They would remember that the army would share a double portion of the general infamy and distress, and that the character of an American officer would become as despicable as it is now glorious.

I confess the appearances in the present instance are disagreeable, but I am convinced they seem to mean more than they really do. The Jersey officers have not been outdone by any others in the qualities either of citizens or soldiers, and I am confident no part of them would seriously intend anything that would be a stain to their former reputation. The gentlemen cannot be in earnest. They have only reasoned wrong about the means of obtaining a good end; and on reconsideration, I hope and flatter myself, they will renounce what must appear improper. At the opening of a campaign, when under marching orders for an important service, their own honor, duty to the public and to themselves, a regard to military propriety, will not suffer them to persist in a measure which would be a violation of them all. It will even wound their delicacy coolly to reflect that they have hazarded a step which has an air of dictating terms to their country by taking advantage of the necessity of the moment. The declaration they have made to the state at so critical a time, that unless they obtain relief in the short period of three days they must be considered out of the service, has very much this aspect. And the seeming relaxation of continuing till the state can have a reasonable time to provide other officers will be thought only a superficial veil.

I am now to request that you will convey my sentiments to the gentlemen concerned and endeavor to make them sensible that they are in an error. The service for which the regiment was intended will not admit of delay. It must at all events march on Monday morning in the first place to this camp, and further directions will be given when it arrives. I am sure I shall not be mistaken in expecting a prompt and cheerful obedience. I am Sir Your most Obedt servt.

To Gouverneur Morris, May 8, 1779 (Excerpt)

As a variety of accidents may disappoint our hopes here, it is indispensable we should make every exertion on our part to check the enemy's progress. This cannot be done to effect if our reliance is solely or principally on militia, for a force continually fluctuating is incapable of any material effort. The states concerned ought by all means to endeavor to draw out men for a length of time. A smaller number on this plan would answer their purpose better. A great deal of expense would be avoided, and agriculture would be much less impeded. It is to be lamented that the remoteness and weakness of this army would make it folly to attempt to send any succor from this quarter. Perhaps for want of knowing the true state of our foreign expectations and prospects of finance, I may be led to contemplate the gloomy side of things. But I confess they appear to me to be in a very disagreeable train. The rapid decay of our currency; the extinction of public spirit; the increasing rapacity of the times; the want of harmony in our councils; the declining zeal of the people; the discontents and distresses of the officers of the army; and I may add, the prevailing security and insensibility to danger—are symptoms in my eye of a most alarming nature. If the enemy have it in their power to press us hard this campaign, I know not what may be the consequence. Our army as it now stands is little more than the skeleton of an army, and I hear of no steps that are taking to give it strength and substance. I hope there may not be great mistakes on this head and that our abilities in general are not overrated. The applications for succor are numerous, but no pains are taken to put it in my power to afford them. When I endeavor to draw together the continental troops for the most essential purposes I am embarrassed with complaints of the exhausted, defenseless situation of particular states and find myself obliged either to resist solicitations made in such a manner and with such a degree of emphasis as scarcely to leave me a choice, or to sacrifice the most obvious principles of military propriety and risk the general safety.

I shall conclude by observing that it is well worthy the ambition of a patriot statesman at this juncture to endeavor to pacify party differences, to give fresh vigor to the springs of government, to inspire the people with confidence, and above all to restore the credit of our currency. With very great regard I am Dr Sir Your most Obed. servant.

To John Jay, President of the Continental Congress, May 10, 1779 (Excerpt)

You give an affecting summary of the causes of the national evil we feel and the still greater we have reason to apprehend. To me it appears that our affairs are in a very delicate situation. And what is not the least to be lamented is that many people think they are in a very flourishing way and seem in a great measure insensible to the danger with which we are threatened. If Britain should be able to make a vigorous campaign in America this summer, in the present depreciation of our money, scantiness of supplies, want of virtue, and want of exertion, 'tis hard to say what may be the consequence.

It is a melancholy consideration that any concerned in the conduct of public affairs should discover an indifference to the state of our currency. Nothing in my opinion can be more manifest than that if something effectual be not done to restore its credit, it will in a short time either cease to circulate altogether or circulate so feebly as to be utterly incapable of drawing out the resources of the country. This is nearly the case now. With every sentiment of esteem & regard I am Dr Sir Yr Most Obedt Ser.

Go: Washington

To the Delaware Nation, May 12, 1779

To the Chief Men, Deputies from the Delaware Nation
Brothers:
I am happy to see you here. I am glad the long journey you have made has done you no harm and that you are in good health. I am glad also you left all our friends of the Delaware Nation well.

Brothers:
I have read your paper. The things you have said are weighty things, and I have considered them well. The Delaware Nation have shown their good will to the United States. They have done wisely, and I hope they will never repent. I rejoice in the new assurances you give of their friendship. The things you now offer to do to brighten the chain prove your sincerity. I am sure Congress will run to meet you and will do everything in their power to make the friendship between the people of those states and their brethren of the Delaware Nation last forever.

Brothers:
I am a warrior. My words are few and plain, but I will make good what I say. 'Tis my business to destroy all the enemies of these states and to protect their friends. You have seen how we have withstood the English for four years, and how their great armies have dwindled away and come to very little, and how what remains of them in this part of our great country are glad to stay upon two or three little islands where the waters and their ships hinder us from going to destroy them. The English, brothers, are a boasting people. They talk of doing a great deal, but they do very little. They fly away on their ships from one part of our country to another, but as soon as our warriors get together, they leave it and go to some other part. They took Boston and Philadelphia, two of our greatest towns; but when they saw our warriors in a great body, ready to fall upon them, they were forced to leave them.

Brothers:
We have till lately fought the English all alone. Now the great king of France is become our good brother and ally. He has taken up the hatchet with us, and we have sworn never to bury it till we have punished the English and made them sorry for all the wicked things they had in their hearts to do against these states. And there are other great kings and nations on the other side of the big waters who love us and wish us well and will not suffer the English to hurt us.

Brothers:

Listen well to what I tell you, and let it sink deep into your hearts. We love our friends and will be faithful to them—as long as they will be faithful to us. We are sure our good brothers the Delawares will always be so. But we have sworn to take vengeance on our enemies—and on false friends. The other day a handful of our young men destroyed the settlement of the Onondagas. They burnt down all their houses, destroyed their grain and horses and cattle, took their arms away, killed several of their warriors and brought off many prisoners and obliged the rest to fly into the woods. This is but the beginning of the troubles which those nations who have taken up the hatchet against us will feel.

Brothers:

I am sorry to hear that you have suffered for want of necessaries, or that any of our people have not dealt justly by you. But as you are going to Congress, which is the great council of the nation and hold all things in their hands, I shall say nothing about the supplies you ask. I hope you will receive satisfaction from them. I assure you I will do everything in my power to prevent your receiving any further injuries and will give the strictest orders for this purpose. I will severely punish any that shall break them.

Brothers:

I am glad you have brought three of the children of your principal chiefs to be educated with us. I am sure Congress will open the arms of love to them and will look upon them as their own children and will have them educated accordingly. This is a great mark of your confidence and of your desire to preserve the friendship between the two nations to the end of time—and to become one people with your brethren of the United States. My ears hear with pleasure the other matters you mention. Congress will be glad to hear them too. You do well to wish to learn our arts and ways of life and above all the religion of Jesus Christ. These will make you a greater and happier people than you are. Congress will do everything they can to assist you in this wise intention and to tie the knot of friendship and union so fast that nothing shall ever be able to loose it.

Brothers:

There are some matters about which I do not open my lips, because they belong to Congress and not to us warriors. You are going to them. They will tell you all you wish to know.

Brothers:

When you have seen all you want to see, I will then wish you a good journey to Philadelphia. I hope you may find there everything your hearts can wish, that when you return home, you may be able to tell your nation good things of us. And I pray God he may make your nation wise and strong, that they may always see their own true interest and have courage to walk in the right path, and that they never may be deceived by lies to do anything against the people of these states, who are their brothers and ought always to be one people with them.

Go: Washington
Commander-in-chief
of all the armies in the
United States of America

To John Armstrong, May 18, 1779 (Excerpt)

Dear Sir,

I have received your favor of the 10th instant and thank you for it. Never was there an observation founded in more truth than yours of my having a choice of difficulties. I cannot say that the resolve of Congress which you allude to has increased them; but with propriety I may observe it has added to my embarrassment in fixing on them; inasmuch as it gives me powers without the means of execution when these ought to be co-equal at least. The cries of the distressed—of the fatherless and the widows—come to me from all quarters. The states are not behindhand in making application for assistance, notwithstanding scarce any one of them that I can find is taking effectual measures to complete its quota of continental troops or have even power or energy enough to draw forth their militia. Each complains of neglect because it gets not what it asks—and conceives that no other suffers like itself because they are ignorant of what others experience, receiving the complaints of their own people only. I have a hard time of it and a disagreeable task. To please everybody is impossible; were I to undertake it I should probably please nobody. If I know myself, I have no partialities. I have from the beginning, and I will to the end, pursue to the best of my judgment and abilities one steady line of conduct for the good of the great whole. This will, under all circumstances, administer consolation to myself, however short I may fall of the expectation of others. But, to leave smaller matters, I am much mistaken if the resolve of Congress hath not an eye to something far beyond our abilities. They are not, I conceive, sufficiently acquainted with the state and strength of the army, of our resources, and how they are to be drawn out. The powers given may be beneficial, but do not let Congress deceive themselves by false expectations founded on a superficial view of the situation and circumstances of things in general and their own troops in particular. For in a word, I give it to you as my opinion that if the reinforcement expected by the enemy should arrive, and no effectual measures be taken to complete our battalions and stop the further depreciation of our money, I do not see upon what ground we are able or mean to continue the contest. We now stand upon the brink of a precipice from whence the smallest help plunges us headlong. At this moment our money does but pass—at what rate I need not add because unsatisfied demands upon the treasury afford too many unequivocal and alarming proofs to stand in need of illustration. Even at this hour everything is in a manner at a stand for want of this money (such as it is), and because many of the states, instead of passing laws to aid the several departments of the army, have done the reverse and hampered the transportation in such a way as to stop the supplies which are indispensably necessary and for want of which we are embarrassed exceedingly. This is a summary of our affairs in general to which I am to add that the officers unable any longer to support themselves in the army are resigning continually, or doing what is even worse: spreading discontent and possibly the seeds of sedition.

You will readily perceive, my good sir, that this is a confidential letter and that, however willing I may be to disclose such matters and such sentiments to particular friends who are entrusted with the government of our great national concerns, I shall be extremely unwilling to have them communicated to any others, as I should feel much compunction if a single word or thought of mine was to create the smallest despair in our own people or feed the hope of the enemy, who I know pursue with avidity every track which leads to a discovery of the sentiments of men in office. Such (men in office I mean) I wish to be impressed—deeply impressed—with the importance of close attention and a vigorous exertion of the means for extricating our finances from the deplorable situation in which they now are. I never was, much less reason have I now, to be afraid of the enemy's arms. But I have no scruple in declaring to you that I have never yet seen the time in which our affairs in my opinion were at so low an ebb as the present; and without a speedy and capital change we shall not be able in a very short time to call out the strength and resources of the country. The hour therefore is certainly come when party differences and disputes should subside, when every man (especially those in office) should with one hand and one heart pull the same way and with their whole strength. Providence has done—and I am persuaded is disposed to do—a great deal for us, but we are not to forget the fable of Jupiter and the Countryman. I am Dr Sir Yr Most Obedt & affe. H. Ser.

Go: W——n

To Colonel Daniel Brodhead, May 21, 1779 (Excerpts)

Dear Sir,

Your favors of the 3rd and 6th instant came to hand the 18th with the papers to which they refer.

The irregularity among the troops occasioned by the inhabitants selling them liquor should be stopped by such means as we have in our power. The establishment of military law where the civil prevails is a measure of extreme necessity, and which I have no authority to recommend. On the present occasion the attention of the officers, strict discipline, and exemplary punishment must be exercised on the soldiers, while on the part of the seller we can only put in practice such seizures as are not legalized[6] by the enclosed general orders ....

The murder of the Delaware young man by the soldier of the Virginia Regiment is an unfortunate affair, particularly at this juncture. The case appears embarrassing as the articles of war are not sufficiently explicit. Exemplary punishment, however, I conceive absolutely necessary to keep the Indians from revenge and preserve the peace of the country. But under your representation this can only be effected by a military process. I am induced therefore to order a court martial on Colonel Gibson's return or, should a field officer be present, when this reaches you. I would imagine the court will find no difficulty in giving a proper decision, as their oath directs them, where doubts shall arise which are not explained by the articles, to act according to their conscience, the best of their understanding, and the custom of war in like cases.

That the punishment may be as extensively known to the Delawares as possible, it should be executed in the presence of some of their principal men. With respect to the design formed to waylay and massacre the Indians of this nation now on a visit of negotiation to Congress, you will take the most effectual and immediate steps for their safe return by affording an escort etc.

Circular to the States, May 22, 1779 (Excerpt)

Sir,

The situation of our affairs at this period appears to me peculiarly critical; and this, I flatter myself, will apologize for that anxiety which impels me to take the liberty of addressing you on the present occasion.

The state of the army in particular is alarming on several accounts; that of its numbers is not among the least. Our battalions are exceedingly reduced, not only from the natural decay incident to the best composed armies, but from the expiration of the term of service for which a large proportion of the men were engaged. The measures hitherto taken to replace them, so far as has come to my knowledge, have been attended with very partial success; and I am ignorant of any others in contemplation that afford a better prospect. A reinforcement expected from Virginia, consisting of new levies and re-enlisted men, is necessarily ordered to the southward. Not far short of one third of our whole force must be detached on a service undertaken by the direction of Congress and essential in itself. I shall only say of what remains that when it is compared with the force of the enemy now actually at New York and Rhode Island, with the addition of the succors they will in all probability receive from England, at the lowest computation it will be found to justify very serious apprehensions and to demand the zealous attention of the different legislatures.

When we consider the rapid decline of our currency, the general temper of the times, the disaffection of a great part of the people, the lethargy that overspreads the rest, the increasing danger to the southern states, we cannot but dread the consequences of any misfortune in this quarter and must feel the impolicy of trusting our security to a want of activity and enterprise in the enemy.

An expectation of peace and an opinion of the enemy's inability to send more troops to this country, I fear, have had too powerful an influence in our affairs. I have never heard anything conclusive to authorize the former, and present appearances are in my opinion against it. The accounts we receive from Europe uniformly announce vigorous preparations to continue the war at least another campaign. The debates and proceedings in Parliament wear this complexion. The public papers speak confidently of large reinforcements destined for America. The minister in his speech asserts positively that reinforcements will be sent over to Sir Henry Clinton, though he acknowledges the future plan of the war will be less extensive than the past. Let it be supposed that the intended succors will not exceed five thousand men. This will give the enemy a superiority very dangerous to our safety, if their strength be properly exerted and our situation is not materially altered for the better.

These considerations and many more that might be suggested point to the necessity of immmediate and decisive exertions to complete our battalions and to make our military force more respectable. I thought it my duty to give an idea of its true state and to urge the attention of the states to a matter in which their safety and happiness are so deeply interested. I hope a concern for the public good will be admitted as the motive and excuse of my importunity.

To Bryan Fairfax, June 30, 1779 (Excerpt)

A contest which appeared last summer and fall to be verging fast to a prosperous end is now likely to be prolonged, and may rage more violently than ever, owing to a want of public virtue. Speculation, peculation, forestalling, monopolizing, with all their concomitants, seem to have taken place of everything else and shows in a clear point of view the depravity of human nature in suffering a thirst for riches to absorb every other consideration and get the better of every other duty.

To Major Henry Lee, July 9, 1779 (Excerpt)

The measure you propose of putting deserters from our army to immediate death would probably tend to discourage the practice. But it ought to be executed with caution and only when the fact is very clear and unequivocal. I think that part of your proposal which respects cutting off their heads and sending them to the light troops had better be omitted. Examples, however severe, ought not to be attended with an appearance of inhumanity, otherwise they give disgust and may excite resistment rather than terror. I am with Great Regard Dr Sir Your most Obedt Servt

G: Washington

To Joseph Reed, President of the Supreme Executive Council of Pennsylvania, July 29, 1779 (Excerpt)

Dear Sir,

I have a pleasure in acknowledging the receipt of your obliging favor of the 15th instant and in finding by it that the author[7] of the queries "Political and Military" has had no great cause to exult in the favorable reception of them by the public.

Without a clue I should have been at no loss to trace the malevolent writer; but I have seen a history of the transaction, and felt a pleasure mingled with pain, at the narration. To stand well in the estimation of one's country is a happiness that no rational creature can be insensible of. To be pursued, first under the mask of friendship, and, when disguise would suit no longer, as an open calumniator with gross misrepresentation and self-known falsehoods, carries an alloy which no temper can bear with perfect composure.

The motives which actuate this gentleman are better understood by himself than me. If he can produce a single instance in which I have mentioned his name (after his trial commenced) where it was in my power to avoid it, and, when it was not, where I have done it with the smallest degree of acrimony or disrespect, I will consent that the world shall view my character in as disreputable a light as he wishes to place it. What cause, then, there is for such a profusion of venom as he is emitting upon all occasions, unless by an act of public duty in bringing him to trial at his own solicitation I have disappointed him and raised his ire, or, conceiving that in proportion as he can darken the shades of my character, he illuminates his own? Whether these, I say, or motives yet more dark and hidden govern him, I shall not undertake to decide, nor have I time to enquire into them at present.

If I had ever assumed the character of a military genius and the officer of experience—if under these false colors I had solicited the command I was honored with—or if, after my appointment, I had presumptuously driven on under the sole guidance of my own judgment and self-will and misfortunes the result of obstinacy and misconduct, not of necessity, had followed—I should have thought myself a proper object for the lash not only of his but the pen of every other writer, and a fit subject of public resentment. But when it is well known that the command, in a manner, was forced upon me, that I accepted it with the utmost diffidence, from a consciousness that it required greater abilities and more experience than I possessed to conduct a great military machine embarrassed, as I knew ours must be, by a variety of complex circumstances, and as it were but little better than a mere chaos, and when nothing more was promised on my part than has been most inviolably performed, it is rather grating to pass over in silence charges which may impress the uninformed, though others know that these charges have neither reason nor truth to support them, and that a simple narrative of facts would defeat all his assertions, notwithstanding they are made with an effrontery which few men do, and for the honor of human nature none ought, to possess.

If this gentleman is envious of my station and conceives that I stand in his way to preferment, I can assure him in most solemn terms that the first wish of my soul is to return to that peaceful retirement and domestic ease and happiness from whence I came. To this end all my labors have been directed, and for this purpose have I been more than four years a perfect slave, endeavoring under as many embarrassing circumstances as ever fell to one man's lot to encounter, and as pure motives as ever man was influenced by, to promote the cause and service I had embarked in.

To John Jay, President of the Continental Congress, September 7, 1779 (Excerpt)

It really appears impossible to reconcile the conduct Britain is pursuing to any system of prudence or policy. For the reasons you assign, appearances are against her deriving aid from other powers; and if it is truly the case that she has rejected the mediation of Spain without having made allies, it will exceed all past instances of her infatuation. Notwithstanding appearances, I can hardly bring myself fully to believe that it is the case, or that there is so general a combination against the interests of Britain among the European powers as to permit them to endanger the political balance. I think it probable enough that the conduct of France in the affairs of the Port[8] and Russia will make an impression on the empress, but I doubt whether it will be sufficient to counter-balance the powerful motives she has to support England. And the Port has been perhaps too much weakened in the last war with Russia to be overfond of renewing it. The emperor is also the natural ally of England, notwithstanding the connections of blood between his family and that of France; and he may prefer reasons of national policy to those of private attachment. 'Tis true his finances may not be in the best state, though one campaign could hardly have exhausted them; but, as Holland looks up to him for her chief protection, if he should be inclined to favor England it may give her councils a decided bias the same way. She can easily supply what is wanting in the article of money, and by their aid give sinews to that confederacy. Denmark is also the natural ally of England; and, though there has lately been a family bickering, her political interest may outweigh private animosity. Her marine assistance would be considerable. Portugal too, though timid and cautious at present, if she was to see connections formed by England able to give her countenance and security would probably declare for her interests. Russia, Denmark, the emperor, Holland, Portugal, and England would form a respectable counterpoise to the opposite scale. Though all the maritime powers of Europe were interested in the independence of this country, as it tended to diminish the overgrown power of Britain, yet they may be unwilling to see too great a preponderancy on the side of her rivals. And when the question changes itself from the separation of America to the ruin of England as a naval power, I should not be surprised at a proportionable change in the sentiments of some of those states which have been heretofore unconcerned spectators or inclining to our side. I suggest these things rather as possible than probable. It is even to be expected that the decisive blow will be struck before the interposition of the allies England may acquire can have effect. But still, as possible events they ought to have their influence and prevent our relaxing in any measures necessary for our safety on the supposition of a speedy peace or removal of the war from the present theater in America.

To Edmund Pendleton, November 1, 1779 (Excerpt)

A new scene, though rather long delayed, is opening to our view, and of sufficient importance to interest the hopes and fears of every well-wisher to his country, and will engage the attention of all America. This I say on a supposition that the delays to the southward and advanced season do not prevent a full and perfect cooperation with the French fleet in this quarter. Be this as it may, everything in the preparatory way that depends upon me is done and doing. To Count D'Estaing, then, and that good Providence which has so remarkably aided us in all our difficulties, the rest is committed.

Stony Point, which has been a bone of contention the whole campaign, and the principal business of it on the part of the enemy, is totally evacuated by them. Rhode Island is also abandoned; and the enemy's whole force is drawn to a point at New York, where neither pains nor labor have been spared to secure the city and harbor, but in their attempts to effect the latter some unexpected disappointments have occurred (in sinking their hulks). This makes them more intent on their land batteries, which are so disposed as to cover the town and the shipping equally.

All lesser matters on both sides are suspended while we are looking to the more important object. The consequences of all these movements are not easy to be foretold. But, another campaign having been wasted, having had their arms disgraced and all their projects blasted, it may be conceived that the enemy, like an enraged monster summoning his whole strength, will make some violent effort, if they should be relieved from their present apprehensions of the French fleet. If they do not detach largely for the West Indies (and I do not see how this is practicable while they remain inferior at sea), they must from the disagreeableness of their situation feel themselves under a kind of necessity of attempting some bold, enterprising stroke to give in some degree éclat to their arms, spirits to the Tories, and hope to the ministry. But I am under no apprehension of a capital injury from any other source than that of the continual depreciation of our money. This indeed is truly alarming and of so serious a nature that every other effort is in vain unless something can be done to restore its credit. Congress, the states individually, and individuals of each state should exert themselves to effect this great end. It is the only hope, the last resource of the enemy, and nothing but our want of public virtue can induce a continuance of the war. Let them once see that, as it is in our power, so it is our inclination and intention to overcome this difficulty, and the idea of conquest or hope of bringing us back to a state of dependence will vanish like the morning dew. They can no more encounter this kind of opposition than the hoar frost can withstand the rays of an all-cheering sun. The liberties and safety of this country depend upon it. The way is plain; the means are in our power. But it is virtue alone that can effect it; for without this, heavy taxes frequently collected (the only radical cure) and loans are not to be obtained. Where this has been the policy (in Connecticut, for instance) the prices of every article have fallen and the money consequently is in demand; but in other states you can scarce get a single thing for it, and yet it is withheld from the public by speculators, while everything that can be useful to the public is engrossed by this tribe of black gentry, who work more effectually against us than the enemy's arms and are a hundred times more dangerous to our liberties and the great cause we are engaged in. My best respects attend Mrs. Pendleton, & with much truth & regard I am Dr Sir Yr Obedt & Affe Servt

Go: Washington

To Major General Robert Howe, November 20, 1779 (Excerpt)

Dear Sir,

Herewith you will receive Mr. Pulteney's lucubrations—and my thanks for the perusal of them. He has made, I perceive, the dependence of America essential to the existence of Great Britain as a powerful nation. This I shall not deny, because I am in sentiment with him in thinking her fallen state in consequence of the separation too obvious to be disputed. It was of magnitude sufficient to have made a wise and just people look before they leaped. But I am glad to find that he has placed the supplies necessary to support that dependence upon three things which I am persuaded will never again exist in his nation: namely, public virtue, public economy, and public union in her grand council.

Stock jobbing, speculation, dissipation, luxury, and venality, with all their concomitants, are too deeply rooted to yield to virtue and the public good. We that are not yet hackneyed in vice—but infants, as it were, in the arts of corruption—and the knowledge of taking advantage of public necessity (though I am much mistaken if we shall not soon become very great adepts at them) find it almost if not quite impossible to preserve virtue enough to keep the body politic and corporate in tolerable tune. It is scarcely to be expected, therefore, that a people who have reduced these things to a system and have actually interwoven them into their constitution should at once become immaculate.

I do not know which rises highest: my indignation or contempt for the sentiments which pervade the ministerial writings of this day. These hireling scribblers labor to describe and prove the ingratitude of America in not breaking faith with France and returning to her allegiance to the Crown of Great Britain after its having offered such advantageous terms of accommodation. Such sentiments as these are insulting to common sense and affrontive to every principle of sound policy and common honesty. Why has she offered these terms? Because after a bloody contest, carried on with unrelenting and savage fury on her part, the issue (which was somewhat doubtful while we stood alone) is now become certain by the aid we derive from our alliance—notwithstanding the manifest advantages of which, and the blood and treasure which have been spent to resist a tyranny which was unremitted as long as there remained a hope of subjugation, we are told with an effrontery altogether unparalleled that every cause of complaint is now done away by the generous offers of a tender parent, that it is ungrateful in us not to accept the proffered terms and impolitic not to abandon a power (dangerous I confess to her but) which held out a saving hand to us in the hour of our distress. What epithet does such sentiment merit? How much should a people possessed of them be despised? From my soul I abhor them! A manly struggle, had it been conducted upon liberal ground, an honest confession that they were unequal to conquest and wished for our friendship, would have had its proper weight. But their cruelties, exercised upon those who have fallen within their power, the wanton depredations committed by themselves and their faithful allies the Indians, their low and dirty practices of counterfeiting our money, forging letters, and condescending to adopt such arts as the meanest villain in private life would blush at being charged with have made me their fixed enemy.

General Orders, January 28, 1780 (Excerpt)

The general is astonished and mortified to find that, notwithstanding the order issued on the 29th of last month, and his exhortation to the officers to prevent it, the inhabitants in the vicinity of camp are absolutely a prey to the plundering and licentious spirit of the soldiery. From their daily complaints, and a formal representation of the magistrates on the subject, a night scarcely passes without gangs of soldiers going out of camp and committing every species of robbery, depredation, and the grossest personal insults. This conduct is intolerable and a disgrace to the army, and if anything can aggravate it it is that these violences are committed on the property and persons of those who, on a very late and alarming occasion, for the want of provisions, manifested the warmest attachment to the army by affording it the most generous and plentiful relief. It has also been reported that when detachments are relieved and are returning to camp, the soldiers straggle, maraud, and plunder in the most shameful and injurious manner. The general trusts and insists that the officers will exert themselves and take effectual measures to prevent all such practices in future.

To Joseph Reed, President of the Supreme Executive Council of Pennsylvania, February 15, 1780

Sir,

I am much indebted to Your Excellency for announcing my election as a member of the Philosophical Society. I feel myself particularly honored by this relation to a society whose successful efforts for promoting useful knowledge have already justly acquired them the highest reputation in the literary world.

I entreat you to present my warmest acknowledgments and to assure them that I shall with zeal embrace every opportunity of seconding their laudable views and manifesting the exalted sense I have of the institution.

The arts and sciences, essential to the prosperity of the state and to the ornament and happiness of human life, have a primary claim to the encouragement of every lover of his country and of mankind. With the greatest respect & esteem I am Sir, Yr Most Obedt Servt.

Go: Washington

To Samuel Huntington, President of the Continental Congress, April 3, 1780 (Excerpt)

Before I conclude, I think it my duty to touch upon the general situation of the army at this juncture. It is absolutely necessary Congress should be apprised of it, for it is difficult to foresee what may be the result, and as very serious consequences are to be apprehended, I should not be justified in preserving silence. There never has been a stage of the war in which the dissatisfaction has been so general or alarming. It has lately in particular instances worn features of a very dangerous complexion. A variety of causes has contributed to this: the diversity in the terms of enlistments, the inequality of the rewards given for entering into the service, but still more the disparity in the provision made by the several states for their respective troops. The system of state supplies, however, in the commencement dictated by necessity, has proved in its operation pernicious beyond description. An army must be raised, paid, subsisted, and regulated upon an equal and uniform principle, or the confusions and discontents are endless. Little less than the dissolution of the army would have been long since the consequence of a different plan, had it not been for a spirit of patriotic virtue both in officers and men of which there are few examples, seconded by the unremitting pains that have been taken to compose and reconcile them to their situation. But these will not be able to hold out much longer against the influence of causes constantly operating and every day with some new aggravation.

Some states, from their internal ability and local advantages, furnish their troops pretty amply not only with clothing but with many little comforts and conveniences; others supply them with some necessaries, but on a more contracted scale; while others have it in their power to do little or nothing at all. The officers and men in the routine of duty mix daily and compare circumstances. Those who fare worse than others of course are dissatisfied and have their resentment excited, not only against their own states but against the confederacy. They become disgusted with a service that makes such injurious distinctions. No arguments can persuade an officer it is justice he should be obliged to pay £ _____ a yard for cloth and other things in proportion while another is furnished at a _____ part of the price. The officers resign, and we have now scarcely a sufficient number left to take care even of the fragments of corps which remain. The men have not this resource; they murmur, brood over their discontents, and have lately shown a disposition to enter into seditious combinations.

A new scene is now opening which I fear will be productive of more troublesome effects than anything that has hitherto taken place. Some of the states have adopted the measure of making good the depreciation of the money to their troops as well for the past as the future. If this does not become general, it is so striking a point that the consequences must be unspeakably mischievous. I enter not into the propriety of this measure in the view of finance but confine myself to its operation upon the army. Neither do I mean to insinuate that the liberality of particular states has been carried to a blamable length. The evil I mean to point out is the inequality of the different provisions, and this is inherent in the present system. It were devoutly to be wished a plan could be adopted by which everything relating to the army could be conducted on a general principle, under the direction of Congress. This alone can give harmony and consistence to our military establishment, and I am persuaded will be infinitely conducive to public economy.

I hope I shall not be thought to have exceeded my duty in the unreserved manner in which I have exhibited our situation. Congress, I flatter myself, will have the goodness to believe that I have no other motives than a zeal for the public service, a desire to give them every necessary information, and an apprehension for the consequences of the evils we now experience. I have the honor to be With the highest respect Yr Excellency's Most Obet & hum. Servant

Go: Washington

To Joseph Jones, May 14, 1780 (Excerpt)

In the present state of our finances, and in the total emptiness of our magazines, a plan must be concerted to bring out the resources of the country with vigor and decision. This I think you will agree with me cannot be effected if the measures to be taken should depend on the slow deliberations of a body so large as Congress, admitting the best disposition in every member to promote the object in view. It appears to me of the greatest importance, and even of absolute necessity, that a *small* committee should be immediately appointed to reside near headquarters, vested with all the powers which Congress have so far as respects the purpose of a full cooperation with the French fleet and army on the *continent*. Their authority should be plenipotentiary to draw out men and supplies of every kind and to give their sanction to any operations which the commander-in-chief may not think himself at liberty to undertake without it, as well beyond as within the limit of these states.

This committee can act with dispatch and energy. By being on the spot it will be able to provide for exigencies as they arise and the better to judge of their nature and urgency. The plans in contemplation may be opened to them with more freedom and confidence than to a numerous body—where secrecy is impossible, where the indiscretion of a single member by disclosing may defeat the project.

I need not enlarge on the advantages of such a measure, as I flatter myself they will occur to you and that you will be ready to propose and give it your support. The conjuncture is one of the most critical and important we have seen; all our prudence and exertions are requisite to give it a favorable issue. Hesitancy and delay would in all probability ruin our affairs. Circumstanced as we are, the greatest good or the greatest ill must result. We shall probably fix the independence of America if we succeed; and if we fail the abilities of the state will have been so strained in the attempt that a total relaxation and debility must ensue, and the worst is to be apprehended.

These considerations should determine Congress to forego all inferior objects and unite with mutual confidence in these measures which seem best calculated to ensure success. There is no man who can be more useful as a member of the committee than General Schuyler. His perfect knowledge of the resources of the country, the activity of his temper, his fruitfulness of expedients, and his sound military sense make me wish above all things he may be appointed. A well-composed committee is of primary importance. I need not hint that the delicacy of these intimations fits them only for your private ear.

The opinion I have of your friendship induces me thus freely and confidentially to impart my sentiments on the occasion, and I shall be very happy you may agree with me in judgment. I am with the greatest esteem & regard Dr Sir Yr Obedt & Affecte Hble Servt

Go: Washington

To Samuel Huntington, President of the Continental Congress, May 27–28, 1780 (Excerpt)

Nothing is further from my wishes than to add in the smallest degree to the distresses or embarrassments of Congress on any occasion, and more particularly on one where I have every reason to fear they have it not in their power to administer the least relief. Duty, however, compels me to add one matter more to those I have already detailed. I have been informed by the two colonels of the Pennsylvania line, in whom I have the utmost confidence, who were called to assist Colonel Meigs to suppress the mutiny on Thursday night, that in the course of their expostulations the troops very pointedly mentioned, besides their distresses for provision, their not being paid for five months and, what is of a still more serious and delicate nature in our present circumstances, they mentioned the great depreciation of the money—its being of little or no value at all, and yet if they should be paid that it would be in this way and according to the usual amount, without an adequate allowance for the depreciation. They were reasoned with and every argument used that these gentlemen and Colonel Meigs could devise either to interest their pride or their passions. They were reminded of their past good conduct, of the late assurances of Congress, of the objects for which they were contending. But their answer was: their sufferings were too great, that they wanted present relief and some present substantial recompence for their service. This matter, I confess, though I have heard of no further uneasiness among the men, has given me infinitely more concern than anything that has ever happened and strikes me as the most important, because we have no means at this time that I know of for paying the troops but in continental money, and as it is evidently impracticable, from the immense quantity it would require, to pay them in this as much as would make up the depreciation. Every possible means in my power will be directed on this and on all occasions, as they ever have been, to preserve order and promote the public service. But in such an accumulation of distresses, amidst such a variety of embarrassments which surround us on all sides, this will be found at least extremely difficult. If the troops could only be comfortably supplied with provisions it would be a great point and such as would—with the event we expect soon to take place: the arrival of the armament from France to our succor—make them forget, or at least forego, many matters which make a part of their anxiety and present complaints. I have the Honor to be with the highest respect & esteem Yr Excellency's Most Obedt st

Go: Washington

To Joseph Reed, President of the Supreme Executive Council of Pennsylvania, May 28, 1780

Dear Sir,

I am much obliged to you for your favor of the 23rd. Nothing could be more necessary than the aid given by your state towards supplying us with provision. I assure you, every idea you can form of our distresses will fall short of the reality. There is such a combination of circumstances to exhaust the patience of the soldiery that it begins at length to be worn out, and we see in every line of the army the most serious features of mutiny and sedition. All our departments, all our operations are at a stand; and, unless a system very different from that which for a long time prevailed be immediately adopted throughout the states, our affairs must soon become desperate beyond the possibility of recovery.

If you were on the spot, my dear sir, if you could see what difficulties surround us on every side, how unable we are to administer to the most ordinary calls of the service, you would be convinced that these expressions are not too strong, and that we have almost ceased to hope. The country in general is in such a state of insensibility and indifference to its interest that I dare not flatter myself with any change for the better.

The committee of Congress in their late address to the several states have given a just picture of our situation. I very much doubt its making the desired impression, and if it does not I shall consider our lethargy as incurable. The present juncture is so interesting that if it does not produce correspondent exertions it will be a proof that motives of honor, public good, and even self-preservation have lost their influence upon our minds. This is a decisive moment—one of the most (I will go further and say the most) important America has seen. The Court of France has made a glorious effort for our deliverance, and if we disappoint its intentions by our supineness we must become contemptible in the eyes of all mankind. Nor can we after that venture to confide that our allies will persist in an attempt to establish what it will appear we want inclination or ability to assist them in.

Every view of our own circumstances ought to determine us to the most vigorous efforts, but there are considerations of another kind that should have equal weight. The combined fleets of France and Spain last year were greatly superior to those of the enemy. The enemy nevertheless sustained no material damage and at the close of the campaign have given a very important blow to our allies. This campaign the difference between the fleets, from every account I have been able to collect, will be very inconsiderable. Indeed, it is far from clear that there will not be an equality. What are we to expect will be the case if there should be another campaign? In all probability, the advantage will be on the side of the English, and then what will become of America? We ought not to deceive ourselves. The maritime resources of Great Britain are more substantial and real than those of France and Spain united. Her commerce is more extensive than that of both her rivals, and it is an axiom that the nation which has the most extensive commerce will always have the most powerful marine. Were these arguments less convincing the fact speaks for itself: her progress in the course of the last year is an incontestable proof.

It is true France in a manner created a fleet in a very short space, and this may mislead us in the judgment we form of her naval abilities. But if they bore any comparison with those of Great Britain, how comes it to pass that with all the force of Spain added she has lost so much ground in so short a time as now to have scarcely a superiority? We should consider what was done by France as a violent and unnatural effort of the government, which for want of sufficient foundation cannot continue to operate proportionable effects.

In modern wars the longest purse must chiefly determine the event. I fear that of the enemy will be found to be so. Though the government is deeply in debt and of course poor, the nation is rich, and their riches afford a fund which will not be easily exhausted. Besides, their system of public credit is such that it is capable of greater exertions than that of any other nation. Speculatists have been a long time foretelling its downfall, but we see no symptoms of the catastrophe being very near. I am persuaded it will at least last out the war, and then in the opinion of many of the best politicians it will be a national advantage. If the war should terminate successfully the Crown will have acquired such influence and power that it may attempt anything, and a bankruptcy will probably be made the ladder to climb to absolute authority. Administration may perhaps wish to drive matters to this issue. At any rate they will not be restrained by an apprehension of it from forcing the resources of the state. It will promote their present purposes, on which their all is at stake; and it may pave the way to triumph more effectually over the constitution. With this disposition I have no doubt that ample means will be found to prosecute the war with the greatest vigor.

France is in a very different position. The abilities of her present financier have done wonders. By a wise administration of the revenues, aided by advantageous loans, he has avoided the necessity of additional taxes. But, I am well informed, if the war continues another campaign he will be obliged to have recourse to the taxes usual in time of war, which are very heavy and which the people of France are not in condition to endure for any duration. When this necessity commences, France makes war on ruinous terms; and England from her individual wealth will find much greater facility in supplying her exigencies.

Spain derives great wealth from her mines, but not so great as is generally imagined. Of late years the profit to government is essentially diminished. Commerce and industry are the best means of a nation, both which are wanting to her. I am told her treasury is far from being so well filled as we have flattered ourselves. She is also much divided on the propriety of the war: there is a strong party against it. The temper of the nation is too sluggish to admit of great exertions. And, though the courts of the two kingdoms are closely linked together, there never has been in any of their wars a perfect harmony of measures, nor has it been the case in this, which has already been no small detriment to the common cause.

I mention these things to show that the circumstances of our allies as well as our own call for peace, to obtain which we must make one great effort this campaign. The present instance of the friendship of the Court of France is attended with every circumstance that can render it important and agreeable, that can interest our gratitude or fire our emulation. If we do our duty, we may even hope to make the campaign decisive on this continent. But we must do our duty in earnest, or disgrace and ruin will attend us. I am sincere in declaring a full persuasion that the succor will be fatal to us if our measures are not adequate to the emergency.

Now, my dear sir, I must observe to you that much will depend on the state of Pennsylvania. She has it in her power to contribute without comparison more to our success than any other state in the two essential articles of flour and transportation. New York, Jersey, Pennsylvania, and Maryland are our flour countries. Virginia went little on this article the last crop (and her resources are called for to the southward). New York by legislative coercion has already given all she could spare for the use of the army. Her inhabitants are left with scarcely a sufficiency for their own subsistence. Jersey from being so long the place of the army's residence is equally exhausted. Maryland has made great exertions, but she can still do something more. Delaware may contribute handsomely in proportion to her extent. But Pennsylvania is our chief dependence. From every information I can obtain, she is at this time full of flour. I speak to you in the language of frankness and as a friend. I do not mean to make any insinuations unfavorable to the state. I am aware of the embarrassments the government labors under from the open opposition of one party and the underhand intrigues of another. I know that with the best dispositions to promote the public service you have been obliged to move with circumspection. But this is a time to hazard and to take a tone of energy and decision. All parties but the disaffected will acquiesce in the necessity and give their support. The hopes and fears of the people at large may be acted upon in such a manner as to make them approve and second your views.

The matter is reduced to a point: either Pennsylvania must give us all the aid we ask of her, or we can undertake nothing, we must renounce every idea of a cooperation, and must confess to our allies that we look wholly to them for our safety. This will be a state of humiliation and littleness against which the feelings of every good American ought to revolt. Yours, I am convinced, will. Nor have I the least doubt that you will employ all your influence to animate the legislature and the people at large. The fate of these states hangs upon it. God grant we may be properly impressed with the consequences.

I wish the legislature could be engaged to vest the executive with plenipotentiary powers. I should then expect everything practicable from your abilities and zeal. This is not a time for formality or ceremony. The crisis in every point of view is extraordinary, and extraordinary expedients are necessary. I am decided in this opinion.

I am happy to hear that you have a prospect of complying with the requisitions of Congress for specific supplies, that the spirit of the city and state seems to revive and the warmth of party decline. These are good omens of our success. Perhaps this is the proper period to unite.

I am obliged to you for the renewal of your assurances of personal regard. My sentiments for you, you are too well acquainted with to make it necessary to tell you with how much esteem & regard I am Dr Sir Yr Most Obedt & Affe Hble Servt

Go: Washington

P.S. I felicitate you on the increase of your family. Mrs. Washington does the same and begs her particular respects and congratulations to Mrs. Reed—to which permit me to add mine.

To Joseph Jones, May 31, 1780 (Excerpt)

Certain I am that unless Congress speaks in a more decisive tone—unless they are vested with powers by the several states competent to the great purposes of war, or assume them as matter of right, and they, and the states respectively, act with more energy than they hitherto have done—our cause is lost. We can no longer drudge on in the old way. By ill-timing the adoption of measures, by delays in the execution of them, or by unwarrantable jealousies, we incur enormous expenses and derive no benefit from them. One state will comply with a requisition of Congress, another neglects to do it, a third executes it by halves, and all differ in the manner, the matter, or so much in point of time that we are always working uphill, and ever shall be (while such a system as the present one, or rather want of one prevails) unable to apply our strength or resources to any advantage.

This, my dear sir, is plain language to a member of Congress; but it is the language of truth and friendship. It is the result of long thinking, close application, and strict observation. I see one head gradually changing into thirteen. I see one army branching into thirteen, and, instead of looking up to Congress as the supreme controlling power of the United States, are considering themselves as dependent on their respective states. In a word, I see the powers of Congress declining too fast for the consequence and respect which is due to them as the grand representative body of America, and am fearful of the consequences of it.

To Anne-César, Chevalier de La Luzerne, June 5, 1780 (Excerpt)

Sir,

My time has been so entirely engrossed in the preliminary arrangements of immediate necessity towards the intended cooperation that I have not been able till now to do myself the honor to thank Your Excellency for your letter of the 21st of May.

We have too many proofs of the generous zeal of your countrymen in the cause of America not to be convinced of it and to feel all that the most grateful sensibility can inspire.

I am happy in believing that the troops and citizens of these states will eagerly embrace every opportunity to manifest their affection to the troops and citizens of your nation, as well as their gratitude and veneration to a prince from whom they have received the most important benefits. Penetrated with a sense of these, I shall think it my duty to cultivate correspondent sentiments as far as my influence extends.

To John Augustine Washington, June 6–July 6, 1780 (Excerpt)

I am glad to find that you did not dispose of your land. The paper currency of this continent has for some time past been upon too fluctuating a scale to receive in return for real property, unless it was to be bartered off immediately for something else of permanent value. To say when the hour of appreciation will arrive is (if not beyond the reach of human ken) very difficult. It depends upon a variety of causes: more virtue, more exertion, more economy, and a better knowledge of our true situation. While the interested man, who makes everything yield to his lust for gain, the speculator, which is only another term for the same thing, and the disaffected, though acting upon different principles to effect the same end, are practicing every art that human craft and cunning can devise to counteract the struggles of the virtuous part of the community, I think our money is upon too unstable a footing and fluctuating to part with land for, when the latter we are certain will become more valuable every day. It ever was my opinion, though candor obliges me to confess it is not consistent with national policy, to have my property as much as possible in lands. I have seen no cause to change this opinion, but abundant reason to confirm me in it, being persuaded that a few years' peace will inundate these states with emigrants and of course enhance the price of land far above the common interest of money.

July 6th 1780.

I began this letter and had written nearly thus far when advice came to me that the enemy had landed at Elizabethtown point and was advancing in force upon us. Unable as we were to oppose them, I thought it best to put on a good countenance and advance towards them, which being done, and the partial engagements which followed being published, make it unnecessary for me to detail them again. It is to be lamented, bitterly lamented, and in the anguish of soul I do lament, that our fatal and accursed policy should bring the 6th of June upon us and not a single recruit to the army, though the consequences were foretold last fall and pressed with as much precision as if the opinion had been the result of inspiration. But it has ever been our conduct and misfortune to slumber and sleep while we should be diligent in preparation—and, when pressed by irresistible necessity and when we can delay no longer, then to bring ourselves to the brink of destruction by expensive and temporary expedients. In a word, we have no system and seem determined not to profit by experience. We are, during the winter, dreaming of independence and peace without using the means to become so. In the spring, when our recruits should be with the army and in training, we have just discovered the necessity of calling for them. And by the fall, after a distressed and inglorious campaign for want of them, we begin to get a few men, which come in just time enough to eat our provisions and consume our stores without rendering any service. Thus it is, one year rolls over another; and without some change we are hastening to our ruin.

To tell a person at the distance of three or four hundred miles that an army reduced almost to nothing (by the expiration of short enlistments) should sometimes be five or six days together without bread, then as many without meat, and, once or twice, two or three without either; that the same army should have had numbers of men in it with scarcely clothes enough to cover their nakedness, and a full fourth of it without even the shadow of a blanket severe as the winter was; and that men under these circumstances were held together, is hardly within the bounds of credibility—but is nevertheless true. It is no difficult matter, therefore, under this view of things (which is not sufficiently colored to the life) to form some idea of my situation.

The states, under an expectation of hourly succor from France, are now called upon in pointed and pressing terms for men and supplies to cooperate with them. But in what manner they will give them, when they will arrive, and what may be the result, the womb of time only can reveal: I cannot. Our whole reinforcement as yet is about 250 men.

To Jonathan Trumbull, Governor of Connecticut, June 27, 1780 (Excerpt)

I can omit no occasion of repeating my earnest entreaties to Your Excellency to use all your influence to forward the measures recommended by the Committee of Cooperation. I assure you with the greatest sincerity and truth that nothing short of them will answer our purpose and that I am fully persuaded, from a general view of European and American affairs, the fate of our cause depends on the exertions of this campaign. The sparing system has been too long tried, till it has brought us to a crisis little less than desperate; and if the opportunity now before us be neglected, I believe it will be too late to retrieve our affairs. These are ideas that I may safely trust to your judgment, though I know they would be slighted by those indolent and narrow politicians who, except at the moment of some signal misfortune, are continually crying all is well, and who, to save a little present expense and avoid some temporary inconvenience (with no ill designs in the main), would protract the war and risk the perdition of our liberties. As I always speak to Your Excellency in the confidence of friendship, I shall not scruple to confess that the prevailing politics, for a considerable time past, have filled me with inexpressible anxiety and apprehension, and have uniformly appeared to me to threaten the subversion of our independence. I hope a period to them is now arrived and that a change of measures will save us from ruin.

To Joseph Reed, President of the Supreme Executive Council of Pennsylvania, July 4, 1780

My Dear Sir,

Motives of friendship, not less than of public good, induce me with freedom to give you my sentiments on a matter which interests you personally as well as the good of the common cause. I flatter myself you will receive what I say in the same spirit which dictates it, and that it will have all the influence circumstances will possibly permit.

The legislature of Pennsylvania has vested you, in case of necessity, with a power of declaring martial law throughout the state, to enable you to take such measures as the exigency may demand. So far the legislature has done its part. Europe, America, the state itself will look to you for the rest. The power vested in you will admit of all the latitude that could be desired, and may be made to mean anything the public safety may require. If it is not exerted proportionably, you will be responsible for the consequences. Nothing, my dear sir, can be more delicate and critical than your situation: a full discretionary power lodged in your hands in conjunction with the council; great expectations in our allies and in the people of this country; ample means in the state for great exertions of every kind; a powerful party, on one hand, to take advantage of every opening to prejudice you, on the other, popular indolence and avarice, averse to every measure inconsistent with present ease and present interest. In this dilemma, there is a seeming danger whatever side you take. It remains to choose that which has least real danger and will best promote the public weal. This, in my opinion, clearly is to exert the powers entrusted to you with a boldness and vigor suited to the emergency.

In general, I esteem it a good maxim that the best way to preserve the confidence of the people durably is to promote their true interest. There are particular exigencies when this maxim has peculiar force. When any great object is in view, the popular mind is roused into expectation and prepared to make sacrifices both of ease and property. If those to whom they confide the management of their affairs do not call them to make these sacrifices and the object is not attained, or they are involved in the reproach of not having contributed as much as they ought to have done towards it, they will be mortified at the disappointment, they will feel the censure, and their resentment will rise against those who, with sufficient authority, have omitted to do what their interest and their honor required. Extensive powers not exercised as far as was necessary have, I believe, scarcely ever failed to ruin the possessor. The legislature and the people, in your case, would be very glad to excuse themselves by condemning you. You would be assailed with blame from every quarter, and your enemies would triumph.

The party opposed to you in the government are making great efforts. I am told the bank established for supplying the army is principally under the auspices of that party. It will undoubtedly give them great credit with the people, and you have no effectual way to counter-balance this but by employing all your influence and authority to render services proportioned to your station. Hitherto, I confess to you frankly my dear sir, I do not think your affairs are in the train which might be wished. And if Pennsylvania does not do its part fully, it is of so much importance in the general scale that we must fail of success or limit our views to mere defense. I have conversed with some gentlemen on the measure of filling your battalions. They seemed to think you could not exceed what the legislature had done for this purpose. I am of very different sentiment. The establishment of martial law implies, in my judgment, the right of calling any part of your citizens into military service, and in any manner which may be found expedient; and I have no doubt the draft may be executed.

I write to you with the freedom of friendship, and I hope you will esteem it the truest mark I could give you of it. In this view, whether you think my observations well founded or not, the motive will, I am persuaded, render them agreeable. In offering my respects to Mrs. Reed, I must be permitted to accompany them with a tender of my very warm acknowledgments to her and you for the civilities and attention both of you have been pleased to show Mrs. Washington, and for the honor you have done me in calling the young Christian by my name. With the greatest regard, I am, dear Sir, &c.

To Fielding Lewis, July 6, 1780 (Excerpt)

The gazettes will have given you an account of the enemy's movements on the 7th and 23rd of last month from Elizabeth Town point and of their having taken post there from the one date to the other. There can be no occasion, therefore, to detail the account in this place. But I may lament in the bitterness of my soul that the fatal policy which has pervaded all our measures from the beginning of the war, and from which no experience however dear bought can change, should have reduced our army to so low an ebb as not to have given a more effectual opposition to those movements than we did, or that we should be obliged to be removing our stores from place to place to keep them out of the way of the enemy instead of driving that enemy from our country. But our weakness invited these insults, and why they did not attempt at least to do more than they did I cannot conceive. Nor will it be easy to make any one at the distance of 400 miles believe that our army, weakened as it is by the expiration of men's enlistments, should at times be five or six days together without meat, then as many without bread, and, once or twice, two or three days together without either. And that, in the same army, there should be numbers of men with scarcely as much clothing as would cover their nakedness, and at least a fourth of the whole with not even the shadow of a blanket, severe as the winter has been. Under these circumstances it is no difficult matter to conceive what a time I must have had to keep up appearances and prevent the most disastrous consequences.

It may be asked how these things have come to pass. The answer is plain and may be ascribed to want of system, not to say foresight—originally (if it is not still the case with some) a fatal jealousy (under our circumstances) of a standing army—by which means we neglected to obtain soldiers for the war when zeal and patriotism ran high and men were eager to engage for a trifle or for nothing, the consequence of which has been that we have protracted the war, expended millions and tens of millions of pounds which might have been saved and have a new army to raise and discipline once or twice a year, and with which we can undertake nothing because we have nothing to build upon, as the men are slipping from us every day by means of their expiring enlistments. To these fundamental errors may be added another which I expect will prove our ruin, and that is the relinquishment of congressional powers to the states individually. All the business is now attempted, for it is not done, by a timid kind of recommendation from Congress to the states, the consequence of which is that, instead of pursuing one uniform system which in the execution shall correspond in time and manner, each state undertakes to determine, first, whether they will comply or not; second, in what manner they will do it; and thirdly, in what time—by which means scarcely any one measure is or can be executed, while great expenses are incurred and the willing and zealous states ruined. In a word, our measures are not under the influence and direction of one council but thirteen, each of which is actuated by local views and politics, without considering the fatal consequences of not complying with plans which the united wisdom of America in its representative capacity have digested, or the unhappy tendency of delay, mutilation, or alteration. I do not scruple to add, and I give it decisively as my opinion, that unless the states will content themselves with a full and well-chosen representation in Congress, and vest that body with absolute powers in all matters relative to the great purposes of war and of general concern (by which the states unitedly are affected), reserving to themselves all matters of local and internal polity for the regulation of order and good government, we are attempting an impossibility, and very soon shall become (if it is not already the case) a many headed monster, a heterogeneous mass, that never will or can steer to the same point. The contest among the different states now is not which shall do most for the common cause, but which shall do least. Hence arise disappointments and delay, one state waiting to see what another will or will not do through fear of doing too much, and, by their deliberations, alterations, and sometimes refusals to comply with the requisitions of Congress, after that Congress have spent months in reconciling (as far as it is possible) jarring interests in order to frame their resolutions as far as the nature of the case will admit upon principles of equality.

There is another source from whence much of our present distress and past difficulties have flowed, and that is the hope and expectation which seizes the states and Congress towards the close of every year that peace must take place in the winter. This never fails to produce an apathy which lulls them into ease and security and involves the most distressing consequences at the opening of every campaign. We may rely upon it that we shall never have peace till the enemy are convinced that we are in a condition to carry on the war. It is no new maxim in politics that for a nation to obtain peace, or ensure it, it must be prepared for war.

But it is time for me to recollect myself and quit a subject which would require a folio volume to elucidate and expose the folly of our measures. To rectify past blunders is impossible, but we might profit by the experience of them, though even here I doubt, as I am furnished with many instances to the contrary.

To Mrs. Esther de Berdt Reed, July 14, 1780

Madam,

I have received with much pleasure—but not till last night—your favor of the 4th specifying the amount of the subscriptions already collected for the use of the American soldiery.

This fresh mark of the patriotism of the ladies entitles them to the highest applause of their country. It is impossible for the army not to feel a superior gratitude on such an instance of goodness.

If I am happy in having the concurrence of the ladies, I would propose the purchasing of course linen, to be made into shirts, with the whole amount of their subscription. A shirt extraordinary to the soldier will be of more service, and do more to preserve his health, than any other thing that could be procured him, while it is not intended, nor shall exclude him, from the usual supply which he draws from the public.

This appears to me to be the best mode for its application; and, provided it is approved of by the ladies, I am happy to find you have been good enough to give us a claim on your endeavors to complete the execution of the design. An example so laudable will certainly be nurtured and must be productive of a favorable issue in the bosoms of the fair in the sister states.

Let me congratulate our benefactors on the arrival of the French fleet off the harbor of Newport on the afternoon of the 10th. It is this moment announced, but without any particulars, as an interchange of signals had only taken place.

I pray the ladies of your family to receive with my compliments my liveliest thanks for the interest they take in my favor. With the most perfect respect and esteem I have the honor to be Madam, Yr Obedt & Hble Serv.

Go: Washington

General Orders, July 20, 1780 (Excerpt)

The commander-in-chief has the pleasure to congratulate the army on the arrival of a large land and naval armament at Rhode Island, sent by His Most Christian Majesty to cooperate with the troops of these states against the common enemy, accompanied with every circumstance that can render it honorable and useful.

The generosity of this succor and the manner in which it is given are a new tie between France and America. The lively concern which our allies manifest for our safety and independence has a claim to the affection of every virtuous citizen. The general with confidence assures the army that the officers and men of the French forces come to our aid animated with a zeal founded in sentiment for us as well as in duty to their prince, and that they will do everything in their power to promote harmony and cultivate friendship. He is equally persuaded that on our part we shall vie with them in their good dispositions, to which we are excited by gratitude as well as by a common interest, and that the only contention between the two armies will be to excel each other in good offices and in the display of every military virtue. This will be the pledge of the most solid advantages to the common cause and of a glorious issue to the campaign.

To Joseph Jones, August 13, 1780

Dear Sir,

The subject of this letter will be confined to a simple point. I shall make it as short as possible and write it with frankness. If any sentiment, therefore, is delivered which might be displeasing to you *as a member of Congress*, ascribe it to the freedom which is taken with you by a friend who has nothing in view but the public good.

In your letter without date, but which came to hand yesterday, an idea is held up, as if the acceptance of General Greene's resignation of the quartermaster department was not all that Congress meant to do with him. If by this it is in contemplation to suspend him from his command in the line (of which he made an express reservation at the time of entering on the other duty), and it is not already enacted, let me beseech you to consider well what you are about before you resolve.

I shall neither condemn nor acquit General Greene's conduct for the act of resignation, because all the antecedent correspondences are necessary to form a right judgment of the matter; and possibly, if the affair is ever brought before the public, you may find him treading on better ground than you seem to imagine. But this by the by. My sole aim at present is to advertise you of what I think would be the consequences of suspending him from his command in the line (a matter distinct from the other) without a proper trial. A procedure of this kind must touch the feelings of every officer. It will show in a conspicuous point of view the uncertain tenure by which they hold their commissions. In a word, it will exhibit such a specimen of power that I question much if there is an officer in the whole line that will hold a commission beyond the end of the campaign, if they do till then. Such an act in the most despotic government would be attended at least with loud complaints.

It does not require, as I am sure with you, argument at this time of day to prove that there is no set of men in the United States (considered as a body) that have made the same sacrifices of their interest in support of the common cause as the officers of the American army; that nothing but a love of their country, of honor, and a desire of seeing their labors crowned with success could possibly induce them to continue one moment in service, that no officer can live upon his pay, that hundreds having spent their little all in addition to their scant public allowance have resigned because they could no longer support themselves as officers, that numbers are, at this moment, rendered unfit for duty for want of clothing, while the rest are wasting their property and some of them verging fast to the gulf of poverty and distress. Can it be supposed that men under these circumstances—who can derive, at best, if the contest ends happily, only the advantages which attend in equal proportion with others—will sit patient under such a precedent? Surely they will not; for the measure, not the man, will be the subject of consideration, and each will ask himself this question: If Congress, by its mere fiat, without inquiry and without trial, will suspend one officer today, an officer of such high rank, may it not be my turn tomorrow, and ought I to put it in the power of any man or body of men to sport with my commission and character, and lay me under the necessity of tamely acquiescing, or by an appeal to the public expose matters which must be injurious to its interests? The suspension of Generals Schuyler and St. Clair, though it was preceded by the loss of Ticonderoga, and which contributed not a little for the moment to excite prejudices against them, was by no means viewed with a satisfactory eye by many discerning men—and though it was in a manner supported by the public clamor. And the one in contemplation, I am almost morally certain, will be generally reprobated by the army. Suffer not, my friend, if it is within the compass of your abilities to prevent it, so disagreeable an event to take place. I do not mean to justify, to countenance, or excuse in the most distant degree any expressions of disrespect which the gentleman in question, if he has used any, may have offered to Congress, no more than I do any unreasonable matters he may have required respecting the quartermaster department. But as I have already observed, my letter is to prevent his suspension, because *I fear*, because *I feel*, it must lead to very disagreeable and injurious consequences. General Greene has his numerous friends out of the army as well as in it; and, from his character and consideration in the world, he might not, when he felt himself wounded in so summary a[9] way, withhold from a discussion that could not, at best, promote the public cause. As a military officer he stands very fair, and very deservedly so, in the opinion of all his acquaintance.

These sentiments are the result of my own reflections on the matter, and I hasten to inform you of them. I do not know that General Greene has ever heard of the matter, and I hope he never may—nor am I acquainted with the opinion of a single officer in the whole army upon the subject, nor will any tone be given by me. It is my wish to prevent the proceeding, for sure I am it cannot be brought to a happy issue if it takes place. I am, &c.

Go. Wn

To Samuel Huntington, President of the Continental Congress, August 20, 1780 (Excerpt)

But while we are meditating offensive operations, which may either not be undertaken at all, or being undertaken may fail, I am persuaded Congress are not inattentive to the present state of the army, and will view in the same light with me the necessity of providing in time against a period, the first of January, when one half of our present force will dissolve. The shadow of an army that will remain will have every motive except mere patriotism to abandon the service, without the hope, which has hitherto supported them, of a change for the better. This is almost extinguished now, and certainly will not outlive the campaign, unless it finds something more substantial to rest upon. This is a truth of which every spectator of the distresses of the army cannot help being convinced. Those at a distance may speculate differently; but on the spot an opinion to the contrary, judging of human nature on the usual scale, would be[10] chimerical. The Honorable the Committee who have seen and heard for themselves will add their testimony to mine, and the wisdom and justice of Congress cannot fail to give it the most serious attention. To me it will appear miraculous if our affairs can maintain themselves much longer in their present train. If either the temper or the resources of the country will not admit of an alteration, we may expect soon to be reduced to the humiliating condition of seeing the cause of America, in America, upheld by foreign arms. The generosity of our allies has a claim to all our confidence and all our gratitude, but it is neither for the honor of America nor for the interest of the common cause to leave the work entirely to them.

It is true our enemies as well as ourselves are struggling with embarrassments of a singular and complicated nature, from which we may hope a great deal. But they have already more than once disappointed the general expectation and displayed resources as extraordinary as unexpected. There is no good reason to suppose those resources yet exhausted. Hitherto they have carried on the war with pretty equal success; and the comparative forces of this campaign are, I believe, less disadvantageous to them than they were the last. At present, indeed, their affairs wear a critical aspect; but there are chances in their favor, and if they escape, their situation will be likely to take a more prosperous turn, and they may continue to prosecute the war with vigor. Their finances are distressed: they have a heavy debt and are obliged to borrow money at an excessive interest. But they have great individual wealth; and while they pay the interest of what they borrow, they will not want credit, nor will they fear to stretch it. A bankruptcy, which may be the result, will perhaps be less terrible to the king and his ministers than giving up the contest. If the measures leading to it enable them to succeed, it will add so much to the influence and power of the Crown as to make that event a ladder to absolute authority—supposed by many to be the object of the present reign. Nor are there wanting enlightened politicians who maintain that a national bankruptcy is not only a necessary consequence but would be a national benefit. When we consider the genius of the present reign and the violent councils by which it has been governed, a system of this kind will be judged less improbable.

As to the domestic dissensions of the enemy—in Ireland—we see they have hitherto not only diverted but have in some measure appeased them; and, by pursuing their plan of taking off the leaders and making plausible concessions to the people, we ought not to be surprised if they keep matters in that country from going to extremity. In England, it is much to be feared the overbearing influence of the Crown will triumph over the opposition to it, and that the next Parliament will be nearly as obsequious as the last. A change of some of the ministry to make way for a few of the principal heads of opposition would perhaps allay the ferment; but even without this, considering the complexion of the British nation for some time past, it is more probable these appearances will terminate in a partial reform than in a revolution favorable to the interests of America. The ministry may be perplexed for a time and may be obliged to make a few sacrifices in favor of public economy, which may finally promote their views by leaving more money in the treasury to be applied to the purposes of the war.

The general disposition of Europe is such as we could wish, but we have no security that it will remain so. The politics of princes are fluctuating, more guided often by a particular prejudice, whim, or interest than by extensive views of policy. The change or caprice of a single minister is capable of altering the whole system of Europe; but, admitting the different courts at this time ever so well fixed in their principles, the death of one of the sovereigns may happen, and the whole face of things be reversed. This ought to be the more attended to as three of the principal potentates are in so advanced an age that it is perhaps more probable one of them should die in the course of a year than that all three should survive it.

The inference from these reflections is that we cannot count upon a speedy end to the war, that it is the true policy of America not to content herself with temporary expedients but to endeavor, if possible, to give consistency and solidity to her measures. An essential step to this will be immediately to devise a plan and put it in execution for providing men in time to replace those who will leave us at the end of the year, for subsisting and making a reasonable allowance to the officers and soldiers.

The plan for this purpose ought to be of general operation and such as will execute itself. Experience has shown that a peremptory draft will be the only effectual one. If a draft for the war, or three years, can be effected it ought to be made on every account; a shorter period than a year is inadmissible.

To one who has been witness to the evils brought upon us by short enlistments, the system appears to have been pernicious beyond description; and a crowd of motives present themselves to dictate a change. It may easily be shown that all the misfortunes we have met with in the military line are to be attributed to this cause. Had we formed a permanent army in the beginning, which by the continuance of the same men in service had been capable of discipline, we never should have had to retreat with a handful of men across the Delaware in '76, trembling for the fate of America, which nothing but the infatuation of the enemy could have saved. We should not have remained all the succeeding winter at their mercy, with sometimes scarcely a sufficient body of men to mount the ordinary guards, liable at every moment to be dissipated if they had only thought proper to march against us. We should not have been under the necessity of fighting at Brandywine with an unequal number of raw troops, and afterwards of seeing Philadelphia fall a prey to a victorious army. We should not have been at Valley Forge with less than half the force of the enemy, destitute of everything, in a situation neither to resist nor to retire. We should not have seen New York left with a handful of men, yet an overmatch for the main army of these states, while the principal part of their force was detached for the reduction of two of them. We should not have found ourselves this spring so weak as to be insulted by five thousand men, unable to protect our baggage and magazines, their security depending on a good countenance and a want of enterprise in the enemy. We should not have been the greatest part of the war inferior to the enemy, indebted for our safety to their inactivity, enduring frequently the mortification of seeing inviting opportunities to ruin them pass unimproved for want of a force which the country was completely able to afford—to see the country ravaged, our towns burnt, the inhabitants plundered, abused, murdered, with impunity, from the same cause.

Nor have the ill effects been confined to the military line: a great part of the embarrassments in the civil flow from the same source. The derangement of our finances is essentially to be ascribed to it. The expenses of the war, and the paper emissions, have been greatly multiplied by it. We have had, a great part of the time, two sets of men to feed and pay: the discharged men going home and the levies coming in. This was more remarkable in '75 and '76. The difficulty and cost of engaging men have increased at every successive attempt—till among the present levies we find there are some who have received a hundred and fifty dollars in specie for five months' service, while our officers are reduced to the disagreeable necessity of performing the duties of drill sergeants to them, and with this mortifying reflection annexed to the business: that by the time they have taught these men the rudiments of a soldier's duty, their term of service will have expired and the work is to recommence with an entire new set.

The consumption of provision, arms, accoutrements, stores of every kind, has been doubled in spite of every precaution I could use, not only from the cause just mentioned, but from the carelessness and licentiousness incident to militia and irregular troops. Our discipline also has been much injured if not ruined by such frequent changes. The frequent calls upon the militia have interrupted the cultivation of the land—of course have lessened the quantity of its produce, occasioned a scarcity, and enhanced the prices. In an army so unstable as ours, order and economy have been impracticable. No person who has been a close observer of the progress of our affairs can doubt that our currency has depreciated without comparison more rapidly from the system of short enlistments than it would have done otherwise.

There is every reason to believe the war has been protracted on this account. Our opposition being less made the successes of the enemy greater. The fluctuation of the army kept alive their hopes, and at every period of the dissolution of a considerable part of it they have flattered themselves with some decisive advantages. Had we kept a permanent army on foot, the enemy would have had nothing to hope for and would in all probability have listened to terms long since.

If the army is left in its present situation, it must continue an encouragement to the efforts of the enemy. If it is put upon a respectable one, it must have a contrary effect—and nothing I believe will tend more to give us peace the ensuing winter. It will be an interesting winter. Many circumstances will contribute to a negotiation. An army on foot not only for another campaign but for several campaigns would determine the enemy to pacific measures and enable us to insist upon favorable terms in forcible language. An army insignificant in numbers, dissatisfied, crumbling into pieces, would be the strongest temptation they could have to try the experiment a little longer. It is an old maxim that the surest way to make a good peace is to be well prepared for war.

I am inclined to hope a draft for the war or three years would succeed. Many incentives of immediate interest may be held up to the people to induce them to submit to it. They must begin to consider the repeated bounties they are obliged to pay as a burden, and be willing to get rid of it by sacrificing a little more, once for all. Indeed, it is probable the bounties may not be much greater in that case than they have been. The people of the states near the seat of war ought to enter into such a plan with alacrity, as it would ease them in a variety of respects—among others by obviating the frequent calls upon the militia.

I cannot forbear returning in this place to the necessity of a more ample and equal provision for the army. The discontents on this head have been gradually matured to a dangerous extremity. There are many symptoms that alarm and distress me. Endeavors are using to unite both officers and men in a general refusal of the money, and some corps now actually decline receiving it. Every method has been taken to counteract it, because such a combination in the army would be a severe blow to our declining currency. The most moderate insist that the accounts of depreciation ought to be liquidated at stated periods and certificates given by government for the sums due. They will not be satisfied with a general declaration that it shall be made good.

This is one instance of complaint; there are others equally serious. Among the most serious is the inequality of the provision made by the several states. Pennsylvania maintains her officers in a decent manner. She has given them half-pay for life. What a wide difference between their situation and that of the officers of every other line in this army, some of whom are actually so destitute of clothing as to be unfit for duty, and obliged for that cause only to confine themselves to quarters. I have often said, and I beg leave to repeat it, the half-pay provision is, in my opinion, the most politic and effectual that can be adopted. On the whole, if something satisfactory be not done, the army (already so much reduced in officers by daily resignations as not to have a sufficiency to do the common duties of it) must either cease to exist at the end of the campaign, or it will exhibit an example of more virtue, fortitude, self-denial, and perseverance than has perhaps ever[11] yet been paralleled in the history of human enthusiasm.

The dissolution of the army is an event that cannot be regarded with indifference. It would bring accumulated distresses upon us. It would throw the people of America into a general consternation. It would discredit our cause throughout the world. It would shock our allies. To think of replacing the officers with others is visionary: the loss of the veteran soldiers could not be repaired. To attempt to carry on the war with militia against disciplined troops would be to attempt what the common sense and common experience of mankind will pronounce to be impracticable. But I should fail in respect to Congress to dwell on observations of this kind in a letter to them.

But, having gone into a detail of our situation, I shall beg leave to make one observation more. It is a thing that has been all along ardently desired by the army that every matter which relates to it should be under the immediate direction and providence of Congress. The contrary has been productive of innumerable inconveniences. Besides the inequality of provision already mentioned, all the confusion we have experienced by irregular appointments and promotions has chiefly originated here; and we are again relapsing into the same chaos. I have daily complaints of palpable mistakes and deviations from those rules on which the tranquility of the service depends, of which I might cite recent instances if it were necessary to trouble Congress with such a detail. I shall, however, mention one in the Jersey line by way of example. A vacancy happened July '79 by Lt. Colonel Brearly's being appointed chief justice of the state. This was not filled till March following, by which the officer entitled to succeed has lost several months' rank in the line of the army. The vacancies his promotion made still continue open to the prejudice of those next in order. And yet (as I have been informed) new appointments have been made by the state on the principle of those vacancies. As this is a fruitful source of discontent it is naturally in my province to point it out; but, if I were to permit myself to touch upon the political consequences, I might easily show that it has[12] a direct tendency to enfeeble our civil union by making us thirteen armies instead of one, and by attaching the troops of each state to that state rather than to the United States. The effects of this spirit begin to be visible. But this is a topic on which I may not be permitted to enlarge.

In this delicate and perplexing conjuncture, which I cannot but contemplate with extreme inquietude, I have thought it my duty to lay my sentiments with freedom—and I hope I have done it with all possible deference before Congress—and to give them the fullest and truest information in my power. I trust they will receive what I have said with all the indulgence which must flow from a conviction that it is dictated by a sincere attachment to their honor and by an anxious concern for the welfare of my country. With the greatest respect I have the honor to be Sir Yr Most Obt Ser.

Go: Washington

Circular to the States, August 27, 1780

Sir,

The Honorable the Committee of Cooperation having returned to Congress, I am under the disagreeable necessity of informing Your Excellency that the army is again reduced to an extremity of distress for want of provision. The greater part of it had been without meat from the 21st to the 26th. To endeavor to obtain some relief, I moved down to this place with a view of stripping the lower parts of the county of its cattle, which after a most rigorous exaction is found to afford between two and three days' supply only, and those consisting of milch cows and calves of one or two years old. When this scanty pittance is consumed, I know not what will be our next resource, as the commissary can give me no certain information of more than 120 head of cattle expected from Pennsylvania and about 150 from Massachusetts. I mean in time to supply our immediate wants.

Military coercion is no longer of any avail, as nothing further can possibly be collected from the country in which we are obliged to take a position without depriving the inhabitants of the last morsel. This mode of subsisting, supposing the desired end could be answered by it, besides being in the highest degree distressing to individuals, is attended with ruin to the morals and discipline of the army. During the few days which we have been obliged to send out small parties to procure provision for themselves, the most enormous excesses have been committed.

It has been no inconsiderable support of our cause to have had it in our power to contrast the conduct of our army with that of the enemy, and to convince the inhabitants that while their rights were wantonly violated by the British troops, by ours they were respected. This distinction must unhappily now cease, and we must assume the odious character of the plunderers instead of the protectors of the people, the direct consequence of which must be to alienate their minds from the army, and insensibly from the cause.

We have not yet been absolutely without flour, but we have this day but one day's supply in camp; and I am not certain that there is a single barrel between this and Trenton. I shall be obliged therefore to draw down one or two hundred barrels from a small magazine which I had endeavored to establish at West Point, for the security of the garrison in case of a sudden investiture.

From the above state of facts, it may be foreseen that this army cannot possibly remain much longer together, unless very vigorous and immediate measures are taken by the states to comply with the requisitions made upon them. The commissary general has neither the means nor the power of procuring supplies. He is only to receive them from the several agents. Without a speedy change of circumstances, this dilemma will be involved: either the army must disband, or what is, if possible, worse, subsist upon the plunder of the people.

I would fain flatter myself that a knowledge of our situation will produce the desired relief—not a relief of a few days, as has generally heretofore been the case, but a supply equal to the establishment of magazines for the winter. If these are not formed before the roads are broken up by the weather, we shall certainly experience the same difficulties and distresses the ensuing winter which we did the last. Although the troops have, upon every occasion hitherto, borne their wants with unparalleled patience, it will be dangerous to trust too often to a repetition of the causes of discontent. I have the honor to be with great Respect Your Excellency's Most obt Servt

Go: Washington

To Samuel Huntington, President of the Continental Congress, September 15, 1780 (Excerpt)

Sir,

I am honored with your letters of the 6th and 8th instant with their enclosures—happy to find that the late disaster in Carolina has not been so great as its first features indicated. This event, however, adds itself to many others to exemplify the necessity of an army—the fatal consequences of depending on militia. Regular troops alone are equal to the exigences of modern war, as well for defense as offense, and whenever a substitute is attempted, it must prove illusory and ruinous. No militia will ever acquire the habits necessary to resist a regular force. Even those nearest the heat of war are only valuable as light troops to be scattered in the woods and plague rather than do serious injury to the enemy. The firmness requisite for the real business of fighting is only to be attained by a constant course of discipline and service. I have never yet been witness to a single instance that can justify a different opinion, and it is most earnestly to be wished the liberties of America may no longer be trusted in any material degree to so precarious a dependence.

General Orders, September 26, 1780 (Excerpt)

Treason of the blackest dye was yesterday discovered! General Arnold, who commanded at West Point—lost to every sentiment of honor, of public and private obligation—was about to deliver up that important post into the hands of the enemy. Such an event must have given the American cause a deadly wound if not a fatal stab. Happily the treason has been timely discovered to prevent the fatal misfortune. The providential train of circumstances which led to it affords the most convincing proof that the liberties of America are the object of divine protection.

At the same time that the treason is to be regretted the general cannot help congratulating the army on the happy discovery. Our enemies, despairing of carrying their point by force, are practicing every base art to effect by bribery and corruption what they cannot accomplish in a manly way.

Great honor is due to the American army that this is the first instance of treason of the kind where many were to be expected from the nature of the dispute. And nothing is so bright an ornament in the character of the American soldiers as their having been proof against all the arts and seduction of an insidious enemy.

Arnold has made his escape to the enemy, but Mr. André, the adjutant general to the British army, who came out as a spy to negotiate the business, is our prisoner.

His Excellency the commander-in-chief has arrived at West Point from Hartford and is now[13] double-taking the proper measures to unravel fully so hellish a plot.

To James Duane, October 4, 1780 (Excerpt)

I thank you, my dear sir, for your letter of the 19th of September. I should have been happy in the information you give me that some progress had been made in the business of raising a permanent army, had it not been intimated to me through other channels that, in the resolutions framed on this article, the fatal alternative of *for one year* has been admitted. In my letter to Congress of the 20th of August I recommended a draft for the war or for three years and say "*a shorter period than one year is inadmissible.*" You will perceive, however, that the general scope of my arguments looks to an army for the war, and any other idea crept in from an apprehension that this plan would not go down. The present juncture is in my opinion peculiarly favorable to a permanent army, and I regret that an opening is given for a temporary one. It also gives me pain to find that the pernicious state system is still adhered to by leaving the reduction, incorporation, etc. of the regiments to the particular states. This is one of the greatest evils of our affairs.

I share with you the pleasure you feel from the measures taken to strengthen the hand of Congress. I am convinced it is essential to our safety that Congress should have an *efficient* power. The want of it must ruin us.

The satisfaction I have in any successes that attend us, or even in the alleviation of misfortunes, is always allayed by a fear that it will lull us into security. Supineness and a disposition to flatter ourselves seem to make parts of our national character. When we receive a check and are not quite undone we are apt to fancy we have gained a victory; and when we do gain any little advantage we imagine it decisive and expect the war is immediately to end. The history of the war is a history of false hopes and temporary expedients. Would to God they were to end here. This winter, if I am not mistaken, will open a still more embarrassing scene than we have yet experienced to the southward. I have little doubt should we not gain a naval superiority that Sir Henry Clinton will detach to the southward to extend his conquests. I am far from being satisfied that we shall be prepared to repel his attempts.

Reflections of this kind to you, my dear sir, are unnecessary. I am convinced you view our affairs on the same scale that I do, and will exert yourself to correct our errors and call forth our resources.

To Brigadier General John Cadwalader, October 5, 1780 (Excerpt)

We are now drawing an inactive campaign to a close, the beginning of which appeared pregnant with events of a favorable complexion. I hoped, but hoped in vain, that a prospect was displaying which would enable me to fix a period to my military pursuits and restore me to domestic life.

The favorable disposition of Spain—the promised succor from France—the combined force in the West Indies—the declaration of Russia (acceded to by other powers of Europe—humiliating to the naval pride and power of Great Britain)—the superiority of France and Spain by sea in Europe—the Irish claims—and British disturbances, formed in the aggregate an opinion in my breast, which is not very susceptible of peaceful dreams, that the hour of deliverance was not far distant, for that, however unwilling Great Britain might be to yield the point, it would not be in her power to continue the contest. But alas! these prospects, flattering as they were, have proved delusory; and I see nothing before us but accumulating distress. We have been half our time without provision and are likely to continue so. We have no magazines, nor money to form them. And in a little time, we shall have no men, if we had money to pay them. We have lived upon expedients till we can live no longer. In a word, the history of the war is a history of false hopes and temporary devices, instead of system and economy.

It is in vain, however, to look back; nor is it our business to do so. Our case is not desperate if virtues exist in the people and there is wisdom among our rulers. But to suppose that this great revolution can be accomplished by a temporary army, that this army will be subsisted by state supplies, and that taxation alone is adequate to our wants is in my opinion absurd, and as unreasonable as to expect an inversion in the order of nature to accommodate things to our views.

If it was necessary, it could easily be proved to any person of a moderate share of understanding that an annual army—or an army raised on the spur of the occasion—besides being unqualified for the end designed is in various ways, which could be enumerated, ten times more expensive than a permanent body of men under good organization and military discipline, which never was, nor never will be the case of new troops. A thousand arguments resulting from experience and the nature of things might also be adduced to prove that the army, if it is to depend upon state supplies, must disband or starve, and that taxation alone (especially at this late hour) cannot furnish the mean to carry on the war. Is it not time, then, to retract from error, and benefit by experience? Or do we want further proof of the ruinous system we have pertinaciously adhered to?

To Lieutenant Colonel John Laurens, October 13, 1780 (Excerpt)

André has met his fate, and with that fortitude which was to be expected from an accomplished man and gallant officer. But I am mistaken if at *this time* Arnold is undergoing the torments of a mental hell. He wants feeling! From some traits of his character which have lately come to my knowledge, he seems to have been so hackneyed in villainy, and so lost to all sense of honor and shame, that while his faculties will enable him to continue his sordid pursuits, there will be no time for remorse.

Circular to the States, October 18, 1780 (Excerpt)

I am religiously persuaded that the duration of the war, and the greatest part of the misfortunes and perplexities we have hitherto experienced, are chiefly to be attributed to the system of temporary enlistments. Had we in the commencement raised an army for the war, such as was within the reach of the abilities of these states to raise and maintain, we should not have suffered those military checks which have so frequently shaken our cause, nor should we have incurred such enormous expenditures as have destroyed our proper currency, and with it all public credit. A moderate, compact force, on a permanent establishment, capable of acquiring the discipline essential to military operations, would have been able to make head against the enemy, without comparison better than[14] the throngs of militia, which at certain periods have not been in the field but in their way to and from the field. For from that want of perseverance, which characterizes all militia, and of that coercion, which cannot be exercised upon them, it has always been found impracticable to detain the greatest part of them in service even for the term for which they have been called out. And this has been commonly so short that we have had, a great proportion of the time, two sets of men to feed and pay: one coming to the army and the other going from it. From this circumstance—and from the extraordinary waste and consumption of provisions, stores, camp equipage, arms, clothes, and every article incident to irregular troops—it is easy to conceive what an immense increase of public expense has been produced from the source of which I am speaking. I might add the diminution of our agriculture, by calling off at critical seasons the laborers employed in it, as has happened in instances without number.

In the enumeration of articles wasted—I mention clothes—it may be objected that the terms of engagement of the levies do not include this article. But if we want service from the men, particularly in the cold season, we are obliged to supply them notwithstanding; and they leave us before the clothes are half worn out.

But there are evils still more striking that have befallen us. The intervals between the dismission of one army and the collection of another have more than once threatened us with ruin, which, humanly speaking, nothing but the supineness or folly of the enemy could have saved us from. How did our cause totter at the close of '76, when, with little more than two thousand men, we were driven before the enemy through the Jerseys, and obliged to take post on the other side of the Delaware to make a show of covering Philadelphia, while in reality nothing was more easy to them, with a little enterprise and industry, than to make their passage good to that city and dissipate the remaining force, which still kept alive our expiring opposition! What hindered them from dispersing our little army and giving a fatal blow to our affairs during all the subsequent winter, instead of remaining in a state of torpid inactivity and permitting us to hover about their quarters, when we had scarcely troops sufficient to mount the ordinary guards? After having lost two battles and Philadelphia in the following campaign, for want of those numbers and that degree of discipline which we might have acquired by a permanent force in the first instance, in what a cruel and perilous situation did we again find ourselves in the winter of '77 at Valley Forge, within a day's march of the enemy, with little more than a third of their strength, unable to defend our position or retreat from it for the want of the means of transportation? What but the fluctuation of our army enabled the enemy to detach so boldly to the southward in '78 and '79, to take possession of two states, Georgia and South Carolina, while we were obliged here to be idle spectators of their weakness—set at defiance by a garrison of six thousand regular troops, accessible everywhere by a bridge which nature had formed, but of which we were unable to take advantage from still greater weakness, apprehensive even for our own safety? How did the same garrison insult the main army of these states the ensuing spring, and threaten the destruction of all our baggage and stores, saved by a good countenance more than by an ability to defend them? And what will be our situation this winter, our army by the 1st of January diminished to little more than a sufficient garrison for West Point, the enemy at full liberty to ravage the country wherever they please, and leaving a handful of men at New York to undertake expeditions for the reduction of other states, which for want of adequate means of defense will, it is much to be dreaded, add to the number of their conquests and to the examples of our want of energy and wisdom?

The loss of Canada to the Union, and the fate of the brave Montgomery, compelled to a rash attempt by the immediate prospect of being left without troops, might be enumerated in the catalogue of evils that have sprung from this fruitful source.

We not only incur these dangers and suffer these losses for want of a constant force equal to our exigencies, but while we labor under this impediment it is impossible there can ever be any order or economy or system in our finances. If we meet with any severe blow, the great exertions which the moment requires to stop the progress of the misfortune oblige us to depart from general principles to run into any expense or to adopt any expedient, however injurious on a large scale, to procure the force and means which the present emergency demands. Everything is thrown into confusion, and the measures taken to remedy immediate evils perpetuate others. The same is the case if particular conjunctures invite us to offensive operations: we find ourselves unprepared, without troops, without magazines, and with little time to provide them. We are obliged to force our resources by the most burdensome methods to answer the end, and after all it is but half answered. The design is announced by the occasional effort, and the enemy have it in their power to counteract and elude the blow. The prices of everything—men provisions, etc.—are raised to a height to which the revenues of no government, much less ours, would suffice. It is impossible the people can endure the excessive burden of bounties for annual drafts and substitutes increasing at every new experiment. Whatever it might cost them, once for all, to procure men for the war would be a cheap bargain.

I am convinced our system of temporary enlistments has prolonged the war and encouraged the enemy to persevere. Baffled while we had an army in the field, they have been constantly looking forward to the period of its reduction as the period to our opposition and the season of their successes. They have flattered themselves with more than the event has justified; for they believed when one army expired, we should not be able to raise another. Undeceived, however, in this expectation by experience, they still remain convinced, and to me evidently on good grounds, that we must ultimately sink under a system which increases our expense beyond calculation, enfeebles all our measures, affords the most inviting opportunities to the enemy, and wearies and disgusts the people. This has doubtless had great influence in preventing their coming to terms, and will continue to operate in the same way. The debates on the ministerial side have frequently manifested the operation of this motive, and it must in the nature of things have had great weight.

The interposition of neutral powers may lead to a negotiation this winter. Nothing will tend so much to make the Court of London reasonable as the prospect of a permanent army in this country, and a spirit of exertion to support it.

It is time we should get rid of an error which the experience of all mankind has exploded, and which our own experience has dearly taught us to reject—the carrying on a war with militia, or (which is nearly the same thing) temporary levies, against a regular, permanent, and disciplined force. The idea is chimerical, and that we have so long persisted in it is a reflection on the judgment of a nation so enlightened as we are, as well as a strong proof of the empire of prejudice over reason. If we continue in the infatuation, we shall deserve to lose the object we are contending for.

America has been almost amused out of her liberties. We have frequently heard the behavior of the militia extolled upon one and another occasion by men who judge only from the surface, by men who had particular views in misrepresenting, by visionary men whose credulity easily swallowed every vague story in support of a favorite hypothesis. I solemnly declare I never was witness to a single instance that can countenance an opinion of militia or raw troops being fit for the real business of fighting. I have found them useful as light parties to skirmish in the woods, but incapable of making or sustaining a serious attack. This firmness is only acquired by habits of discipline and service. I mean not to detract from the merit of the militia. Their zeal and spirit upon a variety of occasions have entitled them to the highest applause, but it is of the greatest importance we should learn to estimate them rightly. We may expect everything from ours that militia is capable of, but we must not expect from them[15] any services for which regulars alone are fit.

The late Battle of Camden is a melancholy comment upon this doctrine. The militia fled at the first fire and left the continental troops surrounded on every side and overpowered with numbers, to combat for safety instead of victory. The enemy themselves have witnessed to their valor.

An ill effect of short enlistments which I have not yet taken notice of is that the constant fluctuation of their men is one of the sources of disgust to the officers. Just when—by great trouble, fatigue, and vexation (with which the training of recruits is attended)—they have brought their men to some kind of order, they have the mortification to see them go home and to know that the same drudgery is to recommence the next campaign. In regiments so constituted, an officer has neither satisfaction nor credit in his command.

Every motive which can arise from a consideration of our circumstances in a domestic or foreign point of view calls upon us to abandon temporary expedients and substitute something durable, systematic, and substantial. This applies to our civil administration as well as to our military establishment. It is as necessary to give Congress, the common head, sufficient power to direct the common forces as it is to raise an army for the war; but I should go out of my province to expatiate on civil affairs. I cannot forbear adding a few more remarks.

Our finances are in an alarming state of derangement. Public credit is almost arrived at its last stage. The people begin to be dissatisfied with the feeble mode of conducting the war and with the ineffectual burdens imposed upon them, which, though light in comparison with what other nations feel, are from their novelty heavy to them. They lose their confidence in government apace. The army is not only dwindling into nothing, but the discontents of the officers as well as the men have matured to a degree that threatens but too general a renunciation of the service at the end of the campaign. Since January last, we have had registered at headquarters more than one hundred and sixty resignations, besides a number of others that never were regularly reported. I speak of the army in this quarter. We have frequently in the course of the campaign experienced an extremity of want. Our officers are in general indecently defective in clothing. Our men are almost naked, totally unprepared for the inclemency of the approaching season. We have no magazines for the winter. The mode of procuring our supplies is precarious, and all the reports of the officers employed in collecting them are gloomy.

These circumstances conspire to show the necessity of immediately adopting a plan that will give more energy to government, more vigor and more satisfaction to the army. Without it we have everything to fear. I am persuaded of the sufficiency of our resources, if properly directed.

Should the requisitions of Congress by any accident not arrive before the legislature is about to rise, I beg leave to recommend that a plan be devised which is likely to be effectual for raising the men that will be required for the war, leaving it to the *executive* to apply it to the quota which Congress will fix. I flatter myself, however, the requisitions will arrive in time.

The present crisis of our affairs appears to me so serious as to call upon me as a good citizen to offer my sentiments freely for the safety of the republic. I hope the motive will excuse the liberty I have taken. I have the honor to be Your Excellency's Most Obedient and very Humble Servant

To George Mason, October 22, 1780 (Excerpt)

We are without money, and have been so for a long time; without provision and forage, except what is taken by impress; without clothing; and shortly shall be (in a manner) without men. In a word, we have lived upon expedients till we can live no longer, and it may truly be said that the history of this war is a history of false hopes and temporary devices instead of system—and economy which results from it.

If we mean to continue our struggles (and it is to be hoped we shall not relinquish our claims) we must do it upon an entire new plan. We must have a permanent force—not a force that is constantly fluctuating and sliding from under us as a pedestal of ice would leave a statue in a summer's day, involving us in expense that baffles all calculation, an expense which no funds are equal to. We must at the same time contrive ways and means to aid our taxes by loans and put our finances upon a more certain and stable footing than they are at present. Our civil government must likewise undergo a reform: ample powers must be lodged in Congress as the head of the federal Union, adequate to all the purposes of war. Unless these things are done, our efforts will be in vain and only serve to accumulate expense, add to our perplexities, and dissatisfy the people without a prospect of obtaining the prize in view. But these sentiments do not appear well in a hasty letter, without digestion or order. I have not time to give them otherwise, and shall only assure you that they are well meant, however crude they may appear. With sincere Affection I am, Dr Sir Yr most Obedt Servt

Go: Washington

To James Duane, December 26, 1780 (Excerpt)

There are two things (as I have often declared) which in my opinion are indispensably necessary to the well-being and good government of our public affairs. These are: greater powers to Congress and more responsibility and permanency in the executive bodies. If individual states conceive themselves at liberty to reject or alter any act of Congress—which, in a full representation of them, has been solemnly debated and decided on—it will be madness in us to think of prosecuting the war. And if Congress suppose that boards, composed of their own body and always fluctuating, are competent to the great business of war (which requires not only close application but a constant and uniform track of thinking and acting) they will most assuredly deceive themselves. Many, many instances might be adduced in proof of this, but to a mind as observant as yours there is no need to enumerate them. One, however, as we *feelingly* experience it, I shall name. It is the want of clothing, when I have every reason to be convinced that the expense which the public is run to in this article would clothe our army as well as any troops in Europe. In place of which we have innumerable objects of most distressing want.

To John Hancock, Governor of Massachusetts, January 5, 1781

Sir,

It is with extreme anxiety and pain of mind I find myself constrained to inform Your Excellency that the event I have long apprehended would be the consequence of the complicated distresses of the army has at length taken place. On the night of the first instant, a mutiny was excited by the non-commissioned officers and privates of the Pennsylvania line, which soon became so universal as to defy all opposition. In attempting to quell this tumult in the first instance some officers were killed, others wounded, and the lives of several common soldiers lost. Deaf to the arguments, entreaties, and utmost efforts of *all their officers* to stop them, they moved off from Morristown, the place of their cantonments, with their arms and six pieces of artillery; and from accounts just received from General Wayne's aide-de-camp, they were still in a body, on their march to Philadelphia, to demand a redress of grievances. At what point this defection will stop, or how extensive it may prove, God only knows. At present the troops at the important posts in this vicinity remain quiet, not being acquainted with this unhappy and alarming affair, but how long they will remain so cannot be ascertained, as they labor under some of the pressing hardships with the troops who have revolted.

The aggravated calamities and distresses that have resulted from the total want of pay for nearly twelve months, the want of clothing at a severe season, and not unfrequently the want of provisions, are beyond description. The circumstances will now point out much more forcibly what ought to be done than anything that can possibly be said by me on the subject.

It is not within the sphere of my duty to make requisitions, without the authority of Congress, from individual states. But at such a crisis as this, and circumstanced as we are, my own heart will acquit me—and Congress, and the states (eastward of this) whom, for the sake of dispatch, I address, I am persuaded will excuse me—when once for all I give it decidedly as my opinion that it is vain to think an army can be kept together much longer under such a variety of sufferings as ours has experienced, and that—unless some immediate and spirited measures are adopted to furnish at least three months' pay to the troops in money which will be of some value to them, and, at the same time, ways and means are devised to clothe and feed them better (more regularly I mean) than they have been—the worst that can befall us may be expected.

I have transmitted Congress a copy of this letter and have in the most pressing manner requested them to adopt the measure which I have above recommended, or something similar to it; and, as I will not doubt of their compliance, I have thought proper to give you this previous notice that you may be prepared to answer the requisitions.

As I have used every endeavor in my power to avert the evil that has come upon us, so will I continue to exert every mean I am possessed of to prevent an extension of the mischief; but I can neither foretell or be answerable for the issue.

That you may have every information that an officer of rank and abilities can give of the true situation of our affairs and the condition and temper of the troops, I have prevailed upon Brigadier General Knox to be the bearer of this letter. To him I beg leave to refer Your Excellency for many matters which would be too tedious for a letter. I have the honor to be With great esteem & respect Your Excellency's Most Obedt Hble servant

Go: Washington

To Lieutenant Colonel John Laurens, January 15, 1781

Dear Sir,

In compliance with your request, I shall commit to writing the result of our conferences on the present state of American affairs, in which I have given you my ideas with that freedom and explicitness which the objects of your commission,[16] my entire confidence in you, and the exigency demand. To me it appears evident:

1st: That—considering the diffused population of these states, the consequent difficulty of drawing together its resources, the composition and temper of a *part* of its inhabitants, the want of a sufficient stock of national wealth as a foundation for revenue, and the almost total extinction of commerce—the efforts we have been compelled to make for carrying on the war have exceeded the natural abilities of this country and by degrees brought it to a crisis, which render immediate and efficacious succors from abroad indispensable to its safety.

2ndly: That, notwithstanding—from the confusion always attendant on a revolution, from our having had governments to frame and every species of civil and military institution to create, from that inexperience in affairs necessarily incident to a nation in its commencement—some errors may have been committed in the administration of our finances to which a part of our embarrassments are to be attributed, yet they are principally to be ascribed to an essential defect of means: to the want of a sufficient stock of wealth, as mentioned in the first article, which, continuing to operate, will make it impossible by any merely interior exertions to extricate ourselves from those embarrassments, restore public credit, and furnish the funds requisite for the support of the war.

3rdly: That experience has demonstrated the impracticability long to maintain a paper credit without funds for its redemption. The depreciation of our currency was, in the main, a necessary effect of the want of those funds; and its restoration is impossible for the same reason, to which the general diffidence that has taken place among the people is an additional, and in the present state of things, an insuperable obstacle.

4thly: That the mode which for want of money has been substituted for supplying the army, by assessing a proportion of the productions of the earth, has hitherto been found ineffectual, has frequently exposed the army to the most calamitous distress, and from its novelty and incompatibility with ancient habits is regarded by the people as burdensome and oppressive, has excited serious discontents, and, in some places, alarming symptoms of opposition. This mode has, besides, many particular inconveniences which contribute to make it inadequate to our wants, and ineligible but as an auxiliary.

5thly: That from the best estimates of the annual expense of the war, and the annual revenues which these states are capable of affording, there is a large balance to be supplied by public credit. The resource of domestic loans is inconsiderable because there are, properly speaking, few monied men, and the few there are can employ their money more profitably otherwise—added to which, the instability of the currency and the deficiency of funds have impaired the public credit.

6thly: That the patience of the army from an almost uninterrupted series of complicated distress is now nearly exhausted, their discontents matured to an extremity which has recently had very disagreeable consequences, and which demonstrates the absolute necessity of speedy relief—a relief not within the compass of our means. You are too well acquainted with all their sufferings: for want of clothing, for want of provisions, for want of pay.

7thly: That the people being dissatisfied with the mode of supporting the war, there is cause to apprehend evils actually felt in the prosecution may weaken those sentiments which began it, founded not on immediate sufferings but in a speculative apprehension of future sufferings from the loss of their liberties. There is danger that a commercial and free people, little accustomed to heavy burdens, pressed by impositions of a new and odious kind, may not make a proper allowance for the necessity of the conjuncture, and may imagine they have only exchanged one tyranny for another.

8thly: That from all the foregoing considerations result:

1st: The absolute necessity of an immediate, ample, and efficacious succor of money, large enough to be a foundation for substantial arrangements of finance, to revive public credit and give vigor to future operations.

2ndly: The vast importance of a decided effort of the allied arms on this continent, the ensuing campaign, to effectuate once for all the great objects of the alliance: the liberty and independence of these states.

Without the first, we may make a feeble and expiring effort the next campaign, in all probability the period to our opposition. With it, we should be in a condition to continue the war as long as the obstinacy of the enemy might require. The first is essential to the last; both combined would bring the contest to a glorious issue, crown the obligations which America already feels to the magnanimity and generosity of her ally, and perpetuate the Union by all the ties of gratitude and affection, as well as mutual advantage, which alone can render it solid and indissoluble.

9thly: That next to a loan of money, a constant naval superiority on these coasts is the object most interesting. This would instantly reduce the enemy to a difficult defensive, and by removing all prospect of extending their acquisitions would take away the motives for prosecuting the war. Indeed, it is not to be conceived how they could subsist a large force in this country if we had the command of the seas to interrupt the regular transmission of supplies from Europe. This superiority (with an aid of money) would enable us to convert the war into a vigorous offensive. I say nothing of the advantages to the trade of both nations, nor how infinitely it would facilitate our supplies. With respect to us, it seems to be one of *two* deciding points; and it appears, too, to be the interest of our allies, abstracted from the immediate benefits to this country, to transfer the naval war to America. The number of ports friendly to them, hostile to the British; the materials for repairing their disabled ships; the extensive supplies towards the subsistence of their fleet, are circumstances which would give them a palpable advantage in the contest of these seas.

10thly: That an additional succor of troops would be extremely desirable. Besides a reinforcement of numbers; the excellence of the French troops; that perfect discipline and order in the corps already sent, which have so happily tended to improve the respect and confidence of the people for our allies; the conciliating disposition and the zeal for the service which distinguish every rank, sure indications of lasting harmony—all these considerations evince the immense utility of an accession of force to the corps now here. Correspondent with these motives, the enclosed minutes of a conference between their Excellencies the Count de Rochambeau, the Chevalier de Ternay, and myself will inform you that an augmentation to fifteen thousand men was judged expedient for the next campaign; and it has been signified to me that an application has been made to the Court of France to this effect. But if the sending so large a succor of troops should necessarily diminish the pecuniary aid which our allies may be disposed to grant, it were preferable to diminish the aid in men. For the same sum of money which would transport from France and maintain here a body of troops with all the necessary apparatus, being put into our hands to be employed by us would serve to give activity to a larger force within ourselves; and its influence would pervade the whole administration.

11thly: That no nation will have it more in its power to repay what it borrows than this. Our debts are hitherto small. The vast and valuable tracts of unlocated lands; the variety and fertility of climates and soils; the advantages of every kind which we possess for commerce, insure to this country a rapid advancement in population and prosperity, and a certainty, its independence being established, of redeeming in a short term of years the comparatively inconsiderable debts it may have occasion to contract.

That, notwithstanding the difficulties under which we labor and the inquietudes prevailing among the people, there is still a fund of inclination and resource in the country equal to great and continued exertions, provided we have it in our power to stop the progress of disgust by changing the present system and adopting another more consonant with the spirit of the nation, and more capable of activity and energy in public measures, of which a powerful succor of money must be the basis. The people are discontented; but it is with the feeble and oppressive mode of conducting the war, not with the war itself. They are not unwilling to contribute to its support, but they are unwilling to do it in a way that renders private property precarious—a necessary consequence of the fluctuation of the national currency and of the inability of government to perform its engagements, oftentimes coercively made. A large majority are still firmly attached to the independence of these states, abhor a reunion with Great Britain, and are affectionate to the alliance with France; but this disposition cannot supply the place of means customary and essential in war, nor can we rely on its duration amidst the perplexities, oppressions, and misfortunes that attend the want of them.

If the foregoing observations are of any use to you, I shall be happy. I wish you a safe and pleasant voyage, the full accomplishment of your mission, and a speedy return, being with Sentiments of perfect friendship regard and affection. Dr Sir Yr Most Obed Ser

General Orders, January 30, 1781 (Excerpt)

The general returns his thanks to Major General Howe for the judicious measures he pursued, and to the officers and men under his command for the good conduct and alacrity with which they executed his orders for suppressing the late mutiny in a part of the New Jersey line. It gave him inexpressible pain to have been obliged to employ their arms upon such an occasion and convinced that they themselves felt all the reluctance which former affection to fellow soldiers could inspire. He considers the patience with which they endured the fatigues of the march through rough and mountainous roads, rendered almost impassable by the depth of the snow, and the cheerfulness with which they performed every other part of their duty as the strongest proof of their fidelity, attachment to the service, sense of subordination, and abhorrence of the principles which actuated the mutineers in so daring and atrocious a departure from what they owed to their country, to their officers, to their oaths, and to themselves.

The general is deeply sensible of the sufferings of the army. He leaves no expedient unessayed to relieve them, and he is persuaded Congress and the several states are doing everything in their power for the same purpose. But while we look to the public for the fulfillment of its engagements, we should do it with proper allowance for the embarrassments of public affairs. We began a contest for liberty and independence ill provided with the means for war, relying on our own patriotism to supply the deficiency. We expected to encounter many wants and distresses, and we should neither shrink from them when they happen nor fly in the face of law and government to procure redress. There is no doubt the public will in the event do ample justice to men fighting and suffering in its defense. But it is our duty to bear present evils with fortitude, looking forward to the period when our country will have it more in its power to reward our services.

History is full of examples of armies suffering with patience extremities of distress which exceed those we have suffered—and this in the cause of ambition and conquest, not in that of the rights of humanity, of their country, of their families, of themselves. Shall we who aspire to the distinction of a patriot army, who are contending for everything precious in society against everything hateful and degrading in slavery, shall we who call ourselves citizens discover less constancy and military virtue than the mercenary instruments of ambition? Those who in the present instance have stained the honor of the American soldiery and sullied the reputation of patient virtues for which they have been so long eminent can only atone for their pusillanimous defection by a life devoted to a zealous and exemplary discharge of their duty. Persuaded that the greater part were influenced by the pernicious advice of a few who probably have been paid by the enemy to betray their associates, the general is happy in the lenity shown in the execution of only two of the most guilty after compelling the whole to an unconditional surrender. And he flatters himself no similar instance will hereafter disgrace our military history. It can only bring ruin in those who are mad enough to make the attempt, for lenity on any future occasion would be criminal and inadmissible.

To Robert R. Livingston, January 31, 1781

Dear Sir,

The disagreeable events which have taken place in the Pennsylvania and Jersey lines, the general discontent of the army for want of pay, clothing, and provisions, added to the usual course of business (which increases with our perplexities) will, I am persuaded, be admitted as a sufficient apology for my not acknowledging the receipt of your confidential and obliging letter of the 8th till now.

To learn from so good authority as your information that the distresses of the citizens of this state are maturing into complaints which are likely to produce serious consequences is a circumstance as necessary to be known as it is unpleasing to hear—and I thank you for the communication. The committees now forming are, at this crisis, disagreeable things; and if they cannot be counteracted, or diverted from their original purposes, may outrun the views of the well-meaning members of them, and plunge this country into deeper distress and confusion than it has hitherto experienced, though I have no doubt but that the same bountiful Providence which has relieved us in a variety of difficulties heretofore will enable us to emerge from them ultimately—and crown our struggles with success.

To trace these evils to their sources is by no means difficult, and errors once discovered are more than half corrected. This I hope is our case at present. But there can be no radical cure till Congress is vested by the several states with full and ample powers to enact laws for general purposes, and till the executive business is placed in the hands of able men and responsible characters. Requisitions then will be supported by law. Jealousies—and those ruinous delays and ill-timed compliances arising from distrust and the fear of doing more than a sister state, will cease. Business will be properly arranged. System and order will take place, and economy must follow—but not till we have corrected the fundamental errors enumerated above.

It would be no difficult matter to prove that less than half the present expenditures (including certificates) is more than sufficient—if we had money, and these alterations were adopted—to answer all our purposes. Taxes of course would be lessened, the burden would be equal and light, and men sharing a common lot would neither murmur nor despond.

The picture you have drawn of the distresses of the people of this state I am persuaded is true; and I have taken the liberty in a late letter, and in as delicate terms as I could express my sentiments, to hint to Congress the propriety of the policy of leaving the resources of this state and Jersey as a kind of reserve—further than this might bring on me the charge of an intermeddler, till I could speak decisively of my own knowledge.

At all times—and under all circumstances—you will please and honor me by a free communication of your sentiments, as I can with much truth assure you that with the greatest esteem and affection, I am—Dr Sir Yr most obedt, and obliged Servant,

Go: Washington

To Samuel Huntington, President of the Continental Congress, February 3, 1781 (Excerpt)

Sir,

I have on different occasions done myself the honor to represent to Congress the inconveniences arising from the want of a proper gradation of punishments in our military code; but as no determination has been communicated to me, I conclude a multiplicity of business may have diverted their attention from the object. As I am convinced a great part of the vices of our discipline springs from this source, I take the liberty again to renew the subject. The highest corporal punishment we are allowed to give is a hundred lashes; between that and death there are no degrees. Instances daily occurring of offenses for which the former is entirely inadequate, courts martial, to preserve some proportion between the crime and the punishment, are obliged to pronounce sentence of death. Capital sentences on this account become more frequent in our service than in any other, so frequent as to render their execution in most cases inexpedient. And it happens from this that greater offenses often escape punishment while lesser are commonly punished, which cannot but operate as an encouragement to the commission of the former.

The inconveniences of this defect are obvious. Congress are sensible of the necessity of punishment in an army, of the justice and policy of a due proportion between the crime and the penalty, and of course of the necessity of proper degrees in the latter. I shall therefore content myself with observing that it appears to me indispensable there should be an extension of the present corporal punishment, and also that it would be useful to authorize courts martial to sentence delinquents to labor at public works—perhaps even for some crimes, particularly desertion, to transfer them from the land to the sea service, where they have less opportunity to indulge their inconstancy. A variety in punishments is of utility as well as a proportion.

The number of lashes may either be indefinite, left to the discretion of the court to fix, or limited to a larger number. In this case I would recommend five hundred.

There is one evil, however, which I shall particularize, resulting from the imperfection of our regulations in this respect. It is the increase of arbitrary punishments. Officers finding discipline cannot be maintained by a regular course of proceeding are tempted to use their own discretion, which sometimes occasions excesses, to correct which the interests of discipline will not permit much rigor. Prompt and therefore arbitrary punishments are not to be avoided in an army, but the necessity for them will be more or less in proportion as the military laws have more or less rigor.

To John Sullivan, February 4, 1781

Dear Sir,

Colonel Armand delivered me your favor of the 29th ultimo last evening, and I thank you for the several communications contained in it. The measure adopted by Congress of appointing a minister of war, finance, and for foreign affairs I think a very wise one. To give efficacy to it, proper characters will, no doubt, be chosen to conduct the business of these departments. How far Colonel Hamilton—of whom you ask my opinion as a financier—has turned his thoughts to that particular study, I am unable to answer because I never entered upon a discussion of this post with him. But this I can venture to advance from a thorough knowledge of him, that there are few men to be found of his age who have a more general knowledge than he possesses, and none whose soul is more firmly engaged in the cause or who exceeds him in probity and sterling virtue.

I am clearly in sentiment with you that our cause only became distressed—and apparently desperate—from an improper management of it, and that errors once discovered are more than half amended. I have no doubt of our abilities or resources, but we must not slumber nor sleep. They never will be drawn forth if we do. Nor will violent exertions which subside with the occasion answer our purposes. It is a provident foresight, a proper arrangement of business, system, and order in the execution that is to be productive of that economy which is to defeat the efforts and hopes of Great Britain. And I am happy—thrice happy, on private as well as public account—to find that these are in train. For it will ease my shoulders of an[17] immense burden which the deranged and perplexed situation of our affairs, and the distresses of every department of the army which concentered in the commander-in-chief, had placed upon them.

I am not less pleased to hear that Maryland has acceded to the Confederation, and that Virginia has relinquished its claim to the land west of the Ohio—which for fertility of soil, pleasantry of clime, and other natural advantages is equal to any known tract of country in the universe of the same extent taking the Great Lakes for its northern boundary.

I wish most devoutly a happy completion to your plan of finance (which you say is near finished)—and much success to your scheme of borrowing coined specie and plate. But in what manner do you propose to apply the latter—as a fund to redeem its value in paper to be emitted, or to coin it? If the latter it will add one more to a thousand other reasons which might be offered in proof of the necessity of vesting legislative or dictatorial powers in Congress to make laws of general utility for the purposes of war etc., that they might prohibit under the pains and penalty of death specie and provisions going into the enemy for goods. The traffic with New York is immense. Individual states will not make it felony, lest (among other reasons) it should not become general; and nothing short of it will ever check, much less stop, a practice which, at the same time that it serves to drain us of our provisions and specie, removes the barrier between us and the enemy, corrupts the morals of our people by a lucrative traffic and by degrees weakens the opposition, affords a mean to obtain regular and perfect intelligence of everything among us, while even in this respect we benefit nothing from a fear of discovery. Men of all descriptions are now indiscriminately engaging in it: Whig, Tory, speculator. By its being practiced by those of the latter class, in a manner with impunity, men who, two or three year ago, would have shuddered at the idea of such connections now pursue it with avidity and reconcile it to themselves (in which their profits plead powerfully) upon a principle of equality with the Tory—who, being actuated by principle (favorable to us), and knowing that a forfeiture of the goods to the informer was all he had to dread, and that this was to be eluded by an agreement to inform against each another, went into the measure without risk.

This is a digression, but the subject is of so serious a nature, and so interesting to our well-being as a nation, that I never expect to see a happy termination of the war, nor great national concerns well conducted in peace, till there is something more than a recommendatory power in Congress. It is not possible in time of war that business can be conducted well without it. The last words, therefore, of my letter and the first wish of my heart concur in favor of it. I am with much esteem and respect Dr Sir Yr obt & Affe Servt

Go: W——n

General Orders, February 18, 1781 (Excerpt)

The general cannot forbear remarking with regret that it is too common for officers on trial to indulge themselves in a vein of invective and abuse as inconsistent with decency as with the respect they owe to themselves and to others. He is sorry that Major Reid has so far forgot himself as to have erred in a more than ordinary degree in this article. The delicacy of an officer's character should make him as delicate in expressing his resentment as in defending his honor.

To Philip Schuyler, February 20, 1781 (Excerpt)

Dear Sir,

The perplexed state of our military affairs generally, and the embarrassments with which I am (or more properly speaking, have been, for they are not so great now as they were) surrounded in this quarter, must apologize for my not acknowledging the receipt of your obliging favor of the 21st ultimo sooner.

It is with peculiar pleasure I hear that Maryland has acceded to the Confederation, and that Virginia has yielded her claim to the country west of Ohio. Great good, I hope, will result from these measures. The first will undoubtedly enable Congress to speak with more decision in their requisitions of the respective states, without which it is physically impossible to prosecute the war with success, great as our expenses are. The other will smooth the way and aid taxation by reconciling jarring interests, removing jealousies, and establishing a fund.

There are other measures lately adopted in Congress with which I am highly pleased: the establishing of ministers (in place of boards) for the departments of war, finance, and foreign affairs. Proper powers to, and a judicious choice of men to fill, these departments will soon lead us to system, order, and economy, without which our affairs, already on the brink of ruin, would soon have been passed redemption. I enjoy by anticipation the benefit of these resolves. I hear with infinite pleasure (though no nomination has yet taken place) that you are generally spoken of for the department of war. At the same time, I learn with pain from Colonel Hamilton that your acceptance of it is doubtful if the choice should fall on you.

I am perfectly aware of all your objections—I feel their force—but they ought not to prevail. Our affairs are brought to an awful crisis. Nothing will recover them but the vigorous exertions of men of abilities who know our wants and the best means of supplying them. These, sir, without a compliment, I think you possess. Why, then, the department being necessary, should you shrink from the duty of it? The greater the chaos, the greater will be your merit in bringing forth order. And to expect to tread the different walks of public life without envy and its concomitants is more than has yet fallen to the lot of humankind.

To express my wishes on the subject, under the prospect of your election, is the cause of my giving you the trouble of a letter at this moment, as I should be exceedingly concerned at your refusal to become the minister of war if the choice should fall on you.

To John Parke Custis, February 28, 1781 (Excerpt)

Dear Custis,

If you will accept a hasty letter in return for yours of last month, I will devote a few moments for this purpose and confine myself to an interesting point or two.

I do not suppose that so young a senator, as you are, little versed in political disquisition, can yet have much influence in a populous assembly composed of gentlemen of various talents and of different views. But it is in your power to be punctual in your attendance (and duty to the trust reposed in you exacts it of you), to hear dispassionately, and determine coolly all great questions.

To be disgusted at the decision of questions because they are not consonant to our own ideas, and to withdraw ourselves from public assemblies, or to neglect our attendance at them upon suspicion that there is a party formed who are inimical to our cause and to the true interest of our country, is wrong, because these things may originate in a difference of opinion. But supposing the fact is otherwise and that our suspicions are well founded, it is the indispensable duty of every patriot to counteract them by the most steady and uniform opposition. This advice is the result of information that you and others, being dissatisfied at the proceedings of the Virginia Assembly and thinking your attendance of little avail (as there is always a majority for measures which you and a minority conceive to be repugnant to the interest of your country), are indifferent about the assembly.

The next and I believe the last thing I shall have time to touch upon is our military establishment. And here, if I thought my conviction of having a permanent force had not ere this flashed upon every man's mind, I could write a volume in support of the utility of it; for no day nor hour arrives unaccompanied with news of some loss, some expense, or some misfortune consequent of the want of it. No operation of war, offensive or defensive, can be carried on for any length of time without it. No funds are adequate to the supplies of a fluctuating army, though it may go under the denomination of a regular one; much less are they competent to the support of militia. In a word, for it is unnecessary to go into all the reasons the subject will admit of, we have brought a cause which might have been happily terminated years ago by the adoption of proper measures to the verge of ruin by temporary enlistments and a reliance on militia. The sums expended in bounties, waste of arms, consumption of military stores, provisions, camp utensils etc., to say nothing of clothing, which temporary soldiers are always receiving and always in want of, are too great for the resources of any nation and prove the fallacy and danger of temporary expedients, which are no more than mushrooms and of as short duration, but leave a sting (that is, a debt which is continually revolving upon us) behind them.

It must be a settled plan, founded in system, order, and economy, that is to carry us triumphantly through the war. Supineness, and indifference to the distresses and cries of a sister state when danger is far off,[18] and a general but momentary resort to arms when it comes to our doors, are equally impolitic and dangerous, and prove the necessity of a controlling power in Congress to regulate and direct all matters of *general* concern. Without it the great business of war never can be conducted at all. While the powers of Congress are only recommendatory, while one state yields obedience and another refuses it, while a third mutilates and adopts the measure in part only, and all vary in time and manner, it is scarcely possible our affairs should prosper or that anything but disappointment can follow the best concerted plan. The willing states are almost ruined by their exertions, distrust and jealousy succeeds to it, hence proceed neglects and ill-timed compliances (one state waiting to see what another will do). This thwarts all our measures after a heavy though ineffectual expense is incurred.

Do not these things show, then, in the most striking point of view the indispensable necessity, the great and good policy, of each state's sending its ablest and best men to Congress—men who have a perfect understanding of the constitution of their country, of its policy and interests—and of vesting that body with competent powers? Our independence depends upon it. Our respectability and consequence in Europe depend upon it. Our greatness as a nation hereafter depends upon it. The fear of giving sufficient powers to Congress for the purposes I have mentioned is futile. Without it, our independence fails and each assembly under its present constitution will be annihilated, and we must once more return to the government of G. Britain—and be made to kiss the rod preparing for our correction. A nominal head, which at present is but another name for Congress, will no longer do. That honorable body, after hearing the interests and views of the several states fairly discussed and explained by their respective representatives, must dictate, not merely recommend and leave it to the states afterwards to do as they please—which, as I have observed before, is in many cases, to do nothing at all.

To Reverend Joseph Willard, March 22, 1781

Sir,

I am much indebted to you for announcing my election as a member of the American Academy of Arts and Sciences. I feel myself particularly honored by this relation to a society whose efforts to promote useful knowledge will, I am persuaded, acquire them a high reputation in the literary world.

I entreat you to present my warmest acknowledgments to that respectable body and to assure them that I shall with zeal embrace every opportunity of seconding their laudable views and manifesting the exalted sense I have of the institution.

The arts and sciences, essential to the prosperity of the state and to the ornament and happiness of human life, have a primary claim to the encouragement of every lover of his country and mankind.

For the polite and flattering terms in which you have been pleased to convey the sentiments of the Academy I beg you to accept my grateful thanks and the assurances of my being with great esteem & respect Sir Yr Most Obedt & Oblig'd Servt

Go: Washington

To Major General John Armstrong, March 26, 1781 (Excerpt)

We ought not to look back unless it is to derive useful lessons from past errors, and for the purpose of profiting by dear bought experience. To inveigh against things that are past and irremediable is unpleasing; but to steer clear of the shelves and rocks we have struck upon is the part of wisdom, equally incumbent on political as other men who have their own little bark, or that of others, to navigate through the intricate paths of life, or the trackless ocean, to the haven of security and rest.

Our affairs are brought to an awful crisis that the hand of Providence, I trust, may be more conspicuous in our deliverance. The many remarkable interpositions of the divine government in the hours of our deepest distress and darkness have been too luminous to suffer me to doubt the happy issue of the present contest. But the period for its accomplishment may be too far distant for a person of my years, whose morning and evening hours, and every moment (unoccupied by business), pant for retirement and for those domestic and rural enjoyments which in my estimation far surpass the highest pageantry of this world.

To John Mathews, June 7, 1781 (Excerpt)

The freedom of your communications is highly pleasing to me. The portrait you have drawn of our affairs is strictly agreeable to the life; and you do me but justice in supposing that my mind is fortified against, or rather prepared for, the most distressing accounts that can be given of them. It would not be the part of friendship, therefore, to conceal any circumstance from an unwillingness to give pain, especially as the knowledge of them to a man determined not to sink under the weight of perplexities may be of the utmost importance. But we must not despair. The game is yet in our own hands. To play it well is all we have to do, and I trust the experience of error will enable us to act better in future. A cloud may yet pass over us. Individuals may be ruined and the country at large or particular states undergo temporary distress. But certain I am that it is in our power to bring the war to a happy conclusion.

To the Magistrates of the City of Philadelphia, December 17, 1781

Gentlemen,

I return you my thanks for this very polite and affectionate address.

As I have ever considered a due support of civil authority essential to the preservation of that liberty for which we are contending, I have from duty as well as from inclination endeavored, so far as possible, to avoid the least violation of it; and I am happy to find that my conduct has met the approbation of those who are appointed guardians of the rights of a free people.

I feel myself highly obliged by your assurance that it will be the pleasing employment of the citizens to render my residence among them agreeable. It shall be my study to merit so kind a mark of their attention and to approve myself. Gentm Yr Most Obedt & Most Hble Servt

Go: Washington

To Thomas Chittenden, January 1, 1782 (Excerpt)

It is not my business, neither do I think it necessary now, to discuss the origin of the right of a number of inhabitants to that tract of country formerly distinguished by the name of the New Hampshire Grants and now known by that of Vermont. I will take it for granted that their right was good, because Congress, by their resolve of the 7th of August, imply it, and by that of the 21st are willing fully to confirm it, provided the new state is confined to certain described bounds. It appears, therefore, to me that the dispute of boundary is the only one that exists, and that that being removed, all further difficulties would be removed also, and the matter terminated to the satisfaction of all parties. Now I would ask you candidly whether the claim of the people of Vermont was not for a long time confined solely or very nearly to that tract of country which is described in the resolve of Congress of the 21st of August last, and whether, agreeable to the tenor of your own letter to me, the late extension of your claim upon New Hampshire and New York was not a more political maneuver than one in which you conceived yourselves justifiable. If my first question be answered in the affirmative, it certainly bars your[19] new claim; and if my second be well founded, your end is answered and you have nothing to do but withdraw your jurisdiction to the confines of your old limits and obtain an acknowledgment of independence and sovereignty, under the resolve of the 21st of August, for so much territory as does not interfere with the ancient established bounds of New York, New Hampshire, and Massachusetts. I persuade myself you will see and acquiesce in the reason, the justice, and indeed the necessity of such a decision.

You must consider, sir, that the point now in dispute is of the utmost political importance to the future union and peace of this great country. The state of Vermont, if acknowledged, will be the first new one admitted into the confederacy and, if suffered to encroach upon the ancient established boundaries of the adjacent ones, will serve as a precedent for others, which it may hereafter be expedient to sell off to make the same unjustifiable demands. Thus, in my private opinion, while it behooves the delegates of the states now confederated to do ample justice to a body of people sufficiently respectable by their numbers and entitled by other claims to be admitted into that confederation, it becomes them also to attend to the interests of their constituents and see that under the appearance of justice to one they do not materially injure the rights of others. I am apt to think this is the prevailing opinion of Congress and that your late extension of claim has, upon the principles I have above mentioned, rather diminished than increased your friends, and that if such extension should be persisted in it will be made a common cause and not considered as only affecting the rights of those states immediately interested in the loss of territory, a loss of too serious a nature not to claim the attention of any people.

There is no calamity within the compass of my foresight which is more to be dreaded than a necessity of coercion on the part of Congress, and consequently every endeavor should be used to prevent the execution of so disagreeable a measure. It must involve the ruin of that state against which the resentment of the others is pointed.

I will only add a few words upon the subject of the negotiations which have been carried on between you and the enemy in Canada and in New York. I will take it for granted, as you assert it, that they were so far innocent that there was never any serious intention of joining Great Britain in their attempts to subjugate your country. But it has had this certain bad tendency: it has served to give some ground to that delusive opinion of the enemy, and upon which they in great measure found their hopes of success, that they have numerous friends among us who only want a proper opportunity to show themselves openly, and that internal disputes and feuds will soon break us in pieces, at the same time the seeds of distrust and jealousy are scattered among ourselves by a conduct of this kind. If you are sincere in your professions, these will be additional motives for accepting the terms which have been offered (and which appear to me equitable) and thereby convincing the common enemy that all their expectations of disunion are vain, and that they have been worsted at their weapon: deception.

As you unbosomed yourself to me, I thought I had the greater right of speaking my sentiments openly and candidly to you. I have done so, and if they should produce the effects which I most sincerely wish, that of an honorable and amicable adjustment of a matter which, if carried to hostile lengths, may destroy the future happiness of my country, I shall have attained my end, while the enemy will be defeated of theirs. Believe me to be with great respect Sir Your most Obt & hume Servt

G. Washington

Circular to the States, January 31, 1782 (Excerpt)

It will, I flatter myself, be unnecessary to recapitulate all the arguments I made use of in the circular letter I had the honor to address to the governors of the several states at the close of the campaign of 1780, in which it must be remembered I took the liberty to urge, from the knowledge I had of our affairs and a series of experience, the policy, the expediency, the necessity of recruiting the army as the only probable means of bringing the war to a speedy and happy conclusion. If those arguments had any influence at that time, if the consequent exertions were crowned with any success, if the present crisis exhibits new and more forcible inducements for still greater efforts, let me point Your Excellency to these considerations. And especially let me recommend, in the warmest terms, that all the fruits of the successes that have been obtained the last campaign may not be thrown away by an inglorious winter of languor and inactivity.

However, at this advanced stage of the war it might seem to be an insult upon the understanding to suppose a long train of reasoning necessary to prove that a respectable force in the field is essential to the establishment of our liberties and independence. Yet, as I am apprehensive the prosperous issue of the combined operation in Virginia may have (as is too common in such cases) the pernicious tendency of lulling the country into a lethargy of inactivity and security, and as I feel my own reputation, as well as the interest, the honor, the glory, and happiness of my country intimately concerned in the event, I will ask the indulgence to speak the more freely on those accounts, and to make some of the observations which the present moment seems to suggest: That the broken and perplexed state of the enemy's affairs, and the successes of the last campaign on our part, ought to be a powerful incitement for vigorous preparations for the next—that, unless we exert ourselves strenuously to profit by these successes, we shall not only lose all the solid advantages that might be derived from them, but we shall become contemptible in our own eyes, in the eyes of our enemy, in the opinion of posterity, and even in the estimation of the whole world, which will consider us as a nation unworthy of prosperity, because we know not how to make a right use of it—that, although we cannot, by the best concerted plans, absolutely command success, although the race is not always to the swift or the battle to the strong, yet, without presumptuously waiting for miracles to be wrought in our favor, it is our *indispensable duty*, with the deepest gratitude to Heaven for the past and humble confidence in its smiles on our future operations, to make use of all the means in our power for our defense and security—that this period is particularly important, because no circumstances since the commencement of the war have been so favorable to the recruiting service as the present, and because it is to be presumed, from the increase of population and the brilliant prospects before us, it is actually in our power to complete the army before the opening of the campaign—that, however flattering these prospects may be, much still remains to be done, which cannot probably be effected unless the army is recruited to the establishment, and consequently the continuance or termination of the war seems principally to rest on the vigor and decision of the states in this interesting point—and finally, that it is our first object of policy under every supposable or possible case to have a powerful army early in the field: for we must suppose the enemy are either disposed "to prosecute the war, or enter into a negotiation for peace"—there is no other alternative. On the former supposition, a respectable army becomes necessary to counteract the enemy and to prevent the accumulating expenses of a lingering war. On the latter, nothing but a decidedly superior force can enable us boldly to claim our rights and dictate the law at the pacification. So that, whatever the disposition of the enemy may be, it is evidently our only interest and economy to act liberally and exert ourselves greatly during the present winter, to cut off at once all the expenses of the war by putting a period to it.

And soon might that day arrive, soon might we hope to enjoy all the blessings of peace, if we could see again the same animation in the cause of our country inspire every breast, the same passion for freedom and military glory impel our youths to the field, and the same disinterested patriotism pervade every rank of men, as was conspicuous at the commencement of this glorious revolution. And I am persuaded only some great occasion was wanting, such as the present moment exhibits, to rekindle the latent sparks of that patriotic fire into a generous flame, to rouse again the unconquerable spirit of liberty, which has sometimes seemed to slumber for a while, into the full vigor of action.

I cannot now conclude this letter without expressing my full expectation that the several states, animated with the noblest principles, and convinced of the policy of complying faithfully with the requisitions, will be only emulous which shall be foremost in furnishing its quota of men; that the calculations of the numbers wanted to fill the deficiency may be[20] so ample, as (allowing for all the casualties and deductions) will be sufficient certainly to complete the battalions; that the measures for this purpose may be so explicit, pointed, and energetic as will inevitably furnish the recruits in season; and that such checks may be established to prevent impositions as to the quality of the men, that no recruits may be accepted but those who are in fact able-bodied and effective. Should any of a different description be sent to the army, they must be rejected, the expenses thrown away, and the service insured, though others are required to fill their places—for it is only deceiving ourselves with having a nominal instead of a real force, and consuming the public provisions and clothing to no effect, by attempting to impose decrepit and improper men or boys upon us as soldiers.

To Philip Schuyler, February 6, 1782 (Excerpt)

Dear Sir,

I have received your favor of the 25th of January enclosing the copy of your letter of the 22nd of October to Major Stark, which, agreeably to your desire, I return by this conveyance. The arguments and reflections respecting the dispute of the Vermontese made use of in that letter appeared so just as well as political as to be particularly calculated to heal the unhappy disturbances and produce a reconciliation. This is one of the many proofs you have given of your ardent desire to put a period to internal contention and unite all the separate and jarring interests in prosecuting the great common cause of America.

I have shown yours of the 21st ultimo to, and conferred with, the minister of foreign affairs. My sentiments, in general, respecting the necessity of perfect unanimity among ourselves, in order to give energy and decision to our collective efforts against the enemy, are too well known to be insisted upon. For I have had frequent occasion to repeat that it was my most fervent wish that all grounds of jealousy and dispute between any districts of inhabitants of the United States which were at variance might be removed by an amicable adjustment of their differences, and that, in my opinion, moderate measures (so long as they can be pursued with propriety) are much more likely than violent ones to produce such a salutary effect. If therefore my public advice in my late circular letter, or my private opinion, which has been given without reserve on every occasion, can be of any avail I am confident the consideration of all other matters would be swallowed up in, or made subservient to, the general good of the whole. But as it has ever been a point of delicacy with me, while acting only in a military character, not to interfere in the civil concerns of the continent or the legislatures, except where they are intimately connected with military matters, I should not think myself at liberty, without deviating from that rule, to intermeddle so far as to dictate particular modes of accommodation (however earnestly I desire it may be effected), especially on a subject which has been under the immediate consideration of Congress itself, whose directions it is my duty as well as inclination to be guided by.

To Major General Alexander McDougall, March 2, 1782

Sir,

I received yesterday your letters of the 8th and 9th of February and have duly noticed the contents of them.

Although the first order for holding the court martial for your trial directed the court to assemble at West Point, yet by an after order of the same day (which I am informed was regularly transmitted from the orderly officer) permission was given for it to be holden at West Point or some convenient place in its vicinity. This was done solely for the greater convenience of all concerned, and I hoped the spirit of accommodating one another would have prevailed so far as to have prevented any trouble on that account.

I have written to General Heath to cause copies of such returns and official papers to be furnished to you as may be necessary in the course of the trial; by this means the difficulty on that head will be obviated.

It would be a matter of great concern to me that a practice should prevail of publishing to the world the opinions which are given in councils of war, as I have always considered the transactions on such occasions to be under the inviolable sanction of secrecy and honor; however, if you judge a copy of the minutes of the council of war, which was held on the 12th of September 1776, essential to your defense, I shall comply with your request, and have given directions to Colonel Varick, my recording secretary, for that purpose. I am Sir Your most Obt Ser.

Go: Washington

To Benjamin Harrison, Governor of Virginia, March 10, 1782 (Excerpt)

Dear Sir,

I sincerely sympathize with you in the arduous task imposed upon you as first magistrate of the state of Virginia, in consequence of the present distressed and embarrassed situation of affairs, which you so pathetically describe in your letter of the 15th of February. For it is well known from experience that in times of war and public calamity, whoever is engaged in the management of public affairs must share largely in the perplexities and troubles of them; but at the same time it must be remembered, besides the gratification which results from a consciousness of having done our duty faithfully, that to struggle nobly with misfortunes, to combat difficulties with intrepidity, and finally to surmount the obstacles which opposed us are stronger proofs of merit, and give a fairer title to reputation, than the brightest scenes of tranquility or the sunshine of prosperity could ever have afforded.

To James McHenry, March 12, 1782 (Excerpt)

Never since the commencement of the present revolution has there been, in my judgment, a period when vigorous measures were more consonant with sound policy than the present. The speech of the British king, and the addresses of the Lords and Commons, are evincive proofs to my mind of two things: namely, their wishes to prosecute the American war and their fears of the consequences. My opinion therefore of the matter is that the minister will obtain supplies for the current year, prepare vigorously for another campaign, and then prosecute the war or treat of peace as circumstances and fortuitous events may justify, and that nothing will contribute more to the first than a relaxation or apparent supineness on the part of these states. The debates upon the address evidently prove what I have here advanced to be true. For these addresses, as explained, are meant to answer any purpose the ministers may have in view. What madness, then, can be greater, or policy and economy worse, than to let the enemy again rise upon our folly and want of exertion? Shall we not be justly chargeable for all the blood and treasure which shall be wasted in a lingering war procrastinated by the false expectation of peace or timid measures for the prosecution of it? Surely we shall. And much is it to be lamented that our endeavors do not at all times accord with our wishes. Each state is anxious to see the end of our warfare accomplished but shrinks when it is called upon for the means, and either withholds them altogether or grants them in such a way as to defeat the end! Such, it is to be feared, will be the case in many instances respecting the requisitions of men and money. I have the pleasure, however, to inform you that the assembly of this state, now sitting, have passed their supply bill without a dissenting voice. And this, a laudable spirit, seems to pervade all the members of that body. But I fear notwithstanding they will be deficient of their quota of men. It is idle at this late period of the war, when enthusiasm is cooled if not done away, when the minds of that class of men who are proper subjects for soldiers are poisoned by the high bounties which have been given, and the knowledge of the distresses of the army so generally diffused through every state, to suppose that our battalions can be completed by voluntary enlistment. The attempt is vain, and we are only deceiving ourselves and injuring the cause by making the experiment. There is no other *effectual* method to get men suddenly but that of classing the people and polling each class to furnish a regiment. Here every man is interested; every man becomes a recruiting officer. If our necessity for men did not press, I should prefer the mode of voluntary enlistment to all others to obtain them. As it does, I am sure it will not answer and that the season for enterprise will be upon us long ere we are ready for the field.

To Colonel Lewis Nicola, May 22, 1782

Sir,

With a mixture of great surprise and astonishment I have read with attention the sentiments you have submitted to my perusal. Be assured, sir, no occurrence in the course of the war has given me more painful sensations than your information of there being such ideas existing in the army as you have expressed and I must view with abhorrence and reprehend with severity. For the present, the communication of them will rest in my own bosom, unless some further agitation of the matter shall make a disclosure necessary.

 I am much at a loss to conceive what part of my conduct could have given encouragement to an address which to me seems big with the greatest mischiefs that can befall my country. If I am not deceived in the knowledge of myself, you could not have found a person to whom your schemes are more disagreeable. At the same time, in justice to my own feeling I must add that no man possesses a more sincere wish to see ample justice done to the army than I do; and as far as my powers and influence, in a constitutional way, extend, they shall be employed to the utmost of my abilities to effect it, should there be any occasion. Let me conjure you, then, if you have any regard for your country, concern for yourself or posterity, or respect for me, to banish these thoughts from your mind and never communicate, as from yourself or anyone else, a sentiment of the like nature. With esteem I am Sir Yr Most Obedt Servt

Go: Washington

The foregoing is an exact copy of a letter which we sealed and sent off to Colonel Nicola at the request of the writer of it.

D. Humphrys, Aide-de-Camp
Jonathan Trumbull, Junior Secretary

To Archibald Cary, June 15, 1782 (Excerpt)

It gives me much pleasure to learn from so good authority as your pen that the Assembly of Virginia is better composed than it has been for several years. Much I think may be expected from it. The path we are to tread is certainly a plain one. The object is full in our view, but it will not come to us. We must work our way to it by proper advances, and the means of doing this is men and money. In vain is it to expect that our aim is to be accomplished by fond wishes for peace. And equally ungenerous as fruitless will it be for one state to depend upon another to bring this to pass; for, if I may be allowed to speak figuratively, our assemblies in politics are to be compared to the wheels of a clock in mechanics. The whole for the general purposes of war should be set in motion by the great wheel (Congress), and if all will do their parts the machine works easy. But a failure in one disorders the whole, and without the large one (which set the whole in motion) nothing can be done. It is by the united wisdom and exertions of the whole, in Congress, who, I presume, do justice to all (but if they fail by being disproportionate in the first instance, it should in my opinion be sought for and remedied in the second, rather than *derange* the whole business of a campaign by the delays incident to contention) that we are to depend upon. Without this, we are no better than a rope of sand and are as easily broken asunder.

I write thus openly and freely to you, my dear sir, because I pant for retirement and am persuaded that an end of our warfare is not to be obtained but by vigorous exertions. The subjugation of America, so far at least as to hold it in a dependent state, is of too much importance to Great Britain to yield the palm to us whilst her resources exist, or our inactivity, want of system, or dependence upon other powers or upon one another prevail. I can truly say that the first wish of my soul is to return speedily into the bosom of that country which gave me birth, and in the sweet enjoyment of domestic pleasures and the company of a few friends to end my days in quiet, when I shall be called from this stage. With great truth and sincerity I am Dr Sir Yr Obedt & Affecte Sev.

Go: Washington

To John Laurens, July 10, 1782 (Excerpt)

I must confess that I am not at all astonished at the failure of your plans.[21] That spirit of freedom which at the commencement of this contest would have gladly sacrificed everything to the attainment of its object has long since subsided, and every selfish passion has taken its place. It is not the public but the private interest which influences the generality of mankind, nor can the Americans any longer boast an exception. Under these circumstances it would rather have been surprising if you had succeeded, nor will you, I fear, succeed better in Georgia.

To Elkanah Watson, August 10, 1782

Gentlemen,

The Masonic ornaments which accompanied your brotherly address of the 23rd of January last, though elegant in themselves, were rendered more valuable by the flattering sentiments and affectionate manner in which they were presented.

If my endeavors to avert the evil with which this country was threatened by a deliberate plan of tyranny should be crowned with the success that is wished, the praise is due to the *Grand Architect* of the Universe, who did not see fit to suffer his superstructures and justice to be subjected to the ambition of the princes of this world, or to the rod of oppression in the hands of any power upon earth.

For your affectionate vows, permit me to be grateful and offer mine for true brothers in all parts of the world, and to assure you of the sincerity with which I am Yrs

Go: Washington

To James McHenry, September 12, 1782 (Excerpt)

Our prospect of peace is vanishing. The death of the Marquis of Rockingham has given a shock to the new administration and disordered its whole system. Fox, Burke, Lord John Cavendish, Lord Keppel (and I believe others) have left it. Earl Shelburne takes the lead as first lord of the treasury, to which office he was appointed by the king in the instant the vacancy happened by the death of Lord Rockingham. This nobleman—Lord Shelburne, I mean—declares that the sun of Great Britain will set the moment American independency is acknowledged and that no man has ever heard him give an assent to the measure. On the other hand, the Duke of Richmond asserts that the ministry, of which Lord Shelburne is one, came into office pledged to each other, and upon the express condition that America should be declared independent, that he will watch him, and the moment he finds him departing therefrom, he will quit administration and give it every opposition in his power. That the king will push the war as long as the nation will find men or money admits not of a doubt in my mind. The whole tenor of his conduct, as well as his last proroguing speech on the 11th of July, plainly indicates it and shows in a clear point of view the impolicy of relaxation on our parts. If we are wise, let us prepare for the worst. There is nothing which will so soon produce a speedy and honorable peace as a state of preparation for war, and we must either do this or lay our account for a patched up inglorious peace, after all the toil, blood, and treasure we have spent. This has been my uniform opinion, a doctrine I have endeavored, amidst the torrent of expectation of an approaching peace, to inculcate. The event, I am sure, will justify me in it. With much truth I am Dr Sir Yr Affecte Hble Servt

Go: Washington

To Thomas Paine, September 18, 1782 (Excerpt)

The measures and the policy of the enemy are at present in great perplexity and embarrassments. But I have my fears whether their necessities (which are the only operating motive with them) are yet arrived to that point which must drive them unavoidably into what they will esteem disagreeable and dishonorable terms of peace—such, for instance, as an absolute, unequivocal admission of American independence on the terms upon which she can accept it.

For this reason, added to the obstinacy of the king, and the probable consonant principles of some of his principal ministers, I have not so full confidence in the success of the present negotiation for peace as some gentlemen entertain.

Should events prove my jealousies to be ill-founded, I shall make myself happy under the mistake, consoling myself with the idea of having erred on the safest side, and enjoying with as much satisfaction as any of my countrymen the pleasing issue of our severe contest.

To Major General Nathanael Greene, September 23, 1782 (Excerpt)

The situation of politics, I mean European, is upon so precarious a footing that I really know not what account to give you of them. Negotiations were still going on at Paris the middle of July, but the prospects of a peace were checked by the death of the Marquis of Rockingham. Doctor Franklin's laconic description of the temper of the British nation seems most apt. They are, says he, unable to carry on the war and too proud to make peace.

To Benjamin Lincoln, Secretary at War, October 2, 1782

My Dear Sir,

Painful as the task is to describe the dark side of our affairs, it sometimes becomes a matter of indispensable necessity. Without disguise or palliation, I will inform you candidly of the discontents which, at this moment, prevail universally throughout the army.

The complaint of evils which they suppose almost remediless are the total want of money or the means of existing from one day to another; the heavy debts they have already incurred; the loss of credit; the distress of their families (i.e. such as are married) at home, and the prospect of poverty and misery before them. It is vain, sir, to suppose that military men will acquiesce *contentedly* with bare rations when those in the civil walk of life (unacquainted with half the hardships they endure) are regularly paid the emoluments of office. While the human mind is influenced by the same passions and has the same inclinations to indulge, it cannot be. A military man has the same turn to sociability as a person in civil life. He conceives himself equally called upon to live up to his rank, and his pride is hurt when circumstances restrain him. Only conceive, then, the mortification they (even the general officers) must suffer when they cannot invite a French officer, a visiting friend, or traveling acquaintance to a better repast than stinking whiskey (and not always that) and a bit of beef without vegetable will afford them.

The officers also complain of other hardships which they think might and ought to be remedied without delay, viz. the stopping promotions where there have been vacancies open for a long time, the withholding commissions from those who are justly entitled to them and have warrants or certificates of their appointments from the executive of their states, and particularly the leaving the compensation for their services in a loose equivocal state, without ascertaining their claims upon the public or making provisions for the future payment of them.

While I premise that, though no one that I have seen or heard of appears opposed to the principle of reducing the army as circumstances may require, yet I cannot help fearing the result of the measure in contemplation under present circumstances, when I see such a number of men, goaded by a thousand stings of reflection on the past and of anticipation on the future, about to be turned into the world, soured by penury and what they call the ingratitude of the public, involved in debts, without one farthing of money to carry them home, after having spent the flower of their days, and, many of them, their patrimonies in establishing the freedom and independence of their country, and suffered everything human nature is capable of enduring on this side of death. I repeat it, in these irritable circumstances, without one thing to sooth their feelings or brighten the gloomy prospects, I cannot avoid apprehending that a train of evils will follow of a very serious and distressing nature. On the other hand, could the officers be placed in as good a situation as when they came into service, the contention, I am persuaded, would be not who should continue in the field but who should retire to private life.

I wish not to heighten the shades of the picture so far as the real life would justify me in doing, or I would give anecdotes of patriotism and distress which have scarcely ever been paralleled, never surpassed, in the history of mankind. But you may rely upon it, the patience and long sufferance of this army are almost exhausted, and that there never was so great a spirit of discontent as at this instant. While in the field I think it may be kept from breaking out into acts of outrage, but when we retire into winter quarters (unless the storm is previously dissipating) I cannot be at ease respecting the consequences. It is high time for a peace.

To you, my dear sir, I need not be more particular in describing my anxiety and the grounds of it. You are too well acquainted from your own service with the real sufferings of the army to require a longer detail. I will therefore only add that exclusive of the common hardships of a military life, our troops have been and still are obliged to perform more services foreign to their proper duty, without gratuity or reward, than the soldiers of any other army—for example, the immense labors expended in doing the duties of artificers in erecting fortifications and military works, the fatigue of building themselves barracks or huts annually, and of cutting and transporting wood for the use of all our posts and garrisons, without any expense whatever to the public.

Of this letter (which from the tenor of it must be considered in some degree of a private nature) you may make such use as you shall think proper. Since the principal objects of it were, by displaying the merits, the hardships, the disposition, and critical state of the army, to give information that might eventually be useful and to convince you with what entire confidence and esteem I am My dear Sir &c.

To James McHenry, October 17, 1782 (Excerpt)

You will recollect the opinion I gave you upon the receipt of Carleton's letter of the 2nd of August to me. Subsequent events, as far as they have come to my knowledge, prove it was well founded; and I wish future ones may not evince that to gain time was all that the British ministry had in view. The impolicy therefore of suffering ourselves to be lulled by expectations of peace, because we wish it, and because it is the interest of G. Britain to hold up the ideas of it, will, more than probably, prove the ruin of our cause, and the disbanding of the army. For it should seem from the conduct the states are pursuing that they do not conceive it necessary for the army to receive anything but hard knocks. To give them pay is a matter which has long been out of the question; and we were upon the point of trying how we could live without subsistence (as the superintendent was no longer able to fulfill his contract with the victualers of the army, and they relinquish it) when, fortunately for us, we met with gentlemen who, for an advanced price per ration, have saved us from starvation or disbandment by giving a credit. Our horses have long been without everything which their own thriftiness could not procure.

Let any man who will allow reason fair play ask himself what must be the inevitable consequence of such policy. Have not military men the same feelings of those in the civil line? Why then should one set receive the constant wages of service and the other be continually without them? Do the former deserve less for their watchings and toil, for enduring heat and cold, for standing in sunshine and in rain, for the dangers they are continually exposed to for the sake of their country, by which means the man in civil life sits quiet under his own vine and fig tree, solacing himself in all the comforts, pleasures, and enjoyments of life, free and unrestrained? Let impartiality answer the question.

These are matters worthy of serious consideration. The patience, the fortitude, the long and great sufferings of this army are unexampled in history. But there is an end to all things, and I fear we are very near one to this—which, more than probably, will oblige me to stick very close to my flock this winter and try, like a careful physician, to prevent, if possible, the disorder's getting to an incurable height. I am Yr very Obedt & Affecte Servt

Go: Washington

To Reverend William Gordon, October 23, 1782

Dear Sir,

I have been honored with your favor of the 2nd instant and thank you for the extract of Mr. Adams's letter.

I never was among the sanguine ones, consequently shall be less disappointed than people of that description if our warfare should continue. From hence (it being the opinion of some men that our expectations have an accordance with our wishes) it may be inferred that mine are for a prolongation of the war. But maugre this doctrine, and the opinion of others that a continuation of the war till the powers of Congress, our political systems, and general form of government are better established. I can say with much truth that there is not a man in America that more fervently wishes for peace and a return to private life than I do. Nor will any man go back to the rural and domestic enjoyments of it with more heartfelt pleasure than I shall. It is painful to me, therefore, to accompany this declaration with an opinion that while the present king can maintain the influence of his Crown and extort men and money from his subjects, so long will the principles by which he is governed push him on in his present wild career. The late change in his ministry is an evidence of this and other changes which convince us, I fear, of the fallacy of our hopes.

It appears to me impracticable for the best historiographer living to write a full and correct history of the present revolution who has not free access to the archives of Congress, those of individual states, the papers of the commander-in-chief and commanding officers of separate departments. Mine, while the war continues, I consider as a species of public property, sacred in my hand and of little service to any historian who has not that general information which is only to be derived with exactitude from the sources I have mentioned. When Congress then shall open their registers and say it is proper for the servants of the public to do so, it will give me much pleasure to afford all the aid to your labors and laudable undertaking which my papers can give. Till one of those periods arrive I do not think myself justified in suffering any inspection of and extracts to be taken from my records. You will please to accept my sincere and grateful thanks for the kind wishes and generous sentiments you express for me. My best respects to Mrs. Gordon. I am Dr Sir Yr Most Obedt and Hble Servt

Go: Washington

To Jonathan Trumbull, Governor of Connecticut, November 13, 1782

Sir,

I do myself the honor to enclose you the extract of a letter which I have lately received from His Excellency the minister of France, on the subject of the amazing quantities of provisions which the enemy draw from the states contiguous to New York. The evil complained of has been long growing and has at length arisen to a height truly alarming. I persuade myself no arguments will be wanting to induce the legislature of your state, at their next sitting, to pay that attention to the matter which its importance deserves.

I have ever been of opinion, and every day's experience convinces me more and more of the truth of it, that nothing short of laws making the supply of the enemy with provisions or stores, or holding any kind of illicit intercourse with them, felony of death will check the evil so justly complained of. A moment's reflection must convince every thinking mind that four such armies as I command would be inadequate to the purpose. The attempt by military coercion alone might prove ruinous. For to guard the immense length of communication from the coast of Monmouth in Jersey eastward would so dissipate my force that every detachment would invite and be at the mercy of the enemy. This observation is too striking to need urging, and shows in the clearest point of view that rigid laws rigidly executed are the only remedies that can be applied, next to a sufficient force to invert the enemy in their post of New York. I have the honor to be with respect and esteem Your Excellency's Most obt and hble servt

Go: Washington

To Major Benjamin Tallmadge, December 10, 1782 (Excerpt)

Dear Sir,

I received your favor of the 8th last evening by express. Though you have not met with the success you deserved and probably would have obtained had the enterprise proceeded, yet I cannot but think your whole conduct in the affair was such as ought to entitle you still more to my confidence and esteem. For however it may be the practice of the world, and those who see objects but partially or through a false medium, to consider that only as meritorious which is attended with success, I have accustomed myself to judge of human actions very differently, and to appreciate them by the manner in which they are conducted more than by the *event*, which it is not in the power of[22] human foresight or prudence to command. In this point of view, I find nothing irreparable, and little to occasion of serious regret, except the wound of the gallant Captain Brewster, from which I earnestly hope he may recover. Another time you will have less opposition from winds and weather, and success will amply compensate for this little disappointment.

To Major General Nathanael Greene, February 6, 1783 (Excerpt)

It is with a pleasure which friendship only is susceptible of, I congratulate you on the glorious end you have put to hostilities in the southern states. The honor and advantages of it, I hope and trust, you will live long to enjoy. When this hemisphere will be equally free is yet in the womb of time to discover—a little while however, 'tis presumed, will disclose the determinations of the British senate with respect to peace or war, as it seems to be agreed on all hands that the present premier (especially if he should find the opposition powerful) intends to submit the decision of these matters to Parliament. The speech, the addresses, and debates for which we are looking in every direction will give a data from which the bright rays of the one or gloomy prospect of the other may be discovered.

If historiographers should be hardy enough to fill the page of history with the advantages that have been gained with unequal numbers (on the part of America) in the course of this contest, and attempt to relate the distressing circumstances under which they have been obtained, it is more than probable that posterity will bestow on their labors the epithet and marks of fiction; for it will not be believed that such a force as Great Britain has employed for eight years in this country could be baffled in their plan of subjugating it by numbers infinitely less, composed of men oftentimes half starved, always in rags, without pay, and experiencing, at times, every species of distress which human nature is capable of undergoing.

General Orders, February 15, 1783 (Excerpt)

The new building being so far finished as to admit the troops to attend public worship therein after tomorrow, it is directed that divine services should be performed there every Sunday by the several chaplains of the New Windsor Cantonment in rotation and in order that the different brigades may have an opportunity of attending at different hours in the same day (whenever the weather and other circumstances will permit, which the brigadiers and commandants of brigades must determine). The general recommends that the chaplains should in the first place consult the commanding officers of their brigades to know what hour will be most convenient and agreeable for attendance, that they will then settle the duty among themselves and report the results to the brigadiers and commandants of brigades, who are desired to give notice in their orders and to afford every aid and assistance in their power for the promotion of that public homage and adoration which are due to the Supreme Being, who has through his infinite goodness brought our public calamities and dangers (in all human probability) very near to a happy conclusion.

The general has been surprised to find in winter quarters that the chaplains have frequently been almost all absent at the same time, under an idea their presence could not be of any utility at that season. He thinks it is proper he should be allowed to judge of that matter himself, and therefore in future no furloughs will be granted to chaplains except in consequence of permission from headquarters; and any who may now be absent without such permission are to be ordered by the commanding officers of their brigades to join immediately, after which not more than one third of the whole number will be indulged with leave of absence at a time. They are requested to agree among themselves upon the time and length of their furloughs before any application shall be made to headquarters on the subject.

The commander-in-chief also desires and expects the chaplains, in addition to their public functions, will in turn constantly attend the hospitals and visit the sick. And while they are thus publicly and privately engaged in performing the sacred duties of their office, they may depend upon his utmost encouragement and support on all occasions, and that they will be considered in a very respectable point of light by the whole army.

To Benjamin Harrison, Governor of Virginia, March 4, 1783 (Excerpt)

What, my dear sir, could induce the state of Virginia to rescind its assent to the impost law? How are the numerous creditors of the public in civil life and the army to be paid if no regular and certain funds are established to discharge the interest of monies borrowed for these purposes? And what tax can be more just or better calculated to answer the end than an impost? The alarm bell, which has been rung with such a tremendous sound by the state of Rhode Island, to show the danger of entrusting Congress with money, is too selfish and futile to require a serious answer. Congress are in fact, the people. They return to them at certain short periods, are amenable at all times for their conduct, and subject to a recall at any moment. What interest, therefore, can a man have under these circumstances distinct from his constituents? Can it be supposed that with design he would form a junto or pernicious aristocracy that would operate against himself, in less than a month, perhaps, after it was established? I cannot conceive it. But from the observations I have made in the course of this war (and my intercourse with the states in their united as well as separate capacities has afforded ample opportunities of judging) I am decided in my opinion that if the powers of Congress are not enlarged and made competent to all general purposes, the blood which has been spilt, the expense that has been incurred, and the distresses which have been felt will avail nothing, and the band, already too weak, which holds us together will soon be broken, when anarchy and confusion will prevail.

I shall make no apology for the freedom of these sentiments. They proceed from an honest heart, although they may be the result of erroneous thinking. They will at least prove the sincerity of my friendship, as they are altogether undisguised. With the greatest esteem and regard I am—Dr Sir Yr most Obed. & Affectt. Hble Servt

Go: Washington

To Alexander Hamilton, March 4, 1783

Dear Sir,

I have received your favor of February and thank you for the information and observations it has conveyed to me. I shall always think myself obliged by a free communication of sentiments and have often thought (but suppose I thought wrong, as it did not accord with the practice of Congress) that the public interest might be benefited if the commander-in-chief of the army was let more into the political and pecuniary state of our affairs than he is. Enterprises and the adoption of military and other arrangements that might be exceedingly proper in some circumstances would be altogether improper in others. It follows, then, by fair deduction that where there is a want of information there must be chance medley; and a man may be upon the brink of a precipice before he is aware of his danger, when a little foreknowledge might enable him to avoid it.

But this by the by.

The hint contained in your letter, and the knowledge I have derived from the public gazettes respecting the non-payment of taxes, contain all the information I have received of the danger that stares us in the face on account of our funds. And so far was I from conceiving that our finances were in so deplorable a state *at this time* that I had imbibed ideas from some source of information or another that, with the prospect of a loan from Holland, we should be able to rub along yet a little farther.

To you, who have seen the danger to which the army has been exposed to a political dissolution for want of subsistence, and the unhappy spirit of licentiousness which it imbibed by becoming in one or two instances its own proveditors, no observations are necessary to evince the fatal tendency of such a measure. But I shall give it as my opinion that it would at this day be productive of civil commotions and end in blood. Unhappy situation, this! God forbid we should be involved in it.

The predicament in which I stand as citizen and soldier is as critical and delicate as can well be conceived. It has been the subject of many contemplative hours. The sufferings of a complaining army on one hand, and the inability of Congress and tardiness of the states on the other, are the forebodings of evil and may be productive of events which are more to be deprecated than prevented. But I am not without hope, if there is such a disposition shown as prudence and policy will dictate to do justice, that your apprehensions in case of peace are greater than there is cause for. In this, however, I may be mistaken, if those ideas which you have been informed are propagating in the army should be extensive—the source of which may be easily traced, as the old leaven, *it is said* (for I have no proof of it), is again beginning to work under a mask of the most perfect dissimulation and apparent cordiality.

Be these things as they may, I shall pursue the same steady line of conduct which has governed me hitherto, fully convinced that the sensible and discerning part of the army cannot be unacquainted (although I never took pains to inform them) of the services I have rendered it on more occasions than one. This, and pursuing the suggestions in your letter, which I am happy to find coincides with my practice for several months past, and which has turned the business of the army into the channel it now is, leaves me under no *great* apprehension of its exceeding the bounds of reason and moderation, notwithstanding the prevailing sentiment therein is that the prospect of compensation for past services will terminate with the war.

The just claims of the army ought and, it is to be hoped will, have their weight with every sensible legislature in the United States if Congress point to their demands, show (if the case is so) the reasonableness of them and the impracticability of complying with them without their aid. In any other point of view, it would, in my opinion, be impolitic to introduce the army on the tapis lest it should excite jealousy and bring on its concomitants. The states cannot, surely, be so devoid of common sense, common honesty, and common policy as to refuse their aid on a full, clear, and candid representation of facts from Congress, more especially if these should be enforced by members of their own body who might demonstrate what the inevitable consequences of failure will lead to.

In my opinion it is a matter worthy of consideration how far an adjournment of Congress for a few months is advisable. The delegates in that case, if they are in unison themselves respecting the great defects of their constitution, may represent them fully and boldly to their constituents. To me, who know nothing of the business which is before Congress, nor of the arcanum, it appears that such a measure would tend to promote the public weal, for it is clearly my opinion, unless Congress have powers competent to all *general* purposes, that the distresses we have encountered, the expense we have incurred, and the blood we have spilt in the course of an eight years war will avail us nothing.

The contents of your letter are known only to myself. Your prudence will be at no less to know what use to make of these sentiments—I am Dr Sir Yrs &c.

G.W.

To Robert Morris, Superintendent of Finance, March 8, 1783

Sir,

Very painful sensations are excited in my mind by your letter of the 27th of February. It is impossible for me to express to you the regret with which I received the information it contains.

I have often reflected, with much solicitude, upon the disagreeableness of your situation and the negligence of the several states in not enabling you to do that justice to the public creditors which their demands require. I wish the step you have taken may sound the alarm to their inmost souls and rouse them to a just sense of their own interest, honor, and credit. But I must confess to you that I have my fears, for as danger becomes further removed from them, their feelings seem to be more callous to those noble sentiments with which I could wish to see them inspired. Mutual jealousies, local prejudices, and misapprehensions have taken such deep root as will not easily be removed.

Notwithstanding the embarrassments which you have experienced, I was in hope that you would have continued your efforts to the close of the war at least. But if your resolutions are absolutely fixed, I assure you I consider the event as one of the most unfortunate that could have fallen upon the states and most sincerely deprecate the sad consequences which I fear will follow. The army, I am sure, at the same time that they entertain the highest sense of your exertions, will lament the step you are obliged to take as a most unfortunate circumstance to them. I am &c.

To Alexander Hamilton, March 12, 1783 (Excerpt)

Dear Sir,

When I wrote to you last, we were in a state of tranquility, but after the arrival of a certain gentleman—who shall be nameless at present[23]—from Philadelphia a storm very suddenly arose with unfavorable prognostics, which, though diverted for a moment, is not yet blown over, nor is it in my power to point to the issue.

The papers, which I send officially to Congress, will supersede the necessity of my remarking on the tendency of them. The notification and address both appeared at the same instant on the day preceding the intended meeting. The first of these I got hold of the same afternoon, the other not till next morning.

There is something very mysterious in this business. It appears reports have been propagated in Philadelphia that dangerous combinations were forming in the army, and this at a time when there was not a syllable of the kind in agitation in camp. It also appears that upon the arrival in camp of the gentleman above alluded to, such sentiments as these were immediately circulated: that it was universally expected the army would not disband until they had obtained justice, that the public creditors looked up to them for redress of their own grievances, would afford them every aid, and even join them in the field if necessary, that some members of Congress wished the measure might take effect, in order to compel the public, particularly the delinquent states, to do justice, with many other suggestions of a similar nature.

From this, and a variety of other considerations, it is firmly believed by some the scheme was not only planned but also digested and matured in Philadelphia; but my opinion shall be suspended till I have better ground to found one on. The matter was managed with great art; for as soon as the minds of the officers were thought to be prepared for the transaction, the anonymous invitations and address to the officers were put in circulation, through every state line in the army. I was obliged therefore—in order to arrest on the spot the foot that stood wavering on a tremendous precipice, to prevent the officers from being taken by surprise while the passions were all inflamed, and to rescue them from plunging themselves into a gulf of civil horror from which there might be no receding—to issue the order of the 11th. This was done upon the principle that it is easier to divert from a wrong and point to a right path than it is to recall the hasty and fatal steps which have been already taken.

It is commonly supposed if the officers had met agreeably to the anonymous summons—with their feelings all alive—resolutions might have been formed the consequences of which may be more easily conceived than described. Now they will have leisure to view the matter more calmly and will act more seriously. It is to be hoped they will be induced to adopt more rational measures and wait a while longer for settlement of their accounts—the postponing of which appears to be the most plausible and almost the only article of which designing men can make an improper use, by insinuating (which they really do) that it is done with design that peace may take place and prevent any adjustment of accounts, which, say they, would inevitably be the case if the war was to cease tomorrow. Or, supposing the best, you would have to dance attendance at public offices at great distances, perhaps, and equally great expenses to obtain a settlement, which would be highly injurious, nay, ruinous to you. This is their language.

Let me beseech you therefore, my good sir, to urge this matter earnestly and without further delay. The situation of these gentleman I do verily believe is distressing beyond description. It is affirmed to me that a large part of them have no better prospects before them than a gaol, if they are turned loose without liquidation of accounts and an assurance of that justice to which they are so worthily entitled. To prevail on the delegates of the states, through whose means these difficulties occur, it may, in my opinion, with propriety be suggested to them, if any disastrous consequences should follow by reason of their delinquency, that they must be answerable to God and their country for the ineffable horror which may be occasioned thereby.

To the Officers of the Army, March 15, 1783[24]

Gentlemen,

By an anonymous summons an attempt has been made to convene you together. How inconsistent with the rules of propriety! how unmilitary! and how subversive of all order and discipline, let the good sense of the army decide.

In the moment of this summons, another anonymous production was sent into circulation, addressed more to the feelings and passions than to the reason and judgment of the army. The author of the piece is entitled to much credit for the goodness of his pen, and I could wish he had as much credit for the rectitude of his heart. For, as men see through different optics and are induced by the reflecting faculties of the mind to use different means to attain the same end, the author of the address should have had more charity than to mark for suspicion the man who should recommend moderation and longer forbearance—or, in other words, who should not think as he thinks and act as he advises. But he had another plan in view, in which candor and liberality of sentiment, regard to justice, and love of country, have no part; and he was right to insinuate the darkest suspicion to effect the blackest designs.

That the address is drawn with great art and is designed to answer the most insidious purposes; that it is calculated to impress the mind with an idea of premeditated injustice in the sovereign power of the United States, and rouse all those resentments which must unavoidably flow from such a belief; that the secret mover of this scheme (whoever he may be) intended to take advantage of the passions while they were warmed by the recollection of past distresses, without giving time for cool, deliberative thinking, and that composure of mind which is so necessary to give dignity and stability to measures, is rendered too obvious by the mode of conducting the business to need other proof than a reference to the proceeding.

Thus much, gentlemen, I have thought it incumbent on me to observe to you, to show upon what principles I opposed the irregular and hasty meeting which was proposed to have been held on Tuesday last, and not because I wanted a disposition to give you every opportunity, consistent with your own honor and the dignity of the army, to make known your grievances. If my conduct heretofore has not evinced to you that I have been a faithful friend to the army, my declaration of it at this time would be equally unavailing and improper. But as I was among the first who embarked in the cause of our common country; as I have never left your side one moment, but when called from you, on public duty; as I have been the constant companion and witness of your distresses, and not among the last to feel and acknowledge your merits; as I have ever considered my own military reputation as inseparably connected with that of the army; as my heart has ever expanded with joy when I have heard its praises, and my indignation has arisen when the mouth of detraction has been opened against it, it can *scarcely be supposed*, at this late stage of the war, that I am indifferent to its interests.

But how are they to be promoted? The way is plain, says the anonymous addresser. If war continues, remove into the unsettled country, there establish yourselves, and leave an ungrateful country to defend itself. But who are they to defend? Our wives, our children, our farms, and other property which we leave behind us. Or, in this state of hostile separation, are we to take the two first (the latter cannot be removed) to perish in a wilderness, with hunger, cold, nakedness? If peace takes place, never sheath your sword, says he, until you have obtained full and ample justice. This dreadful alternative—of either deserting our country in the extremest hour of her distress, or turning our army against it (which is the apparent object, unless Congress can be compelled into an instant compliance)—has something so shocking in it that humanity revolts at the idea. My God! What can this writer have in view by recommending such measures? Can he be a friend to the army? Can he be a friend to this country? Rather, is he not an insidious foe? Some emissary, perhaps from New York, plotting the ruin of both by sowing the seeds of discord and separation between the civil and military powers of the continent? And what a compliment does he pay to our understandings when he recommends measures, in either alternative, impracticable in their nature?

But here, gentlemen, I will drop the curtain, because it would be as imprudent in me to assign my reasons for this opinion as it would be insulting to your conception to suppose you stood in need of them. A moment's reflection will convince every dispassionate mind of the physical impossibility of carrying either proposal into execution.

There might, gentlemen, be an impropriety in my taking notice, in this address to you, of an anonymous production. But the manner in which that performance has been introduced to the army, the effect it was intended to have, together with some other circumstances, will amply justify my observations on the tendency of that writing. With respect to the advice given by the author—to suspect the man who shall recommend moderate measures and longer forbearance—I spurn it, as every man who regards that liberty and reveres that justice for which we contend undoubtedly must. For if men are to be precluded from offering their sentiments on a matter which may involve the most serious and alarming consequences that can invite the consideration of mankind, reason is of no use to us, the freedom of speech may be taken away, and dumb and silent we may be led like sheep to the slaughter.

I cannot, in justice to my own belief and what I have great reason to conceive is the intention of Congress, conclude this address without giving it as my decided opinion that that honorable body entertain exalted sentiments of the services of the army and, from a full conviction of its merits and sufferings, will do it complete justice. That their endeavors to discover and establish funds for this purpose have been unwearied, and will not cease till they have succeeded, I have not a doubt. But, like all other large bodies, where there is a variety of different interests to reconcile, their deliberations are slow. Why, then, should we distrust them and, in consequence of that distrust, adopt measures which may cast a shade over that glory which has been so justly acquired and tarnish the reputation of an army which is celebrated through all Europe for its fortitude and patriotism? And for what is this done? To bring the object we seek for nearer? No! Most certainly, in my opinion, it will cast it at a greater distance.

For myself (and I take no merit in giving the assurance, being induced to it from principles of gratitude, veracity, and justice), a grateful sense of the confidence you have ever placed in me, a recollection of the cheerful assistance and prompt obedience I have experienced from you under every vicissitude of fortune, and the sincere affection I feel for an army I have so long had the honor to command, will oblige me to declare, in this public and solemn manner, that in the attainment of complete justice for all your toils and dangers, and in the gratification of every wish, so far as may be done consistently with the great duty I owe my country and those powers we are bound to respect, you may freely command my services to the utmost of my abilities.

While I give you these assurances and pledge myself in the most unequivocal manner to exert whatever ability I am possessed of in your favor, let me entreat you, gentlemen, on your part not to take any measures which, viewed in the calm light of reason, will lessen the dignity and sully the glory you have hitherto maintained. Let me request you to rely on the plighted faith of your country and place a full confidence in the purity of the intentions of Congress that, previous to your dissolution as an army, they will cause all your accounts to be fairly liquidated, as directed in their resolutions which were published to you two days ago, and that they will adopt the most effectual measures in their power to render ample justice to you for your faithful and meritorious services. And let me conjure you, in the name of our common country, as you value your own sacred honor, as you respect the rights of humanity, and as you regard the military and national character of America, to express your utmost horror and detestation of the man who wishes, under any specious pretenses, to overturn the liberties of our country and who wickedly attempts to open the floodgates of civil discord and deluge our rising empire in blood.

By thus determining and thus acting you will pursue the plain and direct road to the attainment of your wishes. You will defeat the insidious designs of our enemies, who are compelled to resort from open force to secret artifice. You will give one more distinguished proof of unexampled patriotism and patient virtue, rising superior to the pressure of the most complicated sufferings. And you will, by the dignity of your conduct, afford occasion for posterity to say, when speaking of the glorious example you have exhibited to mankind, "had this day been wanting, the world had never seen the last stage of perfection to which human nature is capable of attaining."

Go: Washington

To Elias Boudinot, President of the Confederation Congress, March 18, 1783

Sir,

The result of the proceedings of the grand convention of the officers, which I have the honor of enclosing to Your Excellency for the inspection of Congress, will, I flatter myself, be considered as the last glorious proof of patriotism which will have been given by men who aspired to the distinction of a patriot army, and will not only confirm their claim to the justice, but will increase their title to the gratitude of their country.

Having seen the proceedings on the part of the army terminate with perfect unanimity, and in a manner entirely consonant to my wishes; being impressed with the liveliest sentiments of affection for those who have so long, so patiently, and so cheerfully suffered and fought under my immediate direction; having from motives of justice, duty, and gratitude spontaneously offered myself as an advocate for their rights; and having been requested to write to Your Excellency earnestly entreating the most speedy decision of Congress upon the subjects of the late address from the army to that honorable body; it now only remains for me to perform the task I have assumed and to intercede in their behalf, as I now do, that the sovereign power will be pleased to verify the predictions I have pronounced of, and the confidence the army have reposed in, the justice of their country.

And here I humbly conceive it is altogether unnecessary (while I am pleading the cause of an army which have done and suffered more than any other army ever did in the defense of the rights and liberties of human nature) to expatiate on their *claims* to the most ample compensation for their meritorious services, because they are perfectly known to the whole world, and because (although the topics are inexhaustible) enough has already been said on the subject.

To prove these assertions, to evince that my sentiments have ever been uniform, and to show what my ideas of the rewards in question have always been, I appeal to the archives of Congress and call on those sacred deposits to witness for me. And in order that my observations and arguments in favor of a future adequate provision for the officers of the army may be brought to remembrance again and considered in a single point of view without giving Congress the trouble of having recourse to their files, I will beg leave to transmit herewith an extract from a representation made by me to a committee of Congress so long ago as the 29th of January 1778, and also the transcript of a letter to the president of Congress, dated near Passaic Falls, October 11th, 1780.

That in the critical and perilous moment when the last-mentioned communication was made, there was the utmost danger a dissolution of the army would have taken place unless measures similar to those recommended had been adopted will not admit a doubt. That the adoption of the resolution granting half-pay for life has been attended with all the happy consequences I had foretold so far as respected the good of the service, let the astonishing contrast between the state of the army at this instant and at the former period determine. And that the establishment of funds and security of the payment of all the just demands of the army will be the most certain means of preserving the national faith and future tranquility of this extensive continent is my decided opinion.

By the preceding remarks it will readily be imagined that, instead of retracting and reprehending (from farther experience and reflection) the mode of compensation so strenuously urged in the enclosures, I am more and more confirmed in the sentiment, and if in the wrong, suffer me to please myself with the grateful delusion.

For if, besides the simple payment of their wages, a farther compensation is not due to the sufferings and sacrifices of the officers, then have I been mistaken indeed. If the whole army have not merited whatever a grateful people can bestow, then have I been beguiled by prejudice and built opinion on the basis of error. If this country should not in the event perform everything which has been requested in the late memorial to Congress, then will my belief become vain and the hope that has been excited void of foundation. And "if (as has been suggested for the purpose of inflaming their passions) the officers of the army are to be the only sufferers by this revolution; if retiring from the field they are to grow old in poverty, wretchedness, and contempt; if they are to wade through the vile mire of dependency and owe the miserable remnant of that life to charity, which has hitherto been spent in honor"; then shall I have learned what ingratitude is. Then shall I have realized a tale which will embitter every moment of my future life.

But I am under no such apprehensions. A country rescued by their arms from impending ruin will never leave unpaid the debt of gratitude.

Should any intemperate or improper warmth have mingled itself amongst the foregoing observations, I must entreat Your Excellency and Congress it may be attributed to the effusion of an honest zeal in the best of causes, and that my peculiar situation may be my apology. And I hope I need not on this momentous occasion make any new protestations of personal disinterestedness, having ever renounced for myself the idea of pecuniary reward. The consciousness of having attempted faithfully to discharge my duty and the approbation of my country will be a sufficient recompense for my services. I have the honor to be, with perfect respect, Yr Excellency's Most Obedt Servt

Go: Washington

To Joseph Jones, March 18, 1783

The storm which seemed to be gathering with unfavorable prognostics when I wrote to you last is dispersed, and we are again in a state of tranquility. But do not, my dear sir, suffer this appearance of tranquility to relax your endeavors to bring the requests of the army to a conclusion. Believe me, the officers are too much pressed by their present wants, and are rendered too sore by the recollection of their past sufferings, to be touched much longer upon the string of forbearance in matters wherein they can see no cause for delay. Nor would I have further reliance placed on any influence of mine to dispel other clouds if more should arise from the causes of the last.

By my official letter to Congress, and the papers enclosed in it, you will have a full view of my assurances to and the expectations of the army; and I persuade myself that the well-wishers to both, and of their country, will exert themselves to the utmost to eradicate the seeds of distrust, and give every satisfaction that justice requires and the means which Congress possess will enable them to do.

In a former letter I observed to you that a liquidation of account in order that the balances might be ascertained is the great object of the army, and certainly nothing can be more reasonable. To have these balances discharged at this or in any short period, however desirable, they know is impracticable and do not expect it—although in the meantime they must labor under the pressure of those sufferings which is felt more sensibly by a comparison of circumstances.

The situation of these gentlemen merits[25] the attention of every thinking and grateful mind. As officers, they have been *obliged* to dress and appear in character. To effect this, they have been *obliged* to anticipate their pay or participate their estates. By the first, debts have been contracted. By the latter, their patrimony is injured. To disband men, therefore, under these circumstances, before their accounts are liquidated and the balances ascertained, would be to set open the doors of gaols and then to close them upon seven years faithful and painful services. Under any circumstances which the nature of the case will admit they must be considerable sufferers, because necessity will compel them to part with their certificates for whatever they will fetch to avoid the evil I have mentioned above. And how much this will place them in the hand of unfeeling, avaricious speculators a recurrence to past experience will sufficiently prove.

It may be said by those who have no disposition to compensate the services of the army that the officers have more foresight than to place dependence (in any alternative) upon the strength of their own arm. I will readily concede to these gentlemen that no good could result from such an attempt, but I hope they will be equally candid in acknowledging that much mischief may flow from it, and that nothing is too extravagant to expect from men who conceive they are ungratefully and unjustly dealt by—especially, too, if they can suppose that characters are not wanting to foment every passion which leads to discord, and that there are _____ but, _____ time shall reveal the rest.

Let it suffice that the very attempt would imply a want of justice and fix an indelible stain upon our national character, as the whole world—as well from the enemy's publications (without any intention to serve us) as our own—must be strongly impressed with the sufferings of this army from hunger, cold, and nakedness in almost every stage of the war.

To Benjamin Harrison, Governor of Virginia, March 19, 1783

Dear Sir,

About the first of this month, I wrote you a long letter. I touched upon the state of the army, the situation of public creditors, and wished to know from you, as a friend, what causes had induced the Assembly of Virginia to withdraw their assent to the impost law, and how the continental creditors (without adequate funds) were to come at or obtain security for their money.

I little expected at the time of writing that letter that we were on the eve of an important crisis to this army, when the touchstone of discord was to be applied and the virtue of its members to undergo the severest trial.

You have not been altogether unacquainted, I dare say, with the fears, the hopes, the apprehensions, and the expectations of the army relatively to the provision which is to be made for them hereafter. Although a firm reliance on the integrity of Congress, and a belief that the public would finally do justice to all its servants, and give an indisputable security for the payment of the half-pay of the officers had kept them amidst a variety of sufferings tolerably quiet and contented for two or three years past; yet the total want of pay, the little prospect of receiving any from the unpromising state of the public finances, and the absolute aversion of the states to establish any continental funds for the payment of the debt due to the army did at the close of the last campaign excite greater discontents and threaten more serious and alarming consequences than it is easy for me to describe or you to conceive.

Happily for us, the officers of highest rank and greatest consideration interposed; and it was determined to address Congress in a humble, pathetic, and explicit manner. While the sovereign power appeared perfectly well disposed to do justice, it was discovered the states would enable them to do nothing. And in this state of affairs, after some time spent on the business in Philadelphia, a report was made by the delegates of the army giving a detail of the proceedings. Before this could be fully communicated to the troops, while the minds of all were in a peculiar state of inquietude and irritation, an anonymous writer, who, though he did not boldly step forth and give his name to the world, sent into circulation an address to the officers of the army which in point of composition, in elegance and force of expression, has rarely been equaled in the English language, and in which the dreadful alternative was proposed of relinquishing the service in a body in case the war continued, or retaining their arms in case of peace, until Congress should comply with all their demands. At the same time, seizing the moment when the minds were inflamed by the most pathetic representations, a general meeting of the officers was summoned by another anonymous production.

It is impossible to say what would have been the consequence had the author succeeded in his first plans. But measures having been taken to postpone the meeting so as to give time for cool reflection and counteraction, the good sense of the officers has terminated this affair in a manner which reflects the greatest glory on themselves and demands the highest expressions of gratitude from their country.

The proceedings have this day been reported to Congress and will probably be published for the satisfaction of the good people of these United States. In the meantime, I thought it necessary to give you these particulars, principally with a design to communicate to you, without reserve, my opinion on this interesting subject. For notwithstanding the storm has now passed over, notwithstanding the officers have, in despite of their accumulated sufferings, given the most unequivocal and exalted proofs of patriotism, yet I believe, unless justice shall be done and funds effectually provided for the payment of the debt, the most deplorable and ruinous consequences may be apprehended. Justice, honor, gratitude, policy, everything is opposed to the conduct of driving men to despair of obtaining their just rights after serving seven years a painful life in the field. I say in the *field*, because they have not during that period had anything to shelter them from the inclemency of the seasons but tents and such houses as they could build for themselves.

Convinced of this, and actuated as I am not by private and interested motives but by a sense of duty, a love of justice, and all the feelings of gratitude towards a body of men who have merited infinitely well of their country, I can never conceal or suppress my sentiments. I cannot cease to exert all the abilities I am possessed of to show the evil tendency of procrastinated justice, for I will not suppose it is intended ultimately to withhold it—nor fail to urge the establishment of such adequate and permanent funds as will enable Congress to secure the payment of the public debt on such principles as will preserve the national faith, give satisfaction to the army and tranquility to the public. With great esteem and regard I have the honor to be Dr Sir Yr Most Obedt & H. Ser.

G. W———n

P.S. The author of the anonymous address is yet behind the curtain, and as conjecture may be grounded on error, I will not announce mine at present.

G. W———n

To Lund Washington, March 19, 1783

Dear Lund,

I did not write to you by the last post. I was too much engaged at that time in counteracting a most insidious attempt to disturb the repose of the army and sow the seeds of discord between the civil and military powers of the continent to attend to small matters. The author of this attempt, whoever he may be, is yet behind the curtain; and, as conjectures might be wrong, I shall be silent at present.

The good sense, the virtue, and patient forbearance of the army on this as upon every other trying occasion which has happened to call them into action has again triumphed and appeared with more luster than ever. But if the states will not furnish the supplies required by Congress, thereby enabling the superintendent of finance to feed, clothe, and pay the army; if they suppose the war can be carried on without money, or that money can be borrowed without permanent funds to pay the interest of it; if they have no regard to justice, because it is attended with expense; if gratitude to men who have rescued them from the jaws of danger and brought them to the haven of independence and peace is to subside as danger is removed; if the sufferings of the army, who have borne and forborne more than any other class of men in the United States, expending their health, and many of them their all, in an unremitted service of near eight years in the field, encountering hunger, cold, and nakedness, are to be forgotten; if it is presumed there are no bounds to the patience of the army, or that when peace takes place their claims for pay due and rewards promised may die with the military non-existence of its member; if such, I say, should be the sentiments of the states, and that their conduct, or the conduct of some, does but too well warrant the conclusion, well may another anonymous addresser step forward and, with more effect than the last did, say with him, "You have arms in your hands; do justice to yourselves and never sheath the sword till you have obtained it." How far men who labor under the pressure of accumulated distress and are irritated by a belief that they are treated with neglect, ingratitude, and injustice in the extreme might be worked upon by designing men is worthy of very serious consideration.

But justice, policy, yea, common sense, must tell every man that the creditors of the continent cannot receive payments unless funds are provided for it, and that our national character, if these are much longer neglected, must be stamped with indelible infamy in every nation of the world where the fact is known. I am, &ca

G: Washington

To Arthur Lee, March 29, 1783 (Excerpt)

Dear Sir,

I have been honored with your favor of the 13th and thank you for the information. Your correspondent at Paris had good ground for his opinion, and we have abundant reason to be pleased at the event which he predicted the near approach of. I heartily congratulate you on the conclusion of the war and hope the wisdom of the states will point to that line of policy which will make them a great, a happy people. To accomplish this, local politics and unreasonable jealousies should yield to such a constitution as will embrace the whole and make our Union respectable, lasting. Without it, I think we have spent our time, spilt our blood, and wasted our treasure to very little purpose.

To Robert R. Livingston, Secretary of Foreign Affairs, March 29, 1783 (Excerpt)

Dear Sir,

Your obliging letter of the 24th was delivered me the day before yesterday and accompanied the account of a general peace having been concluded in Europe on the 20th of January last. Most sincerely do I accept your congratulations on this happy event, which has already diffused a general joy through every class of people, and to none more than to the army. It now will be our own fault if we do not enjoy that happiness which we have flattered ourselves this event would bring. To see such measures taken as will effect this is all that remains for me to wish. I shall then enjoy in the bosom of my family a felicity that will amply repay every care.

To Major General Nathanael Greene, March 31, 1783 (Excerpt)

You will give the highest credit to my sincerity when I beg you to accept my warmest and most lively congratulations on this glorious and happy event—an event which crowns all our labors and will sweeten the toils which we have experienced in the course of eight years' distressing war. The army here universally participate in the general joy which this event has diffused; and, from this consideration, together with the late resolutions of Congress for the commutation of the half-pay and for a liquidation of all their accounts, their minds are filled with the highest satisfaction. You will, I am sure, join with me in this additional occasion of joy.

It remains only for the states to be wise and to establish their independence on that basis of inviolable efficacious Union and firm confederation which may prevent their being made the sport of European policy. May Heaven give them wisdom to adopt the measures still necessary for this important purpose.

To Alexander Hamilton, March 31, 1783 (Excerpt)

Dear Sir,

I have duly received your favors of the 17th and 24th ultimo. I rejoice most exceedingly that there is an end to our warfare and that such a field is opening to our view as will, with wisdom to direct the cultivation of it, make us a great, a respectable, and happy people. But it must be improved by other means than state politics and unreasonable jealousies and prejudices; or (it requires not the second sight to see that) we shall be instruments in the hands of our enemies, and those European powers who may be jealous of our greatness, in union to dissolve the Confederation. But to attain this, although the way seems extremely plain, is not so easy.

My wish to see the Union of these states established upon liberal and permanent principles, and inclination to contribute my mite in pointing out the defects of the present constitution, are equally great. All my private letters have teemed with these sentiments, and whenever this topic has been the subject of conversation, I have endeavored to diffuse and enforce them. But how far any further essay by me might be productive of the wished-for end, or appear to arrogate more than belongs to me, depends so much upon popular opinions and the temper and disposition of people, that it is not easy to decide. I shall be obliged to you, however, for the thoughts which you have promised me on this subject, and as soon as you can make it convenient.

No man in the United States is or can be more deeply impressed with the necessity of a reform in our present Confederation than myself. No man, perhaps, has felt the bad effects of it more sensibly; for to the defects thereof and want of powers in Congress may justly be ascribed the prolongation of the war and consequently the expenses occasioned by it. More than half the perplexities I have experienced in the course of my command, and almost the whole of the difficulties and distress of the army, have their origin here. But still, the prejudices of some, the designs of others, and the mere machinery of the majority make address and management necessary to give weight to opinions which are to combat the doctrines of these different classes of men in the field of politics.

To Theodorick Bland, April 4, 1783

Dear Sir,

On Sunday last the Baron de Steuben handed me your obliging favor of the 22nd of March. Permit me to offer you my unfeigned thanks for the clear and candid opinions which you have given me of European politics. Your reasonings upon the conduct of the different powers at war would have appeared conclusive had not the happy event which has been since announced to us, and on which I most sincerely congratulate you, proved how well they were founded.

Peace has given rest to speculative opinions respecting the time and terms of it. The first has come as soon as we could well have expected it under the disadvantages which we labored, and the latter is abundantly satisfactory. It is now the bounden duty of everyone to make the blessings thereof as diffusive as possible.

Nothing would so effectually bring this to pass as the removal of these local prejudices which intrude upon and embarrass that great line of policy which alone can make us a free, happy, and powerful people. Unless our Union can be fixed upon such a basis as to accomplish these, certain I am we have toiled, bled, and spent our treasure to very little purpose.

We have now a national character to establish, and it is of the utmost importance to stamp favorable impressions upon it. Let justice, then, be one of its characteristics, and gratitude another. Public creditors of every denomination will be comprehended in the first. The army in a particular manner will have a claim to the latter. To say that no distinction can be made between the claims of public creditors is to declare that there is no difference in circumstances or that the services of all men are equally alike.

This army is of near eight years standing, six of which they have spent in the field without any other shelter from the inclemency of the seasons than tents or such houses as they could build for themselves without expense to the public. They have encountered hunger, cold, and nakedness. They have fought many battles and bled freely. They have lived without pay, and in consequence of it officers as well as men have subsisted upon their rations. They have often, very often, been reduced to the necessity of eating salt pork or beef, not for a day or a week only, but months together without vegetables or money to buy them or a cloth to wipe on. Many of them to do better, and to dress as officers, have contracted heavy debts or spent their patrimonies. The first see the doors of gaols open to receive them, whilst those of the latter are shut against them. Is there no discrimination then, no extra exertion to be made in favor of men under these peculiar circumstances, in the hour of their military dissolution? Only if no worse cometh of it are they to be turned a drift soured and discontented, complaining of the ingratitude of their country, and under the influence of these passions to become fit subjects for unfavorable impressions and unhappy dissensions. For, permit me to add, though every man in the army feels his distress, it is not every one that will reason to the cause of it.

I would not from the observations here made be understood to mean that Congress should (because I know they cannot, nor does the army expect it) pay the full arrearages due to them till continental or state funds are established for the purpose. They would, from what I can learn, go home contented—nay, *thankful*—to receive what I have mentioned in a more public letter of this date, and in the manner there expressed. And surely this may be effected with proper exertions—or what possibility was there of keeping the army together if the war had continued, when the victualling, clothing, and other expenses of it were to have been added?

Another thing, sir (as I mean to be frank and free in my communications on this subject), I will not conceal from you. It is the dissimilarity in the payments to men in civil and military life. The first receive everything; the other get nothing but bare subsistence. They ask what this is owing to, and reasons have been assigned which, say they, amount to this: that men in civil life have stronger passions and better pretensions to indulge them, or less virtue and regard for their country than us. Otherwise, as we are all contending for the same prize, and equally interested in the attainment of it, why do we not bear the burden equally?

These and other comparisons which are unnecessary to enumerate give a keener edge to their feelings and contribute not a little to sour their tempers. As it is the first wish of my soul to see the war happily and speedily terminated, and those who are now in arms return to citizenship with good dispositions, I think it a duty which I owe to candor and to friendship to point you to such things as my opportunities have given me reason to believe will have a tendency to harmony, and bring them to pass. I shall only add that with much esteem and regard I am—Dr Sir Yr Most Obt & Hble Servt

Go: Washington

To Alexander Hamilton, April 4, 1783

Dear Sir,

The same post which gave me your two letters of the 25th of March handed me one from Colonel Bland on the same point.

Observing that both have been written at the desire of a committee of which you are both members, I have made a very full reply to their subject in my letter which is addressed to Colonel Bland. And, supposing it unnecessary to enter into a complete detail to both, I must beg leave to refer you to Colonel Bland's (a sight of which I have desired him to give you) for a full explanation of my ideas and sentiments.

I read your private letter of the 25th with pain and contemplated the picture it had drawn with astonishment and horror;[26] but I will yet hope for the best. The idea of redress by force is too chimerical to have had a place in the imagination of any serious mind in this army; but there is no telling what unhappy disturbances might result from distress and distrust of justice, and as the fears and jealousies of the army are alive, I hope no resolution will be come to for disbanding or separating the lines till the accounts are liquidated. You may rely upon it, sir, that unhappy consequences would follow the attempt. The suspicions of the officers are afloat, notwithstanding the resolutions which have passed on both sides. Any act, therefore, which can be construed into an attempt to separate them before the accounts are settled will convey the most unfavorable ideas of the rectitude of Congress. Whether well or ill-founded matters not; the consequences will be the same.

I will now, in strict confidence, mention a matter which may be useful for you to be informed of. It is that some men (and leading ones, too) in this army are beginning to entertain suspicions that Congress, or some members of it, regardless of the past sufferings and present distress, maugre the justice which is due to them, and the returns which a grateful people should make to men who certainly have contributed more than any other class to the establishment of independency, are to be made use of as mere puppets to establish continental funds—and that, rather than not succeed in this measure, or weaken their ground, they would make a sacrifice of the army and all its interests.

I have two reasons for mentioning this matter to you. The one is that the army (considering the irritable state it is in, its sufferings and composition) is a dangerous instrument to play with. The other, that every possible means consistent with their own views (which certainly are moderate) should be essayed to get it disbanded without delay. I might add a third. It is that the financier is suspected to be at the bottom of this scheme. If sentiments of this sort should become general, their operation will be opposed to this plan, at the same time that it would increase the present discontents. Upon the whole: disband the army as soon as possible but consult the wishes of it, which really are moderate in the mode and perfectly compatible with the honor, dignity, and justice which is due from the country to it. I am with great esteem & regard Dr Sir Yr Most Obedt Servt

Go: Washington

To Theodorick Bland, April 4, 1783

Sir,

The subject of your private letter is so important and involves so many considerations that I could not hazard my own opinion *only* for a reply. I have therefore communicated its contents to some of the most intelligent, well-informed, and confidential officers, whose judgment I have consulted, and endeavored to collect from them what is the general line and expectation of the army at large respecting the points you mention. And, as this is meant to be equally private and confidential as yours, I shall communicate my sentiments to you without reserve and with the most entire freedom.

The idea of the officers in keeping the army together until settlement of their accounts is effected and *funds established* for their security is perhaps not so extensive as the words of their resolution seem to intimate. When that idea was first expressed, our prospects of peace were distant, and it was supposed that settlement and funds might both be effected before a dissolution of the army would probably take place. They wished, therefore, to have both done at once. But since the expectation of peace is brought so near, however desirable it would be to the officers to have their balances secured to them upon sufficient funds, as well their settlement ascertained, yet it is not in idea that the army should be held together for the sole purpose of enforcing either. Nor do they suppose that by such means they could operate on the *fears* of the civil power or of the people at large. The impracticability as well as the policy of such a mode of conduct is easily discoverable by every sensible, intelligent officer. The thought is reprobated as ridiculous and inadmissible.

Though these are their ideas on the particular point you have mentioned, yet they have their expectations; and they are of a very serious nature and will require all the attention and consideration of Congress to gratify them. These I will endeavor to explain with freedom and candor.

In the first place, I fix it as an *indispensable* measure that previous to the disbanding the army, all their accounts should be completely liquidated and settled and that every person shall be ascertained of the balance due to him. And it is *equally essential* in my opinion that this settlement should be effected with the army in its collected body, without any dispersion of the different lines to their respective states—for in this way the accounts will be drawn into one view, properly digested upon one general system and compared with a variety of circumstances, which will require references upon a much easier plan than to be diffused over all the states. The settlements will be effected with greater ease, in less time, and with much more economy in this than in a scattered situation. At the same time, jealousies will be removed, the minds of the army will be impressed with greater ease and quiet, and they better prepared with good opinions and proper dispositions to fall back into the great mass of citizens.

But after settlement is formed there remains another circumstance of more importance still, and without which it will be of little consequence to have the sums due them ascertained—that is, the payment of one part of the balance. The distresses of officers and soldiers are now driven to the extreme and without this provision will not be lessened by the prospect of dissolution. It is therefore universally expected that three months' pay at least must be given them before they are disbanded. This sum, it is confidently imagined, may be procured and is absolutely indispensable. They are the rather confirmed in a belief of the practicability of obtaining it, as the pay of the army has formed great part of the sum in the estimates which have been made for the expenses of the war. And although this has been obliged to give way to more necessary claims, yet when those demands cease, as many will upon the disbanding the army, the pay will then come into view and have its equal claim to notice. They will not, however, be unreasonable in this expectation. If the whole cannot be obtained before they are dispersed, the receipt of one month in hand, with an absolute assurance of having the other two months in a short time, will be satisfactory. Should Mr. Morris not be able to assure them the two last months from the treasury, it is suggested that it may be obtained in the states, by drafts from him upon their several continental receivers, to be collected by the individual officers and soldiers out of the last year's arrears due from the several states' apportionments, and for which taxes have long since been assessed by the legislatures. This mode, though troublesome to the officer, and perhaps inconvenient for the financier, yet from the necessity of circumstances may be adopted and might be a means of collecting more taxes from the people than would in any other way be done. This is only hinted as an expedient; the financier will take his own measures. But I repeat it as an indispensable point that this sum at least must by some means be procured. Without this provision it will be absolutely impossible for many to get from camp or to return to their friends; and driven to such necessities, it is impossible to foresee what may be the consequences of their not obtaining it—but the worst is to be apprehended. A credit, built by their funds and such others as have been good enough to supply their wants upon the expectation of being refunded at the close of the war, out of the large sum which by their toils in the course of many years' hard service have become due to them from the public, has supported the greatest number of them to the present time, and that debt now remains upon them. But to be disbanded at last, without this little pittance (which is necessary to quit quarters), like a set of beggars, needy, distressed, and without prospect, will not only blast the expectations of their creditors and expose the officers to the utmost indignity and the worst of consequences, but will drive every man of honor and sensibility to the extremest horrors of despair. On the other hand, to give them this sum, however small in comparison of their dues, yet by fulfilling their expectations will sweeten their tempers, cheer their hopes of the future, enable them to subsist themselves till they can cast about for some future means of business. It will gratify their pressing creditors and will throw the officer back with ease and confidence into the bosom of this country and enable him to mix with cordiality and affection among the mass of useful, happy, and contented citizens—an object of the most desirable importance. I cannot, at this point of distance, know the arrangement of the financier, what have been his anticipations, or what his prospects. But the necessity of fulfilling this expectation of the army affects me so exceeding forcibly that I cannot help dwelling upon it. Nor is there in my present apprehension a point of greater consequence or that requires more serious attention. Under this impression, I have thought, if a spirited, pointed, and well-adapted address was framed by Congress and sent to the states on this occasion, that gratitude, justice, honor, national pride, and every consideration would operate upon them to strain every nerve and exert every endeavor to throw into the public treasury a sum equal to this requisition. It cannot be denied, especially when they reflect how small the expectation is compared with the large sum of arrears which is due. And though I know that distinctions are commonly odious and are looked upon with a jealous and envious eye, yet it is impossible that in this case it can have this operation. For whatever the feelings of individuals at large may be in contemplating on their own demands, yet, upon a candid comparison, every man, even the most interested, will be forced to yield to the superior merit and sufferings of the soldier, who for a course of years has contributed his services in the field, not only at the expense of his fortune and former employment, but at the risk of ease, domestic happiness, comfort, and even life. After all these considerations, how must he be struck with the mediocrity of his demand when, instead of the pay due him for four, five, perhaps six years' hard-earned toil and distress, he is content for the present with receiving three months' only, and is willing to risk the remainder upon the same basis of security with the general mass of other public creditors.

Another expectation seems to have possessed the minds of the officers: that, as the objects above mentioned are not the only ones which must occupy the attention of Congress in connection with the army, it may probably be thought advisable that Congress should send to the army a respectable, well-chosen, and well-instructed committee of their own body with liberal powers to confer with the army, to know their sentiments, their expectations, their distresses, their necessities, and the impossibility of their falling back from the soldier to citizenship without some gratification to their most reasonable demands. This would be considered as a compliment. And to add still greater satisfaction and advantage, it is thought very advisable that the secretary at war and the financier should be of this delegation. Previous to a dissolution of the army, many arrangements will doubtless be thought necessary in both those departments to procure a happy and honorable close to the war, and to introduce peace, with a prospect of national glory, stability, and benefit. It is not for me to dictate, but I should suppose that some peace establishment will be necessary. Some posts will be kept up and garrisoned. Arsenals for the deposit of ordnance and military stores will be determined on, and the stores collected and deposited. Arrangements will be necessary for the discharge of the army—at what periods and under what circumstances. The terms of the soldiers' service were on different grounds. Those for the war will suppose, and they have a right to do so, their periods of service to expire at the close of war and proclamation of peace. What period shall be fixed for these? The levy men may be retained while the British force remain in our country if it shall be judged advisable. If I am not consulted in these matters, it will be necessary for me to have an early knowledge of the intentions of Congress on these and many other points. But I can think of no mode so effectual as the one suggested of a committee accompanied by the financier and secretary at war. Plans which to us appear feasible and practicable may be attended with insurmountable difficulties. On the other hand, measures may be adopted at Philadelphia which cannot be carried into execution; but here in the manner proposed something might be hit upon which would accommodate itself to the ideas of both with greater ease and satisfaction than may now be expected, and which could not be effected by writing quires of paper and spending a length of time.

Upon the whole, you will be able to collect from the foregoing sentiments what are the expectations of the army: that they will involve complete settlement and partial payment previous to any dispersion (this they suppose may be done within the time that they must necessarily remain together). Upon the fulfillment of these two, they will readily retire, in full assurance that ample security, at the earliest period and on the best ground it can be had, will be obtained for the remainder of their balances.

If the idea of a committee to visit the army should not be adopted, and you find it necessary to pass any further resolutions, you will easily collect from the foregoing sentiments what will be satisfactory without my troubling you any further. I pray you to communicate the contents of this letter to Colonel Hamilton, from whom I received a request similar to yours. I have the honor to be &c.

To Marquis de Lafayette, April 5, 1783 (Excerpts)

My Dear Marquis,

It is easier for you to conceive than for me to express the sensibility of my heart at the communications in your letter of the 5th of February from Cadiz. It is to these communications we are indebted for the only account yet received of a general pacification. My mind upon the receipt of this news was instantly assailed by a thousand ideas, all of them contending for pre-eminence; but believe me, my dear friend, none could supplant or ever will eradicate that gratitude which has arisen from a lively sense of the conduct of your nation, from my obligations to many illustrious characters of it, among whom (I do yet mean to flatter, when) I place you at the head of them, and from my admiration of the virtues of your august sovereign, who, at the same time that he stands confessed the father of his own people and defender of American rights, has given the most exalted example of moderation in treating with his enemies.

We now stand an independent people and have yet to learn political tactics. We are placed among the nations of the earth and have a character to establish; but how we shall acquit ourselves time must discover. The probability, at least I fear it, is that local or state politics will interfere too much with that most liberal and extensive plan of government which wisdom and foresight, freed from the mist of prejudice, would dictate and that we shall be guilty of many blunders in treading this boundless theater before we shall have arrived at any perfection in this art—in a word, that the experience which is purchased at the price of difficulties and distress will alone convince us that the honor, power, and true interest of this country must be measured by a continental scale, and that every departure therefrom weakens the Union and may ultimately break the band which holds us together. To avert these evils—to form a constitution that will give consistency, stability, and dignity to the Union, and sufficient powers to the great council of the nation for general purposes—is a duty which is incumbent upon every man who wishes well to his country and will meet with my aid as far as it can be rendered in the private walks of life. For hence forward my mind shall be unbent, and I will endeavor to glide gently down the stream of life till I come to that abyss from whence no traveler is permitted to return ....

I have already observed that the determinations of Congress, if they have come to any, respecting the army are yet unknown to me; but as you wish to be informed of *everything* that concerns it, I do, for your satisfaction, transmit authentic documents of some very interesting occurrences which have happened within the last six months. But I ought first to have premised that from accumulated sufferings, and little or no prospect of relief, the discontents of the officers last fall put on the threatening appearance of a total resignation, till the business was diverted into the channel which produced the address and petition to Congress which stands first on the file herewith enclosed. I shall make no comment on these proceedings. To one as well acquainted with the sufferings of the American army as you are, it is unnecessary. It will be sufficient to observe that the more the virtue and forbearance of it are tried, the more resplendent it appears. My hope is that the military exit of this valuable class of the community will exhibit such of proof of the amor patriae as will do them honor in the page of history ....

The scheme, my dear Marquis, which you propose as a precedent to encourage the emancipation of the black people of this country from the bondage in which they are held is a striking evidence of the benevolence of your heart. I shall be happy to join you in so laudable a work but will defer going into a detail of the business till I have the pleasure of seeing you.

To Alexander Hamilton, April 16, 1783

Dear Sir,

My last letter to you was written in a hurry, when I was fatigued by the more public yet confidential letter which (with several others) accompanied it. Possibly I did not on that occasion express myself (in what I intended as a hint) with so much perspicuity as I ought. Possibly, too, what I then dropped might have conveyed more than I intended; for I do not, at this time, recollect the force of my expressions.

My meaning, however, was only to inform that there were different sentiments in the army as well as in Congress respecting continental and state funds, some wishing to be thrown upon their respective states rather than the continent at large for payment, and that if an idea should prevail generally that Congress, or part of its members or ministers bent upon the latter, should *delay* doing them justice, or *hazard* it in pursuit of their favorite object, it might create such divisions in the army as would weaken rather than strengthen the hands of those who were disposed to support continental measures, and might *tend* to defeat the end they themselves had in view by endeavoring to involve the army.

For these reasons I said, or meant to say, the army was a dangerous engine to work with, as it might be made to cut both ways—and, considering the sufferings of it, would, more than probably, throw its weight into that scale which seemed most likely to preponderate towards its immediate relief, without looking forward (under the pressure of present wants) to future consequences with the eyes of politicians. In this light also I meant to apply my observations to Mr. Morris, to whom, or rather to Mr. G. M—— is ascribed, in a great degree, the groundwork of the superstructure which was intended to be raised in the army by the anonymous addresses.

That no man can be more opposed to state funds and local prejudices than myself, the whole tenor of my conduct has been one continual evidence of. No man, perhaps, has had better opportunities to *see* and to *feel* the pernicious tendency of the latter than I have. And I endeavor (I hope not altogether ineffectually) to inculcate them upon the officers of the army upon all proper occasions. But their feelings are to be attended to and soothed and they assured that, if continental funds cannot be established, they will be recommended to their respective states for payment. Justice must be done them.

I should do injustice to report, and what I believe to be the opinion of the army, were I not to inform you that they consider you as a friend, zealous to serve them, and one who has espoused their interests in Congress upon every proper occasion. It is to be wished, as I observed in my letter to Colonel Bland, that Congress would send a committee to the army with plenipotentiary powers. The matters requested of me in your letter of the _____ as chairman of a committee, and many other things, might then be brought to a close with more dispatch and in a happier manner than it is likely they will be by an intercourse of letters at the distance of 150 miles, which takes *our* expresses a week *at least* to go and come. At this moment, being without any instructions from Congress, I am under great embarrassment with respect to the soldiers for the war and shall be obliged more than probably, from the necessity of the case, to exercise my own judgment without waiting for orders as to the discharge of them. If I should adopt measures which events may approve, all will be well. If otherwise, why and by what authority did you do so?

How far a *strong* recommendation from Congress to observe *all* the articles of peace as well as the _____ may imply a suspicion of good faith in the people of this country, I pretend not to judge; but I am much mistaken if something of the kind will not be found wanting, as I already perceive a disposition to carp at and to elude such parts of the treaty as affect their different interests, although you do not find a man who, when pushed, will not acknowledge that upon the whole it is a more advantageous peace than we could possibly have expected. I am Dear Sir with great esteem & regard Yr Most Obedt Servt

Go: Washington

General Orders, April 18, 1783 (Excerpt)

The commander-in-chief orders the cessation of hostilities between the United States of America and the king of Great Britain to be publicly proclaimed tomorrow at 12 o'clock at the new building, and that the proclamation which will be communicated herewith be read tomorrow evening at the head of every regiment and corps of the army—after which the chaplains with the several brigades will render thanks to Almighty God for all his mercies, particularly for his overruling the wrath of man to his own glory and causing the rage of war to cease amongst the nations.

Although the proclamation before alluded to intends only to the prohibition of hostilities and not to the annunciation of a general peace, yet it must afford the most rational and sincere satisfaction to every benevolent mind, as it puts a period to a long and doubtful contest, stops the effusion of human blood, opens the prospect to a more splendid scene, and, like another morning star, promises the approach of a brighter day than hath hitherto illuminated the western hemisphere. On such a happy day, a day which is the harbinger of peace, a day which completes the eighth year of the war, it would be ingratitude not to rejoice, it would be insensibility not to participate in the general felicity.

The commander-in-chief, far from endeavoring to stifle the feelings of joy in his own bosom, offers his most cordial congratulations on the occasion to all the officers of every denomination, to all the troops of the United States in general, and in particular to those gallant and persevering men who had resolved to defend the rights of their invaded country so long as the war should continue. For these are the men who ought to be considered as the pride and boast of the American army—and, who crowned with well-earned laurels, may soon withdraw from the field of glory to the more tranquil walks of civil life.

While the general recollects the almost infinite variety of scenes through which we have passed with a mixture of pleasure, astonishment, and gratitude, while he contemplates the prospects before us with rapture, he cannot help wishing that all the brave men (of whatever condition they may be) who have shared in the toils and dangers of effecting this glorious revolution, of rescuing millions from the hand of oppression, and of laying the foundation of a great empire, might be impressed with a proper idea of the dignified part they have been called to act (under the smiles of Providence) on the stage of human affairs: for, happy, thrice happy shall they be pronounced hereafter who have contributed anything, who have performed the meanest office in creating this stupendous *fabric of freedom and empire* on the broad basis of independency, who have assisted in protesting the rights of human nature and establishing an asylum for the poor and oppressed of all nations and religions.

The glorious task for which we first flew to arms being thus accomplished, the liberties of our country being fully acknowledged and firmly secured by the smiles of *Heaven* on the purity of our cause and the honest exertions of a feeble people (determined to be free) against a powerful nation (disposed to oppress them), and the character of those who have persevered through every extremity of hardship, suffering, and danger being immortalized by the illustrious appellation of the *Patriot Army*—nothing more remains but for the actors of this mighty scene to preserve a perfect, unvarying consistency of character through the very last act, to close the *drama* with applause, and to retire from the military theater with the same approbation of angels and men which have crowned all their former virtuous actions. For this purpose, no disorder or licentiousness must be tolerated. Every considerate and well-disposed soldier must remember it will be absolutely necessary to wait with patience until peace shall be declared or Congress shall be enabled to take proper measures for the security of the public stores, etc. As soon as these arrangements shall be made the general is confident there will be no delay in discharging with every mark of distinction and honor all the men enlisted for the war who will then have faithfully performed their engagements with the public. The general has already interested himself in their behalf, and he thinks he need not repeat the assurances of his disposition to be useful to them on the present and every other proper occasion. In the meantime, he is determined that no military neglects or excesses shall go unpunished while he retains the command of the army. An extra ration of liquor to be issued to *every* man tomorrow to drink perpetual peace, independence, and happiness to the United States of America.

To Alexander Hamilton, April 22, 1783 (Excerpt)

Finding a diversity of opinions respecting the treaty and the line of conduct we ought to observe with prisoners, I requested in precise terms to know from General Lincoln (before I entered on the business) whether we were to exercise our own judgment with respect to the *time* as well as *mode* of releasing them, or were to be confined to the latter. Being informed that we had no option in the first, Congress wishing to be eased of the expense as soon as possible, I acted *solely* on that ground.

At the same time, I scruple not to confess to you that, if this measure was not dictated by necessity, it is, in my opinion, an impolitic one, as we place ourselves in the power of the British before the treaty is definitive. The manner in which peace was first announced, and the subsequent declarations of it, have led the country and army into a belief that it was final. The ratification of the preliminary articles on the 3rd of February so far confirmed this that one consequence resulting from it is the soldiers for the war conceive the term of their services has actually expired. And I believe it is not in the power of Congress or their officers to hold them much, if any, longer; for we are obliged at this moment to increase our guards to prevent rioting and[27] the insults which the officers meet with in attempting to hold them to their duty. The proportion of these men amount to seven elevenths of this army. These we shall lose at the moment the British army will receive, by their prisoners, an augmentation of five or six thousand men.

It is not for me to investigate the causes which induced this measure, nor the policy of these letters—from authority—which gave the tone to the present sentiments. But since they have been adopted we ought, in my opinion, to put a good face upon matters, and by a liberal conduct throughout on our part (freed from appearances of distrust) try if we cannot excite similar dispositions on theirs. Indeed, circumstanced as things *now* are, I wish most fervently that all the troops which are not retained for a peace establishment were to be discharged immediately, or such of them at least as do not incline to await the settlement of their accounts. If they continue here their claims, I can plainly perceive, will increase and our perplexities multiply. A petition is this moment handed to me from the non-commissioned officers of the Connecticut line soliciting half-pay. It is well drawn, I am told; but I did not read it. I sent it back without appearing to understand the contents, because it did not come through the channel of their officers. This may be followed by others, and I mention it to show the necessity—the absolute necessity—of discharging the *war's men* as soon as possible.

I have taken much pains to support Mr. Morris's administration in the army, and in proportion to its numbers I believe he had not more friends anywhere. But if he will neither adopt the mode which has been suggested, point out any other, nor show cause why the first is either impracticable or impolitic (I have heard he objects to it) they will certainly attribute their disappointment to a lukewarmness in him or some design incompatible with their interests. And here, my dear Colonel Hamilton, let me assure you that it would not be more difficult to still the raging billows in a tempestuous gale than to convince the officers of this army of the justice or policy of paying men in civil offices full wages when *they* cannot obtain a sixtieth part of their dues. I am not unapprised of the arguments which are made use of upon this occasion to discriminate the cases; but they really are futile and may be summed up in this: that though both are contending for the same rights and expect equal benefits, yet both cannot submit to the same inconveniences to obtain them. Otherwise, to adopt the language of simplicity and plainness, a ration of salt pork, with or without peas, as the case often is, would support the one as well as the other—and in such a struggle as ours would, in my opinion, be alike honorable in both.

My anxiety to get home increases with the prospect of it, but when is it to happen? I have not heard that Congress have yet had under consideration the lands and other gratuities which at different periods of the war have been promised to the army. Do not these things evince the necessity of a committee's repairing to camp in order to arrange and adjust matters, without spending time in a tedious exchange of letters? Unless something of this kind is adopted, business will be delayed and expenses accumulated—or the army will break up in disorder, go home enraged, complaining of injustice, and committing enormities on the innocent inhabitants in every direction.

I write to you unreservedly. If, therefore, contrary to my apprehensions all these matters are in a proper train, and Mr. Morris has devised means to give the army three months' pay, you will, I am persuaded, excuse my precipitancy and solicitude by ascribing it to an earnest wish to see the war happily and honorably terminated—to my anxious desire of enjoying some repose and the necessity of my paying a little attention to my private concerns, which have suffered considerably in eight years' absence.

To Lieutenant Colonel Tench Tilghman, April 24, 1783

Dear Sir,

I received with much pleasure the kind congratulations contained in your letter of the 25th ultimo from Philadelphia on the honorable termination of the war. No man, indeed, can relish the approaching peace with more heartfelt and grateful satisfaction than myself. A mind always upon the stretch, and tortured with a diversity of perplexing circumstances, needed a respite; and I anticipate the pleasure of a little repose and retirement. It has been happy for me always to have gentlemen about me willing to share my troubles and help me out of difficulties. To none of these can I ascribe a greater share of merit than to you.

I can scarcely form an idea at this moment when I shall be able to leave this place. The distresses of the army for want of money, the embarrassments of Congress, and the consequent delays and disappointments on all sides encompass me with difficulties and produce—every day—some fresh source for uneasiness. But as I now see the port opening to which I have been steering, I shall persevere till I have gained admittance. I will then leave the states to improve their present constitution, so as to make that peace and independency for which we have fought and obtained a blessing to millions yet unborn. But to do this, liberality must supply the place of prejudice; and unreasonable jealousies must yield to that confidence which ought to be placed in the sovereign power of these states. In a word, the constitution of Congress must be competent to the general purposes of government and of such a nature as to bind us together. Otherwise, we may well be compared to a rope of sand and shall as easily be broken—and in a short time become the sport of European politics, although we might have no great inclination to jar among ourselves.

From the intimation in your letter and what I have heard from others, I presume this letter will find you in the state of wedlock. On this happy event I pray you and your lady to accept of my best wishes and sincerest congratulations, in which Mrs. Washington joins hers most cordially. With the most affectionate esteem and regard I am—Dr Sir Yr most obedt Servt

Go: Washington

To Jean de Neufville, April 25, 1783

Sir,

I have been very agreeably favored with your letter of the 25th of February dated from Germany.

The part your states[28] have taken in the causes of the United States of America has inspired the sons of the latter with the happiest presages of a most beneficial connection between the two republics—sister republics—whose similarity of constitutions, interests, and religion bid fair to bind them together by the most lasting ties. The idea gives me peculiar satisfaction. And it is the wish of my heart that the union now commencing may be as durable as it is pleasing—nay, that, grounded in reciprocal interest and affection, it may be perpetual as time.

The distinguished part you have taken in the great events of the present age, and your affection for the interests of happiness of our rising nation, will endear your character with the sons of American freedom, among whom you have long been spoken of with terms of particular veneration and respect.

For the return of those worthy characters, the Baron Vander Capellon and Pensionary Van Berkel, to the affection of their countrymen and their former station and usefulness in your republic, I most sincerely rejoice and beg leave, with great sincerity, to participate in your joy on that happy event, which is a subject of my warmest congratulations to you.

If in any period of my life I can ever be serviceable by myself or friends to the particular interest of yourself or family, you may be assured the occasion will give me the highest satisfaction and will be esteemed among the most fortunate circumstances that shall ever attend me.

To Benjamin Harrison, Governor of Virginia, April 30, 1783

My Dear Sir,

I thank you very sincerely for your kind congratulations on the close of the war and the glorious peace which is held out to us, but not yet made definitive. I return them with great cordiality and heartfelt pleasure and only wish that the business was so far wound up as that I might return to the walks of private life and in retirement enjoy that relaxation and repose which is absolutely necessary for me.

My first wish now is that the states may be wise, that they may improve the advantages which they have obtained, that they may consider themselves individually as parts of the great whole, and not by unreasonable jealousies and unfounded[29] prejudices destroy the goodly fabric we have been eight years laboring to erect. But without more liberality of sentiment and action, I expect but little.

Immediately upon the receipt of your letter of the 31st ultimo, I transmitted the list of your slaves to a gentleman—a worthy, active man—of my acquaintance in New York and requested him to use his endeavors to obtain and forward them to you. All that can be done I am sure he will do, but I have but little expectation that many will be recovered. Several of my own are with the enemy, but I scarce ever bestowed a thought on them. They have so many doors through which they can escape from New York that scarce anything but an inclination to return, or voluntarily surrender themselves, will restore many to their former masters, even supposing every disposition on the part of the enemy to deliver them. With great truth & sincerity I am Dr Sir Yr Most Obt & Affe Ser.

Go: W——n

To Elisha Boudinot, President of the Confederation Congress, May 10, 1783 (Excerpt)

Sir,

Your letter of congratulation contains expressions of too friendly a nature not to affect me with the deepest sensibility. I beg, therefore, you will accept my acknowledgments for them, and that you will be persuaded I can never be insensible of the interest you are pleased to take in my personal happiness, as well as in the general felicity of our country. While I candidly confess I cannot be indifferent to the favorable sentiments which you mention my fellow citizens entertain of my exertions in their service, I wish to express through you the particular obligations I feel myself under to Mr. Smith for the pleasure I have received from the perusal of his elegant *Ode on the Peace*.

The accomplishment of the great object we had in view, in so short a time and under such propitious circumstances, must, I am confident, fill every bosom with the purest joy. And for my own part I will not strive to conceal the pleasure I already anticipate from my approaching retirement to the placid walks of domestic life.

Having no rewards to ask for myself, if I have been so happy as to obtain the approbation of my countrymen, I shall be satisfied. But it still rests with them to complete my wishes by adopting such a system of policy as will ensure the future reputation, tranquility, happiness, and glory of this extensive empire—to which I am well assured nothing can contribute so much as *an inviolable adherence to the principles of the Union*, and a fixed resolution of building *the national faith on the basis of public justice*, without which all that has been done and suffered is in vain, to effect which, therefore, the abilities of every true patriot ought to be exerted with the greatest zeal and assiduity.

Circular to the States, June 8, 1783

Sir,

The great object for which I had the honor to hold an appointment in the service of my country being accomplished, I am now preparing to resign it into the hands of Congress, and to return to that domestic retirement which it is well known I left with the greatest reluctance, a retirement for which I have never ceased to sigh through a long and painful absence, and in which (remote from the noise and trouble of the world) I meditate to pass the remainder of life in a state of undisturbed repose. But before I carry this resolution into effect, I think is a duty incumbent on me to make this, my last official communication, to congratulate you on the glorious events which Heaven has been pleased to produce in our favor, to offer my sentiments respecting some important subjects which appear to me to be intimately connected with the tranquility of the United States, to take my leave of Your Excellency as a public character, and to give my final blessing to that country in whose service I have spent the prime of my life, for whose sake I have consumed so many anxious days and watchful nights, and whose happiness, being extremely dear to me, will always constitute no inconsiderable part of my own.

Impressed with the liveliest sensibility on this pleasing occasion, I will claim the indulgence of dilating the more copiously on the subjects of our mutual felicitation. When we consider the magnitude of the prize we contended for, the doubtful nature of the contest, and the favorable manner in which it has terminated, we shall find the greatest possible reason for gratitude and rejoicing. This is a theme that will afford infinite delight to every benevolent and liberal mind, whether the event in contemplation be considered as the source of present enjoyment or the parent of future happiness. And we shall have equal occasion to felicitate ourselves on the lot which Providence has assigned us, whether we view it in a natural, a political, or a moral point of light.

The citizens of America, placed in the most enviable condition as the sole lords and proprietors of a vast tract of continent, comprehending all the various soils and climates of the world, and abounding with all the necessaries and conveniences of life, are now, by the late satisfactory pacification, acknowledged to be possessed of absolute freedom and independency. They are from this period to be considered as the actors on a most conspicuous theater, which seems to be peculiarly designated by Providence for the display of human greatness and felicity. Here they are not only surrounded with everything which can contribute to the completion of private and domestic enjoyment, but Heaven has crowned all its other blessings by giving a fairer opportunity for political happiness than any other nation has ever been favored with. Nothing can illustrate these observations more forcibly than a recollection of the happy conjuncture of times and circumstances under which our republic assumed its rank among the nations. The foundation of our empire was not laid in the gloomy age of ignorance and superstition, but at an epocha when the rights of mankind were better understood and more clearly defined than at any former period. The researches of the human mind after social happiness have been carried to a great extent, the treasures of knowledge acquired by the labors of philosophers, sages, and legislators, through a long succession of years, are laid open for our use, and their collected wisdom may be happily applied in the establishment of our forms of government. The free cultivation of letters, the unbounded extension of commerce, the progressive refinement of manners, the growing liberality of sentiment, and, above all, the pure and benign light of Revelation, have had a meliorating influence on mankind and increased the blessings of society. At this auspicious period the United States came into existence as a nation, and if their citizens should not be completely free and happy, the fault will be entirely their own.

Such is our situation, and such are our prospects. But notwithstanding the cup of blessing is thus reached out to us, notwithstanding happiness is ours if we have a disposition to seize the occasion and make it our own, yet it appears to me there is an option still left to the United States of America, that it is in their choice and depends upon their conduct whether they will be respectable and prosperous or contemptible and miserable as a nation. This is the time of their political probation. This is the moment when the eyes of the whole world are turned upon them. This is the moment to establish or ruin their national character forever. This is the favorable moment to give such a tone to our federal government as will enable it to answer the ends of its institution. Or this may be the ill-fated moment for relaxing the powers of the Union, annihilating the cement of the Confederation, and exposing us to become the sport of European politick, which may play one state against another to prevent their growing importance and to serve their own interested purposes. For according to the system of policy the states shall adopt at this moment they will stand or fall, and by their confirmation or lapse it is yet to be decided whether the Revolution must ultimately be considered as a blessing or a curse—a blessing or a curse not to the present age alone, for with our fate will the destiny of unborn millions be involved.

With this conviction of the importance of the present crisis, silence in me would be a crime. I will therefore speak to Your Excellency the language of freedom and sincerity without disguise. I am aware, however, that those who differ from me in political sentiment may perhaps remark I am stepping out of the proper line of my duty, and they may possibly ascribe to arrogance or ostentation what I know is alone the result of the purest intention. But the rectitude of my own heart, which disdains such unworthy motives; the part I have hitherto acted in life; the determination I have formed of not taking any share in public business hereafter; the ardent desire I feel and shall continue to manifest of quietly enjoying in private life, after all the toils of war, the benefits of a wise and liberal government, will, I flatter myself, sooner or later convince my countrymen that I could have no sinister views in delivering, with so little reserve, the opinions contained in this address.

There are four things which I humbly conceive are essential to the well-being, I may even venture to say to the existence, of the United States as an independent power.

1st: An indissoluble Union of the states under one federal head.

2ndly: A sacred regard to public justice.

3rdly: The adoption of a proper peace establishment, and

4thly: The prevalence of that pacific and friendly disposition among the people of the United States which will induce them to forget their local prejudices and policies, to make those mutual concessions which are requisite to the general prosperity, and, in some instances, to sacrifice their individual advantages to the interest of the community.

These are the pillars on which the glorious fabric of our independency and national character must be supported. Liberty is the basis, and whoever would dare to sap the foundation or overturn the structure, under whatever specious pretexts he may attempt it, will merit the bitterest execration and the severest punishments which can be inflicted by his injured country.

On the three first articles I will make a few observations, leaving the last to the good sense and serious consideration of those immediately concerned.

Under the first head, although it may not be necessary or proper for me in this place to enter into a particular disquisition of the principles of the Union and to take up the great question which has been frequently agitated, whether it be expedient and requisite for the states to delegate a larger proportion of power to Congress or not, yet it will be a part of my duty, and that of every true patriot, to assert without reserve and to insist upon the following positions: That unless the states will suffer Congress to exercise those prerogatives they are undoubtedly invested with by the constitution, everything must very rapidly tend to anarchy and confusion; that it is indispensable to the happiness of the individual states that there should be lodged somewhere a supreme power to regulate and govern the general concerns of the confederated republic, without which the Union cannot be of long duration; that there must be a faithful and pointed compliance on the part of every state with the late proposals and demands of Congress, or the most fatal consequences will ensue; that whatever measures have a tendency to dissolve the Union, or contribute to violate or lessen the sovereign authority, ought to be considered as hostile to the liberty and independency of America and the authors of them treated accordingly; and lastly, that unless we can be enabled by the concurrence of the states to participate of the fruits of the Revolution and enjoy the essential benefits of civil society, under a form of government so free and uncorrupted, so happily guarded against the danger of oppression as has been devised and adopted by the Articles of Confederation, it will be a subject of regret that so much blood and treasure have been lavished for no purpose, that so many sufferings have been encountered without a compensation, and that so many sacrifices have been made in vain.

Many other considerations might here be adduced to prove that without an entire conformity to the spirit of the Union we cannot exist as an independent power. It will be sufficient for my purpose to mention but one or two which seem to me of the greatest importance. It is only in our united character as an empire that our independence is acknowledged, that our power can be regarded, or our credit supported among foreign nations. The treaties of the European powers with the United States of America will have no validity on a dissolution of the Union. We shall be left nearly in a state of nature, or we may find by our own unhappy experience that there is a natural and necessary progression from the extreme of anarchy to the extreme of tyranny, and that arbitrary power is most easily established on the ruins of liberty abused to licentiousness.

As to the second article, which respects the performance of public justice, Congress have in their late address to the United States almost exhausted the subject. They have explained their ideas so fully and have enforced the obligations the states are under to render complete justice to all the public creditors with so much dignity and energy that in my opinion no real friend to the honor and independency of America can hesitate a single moment respecting the propriety of complying with the just and honorable measures proposed. If their arguments do not produce conviction, I know of nothing that will have greater influence, especially when we recollect that the system referred to, being the result of the collected wisdom of the continent, must be esteemed, if not perfect, certainly the least objectionable of any that could be devised, and that if it shall not be carried into immediate execution a national bankruptcy, with all its deplorable consequences, will take place before any different plan can possibly be proposed and adopted, so pressing are the present circumstances! and such is the alternative now offered to the states!

The ability of the country to discharge the debts which have been incurred in its defense is not to be doubted. An inclination, I flatter myself, will not be wanting. The path of our duty is plain before us. Honesty will be found on every experiment to be the best and only true policy. Let us, then, as a nation be just. Let us fulfill the public contracts which Congress had undoubtedly a right to make for the purpose of carrying on the war with the same good faith we suppose ourselves bound to perform our private engagements. In the meantime, let an attention to the cheerful performance of their proper business as individuals and as members of society be earnestly inculcated on the citizens of America. Then will they strengthen the hands of government and be happy under its protection. Everyone will reap the fruit of his labors; everyone will enjoy his own acquisitions without molestation and without danger.

In this state of absolute freedom and perfect security, who will grudge to yield a very little of his property to support the common interests of society and ensure the protection of government? Who does not remember the frequent declarations at the commencement of the war that we should be completely satisfied if at the expense of one half we could defend the remainder of our possessions! Where is the man to be found who wishes to remain indebted for the defense of his own person and property to the exertions, the bravery, and the blood of others, without making one generous effort to repay the debt of honor and of gratitude? In what part of the continent shall we find any man or body of men who would not blush to stand up and propose measures purposely calculated to rob the soldier of his stipend and the public creditor of his due? And were it possible that such a flagrant instance of injustice could ever happen, would it not excite the general indignation and tend to bring down upon the authors of such measures the aggravated vengeance of Heaven?

If, after all, a spirit of disunion or a temper of obstinacy and perverseness should manifest itself in any of the states; if such an ungracious disposition should attempt to frustrate all the happy effects that might be expected to flow from the Union; if there should be a refusal to comply with the requisitions for funds to discharge the annual interest of the public debts and if that refusal should revive again all those jealousies and produce all those evils which are now happily removed; Congress, who have in all their transactions shown a great degree of magnanimity and justice, will stand justified in the sight of God and man, and the state alone which puts itself in opposition to the aggregate wisdom of the continent and follows such mistaken and pernicious councils will be responsible for all the consequences.

For my own part, conscious of having acted, while a servant of the public, in the manner I conceived best suited to promote the real interests of my country, having in consequence of my fixed belief in some measure pledged myself to the army that their country would finally do them complete and ample justice, and not wishing to conceal any instance of my official conduct from the eyes of the world, I have thought proper to transmit to Your Excellency the enclosed collection of papers relative to the half-pay and commutation granted by Congress to the officers of the army. From these communications my decided sentiment will be clearly comprehended, together with the conclusive reasons which induced me, at an early period, to recommend the adoption of this measure in the most earnest and serious manner. As the proceedings of Congress, the army, and myself are open to all and contain, in my opinion, sufficient information to remove the prejudices and errors which may have been entertained by any, I think it unnecessary to say anything more than just to observe that the resolutions of Congress now alluded to are undoubtedly as absolutely binding upon the United States as the most solemn acts of confederation or legislation. As to the idea which, I am informed, has in some instances prevailed, that the half-pay and commutation are to be regarded merely in the odious light of a pension, it ought to be exploded forever. That provision should be viewed as it really was: a reasonable compensation offered by Congress at a time when they had nothing else to give to the officers of the army for services then to be performed. It was the only means to prevent a total dereliction of the service. It was a part of their hire. I may be allowed to say, it was the price of their blood and of your independency. It is therefore more than a common debt; it is a debt of honor. It can never be considered as a pension or gratuity, nor be canceled until it is fairly discharged.

With regard to a distinction between officers and soldiers, it is sufficient that the uniform experience of every nation of the world, combined with our own, proves the utility and propriety of the discrimination. Rewards in proportion to the aids the public derives from them are unquestionably due to all its servants. In some lines the soldiers have perhaps generally had as ample a compensation for their services by the large bounties which have been paid them as their officers will receive in the proposed commutation. In others, if, besides the donation of lands, the payment of arrearages of clothing and wages (in which articles all the component parts of the army must be on the same footing), we take into the estimate the bounties many of the soldiers have received and the gratuity of one year's full pay which is promised to all, possibly their situation (every circumstance being duly considered) will not be deemed less eligible than that of the officers. Should a farther reward, however, be judged equitable, I will venture to assert no one will enjoy greater satisfaction than myself on seeing an exemption from taxes for a limited time (which has been petitioned for in some instances), or any other adequate compensation or immunity, granted to the brave defenders of their country's cause. But neither the adoption or rejection of this proposition will in any manner affect, much less militate against, the act of Congress by which they have offered five years' full pay in lieu of half-pay for life, which had been before promised to the officers of the army.

Before I conclude the subject of public justice, I cannot omit to mention the obligations this country is under to that meritorious class of veteran non-commissioned officers and privates who have been discharged for inability, in consequence of the resolution of Congress of the 23rd April 1782, on an annual pension for life. Their peculiar sufferings, their singular merits and claims to that provision, need only be known to interest all the feelings of humanity in their behalf. Nothing but a punctual payment of their annual allowance can rescue them from the most complicated misery, and nothing could be a more melancholy and distressing sight than to behold those who have shed their blood or lost their limbs in the service of their country without a shelter, without a friend, and without the means of obtaining any of the necessaries of life or comforts of life, compelled to beg their daily bread from door to door! Suffer me to recommend those of this description belonging to your state to the warmest patronage of Your Excellency and your legislature.

It is necessary to say but a few words on the third topic which was proposed and which regards particularly the defense of the republic. As there can be little doubt but Congress will recommend a proper peace establishment for the United States, in which a due attention will be paid to the importance of placing the militia of the Union upon a regular and respectable footing, if this should be the case, I would beg leave to urge the great advantage of it in the strongest terms. The militia of this country must be considered as the palladium of our security and the first effectual resort, in case of hostility. It is essential, therefore, that the same system should pervade the whole, that the formation and discipline of the militia of the continent should be absolutely uniform, and the same species of arms, accoutrements, and military apparatus should be introduced in every part of the United States. No one who has not learned it from experience can conceive the difficulty, expense, and confusion which result from a contrary system or the vague arrangements which have hitherto prevailed.

If in treating of political points a greater latitude than usual has been taken in the course of this address, the importance of the crisis and the magnitude of the objects in discussion must be my apology. It is, however, neither my wish or expectation that the preceding observations should claim any regard except so far as they shall appear to be dictated by a good intention, consonant to the immutable rules of justice, calculated to produce a liberal system of policy, and founded on whatever experience may have been acquired by a long and close attention to public business. Here I might speak with the more confidence from my actual observations. And if it would not swell this letter (already too prolix) beyond the bounds I had prescribed myself, I could demonstrate to every mind open to conviction that in less time, and with much less expense than has been incurred, the war might have been brought to the same happy conclusion, if the resources of the continent could have been properly drawn forth—that the distresses and disappointments which have very often occurred have in too many instances resulted more from a want of energy in the continental government than a deficiency of means in the particular states—that the inefficacy of measures, arising from the want of an adequate authority in the supreme power, from a partial compliance with the requisitions of Congress in some of the states, and from a failure of punctuality in others, while it tended to damp the zeal of those which were more willing to exert themselves, served also to accumulate the expenses of the war and to frustrate the best concerted plans—and that the discouragement occasioned by the complicated difficulties and embarrassments in which our affairs were by this means involved would have long ago produced the dissolution of any army less patient, less virtuous, and less persevering than that which I have had the honor to command. But while I mention these things, which are notorious facts, as the defects of our Federal Constitution, particularly in the prosecution of a war, I beg it may be understood that as I have ever taken a pleasure in gratefully acknowledging the assistance and support I have derived from every class of citizens, so shall I always be happy to do justice to the unparalleled exertions of the individual states on many interesting occasions.

I have thus freely disclosed what I wished to make known before I surrendered up my public trust to those who committed it to me. The task is now accomplished. I now bid adieu to Your Excellency, as the chief magistrate of your state. At the same time, I bid a last farewell to the cares of office and all the employments of public life.

It remains, then, to be my final and only request that Your Excellency will communicate these sentiments to your legislature at their next meeting and that they may be considered as the legacy of one who has ardently wished on all occasions to be useful to his country and who even in the shade of retirement will not fail to implore the divine benediction upon it.

I now make it my earnest prayer that God would have you and the state over which you preside in his holy protection, that he would incline the hearts of the citizens to cultivate a spirit of subordination and obedience to government, to entertain a brotherly affection and love for one another, for their fellow citizens of the United States at large, and particularly for their brethren who have served in the field—and finally that he would most graciously be pleased to dispose us all to do justice, to love mercy, and to demean ourselves with that charity, humility, and pacific temper of mind which were the characteristics of the Divine Author of our blessed religion, and without a humble imitation of whose example in these things we can never hope to be a happy nation. With the greatest regard and esteem I have the honor to be Sir Your Excellency's Most Obedient and most humble Servant

Go: Washington

To John Augustine Washington, June 15, 1783 (Excerpt)

I wait here with much impatience the arrival of the definitive treaty. This event will put a period not only to my military service but also to my public life, as the remainder of my natural one shall be spent in that kind of ease and repose which a man enjoys that is free from the load of public cares and subject to no other control than that of his own judgment and a proper conduct for the walk of private life.

It is much to be wished (but I think a good deal to be doubted) that the states would adopt a liberal and proper line of conduct for the government of this country. It should be founded in justice. Prejudices, unreasonable jealousies, and narrow policy should be done away. Competent power for all *general* purposes should *be vested* in the sovereignty of the United States, or anarchy and confusion will soon succeed. Liberty, when it degenerates into licentiousness, begets confusion and frequently ends in tyranny or some woeful catastrophe. And to suppose that the affairs of this continent can be conducted by thirteen distinct sovereignties, or by one without adequate powers, are mere solecisms in politics. It is in our united capacity we are known and have a place among the nations of the earth. Depart from this, and the states separately would stand as unknown in the world and as contemptible (comparatively speaking) as an individual county in any one state is to the state itself, and in others, perhaps, has never been heard of and would be as little attended to but for the sport of politicians to answer their sinister views, or the purposes of designing courts, if they should grow jealous of our rising greatness as an empire and wish to play off one state against another. We are a young nation and have a character to establish. It behooves us, therefore, to set out right; for first impressions will be lasting, indeed are all in all. If we do not fulfill our public engagements; if we do not religiously observe our treaties; if we shall be faithless to and regardless of those who have lent their money, given their personal services, and spilt their blood, and who are now returning home poor and penniless; in what light shall we be considered? And that there is but too much reason to apprehend these, none who see the daily publications and will attend to the conduct of some of the states can hardly have any doubt of.

To Elias Boudinot, President of the Confederation Congress, June 17, 1783

Sir,

I have the honor of transmitting to Your Excellency for the consideration of Congress a petition from a large number of officers of the army in behalf of themselves, and such other officers and soldiers of the Continental Army as are entitled to rewards in lands, and may choose to avail themselves of any privileges and grants which shall be obtained in consequence of the present solicitation. I enclose also the copy of a letter from Brigadier General Putnam in which the sentiments and expectations of the petitioners are more fully explained, and in which the ideas of occupying the posts in the western country will be found to correspond very nearly with those I have some time since communicated to a committee of Congress in treating of the subject of a peace establishment. I will beg leave to make a few more observations on the general benefits of the location and settlement now proposed, and then submit the justice and policy of the measure to the wisdom of Congress.

Although I pretend not myself to determine how far the district of unsettled country which is described in the petition is free from the claim of every state, or how far this disposal of it may interfere with the views of Congress, yet it appears to me this is the tract which from its local position and peculiar advantages ought to be first settled in preference to any other whatever; and I am perfectly convinced that it cannot be so advantageously settled by any other class of men as by the disbanded officers and soldiers of the army, to whom the faith of government hath long since been pledged that lands should be granted at the expiration of the war, in certain proportions agreeably to their respective grades.

I am induced to give my sentiments thus freely on the advantages to be expected from this plan of colonization because it would connect our government with the frontiers, extend our settlements progressively, and plant a brave, a hardy, and respectable race of people as our advanced post, who would be always ready and willing (in case of hostility) to combat the savages and check their incursions. A settlement formed by such men would give security to our frontiers. The very name of it would awe the Indians, and more than probably prevent the murder of many innocent families, which frequently, in the usual mode of extending our settlements and encroachments on the hunting grounds of the natives, fall the hapless victims to savage barbarity. Besides the emoluments which might be derived from the peltry trade at our factories, if such should be established, the appearance of so formidable a settlement in the vicinity of their towns (to say nothing of the barrier it would form against our other neighbors) would be the most likely means to enable us to purchase upon equitable terms of the aborigines their right of preoccupancy and to induce them to relinquish our territories and to remove into the illimitable regions of the west.

Much more might be said of the public utility of such a location, as well as of the private felicity it would afford to the individuals concerned in it. I will venture to say it is the most rational and practicable scheme which can be adopted by a great proportion of the officers and soldiers of our army, and promises them more happiness than they can expect in any other way. The settlers, being in the prime of life, inured to hardship, and taught by experience to accommodate themselves in every situation, going in a considerable body, and under the patronage of government, would enjoy in the first instance *advantages* in procuring subsistence and all the necessaries for a comfortable beginning superior to any common class of emigrants, and quite unknown to those who have heretofore extended themselves beyond the Appalachian Mountains. They may expect, after a little perseverance, *competence and independence* for themselves, a pleasant retreat in old age, and the fairest prospects for their children. I have the honor to be Your Excellency's Most Obedt Servant

Go: Washington

To Reverend William Gordon, July 8, 1783 (Excerpt)

I now thank you for your kind congratulations on this event. I feel sensibly the flattering expressions and fervent wishes with which you have accompanied them and make a tender of mine, with much cordiality, in return. It now rests with the confederated powers, by the line of conduct they mean to adopt, to make this country great, happy, and respectable, or to sink it into littleness—worse, perhaps—into anarchy and confusion. For certain I am that unless adequate powers are given to Congress for the *general* purposes of the federal Union, we shall soon molder into dust and become contemptible in the eyes of Europe, if we are not made the sport of their politics. To suppose that the general concerns of this country can be directed by thirteen heads, or one head without competent powers, is a solecism the bad effects of which every man who has had the practical knowledge to judge from that I have is fully convinced of—though none perhaps has felt them in so forcible and distressing a degree. The people at large, and at a distance from the theater of action, who only know that the machine was kept in motion, and that they are at last arrived at the first object of their wishes, are satisfied with the event without investigating the causes of the slow progress to it or of the expenses which have accrued and which they now seem unwilling to pay, great part of which has arisen from the want of energy in the Federal Constitution which I am complaining of, and which I wish to see given to it by a convention of the people, instead of hearing it remarked that as we have worked through an arduous contest with the powers Congress already have (but which, by the by, have been gradually diminishing), why should they be invested with more?

To say nothing of the invisible workings of Providence, which has conducted us through difficulties where no human foresight could point the way, it will appear evident to a close examiner that there has been a concatenation of causes to produce this event, which in all probability at no time or under other circumstances will combine again. We deceive ourselves, therefore, by the mode of reasoning, and, what would be much worse, we may bring ruin upon ourselves by attempting to carry it into practice.

We are known by no other character among nations than as the United States. Massachusetts or Virginia is no better defined, nor any more thought of by foreign powers, than the county[30] of Worcester in Massachusetts is by Virginia, or Gloucester County in Virginia is by Massachusetts (respectable as they are). And yet these counties with as much propriety might oppose themselves to the laws of the state in which they are, as an individual state can oppose itself to the federal government, by which it is or ought to be bound. Each of these counties has, no doubt, its local polity and interests. These should be attended to and brought before their respective legislatures with all the force their importance merits. But when they come in contact with the general interest of the state, when superior considerations preponderate in favor of the whole, their voices should be heard no more. So should it be with individual states when compared to the Union. Otherwise, I think it may properly be asked for what purpose do we farcically pretend to be united? Why do Congress spend months together in deliberating upon, debating, and digesting plans, which are made as palatable and as wholesome to the constitution of this country as the nature of things will admit of, when some states will pay no attention to them and others regard them but partially, by which means all those evils which proceed from delay, unfelt by the whole, while the compliant states are not only suffering by these neglects, but in many instances are injured most capitally by their own exertions, which are wasted for want of the united effort. A hundred thousand men coming one after another cannot move a ten weight, but the united strength of fifty would transport it with ease. So has it been with great part of the expense which has been incurred this war. In a word, I think the blood and treasure which have been spent in it have been lavished to little purpose unless we can be better cemented, and that is not to be effected while so little attention is paid to the recommendations of the sovereign power.

To me it would seem not more absurd to hear a traveler, who was setting out on a long journey, declare he would take no money in his pocket to defray the expenses of it, but rather depend upon chance and charity lest he should misapply it, than are the expressions of so much fear of the powers and means of Congress. For Heaven's sake, who are Congress? Are they not the creatures of the people, amenable to them for their conduct, and dependent from day to day on their bread? Where, then, can be the danger of giving them such powers as are adequate to the great ends of government and to all the general purposes of the Confederation (I repeat the word *general*, because I am no advocate for their having to do with the particular policy of any state, further than it concerns the Union at large). What may be the consequences if they have not these powers I am at no loss to guess, and deprecate the worst; for sure I am, we shall, in a little time, become as contemptible in the great scale of politics as we now have it in our power to be respectable—and that, when the band of Union gets once broken, everything ruinous to our future prospects is to be apprehended. The best that can come of it, in my humble opinion, is that we shall sink into obscurity, unless our civil broils should keep us in remembrance and fill the page of history with the direful consequences of them.

You say that Congress lose time by pressing a mode that does not accord with the genius of the people and will thereby endanger the Union, and that it is the quantum they want. Permit me to ask if the quantum has not already been demanded, whether it has been obtained, and whence proceed the accumulated evils and poignant distresses of many of the public creditors, particularly in the army? For my own part I hesitate not a moment to confess that I see nothing wherein the Union is endangered by the late requisition of that body, but a prospect of much good, justice, and propriety from the compliance with it. I know of no tax more convenient, none so agreeable, as that which every man may pay, or let it alone as his convenience, abilities, or inclination shall prompt. I am therefore a warm friend to the impost.

I can only repeat to you that whenever Congress shall think proper to open the door of their archives to you (which can be best known, and with more propriety discovered, through the delegates of your own state), all my records and papers shall be unfolded to your view; and I shall be happy in your company at Mt. Vernon while you are taking such extracts from them as you may find convenient. It is a piece of respect which I think is due to the sovereign power to let it take the lead in this business (without any interference of mine). And another reason why I choose to withhold mine to this epoch is that I am positive no history of the Revolution can be perfect if the historiographer has not free access to that fund of information. Mrs. Washington joins me in compliments to Mrs. Gordon, and I am Dr Sir—Yr Most Obedt & Most Hble Servt

Go: Washington

To Major John Joiner Ellis, July 10, 1783

Sir,

You profess not to be a panegyrist while you are bestowing the most exalted praise; but, compliments apart, I received your very polite letter of the 25th of March with much pleasure. It recalled to my remembrance some of the pleasing occurrences of my past life and reminded me of the acquaintances I had formed in it, for whom, though separated by time, distance, and political sentiments, I retain the same friendship.

I was opposed to the policy of G.B. and became an enemy to her measures; but I always distinguished between a cause and individuals. And while the latter supported their opinions upon liberal and generous grounds, personally I never could be an enemy to them.

I have only to request, therefore, that you will suffer me to retain that place in your friendship of which you assure me I now hold, that you will accept my sincere thanks for the favorable sentiments you have been pleased to express of me, and will do me the justice to believe that with great esteem and regard I have the honr to be Sir Yr Most Obt & Hble Ser.

Go: Washington

To George William Fairfax, July 10, 1783 (Excerpts)

As the path, after being closed by a long, arduous, and painful contest, is, to use an Indian metaphor, now opened and made smooth, I shall please myself with the hope of hearing from you frequently. And till you forbid me to indulge the wish, I shall not despair of seeing you and Mrs. Fairfax once more the inhabitants of Belvoir, and greeting you both there, the intimate companions of our old age, as you have been of our younger years. I cannot sufficiently express my sensibility for your kind congratulations on the favorable termination of the war, and for the flattering manner in which you are pleased to speak of my instrumentality in effecting a revolution, which I can truly aver was not in the beginning premeditated, but the result of dire necessity brought about by the persecuting spirit of the British government. This no man can speak to with more certainty, or assert upon better ground, than myself, as I was a member of Congress and in the councils of America till the affair at Bunker Hill, and was an attentive observer and witness to those interesting and painful struggles for accommodation and redress of grievances in a constitutional way, which all the world saw and must have approved, except the ignorant, deluded, and designing.

I unite my prayers most fervently with yours for wisdom to these U. States and have no doubt after a little while all errors in the present form of their government will be corrected and a happy temper be diffused through the whole. But like young heirs come a little prematurely, perhaps, to a large inheritance, it is more than probable they will riot for a while—but in this, if it should happen, though it is a circumstance which is to be lamented (as I would have the national character of America be pure and immaculate), will work its own cure, as there is virtue at the bottom ....

I wait with great impatience the arrival of the definitive treaty, that I may quit my military employments and bid adieu to public life, and in the shades of retirement seek that repose and tranquility to which I have been an entire stranger for more than eight years. I wish for it, too, because it will afford me some leisure to attend to an impaired fortune and recover, as it were, from a state of torpidity or suspension—except in the instances of having money paid to me at the depreciated value—my private concerns. My warmest and best affections attend Mrs. Fairfax and yourself—and I am Dr Sir Yr Most Obt & Hble Servt

Go: Washington

To Robert Stewart, August 10, 1783 (Excerpt)

You may be assured, sir, that I should ever feel pleasure in rendering you any service in my power; but I will not be so uncandid as to flatter your expectations or give you any hope of my doing it in the way you seem to expect. In a contest, long, arduous, and painful, which has brought forth the abilities of men in military and civil life, and exposed them, with halters about their necks, not only to common danger, but many of them to the verge of poverty and the very brink of ruin, justice requires, and a grateful government certainly will bestow, those places of honor and profit which necessity must create upon those who have risked life, fortune, and health to support its cause. But, independent of these considerations, I have never interfered in any civil appointments; and I only wait (and with anxious impatience) the arrival of the definitive treaty, that I may take leave of my military employments and, by bidding adieu to public life—forever—enjoy the shades of retirement that ease and tranquility to which, for more than eight years, I have been an entire stranger, and for which a mind which has been constantly on the stretch during that period, and perplexed with a thousand embarrassing circumstances, oftentimes without ray of light to guide it, stands much in need.

Gratitude to a nation to whom I think America owes much, and an ardent desire to see the country and customs of the French people, are strong inducements to make a visit to France. But a consideration more powerful than these will, I dare say, be an insuperable bar to such a tour. An impaired fortune (much injured by this contest) must turn me into those walks of retirement, where perhaps the consciousness of having discharged to the best of my abilities the great trust reposed in me and the duty I owed my country must supply the place of other gratifications and may perhaps afford as rational and substantial entertainment as the gayer scenes of a more enlarged theater.

To George Martin, August 10, 1783

Sir,

So long a course of time as you mention had indeed obscured the remembrance of our former acquaintance, till the letter you have favored me with brought the recollection of your name to my mind. Your good sense has furnished me an apology, should any be needed; and the occasion which introduces this renewal of former times is most pleasing indeed. Your congratulations to our happy-fated country are very agreeable, and your expressions of personal regard for me claim my sincerest thanks, as do your exertions in favor of our righteous cause, now so happily terminated.

I cannot but join with you in my most earnest prayers that these states may be blessed with wisdom equal to the arduous task of rightly forming the establishment of their new empire. And while I thus express my wishes in favor of my native country, I would felicitate the Kingdom of Ireland on their emancipation from British control and extend my pious entreaties that Heaven may establish them in a happy and perpetuated tranquility, enjoying a freedom of legislation and an unconfined extension of trade, that connecting link which binds together the remotest countries.

It is at present very uncertain how far the connection of these states with distant courts may be extended, or what appointments of this nature may be made. Their poverty, with the heavy debt contracted during the period of their troubles, must for a time lead them to economize in every way possible. Nor can I say how far I may be instrumental, should appointments be necessary, in procuring what you wish. I only wait the arrival of the definitive treaty to bid adieu to public life and, in the shades of retirement, to enjoy undisturbed that tranquility and repose which is necessary to unbend and give relaxation to a mind which has been embarrassed by a thousand perplexing circumstances during a painful contest of eight years.

Your poem is very acceptable, as it not only displays your genius, but exhibits sentiments favorable to the liberties of mankind and expressive of the benevolence of your heart. I am &c.

Address to the Confederation Congress, August 26, 1783

Mr. President,

I am too sensible of the honorable reception I have now experienced not to be penetrated with the deepest feelings of gratitude.

Notwithstanding Congress appear to estimate the value of my life beyond any services I have been able to render the U. States, yet I must be permitted to consider the wisdom and unanimity of our national councils, the firmness of our citizens, and the patience and bravery of our troops, which have produced so happy a termination of the war, as the most conspicuous effect of the divine interposition and the surest presage of our future happiness.

Highly gratified by the favorable sentiments which Congress are pleased to express of my past conduct, and amply rewarded by the confidence and affection of my fellow citizens, I cannot hesitate to contribute my best endeavors towards the establishment of the national security, in whatever manner the sovereign power may think proper to direct, until the ratification of the definitive treaty of peace or the final evacuation of our country by the British forces. After either of which events, I shall ask permission to retire to the peaceful shade of private life.

Perhaps, sir, no occasion may offer more suitable than the present to express my humble thanks to God, and my grateful acknowledgments to my country, for the great and uniform support I have received in every vicissitude of fortune, and for the many distinguished honors which Congress have been pleased to confer upon me in the course of the war.

G.W.

To James Duane, September 7, 1783

Sir,

I have carefully perused the papers which you put into my hands relating to Indian affairs.

My sentiments with respect to the proper line of conduct to be observed towards these people coincide precisely with those delivered by General Schuyler, so far as he has gone in his letter of the 29th July to Congress (which, with the other papers, is herewith returned)—and for the reasons he has there assigned. A repetition of them therefore by me would be unnecessary. But independent of the arguments made use of by him, the following considerations have no small weight in my mind.

To suffer a wide extended country to be overrun with land jobbers, speculators, and monopolizers, or even with scattered settlers, is, in my opinion, inconsistent with that wisdom and policy which our true interest dictates, or that an enlightened people ought to adopt, and besides is pregnant of disputes, both with the savages and among ourselves, the evils of which are easier to be conceived than described. And for what? But to aggrandize a few avaricious men to the prejudice of many and the embarrassment of government. For the people engaged in these pursuits, without contributing in the smallest degree to the support of government, or considering themselves as amenable to its laws, will involve it by their unrestrained conduct in inextricable perplexities and, more than probable, in a great deal of bloodshed.

My ideas, therefore, of the line of conduct proper to be observed, not only towards the Indians, but for the government of the citizens of America in their settlement of the western country (which is intimately connected therewith), are simply these.

First, and as a preliminary, that all prisoners of whatever age or sex among the Indians shall be delivered up.

That the Indians should be informed that after a contest of eight years for sovereignty of the country, G. Britain has ceded all the lands of the United States within the limits described by the _____ article of the provisional treaty.

That as they (the Indians), maugre all the advice and admonition which could be given them at the commencement and during the prosecution of the war, could not be restrained from acts of hostility but were determined to join their arms to those of G. Britain and to share their fortune, so, consequently, with a less generous people than Americans they would be made to share the same fate and be compelled to retire along with them beyond the lakes. But, as we prefer peace to a state of warfare; as we consider them as a deluded people; as we persuade ourselves that they are convinced from experience of their error in taking up the hatchet against us, and that their true interest and safety must now depend upon our friendship; as the country is large enough to contain us all; and as we are disposed to be kind to them and to partake of their trade, we will, from these considerations and from motives of compassion, draw a veil over what is past and establish a boundary line between them and us beyond which we will *endeavor* to restrain our people from hunting or settling, and within which they shall not come but for the purposes of trading, treating, or other business unexceptionable in its nature.

In establishing this line, in the first instance, care should be taken neither to yield nor to grasp at too much, but to endeavor to impress the Indians with an idea of the generosity of our disposition to accommodate them, and with the necessity we are under of providing for our warriors, our young people who are growing up, and strangers who are coming from other countries to live among us. And if they should make a point of it or appear dissatisfied at the line we may find it necessary to establish, compensation should be made them for their claims within it.

It is needless for me to express more explicitly, because the tendency of my observations evinces it is my opinion that if the legislature of the state of New York should insist upon expelling the Six Nations from all the country they inhabited previous to the war within their territory (as General Schuyler seems to be apprehensive of), it will end in another Indian war. I have every reason to believe from my inquiries and the information I have received that they will not suffer their country (if it was our policy to take it before we could settle it) to be wrested from them without another struggle. That they would compromise for a part of it I have very little doubt, and that it would be the cheapest way of coming at it I have no doubt at all. The same observations, I am persuaded, will hold good with respect to Virginia or any other state which has powerful tribes of Indians on their frontiers. And the reason of my mentioning New York is because General Schuyler has expressed his opinion of the temper of its legislature, and because I have been more in the way of learning the sentiments of the Six Nations than of any other tribes of Indians on this subject.

The limits being sufficiently extensive (in the new country) to comply with all the engagements of government and to admit such emigrations as may be supposed to happen within a given time, not only from the several states of the Union but from foreign countries, and moreover of such magnitude as to form a distinct and proper government, a proclamation, in my opinion, should issue, making it felony (if there is power for the purpose, and, if not, imposing some very heavy restraint) for any person to survey or settle beyond the line. And the officers commanding the frontier garrison should have pointed and peremptory orders to see that the proclamation is carried into effect.

Measures of this sort would not only obtain peace from the Indians, but would, in my opinion, be the surest means of preserving it. It would dispose of the land to the best advantage, people the country progressively, and check land jobbing and monopolizing (which is now going forward with great avidity), while the door would be open, and the terms known for everyone, to obtain what is reasonable and proper for himself upon legal and constitutional ground.

Every advantage that could be expected or even wished for would result from such a mode of procedure: our settlements would be compact, government well established, and our barrier formidable, not only for ourselves but against our neighbors. And the Indians, as has been observed in General Schuyler's letter, will ever retreat as our settlements advance upon them; and they will be as ready to sell as we are to buy. That it is the cheapest as well as the least distressing way of dealing with them, none who are acquainted with the nature of Indian warfare, and has ever been at the trouble of estimating the expense of one, and comparing it with the cost of purchasing their lands, will hesitate to acknowledge.

Unless some such measures as I have been taken the liberty of suggesting are speedily adopted, one of two capital evils, in my opinion, will inevitably result, and is near at hand: either that the settling, or rather overspreading, the western country will take place by a parcel of banditti who will bid defiance to all authority while they are skimming and disposing of the cream of the country, at the expense of many suffering officers and soldiers who have fought and bled to obtain it, and are now waiting the decision of Congress to point them to the promised reward of their past dangers and toils; or a renewal of hostilities with the Indians, brought about more than probably by this very means.

How far agents for Indian affairs are indispensably necessary I shall not take upon me to decide; but if any should be appointed, their powers, in my opinion, should be circumscribed, accurately defined, and themselves rigidly punished for every infraction of them. A recurrence to the conduct of these people under the British Administration of Indian Affairs will manifest the propriety of this caution, as it will there be found that self-interest was the principle by which their agents were actuated. And to promote this by accumulating lands and passing large quantities of goods through their hands, the Indians were made to speak any language they pleased by their representation, were pacific or hostile as their purposes were most likely to be promoted by the one or the other. No purchase under any pretense whatever should be made by any other authority than that of the sovereign power, or the legislature of the state in which such lands may happen to be. Nor should the agents be permitted directly or indirectly to trade, but to have a fixed and ample salary allowed them as a full compensation for their trouble.

Whether in practice the measure may answer as well as it appears in theory to me, I will not undertake to say. But I think if the Indian trade was carried on, on government account, and with no greater advance than what would be necessary to defray the expense and risk and bring in a small profit, that it would supply the Indians upon much better terms than they usually are, engross their trade, and fix them strongly in our interest, and would be a much better mode of treating them than that of giving presents, where a few only are benefited by them. I confess there is a difficulty in getting a man, or set of men, in whose abilities and integrity there can be a perfect reliance, without which the scheme is liable to such abuse as to defeat the salutary ends which are proposed from it. At any rate, no person should be suffered to trade with the Indians without first obtaining a license and giving security to conform to such rules and regulations as shall be prescribed, as was the case before the war.

In giving my sentiments in the month of May last (at the request of a committee of Congress) on a peace establishment, I took the liberty of suggesting the propriety, which in my opinion there appeared, of paying particular attention to the French and other settlers at Detroit and other parts within the limits of the western country. The perusal of a late pamphlet entitled *Observations on the Commerce of the American States with Europe and the West Indies* impresses the necessity of it more forcibly than ever on my mind. The author of that piece strongly recommends a liberal change in the government of Canada; and though he is too sanguine in his expectations of the benefits arising from it, there can be no doubt of the good policy of the measure. It behooves us, therefore, to counteract them by anticipation. These people have a disposition towards us susceptible of favorable impressions; but as no arts will be left unattempted by the British to withdraw them from our interest, the present moment should be employed by us to fix them in it, or we may lose them forever, and with them the advantages or disadvantages consequent of the choice they may make. From the best information and maps of that country, it would appear that from the mouth of the Great Miami River, which empties into the Ohio, to its confluence with the Mad River, thence by a line to the Miami Fort and Village on the other Miami River, which empties into Lake Erie, and thence by a line to include the settlement of Detroit, would with Lake Erie to the northward peninsula to the eastward and the Ohio to the southward, form a government sufficiently extensive to fulfill all the public engagements, and to receive moreover a large population by emigrants. And to confine the settlement of the new states within these bounds would, in my opinion, be infinitely better even supposing no disputes were to happen with the Indians and that it was not necessary to guard against those other evils which have been enumerated than to suffer the same number of people to roam over a country of at least 500,000 square miles, contributing nothing to the support, but much perhaps to the embarrassment, of the federal government.

Was it not for the purpose of comprehending the settlement of Detroit within the jurisdiction of the new government, a more compact and better shaped district for the line to proceed from the Miami Fort and Village along the river of that name to Lake Erie, leaving in that case the settlement of Detroit and all the territory north of the Rivers Miami and St. Josephs between the Lakes Erie, St. Clair, Huron, and Michigan to form, hereafter, another state equally large compact and water bounded.

At first view it may seem a little extraneous, when I am called upon to give an opinion upon the terms of a peace proper to be made with the Indians, that I should go into the formation of new states. But the settlement of the western country and making a peace with the Indians are so analogous that there can be no definition of the one without involving considerations of the other. For, I repeat it again, and I am clear in my opinion, that policy and economy point very strongly to the expediency of being upon good terms with the Indians and the propriety of purchasing their lands in preference to attempting to drive them by force of arms out of their country—which, as we have already experienced, is like driving the wild beasts of the forest, which will return as soon as the pursuit is at an end and fall perhaps on those that are left there, when the gradual extension of our settlements will as certainly cause the savage as the wolf to retire, both being beasts of prey, though they differ in shape. In a word, there is nothing to be obtained by an Indian war but the soil they live on, and this can be had by purchase at less expense, and without that bloodshed and those distresses which helpless women and children are made partakers of in all kinds of disputes with them.

If there is anything in these thoughts (which I have fully and freely communicated) worthy of attention I shall be happy and am Sir Yr Most Obedt Servt

Go: Washington

To Jean-Baptiste Donatien de Vimeur, Comte de Rochambeau, October 15, 1783 (Excerpt)

With what words, my dear count, shall I express to you the sensibility of a heart which you have warmed by the flattering sentiments that are conveyed in your letters of the 14th of April and 13th of July?

Your sovereign has a claim to my highest admiration, respect, and veneration. Your nation is entitled to all my gratitude—and those individuals of it who have been my companions in war to my friendship and love. Can it be wondered at, then, that I should possess an ardent desire to visit your country? But, as I observed to you in my letter of the 10th of May, it is not yet clear to me that I shall ever have it in my power to accomplish my wishes. My private concerns have been very much deranged by an absence of more than eight years and require particular attention to put them in order.

Congress, from causes which you have doubtless been informed of, and more than probably have seen published, are now sitting at this place. They have fixed upon the Falls of Delaware (at or near Trenton) for their permanent residence and will, I suppose, as soon as possible prepare to establish themselves at it.

I have at their request been with them near two months, and shall remain with them till the definitive treaty arrives, or till New York is evacuated by the British forces, when I shall bid a final adieu to public life and, in the shade of retirement, look back on our past toils with grateful admiration of that benevolent Providence which has raised up so many instruments to accomplish so great a revolution as the one you have had a share in bringing about.

To Armand-Louis de Gontaut Biron, Duc de Lauzun, October 15, 1783 (Excerpt)

New York is not yet evacuated, nor is the definitive treaty arrived. Upon the happening of either of these events I shall bid a final adieu to a military life and, in the shade of retirement, ruminate on the marvelous scenes that are passed, and in contemplating the wonderful workings of that Providence which has raised up so many instruments and such powerful engines (among which your nation stands first) to overthrow the British pride and power by so great a revolution.

Farewell Orders to the Army of the United States, November 2, 1783

The United States in Congress assembled, after giving the most honorable testimony to the merits of the federal armies, and presenting them with the thanks of their country for their long, eminent, and faithful services, having thought proper, by their proclamation bearing date the 18th day of October last, to discharge such part of the troops as were engaged for the war, and to permit the officers on furlough to retire from service from and after tomorrow, which proclamation having been communicated in the public papers for the information and government of all concerned: it only remains for the commander-in-chief to address himself once more, and that for the last time, to the armies of the United States (however widely dispersed the individuals who composed them may be) and to bid them an affectionate, a long farewell.

But before the commander-in-chief takes his final leave of those he holds most dear, he wishes to indulge himself a few moments in calling to mind a slight review of the past. He will then take the liberty of exploring with his military friends their future prospects, of advising the general line of conduct which in his opinion ought to be pursued, and he will conclude the address by expressing the obligations he feels himself under for the spirited and able assistance he has experienced from them in the performance of an arduous office.

A contemplation of the complete attainment (at a period earlier than could have been expected) of the object for which we contended, against so formidable a power, cannot but inspire us with astonishment and gratitude. The disadvantageous circumstances on our part, under which the war was undertaken, can never be forgotten. The singular interpositions of Providence in our feeble condition were such as could scarcely escape the attention of the most unobserving, while the unparalleled perseverance of the armies of the United States through almost every possible suffering and discouragement for the space of eight long years was little short of a standing miracle.

It is not the meaning nor within the compass of this address to detail the hardships peculiarly incident to our service, or to describe the distresses which in several instances have resulted from the extremes of hunger and nakedness, combined with the rigors of an inclement season. Nor is it necessary to dwell on the dark side of our past affairs. Every American officer and soldier must now console himself for any unpleasant circumstances which may have occurred by a recollection of the uncommon scenes in which he has been called to act no inglorious part, and the astonishing events of which he has been a witness—events which have seldom if ever before taken place on the stage of human action, nor can they probably ever happen again. For who has before seen a disciplined army formed at once from such raw materials? Who that was not a witness could imagine that the most violent local prejudices would cease so soon, and that men who came from the different parts of the continent, strongly disposed by the habits of education to despise and quarrel with each other, would instantly become but one patriotic band of brothers? Or who that was not on the spot can trace the steps by which such a wonderful revolution has been effected, and such a glorious period put to all our warlike toils?

It is universally acknowledged that the enlarged prospect of happiness opened by the confirmation of our independence and sovereignty almost exceeds the power of description. And shall not the brave men who have contributed so essentially to these inestimable acquisitions, retiring victorious from the field of war to the field of agriculture, participate in all the blessings which have been obtained? In such a republic, who will exclude them from the rights of citizens and the fruits of their labors? In such a country so happily circumstanced, the pursuits of commerce and the cultivation of the soil will unfold to industry the certain road to competence. To those hardy soldiers who are actuated by the spirit of adventure, the fisheries will afford ample and profitable employment, and the extensive and fertile regions of the west will yield a most happy asylum to those who, fond of domestic enjoyment, are seeking for personal independence. Nor is it possible to conceive that any one of the United States will prefer a national bankruptcy and a dissolution of the Union to a compliance with the requisitions of Congress and the payment of its just debts—so that the officers and soldiers may expect considerable assistance in recommending their civil occupations from the sums due to these from the public, which must and will most inevitably be paid.

In order to effect this desirable purpose, and to remove the prejudices which may have taken possession of the minds of any of the good people of the states, it is earnestly recommended to all the troops that, with strong attachments to the Union, they should carry with them into civil society the most conciliating dispositions and that they should prove themselves not less virtuous and useful as citizens than they have been persevering and victorious as soldiers. What though there should be some envious individuals who are unwilling to pay the debt the public has contracted, or to yield the tribute due to merit, yet let such unworthy treatment produce no invective or any instance of intemperate conduct. Let it be remembered that the unbiased voice of the free citizens of the United States has promised the just reward and given the merited applause. Let it be known and remembered that the reputation of the federal armies is established beyond the reach of malevolence. And let a consciousness of their achievements and fame still incite the men who composed them to honorable actions, under the persuasion that the private virtues of economy, prudence, and industry will not be less amiable in civil life than the more splendid qualities of valor, perseverance, and enterprise were in the field. Everyone may rest assured that much, very much, of the future happiness of the officers and men will depend upon the wise and manly conduct which shall be adopted by these when they are mingled with the great body of the community. And although the general has so frequently given it as his opinion, in the most public and explicit manner, that unless the principles of the federal government were properly supported, and the powers of the Union increased, the honor, dignity, and justice of the nation would be lost forever, yet he cannot help repeating on this occasion so interesting a sentiment, and leaving it as his last injunction to every officer and every soldier who may view the subject in the same serious point of light to add his best endeavors to those of his worthy fellow citizens towards effecting their great and valuable purposes, on which our very existence as a nation so materially depends.

The commander-in-chief conceives little is now wanting to enable the soldier to change the military character into that of the citizen but that steady and decent tenor of behavior which has generally distinguished not only the army under his immediate command, but the different detachments and separate armies through the course of the war. From their good sense and prudence, he anticipates the happiest consequences. And while he congratulates them on the glorious occasion which renders their services in the field no longer necessary, he wishes to express the strong obligations he feels himself under for the assistance he has received from every class—and in every instance. He presents his thanks in the most serious and affectionate manner to the general officers, as well for their counsel on many interesting occasions as for their ardor in promoting the success of the plans he had adopted; to the commandants of regiments and corps, and to the other officers, for their great zeal and attention in carrying his orders promptly into execution; to the staff, for their alacrity and exactness in performing the duties of their several departments; and to the non-commissioned officers and private soldiers, for their extraordinary patience in suffering, as well as their invincible fortitude in action. To the various branches of the army the general takes this last and solemn opportunity of professing his inviolable attachment and friendship. He wishes more than bare professions were in his power, that he was really able to be useful to them all in future life. He flatters himself, however, they will do him the justice to believe that whatever could with propriety be attempted by him has been done. And being now to conclude these his last public orders, to take his ultimate leave, in a short time, of the military character, and to bid a final adieu to the armies he has so long had the honor to command, he can only again offer in their behalf his recommendations to their grateful country and his prayers to the God of armies. May ample justice be done them here, and may the choicest of Heaven's favors, both here and hereafter, attend those who, under the divine auspices, have secured innumerable blessings for others. With these wishes and this benediction, the commander-in-chief is about to retire from service. The curtain of separation will soon be drawn, and the military scene to him will be closed forever.

To the Ministers, Elders, Deacons of the Reformed German Congregation of New York, November 27, 1783

Gentlemen,

The illustrious and happy event on which you are pleased to congratulate and welcome me to this city demands all our gratitude, while the favorable sentiments you have thought proper to express of my conduct entitle you to my warmest acknowledgments.

Disposed at every suitable opportunity to acknowledge publicly our infinite obligations to the Supreme Ruler of the Universe for rescuing our country from the brink of destruction, I cannot fail at this time to ascribe all the honor of our late successes to the same glorious Being. And if my humble exertions have been made in any degree subservient to the execution of the divine purposes, the contemplation of the benediction of Heaven on our righteous cause, the approbation of my virtuous countrymen, and the testimony of my own conscience will be a sufficient reward and augment my felicity beyond anything which the world can bestow.

The establishment of civil and religious liberty was the motive which induced me to the field. The object is attained, and it now remains to be my earnest wish and prayer that the citizens of the United States would make a wise and virtuous use of the blessings placed before them, and that the reformed German Congregation in New York may not only be conspicuous for their religious character but as exemplary in support of our inestimable acquisitions as their reverend minister has been in the attainment of them.

Go: Washington

To the Marine Society of the City of New York, November 29, 1783

Gentlemen,

I consider myself highly honored by the polite attention shown me in your address, and the too partial manner in which you are pleased to express your sense of my public and private conduct. At the same time, I have the pleasure to assure the corporation that I am extremely happy in becoming a member of their humane and excellent institution.

To have conducted as a nation with so much dignity and propriety through the unparalleled difficulties and dangers of an arduous contest, to have accomplished our fondest wishes, and to have fixed the liberties of this country upon the broad and permanent basis of independence, will ever reflect the truest glory on the patriots of the present age and afford the amplest field of description for the future historian.

It would be a mark of great insensibility in me not to partake in the public joy or not to derive an unusual degree of satisfaction from the approbation of good men and lovers of their country. Believe me, gentlemen! I shall return to private life impressed with the most pleasing sensations. A recollection of the happy scene to which I have lately been a witness will attend me in my solitary walks and cheer me in the shade of retirement.

Go: Washington

To the Members of the Volunteer Association and Other Inhabitants of the Kingdom of Ireland Who Have Lately Arrived in the City of New York, December 2, 1783

Gentlemen,

The testimony of your satisfaction at the glorious termination of the late contest, and your indulgent opinion of my agency in it, afford me singular pleasure and merit my warmest acknowledgments.

If the example of the Americans successfully contending in the cause of freedom can be of any use to other nations, we shall have an additional motive for rejoicing at so prosperous an event.

It was not an uninteresting consideration to learn that the Kingdom of Ireland by bold and manly conduct had obtained redress of many of its grievances. And it is much to be wished that the blessings of equal liberty and unrestrained commerce may yet prevail more extensively. In the meantime, you may be assured, gentlemen, that the hospitality and beneficence of your countrymen to our brethren who have been prisoners of war are neither unknown or unregarded.

The bosom of America is open to receive not only the opulent and respectable stranger, but the oppressed and persecuted of all nations and religions, whom we shall welcome to a participation of all our rights and privileges, if by decency and propriety of conduct they appear to merit the enjoyment.

Go: Washington

To the General Assembly of Pennsylvania, December 9, 1783

Gentlemen,

I consider the approbation of the representatives of a free and virtuous people as the most enviable reward that can ever be conferred on a public character.

A sense of duty impelled me to contribute whatever my sword or my pen could effect towards the establishment of our freedom and independence. The smiles of Providence on the united exertions of my fellow citizens have completed our successes. And it remains to be my first and most earnest desire that the United States may profit by the happy occasion, and preserve by wisdom and justice that liberty and honor they have so nobly maintained by arms.

Anticipating the increasing happiness and luster of this growing empire, I shall return to private life with a degree of satisfaction more easily to be conceived than expressed.

As this is the last time I shall have the honor of seeing you gentlemen in my official character, I cannot bid you a final farewell without acknowledging the assistance I have frequently derived from your state, and the pleasure I have lately received from a contemplation of the illustrious example of the legislature in adopting the recommendations of Congress with so much promptness and unanimity. May the representatives and citizens of this commonwealth continue to possess the same good dispositions, and may they be as happy in the enjoyment of peace as it is possible for a wise, just, and united people to be.

To the Merchants of Philadelphia, December 9, 1783

Gentlemen,

The perfect establishment of American independence is indeed an event of such infinite importance as to fill the mind with gratitude and joy, and afford the fairest occasion for mutual congratulations.

The honorable sentiments you are pleased to express respecting the merits of the army, the just idea you entertain of their bravery, sufferings, and magnanimity, and the honest desire you manifest of making an adequate compensation for their services are circumstances highly satisfactory to me, as well as extremely flattering to the gallant men who are more immediately concerned. And I must take the liberty to add that the punctuality of the merchants and other citizens of Philadelphia in raising their proportion of taxes for the support of the war, and their cheerfulness in affording every other assistance in their power, are marks of patriotism which deserve the warmest acknowledgments.

I am happy in having one more opportunity of expressing the personal obligations I feel myself under to you, gentlemen, for your favorable opinion and for the present as well as for every former instance of your polite attention.

Having long since been convinced of the expediency and even necessity of rendering complete justice to all the public creditors, and having at the same time been impressed with a belief that the good sense of my countrymen would ultimately induce them to comply with the requisitions of Congress, I could not avoid being greatly pleased with the example set by the state of Pennsylvania. Nor can I conceal my satisfaction at finding your sentiments coincide so exactly with my own. Let us flatter ourselves that the day is not remote when a wise and just system of polity will be adopted by every state in the Union. Then will national faith be inviolably preserved, public credit durably established, the blessings of commerce extensively diffused, and the reputation of our new-formed empire supported with as much éclat as has been acquired in laying the foundation of it.

To the Militia Officers of the City and Liberties of Philadelphia, December 12, 1783

Gentlemen,

The honorable manner in which you are pleased to notice my return to this city is particularly acceptable to me.

It would have been a proof of the want of patriotism and every social virtue not to have assumed the character of a soldier when the exigency of the public demanded, or not to have returned to the class of citizens when the necessity of farther service ceased to exist. I can therefore claim no merit beyond that of having done my duty with fidelity.

While the various scenes of the war in which I have experienced the timely aid of the militia of Philadelphia recur to my mind, my ardent prayer ascends to Heaven that they may long enjoy the blessings of that peace which has been obtained by the divine benediction on our common exertions.

To the Trustees and Faculty of the University of the State of Pennsylvania, December 13, 1783

Gentlemen,

I experience a singular satisfaction in receiving your congratulations on the establishment of peace and the security of those important interests which were involved in the fate of the war.

Desirous of being considered the friend and (as far as consists with my abilities) the patron of the arts and sciences, I must take the liberty of expressing my sense of the obligations I am under to the trustees and faculty of the University of Pennsylvania for paying me so flattering a compliment, and on so pleasing a subject.

I accept, gentlemen, the honors you have had the goodness to confer upon me with the greatest deference and respect.

May the Revolution prove extensively propitious to the cause of literature. May the tender plants of science which are cultivated by your assiduous care, under the fostering influence of Heaven, soon arrive at an uncommon point of maturity and perfection. And may this university long continue to diffuse throughout an enlightened empire all the blessings of virtue, learning, and urbanity.

To the Learned Professions of Philadelphia, December 13, 1783

Gentlemen,

I entreat you to accept my grateful thanks for your affectionate address and to be assured that the kindness and partiality of your sentiments respecting me, as well as the elegance and urbanity of your expressions, have made an impression on my mind never to be effaced.

Conscious of no impropriety in wishing to merit the esteem of my fellow citizens in general, I cannot hesitate to acknowledge that I feel a certain pleasing sensation in obtaining the good opinion of men eminent for their virtue, knowledge, and humanity. But I am sensible, at the same time, it becomes me to receive with humility the warm commendations you are pleased to bestow on my conduct. For, if I have been led to detest the folly and madness of unbounded ambition, if I have been induced from other motives to draw my sword and regulate my public behavior, or if the management of the war has been conducted upon purer principles, let me not arrogate the merit to human imbecility but rather ascribe whatever glory may result from our successful struggle to a higher and more efficient cause. For the re-establishment of our once violated rights, for the confirmation of our independence, for the protection of virtue, philosophy, and literature, for the present flourishing state of the sciences, and for the enlarged prospect of human happiness, it is our common duty to pay the tribute of gratitude to the greatest and best of Beings.

Though the military scene is now closed and I am hastening with unspeakable delight to the still and placid walks of domestic life, yet even there will my country's happiness be ever nearest to my heart. And, while I cherish the fond idea, I shall still retain a pleasing remembrance of the able support the public has often received from the learned professions, whose prosperity is so essential to the preservation of the liberties, as well as the augmentation of the happiness and glory, of this extensive empire.

To the American Philosophical Society, December 13, 1783

Gentlemen,

While you recall to my mind the honor formerly done me by enrolling my name in the list of the members of your society, you greatly heighten the pleasure of your present congratulations.

For if I know my own inclination, it is to be the friend and associate to men of virtue and philosophical knowledge; or, if I have a wish ungratified, it is that the arts and sciences may continue to flourish with increasing luster.

In the philosophic retreat to which I am retiring, I shall often contemplate with pleasure the extensive utility of your institution. The field of investigation is ample, the benefits which will result to human society from discoveries yet to be made are indubitable, and the task of studying the works of the great Creator inexpressibly delightful.

Go: Washington

Address to the Confederation Congress on Resigning His Commission, December 23, 1783

The great events on which my resignation depended having at length taken place, I have now the honor of offering my sincere congratulations to Congress and of presenting myself before them to surrender into their hands the trust committed to me, and to claim the indulgence of retiring from the service of my country.

Happy in the confirmation of our independence and sovereignty, and pleased with the opportunity afforded the United States of becoming a respectable nation, I resign with satisfaction the appointment I accepted with diffidence—a diffidence in my abilities to accomplish so arduous a task, which, however, was superseded by a confidence in the rectitude of our cause, the support of the supreme power of the Union, and the patronage of Heaven.

The successful termination of the war has verified the more sanguine expectations. And my gratitude for the interposition of Providence and the assistance I have received from my countrymen increases with every review of the momentous contest.

While I repeat my obligations to the army in general, I should do injustice to my own feelings not to acknowledge in this place the peculiar services and distinguished merits of the gentlemen who have been attached to my person during the war. It was impossible the choice of confidential officers to compose my family should have been more fortunate. Permit me, sir, to recommend in particular those who have continued in service to the present moment as worthy of the favorable notice and patronage of Congress.

I consider it an indispensable duty to close this last solemn act of my official life by commending[31] the interests of our dearest country to the protection of Almighty God, and those who have the superintendence of them to his holy keeping.

Having now finished the work assigned me, I retire from the great theater of action, and bidding an affectionate farewell to this august body under whose orders I have so long acted, I here offer my commission and take my leave of all the employments of public life.

Explanatory Notes

1. We have added this word, which was omitted by Washington.
2. This is a reference to Charles Lee.
3. A correction from Washington's "rishes."
4. This is Washington's own capitalization.
5. A reference to the northern part of New Hampshire.
6. Washington here says "are not legalized," although his sense would probably be clearer if the "not" was dropped. He means that the general orders *do* legalize the seizure of liquors in the case of prohibited – and thus *not* legalized – sales.
7. This reference is to General Charles Lee.
8. A reference to the Ottoman Empire.
9. We have added this article.
10. We have added the word "be," which Washington omitted, but which is necessary to his meaning.
11. We have corrected this from Washington's "every."
12. We have corrected this from Washington's "as."
13. We corrected this to "now" from Washington's "no."
14. A correction from Washington's "that."
15. Here we have supplied the word "them," which Washington omitted.
16. Laurens had been named special envoy to France.
17. A correction from Washington's "as."
18. A correction from Washington's "of."
19. A correction from Washington's "you."
20. We have added this word, which Washington had omitted and which is necessary to the sentence.
21. Washington here refers to Laurens's plan to recruit slaves to serve as soldiers for the American army.
22. We have added this word, which Washington had omitted.
23. This reference is to Colonel Walter Stewart, who was involved in the Newburgh conspiracy.
24. These are the celebrated remarks that Washington made to the meeting of officers at Newburgh.
25. A correction from Washington's "merit."
26. A correction from Washington's "honor," which surely cannot be correct.
27. We have added this word, which seems to be necessary to the sentence's meaning.
28. Jean de Neufville was a Dutch merchant.
29. A correction from Washington's "in founded."
30. A correction from Washington's "country."
31. A correction from Washington's "commanding," which is evidently in error.

Fig. 4 Part IV: From Soldier to Statesman: 1783–1788
www.gettyimages.com/detail/news-photo/the-signing-of-the-constitution-of-the-united-states-with-news-photo/525372757?adppopup=true

PART IV

From Soldier to Statesman: 1783–1788

To the Mayor and Commonalty of Alexandria, December 31, 1783

Gentlemen,

Nothing could have contributed more essentially to increase the satisfaction I experience on my return from a successful war to the tranquility of domestic life than your affectionate congratulations.

To find that neither time nor absence have interrupted or diminished the harmony of our happy neighborhood, and that the circumstances are most favorable to the growth and prosperity of your rising town, affords sensations of a very pleasing nature. May the agreeable prospects be soon realized! And may the morals and conduct of the inhabitants of Alexandria ever continue to ensure its felicity.

While your friendly concern for my future welfare demands my best acknowledgments, I beg you will be persuaded, gentlemen, that there is a certain home felt gratification in receiving the approbation and good wishes of those with whom we have been long acquainted and whose friendship we value, which can more easily be conceived than described.

To Jonathan Trumbull, Jr., Governor of Connecticut, January 5, 1784 (Excerpt)

Notwithstanding the jealous and contracted temper which seems to prevail in some of the states, yet I cannot but hope and believe that the good sense of the people will *ultimately* get the better of their *prejudices*, and that order and sound policy—though they do not come so soon as one would wish—will be produced from the present unsettled and deranged state of public affairs. Indeed, I am happy to observe that the political disposition is actually meliorating every day. Several of the states have manifested an inclination to invest Congress with more ample powers. Most of the legislatures appear disposed to do perfect justice; and the assembly of this commonwealth have just complied with the requisitions of Congress, and, I am informed, without a dissentient voice. Everything, my dear Trumbull, will come right at last as we have often prophesied. My only fear is we shall lose a little reputation *first*.

After having passed, with as much prosperity as could be expected, through the career of public life, I have now reached the goal of domestic enjoyment—in which state, I assure you, I find your good wishes most acceptable to me. The family at Mount Vernon joins in the same Complimts & Cordiality to you & yours with which I am—Dr Sir Yr Most Affecte & Obedt Servt

Go: Washington

To Jean de Neufville, January 6, 1784 (Excerpt)

Notwithstanding the embarrassments of our finances, I am also of opinion that justice will ultimately be rendered to all the public creditors. Indeed, it is very much to be regretted that any of our good friends should have suffered from the delay of it. The exigencies have been pressing, and the misfortunes arising therefrom to private individuals perhaps inevitable; but the happy termination of the war will, I trust, soon afford an opportunity of retrieving the public credit and enable Congress and the state of South Carolina to discharge the debts which are due to your house.

To Benjamin Harrison, Governor of Virginia, January 18, 1784 (Excerpt)

That the prospect before us is, as you justly observe, fair, none can deny; but what use we shall make of it is exceedingly problematical. Not but that I believe all things will come right at last. But like a young heir, come a little prematurely to a large inheritance, we shall wanton and run riot until we have brought our reputation to the brink of ruin, and then like him shall have to labor with the current of opinion when *compelled*, perhaps, to do what prudence and common policy pointed out as plain as any problem in Euclid in the first instance.

The disinclination of the individual states to yield competent powers to Congress for the federal government, their unreasonable jealousy of that body and of one another, and the disposition which seems to pervade each of being all-wise and all-powerful within itself, will, if there is not a change in the system, be our downfall as a nation. This is as clear to me as the A, B, C, and I think we have opposed Great Britain and have arrived at the present state of peace and independency to very little purpose if we cannot conquer our own prejudices. The powers of Europe begin to see this, and our newly acquired friends, the British, are already and professedly acting upon this ground, and wisely too, if we are determined to persevere in our folly. They know that individual opposition to their measures is futile, *and boast* that we are not sufficiently united as a nation to give a general one! Is not the indignity alone of this declaration, while we are in the very act of peace-making and conciliation, sufficient to stimulate us to vest more extensive and adequate powers in the sovereign of these United States? For my own part, although I am returned to and am now mingled with the class of private citizens, and like them must suffer all the evils of a tyranny or of too great an extension of federal powers, I have no fears arising from this source in my mind. But I have many and powerful ones indeed which predict the worst consequences from a half starved, limping government that appears to be always moving upon crutches and tottering at every step. Men, chosen as the delegates in Congress are, cannot officially be dangerous. They depend upon the breath—nay, they are so much the creatures of the people under the present constitution that they can have no views (which could possibly be carried into execution), nor any interests, distinct from those of their constituents. My political creed therefore is to be wise in the choice of delegates, support them like gentlemen while they are our representatives, give them competent powers for all federal purposes, support them in the due exercise thereof, and, lastly, to compel them to close attendance in Congress during their delegation. These things under the present mode for and termination of elections, aided by annual instead of constant sessions, would, or I am exceedingly mistaken, make us one of the most wealthy, happy, respectable, and powerful nations that ever inhabited the terrestrial globe. Without them, we shall in my opinion soon be everything which is the direct reverse of them.

To Chevalier Jean de Heintz, January 21, 1784

Sir,

As soon as I had the honor of receiving your letter containing a proposal of the order of the Knights of Divine Providence, I referred the subject of it to the decision of Congress in my letter to that august body dated the 28th of August last, a copy of which is enclosed. Whereupon the United States in Congress assembled were pleased to pass their act of the 5th instant, which is properly authenticated by their secretary, and which I have the honor of transmitting herewith.

Notwithstanding it appears to be incompatible with the principles of our national constitution to admit the introduction of any kind of nobility, knighthood, or distinctions of a similar nature amongst the citizens of our republic, yet I pray you will have the goodness to make known to the illustrious Knights of the Order of Divine Providence that we receive with the deepest gratitude and most perfect respect this flattering mark of their attention and approbation. For the polite manner in which you have communicated the pleasure of the order, you will be pleased to accept my best acknowledgments. I have the honor to be with very great consideration &ca.

G: Washington

To Philip Schuyler, January 21, 1784

Dear Sir,

Your favor of the 20th of December found me, as you conjectured, by that fireside from which I had been too long absent for my own convenience, to which I returned with the greatest avidity the moment my public avocations would permit, and from which I hope never again to be withdrawn.

While I am here solacing myself in my retreat from the busy scenes of life, I am not only made extremely happy by the gratitude of my countrymen in general, but particularly so by the repeated proofs of the kindness and approbation of those who have been more intimately conversant with my public transactions. And I need scarcely add that the favorable opinion of no one is more acceptable than that of yourself.

In recollecting the vicissitudes of fortune we have experienced and the difficulties we have surmounted, I shall always call to mind the great assistance I have frequently received from you, both in your public and private character. May the blessings of peace amply reward your exertions, may you and your family (to whom the compliments of Mrs. Washington and myself are affectionately presented) long continue to enjoy every species of happiness this world can afford. With sentiments of sincere esteem, attachment, and affection I am—Dr Sir Yr Most Obedt & very Hble Servant

Go: Washington

To Marquis de Lafayette, February 1, 1784 (Excerpt)

At length, my dear Marquis, I am become a private citizen on the banks of the Potomac. And under the shadow of my own vine and my own fig tree, free from the bustle of a camp and the busy scenes of public life, I am solacing myself with those tranquil enjoyments of which the soldier, who is ever in pursuit of fame, the statesman, whose watchful days and sleepless nights are spent in devising schemes to promote the welfare of his own, perhaps the ruin of other countries, as if this globe was insufficient for us all, and the courtier, who is always watching the countenance of his prince, in hopes of catching a gracious smile, can have very little conception. I am not only retired from all public employments, but I am retiring within myself and shall be able to view the solitary walk and tread the paths of private life with heartfelt satisfaction. Envious of none, I am determined to be pleased with all. And this, my dear friend, being the order for my march, I will move gently down the stream of life until I sleep with my fathers.

To Comte de Rochambeau, February 1, 1784 (Excerpt)

My Dear Count,

Having resigned my public trust, and with it all my public cares, into the hands of Congress, I now address myself to you in the character of a private citizen on the banks of the Potomac, to which I have been retired (fast locked in frost and snow) since Christmas Eve. The tranquil walks of domestic life are now unfolding to my view and promise a rich harvest of pleasing contemplation, in which, my dear general, you will be one of my most agreeable themes, as I shall recollect with pleasure that we have been contemporaries and fellow laborers in the cause of liberty, and that we have lived together as brothers should do, in harmony and friendship.

I saw all the British forces embarked and on the point of sailing before I left New York about the 4th of December. I then repaired to Congress and surrendered all my public employments into their hands, and am just now beginning to look into the deranged situation of my own private concerns, which I did not permit to come in for any share of my attention during the last nine years of my life.

To the Citizens of Fredericksburg, February 14, 1784

Gentlemen,

With the greatest pleasure I receive in the character of a private citizen the honor of your address.

To a benevolent Providence and the fortitude of a brave and virtuous army, supported by the general exertion of our common country, I stand indebted for the plaudits you now bestow.

The reflection, however, of having met the congratulating smiles and approbation of my fellow citizens for the part I have acted in the cause of liberty and independence cannot fail of adding pleasure to the other sweets of domestic life. And my sensibility of them is heightened by their coming from the respectable inhabitants of the place of my growing infancy and the honorable mention which is made of my revered mother, by whose maternal hand (early deprived of a father) I was led to manhood.

For the expressions of personal affection and attachment, and for your kind wishes for my future welfare, I offer grateful thanks and my sincere prayers for the happiness and prosperity of the corporate town of Fredericksburg.

Go: Washington

To Henry Knox, February 20, 1784 (Excerpt)

I am just beginning to experience that ease and freedom from public cares which, however desirable, take some time to realize; for, strange as it may tell, it is nevertheless true that it was not till lately I could get the better of my usual custom of ruminating, as soon as I waked in the morning, on the business of the ensuing day, and of my surprise, after having revolved many things in my mind, to find that I was no longer a public man or had anything to do with public transactions. I feel now, however, as I conceive a wearied traveler must do, who, after treading many a painful step with a heavy burden on his shoulders, is eased of the latter, having reached the goal to which all the former were directed, and from his house top is looking back and tracing with a grateful eye the meanders by which he escaped the quicksands and mires which lay in his way, and into which none but the all-powerful guide and Great Disposer of human events could have prevented his falling.

To Friedrich Wilhelm August Heinrich Ferdinand von Steuben, March 15, 1784 (Excerpt)

A peace establishment has always two objects in view: the one, present security of posts, of stores, and the public tranquility; the other, to be prepared, if the latter is impracticable, to resist with efficacy the sudden attempts of a foreign or domestic enemy. If we have no occasion for troops for the first purposes, and were certain of not wanting any for the second, then all expense of every nature and kind whatsoever on this score would be equally nugatory and unjustifiable; but while men have a disposition to wrangle and disturb the peace of society, either from ambitious, political, or interested motives, common prudence and foresight require such an establishment as is likely to ensure to us the blessings of peace, although the undertaking should be attended with difficulty, and expense. And I can think of no plan more likely to answer the purpose than the one you have suggested, which (the principles being established) may be enlarged or diminished at pleasure, according to circumstances.

To James Craik, March 25, 1784

Dear Sir,

In answer to Mr. Bowie's request to you, permit me to assure that gentleman that I shall at all times be glad to see him at this retreat; that whenever he is here I will give him the perusal of any public papers antecedent to my appointment to the command of the American army that he may be laying up materials for his work; and, whenever Congress shall have opened *their* archives to any historian for information, that he shall have the examination of all others in my possession which are subsequent thereto; but that till this epoch, I do not think myself at liberty to unfold papers which contain all the occurrences and transactions of my *late* command, first, because I conceive it to be respectful to the sovereign power to let them take the lead in this business, and, next, because I have, upon this principle, refused Doctor Gordon and others who are about to write the history of the Revolution this privilege.

I will frankly declare to you, my dear doctor, that any memoirs of my life, distinct and unconnected with the general history of the war, would rather hurt my feelings than tickle my pride whilst I lived. I had rather glide gently down the stream of life, leaving it to posterity to think and say what they please of me, than by an act of mine to have vanity or ostentation imputed to me. And I will furthermore confess that I was rather surprised into a consent when Doctor Witherspoon (very unexpectedly) made the application than considered the tendency of that consent. It did not occur to me at that moment, from the manner in which the question was propounded, that no history of my life, without a very great deal of trouble indeed, could be written with the least degree of accuracy unless recourse was had to me or to my papers for information, that it would not derive sufficient authenticity without a promulgation of this fact, and that such a promulgation would subject me to the imputation I have just mentioned, which would hurt me the more as I do not think vanity is a trait of my character.

It is for this reason, and candor obliges me to be explicit, that I shall stipulate against the publication of the memoirs Mr. Bowie has in contemplation to give the world till I should see more probability of avoiding the darts which *I think* would be pointed at me on such an occasion. And how far, under these circumstances, it would be worth Mr. Bowie's while to spend time which might be more usefully employed in other matters is with him to consider, as the practicability of doing it efficiently without having free access to the documents of this war, which must fill the most important pages of the memoir, and which for the reasons already assigned cannot be admitted at present, also is. If nothing happens more than I at present foresee, I shall be in Philadelphia on or before the first of May, where 'tis probable I may see Mr. Bowie and converse further with him on this subject. In the meanwhile, I will thank you for communicating these sentiments. I am very truly Your affectionate friend & Servt

G: Washington

To Thomas Jefferson, March 29, 1784 (Excerpts)

My opinion coincides perfectly with yours respecting the practicability of an easy and short communication between the waters of the Ohio and Potomac, of the advantages of that communication and the preference it has over *all* others, and of the policy there would be in this state and Maryland to adopt and render it facile. But I confess to you freely I have no expectation that the public will adopt the measure; for, besides the jealousies which prevail, and the difficulty of proportioning such funds as may be allotted for the purposes you have mentioned, there are two others which in my opinion will be yet harder to surmount. These are (if I have not imbibed too unfavorable an opinion of my countrymen) the impracticability of bringing the great and truly wise policy of this measure to their view and the difficulty of drawing money from them for such a purpose if you could do it. For it appears to me, maugre all the sufferings of the public creditors, breach of public faith, and loss of public reputation, that payment of the taxes which are already laid will be postponed as long as possible! How then are we to expect new ones for purposes more remote? ....

I am not less in sentiment with you respecting the impolicy of this state's grasping at more territory than they are competent to the government of. And for the reasons which you assign, I very much approve of a meridian from the mouth of the Great Kanawha as a convenient and very proper line of separation. But I am mistaken if our chief magistrate will coincide with us in opinion.

I will not enter upon the subject of commerce. It has its advantages and disadvantages, but which of them preponderates is not the question. From trade our citizens *will* not be restrained, and therefore it behooves us to place it in the most convenient channels, under proper regulation—freed, *as much as possible*, from those vices which luxury, the consequence of wealth and power, naturally introduce.

The inertitude which prevails in Congress—and the non-attendance of its members—is discouraging to those who are willing and ready to discharge the trust which is reposed in them, whilst it is disgraceful, in a very high degree, to our country. But I believe the case will never be otherwise so long as that body persist in their present mode of doing business and will hold constant, instead of annual, sessions, against the former of which my mind furnishes me with a variety of arguments, but not one, in times of peace, in favor of the latter.

Annual sessions would always produce a full representation and alertness in business. The delegates, after a recess of eight or ten months, would meet each other with glad countenances. They would be complaisant. They would yield to each other as much as the duty they owed their constituents would permit. And they would have opportunities of becoming better acquainted with the sentiments of them and removing their prejudices during the recess. Men who are always together get tired of each other's company. They throw off[1] the proper restraint. They say and do things which are personally disgusting. This begets opposition, opposition begets faction, and so it goes on till business is impeded, often at a stand. I am sure (having the business prepared by proper boards or a committee) an annual session of two months would dispatch more business than is now done in twelve, and this by a full representation of the Union.

To Antoine-Jean-Louis Le Bègue de Presle Duportail, April 4, 1784 (Excerpt)

Matters in this country, since you left it, remain *nearly* in status quo. It is said, however, a more liberal sentiment is taking place in those states which were most opposed to commutation and the other interests of the army, and that the impost, which has labored so long in them, will certainly pass this spring. This will be a principal move towards restoring public credit and raising our sinking reputation. More competent powers, it is thought, will also be vested, in a little time, in Congress, and that all things will come right after the people *feel* the inconveniences which they might have avoided if they had not been too fond of judging for themselves.

To William Gordon, May 8, 1784

Reverend Sir,

Every aid which can be derived from my official papers I am willing to afford and shall with much pleasure lay before you, whenever the latter can be unfolded with propriety.

It ever has been my opinion, however, that no historian can be possessed of sufficient materials to compile a *perfect* history of the Revolution who has not free access to the archives of Congress, to those of the respective states, to the papers of the commander-in-chief, and to those of the officers who have been employed in separate departments. Combining and properly arranging the information which is to be obtained from these sources must bring to view all the material occurrences of the war. Some things probably will never be known.

Added to this, I have always thought that it would be respectful to the sovereign power of these United States to *follow* rather than to take the lead of them in disclosures of this kind. But if there should be political restraints under which Congress are not inclined at this time to lay open their papers, and these restraints do not in their opinion extend to mine, the same being signified by that honorable body to me, my objections to your request will cease. I shall be happy then, as at all times, to see you at Mount Vernon and will lay before you with cheerfulness my public papers for your information. With great esteem and regard, I am Dr Sir Your Most Obt &c.

G: Washington

To the State Societies of the Cincinnati, May 15, 1784

Gentlemen,

We, the delegates of the Cincinnati, after the most mature and deliberate discussion of the principles and objects of our society, have thought proper to recommend that the enclosed institution of the Society of the Cincinnati, as altered and amended at their first meeting, should be adopted by your state society.

In order that our conduct on this occasion may stand approved in the eyes of the world, that we may not incur the imputations of obstinacy, on the one hand, or levity, on the other, and that you may be induced more cheerfully to comply with our recommendation, we beg leave to communicate the reasons on which we have acted.

Previous to our laying them before you, we hold it a duty to ourselves and to our fellow citizens to declare—and we call Heaven to witness the veracity of our declaration—that in our whole agency on this subject we have been actuated by the purest principles. Notwithstanding we are thus conscious for ourselves of the rectitude of our intentions in instituting or becoming members of this fraternity; and notwithstanding we are confident the highest evidence can be produced from your past, and will be given by your future behavior, that you could not have been influenced by any other motives than those of friendship, patriotism, and benevolence; yet, as our designs in some respects have been misapprehended; as the instrument of our association was, of necessity, drawn up in a hasty manner, at an epocha as extraordinary as it will be memorable in the annals of mankind, when the mind, agitated by a variety of emotions, was not at liberty to attend minutely to every circumstance which respected our social connection, or to digest our ideas into so correct a form as could have been wished; as the original institution appeared, in the opinion of many respectable characters, to have comprehended objects which are deemed incompatible with the genius and spirit of the Confederation; and as, in this case, it would eventually frustrate our purposes and be productive of consequences which we had not foreseen: Therefore, to remove every cause of inquietude, to annihilate every source of jealousy, to designate explicitly the ground on which we wish to stand, and to give one more proof that the late officers of the American army have a claim to be reckoned among the most faithful citizens, we have agreed that the following material alterations and amendments should take place: That the hereditary succession should be abolished; that all interference with political subjects should be done away; and that the funds should be placed under the immediate cognizance of the several legislatures, who should also be requested to grant charters for more effectually carrying our humane designs into execution.

In giving our reasons for the alteration in the first article, we must ask your indulgence while we recall your attention to the original occasion which induced us to form ourselves into a society of friends. Having lived in the strictest habits of amity through the various stages of a war unparalleled in many of its circumstances; having seen the objects for which we contended happily attained; in the moment of triumph and separation, when we were about to act the last pleasing melancholy scene in our military drama—*pleasing*, because we were to leave our country possessed of independence and peace, *melancholy*, because we were to part, perhaps never to meet again; while every breast was penetrated with feelings which can be more easily conceived than described, while every little act of tenderness recurred fresh to the recollection; it was impossible not to wish our friendships should be continued. It was extremely natural to desire they might be perpetuated by our posterity, to the remotest ages. With these impressions and with such sentiments we candidly confess we signed the institution. We know our motives were irreproachable. But, finding it apprehended by many of our countrymen that this would be drawing an unjustifiable line of discrimination between our descendants and the rest of the community, and averse to the creation of unnecessary and unpleasing distinctions, we could not hesitate to relinquish everything but our personal friendships, of which we cannot be divested, and those acts of beneficence which it is our intention should flow from them.

With views equally pure and disinterested, we proposed to use our collective influence in support of that government and confirmation of that Union the establishment of which had engaged so considerable a part of our lives. But, learning from a variety of information that this is deemed an officious and improper interference, and that if we are not charged with having sinister designs, yet we are accused of arrogating too much and assuming the guardianship of the liberties of our country; thus circumstanced, we could not think of opposing ourselves to the concurring opinions of our fellow citizens, however founded, or of giving anxiety to those whose happiness it is our interest and duty to promote.

We come next to speak of the charitable part of our institution, which we esteem the basis of it. By placing your fund in the hands of the legislature of your state and letting them see the application is to the best purposes, you will demonstrate the integrity of your actions as well as the rectitude of your principles. And having convinced them your intentions are only of a friendly and benevolent nature, we are induced to believe they will patronize a design which they cannot but approve, that they will foster the good dispositions and encourage the beneficent acts of those who are disposed to make use of the most effectual and most unexceptionable mode of relieving the distressed. For this purpose, it is to be hoped that charters may be obtained in consequence of the applications which are directed to be made. It is also judged most proper that the admission of members should be submitted to the regulation of such charters, because by thus acting in conformity to the sentiments of government, we not only give another instance of our reliance upon it but of our disposition to remove every source of uneasiness respecting our society.

We trust it has not escaped your attention, gentlemen, that the only objects of which we are desirous to preserve the remembrance are of such a nature as cannot be displeasing to our countrymen or unprofitable to posterity. We have retained, accordingly, those devices which recognize the manner of returning to our citizenship—not as ostentatious marks of discrimination, but as pledges of our friendship and emblems whose appearance will never permit us to deviate from the paths of virtue. And we presume in this place it may not be inexpedient to inform you that these are considered as the most endearing tokens of friendship and held in the highest estimation by such of our allies as have become entitled to them by having contributed their personal services to the establishment of our independence; that those gentlemen who are among the first in rank and reputation have been permitted by their sovereign to hold this grateful memorial of our reciprocal affections; and that this fraternal intercourse is viewed by that illustrious monarch and other distinguished characters as no small additional cement to that harmony and reciprocation of good offices which so happily prevail between the two nations.

Having now relinquished whatever has been found objectionable in our original institution; having, by the deference thus paid to the prevailing sentiments of the community, neither, as we conceive, lessened the dignity nor diminished the consistency of character which it is our ambition to support in the eyes of the present as well as of future generations; having thus removed every possible objection to our remaining connected as a society and cherishing our mutual friendships to the close of life; and having, as we flatter ourselves, retained in its utmost latitude, and placed upon a more certain and permanent foundation, that primary article of our association, which respects the unfortunate; on these two great original pillars, friendship and charity, we rest our institution. And we appeal to your liberality, patriotism, and magnanimity, to your conduct on every other occasion, as well as to the purity of your intentions on the present for the ratification of our proceedings. At the same time, we are happy in expressing a full confidence in the candor, justice, and integrity of the public, that the institution, as now altered and amended, will be perfectly satisfactory, and that acts of legislative authority will soon be passed to give efficacy to your benevolence.

Before we conclude this address, permit us to add that the cultivation of that amity we profess, and the extension of this charity, we flatter ourselves, will be objects of sufficient importance to prevent a relaxation in the prosecution of them. To diffuse comfort and support to any of our unfortunate companions who have seen better days and merited a milder fate; to wipe the tear from the eye of the widow who must have been consigned, with her helpless infants, to indigence and wretchedness, but for this charitable institution; to succor the fatherless; to rescue the female orphan from destruction; to enable the son to emulate the virtues of the father; will be no unpleasing task. It will communicate happiness to others while it increases our own. It will cheer our solitary reflections and sooth our latest moments. Let us, then, prosecute with ardor what we have instituted in sincerity. Let Heaven and our own consciences approve our conduct. Let our actions be the best comment on our words. And let us leave a lesson to posterity that the glory of soldiers cannot be completed without acting well the part of citizens.

Signed by Order
Go: Washington President

To Jonathan Trumbull, Sr., Governor of Connecticut, May 15, 1784 (Excerpt)

It is indeed a pleasure from the walks of private life to view in retrospect all the meanderings of our past labors, the difficulties through which we have waded, and the fortunate haven to which the ship has been brought! Is it possible after this that it should founder? Will not the all-wise and all-powerful director of human events preserve it? I think he will. He may, however (^{2}for wise purposes not discoverable by finite minds), suffer our indiscretions and folly to place our national character low in the political scale. And this, unless more wisdom and less prejudice take the lead in our governments, will most assuredly be the case.

Believe me, my dear sir, there is no disparity in our ways of thinking and acting, though there may happen to be a little in the years we have lived—which places the advantages of the correspondence between us to my account, as I shall benefit more by your experience and observations than you can by mine. No correspondence can be more pleasing than one which originates from similar sentiments and similar conduct through (though not a long war, the importance of it and attainments considered) a painful contest. I pray you therefore to continue me among the number of your friends and to favor me with such observations as shall occur.

To Henry Knox, June 2, 1784 (Excerpt)

It is a real misfortune that in great national concerns the sovereign has not sufficient power to act, or that there should be a contrariety of sentiment among themselves respecting this power. While these matters are in litigation, the public interest is suspended and important advantages are lost. This will be the case respecting the western posts.

To Edward Newenham, June 10, 1784 (Excerpt)

For the honor of these letters, and the favorable sentiments they express of me, you have my sincerest thanks. To stand well in the estimation of good men and honest patriots, whether of this or that clime, or of this or that political way of thinking, has ever been a favorite wish of mine. And to have obtained by such pursuits as duty to my country and the rights of mankind rendered indispensably necessary, the plaudit of Sir Edward Newenham will not be among my smallest felicities. Yes, sir, it was long before you honored me with a line I became acquainted with your name, your worth, and your political tenets; and I rejoice that my own conduct has been such as to acquire your esteem and to be invited to your friendship. I accept it, sir, with the eagerness of a congenial spirit and shall be happy in every opportunity of giving you proofs of its rectitude; but none will be more pleasing to me than the opportunity of welcoming you, or any of your family, to this land of liberty, and to *this* my retreat from the cares of public life, where in homespun and with rural fare we will invite you to our bed and board.

Your intention of making an establishment for one of your sons, either in Pennsylvania or this state, gives me pleasure. If it should be in the latter, or if you should come to this state first, every information or assistance which it may be in my power to give you shall be rendered with great pleasure; and I shall have pleasure also in paying attention to your recommendation of others.

This is an abounding country, and it is as fine as it is extensive. With a little political wisdom, it may become equally populous and happy. Some of the states, having been misled, ran riot for a while, but they are recovering a proper tone again; and I have *no* doubt but that our Federal Constitution will obtain more consistency and firmness every day. We have indeed so plain a road before us that it must be worse than ignorance if we miss it.

To James Madison, June 12, 1784

Dear Sir,

Can nothing be done in our assembly for poor Paine? Must the merits and services of *Common Sense* continue to glide down the stream of time unrewarded by this country? His writings certainly have had a powerful effect on the public mind; ought they not then to meet an adequate return? He is poor! He is chagrined!—and almost, if not altogether, in despair of relief.

New York, it is true, not the least distressed nor best able state in the Union, has done something for him. This kind of provision he prefers to an allowance from Congress. He has reasons for it, which to him are conclusive, and such, I think, as would have weight with others. His views are moderate: a decent independency is, I believe, all he aims at. Should he not obtain this? If you think so, I am sure you will not only move the matter but give it your support. For me, it only remains to feel for his situation and to assure you of the sincere esteem and regard with which I have the honor to be Dr Sir, Yr most obedt Hble Servt

Go: Washington

To the Virginia Legislature, July 15, 1784

Gentlemen,

With feelings which are more easy to be conceived than expressed, I meet and reciprocate the congratulations of the representatives of this commonwealth on the final establishment of peace.

Nothing can add more to the pleasure which arises from a conscientious discharge of public trust than the approbation of one's country. To have been, under a vicissitude of fortune, amidst the difficult and trying scenes of an arduous conflict, so happy as to meet this is in my mind to have attained the highest honor; and the consideration of it in my present peaceful retirement will heighten all my domestic enjoyments and constitute my greatest felicity.

I should have been truly wanting in duty, and must have frustrated the great and important object for which we resorted to arms, if, seduced by a temporary regard of fame, I had suffered the paltry love of it to have interfered with my country's welfare, the interest of which was the only inducement which carried me to the field, or permitted the rights of civil authority, though but for a moment, to be violated and infringed by a power meant originally to rescue and confirm them.

For those rewards and blessings which you have invoked for me in this world, and for the fruition of that happiness which is to come, you have, gentlemen, all my thanks and all my gratitude. I wish I could ensure them to you and the state you represent a hundred fold.

G. Washington

To Jacob Read, August 11, 1784 (Excerpt)

Dear Sir,

I return the letter you were so obliging as to send me and thank you for the perusal of it. No copy has been taken, nor will any part of its contents transpire from me.

Although Mr. L's[3] intelligence may come from a man of information, and though it is undoubted that the British cabinet wish to recover the United States to a dependence on that government, yet I can scarcely think they ever expect to see it realized, or that they have any plan in contemplation by which it is to be attempted—unless our want of wisdom and perseverance in error should in their judgment render the effort certain.

The affairs of Ireland, if our accounts from thence are to be relied on, are in too turbulent a state to suffer G. Britn to enter very soon into another war with America, even if her finances were on a more respectable footing than I believe them to be. And her prospect of success must diminish as our population increases and the governments become more consistent—without the last of which, indeed, anything may be apprehended.

It is, however, as necessary for the sovereign in council as it is for a general in the field not to despise information, but to hear all, compare all, combine them with other circumstances, and take measures accordingly. Nothing, I acknowledge, would sooner induce me to give credit to a hostile intention on the part of G. Britain than their continuing (without the shadow of reason, for I really see none they have) to withhold the western posts on the American side of the line from us and sending, as the gazettes mention, Sir Guy Carleton over as viceroy to their possessions in America, which it seems is to undergo a new organization.

The opinion I have here given you will readily perceive is founded upon the idea I entertain of the temper of Ireland, the imbecility of G.B., and her internal divisions. For it is with pain I add that I think our affairs are under wretched management and that our conduct, if Great B. was in circumstances to take advantage of it, would bid her hope everything, while other powers might expect little from the wisdom or exertion of these states.

Diary Entry, October 4, 1784 (Excerpt)

Hitherto, the people of the western country having had no excitements to industry, labor very little. The luxuriancy of the soil, with very little culture, produces provisions in abundance. These supply the wants of the increasing population; and the Spaniards, when pressed by want, have given high prices for flour. Other articles they reject, and at times (contrary, I think, to sound policy) shut their ports against them altogether. But let us open a good communication with the settlements west of us, extend the inland navigation as far as it can be done with convenience, and show them by this means how easy it is to bring the produce of their lands to our markets, and see how astonishingly our exports will be increased and these states benefited in a commercial point of view—which alone is an object of such magnitude as to claim our closest attention. But when the subject is considered in a political point of view, it appears of much greater importance.

No well-informed mind need be told that the flanks and rear of the United territory are possessed by other powers, and formidable ones too, nor how necessary it is to apply the cement of interest to bind all parts of it together by one indissolvable band—particularly the middle states with the country immediately back of them. For what ties, let me ask, should we have upon those people, and how entirely unconnected should we be with them, if the Spaniards on their right, or Great Britain on their left, instead of throwing stumbling blocks in their way, as they now do, should invite their trade and seek alliances with them? What, when they get strength, which will be sooner than is generally imagined (from the emigration of foreigners who can have no predilection for us, as well as from the removal of our own citizens), may be the consequence of their having formed such connections and alliances requires no uncommon foresight to predict.

The western settlers, from my own observation, stand as it were on a pivot; the touch of a feather would almost incline them any way. They looked down the Mississippi until the Spaniards (very impoliticly, I think, for themselves) threw difficulties in the way, and for no other reason that I can conceive than because they glided gently down the stream, without considering perhaps the tediousness of the voyage back and the time necessary to perform it in, and because they have no other means of coming to us but by a long land transportation and unimproved roads.

A combination of circumstances makes the present conjuncture more favorable than any other to fix the trade of the western country to our markets. The jealous and untoward disposition of the Spaniards on one side, and the private views of some individuals, coinciding with the policy of the Court of G. Britain on the other, to retain the Posts of Oswego, Niagara, Detroit, etc. (which, though done under the letter of the treaty, is certainly an infraction of the spirit of it and injurious to the Union) may be improved to the greatest advantage by this state if she would open her arms and embrace the means which are necessary to establish it. The way is plain; and the expense, comparatively speaking, deserves not a thought, so great would be the prize. The western inhabitants would do their part towards accomplishing it. Weak as they now are, they would, I am persuaded, meet us halfway rather than be driven into the arms of, or be in any wise dependent upon, foreigners, the consequence of which would be a separation or a war.

The way to avoid both, happily for us, is easy, and dictated by our clearest interests. It is to open a wide door and make a smooth way for the produce of that country to pass to our markets before the trade may get into another channel. This, in my judgment, would dry up the other sources; or, if any part should flow down the Mississippi from the falls of the Ohio, in vessels which may be built—fitted for sea and sold with their cargoes the proceeds, I have no manner of doubt, will return this way; and that it is better to prevent an evil than to rectify a mistake none can deny; commercial connections, of all others, are most difficult to dissolve—if we wanted proof of this, look to the avidity with which we are renewing, after a total suspension of eight years, our correspondence with Great Britain; So, if we [Virginians] are supine, and suffer without a struggle the settlers of the western country to form commercial connections with the Spaniards, Britons, or with any of the states in the Union we shall find it a difficult matter to dissolve them although a better communication should, thereafter, be presented to them. Time only could effect it; such is the force of habit!

To Benjamin Harrison, Governor of Virginia, October 10, 1784

Dear Sir,

Upon my return from the western country a few days ago, I had the pleasure to receive your favor of the 17th ultimo. It has always been my intention to pay my respects to you before the chance of *another* early and hard winter should make a warm fireside too comfortable to be relinquished. And I shall feel an additional pleasure in offering this tribute of friendship and respect to you by having the company of the Marquis de Lafayette, when he shall have revisited this place from his eastern tour, now every day to be expected.

I shall take the liberty now, my dear sir, to suggest a matter which would (if I am not too shortsighted a politician) mark your administration as an important era in the annals of this country, if it should be recommended by you and adopted by the assembly.

It has been long my decided opinion that the shortest, easiest, and least expensive communication with the invaluable and extensive country back of us would be by one or both of the rivers of this state which have their sources in the Appalachian Mountains. Nor am I singular in this opinion. Evans, in his map and analysis of the middle colonies, which (considering the early period at which they were given to the public) are done with amazing exactness, and Hutchins since, in his topographical description of the western country (good part of which is from actual surveys), are decidedly of the same sentiments, as indeed are all others who have had opportunities and have been at the pains to investigate and consider the subject.

But that this may not stand as mere matter of opinion or assertion, unsupported by facts (such at least as the best maps now extant, compared with the oral testimony, which my opportunities in the course of the war have enabled me to obtain), I shall give you the different routes and distances from Detroit, by which all the trade of the northwestern parts of the united territory must pass, unless the Spaniards, contrary to their present policy, should engage part of it, or the British should attempt to force nature by carrying the trade of the upper lakes by the River Outaouais into Canada, which I scarcely think they will or could effect. Taking Detroit, then (which is putting ourselves in as unfavorable a point of view as we can be well placed, because it is upon the line of the British territory), as a point by which, as I have already observed, all that part of the trade must come, it appears from the statement enclosed that the tide-waters of this state are nearer to it by 168 miles than that of the River St. Lawrence, or than that of the Hudson at Albany by 176 miles.

Maryland stands upon similar ground with Virginia. Pennsylvania, although the Susquehanna is an unfriendly water, much impeded it is said with rocks and rapids, and nowhere communicating with those which lead to her capital, have it in contemplation to open a communication between Toby's Creek (which empties into the Allegheny River, 95 miles above Fort Pitt) and the west branch of Susquehanna, and to cut a canal between the waters of the latter and the Schuylkill, the expense of which is easier to be conceived than estimated or described by me. A people, however, who are possessed of the spirit of commerce, who see and who will pursue their advantages, may achieve almost anything. In the meantime, under the uncertainty of these undertakings, they are smoothing the roads and paving the ways for the trade of that western world. That New York will do the same so soon as the British garrisons are removed, which are at present insurmountable obstacles in *their* way, no person who knows the temper, genius, and policy of those people as well as I do can harbor the smallest doubt.

Thus much with respect to rival states. Let me now take a short view of our own; and, being aware of the objections which are in the way, I will enumerate in order to contrast them with the advantages.

The first and principal one is the *unfortunate jealousy* which ever has and, it is to be feared, ever will prevail lest one part of the state should obtain an advantage over the other part (as if the benefits of trade were not diffusive and beneficial to all). Then follow a train of difficulties, viz.—that our people are already heavily taxed; that we have no money; that the advantages of this trade are remote; that the most *direct* route for it is through *other* states, over whom we have no control; that the routes over which we have control are as distant as either of those which lead to Philadelphia, Albany, or Montreal; that a sufficient spirit of commerce does not pervade the citizens of this commonwealth; that we are in fact doing for others what they ought to do for themselves.

Without going into the investigation of a question which has employed the pens of able politicians, namely, whether trade with foreigners is an advantage or disadvantage to a country: This state, as a part of the confederated states (all of whom have the spirit of it very strongly working within them), must adopt it or submit to the evils arising therefrom without receiving its benefits. Common policy therefore points clearly and strongly to the propriety of our enjoying all the advantages which nature and our local situation afford us and evinces clearly that unless this spirit could be totally eradicated in other states as well as in this, and every man made to become either a cultivator of the land or a manufacturer of such articles as are prompted by necessity, such stimuli should be employed as will force this spirit by showing to our countrymen the superior advantages we possess beyond others and the importance of being upon a footing with our neighbors.

If this is fair reasoning, it ought to follow as a consequence that we should do our part towards opening the communication with the fur and peltry trade of the lakes and for the produce of the country which lies within, and which will—so soon as matters are settled with the Indians, and the terms on which Congress mean to dispose of the land, and found to be favorable, are announced—settle faster than any other ever did or anyone would imagine. This, then, when considered in an interested point of view, is alone sufficient to excite our endeavors. But in my opinion, there is a political consideration for so doing which is of still greater importance.

I need not remark to you, sir, that the flanks and rear of the United States are possessed by other powers—and formidable ones, too—nor how necessary it is to apply the cement of interest to bind all parts of the Union together by indissoluble bonds, especially that part of it which lies immediately west of us, with the middle states. For, what ties, let me ask, should we have upon those people? How entirely unconnected with them shall we be, and what troubles may we not apprehend, if the Spaniards on their right and Great Britain on their left, instead of throwing stumbling blocks in their way as they now do, should hold out lures for their trade and alliance? What, when they get strength, which will be sooner than most people conceive (from the emigration of foreigners who will have no particular predilection towards us, as well as from the removal of our own citizens), will be the consequence of their having formed close connections with both or either of those powers in a commercial way? It needs not, in my opinion, the gift of prophecy to foretell.

The western settlers (I speak now from my own observation) stand as it were upon a pivot: the touch of a feather would turn them any way. They have looked down the Mississippi until the Spaniards (very impoliticly, I think, for themselves) threw difficulties in their way; and they looked that way for no other reason than because they could glide gently down the stream, without considering, perhaps, the fatigues of the voyage back again and the time necessary to perform it in, and because they have no other means of coming to us but by a long land transportation and unimproved roads. These causes have hitherto checked the industry of the present settlers; for, except the demand for provisions, occasioned by the increase of population, and a little flour which the necessities of Spaniards compel them to buy, they have no excitements to labor. But smooth the road once and make easy the way for them, and then see what an influx of articles will be poured in upon us, how amazingly our exports will be increased by them, and how amply we shall be compensated for any trouble and expense we may encounter to effect it.

A combination of circumstances makes the present conjuncture more favorable for Virginia than for any other state in the Union to fix these matters. The jealous and untoward disposition of the Spaniards on one hand, and the private views of some individuals coinciding with the general policy of the Court of Great Britain, on the other, to retain as long as possible the posts of Detroit, Niagara, Oswego, etc. (which, though they are done under the letter of the treaty, is certainly an infraction of the spirit of it, and injurious to the Union) may be improved to the greatest advantage by this state, if she would open her avenues to the trade of that country and embrace the present moment to establish it. It only wants a beginning. The western inhabitants would do their part towards its execution. Weak as they are, they would meet us at least halfway, rather than be driven into the arms of, or be made dependent upon foreigners, which would, eventually, either bring on a separation of them from us or a war between the United States and one or the other of those powers—most probably with the Spaniards. The preliminary steps to the attainment of this great object would be attended with very little expense and might, at the same time that it served to attract the attention of the western country, and to convince the wavering inhabitants thereof of our disposition to connect ourselves with them and to facilitate their commerce with us, would be a mean of removing those jealousies which otherwise might take place among ourselves.

These, in my opinion, are: to appoint commissioners who from their situation, integrity, and abilities can be under no suspicion of prejudice or predilection to one part more than to another; let these commissioners make an actual survey of James River and Potomac from tide-water to their respective sources; note with great accuracy the kind of navigation and the obstructions in it, the difficulty and expense attending the removal of these obstructions, the distances from place to place through the whole extent, and the nearest and best portages between these waters and the streams capable of improvement which run into the Ohio; traverse these in like manner to *their* junction with the Ohio, and with equal accuracy. The navigation of this river (i.e. the Ohio) being well known, they will have less to do in the examination of it; but, nevertheless, let the courses and distances of it be taken to the mouth of the Muskingum, and up that river (notwithstanding it is in the ceded lands) to the carrying place with Cuyahoga, down Cuyahoga to Lake Erie, and thence to Detroit. Let them do the same with Big Beaver Creek, although part of it is in the state of Pennsylvania, and with the Scioto also. In a word, let the waters east and west of the Ohio, which invite our notice by their proximity and the ease with which land transportation may be had between them and the lakes on one side, and the Rivers Potomac and James on the other, be explored, accurately delineated, and a correct and connected map of the whole be presented to the public. These things being done, I shall be mistaken if prejudice does not yield to facts, jealousy to candor, and, finally, that reason and nature thus aided will dictate what is right and proper to be done.

In the meanwhile, if it should be thought that the lapse of time which is necessary to effect this work may be attended with injurious consequences, could not there be a sum of money granted towards opening the best or, if it should be deemed *more eligible,* two of the nearest communications, one to the northward and another to the southward, with the settlements to the westward? And an act be passed (if there should not appear a manifest disposition in the assembly to make it a public undertaking) to incorporate and encourage private adventurers, if any should associate, and solicit the same, for the purpose of extending the navigation of Potomac or James River? And, in the former case, to request the concurrence of Maryland in the measure? It will appear from my statement of the different routes (and as far as my means of information have extended, I have done it with the utmost candor) that all the produce of the settlements about Fort Pitt can be brought to Alexandria by the Yohoghaney in 304 miles, whereof only 31 is land transportation. And by the Monongahela and Cheat River in 360 miles, 20 only of which are land carriage. Whereas the common road from Fort Pitt to Philadelphia is 320 miles, all land transportation, or 476 miles, if the Ohio, Toby's Creek, Susquehanna, and Schuylkill are made use of for this purpose—how much of this by land I know not, but from the nature of the country it must be very considerable. How much the interests and feelings of people thus circumstanced would be engaged to promote it requires no illustration.

For my own part, I think it highly probable that upon the strictest scrutiny (if the falls of the Great Kanawha can be made navigable, or a short portage had there) it will be found of equal importance and convenience to improve the navigation of both the James and Potomac. The latter I am fully persuaded affords the nearest communication with the lakes; but James River may be more convenient for all the settlers below the mouth of the Great Kanawha, and for some distance, perhaps, above and west of it. For I have *no* expectation that any part of the trade above the falls of the Ohio will go down that river and the Mississippi, much less that the returns will ever come up them, unless our want of foresight and good management is the occasion of it. Or, upon trial, if it should be found that these rivers, from the before-mentioned falls, will admit the descent of sea vessels, in which case, and the navigation of the former's becoming free, it is probable that both vessels and cargoes will be carried to foreign markets and sold; but the returns for them will never, in the natural course of things, ascend the long and rapid current of that river, which with the Ohio to the falls, in their meanderings, is little if any short of 2,000 miles. Upon the whole, the object, in my estimation, is of vast commercial and political importance. In these lights I think posterity will consider it, and regret (if our conduct should give them cause) that the present favorable moment to secure so great a blessing for them was neglected.

One thing more remains, which I had like to have forgot, and that is the supposed difficulty of obtaining a passage through the state of Pennsylvania. How an application to its legislature would be relished, in the first instance, I will not undertake to decide; but of one thing I am almost certain, such an application would place that body in a very delicate situation. There are in the state of Pennsylvania at least 100,000 souls west of the Laurel Hill, who are groaning under the inconveniencies of a long land transportation. They are wishing, indeed they are looking for, the improvement and extension of inland navigation; and if this cannot be made easy for them, to Philadelphia (at any rate it must be lengthy), they will seek a mart elsewhere—the consequence of which would be that the state, though contrary to the policy and interests of its seaports, must submit to the loss of so much of its trade, or hazard not only the trade but the loss of the settlement also. For an opposition on the part of government to the extension of water transportation, so consonant with the essential interests of a large body of people, or any extraordinary impositions upon the exports or imports to or from another state, would ultimately bring on a separation between its eastern and western settlements—towards which there is not wanting a disposition at this moment in that part of it which is beyond the mountains.

I consider Rumsey's discovery for working boats against stream by mechanical powers (principally) as not only a very fortunate invention for these states in general, but as one of those circumstances which have combined to render the present epocha favorable above all others for fixing, if we are disposed to avail ourselves of them, a large portion of the trade of the western country in the bosom of this state irrevocably.

Lengthy as this letter is, I intended to have written a fuller and more digested one upon this important subject, but have met with so many interruptions since my return home as almost to have precluded my writing at all. What I now give is crude; but if you are in sentiment with me, I have said enough. If there is not an accordance of opinion, I have said too much; and all I pray in the latter case is that you will do me the justice to believe my motives are pure, however erroneous my judgment may be on this matter, and that I am with the most perfect esteem & friendship Dr Sir Yrs &c. &c. &c.

G: Washington

To Jacob Read, November 3, 1784 (Excerpt)

It is much to be regretted that the slow determinations of Congress involve many evils. It is much easier to avoid mischiefs than to apply remedies after they have happened. Had Congress paid an earlier attention to, or decided sooner on, Indian affairs, matters would have been in a more favorable train than they now are. And if they are longer delayed, they will grow worse. Twelve months ago, the Indians would have listened to propositions of *any kind* with more readiness than they will do now. The terms of peace frightened them, and they were disgusted with Great Britain for making such. Bribery and every address which British art could devise have been practiced since to sooth them, to estrange them from us, and to secure their trade.

To what other causes can be ascribed their holding our western posts so long after the ratification of the treaty, contrary to the spirit though they do it under the letter of it. To remove their garrisons and stores is not the work of a week. For if report be true, they have only to shift them to the opposite side of the line. But it is now more than a year since I foretold what has happened; and I shall not be surprised if they leave us *no* posts to occupy. For if they *mean* to surrender them *at all*, they may fix upon a *season* or appoint a short day perhaps for the evacuation, which would preclude all relief, especially as I believe you are in no condition to possess them. To do it properly requires time. Ordnance, stores, provisions, and other articles, no more than garrisons, are to be established in a moment, even where boats and other conveniences (of which I dare say you are deficient) are at hand to transplant them. Supposing this to be the case, there will be an interregnum during which the works will be left without guards, and being obnoxious to British policy and Indian prejudices, will, by *accidental* fires, or Indian drunkenness, end in conflagration.

There is a matter which, though it does not come before Congress wholly, is in my opinion of great political importance and ought to be attended to in time. It is to prevent the trade of the western territory from settling in the hands either of the Spaniards or British. If either of these happen, there is a line of separation at once drawn between the eastern and western country, the consequences of which may be fatal. To tell any man of information how fast the latter is settling; how much more rapidly it will settle by means of foreign emigrants, who can have no particular predilection for us; of the vast fertility of the soil and the population the country is competent to would be futile—and equally nugatory to observe that it is by the cement of interest only we can be held together. If, then, the trade of that country should flow through the Mississippi or St. Lawrence, if the inhabitants thereof should form commercial connections, which lead, we know, to intercourse of other kinds, they would in a few years be as unconnected with us, indeed more so, than we are with South America, and would soon be alienated from us.

It may be asked how we are to prevent this? Happily for us, the way is plain; and our *immediate* interests, as well as remote political advantages, point to it, whilst a combination of circumstances renders the present epocha more favorable than any other to accomplish them. Extend the inland navigation of the eastern waters, communicate them as near as possible (by excellent roads) with those which run to the westward, open these to the Ohio and such others as extend from the Ohio towards Lake Erie, and we shall not only draw the produce of the western settlers, but the fur and peltry trade of the lakes also, to our ports (being the nearest and easiest of transportation), to the amazing increase of our exports, while we bind those people to us by a chain which never can be broken.

This is no utopian scheme. It can be demonstrated as fully as facts can ascertain anything that not only the produce of the Ohio and its waters, at least to the falls, but those of the lakes also, as far even as that of the Wood, may be brought to the seaports of the United States by routes shorter, easier, and less expensive than they can be carried to Montreal or New Orleans, if we would be at a little trouble and expense to open them. I will acknowledge that the most essential part of this business comes more properly before individual states than the Union. But there is one part of it which lies altogether with the latter, and that is to have actual surveys of the western territory, more especially of the rivers which empty into the Ohio on the northwest side thereof, which have the easiest and best communications with Lake Erie, reporting the nature of these waters, the practicability of their navigation, and expense in opening of them. This, in my opinion, is an important business and admits of no delay. It would show the value of those lands more clearly. It would attract the attention of the settlers and the traders. It would give the tone and fix ideas that at present are as floating as chaos.

You see, sir, I have obeyed your commands. My sentiments are delivered with freedom. The worst construction they will admit of is that they are errors of judgment. For sure I am I have no private views that can be promoted by the adoption of them. Mrs. Washington thanks you for your polite remembrance of her and joins me in best respects. I am with esteem & regard Dr Sir Yr most Obt Hble Servt

Go: Washington

To Officials of the City of Richmond, November 15, 1784

Gentlemen,

I derive great honor from your congratulatory address, the language of which is too flattering not to have excited my utmost gratitude.

To the smiles of Heaven, to a virtuous and gallant army, and to the exertions of my fellow citizens of the Union (not to superior talents of mine) are to be ascribed the blessings of that liberty, independence, and peace of which we are all now in the enjoyment. Whilst these are afforded us, and while the advantages of commerce are not only offered but are soliciting our acceptance, it must be our own fault indeed if we do not make them productive of a rich and plenteous harvest—and of that national honor and glory which should be characteristic of a young and rising empire.

That this growing city may enjoy all the benefits which are to be derived from them in the fullest extent, that it may improve such as nature has bestowed, and that it may soon be ranked among the first in the Union for population, commerce, and wealth, is my sincere and fervent wish.

Go: Washington

To George Clinton, Governor of New York, November 25, 1784 (Excerpt)

It gives me great pleasure to learn from yourself that the state over which you preside is tranquil. Would to God it may ever remain so, and that all others would follow the example. Internal dissensions and jarring with our neighbors are not only productive of mischievous consequences as it respects ourselves, but have a tendency to lessen our national character and importance in the eyes of European powers. If anything can, this will expose us to their intriguing politics and may shake the Union.

To Henry Knox, December 5, 1784 (Excerpt)

I am now endeavoring to stimulate my countrymen to the extension of the inland navigation of the Rivers Potomac and James—thereby, and a short land transportation, to connect the western territory by strong commercial bands with this. I hope I shall succeed, more on account of its political importance than the commercial advantages which would result from it, although the latter is an immense object. For if this country, which will settle faster than any other ever did (and chiefly by foreigners who can have no particular predilection for *us*), cannot by an easy communication be drawn this way, but are suffered to form commercial intercourses (which lead, we all know, to others) with the Spaniards on their right and rear, or the British on their left, they will become a distinct people from us, have different views, different interests, and instead of adding strength to the Union may, in case of a rupture with either of those powers, be a formidable and dangerous neighbor.

After much time spent (charity directs us to suppose, in duly considering the matter) a treaty has at length been held with the Six Nations at Fort Stanwix, much to the advantage, it is said, of the United States, but to the great disquiet of that of New York—fruitlessly, it is added by some, who assert that the deputies on the part of the Indians were not properly authorized to treat. How true this may be, I will not pretend to decide. But certain it is, in my opinion, that there is a kind of fatality attending all our public measures: inconceivable delays, particular states counteracting the plans of the United States when submitted to them, opposing each other upon all occasions, torn by internal disputes, or supinely negligent and inattentive to everything which is not local and self-interesting (and very often shortsighted in these), make up our system of conduct. Would to God our own countrymen who are entrusted with the management of the political machine could view things by that large and extensive scale upon which it is measured by foreigners and by the statesmen of Europe, who see what we might be and predict what we shall come to. In fact, our federal government is a name without substance. No state is longer bound by its edicts than it suits *present* purposes, without looking to the consequences. How then can we fail in a little time becoming the sport of European politics and the victims of our own folly.

To George Chapman, December 15, 1784

Sir,

Not until within a few days have I been honored with your favor of the 27th of September 1783, accompanying your treatise on education.

My sentiments are perfectly in unison with yours, sir, that the best means of forming a manly, virtuous, and happy people will be found in the right education of youth. Without this foundation, every other means, in my opinion, must fail; and it gives me pleasure to find that gentlemen of your abilities are devoting their time and attention in pointing out the way. For your lucubrations on this subject, which you have been so obliging as to send me, I pray you to accept my thanks and an expression of the pleasure I felt at the declaration of your intention to devote a further portion of your time in so useful a study.

Of the importance of education our assemblies, happily, seem fully impressed; they are[4] establishing new, and giving further endowments to the old, seminaries of learning, and, I persuade myself, will leave nothing unessayed to cultivate literature and useful knowledge for the purpose of qualifying the rising generation for patrons of good government, virtue, and happiness. I have the honor to be &c.

G: Washington

To Samuel Chase, January 5, 1785 (Excerpt)

The attention which your assembly is giving to the establishment of public schools for the encouragement of literature does them great honor. To accomplish this ought to be one of our first endeavors. I know of no object more interesting. We want something to expand the mind and make us think with more liberality and act with sounder policy than most of the states do. We should consider that we are not now in leading strings. It behooves us therefore to look well to our ways. My best wishes attend the ladies of your family. I am, Dr Sir Yr mo. obt Servt

G: Washington

To Benjamin Harrison, January 22, 1785

My Dear Sir,

It is not easy for me to decide by which my mind was most affected upon the receipt of your letter of the 6th instant—surprise or gratitude. Both were greater than I have words to express. The attention and good wishes which the assembly have evidenced by their act for vesting in me 150 shares in the navigation of each of the Rivers Potomac and James is more than mere compliment; there is an unequivocal and substantial meaning annexed. But believe me, sir, notwithstanding these, no circumstance has happened to me since I left the walks of public life which has so much embarrassed me. On the one hand, I consider this act, as I have already observed, as a noble and unequivocal proof of the good opinion, the affection, and disposition of my country to serve me. And I should be hurt if by declining the acceptance of it my refusal should be construed into disrespect, or the smallest slight put upon the generous intention of the country, or that an ostentatious display of disinterestedness or public virtue was the source of the refusal.

On the other hand, it is really my wish to have my mind, and the actions which are the result of contemplation, as free and independent as the air, that I may be more at liberty (in things which my opportunities and experience have brought me to the knowledge of) to express my sentiments and, if necessary, to suggest what may occur to me under the fullest conviction that, although my judgment may be arraigned, there will be no suspicion that sinister motives had the smallest influence in the suggestion. Not content, then, with the bare consciousness of my having, in all this navigation business, acted upon the clearest conviction of the political importance of the measure, I would wish that every individual who may hear that it was a favorite plan of mine may know also that I had no other motive for promoting it than the advantage I conceived it would be productive of to the Union, and to this state in particular, by cementing the eastern and western territory together, at the same time that it will give vigor and increase to our commerce and be a convenience to our citizens.

How would this matter be viewed, then, by the eye of the world, and what would be the opinion of it, when it comes to be related that George Washington exerted himself to effect this work, and George Washington has received 20,000 dollars and £5,000 sterling of the public money as an interest therein? Would not this in the estimation of it (if I am entitled to any merit for the part I have acted, and without it there is no foundation for the act) deprive me of the principal thing which is laudable in my conduct? Would it not, in some respects, be considered in the same light as a pension? And would not the apprehension of this make me more reluctantly offer my sentiments in future? In a word, under whatever pretense, and however customary these gratuitous gifts are made in other countries, should I not thenceforward be considered as a dependent?—one moment's thought of which would give me more pain than I should receive pleasure from the product of all the tolls, was every farthing of them vested in me, although I consider it as one of the most certain and increasing estates in the country.

I have written to you with an openness becoming our friendship. I could have said more on the subject, but I have already said enough to let you into the state of my mind. I wish to know whether the ideas I entertain occurred to and were expressed by any member in or out of the house. Upon the whole, you may be assured my dear sir, that my mind is not a little agitated. I want the best information and advice to settle it. I have no inclination (as I have already observed) to avail myself of the generosity of the country. Nor do I want to appear ostentatiously disinterested (for more than probable my refusal would be ascribed to this motive), or that the country should harbor an idea that I am disposed to set little value on her favors—the manner of granting which is as flattering as the grant is important. My present difficulties, however, shall be no impediment to the progress of the undertaking. I will receive the full and frank opinions of my friends with thankfulness. I shall have time enough between this and the sitting of the next assembly to consider the tendency of the act—and in this, as in all other matters, will endeavor to decide for the best.

My respectful compliments and best wishes, in which Mrs. Washington and Fanny Bassett (who is much recovered) join, are offered to Mrs. Harrison and the rest of your family. It would give us great pleasure to hear that Mrs. Harrison had her health restored to her. With every sentiment of esteem, regard, and friendship, I am My Dr Sir &c. &c.

G: Washington

To Richard Henry Lee, President of the Confederation Congress, February 8, 1785 (Excerpt)

Towards the latter part of the year 1783, I was honored with a letter from the Countess of Huntingdon, briefly reciting her benevolent intention of spreading Christianity among the tribes of Indians inhabiting our western territory and expressing a desire that my advice and assistance might be afforded her to carry this charitable design into execution. I wrote her Ladyship for answer that it would by no means comport with the plan of retirement I had promised myself to take an active or responsible part in this business, and that it was my belief there would be no other way to effect her pious and benevolent design but by first reducing these people to a state of greater civilization, but that I would give every aid in my power, consistent with that ease and tranquility I meant to devote the remainder of my life to facilitate her views. Since this I have been favored with other letters from her, and a few days ago, under cover from Sir James Jay, I received the papers herewith enclosed.

As the plan contemplated by Lady Huntingdon, according to the outlines exhibited, is not only unexceptionable in its design and tendency, but has humanity and charity for its object—and may, as I conceive, be made subservient to valuable political purposes—I take the liberty of laying the matter before you for your free and candid sentiments thereon. The communication I make of this matter to you, sir, is in a private way; but you are at full liberty to communicate the plan of Lady Huntingdon to the members individually, or officially to Congress, as the importance and propriety of the measure may strike you.

My reasons for it are these. First, I do not believe that any of the states to whom she has written (unless it may be New York) are in circumstances, since their cession of territory, to comply with the requisition respecting emigration; for it has been privately hinted to me (and ought not to become a matter of public notoriety) that notwithstanding the indefinite expressions of the address respecting the numbers or occupations of the emigrants (which was purposely omitted, to avoid giving alarms in England), the former will be great and the useful artisans among them many. Second, because such emigration, if it should accomplish the object in view, besides the humane and charitable purposes which would thereby be answered, would be of immense political consequence. And even if this should not succeed to her Ladyship's wishes, it must nevertheless be of considerable importance from the increase of population by orderly and well-disposed characters, who would at once form a barrier and attempt the conversion of the savages without any expense to the Union.

I see but one objection to a compact, unmixed, and powerful settlement of this kind (if it should ever become so)—the weight of which you will judge of. It is (and her Ladyship seems to have been aware of it, and endeavors to guard against it) placing a people, in a body, upon our exterior (contiguous to Canada), who may bring with them strong prejudices against us and our forms of government and equally strong attachments to the country and constitution they leave, without the means, being detached and unmixed with citizens of different sentiments, of having them eradicated.

Her Ladyship has spoken so sensibly and feelingly on the religious and benevolent purposes of the plan that no language of which I am possessed can add aught to enforce her observations. And no place, in my opinion, bids so fair to answer her views as that spot in Hutchins's map marked Miami Village and Fort. From hence there is a communication to all parts by water, and at which, in my judgment, there ought to be a post.

To Patrick Henry, Governor of Virginia, February 27, 1785

Dear Sir,

I have had the honor to receive Your Excellency's letter of the 5th, enclosing the act of the legislature for vesting in me and my heirs fifty shares in the navigation of each of the Rivers Potomac and James. For your trouble and attention in forwarding the act you will please to accept my thanks, whilst to the assembly for passing it, these with all my gratitude are due. I shall ever consider this act as an unequivocal and substantial testimony of the approving voice of my country for the part I have acted on the American theater and shall feast upon the recollection of it as often as it occurs to me; but this is all I can or mean to do. It was my first declaration in Congress after accepting my military appointment that I would not receive anything for such services as I might be able to render the cause in which I had embarked. It was my fixed determination when I surrendered that appointment never to hold any other office under government by which emolument might become a necessary appendage, or, in other words, which should withdraw me from the necessary attention which my own private concerns indispensably required—nor to accept of any pecuniary acknowledgment for what had passed. From this resolution my mind has never yet swerved. The act, therefore, which Your Excellency enclosed is embarrassing to me. On the one hand, I should be unhappy if my non-acceptance of the shares should be considered as a slight of the favors the magnitude of which I think very highly of, or disrespectful to the generous intention of my country. On the other, I should be equally hurt if motives of pride or an ostentatious display of disinterestedness should be ascribed to the action. None of these have existence in my breast, and none of them would I have imputed to me whilst I am indulging the bent of my inclination by acting independent of rewards for occasional and accidental services. Besides, may not the plans be affected, unless some expedient can be hit upon to avoid the shock which may be sustained by withdrawing so many shares from them?

Under these circumstances, and with this knowledge of my wishes and intention, I would thank Your Excellency for your frank and full opinion of this matter, in a friendly way as this letter to you is written and I hope will be considered. I am &c. &c.

G: Washington

To Hugh Williamson, March 15, 1785 (Excerpt)

I thank you, sir, for your account of the last Indian treaty. I had received a similar one before, but do not comprehend by what line it is our northern limits are to be fixed.

Two things seem naturally to result from this treaty. The terms on which the ceded lands are to be disposed of and the mode of settling them. The first, in my opinion, ought not to be delayed. The second ought not to be too diffusive. Compact and progressive seating will give strength to the Union, admit law and good government, and federal aids at an early period. Sparse settlements in *several* new states, or in a large territory for one state, will have the direct contrary effects—and whilst it opens a large field to land jobbers and speculators, who are prowling about like wolves in every shape, will injure the real occupants and useful citizens, and consequently, the public interest. If a tract of country of convenient size for a new state contiguous to the present settlements on the Ohio is laid off, and a certain proportion of the land therein actually seated or at least granted before any other state is marked out and no land suffered to be had beyond the limits of it, we shall, I conceive, derive great political advantages from such a line of conduct, and without it may be involved in much trouble and perplexity before any new state will be well organized or can contribute anything to the support of the Union. I have the honor to be Sir Yr Most Obt Hble Sert

Go: Washington

To James Duane, April 10, 1785 (Excerpt)

It is painful to hear that a state which used to be foremost in acts of liberality, and its exertion to establish our federal system upon a broad bottom and solid ground, is contracting her ideas and pointing them to local and independent measures which, if persevered in, must sap the constitution of these states (already too weak), destroy our national character, and render us as contemptible in the eyes of Europe as we have it in our power to be respectable. It should seem as if the impost of five percent would never take place, for no sooner does an obstinate state begin to relent and adopt the recommendation of Congress, but some other runs restive, as if there was a combination among them to defeat the measure.

From the latest European accounts, it is probable an accommodation will take place between the emperor and the Dutch. But to reverberate news to a man at the source of intelligence would be idle—therefore mum. The Dutch I conceive are too much attached to their possessions and their wealth, if they could yield to the pangs of parting with their country, to adopt the plan you hinted to Mr. Van Berckel. The nations of Europe are ripe for slavery. A thirst after riches, a promptitude to luxury, and a sinking into venality, with their concomitants, untune them for manly exertions and virtuous sacrifices.

To William Carmichael, June 10, 1785 (Excerpt)

Great Britain, viewing with eyes of chagrin and jealousy the situation of this country, will not, for some time yet if ever, pursue a liberal policy towards it. But unfortunately *for her*, the conduct of her ministers defeats[5] their own ends. Their restriction of our trade with them will facilitate the enlargement of congressional powers in commercial matters more than half a century would otherwise have effected. The mercantile interests of this country are uniting as one man to vest the federal government with ample powers to regulate trade and to counteract the selfish views of other nations. This may be considered as another proof that this country will ever unite in opposition to unjust or ungenerous measures, whensoever or from whomsoever they are offered. I have the honor to be &c.

G: Washington

To William Goddard, June 11, 1785

Sir,

On the 8th instant I received the favor of your letter of the 30th of May. In answer to it I can only say that your own good judgment must direct you in the publication of the manuscript papers of General Lee. I can have no request to make concerning the work.

I never had a difference with that gentleman but on public ground, and my conduct towards him upon this occasion was such only as I conceived myself indispensably bound to adopt in discharge of the public trust reposed in me. If this produced in him unfavorable sentiments of me, I yet can never consider the conduct I pursued with respect to him either wrong or improper, however I may regret that it may have been differently viewed by him, and that it excited his censure and animadversions. Should there appear in General Lee's writings anything injurious or unfriendly to me, the impartial and dispassionate world must decide how far I deserved it from the general tenor of my conduct.

I am gliding down the stream of life and wish, as is natural, that my remaining days may be undisturbed and tranquil; and, conscious of my integrity, I would willingly hope that nothing would occur tending to give me anxiety. But should anything present itself in this or in any other publication, I shall never undertake the painful task of recrimination. Nor do I know that I shall even enter upon my justification.

I consider the communication you have made as a mark of great attention and the whole of your letter as a proof of your esteem. I am &c.

G: Washington

To George William Fairfax, June 30, 1785 (Excerpt)

The information which you have given of the disposition of a certain court coincides precisely with the sentiments I had formed of it from my own observations upon many late occurrences, and from a combination of circumstances. With respect to ourselves, I wish I could add that as much wisdom had pervaded our councils as reason and common policy most evidently dictated; but the truth is, the people must feel before they will see, consequently are brought slowly into measures of public utility. Past experience, or the admonitions of a few, have but little weight where ignorance, selfishness, and design possess the major part. But evils of this nature work their own cure, though the remedy comes slower than those who foresee, or think they foresee, the danger attempt to effect. With respect to the commercial system which G.B. is pursuing with this country, the ministers, in this as in other matters, are defeating their own ends by facilitating those powers in Congress which will produce a counter action of their plans, and which half a century without would not have invested that body with. The restriction of our trade, and the additional duties which are imposed upon many of our staple commodities, have put the commercial people of this country in motion. They now see the indispensable necessity of a general controlling power and are addressing their respective assemblies to grant this to Congress. Before this, every state thought itself competent to regulate its own trade and were verifying the observations of Lord Sheffield, who supposed we never could agree upon any general plan. But those who will go a little deeper into matters than His Lordship seems to have done will readily perceive that in any measure where the federal interest is touched, however wide apart the politics of individual states may be, yet as soon as it is discovered they will always unite to effect a common good.

To David Humphreys, July 25, 1785 (Excerpt)

As the complexion of European politics seem now (from the letters I have received from the Marquises de Lafayette and Chastellux, the Chevalier de La Luzerne, etc.) to have a tendency to peace, I will say nothing of war, nor make any animadversions upon the contending powers—otherwise I might possibly have added that the retreat from it seemed impossible, after the explicit declarations of the parties.

My first wish is to see this plague to mankind banished from the earth and the sons and daughters of this world employed in more pleasing and innocent amusements than in preparing implements and exercising them for the destruction of the human race. Rather than quarrel about territory, let the poor, the needy, and oppressed of the earth, and those who want land, resort to the fertile plains of our western country, to the second land of promise, and there dwell in peace, fulfilling the first and great commandment.

In a former letter I informed you, my dear Humphreys, that if I had talents for it, I have not leisure to devote my time and thoughts to commentaries. I am conscious of a defective education and want of capacity to fit me for such an undertaking. What with company, letters, and other matters, many of them extraneous, I have not yet been able to arrange my own private concerns so as to rescue them from that disordered state into which they have been thrown by the war, and to do which is become indispensably necessary for my support, whilst I remain on this stage of human action.

The sentiment of your last letter on this subject gave me great pleasure. I should indeed be pleased to see you undertake this business. Your abilities as a writer; your discernment respecting the principles which led to the decision by arms; your personal knowledge of many facts as they occurred in the progress of the war; your disposition to justice, candor, and impartiality; and your diligence in investigating truth, combining, fits you, in the vigor of life, for this task. And I should with great pleasure not only give you the perusal of all my papers, but any oral information of circumstances which cannot be obtained from the latter, that my memory will furnish. And I can with great truth add that my house would not only be at your service during the period of your preparing this work, but (and without an unmeaning compliment I say it) I should be exceedingly happy if you would make it your home. You might have an apartment to yourself in which you could command your own time. You would be considered and treated as one of the family, and would meet with that cordial reception and entertainment which are characteristic of the sincerest friendship.

To reverberate European news would be idle, and we have little of a domestic kind worthy of attention. We have held treaties, indeed, with the Indians; but they were so unseasonably delayed that these people from our last accounts from the westward are in a discontented mood, supposed by many to be instigated thereto by our late enemy, now, to be sure, good and fast friends, who, from anything I can learn, under the indefinite expression of the treaty, hold and seem resolved to retain possession of our western posts. Congress have also, after long and tedious deliberation, passed an ordinance for laying of the western territory into states and for disposing of the land, but in a manner and on terms which few people (in the southern states) conceive can be accomplished. Both sides are sure, and the event is appealed to. Time must decide. It is to be regretted, however, that local politics and self-interested views obtrude themselves into every measure of public utility. But on such characters be the obloquy. My attention is more immediately engaged in a project which I think is big with great political as well as commercial consequences to these states, especially the middle ones. It is, by removing the obstructions and extending the inland navigations of our rivers, to bring the states on the Atlantic in close connection with those forming to the westward, by a short and easy land transportation. Without this is effected, I can readily conceive that the western settlers will have different views, separate interests, and other connections.

To Marquis de Lafayette, July 25, 1785 (Excerpts)

I now congratulate you—and my heart does it more effectually than my pen—on your safe arrival at Paris from your voyage to this country, and on the happy meeting with Madame Lafayette and your family in good health. May the blessing of this long continue to them, and may every day add increase of happiness to yourself. As the clouds which overspread your hemisphere are dispersing, and peace with all its concomitants is dawning upon your land, I will banish the sound of war from my letter. I wish to see the sons and daughters of the world in peace and busily employed in the more agreeable amusement of fulfilling the first and great commandment, *increase and multiply*, as an encouragement to which we have opened the fertile plains of the Ohio to the poor, the needy, and the oppressed of the earth. Anyone, therefore, who is heavy laden or who wants land to cultivate may repair thither and abound, as in the land of promise, with milk and honey. The ways are preparing, and the roads will be made easy, through the channels of Potomac & James River ....

Great Britain in her commercial policy is acting the same unwise part with respect to herself which seems to have influenced all her councils, and thereby is defeating her own ends. The restriction of our trade, and her heavy imposts on the staple commodities of this country, will, I conceive, immediately produce powers in Congress to regulate the trade of the Union—which, more than probably, would not have been obtained without in half a century. The mercantile interests of the whole Union are endeavoring to effect this and will no doubt succeed. They see the necessity of a controlling power and the futility, indeed the absurdity, of each state's enacting laws for this purpose, independent of one another. This will be the case also, after a while, in all matters of common concern. It is to be regretted, I confess, that democratical states must always *feel* before they can *see*. It is this that makes their governments slow. But the people will be right at last.

Congress, after long deliberation, have at length agreed upon a mode for disposing of the lands of the United States in the western territory. It may be a good one, but it does not comport with my ideas. The ordinance is long, and I have none of them by me, or I would send one for your perusal. They seem in this instance, as in almost every other, to be surrendering the little power they have to the states individually, which gave it to them. Many think the price which they have fixed upon the lands too high, and all to the southward, I believe, that disposing of them in townships and by square miles alternately will be a great let to the sale. But experience, to which there is an appeal, must decide.

To Edmund Randolph, July 30, 1785 (Excerpt)

Dear Sir,

Although it is not my intention to derive any pecuniary advantage from the generous vote of the assembly of this state, consequent of its gratuitous gift of fifty shares in each of the navigations of the Rivers Potomac and James, yet, as I consider these undertakings as of vast political and commercial importance to the states on the Atlantic, especially to those nearest the center of the Union and adjoining the western territory, I can let no act of mine impede the progress of the work. I have therefore come to the determination to hold the shares which the treasurer was directed to subscribe on my account in trust for the use and benefit of the public, unless I shall be able to discover, before the meeting of the assembly, that it would be agreeable to it to have the product of the tolls arising from these shares applied as a fund on which to establish two charity schools, one on each river, for the education and support of the children of the poor and indigent of this country who cannot afford to give it, particularly the children of those men of this description who have fallen in defense of the rights and liberties of it. If the plans succeed, of which I have no doubt, I am sure it will be a very productive and increasing fund and the monies thus applied will be a beneficial institution.

I am aware that my non-acceptance of these shares will have various motives ascribed to it, among which an ostentatious display of disinterestedness, perhaps the charge of disrespect or slight of the favors of my country, may lead the van. But under a consciousness that my conduct herein is not influenced by considerations of this nature, and that I shall act more agreeably to my own feelings and more consistent with my early declarations by declining to accept them, I shall not only hope for indulgence but a favorable interpretation of my conduct. My friends, I persuade myself, will acquit me; the world, I hope, will judge charitably.

To William Grayson, August 22, 1785 (Excerpt)

I thank you for the several articles of intelligence contained in your letter, and for the propositions respecting a coinage of gold, silver, and copper—a measure which, in my judgment, is become indispensably necessary. Mr. Jefferson's ideas upon this subject are plain and simple, well adapted, I think, to the nature of the case, as he has exemplified by the plan. Without a coinage, or some stop can be put to the cutting and clipping of money, our dollars, pistareens, etc. will all be converted (as Teague says) into five quarters; and a man must travel with a pair of money scales in his pocket or run the risk of receiving gold at one fourth more by count than weight.

I have ever been a friend to adequate congressional powers, consequently wish to see the 9th Article of the Confederation amended and extended. Without these powers we cannot support a national character and must appear contemptible in the eyes of Europe. But to you, my dear sir, I will candidly confess that, in my opinion, it is of little avail to give these to Congress. The members seem so much afraid of exerting those which they already have that no opportunity is slipped of *surrendering* or *referring* the exercise of them to the states individually. Witness your late ordinance respecting the dispersal of the western lands, in which no state with the smallest propriety could have obtruded an interference.

To Richard Henry Lee, President of the Confederation Congress, August 22, 1785 (Excerpt)

It is to be hoped that our minister at the Court of London will bring that government to an explanation respecting the western posts, which it still retains on the American side of the line, contrary to the spirit, if not to the letter, of the treaty. My opinion from the first, and so I declared it, was that these posts would be detained from us as long as they could be held under any pretense whatsoever. I have not changed it, though I wish for cause to do so, as it may ultimately become a serious matter. However singular the opinion may be, I cannot divest myself of it, that the navigation of the Mississippi, *at this time*, ought to be no object with us. On the contrary, till we have a little time allowed to open and make easy the ways between the Atlantic states and the western territory, the obstructions had better remain.

There is nothing which binds one country or one state to another but interest. Without this cement, the western inhabitants (which more than probably will be composed in a great degree of foreigners) can have no predilection for us; and a commercial connection is the only tie we can have upon them. It is clear to me that the trade of the lakes, and of the River Ohio as low as the Great Kanawha (if not to the falls), *may* be brought to the ports on the Atlantic easier and cheaper (taking the *whole* voyage together) than it can be carried to New Orleans. But once open the door to the latter before the obstructions are removed from the former, let commercial connections (which lead to others) be formed and the habit of that trade be well established, and it will be found no easy matter to divert it. And vice versa: When the settlements are stronger and more extended to the westward, the navigation of the River Mississippi will be an object of importance; and we shall be able then (reserving our claim) to speak a more efficacious language than policy, I think, should dictate at present.

I never have, and I hope never shall, hear any serious mention of a paper emission in this state. Yet such a thing may be in agitation. Ignorance and design are productive of much mischief. The first is the tool of the latter and are often set to work as suddenly as unexpectedly. Those with whom I have conversed on this subject in this part of the state reprobate the idea exceedingly.

To James McHenry, August 22, 1785 (Excerpt)

As I have ever been a friend to adequate powers in Congress, without which it is evident to me we never shall establish a national character or be considered on a respectable footing by the powers of Europe, I am sorry I cannot agree with you in sentiment not to enlarge them for the regulation of commerce. I have neither time nor abilities to enter upon a full discussion of this subject; but it should seem to me that your arguments against it—principally that some states may be more benefited than others by a commercial regulation—applies to every matter of general utility. For where is the case in which this argument may not be used in a greater or less degree? We are either a United people under one head and for federal purposes, or we are thirteen independent sovereignties, eternally counteracting each other. If the former, whatever such a majority of the states as the constitution requires conceives to be for the benefit of the whole should, in my humble opinion, be submitted to by the minority. Let the southern states always be represented; let them act more in unison; let them declare freely and boldly what is for the interest and what is prejudicial to their constituents; and there will, there must, be an accommodating spirit. In the establishment of an act for navigation, this in a particular manner ought and will doubtless be attended to. And if the assent of nine (or, as some propose, of eleven) states is necessary to give validity to a commercial system, it ensures this measure, or the act cannot be obtained. Wherein, then, lies the danger? But if your fears are in danger of being realized, cannot certain provisos in the law guard against the evil? I see no difficulty in this if the southern delegates would give their attendance in Congress and follow the example, if such a one should beset them, of hanging together to counteract combinations.

I confess to you candidly that I can foresee no evil greater than disunion—than those unreasonable jealousies (I say *unreasonable* because I would have a proper jealousy always awake, and the United States always upon the watch, to prevent individual states from infracting the constitution with impunity) which are continually poisoning our minds and filling them with imaginary evils, to the prevention of real ones. As you have asked the question, I answer I do not know that we can enter a war of imposts with G. Britain or any other foreign power; but we are certain that this war has been waged against us by the former, *professedly* upon a belief that we never could unite in opposition to it. And I believe there is no way of putting an end to—at least of stopping the increase of—it but to convince them of the contrary. Our trade in all points of view is as essential to G.B. as hers is to us. And she will exchange it upon reciprocal and liberal terms if an advantage is not to be obtained. It can hardly be supposed, I think, that the carrying business will devolve wholly on the states you have named or remain long with them if it should—for either G.B. will depart from her present selfish system, or the policy of the southern states in forming a general act of navigation, or by laws individually passed by their respective legislatures, will devise ways and means to encourage seamen for the transportation of their own produce or for the encouragement of manufactures. But admitting the contrary, if the Union is considered as permanent, and on this I presume all superstructures are built, had we not better encourage seamen among ourselves with less imports than divide it with foreigners and, by increasing them, ruin our merchants and greatly injure the mass of our citizens?

To sum up the whole, I foresee, or think I do it, many advantages which will result from giving powers of this kind to Congress (if a sufficient number of states are required to exercise them) without any evil save those which may proceed from inattention or want of wisdom in the formation of the act—whilst without them we stand, I conceive, in a ridiculous point of view in the eyes of the nations of the earth, with whom we are attempting to enter into commercial treaties without means of carrying them into effect, and who must see and feel that the Union or the states individually are sovereigns as it best suits their purposes. In a word, that we are one nation today and thirteen tomorrow. Who will treat with us on such terms?

To François-Jean de Beauvoir Chastellux, September 5, 1785 (Excerpt)

It gives me great pleasure to find by my last letters from France that the dark clouds which hung over your hemisphere are vanishing before the all-cheering sunshine of peace. My first wish is to see the blessings of it diffused through all countries and among *all* ranks in every country, and that we should consider ourselves as the children of a common parent and be disposed to acts of brotherly kindness towards one another. In that case all restrictions of trade would vanish. We should take your wines, your fruits, and surplusage of other articles and give you in return our oils, our fish, tobacco, naval stores, etc. And in like manner we should exchange produce with other countries, to our reciprocal advantage. The globe is large enough; why then need we wrangle for a small spot of it? If one country cannot contain us, another should open its arms to us. But these halcyon days (if they ever did exist) are now no more. A wise Providence, I presume, has ordered it otherwise, and we must go in the old way disputing—and now and then fighting—until the globe itself is dissolved.

To Richard Varick, September 26, 1785 (Excerpt)

Dear Sir,

Mr. Taylor brought me your favor of the 28th ultimo, and I have received your other letter of the 2nd of December. For both I thank you, as also for the proceedings of the Mayor's Court in the case of Rutgers and Waddington, enclosed in the latter. I have read this with attention, and though I pretend not to be a competent judge of the law of nations, or of the act of your assembly, nor of the spirit of the Confederation, in their niceties, yet it should seem to me that the interpretation of them by the court is founded in reason and common sense, which is or ought to be the foundation of all law and government.

To George Mason, October 3, 1785

Dear Sir,

I have this moment received yours of yesterday's date enclosing a memorial and remonstrance against the assessment bill, which I will read with attention. At present I am unable to do it on account of company. The bill itself I do not recollect ever to have read—with attention I am certain I never did—but will compare them together.

Although no man's sentiments are more opposed to *any kind* of restraint upon religious principles than mine are, yet I must confess that I am not amongst the number of those who are so much alarmed at the thoughts of making people pay towards the support of that which they profess if of the denominations of Christians, or declare themselves Jews, Mahometans, or otherwise and thereby obtain proper relief. As the matter now stands, I wish an assessment had never been agitated, and, as it has gone so far, that the bill could die an easy death—because I think it will be productive of more quiet to the state than by enacting it into a law, which, in my opinion, would be impolitic, admitting there is a decided majority for it, to the disgust of a respectable minority. In the first case the matter will soon subside. In the latter it will rankle and perhaps convulse the state. The dinner bell rings, and I must conclude with an expression of my concern for your indisposition. Sincerely and affectionately I am &c. &c.

G: Washington

To James Warren, October 7, 1785 (Excerpt)

Dear Sir,

The assurances of your friendship, after a silence of more than six years, are extremely pleasing to me. Friendships formed under the circumstances that ours commenced are not easily eradicated, and I can assure you that mine has undergone no diminution. Every occasion, therefore, of renewing it will give me pleasure; and I shall be happy at all times to hear of your welfare.

The war, as you have very justly observed, has terminated most advantageously for America; and a large and glorious field is presented to our view. But I confess to you, my dear sir, that I do not think we possess wisdom or justice enough to cultivate it properly. Illiberality, jealousy, and local policy mix too much in all our public councils for the good government of the Union. In a word, the Confederation appears to me to be little more than an empty sound and Congress a nugatory body, the ordinances of it being very little attended to.

To me it is a solecism in politics, indeed it is one of the most extraordinary things in nature, that we should confederate for national purposes and yet be afraid to give the rulers thereof—who are the creatures of our own making, appointed for a limited and short duration, who are amenable for every action, recallable at any moment, and subject to all the evils they may be instrumental in producing—sufficient powers to order and direct the affairs of that nation.

By such policy as this the wheels of government are clogged and our brightest prospects, and that high expectation which was entertained of us by the wondering world, are turned into astonishment. And from the high ground on which we stood we are descending into the valleys of confusion and darkness. That we have it in our power to be one of the most respectable nations upon earth admits not, in my humble opinion, of a doubt, if we would pursue a wise, just, and liberal policy towards one another, and would keep good faith with the rest of the world. That our resources are ample and increasing none can deny. But whilst they are grudgingly applied, or not applied at all, we give the vital stab to public credit and must sink into contempt in the eyes of Europe.

It has long been a speculative question amongst philosophers and wise men whether foreign commerce is of advantage to any country—that is, whether the luxury, effeminacy, and corruption which are introduced by it are counter-balanced by the conveniencies and wealth of which it is productive. But the right decision of this question is of very little importance to us. We have abundant reason to be convinced that the spirit of trade which pervades these states is not to be restrained. It behooves us, therefore, to establish it upon just principles; and this, any more than other matters of national concern, cannot be done by thirteen heads, differently constructed. The necessity, therefore, of a controlling power is obvious, and why it should be withheld is beyond comprehension.

The agricultural society lately established in Philadelphia promises extensive usefulness, if it is prosecuted with spirit. I wish most sincerely that every state in the Union would institute similar ones, and that these societies would correspond fully and freely with each other and communicate all useful discoveries founded on practice, with a due attention to climate, soil, and seasons, to the public.

To Patrick Henry, Governor of Virginia, October 29, 1785

Sir,

Your Excellency having been pleased to transmit me a copy of the act appropriating to my benefit certain shares in the companies for opening the navigation of James and Potomac Rivers, I take the liberty of returning to the General Assembly through your hands the profound and grateful acknowledgments inspired by so signal a mark of their beneficent intentions towards me. I beg you, sir, to assure them that I am filled on this occasion with every sentiment which can flow from a heart warm with love for my country, sensible to every token of its approbation and affection, and solicitous to testify in every instance a respectful submission to its wishes.

With these sentiments in my bosom, I need not dwell on the anxiety I feel in being obliged, in this instance, to decline a favor which is rendered no less flattering by the manner in which it is conveyed than it is affectionate in itself.

In explaining this obligation, I pass over a comparison of my endeavors in the public service with the many honorable testimonies of approbation which have already so far overrated and overpaid them, reciting one consideration only which supersedes the necessity of recurring to every other.

When I was first called to the station with which I was honored during the late conflict for our liberties, to the diffidence which I had so many reasons to feel in accepting it, I thought it my duty to join a firm resolution to shut my hand against every pecuniary recompence. To this resolution I have invariably adhered. From this resolution (if I had the inclination) I do not consider myself at liberty to depart.

Whilst I repeat, therefore, my fervent acknowledgments to the legislature for their very kind sentiments and intentions in my favor, and at the same time beg them to be persuaded that a remembrance of this singular proof of their goodness towards me will never cease to cherish returns of the warmest affection and gratitude, I must pray that their act, so far as it has for its object my personal emolument, may not have its effect. But if it should please the General Assembly to permit me to turn the destination of the fund vested in me from my private emoluments to objects of a public nature, it will be my study in selecting these to prove the sincerity of my gratitude for the honor conferred on me by preferring such as may appear most subservient to the enlightened and patriotic views of the legislature. With great respect and considn I have the honor to be Yr Excellency's Most Obedt Hble Servt

Go: Washington

To David Humphreys, October 30, 1785 (Excerpt)

Nothing new has happened since my last; nor is it probable anything interesting will happen until the different assemblies convene. Congress, as usual, are proceeding very slowly in their business—and, shameful as it is, are often at a stand for want of a sufficient representation. The states have been addressed by them on the subject, but what will be the effect I know not. To me there appears such lassitude in our public councils as is truly shocking and must clog the wheels of government, which, under such circumstances, will either stop altogether or will be moved by ignorance or a few designing men.

To Edward Newenham, November 25, 1785 (Excerpt)

The opposition which the virtuous characters of Ireland have given to the attempts of a British administration's interfering with its manufactures, fettering its commerce, restraining the liberties of its subjects by their plan of reform, etc., etc., will hand their names to posterity with that veneration and respect to which their amor patriae entitles them.

Precedents, as you justly observe, are dangerous things. They form the arm which first arrests the liberties and happiness of a country. In the first approaches they may indeed assume the garb of plausibility and moderation, and are generally spoken of by the movers as a *chip in porridge* (to avoid giving alarm), but soon are made to speak a language equally decisive and irresistible, which shows the necessity of opposition in the first attempts to establish them, let them appear under what guise or courtly form they may, and proves too that vigilance and watchfulness can scarcely be carried to an excess in guarding against the insidious arts of a government founded in corruption.

I do not think there is as much wisdom and sound policy displayed in the different legislatures of these states as might be, yet I hope everything will come right at last. In republican governments, it too often happens that the people (not always seeing) must *feel* before they act. This is productive of errors and temporary evils, but generally these evils are of a nature to work their own cure.

To James Madison, November 30, 1785 (Excerpt)

My Dear Sir,

Receive my thanks for your obliging communications of the 11th. I hear with much pleasure that the assembly are engaged seriously in the consideration of the revised laws. A short and simple code, in my opinion, though I have the sentiments of some of the gentlemen of the long robe against me, would be productive of happy consequences and redound to the honor of this or any country which shall adopt such.

I hope the resolutions which were published for the consideration of the house, respecting the reference to Congress for the regulation of a commercial system, will have passed. The proposition in my opinion is so self-evident that I confess I am at a loss to discover wherein lies the weight of the objection to the measure. We are either a united people, or we are not. If the former, let us, in all matters of general concern, act as a nation, which have national objects to promote and a national character to support. If we are not, let us no longer act a farce by pretending to it. For whilst we are playing a double game, or playing a game between the two, we never shall be consistent or respectable but may be the dupes of some powers and, most assuredly, the contempt of all. In any case it behooves us to provide good militia laws and look well to the execution of them. But if we mean by our conduct that the states shall act independently of each other, it becomes indispensably necessary, for therein will consist our strength and respectability in the Union.

It is much to be wished that public faith may be held inviolate. Painful is it even in thought that attempts should be made to weaken the bands of it. It is a dangerous experiment. Once slacken the reins and the power is lost. And it is questionable with me whether the advocates of the measure foresee all the consequences of it. It is an old adage that honesty is the best policy. This applies to public as well as private life, to states as well as individuals. I hope the port and assize bills no longer sleep but are awakened to a happy establishment. The first, with some alterations, would in my judgment be productive of great good to this country. Without it, the trade thereof I conceive will ever labor and languish. With respect to the second, if it institutes a speedier administration of justice, it is equally desirable.

To David Stuart, November 30, 1785 (Excerpt)

Dear Sir,

Your favor of the 16th came duly to hand, and I thank you for its several communications. The resolutions which were published for consideration, vesting Congress with powers to regulate the commerce of the Union, have I hope been acceded to. If the states individually were to attempt this, an abortion or a many headed monster would be the issue. If we consider ourselves, or wish to be considered by others, as a united people, why not adopt the measures which are characteristic of it and support the honor and dignity of one? If we are afraid to trust one another under qualified powers, there is an end of the Union. Why then need we be solicitous to keep up the farce of it?

To Henry Lee, Jr., April 5, 1786 (Excerpt)

My sentiments with respect to the federal government are very well known—publicly and privately have they been communicated without reserve. But my *opinion* is that there is more wickedness than ignorance in the conduct of the states, or, in other words, in the conduct of those who have too much influence in the fabrication of our laws, and that till the curtain is withdrawn, and the private views and selfish principles upon which these men act are exposed to public notice and resentment, I have little hopes of amendment without another convulsion. The picture of our affairs as drawn by the committee, approved by Congress, and handed to the public, did not at all surprise me. Before that report appeared, though I could not go into the minutiae of matters, I was more certain of the aggregate of our distresses than I am now of the remedy which will be applied. And without the latter, I do not see upon what ground your agent at the Court of Morocco and the other at Algiers are to treat, unless, having to do with new hands, they mean to touch the old string again and make them dance a while to the tune of promises.

To Robert Morris, April 12, 1786

Dear Sir,

I give you the trouble of this letter at the instance of Mr. Dalby of Alexandria, who is called to Philadelphia to attend what he conceives to be a vexatious lawsuit respecting a slave of his, which a society of Quakers in the city (formed for such purposes) have attempted to liberate. The merits of this case will no doubt appear upon trial. But from Mr. Dalby's statement[6] of the matter, it should seem that this society is not only acting repugnant to justice so far as its conduct concerns strangers, but, in my opinion, extremely impoliticly with respect to the state—the city in particular—without being able (but by acts of tyranny and oppression) to accomplish their own ends. He says the conduct of this society is not sanctioned by law. Had the case been otherwise, whatever my opinion of the law might have been, my respect for the policy of the state would on this occasion have appeared in my silence, because against the penalties of promulgated laws one may guard. But there is no avoiding the snares of individuals or of private societies. And if the practice of this society of which Mr. Dalby speaks is not discountenanced, none of those whose *misfortune* it is to have slaves as attendants will visit the city if they can possibly avoid it, because by so doing they hazard their property, or they must be at the expense (and this will not always succeed) of providing servants of another description for the trip.

I hope it will not be conceived from these observations that it is my wish to hold the unhappy people who are the subject of this letter in slavery. I can only say that there is not a man living who wishes more sincerely than I do to see a plan adopted for the abolition of it. But there is only one proper and effectual mode by which it can be accomplished, and that is by legislative authority—and this, as far as my suffrage will go, shall never be wanting.

But when slaves who are happy and content to remain with their present masters are tampered with and seduced to leave them; when masters are taken at unawares by these practices; when a conduct of this sort begets discontent on one side and resentment on the other; and when it happens to fall on a man whose purse will not measure with that of the society, and he loses his property for want of means to defend it; it is oppression in the latter case and not humanity in any, because it introduces more evils than it can cure.

I will make no apology for writing to you on this subject; for if Mr. Dalby has not misconceived the matter, an evil exists which requires a remedy. If he has, my intentions have been good, though I may have been too precipitate in this address. Mrs. Washington joins me in every good and kind wish for Mrs. Morris and your family, and I am &c.

G: Washington

To Marquis de Lafayette, May 10, 1786 (Excerpt)

The account given of your tour through Prussia and other states of Germany to Vienna and back—and of the troops which you saw reviewed, in the pay of those monarchs, at different places—is not less pleasing than it is interesting, and must have been as instructive as entertaining to yourself. Your reception at the Courts of Berlin, Vienna, and elsewhere must have been pleasing to you. To have been received by the king of Prussia and Prince Henry, his brother (who as soldiers and politicians can yield the palm to none), with such marks of attention and distinction was as indicative of their discernment as it is of your merit, and will increase my opinion of them. It is to be lamented, however, that great characters are seldom without a blot. That one man should tyrannize over millions will always be a shade in that of the former, whilst it is pleasing to hear that a due regard to the rights of mankind is characteristic of the latter. I shall revere and love him for this trait of his character. To have viewed the several fields of battle over which you passed could not, among other sensations, have failed to excite this thought: here have fallen thousands of gallant spirits to satisfy the ambition of or to support their sovereigns perhaps in acts of oppression or injustice!—melancholy reflection! For what wise purposes does Providence permit this? Is it as a scourge for mankind, or is it to prevent them from becoming too populous? If the latter, would not the fertile plains of the western world receive the redundancy of the old?

For the several articles of intelligence with which you have been so good as to furnish me, and for your sentiments on European politics, I feel myself very much obliged. On these I can depend. Newspaper accounts are too sterile, vague, and contradictory on which to form any opinion or to claim even the smallest attention. The account of and observations which you have made on the policy and practice of Great Britain at the other Courts of Europe respecting those states I was but too well informed and convinced of before. Unhappily for us, though their accounts are greatly exaggerated, yet our conduct has laid the foundation for them. It is one of the evils of democratical governments that the people, not always seeing and frequently misled, must often feel before they can act right. But then evils of this nature seldom fail to work their own cure. It is to be lamented, nevertheless, that the remedies are so slow and that those who may wish to apply them seasonably are not attended to before they suffer in person, in interest, and in reputation. I am not without hopes that matters will soon take a favorable turn in the Federal Constitution. The discerning part of the community have long since seen the necessity of giving adequate powers to Congress for national purposes, and the ignorant and designing must yield to it 'ere long. Several late acts of the different legislatures have a tendency thereto. Among these, the impost, which is now acceded to by every state in the Union (though clogged a little by that of New York), will enable Congress to support the national credit in pecuniary matters better than it has been, whilst a measure in which this state has taken the lead at its last session will, it is to be hoped, give efficient powers to that body for all commercial purposes. This is a nomination of some of its first characters to meet other commissioners from the several states in order to consider of and decide upon such powers as shall be necessary for the sovereign power of them to act under, which are to be reported to the respective legislatures at their autumnal sessions for, it is to be hoped, final adoption, thereby avoiding those tedious and futile deliberations which result from recommendations and partial concurrences, at the same time that it places it at once in the power of Congress to meet European nations upon decisive and equal ground. All the legislatures which I have heard from have come into the proposition and have made very judicious appointments. Much good is expected from this measure, and it is regretted by many that more objects were not embraced by the meeting. A general convention is talked of by many for the purpose of revising and correcting the defects of the federal government; but whilst this is the wish of some, it is the dread of others from an opinion that matters are not yet sufficiently ripe for such an event.

The British still occupy our posts to the westward and will, I am persuaded, continue to do so under one pretense or another, no matter how shallow, as long as they can. Of this, from some circumstances which had occurred, I have been convinced since August 1783, and gave it as my opinion at that time, if not officially to Congress as the sovereign, at least to a number of its members that they might act accordingly. It is indeed evident to me that they had it in contemplation to do this at the time of the treaty. The expression of the article which respects the evacuation of them, as well as the tenor of their conduct since relative to this business, is strongly masked with deception. I have not the smallest doubt but that every secret engine in their power is continually at work to inflame the Indian mind, with a view to keep it at variance with these states for the purpose of retarding our settlements to the westward and depriving us of the fur and peltry trade of that country.

To John Jay, Secretary of Foreign Affairs, May 18, 1786 (Excerpt)

I coincide perfectly in sentiment with you, my dear sir, that there are errors in our national government which call for correction—loudly I will add. But I shall find myself happily mistaken if the remedies are at hand. We are certainly in a delicate situation, but my fear is that the people are not yet sufficiently misled to retract from error! To be plainer, I think there is more wickedness than ignorance mixed with our councils. Under this impression, I scarcely know what opinion to entertain of a general convention. That it is necessary to revise and amend the Articles of Confederation, I entertain *no* doubt; but what may be the consequences of such an attempt is doubtful. Yet something must be done, or the fabric must fall. It certainly is tottering! Ignorance and design are difficult to combat. Out of these proceed illiberality, *improper* jealousies, and a train of evils which oftentimes, in republican governments, must be sorely felt before they can be removed. The former, that is, ignorance, being a fit soil for the latter to work in, tools are employed which a generous mind would disdain to use, and which nothing but time, and their own puerile or wicked productions, can show the inefficacy and dangerous tendency of. I think often of our situation and view it with concern. From the high ground on which we stood, from the plain path which invited our footsteps, to be so fallen!—so lost!—is really mortifying. But virtue, I fear, has, in a great degree, taken its departure from our land, and the want of disposition to do justice is the source of the national embarrassments. For under whatever guise or colorings are given to them, this, I apprehend, is the origin of the evils we now feel and probably shall labor for some time yet. With respectful complimts to Mrs. Jay, and sentiments of sincere friendship, I am Dear Sir Yr most Obedt Hble Servt

Go: Washington

To William Grayson, July 26, 1786 (Excerpts)

Is it not among the most unaccountable things in nature that the representation of a great country should generally be so thin as not to be able to execute the functions of government? To what is this to be ascribed? Is it the result of political maneuver in some states, or is it owing to supineness or want of means?

Be the causes what they may, it is shameful and disgusting. In a word, it hurts us. Our character as a nation is dwindling; and what it must come to if a change should not soon take place, our enemies have foretold. For in truth we seem either not capable, or not willing to take care of ourselves ....

It is good policy at all times to place one's adversary in the wrong. Had we observed good faith and the western posts had then been withheld from us by G. Britain, we might have appealed to God and man for justice; and if there are any guarantees to the treaty, we might have called upon them to see it fulfilled. But now we cannot do this—though clear I am that the reasons assigned by the British ministry are only ostensible, and that the posts, under one pretense or another, were intended to have been detained, though no such acts had ever passed. But how different would our situation have been under such circumstances? With very sincere regard and Affection, I am Dr Sir, &ca

G: Washington

To Comte de Rochambeau, July 31, 1786 (Excerpt)

It must give pleasure to the friends of humanity, even in this distant section of the globe, to find that the clouds which threatened to burst in a storm of war in Europe have dissipated and left a still brighter political horizon. It is also to be hoped that something will turn up to prevent, even at the death of the elector of Bavaria or the king of Prussia, the effusion of human blood for the acquisition of a little territory.

As the rage of conquest, which in the times of barbarity stimulated nations to blood, has in a great degree ceased; as the objects which formerly gave birth to wars are daily diminishing; and as mankind are becoming more enlightened and humanized; I cannot but flatter myself with the pleasing prospect that more liberal policies and more pacific systems will take place amongst them. To indulge this idea affords a soothing consolation to a philanthropic mind, insomuch that, although it should be founded in illusion, one would hardly wish to be divested of an error so grateful in itself and so innocent in its consequences.

The treaty of amity which has lately taken place between the king of Prussia and the United States marks a new era in negotiation. It is perfectly original in many of its articles. It is the most liberal treaty which has ever been entered into between independent powers; and should its principles be considered hereafter as the basis of connection between nations, it will operate more fully to produce a general pacification than any measure hitherto attempted amongst mankind. Superadded to this, we may safely assert that there is at present less war in the world than ever has been at any former period.

The British continue to hold the posts ceded by the late treaty of peace to the United States. Each of these powers does not hesitate to criminate the other by alleging some infractions of that treaty. How the matter will terminate, time must disclose. Everything remains tranquil on this side of the Atlantic, except that the savages sometimes commit a few trifling ravages on the frontiers.

To Thomas Jefferson, August 1, 1786 (Excerpt)

We have no news of importance; and if we had I should hardly be in the way of learning it, as I divide my time between the superintendence of opening the navigations of our rivers and attention to my private concerns. Indeed, I am too much secluded from the world to know with certainty what sensation the refusal of the British to deliver up the western posts has made on the public mind. I fear the edge of its sensibility is somewhat blunted. Federal measures are not yet universally adopted. New York, which was as well disposed a state as any in the Union, is said to have become in a degree Anti-Federal. Some other states are, in my opinion, falling into very foolish and wicked plans of emitting paper money. I cannot, however, give up my hopes and expectations that we shall ere long adopt a more liberal system of policy. What circumstances will lead, or what misfortunes will compel us, to it is more than can be told without the spirit of prophecy.

In the meantime, the people are industrious, economy begins to prevail, and our internal governments are, in general, tolerably well administered.

You will probably have heard of the death of General Greene before this reaches you, in which case you will, in common with your countrymen, have regretted the loss of so great and so honest a man. General McDougall, who was a brave soldier and a disinterested patriot, is also dead. He belonged to the legislature of his state, the last act of his life was (after being carried on purpose to the senate) to give his voice against the emission of a paper currency. Colonel Tilghman, who was formerly of my family, died lately and left as fair a reputation as ever belonged to a human character. Thus some of the pillars of the Revolution fall. Others are moldering by insensible degrees. May our country never want props to support the glorious fabric! With sentiments of the highest esteem and regard, I have the honor to be Dear Sir Yr Most Obedt & very Hble Servt

Go: Washington

To Anne-César, Chevalier de La Luzerne, August 1, 1786 (Excerpt)

I wish I had it in my power to inform you that the several states had fully complied with all the wise requisitions which Congress has made to them on national subjects. But, unfortunately for us, this is not yet the case—although for my own part I do not cease to expect that this just policy will ultimately take effect. It is not the part of a good citizen to despair of the republic; nor ought we to have calculated that our young governments would have acquired, in so short a period, all the consistency and solidity which it has been the work of ages to give to other nations. All the states, however, have at length granted the impost, though unhappily some of them have granted it under such qualifications as have hitherto prevented its operation. The greater part of the Union seems to be convinced of the necessity of federal measures and of investing Congress with the power of regulating the commerce of the whole. The reasons you offer on this subject are certainly forcible, and I cannot but hope will 'ere long have their due efficacy.

In other respects our internal governments are daily acquiring strength. The laws have their fullest energy. Justice is well administered. Robbery, violence, or murder are not heard of from New Hampshire to Georgia. The people at large (as far as I can learn) are more industrious than they were before the war. Economy begins, partly from necessity and partly from choice and habit, to prevail. The seeds of population are scattered over an immense tract of western country. In the old states, which were the theaters of hostility, it is wonderful to see how soon the ravages of war are repaired. Houses are rebuilt, fields enclosed, stocks of cattle which were destroyed are replaced, and many a desolated territory assumes again the cheerful appearance of cultivation. In many places the vestiges of conflagration and ruin are hardly to be traced. The arts of peace, such as clearing of rivers, building of bridges, establishing conveniences for traveling, etc., are assiduously promoted. In short, the foundation of a great empire is laid, and I please myself with a persuasion that Providence will not leave its work imperfect.

I am sensible that the picture of our situation which has been exhibited in Europe since the peace has been of a very different complexion, but it must be remembered that all the unfavorable features have been much heightened by the medium of the English newspapers through which they have been represented.

The British still continue to hold the posts on our frontiers and affect to charge us with some infractions of the treaty. On the other hand, we retort the accusation. What will be the consequences is more than I can pretend to predict. To me, however, it appears that they are playing the same foolish game in commerce that they have lately done in war, that their ill-judged impositions will eventually drive our ships from their ports, wean our attachments to their manufactures, and give to France decided advantages for a commercial connection with us. To strengthen the alliance and promote the interests of France and America will ever be the favorite object of him who has the honor to subscribe himself, with every sentiment of attachment, &c. &c.

G: Washington

To John Jay, Secretary of Foreign Affairs, August 15, 1786

Dear Sir,

I have to thank you very sincerely for your interesting letter of the 27th of June, as well as for the other communications you had the goodness to make at the same time.

I am sorry to be assured, of what indeed I had little doubt before, that we have been guilty of violating the treaty in some instances. What a misfortune it is the British should have so well grounded a pretext for their palpable infractions! And what a disgraceful part, out of the choice of difficulties before us, are we to act!

Your sentiments that our affairs are drawing rapidly to a crisis accord with my own. What the event will be is also beyond the reach of my foresight. We have errors to correct. We have probably had too good an opinion of human nature in forming our confederation. Experience has taught us that men will not adopt and carry into execution measures the best calculated for their own good without the intervention of a coercive power. I do not conceive we can exist long as a nation without having lodged somewhere a power which will pervade the whole Union in as energetic a manner as the authority of the different state governments extends over the several states. To be fearful of vesting Congress, constituted as that body is, with ample authorities for national purposes appears to me the very climax of popular absurdity and madness. Could Congress exert them for the detriment of the public without injuring themselves in an equal or greater proportion? Are not their interests inseparably connected with those of their constituents? By the rotation of appointment must they not mingle frequently with the mass of citizens? Is it not rather to be apprehended, if they were possessed of the powers before described, that the individual members would be induced to use them on many occasions very timidly and inefficaciously for fear of losing their popularity and future election? We must take human nature as we find it. Perfection falls not to the share of mortals. Many are of opinion that Congress have too frequently made use of the suppliant humble tone of requisition in applications to the states when they had a right to assume their imperial dignity and command obedience. Be that as it may, requisitions are a perfect nihility where thirteen sovereign, independent, disunited states are in the habit of discussing and refusing compliance with them at their option.

Requisitions are actually little better than a jest and a byword throughout the land. If you tell the legislatures they have violated the treaty of peace and invaded the prerogatives of the confederacy they will laugh in your face. What, then, is to be done? Things cannot go on in the same train forever. It is much to be feared, as you observe, that the better kind of people, being disgusted with the circumstances, will have their minds prepared for any revolution whatever. We are apt to run from one extreme into another. To anticipate and prevent disastrous contingencies would be the part of wisdom and patriotism.

What astonishing changes a few years are capable of producing! I am told that even respectable characters speak of a monarchical form of government without horror. From thinking proceeds speaking; thence to acting is often but a single step. But how irrevocable and tremendous! What a triumph for the advocates of despotism to find that we are incapable of governing ourselves and that systems founded on the basis of equal liberty are merely ideal and fallacious! Would to God that wise measures may be taken in time to avert the consequences we have but too much reason to apprehend.

Retired as I am from the world, I frankly acknowledge I cannot feel myself an unconcerned spectator. Yet having happily assisted in bringing the ship into port and having been fairly discharged, it is not my business to embark again on a sea of troubles. Nor could it be expected that my sentiments and opinions would have much weight on the minds of my countrymen. They have been neglected, though given as a last legacy in the most solemn manner. I had then perhaps some claims to public attention. I consider myself as having none at present. With sentiments of sincere esteem and friendship I am, my dear Sir, Yr most Obedt & Affecte Hble Servant

Go: Washington

To Marquis de Lafayette, August 15, 1786 (Excerpt)

My Dear Marquis,

I will not conceal that my numerous correspondences are daily becoming irksome to me; yet I always receive your letters with augmenting satisfaction, and therefore rejoice with you in the measures which are likely to be productive of a more frequent intercourse between our two nations. Thus, motives of a private as well as of a public nature conspire to give me pleasure in finding that the active policy of France is preparing to take advantage of the supine stupidity of England with respect to our commerce.

While the latter by its impolitic duties and restrictions is driving our ships incessantly from its harbors, the former seems by the invitations it is giving to stretch forth the friendly hand to invite them into its ports. I am happy in a conviction that there may be established between France and the U.S. such a mature intercourse of good offices and reciprocal interests as cannot fail to be attended with the happiest consequences. Nations are not influenced as individuals may be by disinterested friendships, but when it is their interest to live in amity, we have little reason to apprehend any rupture. This principle of union can hardly exist in a more distinguished manner between two nations than it does between France and the United States. There are many articles of manufacture which we stand absolutely in need of and shall continue to have occasion for so long as we remain an agricultural people, which will be while lands are so cheap and plenty, that is to say, for ages to come. In the meantime, we shall have large quantities of timber, fish, oil, wheat, tobacco, rice, indigo, etc. to dispose of. Money we have not. Now it is obvious that we must have recourse for the goods and manufactures we may want to the nation which will enable us to pay for them by receiving our produce in return. Our commerce with any of the great manufacturing kingdoms of Europe will therefore be in proportion to the facility of making remittance which such manufacturing nations may think proper to afford us. On the other hand, France has occasion for many of our productions and raw materials. Let her judge whether it is most expedient to receive them by direct importation and to pay for them in goods, or to obtain them through the circuitous channel of Britain and to pay for them in money as she formerly did. I know that Britain arrogantly expects we will sell our produce wherever we can find a market and bring the money to purchase goods from her. I know that she vainly hopes to retain what share she pleases in our trade, in consequence of our prejudices in favor of her fashions and manufactures. But these are illusions which will vanish and disappoint her, as the dreams of conquest have already done. Experience is constantly teaching us that these predilections were founded in error. We find the quality and price of the French goods we receive in many instances to be better than the quality and price of the English. Time and a more thorough acquaintance with the business may be necessary to instruct your merchants in the choice and assortment of goods necessary for such a country. As to an ability for giving credit, in which the English merchants boast a superiority, I am confident it would be happy for America if the practice could be entirely abolished.

However unimportant America may be considered at present, and however Britain may affect to despise her trade, there will assuredly come a day when this country will have some weight in the scale of empires. While connected with us as colonies only, was not Britain the first power in the world? Since the dissolution of that connection, does not France occupy the same illustrious place? Your successful endeavors, my dear Marquis, to promote the interests of your two countries (as you justly call them) must give you the most unadulterated satisfaction. Be assured the measures which have been lately taken with regard to the two articles of *oil and tobacco* have tended very much to endear you to your fellow citizens on this side of the Atlantic.

Although I pretend to no peculiar information respecting commercial affairs, nor any foresight into the scenes of futurity, yet, as the member of an infant empire, as a philanthropist by character, and (if I may be allowed the expression) as a citizen of the great republic of humanity at large, I cannot help turning my attention sometimes to this subject. I would be understood to mean, I cannot avoid reflecting with pleasure on the probable influence that commerce may hereafter have on human manners and society in general. On these occasions I consider how mankind may be connected like one great family in fraternal ties. I indulge a fond, perhaps an enthusiastic, idea that as the world is evidently much less barbarous than it has been, its melioration must still be progressive—that nations are becoming more humanized in their policy—that the subjects of ambition and causes for hostility are daily diminishing—and, in fine, that the period is not very remote when the benefits of a liberal and free commerce will pretty generally succeed to the devastations and horrors of war. Some of the late treaties which have been entered into, and particularly that between the king of Prussia and the United States, seem to constitute a new era in negotiation and to promise the happy consequences I have just now been mentioning.

But let me ask you, my dear Marquis, in such an enlightened, in such a liberal age, how is it possible the great maritime powers of Europe should submit to pay an annual tribute to the little piratical states of Barbary? Would to Heaven we had a navy able to reform those enemies to mankind or crush them into non-existence.

I forbear to enter into a discussion of our domestic politics, because there is little interesting to be said upon them; and perhaps it is best to be silent, since I could not disguise or palliate where I might think them erroneous. The British still hold the frontier posts and are determined to do so. The Indians commit some trifling ravages, but there is nothing like a general or even open war. You will have heard what a loss we have met with by the death of poor General Greene. General McDougall and Colonel Tilghman are also dead.

To John Francis Mercer, September 9, 1786 (Excerpt)

Dear Sir,

Your favor of the 20th ultimo did not reach me till about the first instant. It found me in a fever, from which I am now but sufficiently recovered to attend to business. I mention this to show that I had it not in my power to give an answer to your propositions sooner.

With respect to the first, I never mean (unless some particular circumstances should compel me to it) to possess another slave by purchase, it being among my first wishes to see some plan adopted by the legislature by which slavery in this country may be abolished by slow, sure, and imperceptible degrees.

To Bushrod Washington, September 30, 1786 (Excerpt)

Generally speaking, I have seen as much evil as good result from such societies as you describe the constitution of yours to be. They are a kind of imperium imperio, and as often clog as facilitate public measures. I am no friend to instructions, except in local matters which are wholly or in a great measure confined to the county of the delegate. To me, it appears a much wiser and more politic conduct to choose able and honest representatives and leave them in all national questions to determine from the evidence of reason and the facts which shall be adduced, when internal and external information is given to them in a collective state. What certainty is there that societies in a corner or remote part of a state can possess all that knowledge which is necessary for them to decide on many important questions which may come before an assembly? What reason is there to expect that the society itself may be accordant in opinion on such subjects? May not a few members of this society (more sagacious and designing than the rest) direct the measures of it to private views of their own? May not this embarrass an honest, able delegate who hears the voice of his country from all quarters, and thwart public measures?

These are first thoughts, but I give no decided opinion. Societies nearly similar to such as you speak of have lately been formed in Massachusetts Bay. What has been the consequence? Why they have declared the Senate useless, many other parts of the constitution unnecessary, salaries of public officers burdensome, etc. To point out the defects of the constitution in a decent way (if any existed) was proper enough, but they have done more. They first vote the courts of justice in the present circumstances of the state oppressive, and next, by violence, stop them, which has occasioned a very solemn proclamation and appeal from the governor to the people. You may say that no such matters are in contemplation by your society. Granted. A snowball gathers by rolling. Possibly a line may be drawn between occasional meetings for special purposes, and a standing society to direct with local views and partial information the affairs of the nation, which cannot be well understood but by a large and comparative view of circumstances. Where is this so likely to enter as in the general assembly of the people? What figure then must a delegate make who comes there with his hands tied and his judgment forestalled? His very instructors, perhaps (if they had nothing sinister in view), were they present at all the information and arguments which would come forward, might be the first to change sentiments.

To Henry Lee, Jr., October 31, 1786 (Excerpt)

The picture which you have drawn, and the accounts which are published, of the commotions and temper of numerous bodies in the eastern states, are equally to be lamented and deprecated. They exhibit a melancholy proof of what our transatlantic foes have predicted, and of another thing, perhaps, which is still more to be regretted and is yet more unaccountable: that mankind left to themselves are unfit for their own government. I am mortified beyond expression whenever I view the clouds which have spread over the brightest morn that ever dawned upon any country. In a word, I am lost in amazement when I behold what intriguing the interested views of desperate characters, jealousy, and ignorance of the minor part are capable of effecting as a scourge on the major part of our fellow citizens of the Union. For it is hardly to be imagined that the great body of the people, though they will not act, can be so enveloped in darkness or shortsighted as not to see the rays of a distant sun through all this mist of intoxication and folly.

You talk, my good sir, of employing influence to appease the tumults in Massachusetts. I know not where that influence is to be found, and, if attainable, that it would be a proper remedy for the disorders. Influence is no government. Let us have one by which our lives, liberties, and properties will be secured; or let us know the worst at once. Under these impressions, my humble opinion is that there is a call for decision. Know precisely what the insurgents aim at. If they have real grievances, redress them *if possible*, or acknowledge the justice of their complaints and your inability of doing it in the present moment. If they have not, employ the force of government against them at once. If this is inadequate, *all* will be convinced that the superstructure is bad or wants support. To be more exposed in the eyes of the world, and more contemptible than we already are, is hardly possible. To delay one or the other of these is to exasperate in one case and to give confidence in the other and will add to their numbers. For like snowballs, such bodies increase by every movement unless there is something in the way to obstruct and crumble them before the weight is too great and irresistible.

These are my sentiments. Precedents are dangerous things. Let the reins of government then be braced in time and held with a steady hand, and every violation of the constitution be reprehended. If defective, let it be amended, but not suffered to be trampled on whilst it has an existence.

To James Madison, November 5, 1786

My Dear Sir,

I thank you for the communications in your letter of the first instant. The decision of the house on the question respecting a paper emission is portentous, I hope, of an auspicious session. It may certainly be classed among the important questions of the present day and merited the serious consideration of the assembly. Fain would I hope that the great and most important of all objects—the federal government—may be considered with that calm and deliberate attention which the magnitude of it so loudly calls for at this critical moment.

Let prejudices, unreasonable jealousies, and local interest yield to reason and liberality. Let us look to our national character and to things beyond the present period. No morn ever dawned more favorable than ours did—and no day was ever more clouded than the present! Wisdom and good examples are necessary at this time to rescue the political machine from the impending storm. Virginia has now an opportunity to set the latter, and has enough of the former, I hope, to take the lead in promoting this great and arduous work. Without some alteration in our political creed, the superstructure we have been seven years raising at the expense of much blood and treasure must fall. We are fast verging to anarchy and confusion! A letter which I have just received from General Knox, who had just returned from Massachusetts (whither he had been sent by Congress consequent of the commotion in that state) is replete with melancholy information of the temper and designs of a considerable part of that people. Among other things, he says "their creed is that the property of the United States has been protected from confiscation of Britain by the joint exertions of *all*, and therefore ought to be the *common property* of all. And he that attempts opposition to this creed is an enemy to equity and justice, and ought to be swept from off the face of the Earth." Again: "They are determined to annihilate all debts public and private, and have agrarian laws, which are easily effected by the means of unfunded paper money, which shall be a tender in all cases whatever." He adds: "The numbers of these people amount in Massachusetts to about one fifth part of several populous counties, and to them may be collected people of similar sentiments from the States of Rhode Island, Connecticut, and New Hampshire, so as to constitute a body of twelve or fifteen thousand desperate and unprincipled men. They are chiefly of the young and active part of the community."

How melancholy is the reflection that in so short a space we should have made such large strides towards fulfilling the prediction of our transatlantic foes!—"leave them to themselves, and their government will soon dissolve." Will not the wise and good strive hard to avert this evil? Or will their supineness suffer ignorance and the arts of self-interested, designing, disaffected, and desperate characters to involve this rising empire in wretchedness and contempt? What stronger evidence can be given of the want of energy in our governments than these disorders? If there exists not a power to check them, what security has a man of life, liberty, or property? To you, I am sure I need not add aught on this subject. The consequences of a lax or inefficient government are too obvious to be dwelt on. Thirteen sovereignties pulling against each other, and all tugging at the federal head, will soon bring ruin on the whole; whereas a liberal and energetic constitution, well guarded and closely watched to prevent encroachments, might restore us to that degree of respectability and consequence to which we had a fair claim and the brightest prospect of attaining. With sentiments of the sincerest esteem and regard I am—Dear Sir Yr Most Obedt & Affecte Hble Servt

Go: Washington

To Bushrod Washington, November 15, 1786

Dear Bushrod,

Your letter of the 31st of October in reply to mine of the 30th of September came safe to hand.

It was not the intention of my former letter either to condemn or give my voice in favor of the patriotic society of which you are a member. I offered observations, under the information you gave of it, the weight of which were to be considered. As first thoughts they were undigested and might be very erroneous.

That representatives ought to be the mouth of their constituents I do not deny; nor do I mean to call in question the right of the latter to instruct them. It is to the embarrassment into which they may be thrown by these instructions in national matters that my objection lies. In speaking of national matters, I look to the federal government, which in my opinion it is the interest of every state to support. And to do it, as there are a variety of interests in the Union, there must be a yielding of the parts to coalesce the whole. Now a county, a district, or even a state might decide on a measure, though apparently for the benefit of it in its separate and unconnected state, which may be repugnant to the interest of the nation, and eventually to the state itself, as a part of the Confederation. If, then, members go instructed to the assembly from the different districts, all the requisitions of Congress repugnant to the sense of them—and all the lights which they may receive from the communications of that body to the legislature—must be unavailing, although the nature and necessity of them when the reasons therefore are expounded are as self-evident as our existence. In local matters, which concern the district, or in things which respect the internal police of the state, there may be no impropriety in instructions. In national matters also, the sense (under the view they have of them) but not the law of the district may be given, leaving the delegates to judge from the nature of the case and the evidence before them, which can only be received from Congress to the executive and will be brought before them in their assembled capacity.

The instructions of your society, as far as they have gone, accord with my sentiments, except in the article of commutables. Here, if I understand the meaning and design of the clause, I disagree to it most clearly. For if the intention of it is to leave it optional in the person taxed to pay any staple commodity (tobacco would be least exceptionable) in lieu of specie, the people will be burdened, a few speculators enriched, and the public not benefited. Have we not had a recent and glaring instance of this in the course of the war in the provision tax? Did not the people pay this in some way or other, perhaps badly, and was the army, for whose benefit it was laid, the better for it? Can any instance be given where the public has sold tobacco, hemp, flour, or any other commodity upon as good terms as individuals have done? Who is this to serve? Is there a man to be found who, having any of the staple commodities to sell, will say he cannot get a reasonable price for them? Must there not be places of deposit for these commutables? Collectors, storekeepers, etc., etc., employed? Rely on it, these will sink one half the tax and a parcel of speculators will possess themselves of the other half, to the injury of the people and deception of the public. It is to similar measures of this we owe the present depravity of morals and abound in so many designing characters.

Among the great objects which you took into consideration at your meeting in Richmond, how came it to pass that you never turned your eyes towards the inefficiency of the federal government, so as to instruct your delegates to accede to the propositions of the commissioners lately convened at Annapolis, or to devise some other mode to give it that energy which is necessary to support a national character? Every man who considers the present constitution of it, and sees to what it is verging, trembles and deprecates the event. The fabric which took nine years (at the expense of much blood and treasure) to erect now totters to the foundation, and without support must soon fall.

The determination of your society to promote frugality and industry by example, to encourage manufactures, and to discountenance dissipation is highly praiseworthy—these and premiums for the most useful discoveries in agriculture within your district. The most profitable course of cropping and the best method of fencing to save timber etc. would soon make you a rich and happy people. With every good wish for you and yours in which your aunt joins me I am—Dear Bushrod Yr Affecte

Go: Washington

To Edmund Randolph, November 19, 1786

Dear Sir,

It gave me great pleasure to hear that the voice of the country had been directed to you as chief magistrate of this commonwealth, and that you had accepted the appointment.

Our affairs seem to be drawing to an awful crisis. It is necessary therefore that the abilities of every man should be drawn into action in a public line, to rescue them, if possible, from impending ruin. As no one seems more fully impressed with the necessity of adopting such measures than yourself, so none is better qualified to be entrusted with the reins of government. I congratulate you on this occasion, and with sincere regard and respect am, Dr Sir, &c. &c.

G: Washington

To David Stuart, November 19, 1786 (Excerpt)

It gives me sincere pleasure to find that the proceedings of the present assembly are marked with wisdom, liberality, and justice. These are the surest walks to public and private happiness—the display of which by so respectable a part of the Union, at so important a crisis, will, I hope, be influential and attended with happy consequences.

However delicate the revision of the federal system may appear, it is a work of indispensable necessity. The present constitution is inadequate. The superstructure totters to its foundations, and without helps will bury us in its ruins. Although I never more intended to appear on a public theater, and had in a public manner bid adieu to public life, yet, if the voice of my country had called me to this important duty, I might, in obedience to the repeated instances of its affection and confidence, have dispensed with these objections; but another now exists which would render my acceptance of this appointment impracticable, with any degree of consistency. It is this. The triennial General Meeting of the Society of the Cincinnati is to be holden in Philadelphia the first Monday in May next. Many reasons combining—some of a public, some of a private nature—to render it unpleasing and inconvenient for me to attend it, I did on the 31st ultimo address a circular letter to the state societies, informing them of my intention not to be there and desiring that I might no longer be rechosen president. The vice president (Gates) has also been informed thereof, that the business of the meeting might not be impeded on account of my absence. Under these circumstances, I could not be in Philadelphia precisely at the same moment on another occasion, without giving offense to a worthy and respectable part of the American community, the late officers of the American army.

To James Madison, December 16, 1786 (Excerpt)

My Dear Sir,

Your favor of the 7th came to hand the evening before last. The resolutions which you say are inserted in the papers I have not yet seen. The latter come irregularly, though I am a subscriber to Hayes's *Gazette*.

Besides the reasons which are assigned in my circular letter to the several State Societies of the Cincinnati for my non-attendance at the next General Meeting to be holden in Philadelphia the first Monday of May, there exists one of a political nature which operates more *forcibly* on my mind than all the others and which, in confidence, I will now communicate to you.

When this Society was first formed, I am persuaded not a member of it conceived that it would give birth to those jealousies, or be chargeable with those dangers (real or imaginary), with which the minds of many, and some of respectable characters, were filled. The motives which induced the officers to enter into it were, I am confident, truly and frankly recited in the Institution—one of which, indeed the principal, was to establish a charitable fund for the relief of such of their compatriots, the widows, and dependents of them as were fit subjects for their support, and for whom no *public* provision had been made. But the trumpet being sounded, the alarm was spreading far and wide. I readily perceived therefore that, unless a modification of the plan could be effected (to annihilate the Society altogether was impracticable, on account of the foreign officers who had been admitted), irritations would arise which would soon draw a line between the Society and their fellow citizens. To prevent this—to conciliate the affections and to convince the world of the purity of the plan—I exerted myself and with much difficulty effected the changes which appeared in the recommendation from the General Meeting to those of the states, the accomplishment of which was not easy. And I have since heard that whilst some states acceded to the recommendation, others are not disposed thereto, alleging that unreasonable prejudices and ill-founded jealousies ought not to influence a measure laudable in its institution and salutary in its objects and operation. Under these circumstances, there will be no difficulty in conceiving that the part I should have had to have acted would have been delicate. On the one hand, I might be charged with dereliction to the officers, who had nobly supported and had treated me with uncommon marks of attention and attachment, on the other, with supporting a measure incompatible (some say) with republican principles. I thought it best therefore, without assigning this (the principal reason), to decline the presidency and to excuse my attendance at the meeting on the ground, which is firm and just: the necessity of paying attention to my private concerns, the conformity to my determination of passing the remainder of my days in a state of retirement, and to indisposition occasioned by rheumatic complaints with which, at times, I am a good deal afflicted—professing at the same time my entire approbation of the Institution as altered, and the pleasure I feel at the subsidence of those jealousies which yielded to the change, presuming on the general adoption of them.

I have been thus particular to show that under circumstances like these I should feel myself in an awkward situation to be in Philadelphia on another public occasion during the sitting of this Society. That the present era is pregnant of great and *strange* events, none who will cast their eyes around them can deny. What may be brought forth between this and the first of May to remove the difficulties which at present labor in my mind against the acceptance of the honor which has lately been conferred on me by the assembly is not for me to predict. But I should think it incompatible with that candor which ought to characterize an honest mind not to declare that under my present view of the matter I should be too much embarrassed by the meetings of these two bodies in the same place in the same moment (after what I have written) to be easy in the situation, and consequently that it would be improper to let my appointment stand in the way of any other.

Of this, you who have had the whole matter fully before you will judge; for having received no other than private intimation of my election, and unacquainted with the formalities which are or ought to be used on these occasions, silence may be deceptious or considered as disrespectful. The imputation of both or either I would wish to avoid. This is the cause of the present disclosure, immediately on the receipt of your letter, which has been locked up by ice; for I have had no communication with Alexandria for many days, till the day before yesterday.

To Edmund Randolph, Governor of Virginia, December 21, 1786

Sir,

I had not the honor of receiving Your Excellency's favor of the 6th, with its enclosures, till last night.

Sensible as I am of the honor conferred on me by the General Assembly in appointing me one of the deputies to a Convention proposed to be held in the City of Philadelphia in May next, for the purpose of revising the Federal Constitution, and desirous as I am on all occasions of testifying a ready obedience to the calls of my country, yet, sir, there exists at this moment circumstances which I am persuaded will render my acceptance of this fresh mark of confidence incompatible with other measures which I had previously adopted, and from which, seeing little prospect of disengaging myself, it would be disingenuous not to express a wish that some other character, on whom greater reliance can be had, may be substituted in my place, the probability of my non-attendance being too great to continue my appointment.

As no mind can be more deeply impressed than mine is with the awful situation of our affairs—resulting in a great measure from the want of efficient powers in the federal head and due respect to its ordinances—so, consequently, those who do engage in the important business of removing these defects will carry with them every good wish of mine, which the best dispositions towards the attainment can bestow. I have the honr to be with very grt respect—Your Excelly's Most Obedt Hble Servt

Go: Washington

To David Humphreys, December 26, 1786 (Excerpt)

I had hardly dispatched my circular letters to the several State Societies of the Cincinnati when I received letters from some of the principal members of our assembly, expressing a wish that they might be permitted to name me as one of the deputies to the Convention proposed to be held at Philadelphia, the first of May next. I immediately wrote to my particular friend Madison (and similarly to the rest) the answer contained in the extract No. 1. In reply I got No. 2. This obliged me to be *more* explicit and confidential with him on points which a recurrence to the conversations we have had on this subject will bring to your mind without my hazarding the recital of them in a letter. Since this interchange, I have received from the governor the letter No. 4 to whom I returned the answer No. 5. If this business should be further pressed (which I hope it will not, as I have no inclination to go), what had I best do? *You*, as an *indifferent person*—and one who is much better acquainted with the sentiments and views of the Cincinnati than I am (for in this state, where the recommendations of the General Meeting have been acceded to, hardly anything is said about it), as also with the temper of the people and the state of politics at large—can determine upon fuller evidence and better ground than myself, especially as you will know in what light the states to the eastward consider *the Convention* and the measures they are pursuing to contravene or give efficacy to it. On the last occasion, only five states were represented—none east of New York. Why the New England governments did not appear I am yet to learn; for of all others the distractions and turbulent temper of their people would, I should have thought, have afforded the strongest evidence of the *necessity* of competent powers somewhere. That the federal government is nearly, if not quite, at a stand none will deny. The question then is: can it be propped, or shall it be annihilated? If the former, the proposed Convention is an object of the first magnitude and should be supported by all the friends of the present constitution. In the other case, if, on a full and dispassionate revision thereof, the continuances shall be adjudged impracticable or unwise, would it not be better for such a meeting to suggest some other to avoid, if possible, civil discord or other impending evils? Candor, however, obliges me to confess that, as we could not remain quiet more than three or four years (in time of peace) under the constitutions of our own choice, which it was believed, in many instances, were formed with deliberation and wisdom, I see little prospect either of our agreeing upon any other, or that we should remain long satisfied under it if we could. Yet I would wish to see *anything* and everything essayed to prevent the effusion of blood and to avert the humiliating and contemptible figure we are about to make in the annals of mankind.

If this second attempt to convene the states for the purposes proposed in the report of the partial representation at Annapolis in September last should also prove abortive, it may be considered as an unequivocal proof that the states are not likely to agree in any general measure which is to pervade the Union, and consequently that there is an end put to federal government. The states, therefore, who make this last dying essay to avoid the misfortune of a dissolution would be mortified at the issue; and their deputies would return home chagrined at their ill success and disappointment. This would be a disagreeable predicament for any of them to be in, but more particularly so for a person in my situation. If no further application is made to me, of course I do not attend. If there is, I am under no obligation to do it; but as I have had so many proofs of your friendship, know your abilities to judge, and your opportunities of learning the politics of the day on the points I have enumerated, you would oblige me by a *full and confidential* communication of your sentiments thereon.

Peace and tranquility prevail in this state. The assembly, by a very great majority, and in very emphatical terms, have rejected an application for paper money and spurned the idea of fixing the value of military certificates by a scale of depreciation. In some other respects, too, the proceedings of the present session have been marked with justice and a strong desire of supporting the federal system.

To Henry Knox, December 26, 1786 (Excerpt)

Lamentable as the conduct of the insurgents of Massachusetts is, I am exceedingly obliged to you for the advices respecting them, and pray you most ardently to continue the account of their proceedings, because I can depend upon them from you without having my mind bewildered with those vague and contradictory reports which are handed to us in newspapers, and which please one hour only to make the moments of the next more bitter.

I feel, my dear General Knox, infinitely more than I can express to you, for the disorders which have arisen in these states. Good God! Who besides a Tory could have foreseen, or a Briton predicted, them! Were these people wiser than others, or did they judge of us from the corruption and depravity of their own hearts? The latter, I am persuaded, was the case, and that, notwithstanding the boasted virtue of America, we are far gone in everything ignoble and bad. I do assure you that even at this moment, when I reflect on the present posture of our affairs, it seems to me to be like the vision of a dream. My mind does not know how to realize it as a thing in actual existence, so strange, so wonderful does it appear to me! In this, as in most other matters, we are too slow. When this spirit first dawned, probably it might easily have been checked; but it is scarcely within the reach of human ken at this moment, to say when, where, or how it will end. There are combustibles in every state which a spark may set fire to. In this state a perfect calm prevails at present, and a prompt disposition to support and give energy to the federal system is discovered, if the unlucky stirring of the dispute respecting the navigation of the Mississippi does not become a leaven that will ferment and sour the mind of it.

The resolutions of the present session respecting a paper emission, military certificates, etc., have stamped justice and liberality on the proceedings of the assembly; and by a late act it seems very desirous of a general convention to revise and amend the Federal Constitution. Apropos, what prevented the eastern states from attending the September meeting at Annapolis? Of all the states in the Union, it should have seemed to me, that a measure of this sort (distracted as they were with internal commotions and experiencing the want of energy in government) would have been most pleasing to them. What are the prevailing sentiments of the one now proposed to be held at Philadelphia in May next, and how will it be attended? You are at the fountain of intelligence and where the wisdom of the nation, it is to be presumed, has concentered, consequently better able (as I have had abundant experience of your intelligence, confidence, and candor) to solve these questions. The Maryland Assembly has been violently agitated by the question for a paper emission. It has been carried in the House of Delegates, but what has or will be done with the bill in the Senate I have not yet heard. The partisans in favor of the measure in the lower house threaten, it is said, a secession if it is rejected by that branch of the legislature. Thus are we advancing.

In regretting, which I have often done with the deepest sorrow, the death of our much lamented friend, General Greene, I have accompanied it of late with a query: whether he would not have preferred such an exit to the scenes which it is more than probable many of his compatriots may live to bemoan.

In both your letters you intimate that the men of reflection, principle, and property in New England, feeling the inefficacy of their present government, are contemplating a change; but you are not explicit with respect to the nature of it. It has been supposed that the Constitution of the state of Massachusetts was amongst the most energetic in the Union; may not these disorders then be ascribed to an indulgent exercise of the powers of administration? If your laws authorized, and your powers were adequate to, the suppression of these tumults in the first appearance of them, delay and temporizing expedients were, in my opinion, improper. These are rarely well applied, and the same causes would produce similar effects in any form of government, if the powers of it are not enforced. I ask this question for information; I know nothing of the facts.

That G.B. will be an unconcerned spectator of the present insurrections (if they continue) is not to be expected. That she is at this moment sowing the seeds of jealousy and discontent among the various tribes of Indians on our frontier admits of no doubt in my mind. And that she will improve every opportunity to foment the spirit of turbulence within the bowels of the United States, with a view of distracting our governments and promoting divisions, is, with me, not less certain. Her first maneuvers will, no doubt, be covert, and may remain so till the period shall arrive when a decided line of conduct may avail her. Charges of violating the treaty and other pretexts will not then be wanting to color overt acts, tending to effect the great objects of which she has long been in labor. A man is now at the head of their American affairs well calculated to conduct measures of this kind, and more than probably was selected for the purpose. We ought not therefore to sleep nor to slumber. Vigilance in the watching, and vigor in acting, is, in my opinion, become indispensably necessary. If the powers are inadequate, amend or alter them; but do not let us sink into the lowest state of humiliation and contempt and become a byword in all the earth. I think with you that the spring will unfold important and distressing scenes, unless much wisdom and good management is displayed in the interim. Adieu. Be assured no man has a higher esteem and regard for you than I have—none more sincerely Your friend, and More Affectly yr Hble Servt

Go: Washington

To Thomas Johnson, December 28, 1786 (Excerpt)

The lesson you seem fearful of learning will most assuredly be taught us. The strides we have already taken, and are now making, to corruption are inconceivably great. And I shall be exceedingly but very agreeably disappointed if next spring does not display scenes which will astonish the world. Nothing, I am certain, but the wisest councils and the most vigorous exertions can avert them.

To Jabez Bowen, January 9, 1787 (Excerpt)

I have been long since fully convinced of the necessity of granting to Congress more ample and extensive powers than they at present possess. The want of power and energy in that body has been severely felt in every part of the United States. The disturbances in New England, the declining state of our commerce, and the general languor which seems to pervade the Union are in a great measure (if not entirely) owing to the want of proper authority in the supreme council. The extreme jealousy that is observed in vesting Congress with adequate powers has a tendency rather to destroy than confirm our liberties. The wisest resolutions cannot produce any good unless they are supported with energy. They are only applauded, but never followed.

Paper money has had the effect in your state that it ever will have: to ruin commerce, oppress the honest, and open a door to every species of fraud and injustice.

I am entirely in sentiment with you, sir, of the necessity there is to adopt some measures for the support of our national peace and honor. The present situation of our public affairs demands the exertion and influence of every good and honest citizen in the Union to tranquilize disturbances, retrieve our credit, and place us upon a respectable footing with other nations.

To Henry Knox, February 3, 1787

My Dear Sir,

I feel myself exceedingly obliged to you for the full and friendly communications in your letters of the 14th, 21st, 25th ultimo and shall (critically, as matters are described in the latter) be extremely anxious to know the issue of the movements of the forces that were assembling, the one to support, the other to oppose the constitutional rights of Massachusetts. The moment is, indeed, important! If government shrinks, or is unable to enforce its laws, fresh maneuvers will be displayed by the insurgents, anarchy and confusion must prevail, and everything will be turned topsy turvy in that state, where it is not probable the mischiefs will terminate.

In your letter of the 14th, you express a wish to know my intention respecting the Convention proposed to be held at Philadelphia in May next. In *confidence* I inform you that it is not, at this time, my purpose to attend it. When this matter was first moved in the assembly of this state, some of the principal characters of it wrote to me requesting to be permitted to put my name in the delegation. To this I objected. They again pressed; and I again refused, assigning among other reasons my having declined meeting the Society of the Cincinnati at that place about the same time, and that I thought it would be disrespectful to that body (to whom I owed much) to be there on any other occasion. Notwithstanding these intimations, my name was inserted in the act and an official communication thereof made by the executive to me, to whom, at the same time that I expressed my sense of the confidence reposed in me, I declared that, as I saw no prospect of my attending, it was my wish that my name might not remain in the delegation to the exclusion of another. To this I have been requested, in emphatical terms, not to decide absolutely, as no inconvenience would result from the non-appointment of another, at least for some time. Thus the matter stands, which is the reason of my saying to you in *confidence* that at present I retain my first intention—not to go. In the meanwhile, as I have the fullest conviction of your friendship for and attachment to me, know your abilities to judge and your means of information, I shall receive any communications from you respecting this business with thankfulness. My first wish is to do for the best and to act with propriety; and you know me too well to believe that reserve or concealment of any circumstance or opinion would be at all pleasing to me.

The legality of this Convention I do not mean to discuss, nor how problematical the issue of it may be. That powers are wanting, none can deny. Through what medium they are to be derived, will, like other matters, engage public attention. That which takes the shortest course to obtain them will, in my opinion, under present circumstances, be found best. Otherwise, like a house on fire, whilst the most regular mode of extinguishing it is contending for, the building is reduced to ashes. My opinion of the energetic wants of the federal government are well known. Publicly and privately, I have declared it; and however constitutionally it may be for Congress to point out the defects of the federal system, I am strongly inclined to believe that it would not be found the most efficacious channel for the recommendation, more especially the alterations, to flow—for reasons too obvious to enumerate.

The system on which you seem disposed to build a national government is certainly more energetic and, I dare say, in every point of view is more desirable than the present one, which, from experience, we find is not only slow, debilitated, and liable to be thwarted by every breath, but is defective in that secrecy which for the accomplishment of many of the most important national purposes is indispensably necessary. And besides, having the legislative, executive, and judiciary departments concentered is exceptionable. But at the same time I give this opinion, I believe that the political machine will yet be much tumbled and tossed, and possibly be wrecked altogether, before such a system as you have defined will be adopted. The darling sovereignties of the states individually, the governors elected and elect, the legislators, with a long train of etcetera, whose political consequence will be lessened if not annihilated, would give their weight of opposition to such a revolution. But I may be speaking without book, for scarcely ever going off my own farms, I see few people who do not call upon me, and am very little acquainted with the sentiments of the great world. Indeed, after what I have seen, or rather after what I have heard, I shall be surprised at nothing. For if, three years ago, any person had told me that at this day I should see such a formidable rebellion against the laws and constitutions of our own making as now appears, I should have thought him a bedlamite—a fit subject for a mad house. Adieu. You know how much and how sincerely I am, ever, Yr Affecte & most Obedt Servant

Go: Washington

Mrs. Washington joins me in every good wish for yourself, Mrs. Knox, and the family.

To Thomas Stone, February 16, 1787

Dear Sir,

Your favor of the 30th ultimo came duly to hand. To give an opinion in a cause of so much importance as that which has warmly agitated two branches of your legislature, and which, from the appeal that is made, is likely to create great and perhaps dangerous divisions, is rather a delicate matter. But as this diversity of opinion is on a subject which has, I believe, occupied the minds of most men, and as my sentiments thereon have been fully and decidedly expressed long before the assembly either of Maryland or this state were convened, I do not scruple to declare that, if I had a voice in your legislature, it would have been given decidedly against a paper emission, upon the general principles of its utility, as a representative, and the necessity of it as a medium. And as far as I have been able to understand its advocates (for the two papers you sent me were the same and contained no reasons of the House of Delegates for the local want of it in your state, though I have seen and given them a cursory reading elsewhere), I should have been very little less opposed to it.

To assign reasons for this opinion would be as unnecessary as tedious. The ground has been so often trod that a place hardly remains untouched. But, in a word, the necessity arising from a want of specie greater than it really is, I contend that it is by the substance, not with the shadow of a thing, we are to be benefited. The wisdom of man, in my humble opinion, cannot at this time devise a plan by which the credit of paper money would be long supported. Consequently, depreciation keeps pace with the quantum of the emission, and articles for which it is exchanged rise in a greater ratio than the sinking value of the money. Wherein, then, is the farmer, the planter, the artisan benefited? The debtor may be, because, as I have observed, he gives the shadow in lieu of the substance; and in proportion to his gain, the creditor or the body politic suffer. For whether it be a legal tender or not, it will, as hath been observed very truly, leave no alternative—it must be that or nothing. An evil equally great is the door it immediately opens for speculation, by which the least designing and perhaps most valuable part of the community are preyed upon by the more knowing and crafty speculators. But, contrary to my intention and declaration, I am offering reasons in support of my opinion—reasons, too, which of all others are least pleasing to the advocates for paper money. I shall therefore only observe, generally, that so many people have suffered by former emissions, that, like a burnt child who dreads the fire, no person will touch it who can possibly avoid it. The natural consequence of which will be that the specie which remains unexported will be instantly locked up. With my great esteem and regard—I am Dr Sir your most obed. Servant

G. Washington

To Benjamin Lincoln, Jr., February 24, 1787 (Excerpt)

I am much obliged to you for the account of the political situation of your state which you gave me, and am very happy to find, by later advices, that matters are soon likely to terminate entirely in favor of government by the suppression of the insurgents. And it adds much to the satisfaction which these accounts give that it may be effected with so little bloodshed. I hope some good may come out of so much evil, by giving energy and respectability to the government.

General Lincoln's situation must have been very painful, to be obliged to march against those men whom he had heretofore looked upon as his fellow citizens, and some of whom had, perhaps, been his companions in the field; but as they had, by their repeated outrages, forfeited all the rights of citizenship, his duty and patriotism must have got the better of every other consideration and led him with alacrity to support the government.

To Henry Knox, February 25, 1787 (Excerpt)

Accept, my dear General Knox, my affectionate thanks for your obliging favors of the 29th, 30th, & 31st of January and 1st, 8th, and 12th of the present month.

They were, indeed, exceedingly satisfactory and relieving to my mind, which has been filled with great and anxious uneasiness for the issue of General Lincoln's operations and the dignity of government.

On the prospect of the happy termination of this insurrection I sincerely congratulate you, hoping that good may result from the cloud of evils which threatened not only the hemisphere of Massachusetts but, by spreading its baneful influence, the tranquility of the Union. Surely Shays must be either a weak man—the dupe of some characters who are yet behind the curtain—or has been deceived by his followers. Or, which may yet be more likely, he did not conceive that there was energy enough in the government to bring matters to the crisis to which they have been pushed. It is to be hoped the General Court of that state concurred in the report of the committee that a rebellion did actually exist. This would be decisive and the most likely means of putting the finishing stroke to the business.

We have nothing new in this quarter except the dissensions which prevailed in, and occasioned the adjournment of, the Assembly of Maryland, that an appeal might be made to the people for their sentiments on the conduct of their representatives in the Senate and delegates respecting a paper emission, which was warmly advocated by the latter and opposed by the former—and which may be productive of great, and perhaps dangerous, divisions. Our affairs, generally, seem really to be approaching to some awful crisis. God only knows what the result will be. It shall be my part to hope for the best, as to see this country happy whilst I am gliding down the stream of life in tranquil retirement is so much the wish of my soul, that nothing on this side Elysium can be placed in competition with it.

To Henry Knox, March 8, 1787 (Excerpt)

The observations contained in your letter of the 22nd ultimo (which came duly to hand) respecting the disfranchisement of a number of the citizens of Massachusetts for their rebellious conduct may be just. And yet, without exemplary punishment, similar disorders may be excited by other ambitious and discontented characters. Punishment, however, ought to light on the principals.

I am glad to hear that Congress are about to remove some of the stumbling blocks which lay in the way of the proposed Convention. A Convention I wish to see tried—after which, if the present government is not efficient, conviction of the propriety of a change will disseminate through every rank and class of people and may be brought about in peace—till which, however necessary it may appear in the eyes of the more discerning, my opinion is that it cannot be effected without great contention and much confusion. It is among the evils, and perhaps is not the smallest, of democratical governments that the people must *feel* before they will *see*. When this happens, they are roused to action. Hence it is that this form of government is so slow. I am indirectly and delicately pressed to attend this Convention. Several reasons are opposed to it in my mind, and not the least my having declined attending the General Meeting of the Cincinnati, which is to be holden in Philadelphia at the same time, on account of the disrespect it might seem to offer to that Society to be there on another occasion. A thought, however, has lately run through my mind, which is attended with embarrassment. It is, whether my non-attendance in this Convention will not be considered as a dereliction to republicanism—nay more—whether other motives may not (however injuriously) be ascribed to me for not exerting myself on this occasion in support of it. Under these circumstances let me pray you, my dear sir, to inform me confidentially what the public expectation is on this head—that is, whether I will or ought to be there? You are much in the way of obtaining this knowledge, and I can depend upon your friendship, candor, and judgment in the communication of it, as far as it shall appear to you. My final determination (if what I have already given to the executive of this state is not considered in that light) cannot be delayed beyond the time necessary for your reply. With great truth I am yrs most Affectly

Go: Washington

To John Jay, March 10, 1787 (Excerpt)

Dear Sir,

How far the revision of the federal system and giving more adequate powers to Congress may be productive of an efficient government I will not, under my present view of the matter, presume to decide. That many inconveniencies result from the present form, none can deny. Those enumerated in your letter are so obvious and sensibly felt that no logic can controvert, nor is it probable that any change of conduct will remove, them. And that all attempts to alter or amend it will be like the propping of a house which is ready to fall, and which no shores can support (as many seem to think), may also be true.

But is the public mind matured for such an important change as the one you have suggested? What would be the consequences of a premature attempt?

My opinion is that this country have yet to *feel* and *see* a little more before it can be accomplished. A thirst for power, and the bantling—I had like to have said monster—sovereignty which have taken such fast hold of the states individually, will, when joined by the many whose personal consequence in the line of state politics will in a manner be annihilated, form a strong phalanx against it. And when to these the few who can hold posts of honor or profit in the national government are compared with the many who will see but little prospect of being noticed, and the discontents of others who may look for appointments, the opposition would be altogether irresistible till the mass as well as the more discerning part of the community shall see the necessity.

Among men of reflection few will be found, I believe, who are not *beginning* to think that our system is better in theory than practice—and that, notwithstanding the boasted virtue of America, it is more than probable we shall exhibit the last melancholy proof that mankind are not competent to their own government without the means of coercion in the sovereign.

Yet I would try what the wisdom of the proposed Convention will suggest and what can be effected by their councils. It may be the last peaceable mode of essaying the practicability of the present form, without a greater lapse of time than the exigency of our affairs will admit. In strict propriety a Convention so holden may not be legal. Congress, however, may give it a coloring by recommendation, which would fit it more to the taste, without proceeding to a definition of powers. This, however constitutionally it might be done, would not, in my opinion, be expedient; for delicacy on the one hand, and jealousy on the other, would produce a mere nihil.

To Benjamin Lincoln, March 23, 1787 (Excerpt)

My Dear Sir,

Ever since the disorders in your state began to grow serious, I have been particularly anxious to hear from that quarter. General Knox has from time to time transmitted to me the state of affairs as they came to his hands; but nothing has given such full and satisfactory information as the particular detail of events which you have been so good as to favor me with, and for which you will please to accept my warmest and most grateful acknowledgments.

Permit me also, my dear sir, to offer you my sincerest congratulations upon your success. The suppression of those tumults and insurrections with so little bloodshed is an event as happy as it was unexpected. It must have been peculiarly agreeable to you, being placed in so delicate and critical a situation.

I am extremely happy to find that your sentiments upon the disfranchising act are such as they are. Upon my first seeing it I formed an opinion perfectly coincident with yours—viz. that measures more *generally* lenient might have produced equally as good an effect without entirely alienating the affections of the people from the government. As it now stands, it affects a large body of men; some of them, perhaps, it deprives of the means of gaining a livelihood. The friends and connections of those people will feel themselves wounded in a degree; and I think it will rob the state of a number of its inhabitants, if it produces nothing worse.

To Edmund Randolph, Governor of Virginia, March 28, 1787 (Excerpt)

It was the decided intention of the letter I had the honor of writing to Your Excellency the 21st of December last to inform you that it would not be convenient for me to attend the Convention proposed to be holden in Philadelphia in May next. And I had entertained hopes that another had been, or soon would be, appointed in my place, inasmuch as it is not only inconvenient for me to leave home, but because there will be, I apprehend, too much cause to charge my conduct with inconsistency in again appearing on a public theater after a public declaration to the contrary, and because it will, I fear, have a tendency to sweep me back into the tide of public affairs, when retirement and ease is so essentially necessary for and is so much desired by me.

However, as my friends, with a degree of solicitude which is unusual, seem to wish my attendance on this occasion, I have come to a resolution to go if my health will permit, provided, from the lapse of time between the date of Your Excellency's letter and this reply, the executive may not—the reverse of which would be highly pleasing to me—have turned its thoughts to some other character. For independently of all other considerations, I have, of late, been so much afflicted with a rheumatic complaint in my shoulder that at times I am hardly able to raise my hand to my head or turn myself in bed. This, consequently, might prevent my attendance and eventually a representation of the state, which would afflict me more sensibly than the disorder which occasioned it.

If, after the expression of these sentiments, the executive should consider me as one of the delegates, I would thank Your Excellency for the earliest advice of it, because if I am able and should go to Philadelphia I shall have some previous arrangements to make, and would set off[7] for that place the first or second day of May, that I may be there in time to account, personally, for my conduct to the General Meeting of the Cincinnati, which is to convene on the first Monday of that month. My feelings would be much hurt if that body should otherwise ascribe my attendance on the one and not on the other occasion to a disrespectful inattention to the Society, when the fact is that I shall ever retain the most lively and affectionate regard for the members of which it is composed, on account of their attachment to and uniform support of me upon many trying occasions, as well as on account of their public virtues, patriotism, and sufferings.

I hope Your Excellency will be found among the *attending* delegates. I should be glad to be informed who the others are—and cannot conclude without once more, and in emphatical terms, praying that if there is not a *decided* representation in *prospect* without me, that another, for the reason I have assigned, may be chosen in my room without ceremony and without delay. For it would be unfortunate indeed if the state which was the mover of this Convention should be unrepresented in it. With great respect I have the honor to be Yr Excelly's Most Obedt Ser.

Go: Washington

To James Madison, March 31, 1787 (Excerpt)

I am glad to find that Congress have recommended to the states to appear in the Convention proposed to be holden in Philadelphia in May. I think the reasons in favor have the preponderancy of those against the measure. It is idle in my opinion to suppose that the sovereign can be insensible of the inadequacy of the powers under which it acts—and that seeing, it should not recommend a revision of the federal system, when it is considered by many as the *only* constitutional mode by which the defects can be remedied. Had Congress proceeded to a delineation of the powers, it might have sounded an alarm; but as the case is, I do not conceive that it will have that effect.

From the acknowledged abilities of the secretary for foreign affairs I could have had no doubt of his having ably investigated the infractions of the treaty on both sides. Much is it to be regretted, however, that there should have been any on ours. We seem to have forgotten, or never to have learnt, the policy of placing one's enemy in the wrong. Had we observed good faith on our part, we might have told our tale to the world with a good grace; but complaints illy become those who are found to be the first aggressors.

I am fully of opinion that those who lean to a monarchical government have either not consulted the public mind, or that they live in a region where the leveling principles in which they were bred, being entirely eradicated, is much more productive of monarchical ideas than are to be found in the southern states, where, from the habitual distinctions which have always existed among the people, one would have expected the first generation and the most rapid growth of them. I also am clear that even admitting the utility—nay, necessity of the form—yet that the period is not arrived for adopting the change without shaking the peace of this country to its foundation.

That a thorough reform of the present system is indispensable none who have capacities to judge will deny. And with hand and heart I hope the business will be essayed in a full Convention. After which, if more powers and more decision are not found in the existing form; if it still wants energy and that secrecy and dispatch (either from the non-attendance or the local views of its members) which is characteristic of good government; and if it shall be found (the contrary of which, however, I have always been more afraid of than of the abuse of them) that Congress will upon all proper occasions exercise the powers with a firm and steady hand, instead of frittering them back to the individual states, where the members, in place of viewing themselves in their national character, are too apt to be looking—I say after this essay is made, if the system proves inefficient, conviction of the necessity of a change will be disseminated among all classes of the people. Then, and not till then, in my opinion can it be attempted without involving all the evils of civil discord.

I confess, however, that my opinion of public virtue is so far changed that I have my doubts whether any system without the means of coercion in the sovereign will enforce obedience to the ordinances of a general government, without which everything else fails. Laws or ordinances unobserved, or partially attended to, had better never have been made, because the first is a mere nihil and the 2nd is productive of much jealousy and discontent. But the kind of coercion, you may ask? This indeed will require thought, though the non-compliance of the states with the late requisition is an evidence of the necessity.

It is somewhat singular that a state (New York) which used to be foremost in all federal measures should now turn her face against them in almost every instance.

I fear the state of Massachusetts has exceeded the bounds of good policy in its disfranchisements. Punishment is certainly due to the disturbers of a government, but the operations of this act are too extensive. It embraces too much and probably may give birth to new, instead of destroying the old, leaven.

Some acts passed at the last session of our assembly respecting the trade of this country have given great and general discontent to the merchants of it. An application from the whole body of those at Norfolk has been made, I am told, to convene the assembly.

I had written thus far, and was on the point of telling you how much I am your obliged servant, when your favor of the 18th calls upon me for additional acknowledgments.

I thank you for the Indian vocabulary, which I dare say will be very acceptable in a general comparison. Having taken a copy, I return you the original with thanks.

It gives me pleasure to hear that there is a probability of a full representation of the states in convention; but if the delegates come to it under fetters, the salutary ends proposed will, in my opinion, be greatly embarrassed and retarded, if not altogether defeated. I am anxious to know how this matter really is, as my wish is that the Convention may adopt no temporizing expedient, but probe the defects of the constitution to the bottom and provide radical cures, whether they are agreed to or not. A conduct like this will stamp wisdom and dignity on the proceedings and be looked to as a luminary, which sooner or later will shed its influence.

I should feel pleasure, I confess, in hearing that Vermont is received into the Union upon terms agreeable to all parties. I took the liberty years ago to tell some of the first characters in the state of New York that sooner or later it would come to that, that the longer it was delayed the terms on their part would probably be more difficult, and that the general interest was suffering by the suspense in which the business was held, as the asylum which it afforded was a constant drain from the army in place of an aid which it offered to afford, and, lastly, considering the proximity of it to Canada, if they were not with us they might become a sore thorn in our sides, which I verily believe would have been the case if the war had continued. The western settlements, without good and wise management of them, may be equally troublesome. With sentiments of the sincerest friendship I am—Dear Sir Yr Affecte Servt

Go: Washington

To Henry Knox, April 2, 1787

My Dear Sir,

The early attention which you were so obliging as to pay to my letter of the 8th ultimo is highly pleasing and flattering to me. Were you to continue to give me information on the same point, you would add to the favor, as I see, or think I see, reasons for and against my attendance in convention so near an equilibrium as will cause me to determine upon either with diffidence. One of the reasons against it is an apprehension that all the states will not appear and that some of them, being unwillingly drawn into the measure, will send their delegates so fettered as to embarrass and perhaps render nugatory the whole proceedings. In either of these circumstances—that is, a partial representation or cramped powers—I should not like to be a sharer in this business. If the delegates come with such powers as will enable the Convention to probe the defects of the constitution to the bottom and point out radical cures, it would be an honorable employment; but otherwise, it is desirable to avoid it. And these are matters you may possibly come at by means of your acquaintances among the delegates in Congress, who undoubtedly know what powers are given by their respective states. You also can inform me what the prevailing opinion with respect to my attendance or non-attendance is; and I would sincerely thank you for the confidential communication of it.

If I should attend the Convention, I will be in Philadelphia previous to the meeting of the Cincinnati, where I shall hope and expect to meet you and some others of my particular friends the day before, in order that I may have a free and unreserved conference with you on the subject of it. For I assure you this is, in my estimation, a business of a delicate nature. That the design of the institution was pure I have not a particle of doubt. That it may be so still is perhaps equally unquestionable. But, query, are not the subsidence of the jealousies of it to be ascribed to the modification which took place at the last general meeting? Are not these rejected in toto by some of the state societies and partially acceded to by others? Has any state so far overcome its prejudices as to grant a charter? Will the modifications and alterations be insisted on or given up in the next meeting? If the first, will it not occasion warmths and divisions? If the latter, and I should remain at the head of this order, in what light would my signature appear in contradictory recommendations? In what light would the versatility appear to the foreign members, who perhaps are acting agreeably to the recommendations of the last general meeting? These and other matters which may be agitated will, I fear, place me in a disagreeable predicament if I should preside, and were among the causes which induced me to decline the honor of it, previously to the meeting. Indeed, my health is become very precarious. A rheumatic complaint which has followed me more than six months is frequently so bad that it is with difficulty I can, at times, raise my hand to my head or turn myself in bed. This, however smooth and agreeable other matters might be, might almost in the moment of my departure prevent my attendance on either occasion.

I will not at present touch on any other parts of your letter, but would wish you to ponder on all these matters and write to me as soon as you can. With the most sincere friendship I am My dear Sir Yr affecte Serv

Go: Washington

To Edmund Randolph, Governor of Virginia, April 9, 1787 (Excerpt)

It gives me pleasure to find by your letter that there will be so full a representation from this state. If the case had been otherwise, I would in emphatical terms have urged again that, rather than depend upon my going, another might be chosen in my place. For as a friend, and in confidence, I declare to you that my assent is given contrary to my judgment, because the act will, I apprehend, be considered as inconsistent with my public declaration delivered in a solemn manner at an interesting era in[8] my life never more to intermeddle in public matters. This declaration not only stands on the files of Congress, but is, I believe, registered in almost all the gazettes and magazines that are published. And what adds to the embarrassment is I had, previous to my appointment, informed by circular letter the several State Societies of the Cincinnati of my intention to decline the presidency of that order and excused myself from attending the next general meeting at Philadelphia on the first Monday in May, assigning reasons for so doing which apply as well in the one case as the other. Add to these, I very much fear that all the states will not appear in convention, and that some of them will come fettered so as to impede rather than accelerate the great ends of their calling which, under the peculiar circumstances of my case, would place me in a disagreeable situation which no other member present would stand in. As I have yielded, however, to what appeared to be the earnest wishes of my friends, I will hope for the best, and can assure you of the sincere and affectionate regard with which I am Dr Sir yr Obed. Servant

G. Washington

To Thomas Jefferson, Minister to France, May 30, 1787 (Excerpt)

The business of this Convention is as yet too much in embryo to form any opinion of the result. Much is expected from it by some, but little by others, and nothing by a few. That something is necessary all will agree; for the situation of the general government (if it can be called a government) is shaken to its foundation, and liable to be overset by every blast. In a word, it is at an end, and, unless a remedy is soon applied, anarchy and confusion will inevitably ensue. But, having greatly exceeded the bounds of a letter already, I will only add assurances of that esteem, regard, and respect with which I have the honor to be Dear Sir Yr Most Obedt & Very Hble Servt

Go: Washington

To David Stuart, July 1, 1787 (Excerpt)

Rhode Island, from our last accounts, still persevere in that impolitic, unjust, and, one might add without much impropriety, scandalous conduct which seems to have marked all her public councils of late. Consequently, no representation is yet here from thence. New Hampshire, though delegates have been appointed, is also unrepresented. Various causes have been assigned—whether well or ill-founded I shall not take upon me to decide. The fact, however, is that they are not here. Political contests and want of money are amidst the reasons assigned for the non-attendance of the members.

As the rules of the Convention prevent me from relating any of the proceedings of it, and the gazettes contain more fully than I could detail other occurrences of public nature, I have little to communicate to you on the article of news. Happy, indeed, would it be if the Convention shall be able to recommend such a firm and permanent government for this Union as all who live under it may be secure in their lives, liberty, and property; and thrice happy would it be if such a recommendation should obtain. Everybody wishes, everybody expects something from the Convention; but what will be the final result of its deliberation, the book of fate must disclose. Persuaded I am that the primary cause of all our disorders lies in the different state governments, and in the tenacity of that power which pervades the whole of their systems. Whilst independent sovereignty is so ardently contended for, whilst the local views of each state and separate interests by which they are too much governed will not yield to a more enlarged scale of politics, incompatibility in the laws of different states and disrespect to those of the general government must render the situation of this great country weak, inefficient, and disgraceful. It has already done so, almost to the final dissolution of it. Weak at home and disregarded abroad is our present condition, and contemptible enough it is. Entirely unnecessary was it to offer any apology for the sentiments you were[9] so obliging as to offer me. I have had no wish more ardent (through the whole progress of this business) than that of knowing what kind of government is best calculated for us to live under. No doubt there will be a diversity of sentiment on this important subject; and to inform the judgment it is necessary to hear all arguments that can be advanced. To please all is impossible, and to attempt it would be vain. The only way, therefore, is, under all the views in which it can be placed, and with a due consideration to circumstances, habits, etc., etc., to form such a government as will bear the scrutinizing eye of criticism, and trust it to the good sense and patriotism of the people to carry it into effect. Demagogues—men who are unwilling to lose any of their state consequence—and interested characters in each will oppose any general government; but ought these not to be regarded, right and justice, it is to be hoped, will at length prevail.

To Alexander Hamilton, July 10, 1787

Dear Sir,

I thank you for your communication of the 3rd. When I refer you to the state of the councils which prevailed at the period you left this city and add that they are now, if possible, in a worse train than ever, you will find but little ground on which the hope of a good establishment can be formed. In a word, I *almost* despair of seeing a favorable issue to the proceedings of the Convention, and do therefore repent having had any agency in the business.

The men who oppose a strong and energetic government are, in my opinion, narrow minded politicians or are under the influence of local views. The apprehension expressed by them that the people will not accede to the form proposed is the *ostensible*, not the *real*, cause of the opposition. But admitting that the present sentiment is as they prognosticate, the question ought nevertheless to be: is it or is it not the best form? If the former, recommend it, and it will assuredly obtain maugre opposition.

I am sorry you went away. I wish you were back. The crisis is equally important and alarming, and no opposition under such circumstances should discourage exertions till the signature is fixed. I will not at this time trouble you with more than my best wishes and sincere regards. I am Dear Sir Yr obedt Servt

Go: Washington

To Marquis de Lafayette, August 15, 1787 (Excerpt)

Newspaper accounts inform us that the session of the Assembly of Notables is ended; and you have had the goodness (in your letter of the 5th of May) to communicate some of the proceedings to me, among which is that of the interesting motion made by yourself respecting the expenditure of public money by Monsieur de Calonne, and the consequence thereof. The patriotism with which this nation was dictated throws a luster on the action which cannot fail to dignify the author; and I sincerely hope, with you, that much good will result from the deliberations of so respectable a council. I am not less ardent in my wish that you may succeed in your plan of toleration in religious matters. Being no bigot myself to any mode of worship, I am disposed to indulge the professors of Christianity in the church that road to Heaven which to them shall seem the most direct, plainest, easiest, and least liable to exception.

To Henry Knox, August 19, 1787 (Excerpt)

My Dear Sir,

By slow—I wish I could add "and sure"[10]—movements, the business of the Convention progresses; but to say when it will end, or what will be the result, is more than I can venture to do, and therefore shall hazard no opinion thereon. If, however, *some* good does not proceed from the session, the defects cannot with propriety be charged to the hurry with which the business has been conducted. Yet many things may be forgot, some of them not well digested, and others become a mere nullity. Notwithstanding which I wish a disposition may be found in Congress, the several states' legislatures, and the community at large to adopt the government which may be agreed on in Convention, because I am fully persuaded it is the best that can be obtained at the present moment, under such diversity of ideas as prevail.

Diary Entry, September 17, 1787

Monday 17th. Met in Convention when the Constitution received the unanimous assent of eleven states and Colonel Hamilton's from New York (the only delegate from thence in Convention) and was subscribed to by every member present except Governor Randolph and Colonel Mason from Virginia and Mr. Gerry from Massachusetts. The business being thus closed, the members adjourned to the City Tavern, dined together, and took a cordial leave of each other, after which I returned to my lodgings, did some business with and received the papers from the secretary of the Convention, and retired to meditate on the momentous work which had been executed after not less than five, for a large part of the time six, and sometimes seven hours sitting every day, Sundays, and the ten days' adjournment, to give a committee opportunity and time to arrange the business, for more than four months.[11]

To the President of Congress, September 17, 1787

We have now the honor to submit to the consideration of the United States in Congress assembled that Constitution which has appeared to us the most advisable.

The friends of our country have long seen and desired that the power of making war, peace, and treaties, that of levying money and regulating commerce, and the correspondent executive and judicial authorities, should be fully and effectually vested in the general government of the Union. But the impropriety of delegating such extensive trust to one body of men is evident. Hence results the necessity of a different organization.

It is obviously impracticable in the federal government of these states to secure all rights of independent sovereignty to each and yet provide for the interest and safety of all. Individuals entering into society must give up a share of liberty to preserve the rest. The magnitude of the sacrifice must depend as well on situations and circumstances as on the object to be obtained. It is at all times difficult to draw with precision the lines between those rights which must be surrendered and those which may be reserved. And on the present occasion, this difficulty was increased by a difference among the several states as to their situation, extent, habits, and particular interests.

In all our deliberations on this subject, we kept steadily in our view that which appears to us the greatest interest of every true American: the consolidation of our Union, in which is involved our prosperity, felicity, safety, perhaps our national existence. This important consideration, seriously and deeply impressed on our minds, led each state in the Convention to be less rigid on points of inferior magnitude than might have been otherwise expected. And thus the Constitution which we now present is the result of a spirit of amity and of that mutual deference and concession which the peculiarity of our political situation rendered indispensable.

That it will meet the full and entire approbation of every state is not perhaps to be expected. But each will doubtless consider that had her interests been alone consulted, the consequences might have been particularly disagreeable or injurious to others. That it is liable to as few exceptions as could reasonably have been expected we hope and believe. That it may promote the lasting welfare of that country so dear to us all, and secure her freedom and happiness, is our most ardent wish.

To Marquis de Lafayette, September 18, 1787

My Dear Marquis,

In the midst of hurry, and in the moment of my departure from this city, I address this letter to you. The principal, indeed the only, design of it is to fulfill the promise I made that I would send you the proceedings of the Federal Convention as soon as the business of it was closed. More than this, circumstanced as I am at present, is not in my power to do. Nor am I inclined to attempt it, as the enclosure must speak for itself and will occupy your thoughts for some time.

It is the production of four months' deliberation. It is now a child of fortune, to be fostered by some and buffeted by others. What will be the general opinion on or the reception of it is not for me to decide, nor shall I say anything for or against it. If it be good, I suppose it will work its way good; if bad, it will recoil on the framers. My best wishes attend you and yours, and with the sincerest friendship and most affectionate regard I am ever yours

G. Washington

To Benjamin Harrison, September 24, 1787

Dear Sir,

In the first moments after my return, I take the liberty of sending you a copy of the Constitution which the Federal Convention has submitted to the people of these states.

I accompany it with no observations. Your own judgment will at once discover the good and the exceptionable parts of it. And your experience of the difficulties which have ever arisen when attempts have been made to reconcile such variety of interests and local prejudices as pervade the several states will render explanation unnecessary. I wish the Constitution which is offered had been made more perfect, but I sincerely believe it is the best that could be obtained at this time. And, as a constitutional door is opened for amendment hereafter, the adoption of it under present circumstances of the Union is, in my opinion, desirable.

From a variety of concurring accounts it appears to me that the political concerns of this country are, in a manner, suspended by a thread; that the Convention has been looked up to by the reflecting part of the community with a solicitude which is hardly to be conceived; and that, if nothing had been agreed on by that body, anarchy would soon have ensued, the seeds being richly sown in every soil. I am &c.

G. Washington

To David Humphreys, October 10, 1787 (Excerpt)

The Constitution that is submitted is not free from imperfections; but there are as few radical defects in it as could well be expected, considering the heterogeneous mass of which the Convention was composed and the diversity of interests which were to be reconciled. A constitutional door being opened for future alterations and amendments, I think it would be wise in the people to adopt what is offered to them. And I wish it may be by as great a majority of them as in the body that decided on it. But this is hardly to be expected, because the importance and sinister views of too many characters will be affected by the change. Much will depend, however, on literary abilities and the recommendation of it by good pens, should it be openly, I mean publicly, attacked in the gazettes. Go matters however as they may, I shall have the consolation to reflect that no objects but the public good, and that peace and harmony which I wished to see prevail in the Convention, ever obtruded, even for a moment, in my mind during the whole session, lengthy as it was. What reception this state will give to the proceedings (through the great territorial extent of it) I am unable to inform you. In these parts of it, it is advocated beyond my expectation. The great opposition, if great is given, will come from the counties southward and westward, from whence I have not as yet heard much that can be depended on.

I condole with you on the loss of your parents; but, as they lived to a good old age, you could not be unprepared for the shock, though there is something painful in bidding an adieu to those we love or revere, when we know it is a final one. Reason, religion, and philosophy may soften the anguish; but time alone can eradicate it.

To James Madison, October 10, 1787 (Excerpt)

My Dear Sir,

I thank you for your letter of the 30th ultimo. It came by the last post. I am better pleased that the proceedings of the Convention is handed from Congress by a unanimous vote (feeble as it is) than if it had appeared under stronger marks of approbation without it. This apparent unanimity will have its effect. Not everyone has opportunities to peep behind the curtain; and as the multitude often judge from externals, the appearance of unanimity in that body on this occasion will be of great importance.

To Henry Knox, October 15, 1787 (Excerpt)

The Constitution is now before the judgment seat. It has, as was expected, its adversaries and its supporters. Which will preponderate is yet to be decided. The former, it is probable, will be most active, because the major part of them, it is to be feared, will be governed by sinister and self-important considerations on which no arguments will work conviction. The opposition from another class of them (if they are men of reflection, information, and candor) may perhaps subside in the solution of the following plain but important questions. 1. Is the Constitution which is submitted by the Convention preferable to the government (if it can be called one) under which we now live? 2. Is it probable that more confidence will, at this time, be placed in another convention (should the experiment be tried) than was given to the last, and is it likely that there would be a better agreement in it? Is there not a constitutional door open for alterations and amendments, and is it not probable that real defects will be as readily discovered after as before trial? And will not posterity be as ready to apply the remedy as ourselves, if there is occasion for it, when the mode is provided? To think otherwise will, in my judgment, be ascribing more of the amor patria, more wisdom, and more foresight to ourselves than I conceive we are entitled to.

It is highly probable that the refusal of our governor and Colonel Mason to subscribe to the proceedings of the Convention will have a bad effect in this state; for, as you well observe, they *must* not only assign reasons for the justification of their conduct, but it is highly probable these reasons will appear in terrific array, with a view to alarm the people. Some things are already addressed to their fears and will have their effect. As far, however, as the sense of *this* part of the country has been taken, it is strongly in favor of the proposed Constitution. Further I cannot speak with precision. If a powerful opposition is given to it, the weight thereof will, I apprehend, come from the southward of James River and from the western counties.

To David Stuart, November 5, 1787 (Excerpt)

With respect to the payment of British debts, I would fain hope (let the eloquence or abilities of any man or set of men in opposition be they what they may) that the good sense of this country will never suffer a violation of a public treaty, nor pass acts of injustice to individuals. Honesty in states, as well as in individuals, will ever be found the soundest policy.

To Bushrod Washington, November 9, 1787

Dear Bushrod,

In due course of post I received your letters of the 19th & 26th ultimo—and since, the one which you committed to the care of Mr. Powell. I thank you for the communications therein, and for a continuation, in matters of importance, I shall be obliged to you.

That the assembly would afford the people an opportunity of deciding on the proposed Constitution I had hardly a doubt. The only question with me was whether it would go forth under favorable auspices or be branded with the mark of disapprobation. The opponents, I expected (for it has ever been that the adversaries to a measure are more active than its friends), would endeavor to give it an unfavorable complexion, with a view to bias the public mind. This, evidently, is the case with the writers in opposition; for their objections are better calculated to alarm the fears than to convince the judgment of their readers. They build them upon principles which do not exist in the Constitution, which the known and literal sense of it does not support them in—and this, too, after being flatly told that they are treading on untenable ground, and after an appeal has been made to the letter and spirit thereof for proof, and then, as if the doctrine was incontrovertible, draw such consequences as are necessary to rouse the apprehensions of the ignorant and unthinking. It is not the interest of the major part of these characters to be convinced, nor will their local views yield to arguments which do not accord with their present or future prospects. And yet a candid solution of a single question, to which the understanding of almost every man is competent, must decide the point in dispute: namely, is it best for the states to unite or not to unite?

If there are men who prefer the latter, then unquestionably the Constitution which is offered must, in their estimation, be inadmissible from the first word to the last signature, inclusively. But those who may think differently, and yet object to parts of it, would do well to consider that it does not lie with *one* state, nor with a *minority* of the states, to superstruct a constitution for the *whole*. The separate interests, as far as it is practicable, must be consolidated; and local views, as far as the general good will admit, must be attended to. Hence it is that *every* state has some objection to the *proposed* form, and that these objections are directed to different points. That which is most pleasing to one is obnoxious to another, and vice versa. If, then, the union of the whole is a desirable object, the parts which compose it must yield a little in order to accomplish it; for without the latter, the former is unattainable. For I again repeat it, that not a single state nor a minority of the states can force a constitution on the majority. But admitting they had (from their importance) the power to do it, will it not be granted that the attempt would be followed by civil commotions of a very serious nature? But to sum up the whole, let the opponents of the proposed Constitution *in this state* be asked (it is a question they ought certainly to have asked themselves): What line of conduct they would advise it to adopt, if nine other states should accede to it, of which I think there is little doubt? Would they recommend that it should stand on its own basis, separate and distinct from the rest? Or would they connect it with Rhode Island, or even, say, two others, checkerwise, and remain with them as outcasts from the society, to shift for themselves? Or will they advise a return to our former dependence on Great Britain for their protection and support? Or, lastly, would they prefer the mortification of coming in when they will have no credit therefrom? I am sorry to add in this place that Virginians entertain too high an opinion of the importance of their own country. In extent of territory, in number of inhabitants (*of all descriptions*), and in wealth, I will readily grant that it certainly stands first in the Union; but in point of strength, it is comparatively weak. To this point, my opportunities authorize me to speak decidedly; and sure I am, in every point of view in which the subject can be placed, it is not (considering also the geographical situation of the state) more the interest of any one of them to confederate than it is the one in which we live.

The warmest friends to and the best supporters of the Constitution do not contend that it is free from imperfections, but these were not to be avoided. And they are convinced, if evils are likely to flow from them, that the remedy must come thereafter, because in the present moment it is not to be obtained. And as there is a constitutional door open for it, I think the people (for it is with them to judge) can, as they will have the aid of experience on their side, decide with as much propriety on the alterations and amendments which shall be found necessary as ourselves. For I do not conceive that we are more inspired, have more wisdom, or possess more virtue than those who will come after us. The power under the Constitution will always be with the people. It is entrusted for certain defined purposes and for a certain limited period to representatives of their own choosing; and whenever it is exercised contrary to their interests, or not according to their wishes, their servants can and undoubtedly will be recalled. There will not be wanting those who will bring forward complaints of maladministration whensoever they occur. To say that the Constitution *may be strained*, and an *improper* interpretation given to some of the clauses or articles of it, will apply to any that can be framed—in a word, renders any one nugatory, for not one more than another can be binding if the spirit and letter of the expression is disregarded. It is agreed on all hands that no government can be well administered without powers; and yet the instant these are delegated, although those who are entrusted with the administration are taken from the people, return shortly to them again, and must feel the bad effect of oppressive measures, the persons holding them, as if their natures were immediately metamorphosed, are denominated tyrants, and no disposition is allowed them but to do wrong. Of these things in a government so constituted and guarded as the proposed one is, I can have no idea, and do firmly believe that whilst many ostensible reasons are held out against the adoption of it, the true ones are yet behind the curtain, not being of a nature to appear in open day. I believe further, supposing these objections to be founded in purity itself, that as great evils result from too much jealousy as from the want of it. And I adduce several of the constitutions of these states as proof thereof. No man is a warmer advocate for *proper* restraints and *wholesome* checks in every department of government than I am, but neither my reasoning nor my experience has yet been able to discover the propriety of preventing men from doing good because there is a possibility of their doing evil.

If Mr. Ronald can place the finances of this country upon so respectable a footing as he has intimated, he will deserve its warmest and most grateful thanks. In the attempt, my best wishes—which is all I have to offer—will accompany him.

I hope there remains virtue enough in the assembly of this state to preserve inviolate public treaties and private contracts. If these are infringed, farewell to respectability and safety in the government.

I never possessed a doubt—but if any had ever existed in my breast, reiterated proofs would have convinced me—of the impolicy of all commutable taxes. If wisdom is not to be acquired from experience, where is it to be found? But why ask the question? Is it not believed by everyone that these are time-serving jobs by which a few are enriched at the public expense! But whether the plan originates for this purpose or is the child of ignorance, oppression is the result.

You have, I find, broke the ice (as the saying is). One piece of advice only I will give you on the occasion (if you mean to be a respectable member, and to entitle yourself to the ear of the house) and that is: Except in local matters which respect your constituents, and to which you are obliged by duty to speak, rise but seldom. Let this be on important matters, and then make yourself thoroughly acquainted with the subject. Never be agitated by *more than* a decent *warmth*, and offer your sentiments with modest diffidence. Opinions thus given are listened to with more attention than when delivered in a dictatorial style. The latter, if attended to at all, although they may *force* conviction, are sure to convey disgust also.

Your aunt and the family here join me in every good wish for you. And I am with sentiments of great regd and Affecte—Yours

Go: Washington

To Alexander Hamilton, November 10, 1787 (Excerpt)

Dear Sir,

I thank you for the pamphlet and for the gazette contained in your letter of the 30th ultimo. For the remaining numbers of Publius I shall acknowledge myself obliged, as I am persuaded the subject will be well handled by the author.

The new Constitution has, as the public prints will have informed you, been handed to the people of this state by a unanimous vote of the assembly; but it is not to be inferred from hence that its opponents are silenced. On the contrary, there are many, and some powerful, ones—some of whom, it is said, by *overshooting* the mark have lessened their weight. Be this as it may, their assiduity stands unrivaled, whilst the friends to the Constitution content themselves with barely avowing their approbation of it. Thus stands the matter with *us* at present; yet my opinion is that the major voice is favorable.

To Catherine Sawbridge Macaulay Graham, November 16, 1787 (Excerpt)

You will undoubtedly, before you receive this, have an opportunity of seeing the plan of government proposed by the Federal Convention for the United States. You will very readily conceive, madam, the difficulties which the Convention had to struggle against, the various and opposite interests which were to be conciliated, the local prejudices which were to be subdued, the diversity of opinions and sentiments which were to be reconciled. And, in fine, the sacrifices which were necessary to be made on all sides for the general welfare combined to make it a work of so intricate and difficult a nature that I think it is much to be wondered at that anything could have been produced with such unanimity as the Constitution proposed.

It is now submitted to the consideration of the people and waits their decision. The legislatures of the several states which have been convened since the Constitution was offered have readily agreed to the calling a convention in their respective states—some by a unanimous vote, and others by a large majority. But whether it will be adopted by the people or not remains yet to be determined. Mrs. Washington and the rest of the family join me in compliments and best wishes for you and Mr. Graham. I have the honor to be madam—Yr Most Obedt & Very Hble Servant

Go: Washington

To David Stuart, November 30, 1787 (Excerpt)

Dear Sir,

Your favor of the 14th came duly to hand. I am sorry to find by it that the opposition is gaining strength. At this, however, I do not wonder. The adversaries to a measure are generally, if not always, more active and violent than the advocates, and frequently employ means which the others do not to accomplish their ends.

I have seen no publication yet that ought, in my judgment, to shake the proposed government in the mind of an impartial public. In a word, I have hardly seen any that is not addressed to the passions of the people and obviously calculated to rouse their fears. Every attempt to amend the Constitution at this time is, in my opinion, idly vain. If there are characters who prefer disunion or separate confederacies to the general government which is offered to them, their opposition may, for aught I know, proceed from principle. But as nothing in my conception is more to be deprecated than a disunion or these separate confederacies, my voice, as far as it will extend, shall be offered in favor of the latter.

That there are some writers (and others perhaps who may not have written) who wish to see these states divided into several confederacies is pretty evident. As an antidote to these opinions, and in order to investigate the ground of objections to the Constitution which is submitted to the people, the *Federalist*, under the signature of Publius, is written. The numbers which have been published I send you. If there is a printer in Richmond who is really well disposed to support the new Constitution, he would do well to give them a place in his paper. They are (I think I may venture to say) written by able men, and before they are finished will, if I mistake not, place matters in a true point of light. Although I am acquainted with some of the writers who are concerned in this work, I am not at liberty to disclose their names, nor would I have it known that they are sent by me to you for promulgation.

To James Madison, December 7, 1787 (Excerpt)

My Dear Sir,

Since my last to you I have been favored with your letters of the 28th of October and 18th of November. With the last came seven numbers of the *Federalist*, under the signature of Publius. For these I thank you. They are forwarded to a gentleman in Richmond for republication. The doing of which, in this state, will, I am persuaded, have a good effect, as there are certainly characters in it who are no friends to a general government—perhaps I might go further and add, who would have no great objection to the introduction of anarchy and confusion.

The solicitude to know what the several state legislatures would do with the Constitution is now transferred to the several conventions thereof, the decisions of which, being more interesting and conclusive, are consequently more anxiously expected than the other. What Pennsylvania and Delaware have done or will do must soon be known. Other conventions are treading closely on their heels; but what the three southern states have done, or in what light the new Constitution is viewed by them, I have not been able to learn. North Carolina, it is said (by some accounts from Richmond), will be governed in a great measure by the conduct of Virginia. The pride of South Carolina will not, I conceive, suffer this influence to operate in her councils; and the disturbances in Georgia will, or at least ought to, show the people of it the propriety of a strict union and the necessity there is for a general government.

If these, with the states eastward and northward of us, should accede to the proposed plan, I think the citizens of this state will have no cause to bless the opponents of it here, if they should carry their point.

To Edward Newenham, December 25, 1787 (Excerpt)

The public attention here is at present wholly employed in considering and animadverting upon the form of government proposed by the late Convention for these states. The inefficacy of our present general system is acknowledged on all hands; and the proposed one has its opponents, but they bear so small a proportion to its friends that there is little or no doubt of its taking place. Three states have already decided in its favor—two unanimously and the other by a majority of two to one. These are the only states whose conventions have as yet determined upon the subject, but from every information the others will be found pretty fully in sentiment with them. The establishment of an energetic general government will disappoint the hopes and expectations of those who are unfriendly to this country, give us a national respectability, and enable us to improve those commercial and political advantages which nature and situation have placed within our reach.

To Thomas Jefferson, Minister to France, January 1, 1788 (Excerpt)

I did myself the honor to forward to you the plan of government formed by the Convention the day after that body rose, but was not a little disappointed, and mortified indeed (as I wished to make the first offering of it to you), to find by a letter from Commodore Jones, dated in New York the 9th of November, that it was, at that time, in his possession. You have undoubtedly received it or some other 'ere now and formed an opinion upon it. The public attention is, at present, wholly engrossed by this important subject. The legislatures of those states (Rhode Island excepted) which have met since the Constitution has been formed have readily assented to its being submitted to a convention chosen by the people. Pennsylvania, New Jersey, and Delaware are the only states whose conventions have as yet decided upon it. In the former it was adopted by 46 to 23, and in the two latter unanimously. Connecticut and Massachusetts are to hold their conventions on the 1st and 2nd Tuesdays of this month, Maryland in April, Virginia in June, and upon the whole it appears, so far as I have had an opportunity of learning the opinions of the people in the several states, that it will be received. There will undoubtedly be more or less opposition to its adoption in most of the states, and in none a more formidable one than in this, as many influential characters here have taken a decided part against it, among whom are Mr. Henry, Colonel Mason, Governor Randolph, and Colonel R. H. Lee. But from every information which I have been able to obtain I think there will be a majority in its favor, notwithstanding their dissension. In New York a considerable opposition will also be given.

    I am much obliged to you, my dear sir, for the account which you gave me of the general state of affairs in Europe. I am glad to hear that the Assemblée des Notables has been productive of good in France. The abuse of the finances being disclosed to the king and the nation must open their eyes and lead to the adoption of such measures as will prove beneficial to them in future. From the public papers it appears that the parliaments of the several provinces, and particularly that of Paris, have acted with great spirit and resolution. Indeed, the rights of mankind, the privileges of the people, and the true principles of liberty seem to have been more generally discussed and better understood throughout Europe since the American Revolution than they were at any former period.

    Although the finances of France and England were such as led you to suppose, at the time you wrote to me, would prevent a rupture between those two powers, yet, if we credit the concurrent accounts from every quarter, there is little doubt but that they have commenced hostilities before this. Russia and the Porte have formally begun the contest, and from appearances (as given to us) it is not improbable but that a pretty general war will be kindled in Europe. Should this be the case, we shall feel more than ever the want of an efficient general government to regulate our commercial concerns, to give us a national respectability, and to connect the political views and interests of the several states under one head in such a manner as will effectually prevent them from forming separate, improper, or indeed any, connection with the European powers which can involve them in their political disputes. For our situation is such as makes it not only unnecessary but extremely imprudent for us to take a part in their quarrels. And whenever a contest happens among them, if we wisely and properly improve the advantages which nature has given us, we may be benefited by their folly—provided we conduct ourselves with circumspection and under proper restriction, for I perfectly agree with you that an extensive speculation, a spirit of gambling, or the introduction of anything which will divert our attention from agriculture must be extremely prejudicial if not ruinous to us. But I conceive under an energetic general government such regulations might be made and such measures taken as would render this country the asylum of pacific and industrious characters from all parts of Europe, would encourage the cultivation of the earth by the high price which its products would command, and would draw the wealth and wealthy men of other nations into our own bosom by giving security to property and liberty to its holders. I have the honor to be with great esteem & regard Dear Sir Yr Most Obedt & Most Hble Servt

Go: Washington

To Edmund Randolph, Governor of Virginia, January 8, 1788 (Excerpt)

The diversity of sentiments upon the important matter which has been submitted to the people was as much expected as it is regretted by me. The various passions and medium by which men are influenced are concomitants of fallibility—engrafted into our nature for the purposes of unerring wisdom. But had I entertained a latent hope (at the time you moved to have the Constitution submitted to a second convention) that a more perfect form would be agreed to—in a word, that any Constitution would be adopted under the impressions and instructions of the members, the publications which have taken place since would have eradicated every form of it. How do the sentiments of the influential characters in *this* state who are opposed to the Constitution, and have favored the public with their opinions, quadrate with each other? Are they not at variance on some of the most important points? If the opponents in the *same* state cannot agree in *their* principles, what prospect is there of a coalescence with the advocates of the measure when the different views and jarring interests of so wide and extended an empire are to be brought forward and combated?

To my judgment, it is more clear than ever that an attempt to amend the Constitution which is submitted would be productive of more heat and greater confusion than can well be conceived. There are some things in the new form, I will readily acknowledge, which never did, and I am persuaded never will, obtain my *cordial* approbation; but I then did conceive, and now do most firmly believe, that, in the aggregate it is the best Constitution that can be obtained at this epocha, and that this or a dissolution of the Union awaits our choice, and are the only alternatives before us. Thus believing, I had not, nor have I now, any hesitation in deciding on which to lean.

I pray your forgiveness for the expression of these sentiments. In acknowledging the receipt of your letter on this subject, it was hardly to be avoided, although I am well disposed to let the matter rest entirely on its own merits—and men's minds to their own workings. With very great esteem & regard—I am &c.

G. Washington

To Comte de Rochambeau, January 8, 1788 (Excerpt)

I now begin to hope that the period is not very distant when this country will make a more respectable figure in the eyes of Europe than it has hitherto done. The Constitution formed by the late Convention appears, as far as my information extends, to be highly acceptable to the people of these states. Jersey, Delaware, and Pennsylvania having already decided in its favor, the two former unanimously and the latter by a majority of two to one, the conventions in the other states have not yet determined upon it, but their dispositions are very favorable. Whenever this government is established we shall regain thus confidence and credit among the European powers which a want of energy in the present Confederation has deprived us of, and shall likewise feel the benefit of those commercial and political advantages which our situation holds out to us. This event must be extremely pleasing to every friend of humanity and peculiarly so to you and others, who must feel interested in the happiness and welfare of this country, from the part which you took in establishing her liberty and independence.

To Nicholas Simon van Winter and Lucretia Wilhelmina van Winter, January 8, 1788

I have received your letter of the 26th of February accompanied by a poem entitled Germanicus. I consider your sending the latter to me as a mark of polite attention which merits my warmest acknowledgment; and I beg you to accept my thanks for that, as well as for the many obliging expressions in your letter.

The muses have always been revered in every age, and in all countries where letters and civilization have made any progress. As they tend to alleviate the misfortunes and soften the sorrows of life, they will ever be respected by the humane and virtuous. I am Yr most obedt Hble Servt

Go: Washington

To Richard Butler, January 10, 1788 (Excerpt)

Dear Sir,

I have received your letter of the 30th of November, accompanied by the Indian vocabulary which you have been so obliging as to forward to me. I am so far from thinking any apology necessary on your part for not having furnished me with the vocabulary at an earlier period that I assure you it is a matter of surprise to me to find that you have been able to complete a work of such difficulty and magnitude as this appears to be in so short a time, under the pain which you must have suffered and the delays occasioned by your misfortune in breaking your leg.

The pleasing satisfaction which you must enjoy from a reflection that you have exerted yourself to throw light upon the original history of this country, to gratify the curiosity of the philosopher, and to forward the researches into the probable connection and communication between the northern parts of America and those of Asia, must make you a more ample compensation for the laborious task which you have executed than my warmest acknowledgments, which, however I must beg you to accept.

The observations contained in your letter respecting the different tribes of Indians inhabiting the western country, the traditions which prevail among them, and the reasoning deduced therefrom, are very valuable and may lead to some useful discoveries. Those works which are found upon the Ohio, and other traces of the country's being once inhabited by a race of people more ingenious, at least, if not more civilized than those who at present dwell there, have excited the attention and inquiries of the curious to learn from whence they came, whither they are gone, and something of their history. Any clue, therefore, which can lead to a knowledge to these must be gratefully received.

To Marquis de Lafayette, January 10, 1788 (Excerpt)

It is with great pleasure I transmit to you by this conveyance a vocabulary of the Shawanese and Delaware languages. Your perfect acquaintance with General Richard Butler, the same worthy officer who served under your orders, and who has taken the trouble to compile them, supersedes the necessity of my saying anything in support of their veracity and correctness. I likewise send a shorter specimen of the language of the southern Indians. It was procured by that ingenious gentleman, the Honorable Mr. Hawkins, a member of Congress from North Carolina, and lately a commissioner from the United States to Indians of the south. I heartily wish the attempt of that singular great character, the Empress of Russia, to form a universal dictionary may be attended with the merited success. To know the affinity of tongues seems to be one step towards promoting the affinity of nations. Would to God the harmony of nations was an object that lay nearest to the hearts of sovereigns, and that the incentives to peace (of which commerce and facility of understanding each other are not the most inconsiderable) might be daily increased! Should the present or any other efforts of mine to procure information respecting the different dialects of the aborigines in America serve to reflect a ray of light on the obscure subject of language in general, I shall be highly gratified. For I love to indulge the contemplation of human nature in a progressive state of improvement and melioration. And if the idea would not be considered as visionary and chimerical, I could fondly hope that the present plan of the great Potentate of the north might, in some measure, lay the foundation for that assimilation of language which, producing assimilation of manners and interests, should one day remove many of the causes of hostility from amongst mankind.

At this moment, however, it appears by the current of intelligence from your side of the Atlantic that but too many motives and occasions exist for interrupting the public tranquility. A war between the Russians and Turks, we learn, has broken out. How far or in what manner this may involve other nations seems to us, at this distance, uncertain. Extraordinary speculations and expectations arise from the conduct of the king of Prussia in the Dutch and the emperor of Germany in the Austrian Netherlands. Nothing as yet has come to our knowledge which indicates with certainty whether hostilities will take place between France and England, or, in that event, how extensively the flames of war will spread. We are apprehensive we have but too much reason to bewail the fate of the Dutch patriots.

To guard against the similar calamities of domestic discord or foreign interposition, and effectually to secure our liberties, with all the benefits of an efficient government, is now the important subject that engrosses the attention of all our part of America. You will doubtless have seen in the public papers in what manner the new Constitution has been attacked and defended. There have been some compositions published in its defense which I think will at least do credit to American genius. I dare say its principles and tendencies have also before this time been amply discussed in Europe. Here, that is in United America, it is strongly advocated by a very great and decided majority. The conventions in the states of Jersey and Delaware have *unanimously* adopted it, and that of Pennsylvania by a majority of two to one. No other state has yet had an opportunity of deciding. New England (with the exception of Rhode Island, which seems itself, politically speaking, to be an exception from all that is good), it is believed, will cheerfully and fully accept it. And there is little doubt but that the three southern states will do the same. In Virginia and New York its fate is somewhat more questionable, though, in my private opinion, I have no hesitation to believe there will be a clear majority in its favor in the former. Of the latter, I can say nothing from my own knowledge. Its advocates there generally conclude that they shall carry it.

Upon this summary view, you will perceive, my dear Marquis, the highest probability exists that the proposed Constitution will be adopted by more than nine states, by some period early in the coming summer.

To Marquis de Lafayette, February 7, 1788 (Excerpt)

I shall myself be happy in forming an acquaintance and cultivating a friendship with the new Minister Plenipotentiary of France, whom you have commended as "a sensible and honest man." These are qualities too rare and too precious not to merit one's particular esteem. You may be persuaded he will be well received by the Congress of the United States, because they will not only be influenced in their conduct by his individual merits, but also by their affection for the nation of whose sovereign he is the representative. For it is an undoubted fact that the people of America entertain a grateful remembrance of past services as well as a favorable disposition for commercial and friendly connections with your nation.

You appear to be, as might be expected from a real friend to this country, anxiously concerned about its present political situation. So far as I am able, I shall be happy in gratifying that friendly solicitude. As to my sentiments with respect to the merits of the new Constitution, I will disclose them without reserve (although by passing through the post offices they should become known to all the world) for, in truth, I have nothing to conceal on that subject. It appears to me, then, little short of a miracle that the delegates from so many different states (which states you know are also different from each other in their manners, circumstances, and prejudices) should unite in forming a system of national government so little liable to well-founded objections. Nor am I yet such an enthusiastic, partial, or undiscriminating admirer of it as not to perceive it is tinctured with some real (though not radical) defects. The limits of a letter would not suffer me to go fully into an examination of them, nor would the discussion be entertaining or profitable; I therefore forbear to touch upon it. With regard to the two great points (the pivots on which the whole machine must move) my creed is simply:

1st: That the general government is not invested with more powers than are indispensably necessary to perform the functions of a good government, and, consequently, that no objection ought to be made against the quantity of power delegated to it.

2ly: That these powers (as the appointment of all rulers will forever arise from and, at short stated intervals, recur to the free suffrage of the people) are so distributed among the legislative, executive, and judicial branches, into which the general government is arranged, that it can never be in danger of degenerating into a monarchy, an oligarchy, an aristocracy, or any other despotic or oppressive form, so long as there shall remain any virtue in the body of the people.

I would not be understood, my dear Marquis, to speak of consequences which may be produced in the revolution of ages by corruption of morals, profligacy of manners, and listlessness for the preservation of the natural and unalienable rights of mankind, nor of the successful usurpations that may be established at such an unpropitious juncture upon the ruins of liberty, however providently guarded and secured, as these are contingencies against which no human prudence can effectually provide. It will at least be a recommendation to the proposed Constitution that it is provided with more checks and barriers against the introduction of tyranny, and those of a nature less liable to be surmounted, than any government hitherto instituted among mortals hath possessed. We are not to expect perfection in this world; but mankind, in modern times, have apparently made some progress in the science of government. Should that which is now offered to the people of America be found an experiment less perfect than it can be made, a constitutional door is left open for its amelioration. Some respectable characters have wished that the states, after having pointed out whatever alterations and amendments may be judged necessary, would appoint another federal convention to modify it upon these documents. For myself, I have wondered that sensible men should not see the impracticability of the scheme. The members would go fortified with such instructions that nothing but discordant ideas could prevail. Had I but slightly suspected (at the time when the late Convention was in session) that another convention would not be likely to agree upon a better form of government, I should now be confirmed in the fixed belief that they would not be able to agree upon any system whatever. So many—I may add, such contradictory and, in my opinion, unfounded—objections have been urged against the system in contemplation, many of which would operate equally against every efficient government that might be proposed. I will only add, as a farther opinion founded on the maturest deliberation, that there is no alternative, no hope of alteration, no intermediate resting place between the adoption of this and a recurrence to an unqualified state of anarchy, with all its deplorable consequences.

Since I had the pleasure of writing to you last, no material alteration in the political state of affairs has taken place to change the prospect of the Constitution's being adopted by nine states or more. Pennsylvania, Delaware, Jersey, and Connecticut have already done it. It is also said Georgia has acceded. Massachusetts, which is perhaps thought to be rather more doubtful than when I last addressed you, is now in convention.

To Eléanor-François-Elie Moustier, February 7, 1788 (Excerpt)

The fidelity, honor, and bravery of the troops of your nation, to which I have been a witness; the enlightened sentiments of patriotism and the delicate feelings of friendship which have actuated great numbers of your compatriots, with whom I may boast the happiness of being intimately connected; and above all that lively interest which your illustrious monarch and his faithful subjects took in the success of the American arms and the confirmation of our independence have endeared the national character to me, formed attachments, and left impressions which no distance in time or contingency in event can possibly remove. Though but a private citizen myself, and in a measure secluded from the world, I am conscious the assertion will be founded while I venture to affirm such are the feelings and such the affections of the American people.

To Benjamin Lincoln, February 11, 1788 (Excerpt)

My Dear Sir,

As you must be convinced that whatever affects your happiness or welfare cannot be indifferent to me, I need not tell you that I was most sensibly affected by your letter of the 20th of January. Yes, my dear sir, I sincerely condole with you the loss of a worthy, amiable, and valuable son! Although I had not the happiness of a personal acquaintance with him, yet the character which he sustained, and his near connection with you, are to me sufficient reasons to lament his death.

It is unnecessary for me to offer any consolation on the present occasion; for to a mind like yours it can only be drawn from that source which never fails to give a bountiful supply to those who reflect justly. Time alone can blunt the keen edge of afflictions. Philosophy and religion hold out to us such hopes as will, upon proper reflection, enable us to bear with fortitude the most calamitous incidents of life; and these are all that can be expected from the feelings of humanity, and all which they will yield.

I thank you, my dear sir, for the information you forwarded me of the proceedings of your convention. It is unhappy that a matter of such high importance cannot be discussed with that candor and moderation which would throw[12] light on the subject and place its merits in a proper point of view. But in an assembly so large as your convention must be, and composed of such various and opposite characters, it is almost impossible but that some things will occur which would rouse the passions of the most moderate man on earth. It is, however, to be hoped that your final decision will be agreeable to the wishes of good men and favorable to the Constitution.

To James Madison, March 2, 1788

My Dear Sir,

The decision of Massachusetts, notwithstanding its concomitants, is a severe stroke to the opponents of the proposed Constitution in this state, and with the favorable determinations of the states which have gone before, and such as are likely to follow after, will have a powerful operation on the minds of men who are not actuated more by disappointment, passion, and resentment than they are by moderation, prudence, and candor. Of the first description, however, it is to be lamented that there are too many—and among them *some* who would hazard *every* thing rather than their opposition should fail, or the sagacity of their prognostications should be impeached by an issue contrary to their predictions.

The determination you have come to will give pleasure to your friends. From those in your own county you will learn with more certainty than from me the expediency of your attending the election in it. With *some*, to have differed in sentiment is to have passed the rubicon of their friendship, although you should go no further. With others (for the honor of humanity) I hope there is more liberality. But the consciousness of having discharged that duty which we owe to our country is superior to all other considerations, and will place smaller matters in a secondary point of view.

His Most Christian Majesty speaks and acts in a style not very pleasing to republican ears or to republican forms; nor do I think this language is altogether so to the temper of his own subjects at *this* day. Liberty, when it begins to take root, is a plant of rapid growth. The checks he endeavors to give it, however warrantable by ancient usage, will, more than probably, kindle a flame which may not easily be extinguished, though for a while it may be smothered by the armies at his command and the nobility in his interest. When the people are oppressed with taxes and have cause to suspect that there has been a misapplication of their money, the language of despotism is but illy brooked. This and the mortification which the pride of the nation has sustained in the affairs of Holland (if one may judge from appearances) may be productive of events which prudence will not mention.

Tomorrow the elections for delegates to the convention of this state commences—and, as they will tread close on the heels of each other, this month becomes interesting and important. With the most friendly sentiments and affectionate regards, I am, My dear Sir Your Obedient

Go: Washington

To Eléanor-François-Elie Moustier, March 26, 1788 (Excerpt)

While I am highly gratified with the justice you do me in appreciating the friendly sentiments I entertain for the French nation, I cannot avoid being equally astonished and mortified in learning that you had met with any subject of discontent or inquietude since your arrival in America. Be assured, sir, as nothing could have been more unexpected, so nothing can now give me greater pleasure than to be instrumental in removing (as far as might be in the power of a private citizen as I am) every occasion of uneasiness that may have occurred. I have even hoped, from the short time of your residence here, and the partial acquaintance you may have had with the characters of the persons, that a natural distance in behavior and reserve in address may have appeared as intentional coldness and neglect. I am sensible that the apology itself, though it should be well founded, would be but an indifferent one, yet it would be better than none, while it served to prove that it is our misfortune not to have the same cheerfulness in appearance and facility in deportment which some nations possess. And this I believe in a certain degree to be a real fact, and that such a reception is sometimes given by individuals as may affect a foreigner with very disagreeable sensations, when not the least shadow of an affront is intended.

As I know the predilections of most of our leading characters for your nation; as I had seen the clearest proofs of affection for your king given by the people of this country on the birth of the Dauphin; as I had heard before the receipt of your letter that you had been received at your public audience by Congress with all the marks of attention which had ever been bestowed upon a representative of any sovereign power; and as I found that your personal character stood in the fairest point of light; I must confess, I could not have conceived that there was one person in public office in the United States capable of having treated with indifference, much less with indignity, the representative from a court with which we have ever been upon the most friendly terms. And confident I am that it is only necessary for such conduct to be known to be detested.

But in the mean, so ardently do I wish to efface any ill impressions that may have been made upon Your Excellency's mind to the prejudice of the public by individuals that I must again repeat that I am egregiously deceived if the people of this country are not in general extremely well affected to France. The prejudices against that kingdom had been so riveted by our English connection and English policy that it was some time before our people could entirely get the better of them. This, however, was thoroughly accomplished in the course of the war—and I may venture to say that a greater revolution never took place in the sentiments of one people respecting another. Now as none of their former attachments have been revived for Britain, and as no subject of uneasiness has turned up with respect to France, any disgust or enmity to the latter would involve a mystery beyond my comprehension. For I had always believed that some apparent cause, powerful in its nature and progressive in its operation, must be employed to produce a change in national sentiments. But no prejudice has been revived, no jealousy excited, no interest adduced, and, in short, no cause has existed (to my knowledge) which could have wrought a revolution unfriendly to your nation. If one or a few persons in New York have given a different specimen of thinking and acting, I rely too much upon your candor to apprehend that you will impute it to the American people at large.

I am happy to learn that Your Excellency is meditating to strengthen the commercial ties that connect the two nations, and that your ideas of effecting it by placing the arrangements upon the basis of mutual advantage coincide exactly with my own. Treaties which are not built upon reciprocal benefits are not likely to be of long duration. Warmly as I wish to second your views, it is a subject of regret that my little acquaintance with commercial affairs and my seclusion from public life have not put me in a state of preparation to answer your several questions with accuracy. I will endeavor to inform myself of the most interesting particulars & shall take a pleasure in communicating the result.

To Henry Knox, March 30, 1788 (Excerpt)

The conduct of the state of New Hampshire has baffled all calculation, and happened extremely mal-apropos for the election of delegates to the convention of this state. For be the *real* cause of the adjournment to so late a day what it may, the Anti-Federal party with us do not scruple to declare that it was done to await the issue of this convention before it would decide—and add that if this state should reject it, all those which are to follow will do the same, and consequently the Constitution cannot obtain, as there will be only eight states in favor of the measure.

Had it not been for this untoward event, the opposition in this state would have proved entirely unavailing, notwithstanding the unfair conduct (I might have bestowed a harsher epithet without doing injustice) which has been practiced to rouse the fears and to inflame the passions of the people. What will be the result *now* is difficult for me to say with any degree of certainty, as I have seen but a partial return of the delegates, and not well acquainted with the political sentiments even of those few. In the northern part of the state the tide of sentiment—I know—is *generally* in favor of the proposed system. In the southern part—*I am told*—it is the reverse. While the middle, it is said, is pretty much divided. The Kentucky district will have great weight in deciding this question; and the idea of its becoming an impediment to its separation has got hold of them, while no pains is spared to inculcate a belief that the government proposed will, without scruple or delay, barter away the right of navigation to the River Mississippi.

The postponement in New Hampshire will also unquestionably give strength and vigor to the opposition in New York, and possibly will render Rhode Island more backward than she otherwise would have been, if all the New England states had *finally* decided in favor of the measure.

To John Armstrong, April 25, 1788 (Excerpt)

I well remember the observation you made in your letter to me of last year, "that my domestic retirement must suffer an interruption." This took place, notwithstanding it was utterly repugnant to my feelings, my interest, and my wishes. I sacrificed every private consideration and personal enjoyment to the earnest and pressing solicitations of those who saw and knew the alarming situation of our public concerns, and had no other end in view but to promote the interest of their country, and conceiving that under those circumstances, and at so critical a moment, an absolute refusal to act might, on my part, be construed as a total dereliction of my country, if imputed to no worse motives. Although you say the same motives induce you to think that another tour of duty of this kind will fall to my lot, I cannot but hope that you will be disappointed, for I am so wedded to a state of retirement and find the occupations of a rural life so congenial with my feelings, that to be drawn unto public at this[13] advanced age would be a sacrifice that could admit of no compensation.

Your remarks on the impressions which will be made on the manners and sentiments of the people by the example of those who are first called to act under the proposed government are very just, and I have no doubt but (if the proposed Constitution obtains) those persons who are chosen to administer it will have wisdom enough to discern the influence which their examples as rulers and legislators may have on the body of the people, and will have virtue enough to pursue that line of conduct which will most conduce to the happiness of their country. And as the first transactions of a nation, like those of an individual upon his entrance into life, make the deepest impression and are to form the leading traits in its character, they will undoubtedly pursue those measures which will best tend to the restoration of public and private faith and of consequence promote our national respectability and individual welfare.

That the proposed Constitution will admit of amendments is acknowledged by its warmest advocates, but to make such amendments as may be proposed by the several states the condition of its adoption would, in my opinion, amount to a complete rejection of it. For upon examination of the objections which are made by the opponents in different states and the amendments which have been proposed, it will be found that what would be a favorite object with one state is the very thing which is strenuously opposed by another. The truth is, men are too apt to be swayed by local prejudices, and those who are so fond of amendments which have the particular interest of their own state in view cannot extend their ideas to the general welfare of the Union. They do not consider that for every sacrifice which they make, they receive an ample compensation by the sacrifices which are made by other states for their benefit, and that those very things which they give up will operate to their advantage through the medium of the general interest. In addition to these considerations it should be remembered that a constitutional door is open for such amendments as shall be thought necessary by nine states. When I reflect upon these circumstances I am surprised to find that any person who is acquainted with the critical state of our public affairs, and knows the variety of views, interests, feelings, and prejudices which must be consulted and conciliated in framing a general government for these states, and how little propositions in themselves so opposite to each other will tend to promote that desirable an end, can wish to make amendments the ultimatum for adopting the offered system.

I am very glad to find that the opposition in your state, however formidable it has been represented, is, generally speaking, composed of such characters as cannot have an extensive influence. Their forte, as well as that of those of the same class in other states, seems to lie in misrepresentation and a desire to inflame the passions and to alarm the fears by noisy declamation rather than to convince the understanding by some arguments or fair and impartial statements. Baffled in their attacks upon the Constitution, they have attempted to vilify and debase the characters who formed it; but even here I trust they will not succeed. Upon the whole I doubt whether the opposition to the Constitution will not ultimately be productive of more good than evil. It has called forth in its defense abilities (which would not perhaps have been otherwise exerted) that have thrown new lights upon the science of government. They have given the rights of man a full and fair discussion, and have explained them in so clear and forcible a manner as cannot fail to make a lasting impression upon those who read the best publications on the subject, and particularly the pieces under the signature of Publius. There will be a greater weight of abilities opposed to the system in the convention of this state than there has been in any other, but notwithstanding the unwearied pains which have been taken and the vigorous efforts which will be made in the convention to prevent its adoption, I have not the smallest doubt but it will obtain here.

I am sorry to hear that the college in your neighborhood is in so declining a state as you represent it, and that it is likely to suffer a farther injury by the loss of Dr. Nisbet, whom you are afraid you shall not be able to support in a proper manner on account of the scarcity of cash, which prevents parents from sending their children hither. This is one of the numerous evils which arise from the want of a general regulating power; for in a country like this, where equal liberty is enjoyed, where every man may reap his own harvest, which by proper attention will afford him much more than what is necessary for his own consumption, and where there is so ample a field for every mercantile and mechanical exertion, if there cannot be money found to answer the common purposes of education, not to mention the necessary commercial circulation, it is evident that there is something amiss in the ruling political power which requires a steady, regulating, and energetic hand to connect and control. That money is not to be had, every man's experience tells him, and the great fall in the price of property is an unequivocal and melancholy proof of it—when, if that property was well secured, faith and justice well preserved, a stable government well administered, and confidence restored, the tide of population and wealth would flow to us from every part of the globe and, with a due sense of the blessing, make us the happiest people upon earth. With sentiments of very great esteem and regard I am Dr Sir &c.

Go. Washington

To François-Jean de Beauvoir Chastellux, April 25, 1788 (Excerpt)

My Dear Marquis,

In reading your very friendly and acceptable letter of the 21st of December 1787, which came to hand by the last mail, I was, as you may well suppose, not less delighted than surprised to come across that plain American word—"my wife." A wife! Well, my dear Marquis, I can hardly refrain from smiling to find you are caught at last. I saw by the eulogium you often made on the happiness of domestic life in America that you had swallowed the bait and that you would as surely be taken (one day or another), as you were a philosopher and a soldier. So your day has, at length, come. I am glad of it with all my heart and soul. It is quite good enough for you. Now you are well served for coming to fight in favor of the American rebels, all the way across the Atlantic Ocean, by catching that terrible contagion—domestic felicity—which time, like the smallpox or the plague, a man can have only once in his life, because it commonly lasts him (at least with us in America—I don't know how you manage these matters in France) for his whole life time. And yet after all the maledictions you so richly merit on the subject, the worst wish which I can find in my heart to make against Madame de Chastellux and yourself is that you may neither of you ever get the better of this same—domestic felicity—during the entire course of your mortal existence.

If so wonderful an event should have occasioned me, my dear Marquis, to have written in a strange style, you will understand me as clearly as if I had said (what, in plain English, is the simple truth), do me the justice to believe that I take a heartfelt interest in whatsoever concerns your happiness. And in this view, I sincerely congratulate you on your auspicious matrimonial connection. I am happy to find that Madame de Chastellux is so intimately connected with the Duchess of Orleans, as I have always understood that this noble lady was an illustrious pattern of connubial love, as well as an excellent model of virtue in general.

While you have been making love, under the banner of Hymen, the great personages in the north have been making war, under the inspiration, or rather under the infatuation, of Mars. Now, for my part, I humble conceive you have had much the best and wisest of the bargain. For certainly it is more consonant to all the principles of reason and religion (natural and revealed) to replenish the earth with inhabitants rather than to depopulate it by killing those already in existence. Besides, it is time for the age of knight-errantry and mad-heroism to be at an end. Your young military men, who want to reap the harvest of laurels, don't care (I suppose) how many seeds of war are sown. But for the sake of humanity, it is devoutly to be wished that the manly employment of agriculture and the humanizing benefits of commerce would supersede the waste of war and the rage of conquest, that the swords might be turned into plowshares, the spears into pruning hooks, and, as the scripture expresses it, the nations learn war no more.

Now I will give you a little news from this side of the water, and then finish. As for us, we are plodding on in the dull road of peace and politics. We who live in these ends of the earth only hear of the rumours of war, like the roar of distant thunder. It is to be hoped our remote local situation will prevent us from being swept into its vortex.

The Constitution, which was proposed by the Federal Convention, has been adopted by the States of Massachusetts, Connecticut, Jersey, Pennsylvania, Delaware, and Georgia. No state has rejected it. The convention of Maryland is now setting and will probably adopt it, as that of South Carolina is expected to do in May. The other conventions will assemble early in the summer. Hitherto there has been much greater unanimity in favor of the proposed government than could have been reasonably expected. Should it be adopted (and I think it will be), America will lift up her head again and in a few years become respectable among the nations. It is a flattering and consolatory reflection that our rising republics have the good wishes of all the philosophers, patriots, and virtuous men in all nations, and that they look upon us as a kind of asylum for mankind. God grant that we may not disappoint their honest expectations by our folly or perverseness! With sentiments of the purest attachment and esteem I have the honor to be My dear Marquis Yr most obedient and Most humble Servant

Go. Washington

To Marquis de Lafayette, April 28, 1788 (Excerpt)

This I lay out to be a letter of politics. We are looking anxiously across the Atlantic for news, and you are looking anxiously back again for the same purpose. It is an interesting subject to contemplate how far the war, kindled in the north of Europe, may extend its conflagrations, and what may be the result before its extinction. The Turk appears to have lost his old and acquired a new connection. Whether England has not, in the hour of her pride, overacted her part and pushed matters too far for her own interest, time will discover; but, in my opinion (though from my distance and want of minute information I should form it with diffidence) the affairs of that nation cannot long go on in the same prosperous train. In spite of expedients and in spite of resources, the paper bubble will one day burst. And it will whelm many in the ruins. I hope the affairs of France are gradually sliding into a better state. Good effects may and I trust will ensue, without any public convulsion. France, were her resources properly managed and her administrations wisely conducted, is (as you justly observe) much more potent in the scale of empire than her rivals at present seem inclined to believe.

I notice with pleasure the additional immunities and facilities in trade which France has granted by the late royal arret to the United States. I flatter myself it will have the desired effect in some measure of augmenting the commercial intercourse. From the productions and wants of the two countries, their trade with each other is certainly capable of great amelioration, to be actuated by a spirit of unwise policy. For so surely as ever we shall have an efficient government established, so surely will that government impose retaliating restrictions, to a certain degree, upon the trade of Britain. At present, or under our existing form of Confederation, it would be idle to think of making commercial regulations on our part. One state passes a prohibitory law respecting some article; another state opens wide the avenue for its admission. One assembly makes a system; another assembly unmakes it. Virginia, in the very last session of her legislature, was about to have passed some of the most extravagant and preposterous edicts on the subject of trade that ever stained the leaves of a legislative code. It is in vain to hope for a remedy of these and innumerable other evils, until a general government shall be adopted.

The convention of six states only have as yet accepted the new Constitution. No one has rejected it. It is believed that the convention of Maryland, which is now in session, and that of South Carolina, which is to assemble on the 12th of May, will certainly adopt it. It is, also, since the elections of members for the convention have taken place in this state, more general believed that it will be adopted here than it was before those elections were made. There will, however, be powerful and eloquent speeches on both sides of the question in the Virginia convention. But as Pendleton, Wythe, Blair, Madison, Jones, Nicholas, Innis, and many other of our first characters will be advocates for its adoption, you may suppose the weight of abilities will rest on that side. Henry and Mason are its great adversaries. The governor, if he opposes it at all, will do it feebly.

On the general merits of this proposed Constitution, I wrote to you some time ago my sentiments pretty freely. That letter had not been received by you when you addressed to me the last of yours which has come to my hands. I had never supposed that perfection could be the result of accommodation and mutual concession. The opinion of Mr. Jefferson and yourself is certainly a wise one, that the Constitution ought by all means to be accepted by nine states before any attempt should be made to procure amendments. For if that acceptance shall not previously take place, men's minds will be so much agitated and soured that the danger will be greater than ever of our becoming a disunited people. Whereas, on the other hand, with prudence in temper and a spirit of moderation, every essential alteration may, in the process of time, be expected.

You will doubtless have seen that it was owing to this conciliatory and patriotic principle that the convention of Massachusetts adopted the Constitution in toto, but recommended a number of specific alterations and quieting explanations, as an early, serious, and unremitting subject of attention. Now, although it is not to be expected that every individual in society will or can ever be brought to agree upon what is, exactly, the best form of government, yet there are many things in the Constitution which only need to be explained in order to prove equally satisfactory to all parties. For example, there was not a member of the Convention, I believe, who had the least objection to what is contended for by the advocates for a *bill of rights* and *trial by jury*. The first, where the people evidently retained everything which they did not in express terms give up, was considered nugatory, as you will find to have been more fully explained by Mr. Wilson and others. And as to the second, it was only the difficulty of establishing a mode which should not interfere with the fixed modes of any of the states that induced the Convention to leave it as a matter of future adjustment.

There are other points on which opinions would be more likely to vary— as, for instance, on the ineligibility of the same person for president after he should have served a certain course of years. Guarded so effectually as the proposed Constitution is in respect to the prevention of bribery and undue influence in the choice of president, I confess I differ widely myself from Mr. Jefferson and you as to the necessity or expediency of rotation in that appointment. The matter was fairly discussed in the Convention, and to my full convictions, though I cannot have time or room to sum up the arguments in this letter. There cannot, in my judgment, be the least danger that the president will by any practicable intrigue ever be able to continue himself one moment in office, much less perpetuate himself in it—but in the last stage of corrupted morals and political depravity. And even then there is as much danger that any other species of domination would prevail—though when a people shall have become incapable of governing themselves and fit for a master, it is of little consequence from what quarter he comes.

Under an extended view of this part of the subject, I can see no propriety in precluding ourselves from the services of any man who on some great emergency shall be deemed universally most capable of serving the public. In answer to the observations you make on the probability of my election to the presidency (knowing me as you do), I need only say that it has no enticing charms and no fascinating allurements for me. However, it might not be decent for me to say I would refuse to accept or even to speak much about an appointment which may never take place. For in so doing, one might possibly incur the application of the moral resulting from that fable in which the fox is represented as inveighing against the sourness of the grapes because he could not reach them. All that it will be necessary to add, my dear Marquis, in order to shew my decided predilection is that (at my time of life and under my circumstances) the increasing infirmities of nature and the growing love of retirement do not permit me to entertain a wish beyond that of living and dying an honest man on my own farm. Let those follow the pursuits of ambition and fame who have a keener relish for them, or who may have more years in store for the enjoyment!

To Samuel Griffin, April 30, 1788 (Excerpt)

Influenced by a heartfelt desire to promote the cause of science in general and the prosperity of the College of William and Mary in particular, I accept the office of chancellor in the same, and request you will be pleased to give official notice thereof to the learned body who have thought proper to honor me with the appointment. I consider fully in their strenuous endeavors for placing the system of education on such a basis as will render it most beneficial to the state and the republic of letters, as well as to the more extensive interests of humanity and religion. In return, they will do me the justice to believe that I shall not be tardy in giving my cheerful concurrence to such measures as may be best calculated for the attainment of those desirable and important objects.

To Marquis de Lafayette, May 28, 1788 (Excerpt)

Notwithstanding you are acquainted with Mr. Barlow[14] in person, and with his works by reputation, I thought I would just write you a line by him in order to recommend him the more particularly to your civilities. Mr. Barlow is considered by those who are good judges to be a genius of the first magnitude, and to be one of those bards who hold the keys of the gate by which patriots, sages, and heroes are admitted to immortality. Such are your ancient bards, who are both the priest and doorkeepers to the temple of fame, and these, my dear Marquis, are no vulgar functions. Men of real talents in arms have commonly approved themselves patriots of the liberal arts and friends to the poets of their own as well as former times. In some instances, by acting reciprocally, heroes have made poets and poets heroes. Alexander the Great is said to have been enraptured with the poems of Homer and to have lamented that he had not a rival muse to celebrate his actions. Julius Caesar is well known to have been a man of a highly cultivated understanding and taste. Augustus was the professed and munificent rewarder of poetical merit—nor did he lose the return of having his achievements immortalized in song. The Augustan age is proverbial for intellectual refinement and elegance in composition; in it the harvest of laurels and bays was wonderfully mingled together. The age of your Louis the Fourteenth, which produced a multitude of great poets and great captains, will never be forgotten; nor will that of Queen Ann in England, for the same cause, ever cease to reflect a luster upon the kingdom. Although we are yet in our cradle as a nation, I think the efforts of the human mind with us are sufficient to refute (by incontestable facts) the doctrines of those who have asserted that everything degenerates in America. Perhaps we shall be found, at this moment, not inferior to the rest of the world in the performances of our poets and painters, notwithstanding many of the incitements are wanting which operate powerfully among older nations. For it is generally understood that excellence in those sister arts has been the result of easy circumstances, public encouragements, and an advanced stage of society. I observe that the critics in England who speak highly of the American poetical geniuses (and their praises may be the more relied upon as they seem to be reluctantly exhorted) are not pleased with the tribute of applause which is paid to your nation. It is a reason why they should be the more caressed by your nation. I hardly know how it is that I am drawn thus far in observations on a subject so foreign from those in which we are mostly engaged, farming and politics, unless because I had little news to tell you.

Since I had the pleasure of writing to you by the last packet, the convention of Maryland has ratified the Federal Constitution by a majority of 63 to 11 voices. That makes the seventh state which has adopted it. Next Monday the convention in Virginia will assemble. We have still good hopes of its adoption here, though by no great plurality of votes. South Carolina has probably decided favorably before this time. The plot thickens fast. A few short weeks will determine the political fate of America for the present generation and probably produce no small influence on the happiness of society through a long succession of ages to come. Should everything proceed with harmony and consent according to our actual wishes and expectations, I will confess to you sincerely, my dear Marquis, it will be so much beyond anything we had a right to imagine or expect eighteen months ago that it will demonstrate as visibly the finger of Providence, as any possible event in the course of human affairs can ever designate it. It is impracticable for you or anyone who has not been on the spot to realize the change in men's minds and the progress towards rectitude in thinking and acting which will then have been made.

To Francis van der Kemp, May 28, 1788 (Excerpt)

Sir,

The letter which you did me the favor to address to me on the 15th of this instant from New York has been duly received, and I take the speediest occasion to welcome your arrival on the American shore.

I had always hoped that this land might become a safe and agreeable asylum to the virtuous and persecuted part of mankind, to whatever nation they might belong. But I shall be the more particularly happy if this country can be, by any means, useful to the patriots of Holland, with whose situation I am peculiarly touched, and of whose public virtue I entertain a great opinion.

You may rest assured, sir, of my best and most friendly sentiments of your suffering compatriots, and that, while I deplore the calamities to which many of the most worthy members of your community have been reduced by the late foreign interposition in the interior affairs of the United Netherlands, I shall flatter myself that many of them will be able with the wrecks of their fortunes, which may have escaped the extensive devastation, to settle themselves in comfort, freedom, and ease in some corner of the vast regions of America. The spirit of the religions and the genius of the political institutions of this country must be an inducement. Under a good government (which I have no doubt we shall establish) this country certainly promises greater advantages than almost any other to persons of moderate property who are determined to be sober, industrious, and virtuous members of society. And it must not be concealed that a knowledge that these are the general characteristics of your compatriots would be a principal reason to consider their advent as a valuable acquisition to our infant settlements. If you should meet with as favorable circumstances as I hope will attend your first operations, I think it probable that your coming will be the harbinger for many more to adventure across the Atlantic.

To James Madison, June 8, 1788 (Excerpt)

My Dear Sir,

I am much obliged by the few lines you wrote to me on the 4th; and, though it is yet too soon to rejoice, one cannot avoid being pleased at the auspicious opening of the business of your convention. Though an ulterior opinion of the decision of this state on the Constitution would at any time previous to the discussion of it in the convention have been premature, yet I have never despaired of its adoption here. What I have mostly apprehended is that the insidious arts of its opposers to alarm the fears and to inflame the passions of the multitude may have produced instructions to the delegates that would shut the door against argument and be a bar to the exercise of the judgment. If this is not the case I have no doubt but that the good sense of this country will prevail against the local views of designing characters and the arrogant opinions of chagrined and disappointed men. The decision of Maryland and South Carolina by such large majorities and the moral certainty of the adoption by New Hampshire will make *all* except desperate men look before they leap into the dark consequences of rejection.

The ratification by eight states without a negative; by three of them unanimously; by six against one in another; by three to one in another; by two for one in two more; and by *all* the weight of *abilities* and *property* in the other; is enough, one would think, to produce a cessation of opposition. I do not mean that number alone is sufficient to produce conviction in the mind, but I think it is enough to produce some change in the conduct of any man who entertains a doubt of his infallibility.

To David Stuart, June 8, 1788 (Excerpt)

Dear Sir,

I have received your favor of the 4th and am happy to find that matters so far as you had proceeded had assumed an auspicious aspect. I hope the good sense of the country will be superior to and overcome the local views of some, and the arrogant and malignant pride of others. The decided majority by which the proposed Constitution was ratified in South Carolina, and the almost absolute certainty of its adoption in New Hampshire, will contribute more than a little to dispel the mist which may have blinded the eyes of the wavering (if they have minds open to conviction and capable of foreseeing the consequences of rejection and separation) and must, one would think, turn them into the right road.

To Marquis de Lafayette, June 18, 1788 (Excerpt)

There seems to be a great deal of bloody work cut out for this summer in the north of Europe. If war, want, and plague are to desolate those huge armies that are assembled, who that has the feelings of a man can refrain from shedding a tear over the miserable victims of regal ambition? It is really a strange thing that there should not be room enough in the world for men to live without cutting one another's throats. As France, Spain, and England have hardly recovered from the wounds of the late war, I would fain hope they will hardly be dragged into this. However, if the war should be protracted (and not end in a campaign, as you intimate it possibly may) there seems to be a probability of other powers being engaged on one side or the other. By the British papers (which are our principal source of intelligence, though not always to be relied upon, as you know) it appears that the Spaniards are fitting out a considerable fleet and that the English ministry have prohibited the subjects of their kingdom from furnishing transports for the Empress of Russia. France must be too intent on its own domestic affairs to wish to interfere; and all have not heard that the king of Prussia, since his exports in Holland, has taken it into his head to meddle with other people's business. I cannot say that I am sorry to hear that the Algerines and other piratical powers are about to assist the Porte, because I think Russia will not forget and that she will take some leisure moment, just to keep her fleets in exercise, for exterminating those nests of miscreants.

I like not much the situation of affairs in France. The bold demands of the parliaments and the decisive tone of the king show that but little more irritation would be necessary to blow up the spark of discontent into a flame that might not easily be quenched. If I were to advise, I would say that great moderation should be used on both sides. Let it not, my dear Marquis, be considered as a derogation from the good opinion that I entertain of your prudence when I caution you, as an individual desirous of signalizing yourself in the cause of your country and freedom, against running into extremes and prejudicing your cause. The king—though I think from everything I have been able to learn he is really a good-hearted, though a warm-spirited, man—if thwarted injudiciously in the execution of prerogatives that belonged to the Crown, and in plans which he conceives calculated to promote the national good, may disclose qualities he has been little thought to possess. On the other hand, such a spirit seems to be awakened in the kingdom as, if managed with extreme prudence, may produce a gradual and tacit revolution much in favor of the subjects, by abolishing Lettres de Cachet and defining more accurately the powers of government. It is a wonder to me there should be found a single monarch who does not realize that his own glory and felicity must depend on the prosperity and happiness of his people. How easy is it for a sovereign to do that which shall not only immortalize his name, but attract the blessings of millions.

In a letter I wrote you a few days ago by Mr. Barlow (but which might not possibly have reached New York until after his departure) I mentioned the accession of Maryland to the proposed government and gave you the state of politics, to that period. Since which the convention of South Carolina has ratified the Constitution by a great majority. That of this state has been setting almost three weeks, and so nicely does it appear to be balanced that each side asserts that it has a preponderancy of votes in its favor. It is probable, therefore, the majority will be small, let it fall on which ever part it may. I am inclined to believe it will be in favor of the adoption. The convention of New York and New Hampshire assemble both this week—a large proportion of members, with the governor at their head, in the former are said to be opposed to the government in contemplation. New Hampshire, it is thought, will adopt it without much hesitation or delay. It is a little strange that the men of large property in the south should be more afraid that the Constitution will produce an aristocracy or a monarchy than[15] the genuine democratical people of the east. Such are our actual prospects. The accession of one state more will complete the number which, by the constitutional provision, will be sufficient in the first instance to carry the government into effect.

And then I expect that many blessings will be attributed to our new government which are now taking their rise from that industry and frugality into the practice of which the people have been forced from necessity. I really believe that there never was so much labor and economy to be found before in the country as at the present moment. If they persist in the habits they are acquiring, the good effects will soon be distinguishable. When the people shall find themselves secure under an energetic government, when foreign nations shall be disposed to give us equal advantages in commerce from dread of retaliation, when the burdens of the war shall be in a manner done away by the sale of western lands, when the seeds of happiness which are sown here shall begin to expand themselves, and when everyone (under his own vine and fig tree) shall begin to taste the fruits of freedom, then all these blessings (for all these blessings will come) will be referred to the fostering influence of the new government—whereas many causes will have conspired to produce them. You see I am not less enthusiastic than ever I have been, if a belief that peculiar scenes of felicity are reserved for this country is to be denominated enthusiasm. Indeed, I do not believe that Providence has done so much for nothing. It has always been my creed that we should not be left as an awful monument to prove "that mankind, under the most favorable circumstances for civil liberty and happiness, are unequal to the task of governing themselves, and therefore made for a master."

To Richard Henderson, June 19, 1788

Sir,

Your favor of the 5th instant was lodged at my house, while I was absent on a visit to my mother. I am now taking the earliest opportunity of noticing its contents and those of its enclosure. Willing as I am to give satisfaction so far as I am able to every reasonable inquiry[16] (and this is certainly not only so, but may be highly important and interesting), I must, however, rather deal in general than particular observations—as I think you will be able, from the length of your residence in the country and the extensiveness of your acquaintance with its affairs, to make the necessary applications and add the proper details. Nor would I choose that my interference in the business should be transmitted, lest, in a malicious world, it might be represented that I was officiously using the arts of seduction to depopulate other countries for the sake of peopling our own.

In the first place, it is a point conceded that America, under an efficient government, will be the most favorable country of any in the world for persons of industry and frugality, possessed of a moderate capital, to inhabit. It is also believed that it will not be less advantageous to the happiness of the lowest class of people because of the equal distribution of property, the great plenty of unoccupied lands, and the facility of procuring the means of subsistence. The scheme of purchasing a good tract of freehold estate and bringing out a number of able-bodied men, indented for a certain time, appears to be indisputably a rational one. All the interior arrangements of transferring the property and commencing the establishment you are as well acquainted with as I can possibly be. It might be considered as a point of more difficulty to decide upon the place which should be most proper for a settlement. Although I believe that emigrants from other countries to this, who shall be well disposed and conduct themselves properly, would be treated with equal friendship and kindness in all parts of it, yet in the old settled states, land is so much occupied and the value so much enhanced by the contiguous cultivation that the price would in general be an objection. The land in western country, or that on the Ohio, like all others, has its advantages and disadvantages. The neighborhood of the savages and the difficulty of transportation were the great objections. The danger of the first will soon cease by the strong establishments now taking place. The inconveniencies of the second will be, in a great degree, remedied by opening the internal navigation. No colony in America was ever settled under such favorable auspices as that which has just commenced at the Muskingum Information; property and strength will be its characteristics. I know many of the settlers personally and that there never were men better calculated to promote the welfare of such a community.

If I was a young man, just preparing to begin the world, or if advanced in life and had a family to make a provision for, I know of no country where I should rather fix my habitation than in some part of that region, for which the writer of the queries seems to have a predilection. He might be informed that his namesake and distant relation, General St. Clair, is not only in high repute, but that he is governor of all the territory westward of the Ohio, and that there is a gentleman (to wit, Mr. Joel Barlow) come from New York by the last French packet, who will be in London in the course of this year, and who is authorized to dispose of a very large body of land in that country. The author of the queries may then be referred to the "Information for those who would wish to remove to America," published in Europe in the year 1784 by the great philosopher Dr. Franklin. Short as it is, it contains almost everything that needs to be known on the subject of migrating to this country. You may find that excellent little treatise in *Carey's American Museum* for September 1787. It is worthy of being republished in Scotland and every other part of Europe.

As to the European publications respecting the United States, they are commonly very defective. The Abbe Raynale is quite erroneous. Guthrie, though somewhat better informed, is not absolutely correct. There is now "an American Geography preparing for the press by a Mr. Morse of New Haven in Connecticut" which, from the pains the author has taken in traveling through the states and acquiring information from the principal characters in each, will probably be much more exact and useful. Of books at present existing, Mr. Jefferson's *Notes on Virginia* will give the best idea of this part of the continent to a foreigner. And the *American Farmer's Letters*—written by Mr. Crevecoeur (commonly called Mr. St. John), the French consul in New York (who actually resided 20 years as a farmer in that state), will afford a great deal of profitable and amusive information respecting the *private life* of the Americans, as well as the progress of agriculture, manufactures, and arts in their country. Perhaps the picture he gives, though founded in fact, is in some instances embellished with rather too flattering circumstances—I am &ca

Go. Washington

To John Lathrop, June 22, 1788

Reverend and Respected Sir,

Your acceptable favor of the 16th of May, covering a recent publication of the proceedings of the Humane Society, has, within a few days past, been put into my hands.

I observe with singular satisfaction the cases in which your benevolent institution has been instrumental in recalling some of our fellow creatures (as it were) from beyond the gates of eternity and has given occasion for the hearts of parents and friends to leap for joy. The provision made for shipwrecked mariners is also highly estimable in the view of every philanthropic mind and greatly consolatory to that suffering part of the community. These things will draw upon you the blessings of those who were nigh to perish. These works of charity and good will towards men reflect, in my estimation, great luster upon the authors and presage an era of still farther improvements. How pitiful, in the eye of reason and religion, is that false ambition which desolates the world with fire and sword for the purposes of conquest and fame, when compared to the milder virtues of making our neighbors and our fellow men as happy as their frail conditions and perishable natures will permit them to be!

I am happy to find that the proposed general government meets with your approbation—as indeed it does with *that* of most disinterested and discerning men. The convention of this state is now in session, and I cannot but hope that the Constitution will be adopted by it—though not without considerable opposition. I trust, however, that the commendable example exhibited by the minority in your state will not be without its salutary influence in this. In truth it appears to me that (should the proposed government be generally and harmoniously adopted) it will be a new phenomenon in the political and moral world, and an astonishing victory gained by enlightened reason over brutal force. I have the honor to be with very great consideration Reverd & respected Sir Yr Most Obedt & Hble Sert

Go: Washington

To Mathew Carey, June 25, 1788

Sir,

Although I believe *The American Museum* published by you has met with extensive, I may say, with universal approbation from competent judges, yet I am sorry to find by your favor of the 19th that in a pecuniary view it has not equaled your expectations.

A discontinuance of the publication for want of proper support would, in my judgment, be an impeachment on the understanding of this country. For I am of opinion that the work is not only eminently calculated to disseminate political, agricultural, philosophical, and other valuable information, but that it has been uniformly conducted with taste, attention, and propriety. If to these important objects be superadded the more immediate design of rescuing public documents from oblivion, I will venture to pronounce as my sentiment that a more useful literary plan has never been undertaken in America, or one more deserving public encouragement. By continuing to prosecute that plan with similar assiduity and discernment, the merit of your *Museum* must ultimately become as well known in some countries of Europe as on this continent, and can scarcely fail of procuring an ample compensation for your trouble and expense.

For myself, I entertain a high idea of the utility of periodical publications, insomuch that I could heartily desire copies of the *Museum* and magazines, as well as common gazettes, might be spread through every city, town, and village in America. I consider such easy vehicles of knowledge more happily calculated than any other to preserve the liberty, stimulate the industry, and meliorate the morals of an enlightened and free people. With sincere wishes for the success of your undertaking in particular, and for the prosperity of the typographical art in general, I am—Sir Yr Most Obedt & Most Hble Servt

Go: Washington

To Charles Cotesworth Pinckney, June 28, 1788

Dear Sir,

I had the pleasure to receive, a day or two ago, your obliging letter of the 24th of last month, in which you advise me of the ratification of the Federal Constitution by South Carolina. By a more rapid water conveyance, that good news had some few days before arrived at Baltimore, so as to have been very opportunely communicated to the convention of this state, in session at Richmond. It is with great satisfaction I have it now in my power to inform you that, on the 25th instant, the delegates of Virginia adopted the Constitution, in toto, by a division of 89 in favor of it to 79 against it, and that, notwithstanding the majority is so small, yet, in consequence of some conciliatory conduct and recommendatory amendments, a happy acquiescence, it is said, is likely to terminate the business here in as favorable a manner as could possibly have been expected.

No sooner had the citizens of Alexandria (who are federal to a man) received the intelligence by the mail last night than they determined to devote this day to festivity. But their exhilaration was greatly increased and a much keener zest given to their enjoyment by the arrival of an express (two hours before day) with the news that the convention of New Hampshire had, on the 21st instant, acceded to the new confederacy by a majority of 11 voices, that is to say, 57 to 46.

Thus the citizens of Alexandria, when convened, constituted the first public company in America which had the pleasure of pouring libation to the prosperity of the ten states that had actually adopted the general government. The day itself is memorable for more reasons than one. It was recollected that this day is the anniversary of the battles of Sullivan's Island and Monmouth. I have just returned from assisting at the entertainment and mention these details, unimportant as they are in themselves, the rather because I think we may rationally indulge the pleasing hope that the Union will now be established upon a durable basis, and that Providence seems still disposed to favor the members of it with unequalled opportunities for political happiness.

From the local situation as well as the other circumstances of North Carolina, I should be truly astonished if that state should withdraw itself from the Union. On the contrary, I flatter myself with *a confident expectation* that more salutary counsels will certainly prevail. At present there is more doubt how the question will be immediately disposed of in New York. For it seems to be understood that there is a majority in the convention opposed to the adoption of the new federal system. Yet it is hardly to be supposed (or rather in my judgment it is irrational to suppose) they will reject a government which, from an unorganized embryo ready to be stifled with a breath, has now in the maturity of its birth assumed a confirmed bodily existence. Or, to drop the metaphor, the point in debate has, at least, shifted its ground from policy to expediency. The decision often states cannot be without its operation.[17] Perhaps the wisest way, in this crisis, will be not to attempt to accept or reject but to adjourn until the people in some parts of the state can consider the magnitude of the question and of the consequences involved in it more coolly and deliberately. After New York shall have acted, then only one little state will remain. Suffice it to say, *it is universally believed that the scales are ready to drop from the eyes and the infatuation to be removed from the heart of Rhode Island.* May this be the case, before that inconsiderate people shall have filled up the measure of inequity before it shall be too late! Mrs. Washington and all with us desire their best compliments may be presented to Mrs. Pinckney and yourself. Wishing that mine may also be made acceptable to you both, I am &c.

Go. Washington

To Benjamin Lincoln, June 29, 1788

My Dear Sir,

I beg you will accept my thanks for the communications handed to me in your letter of the 3rd instant. And my congratulations on the increasing good dispositions of the citizens of your state, of which the late elections are strongly indicative.

No one can rejoice more than I do at every step taken by the people of this great country to preserve the Union, establish good order and government, and to render the nation happy at home and respected abroad. No country upon earth ever had it more in its power to attain these blessings than United America. Wondrously strange then, and much to be regretted indeed would it be, were we to neglect the means and to stray from the road to which the finger of Providence has so manifestly pointed. I cannot believe it will ever come to pass! The great Author of all good has not conducted us so far on the road to happiness and glory to withdraw from us, in the hour of need, his beneficent support. By folly and misconduct (proceeding from a variety of causes) we may now and then get bewildered, but I hope and trust that there is good sense and virtue enough left to bring us back into the right way before we shall be entirely lost.

Before this letter can have reached you, you will have heard of the ratification of the proposed Constitution by this state, without previous amendments. The final question was taken the 25th—Ayes 89, Noes 79. But something recommendatory or declaratory of the rights of the people, it is said, will follow, so as not to affect the preceding decision. This account, and the news of the adoption by New Hampshire, arrived in Alexandria nearly about the same time on Friday evening and, as you may easily conceive, gave cause for great rejoicing among the inhabitants, who have not, I believe, an Anti-Federalist among them.

Our accounts from Richmond are that the debates (through all the different stages of the business, though long and animated) were conducted with great dignity and temper, that the final decision exhibited an awful and solemn scene, and that there is reason to expect a perfect acquiescence thereto by the minority. Not only from the good sense and conduct of that body during the session, but from the declaration of Mr. Henry, the great leader of the opposition, to the effect that though he cannot be reconciled to the Constitution in its present form, and shall give it every *constitutional* opposition in his power, yet that he will submit to it peaceably, as he thinks every good citizen ought to do when it is in exercise, and that he will, both by precept and example, endeavor to inculcate this doctrine.

But little doubt is *now* entertained *here* of the ratification of the proposed Constitution by the state of North Carolina. And however great the opposition to it may be in that of New York, the leaders thereof will, I should conceive, consider the consequences of rejection well, before it is given. With respect to Rhode Island, the power that governs there has so far baffled all calculation on this subject that no man will hazard an opinion on their proceedings lest he should be suspected of participating in its frenzy. You have every good wish of this family—and the sincere regard of your Affecte friend & Servt

Go: Washington

To John Jay, Secretary of Foreign Affairs, July 18, 1788 (Excerpt)

It is extremely to be lamented that a new arrangement in the post office, unfavorable to the circulation of intelligence, should have taken place at the instant when the momentous question of a general government was to come before the people. I have seen no good apology, not even in Mr. Hazard's publication, for deviating from the old custom of permitting printers to exchange their papers by the mail. That practice was a great public convenience and gratification. If the privilege was not from convention an original right, it had from prescription strong pretensions for continuance, especially at so interesting a period. The interruption in that mode of conveyance has not only given great concern to the friends of the Constitution, who wished the public to be possessed of everything that might be printed on both sides of the question, but it has afforded its enemies very plausible pretext for dealing out their scandals and exciting jealousies by inducing a belief that the suppression of intelligence at that critical juncture was a wicked trick of policy, contrived by an aristocratic junto. Now, if the postmaster general (with whose character I am unacquainted and therefore would not be understood to form an unfavorable opinion of his motives) has any candid advisers who conceive that he merits the public employment, they ought to counsel him to wipe away the aspersion he has incautiously brought upon a good cause. If he is unworthy of the office he holds, it would be well that the ground of a complaint, apparently so general, should be inquired into, and, if founded, redressed through the medium of a better appointment. It is a matter, in my judgment, of primary importance that the public mind should be relieved from inquietude on this subject. I know it is said that the irregularity or defect has happened accidentally, in consequence of the contract for transporting the mail on horseback, instead of having it carried in the *stages*. But I must confess, I could never account, upon any satisfactory principles, for the inveterate enmity with which the postmaster general is asserted to be actuated against that valuable institution. It has often been understood by wise politicians and enlightened patriots that giving a facility to the means of traveling for strangers and of intercourse for citizens was an object of legislative concern and a circumstance highly beneficial to any country. In England, I am told, they consider the mail coaches as a great modern improvement in their post office regulations. I trust we are not too old or too proud to profit by the experience of others. In this article, the materials are amply within our reach.

I am taught to imagine that the horses, the vehicles, and the accommodations in America (with very little encouragement) might in a short period become as good as the same articles are to be found in any country of Europe—and, at the same time, I am sorry to learn that the line of stages is at present interrupted in some parts of New England and totally discontinued at the southward.

To John Langdon, President of New Hampshire, July 20, 1788

Dear Sir,

I had the satisfaction to receive regularly your favor of the 21st ultimo announcing the adoption of the federal government by the convention of New Hampshire. You will already have been informed through the ordinary channels of communication that the same event took effect in this state a few days afterwards. And I am happy to say that, so far as I have been able to learn, a spirit of harmony and acquiescence obtained among the large and respectable minority in as great a degree as could possibly have been expected.

If we may calculate upon rectitude in the views and prudence in the conduct of the leading characters throughout the states, accompanied by industry and honesty in the mass of the people, we may assuredly anticipate a new era, and perhaps we shall not deceive ourselves by expecting a more happy one than hath before appeared on this checkered scene of existence. But we ought not to be too sanguine or to expect that we shall be entirely exempted from the ills which fall to the lot of humanity.

With congratulations to Your Excellency on your elevation to the chief magistracy of your state, and with sentiments of consideration and respect, I remain Sir—Your Excellency's Most Obedt Hble Servt

Go: Washington

To Jonathan Trumbull, Jr., July 20, 1788

Dear Sir,

I have received your favor of the 20th of June and thank you heartily for the confidential information contained in it. The character given of a certain great personage, who is remarkable for neither forgetting or forgiving, I believe to be just. What effect the addition of such an extraordinary weight of power and influence as the arrangement of the East India affairs gives to one branch of the British government cannot be certainly foretold; but one thing is certain, that is to say, it will always be wise for America to be prepared for events. Nor can I refrain from indulging the expectation that the time is not very distant when it shall be more in the power of the United States than it hath hitherto been to be forearmed as well as forewarned against the evil contingencies of European politics.

You will have perceived from the public papers that I was not erroneous in my calculation that the Constitution would be accepted by the convention of this state. The majority, it is true, was small; and the minority respectable in many points of view. But the greater part of the minority here, as in most other states, have conducted themselves with great prudence and political moderation, insomuch that we may anticipate a pretty general and harmonious acquiescence. We shall impatiently wait the result from New York and North Carolina. The other state which has not yet acted is nearly out of the question. As the infamy of the conduct of Rhode Island outgoes all precedent, so the influence of her counsels can be of no prejudice. There is no state or description of men but would blush to be involved in a connection with the paper money junto of that anarchy. God grant that the honest men may acquire an ascendency before irrevocable ruin shall confound the innocent with the guilty.

I am happy to hear from General Lincoln and others that affairs are taking a good turn in Massachusetts. But the triumph of salutary and liberal measures over those of an opposite tendency seems to be as complete in Connecticut as in any state and affords a particular subject for congratulation. Your friend Colonel Humphreys informs me, from the wonderful revolution of sentiment in favor of federal measures and the marvelous change for the better in the elections of your state, that he shall begin to suspect that miracles have not ceased. Indeed, for myself, since so much liberality has been displayed in the construction and adoption of the proposed general government, I am almost disposed to be of the same opinion. Or at least we may, with a kind of grateful and pious exultation, trace the finger of Providence through those dark and mysterious events which first induced the states to appoint a general convention and then led them one after another (by such steps as were best calculated to effect the object) into an adoption of the system recommended by that general convention—thereby, in all human probability, laying a lasting foundation for tranquility and happiness, when we had but too much reason to fear that confusion and misery were coming rapidly upon us.

That the same good Providence may still continue to protect us and prevent us from dashing the cup of national felicity just as it has been lifted to our lips, is the earnest prayer of My dear Sir Your faithful friend & Affectionate Servt

Go: Washington

To James McHenry,
July 31, 1788

Dear Sir,

In reply to your recent favor, which has been duly received, I can only observe that, as I never go from home except when I am obliged by necessary avocations, and as I meddle as little as possible with politics that my interference may not give occasion for impertinent imputations, so I am less likely than almost any person to have been informed of the circumstance to which you allude. That some of the leading characters among the opponents of the proposed government have not laid aside their ideas of obtaining great and essential changes through a constitutional opposition (as they term it) may be collected from their public speeches. That others will use more secret and, perhaps, insidious means to prevent its organization may be presumed from their previous conduct on the subject. In addition to this probability, the casual information received from visitants at my house would lead me to expect that a considerable effort will be made to procure the election of Anti-Federalists to the first Congress, in order to bring the subject immediately before the state legislators, to open an extensive correspondence between the minorities for obtaining alterations, and in short to undo all that has been done. It is reported that a respectable neighbor of mine has said the Constitution cannot be carried in execution without great amendments. But I will freely do the opposition with us the justice to declare that I have heard of no cabals or canvassings respecting the elections. It is said to be otherwise on your side of the river. By letters from the eastern states, I am induced to believe the minorities have acquiesced not only with a good grace, but also with a serious design to give the government a fair chance to discover its operation by being carried into effect. I hope and trust that the same liberal disposition prevails with a large proportion of the same description of men in this state. Still, I think there will be great reason for those who are well affected to the government to use their utmost exertions that the worthiest citizens may be appointed to the two houses of the first Congress, and, where state elections take place previous to this choice, that the same principle govern in these also. For much will doubtless depend on their prudence in conducting business at the beginning, and reconciling discordant dispositions to a reasonable acquiescence with candid and honest measures. At the same time, it will be a point of no common delicacy to make provision for effecting such explanations and amendments as might be really proper and generally satisfactory, without producing or at least fostering such a spirit of innovation as will overturn the whole system.

I earnestly pray that the Omnipotent Being who hath not deserted the cause of America in the hour of its extremest hazard will never yield so fair a heritage of freedom a prey to anarchy or despotism. With sentiments of real regard I am Dr Sir &ca

Go. Washington

To James Madison, August 3, 1788 (Excerpt)

The place proper for the new Congress to meet at will unquestionably undergo (if it has not already done it) much investigation, but there are certain things which are so self-evident in their nature as to speak for themselves. This, possibly, may be one. Where the true point lays I will not undertake to decide, but there can be no hesitation I conceive in pronouncing one thing: that in all societies, if the bond or cement is strong and interesting enough to hold the body together, the several parts should submit to the inconveniencies for the benefits which they derive from the conveniencies of the compact.

To Thomas Nelson, Jr., August 3, 1788 (Excerpt)

Far, very far indeed, was it from my intention to embarrass you by the letter which enclosed the proceedings of the general convention—and still farther was it from my wish that the communication should be received in any other light than as an instance of my attention and friendship. I was well aware that the adoption or rejection of the Constitution would, as it ought to, be decided upon according to its merits and agreeably to the circumstances to which our public affairs had arriven. That all questions of this kind are, ever will, and perhaps ought to be (to accomplish the designs of infinite wisdom) viewed through different mediums by different men is as certain as that they have existence. All that can be expected in such cases therefore is charity, mutual forbearance, and acquiescence in the general voice, which, though it may be wrong, is presumably right.

To Charles Pettit, August 16, 1788

Sir,

I have to acknowledge with much sensibility the receipt of your letter, dated the 5th instant, in which you offer your congratulations on the prospect of an established government, whose principles seem calculated to secure the benefits of society to the citizens of the United States, and in which you also give a more accurate state of federal politics in Pennsylvania than I had before received. It affords me unfeigned satisfaction to find that the acrimony of parties is much abated.

Doubtless there are defects in the proposed system which may be remedied in a constitutional mode. I am truly pleased to learn that those who have been considered as its most violent opposers will not only acquiesce peaceably but cooperate in its organization and content themselves with asking amendments in the manner prescribed by the Constitution. The great danger, in my view, was that everything might have been thrown into the last stage of confusion before any government whatsoever could have been established, and that we should have suffered a political shipwreck without the aid of one friendly star to guide us into port. Every real patriot must have lamented that private feuds and local politics should have unhappily insinuated themselves into, and in some measure obstructed, the discussion of a great national question. A just opinion that the people when rightly informed will decide in a proper manner ought certainly to have prevented all intemperate or precipitate proceedings on a subject of so much magnitude. Nor should a regard to common decency have suffered the zealots in the minority to have stigmatized the authors of the Constitution as conspirators and traitors. However unfavorably individuals, blinded by passion and prejudice, might have thought of the characters which composed the Convention, the election of those characters by the legislatures of the several states and the reference of their proceedings to the free determination of their constituents did not carry the appearance of *a private combination to destroy the liberties of their country*.

Nor did the outrageous disposition which some indulged in traducing and vilifying the members seem much calculated to produce concord or accommodation.

For myself, I expected not to be exempted from obloquy any more than others. It is the lot of humanity.

But if the shafts of malice had been aimed at me in ever so pointed a manner, on this occasion, involved as I was in a consciousness of having acted in conformity to what I believed my duty, they would have fallen blunted from their mark. It is known to some of my countrymen and can be demonstrated to the conviction of all that I was in a manner constrained to attend the general convention in compliance with the earnest and pressing desires of many of the most respectable characters in different parts of the continent.

At my age, and in my circumstances, what sinister object or personal emolument had I to seek after in this life? The growing infirmities of age and the increasing love of retirement daily confirm my decided predilection for domestic life. And the great searcher of human hearts is my witness, that I have no wish which aspires beyond the humble and happy lot of living and dying a private citizen on my own farm.

Your candor and patriotism in endeavoring to moderate the jealousies and remove the prejudices which a particular class of citizens had conceived against the new government are certainly very commendable, and must be viewed as such by all true friends to their country. In this description I shall fondly hope I have a right to comprehend myself, and shall conclude by professing the grateful sense of your favorable opinion for me, with which I am, Sir, Your Most Obedient Servant

George Washington

To William Tudor, August 18, 1788 (Excerpt)

The troubles in your state may, as you justly observe, have operated in proving to the comprehension of many minds the necessity of a more efficient government. A multiplicity of circumstances, scarcely yet investigated, appears to have *cooperated* in bringing about the great and, I trust, the happy revolution that is on the eve of being accomplished. It will not be uncommon that these things, which were considered at the moment as real ills, should have been no inconsiderable causes in producing positive and permanent national felicity. For it is thus that Providence works in the mysterious course of events "from seeming evil still educing good."

I was happy to hear from several respectable quarters that liberal policy and federal sentiments had been rapidly increasing in Massachusetts for some time past. It gives me an additional pleasure to find that labor is becoming more productive and commerce more flourishing among the citizens.

To Alexander Hamilton, August 28, 1788

Dear Sir,

I have had the pleasure to receive your letter dated the 13th, accompanied by one addressed to General Morgan. I will forward the letter to General Morgan by the first conveyance, and add my particular wishes that he would comply with the request contained in it. Although I can scarcely imagine how the watch of a British officer, killed within their lines, should have fallen into his hands (who was many miles from the scene of action), yet, if it so happened, I flatter myself there will be no reluctance or delay in restoring it to the family.

As the perusal of the political papers under the signature of Publius has afforded me great satisfaction, I shall certainly consider them as claiming a most distinguished place in my library. I have read every performance which has been printed on one side and the other of the great question lately agitated (so far as I have been able to obtain them) and, without an unmeaning compliment, I will say that I have seen no other so well calculated (in my judgment) to produce conviction on an unbiased mind as the *production* of your *triumvirate*. When the transient circumstances and fugitive performances which attended this *crisis* shall have disappeared, that work will merit the notice of posterity, because in it are candidly discussed the principles of freedom and the topics of government, which will be always interesting to mankind so long as they shall be connected in civil society.

The circular letter from your convention, I presume, was the equivalent by which you obtained an acquiescence in the proposed Constitution. Notwithstanding I am not very well satisfied with the tendency of it, yet the federal affairs have proceeded, with few exceptions, in so good a train that I hope the political machine may be put in motion without much effort or hazard of miscarrying.

On the delicate subject with which you conclude your letter, I can say nothing, because the event alluded to may never happen, and because, in case it should occur, it would be a point of prudence to defer forming one's ultimate and irrevocable decision so long as new data might be afforded for one to act with the greater wisdom and propriety. I would not wish to conceal my prevailing sentiment from you. For you know me well enough, my good sir, to be persuaded that I am not guilty of affectation[18] when I tell you, it is my great and sole desire to live and die in peace and retirement on my own farm. Were it even indispensable, a different line of conduct should be adopted. While you and some others who are acquainted with my heart would *acquit*, the world and posterity might probably *accuse* me of *inconsistency* and *ambition*. Still I hope I shall always possess firmness and virtue enough to maintain (what I consider the most enviable of all titles) the character of an *honest man*, as well as prove (what I desire to be considered in reality) that I am, with great sincerity & esteem, Dear Sir Your friend and Most obedient Hble Servt

Go: Washington

To Benjamin Lincoln, August 28, 1788

My Dear Sir,

I received with your letter of the 9th instant one from Mr. Minot and also his *History of the Insurrections in Massachusetts*. The work seems to be executed with ingenuity, as well as to be calculated to place facts in a true point of light, obviate the prejudices of those who were unacquainted with the circumstances, and answer good purposes in respect to our government in general. I have returned him my thanks for his present by this conveyance.

The public appears to be anxiously waiting for the decision of Congress respecting the place for convening the National Assembly under the new government, and the ordinance for its organization. Methinks it is a great misfortune that local interests should involve themselves with federal concerns at this moment.

So far as I am able to learn, federal principles are gaining ground considerably. The declaration of some of the most respectable characters in this state (I mean of those who were opposed to the government) is now explicit that they will give the Constitution (as it has been fairly discussed) a fair chance by affording it all the support in their power. Even in Pennsylvania the minority, who were more violent than in any other place, say they will only seek for amendments in the mode pointed out by the Constitution itself.

I will, however, just mention by way of *caveat* there are suggestions that attempts will be made to procure the election of a number of Anti-Federal characters to the first Congress, in order to embarrass the wheels of government and produce premature alterations in the Constitution. How far these hints, which have come through different channels, may be well or ill-founded, I know not; but it will be advisable, I should think, for the Federalists to be on their guard so far as not to suffer any secret machinations to prevail without taking measures to frustrate them. That many amendments and explanations might and should take place I have no difficulty in conceding; but I will confess that my apprehension is that the New York circular letter is intended to bring on a general convention at too early a period, and, in short, by referring the subject to the legislatures, to set everything afloat again. I wish I may be mistaken in imagining that there are persons who, upon finding they could not carry their point by an open attack against the Constitution, have some sinister designs to be silently effected if possible. But I trust in that Providence which has saved us in six troubles, yea, in seven, to rescue us again from any imminent though unseen dangers. Nothing, however, on our part ought to be left undone. I conceive it to be of unspeakable importance that whatever there be of wisdom and prudence and patriotism on the continent should be concentered in the public councils at the first outset.

Our habits of intimacy will render an apology unnecessary—Heaven is my witness, that an inextinguishable desire the felicity of my country may be promoted is my only motive in making these observations. With sincere attachment & esteem I am—My dear Sir, Yr Most Obedt & Affecte Servt

Go: Washington

To George Richards Minot, August 28, 1788

Sir,

Your favor of the 7th of this month has been duly received, and I lose no time before I acknowledge the obligations under which you have placed me by offering the copy of your *History* as a present. Aside of the honorable testimony of my friend General Lincoln, the intrinsic merit of the work (so far as I am able to form a judgment from its perspicuity and impartiality) carries a sufficient recommendation.

The series of events which followed from the conclusion of the war forms a link of no ordinary magnitude in the chain of the American annals. That portion of domestic history which you have selected for your narrative deserved particularly to be discussed and set in its proper point of light while materials for the purpose were attainable. Nor was it unbecoming or unimportant to enlighten the Europeans, who seem to have been extremely ignorant with regard to these transactions. While I comprehend fully the difficulty of stating facts on the spot, amidst the living actors and recent animosities, I approve the more cordially that candor with which you appear to have done it.

I will only add that I always feel a singular satisfaction in discovering proofs of talents and patriotism in those who are soon to take the parts of the generation which is now hastening to leave the stage—and that, with wishes for your prosperity, I remain, Sir Your most obedt & very humble Servant

Go. Washington

To Joseph Mandrillon, August 29, 1788

Sir,

I have lately received with a grateful sensibility the miscellaneous collection in verse and prose which you have had the goodness to send to me, accompanied by your letter under date of May the 24th—for both of which I pray you to accept my warmest thanks.

But, sir, I consider you as a patriot of the world, earnestly solicitous for the freedom and prosperity of all nations. And I should do injustice to my feelings not to go beyond common expressions of personal civility in testifying my sense of the uniform and able exertions you have made in favor of the cause and reputation of the United States of America. Your honest endeavors to confute the erroneous reports that had been scattered in Europe respecting the partial commotions in Massachusetts were truly laudable and merit the applause of every patriot. As I know of no European character better calculated or more disposed to make good use of authentic *History of the Insurrections in Massachusetts*. It possesses the merit of being written with simplicity and impartiality, and will tend to destroy the idle opinions that were propagated in the English newspapers on the subject. All the accounts of our being in great jeopardy from a war with the savages are equally groundless and seem principally designed to deter people from migrating to America.

We flatter ourselves your patriotic wishes and sanguine hopes respecting the political felicity of this country will not prove abortive. We hope, from the general acquiescence of the states so far, with small exceptions, in the proposed Constitution that the foundation is laid for the enjoyment of much purer civil liberty and greater public happiness than have hitherto been the portion of mankind. And we trust the western world will yet verify the predictions of its friends and prove an asylum for the persecuted of all nations. With sentiments of great esteem and respect, I have the honor to be yours &c.

Go. Washington

To Edward Newenham, August 29, 1788 (Excerpt)

I am heartily glad to find that the prosperity of Ireland is on the increase. It was afflicting for the philanthropic mind to consider the mass of people, inhabiting a country naturally fertile in productions and full of resources, sunk to an abject degree of penury and depression. Such has been the picture we have received of the peasantry. Nor do their calamities seem to be entirely removed yet, as we may gather from the spirited speech of Mr. Gratton on the commutation of tithes.[19] But I hope, ere long, matters will go right there and in the rest of the world. For instead of the disconsolatory idea that everything is growing worse, I would fain cheer myself with a hope that everything is beginning to mend. As you observe, if Ireland was 500 miles farther distant from Great Britain, the case with respect to the former would be as speedily as materially changed for the better.

But what shall we say of wars and the appearances of wars in the rest of the world? Mankind are not yet ripe for the millennial state. The affairs of some of the greatest potentates appear to be very much embroiled in the north of Europe. The question is whether the Turks will be driven out of Europe or not? One would suppose, if discipline and arrangement are to be calculated upon in preference to ignorance and brutal force, that the Porte must recede before the two imperial powers. But in the game of war there are so many contingencies that often prevent the most probable events from taking place, and in the present instance there are so many causes that may kindle the hostile conflagration into a general flame, that we need not be over hasty and sanguine in drawing our conclusions. Let us see how far the sparks of hostility have been scattered. The almost open rupture between the emperor of Germany and his subjects in the Low Countries; the interference of Prussia in Holland and the disordered condition of that republic; the new alliances on the part of that republic with England and Prussia; the humiliating dereliction (or rather sacrifice) which France has been obliged to make of the Dutch patriots in consequence of the derangement of her finances; the troubles, internally, which prevail in France, together with the ill-temper she must feel towards England on account of the terms lately dictated by the latter; the animosity of Britain and Morocco, in conjunction with several smaller subjects of national discussion; leave but too much ground to apprehend that the tranquility of Europe will not be of long continuance. I hope the United States of America will be able to keep disengaged from the labyrinth of European politics and wars and that before long they will, by the adoption of a good national government, have become respectable in the eyes of the world so that none of the maritime owners, especially none of those who hold possessions in the new world or the West Indies, shall presume to treat them with insult or contempt. It should be the policy of United America to administer to their wants without being engaged in their quarrels. And it is not in the ability of the proudest and most potent people on earth to prevent us from becoming a great, a respectable, and a commercial nation, if we shall continue united and faithful to ourselves.

Your solicitude that an efficient and good government may be established in this country, in order that it may enjoy felicity at home and respectability abroad, serves only to confirm me in the opinion I have always entertained of your disinterested and ardent friendship for this land of freedom. It is true that, for the want of a proper confederation, we have not yet been in a situation fully to enjoy those blessings which God and Nature seemed to have intended for us. But I begin to look forward, with a kind of political faith, to scenes of national happiness which have not heretofore been offered for the fruition of the most favored nations. The natural, political, and moral circumstances of our nascent empire justify the anticipation. We have an almost unbounded territory, whose natural advantages for agriculture and commerce equal those of any on the globe. In a civil point of view, we have the unequalled privilege of choosing our own political institutions and of improving upon the experience of mankind in the formation of a confederated government where due energy will not be incompatible with the unalienable rights of freemen. To complete the picture, I may observe that the information and morals of our citizens appear to be peculiarly favorable for the introduction of such a plan of government as I have just now described.

Although there were some few things in the Constitution recommended by the Federal Convention to the determination of the people which did not fully accord with my wishes; yet, having taken every circumstance seriously into consideration, I was convinced it approached nearer to perfection than any government hitherto instituted among men. I was also convinced that nothing but a genuine spirit of amity and accommodation could have induced the members to make those mutual concessions and to sacrifice (at the shrine of enlightened liberty) those local prejudices, which seemed to oppose an insurmountable barrier, to prevent them from harmonizing in any system whatsoever.

But so it has happened by the good pleasure of Providence, and the same happy disposition has been diffused and fostered among the people at large. You will permit me to say that a greater drama is now acting on this theater than has heretofore been brought on the American stage, or any other in the world. We exhibit at present the novel and astonishing spectacle of a whole people deliberating calmly on what form of government will be most conducive to their happiness, and deciding with an unexpected degree of unanimity in favor of a system which they conceive calculated to answer the purpose.

It is only necessary to add for your satisfaction that, as all the states which have yet acted, and which are ten in number, have adopted the proposed Constitution, and as the concurrence of nine states was sufficient to carry it into effect in the first instance, it is expected the government will be in complete organization and execution before the commencement of the ensuing year.

To Thomas Jefferson, Minister to France, August 31, 1788 (Excerpt)

I do not pretend to judge how far the flames of war, which are kindled in the north of Europe, may be scattered or how soon they will be extinguished. The European politics have taken so strange a turn, and the nations formerly allied have become so curiously severed, that there are fewer sure premises for calculation than are usually afforded, even on that precarious and doubtful subject. But it appears probable to me that peace will either take place this year, or hostility be greatly extended in the course of the next. The want of a hearty cooperation between the two imperial powers against the Porte, or the failure of success from any other cause, may accelerate the first contingency. The irritable state into which several of the other potentates seem to have been drawn may open the way to the second. Hitherto the event of the contest has proved different from the general expectation. If, in our speculations, we might count upon discipline, system, and resource, and certainly these are the articles which generally give decisive advantages in war, I had thought full—surely the Turks must, at least, have been driven out of Europe. Is it not unaccountable that the Russians and Germans combined are not able to effect so much as the former did alone in the late war? But perhaps these things are all for the best and may afford room for pacification.

I am glad our Commodore Paul Jones has got employment, and heartily wish him success. His new situation may possibly render his talents and services more useful to us at some future day. I was unapprised of the circumstances which you mention, that Congress had once in contemplation to give him promotion. They will judge now how far it may be expedient.

By what we can learn from the late foreign gazettes, affairs seem to have come to a crisis in France, and I hope are beginning to meliorate. Should the contest between the king and the parliaments result in a well-constituted National Assembly, it must ultimately be a happy event for the kingdom. But I fear that kingdom will not recover its reputation and influence with the Dutch for a long time to come. Combinations appear also to be forming in other quarters. It is reported by the last European accounts that England has actually entered into a treaty with Prussia, and that the French ambassador at the Court of London has asked to be informed of its tenor. In whatever manner the nations of Europe shall endeavor to keep up their prowess in war and their balance of power in peace, it will be obviously our policy to cultivate tranquility at home and abroad, and extend our agriculture and commerce as far as possible.

I am much obliged by the information you give respecting the credit of different nations among the Dutch money-holders, and fully accord with you with regard to the manner in which our own ought to be used. I am strongly impressed with the expediency of establishing our national faith beyond imputation, and of having recourse to loans only on critical occasions. Your proposal for transferring the whole foreign debt to Holland is highly worthy of consideration. I feel mortified that there should have been any just ground for the clamor of the foreign officers who served with us; but, after having received a quarter of their whole debt in specie and their interest in the same for some time, they have infinitely less reason for complaint than our native officers, of whom the suffering and neglect have only been equaled by their patience and patriotism. A great proportion of the officers and soldiers of the American army have been compelled by indigence to part with their securities for one eighth of the nominal value. Yet their conduct is very different from what you represent that of the French officers to have been.

The merits and defects of the proposed Constitution have been largely and ably discussed. For myself, I was ready to have embraced any tolerable compromise that was competent to save us from impending ruin. And I can say there are scarcely any of the amendments which have been suggested to which I have *much* objection, except that which goes to the prevention of direct taxation—and that, I presume, will be more strenuously advocated and insisted upon hereafter than any other. I had indulged the expectation that the new government would enable those entrusted with its administration to do justice to the public creditors and retrieve the national character. But if no means are to be employed but requisitions, that expectation was vain and we may as well recur to the old Confederation. If the system can be put in operation without touching much the pockets of the people, perhaps it may be done; but in my judgment, infinite circumspection and prudence are yet necessary in the experiment. It is nearly impossible for anybody who has not been on the spot to conceive (from any description) what the delicacy and danger of our situation have been. Though the peril is not passed entirely, thank God the prospect is somewhat brightening! You will probably have heard before the receipt of this letter that the general government has been adopted by eleven states, and that the actual Congress have been prevented from issuing their ordinance for carrying it into execution, in consequence of a dispute about the place at which the future Congress shall meet. It is probable that Philadelphia or New York will soon be agreed upon.

I will just touch on the bright side of our national state before I conclude, and we may perhaps rejoice that the people have been ripened by misfortune for the reception of a good government. They are emerging from the gulf of dissipation and debt into which they had precipitated themselves at the close of the war. Economy and industry are evidently gaining ground. Not only agriculture but even manufactures are much more attended to than formerly. Notwithstanding the shackles under which our trade in general labors, commerce to the East Indies is prosecuted with considerable success. Salted provisions and other produce (particularly from Massachusetts) have found an advantageous market there. The voyages are so much shorter and the vessels are navigated at so much less expense that we hope to rival and supply (at least through the West Indies) some part of Europe with commodities from thence. This year the exports from Massachusetts have amounted to a great deal more than their imports. I wish this was the case everywhere.

To Annis Boudinot Stockton, August 31, 1788

I have received and thank you very sincerely, my dear madam, for your kind letter of the 3rd instant. It would be in vain for me to think of acknowledging in adequate terms the delicate compliments which, though expressed in plain prose, are evidently inspired by the Muse of Morven. I know not by what fatality it happens that even philosophical sentiments come so much more gracefully (forcibly, I might add) from your sex than my own. Otherwise I should be strongly disposed to dispute your Epicurean position concerning the economy of pleasures. Perhaps, indeed, upon a self-interested principle—because I should be conscious of becoming a gainer by a different practice. For, to tell you the truth, I find myself altogether interested in establishing in theory what I feel in effect, that we can never be cloyed with the pleasing compositions of our female friends.

You see how selfish I am, and that I am too much delighted with the result to perplex my head much in seeking for the cause. But with Cicero in speaking respecting his belief of the immortality of the soul, I will say, if I am in a grateful delusion, it is an innocent one, and I am willing to remain under its influence. Let me only annex one hint to this part of the subject: while you may be in danger of appreciating the qualities of your friend too highly, you will run no hazard in calculating upon his sincerity or in counting implicitly on the reciprocal esteem and friendship which he entertains for yourself.

The felicitations you offer on the present prospect of our public affairs are highly acceptable to me, and I entreat you to receive a reciprocation from my part. I can never trace the concatenation of causes which led to these events without acknowledging the mystery and admiring the goodness of Providence. To that superintending Power alone is our retraction from the brink of ruin to be attributed. A spirit of accommodation was happily infused into the leading characters of the continent, and the minds of men were gradually prepared by disappointment for the reception of a good government. Nor would I rob the fairer sex of their share in the glory of a revolution so honorable to human nature, for, indeed, I think you ladies are in the number of the best patriots America can boast.

And now that I am speaking of your sex, I will ask whether they are not capable of doing something towards introducing federal fashions and national manners? A good general government, without good morals and good habits, will not make us a happy people; and we shall deceive ourselves if we think it will. A good government will, unquestionably, tend to foster and confirm those qualities on which public happiness must be engrafted. Is it not shameful that we should be the sport of European whims and caprices? Should we not blush to discourage our own industry and ingenuity by purchasing foreign superfluities and adopting fantastic fashions, which are, at best, ill-suited to our stage of society? But I will preach no longer on so unpleasant a subject, because I am persuaded that you and I are both of a sentiment, and because I fear the promulgation of it would work no reformation.

You know me well enough, my dear madam, to believe me sufficiently happy at home to be intent upon spending the residue of my days there. I hope that you and yours may have the enjoyment of your health as well as Mrs. Washington and myself; that enjoyment, by the divine benediction, adds much to our temporal felicity. She joins with me in desiring our compliments may be made acceptable to yourself and children. It is with the purest sentiment of regard and esteem I have always the pleasure to subscribe myself, Dear Madam, Your sincere friend and Obedt Humble Servt

Go: Washington

To William Barton, September 7, 1788 (Excerpt)

Imperfectly acquainted with the subject as I profess myself to be, and persuaded of your skill as I am, it is far from my design to intimate an opinion that heraldry, coat-armor, etc., might not be rendered conducive to public and private uses with us, or that they can have any tendency unfriendly to the purest spirit of republicanism. On the contrary, a different conclusion is deducible from the practice of Congress and the states, all of which have established some kind of armorial devices to authenticate their official instruments. But, sir, you must be sensible that political sentiments are very various among the people in the several states, and that a formidable opposition to what appears to be the prevailing sense of the Union is but just declining into peaceable acquiescence. While, therefore, the minds of a certain portion of the community (possibly from turbulent or sinister views) are, or affect to be, haunted with the very specter of innovation; while they are indefatigably striving to make the credulity of the less-informed part of the citizens subservient to their schemes, in believing that the proposed general government is pregnant with the seeds of discrimination, oligarchy, and despotism; while they are clamorously endeavoring to propagate an idea that those whom they wish invidiously to designate by the name of the "well-born" are meditating in the first instance to distinguish themselves from their compatriots, and to wrest the dearest privileges from the bulk of the people; and while the apprehensions of some who have demonstrated themselves the sincere, but too jealous, friends of liberty, are feelingly alive to the effects of the actual revolution, and too much inclined to coincide with the prejudices above described; it might not, perhaps, be advisable to stir any question that would tend to reanimate the dying embers of faction or blow the dormant spark of jealousy into an inextinguishable flame. I need not say that the deplorable consequences would be the same, allowing there should be no real foundation for jealousy, in the judgment of sober reason, as if there were demonstrable, even palpable, causes for it.

I make these observations with the greater freedom, because I have once been a witness to what I conceived to have been a most unreasonable prejudice against an innocent institution, I mean the Society of the Cincinnati. I was conscious that my own proceedings on that subject were immaculate. I was also convinced that the members, actuated by motives of sensibility, charity, and patriotism, were doing a laudable thing in erecting that memorial of their common services, sufferings, and friendships. And I had not the most remote suspicion that our conduct therein would have been unprofitable or unpleasing to our countrymen. Yet have we been virulently traduced as to our designs; and I have not even escaped being represented as shortsighted in not foreseeing the consequences, or wanting in patriotism for not discouraging an establishment calculated to create distinctions in society and subvert the principles of a republican government. Indeed, the phantom seems now to be pretty well laid, except on certain occasions, when it is conjured up by designing men to work their own purposes upon terrified imaginations. You will recollect there have not been wanting, in the late political discussions, those who were hardy enough to assert that the proposed general government was the wicked and traitorous fabrication of the Cincinnati.

At this moment of general agitation and earnest solicitude, I should not be surprised to hear a violent outcry raised by those who are hostile to the new Constitution that the proposition contained in your paper had verified their suspicions and proved the design of establishing unjustifiable discriminations. Did I believe that to be the case, I should not hesitate to give it my hearty disapprobation. But I proceed on other grounds. Although I make not the clamor of credulous, disappointed, or unreasonable men the criterion of truth, yet I think their clamor might have an ungracious influence at the present critical juncture; and, in my judgment, some respect should not only be paid to prevalent opinions, but even some sacrifices might innocently be made to well-meant prejudices in a popular government. Nor could we hope the evil impression would be sufficiently removed, should your account and illustrations be found adequate to produce conviction on candid and unprejudiced minds. For myself, I can readily acquit you of having any design of facilitating the setting up an "Order of Nobility." I do not doubt the rectitude of your intentions. But, under the existing circumstances, I would willingly decline the honor you have intended me by your polite inscription, if there should be any danger of giving serious pretext, however ill-founded in reality, for producing or confirming jealousy and dissension in a single instance, where harmony and accommodation are most essentially requisite to our public prosperity, perhaps to our national existence.

My remarks, you will please to observe, go only to the expediency, not to the merits, of the proposition. What may be necessary and proper hereafter, I hold myself incompetent to decide, as I am but a private citizen. You may, however, rest satisfied that your composition is calculated to give favorable impressions of the science, candor, and ingenuity with which you have handled the subject, and that, in all personal considerations, I remain with great esteem, Sir, your most obedient, &c.

To Henry Lee, Jr., September 22, 1788 (Excerpt)

Private

Dear Sir,

Your letter of the 13th instant was of so friendly and confidential a complexion as to merit my early attention and cordial acknowledgments.

I am glad Congress have at last decided upon an ordinance for carrying the new government into execution. In my mind, the place for the meeting of the new Congress was not an object of such very important consequence; but I greatly fear that the question entailed upon that body, respecting their permanent residence, will be pregnant with difficulty and danger. God grant that true patriotism and a spirit of moderation may exclude a narrow locality and all ideas unfriendly to the Union from every quarter.

Your observations on the solemnity of the crisis and its application to myself bring before me subjects of the most momentous and interesting nature. In our endeavors to establish a new general government, the contest, nationally considered, seems not to have been so much for glory as existence. It was for a long time doubtful whether we were to survive as an independent republic, or decline from our federal dignity into insignificant and wretched fragments of empire. The adoption of the Constitution so extensively, and with so liberal an acquiescence on the part of the minorities in general, promised the former—until, lately, the circular letter of New York carried, in my apprehension, an unfavorable if not an insidious tendency to a contrary policy. I will hope for the best, but before you mentioned it, I could not help fearing it would serve as a standard to which the disaffected might resort. It is now evidently the part of all honest men who are friends to the new Constitution to endeavor to give it a chance to disclose its merits and defects by carrying it fairly into effect in the first instance. For it is to be apprehended that, by an attempt to obtain amendments before the experiment has been candidly made, "more is meant than meets the ear"—that an intention is concealed to accomplish slyly what could not have been done openly—to undo all that has been done. If the fact so exists that a kind of combination is forming to stifle the government in embryo, it is a happy circumstance that the design has become suspected. Preparation should be the sure attendant upon forewarning. Probably, prudence, wisdom, and patriotism were never more essentially necessary than at the present moment. And so far as it can be done in an irreproachable direct manner, no effort ought to be left unessayed to procure the election of the best possible characters to the new Congress. On their harmony, deliberation, and decision everything will depend. I heartily wish Mr. Madison was in our assembly, as I think, with you, it is of unspeakable importance Virginia should set out in her federal measures under right auspices.

The principal topic of your letter is, to me, a point of great delicacy indeed, insomuch that I can scarcely, without some impropriety, touch upon it. In the first place, the event to which you allude may never happen—amongst other reasons—because, if the partiality of my fellow citizens conceives it to be a mean by which the sinews of the new government would be strengthened, it will of consequence be obnoxious to those who are in opposition to it, many of whom unquestionably will be placed among the electors. This consideration alone would supersede the expediency of announcing any definitive and irrevocable resolution. You are among the small number of those who know my invincible attachment to domestic life, and that my sincerest wish is to continue in the enjoyment of it, solely, until my final hour. But the world would be neither so well instructed or so candidly disposed as to believe me to be uninfluenced by sinister motives, in case any circumstance should render a deviation from the line of conduct I had prescribed myself indispensable. Should the contingency you suggest take place, and (for argument sake alone let me say) should my unfeigned reluctance to accept the office be overcome by a deference for the reasons and opinions of my friends, might I not, after the declarations I have made (and Heaven knows they were made in the sincerity of my heart), in the judgment of the impartial world and of posterity be chargeable with levity and inconsistency, if not with rashness and ambition? Nay, farther, would there not even be some apparent foundation for the two former charges? Now justice to myself and tranquility of conscience require that I should act a part, if not above imputation, at least capable of vindication. Nor will you conceive me to be too solicitous for reputation. Though I prize, as I ought, the good opinion of my fellow citizens; yet, if I know myself, I would not seek or retain popularity at the expense of one social duty or moral virtue. While doing what my conscience informed me was right, as it respected my God, my country, and myself, I could despise all the party clamor and unjust censure which must be expected from some whose personal enmity might be occasioned by their hostility to the government. I am conscious that I fear alone to give any real occasion for obloquy, and that I do not dread to meet with unmerited reproach. And certain I am, whensoever I shall be convinced the good of my country requires my reputation to be put in risk, regard for my own fame will not come in competition with an object of so much magnitude. If I declined the task, it would be upon quite another principle. Notwithstanding my advanced season of life, my increasing fondness for agricultural amusements, and my growing love of retirement augment and confirm my decided predilection for the character of a private citizen, yet it would be no one of these motives, nor the hazard to which my former reputation might be exposed, or the terror of encountering new fatigues and troubles that would deter me from an acceptance, but a belief that some other person, who had less pretense and less inclination to be excused, could execute all the duties full as satisfactorily as myself. To say more would be indiscreet, as a disclosure of a refusal beforehand might incur the application of the fable in which the fox is represented as undervaluing the grapes he could not reach. You will perceive, my dear sir, by what is here observed (and which you will be pleased to consider in the light of a confidential communication) that my inclinations will dispose and decide me to remain as I am, unless a clear and insurmountable conviction should be impressed on my mind that some very disagreeable consequences must in all human probability result from the indulgence of my wishes.

To James Madison, September 23, 1788 (Excerpt)

Upon mature reflection, I think the reasons you offer in favor of Philadelphia as the place for the first meeting of Congress are conclusive, especially when the farther agitation of the question respecting its permanent residence is taken into consideration. But I cannot, however, avoid being satisfied that the minority should have acquiesced in any place rather than to have prevented the system from being carried into effect. The delay had already become the source of clamors and might have given advantages to the Anti-Federalists. Their expedient will now probably be an attempt to procure the election of so many of their own junto under the new government as by the introduction of local and embarrassing disputes to impede or frustrate its operation.

In the meantime, it behooves all the advocates of the Constitution, forgetting partial and smaller considerations, to combine their exertions for collecting the wisdom and virtue of the continent to one center, in order that the republic may avail itself of the opportunity for escaping from anarchy, division, and the other great national calamities that impended. To be shipwrecked in sight of the port would be the severest of all possible aggravations to our misery, and I assure you I am under painful apprehensions from the single circumstance of Mr. H— —'s[20] having the whole game to play in the assembly of this state and the effect it may have on others. It should be counteracted if possible. With sentiments of the highest esteem and regard I am— My dear Sir Your Affectionate Hble Servt

Go: Washington

Explanatory Notes

1 A correction from Washington's "of."
2 We have provided this seemingly missing parenthesis.
3 A reference to Henry Laurens.
4 We added this word, which Washington had omitted.
5 A correction from Washington's "defeat."
6 A correction from Washington's "state."
7 A correction from Washington's "of."
8 A correction from Washington's "if."

9 Corrected from Washington's "ware."
10 We have added these quotation marks because they help to clarify Washington's meaning.
11 Here we have left Washington's diary entry exactly as he wrote it, but it would appear that he should have used the word "excepted" after the word "adjournment," since the Convention did not meet on Sundays or during periods of adjournment.
12 A correction from Washington's "through."
13 A correction from Washington's "the."
14 A reference to Joel Barlow, the American poet and diplomat who also won French citizenship and served in the National Assembly during France's revolutionary period.
15 A correction from Washington's "then."
16 A correction from Washington's "enquire."
17 Washington's meaning in this sentence is very obscure, but we cannot think of an alternate rendering. He had capitalized "states" in the original, so he was likely referring to the state governments.
18 A correction from Washington's "affection."
19 A correction from Washington's "tithe."
20 A reference to Patrick Henry.

Index

Page numbers in *italics* indicate figures. Dates in parentheses refer to dates of writings.

agrarian law, 546–47
agriculture
    advice on investing in land (June 6–July 6, 1780), 291–92
    suggestion to take advantage of harvest (November 15, 1784), 493
    that agriculture and manufactures are gaining ground (August 31, 1788), 662–63
    wish that agriculture and commerce would supersede the waste of war (April 25, 1788), 619–20
alcohol, 265
Alexander, William (Lord Stirling), 132
Alexander the Great, 625–26
Alexandria, Virginia
    no Anti-Federalists among the inhabitants of (June 29, 1788), 638–39
    satisfaction on return to domestic life in (December 31, 1783), 455
Algeria, 630–31
Allegheny River, 486–90
allegiance
    oath of. *see* oath of allegiance
    recommended measures to induce persons to return from aligning with the enemy (June 3, 1777), 141–42
Allen, William B., 2
American Academy of Arts and Sciences, 341
American colonies
    request to unite in face of French and Indian advance (April 9, 1756), 17
    support for preventing Intolerable Acts against (August 24, 1774), 43–44
American Farmer's Letters (Crevecoeur), 633
The American Museum, 635
American Philosophical Society
    honor of election to membership in (February 15, 1780), 279
    intention to be friend and associate to (December 13, 1783), 448
American Revolutionary War
    alliance with France, 4, 164–65, 209–11, 217, 220, 224
        gratitude and pledge of good offices (July 20, 1780), 299
        gratitude and veneration for (June 5, 1780), 290
        recommendation for small committee to oversee cooperation (May 14, 1780), 282–83
        state of preparations for cooperation (November 1, 1779), 274–75
        statement of situation (May 28, 1780), 285–88
    alliance with Spain (May 28, 1780), 285–88
    assurances of success, 151–52, 156
    Battle of Brandywine, 304–7
    Battle of Camden, 319–20
    Battle of Monmouth, 636–37
    Battle of Sullivan's Island, 636–37
    Battle of Trenton, 113–14
    Battles of Lexington and Concord, 48
    Battles of Saratoga, 159
    Bunker Hill fight, 87–88

American Revolutionary War (cont.)
  cautions against ending without another desperate effort on the part of the enemy (March 15, 1779), 244–45
  cautions against expectations of peace (October 17, 1782), 363
  cautions regarding joint engagements with France (November 11, 1778), 230
  cautions regarding joint expedition against Canada (November 14, 1778), 230
  certainty of loss (May 31, 1780), 289
  cessation of hostilities
    congratulations and hope for new measures of government (March 29, 1783), 388
    congratulations and hope for respectable constitution (March 29, 1783), 387
    congratulations and hope for the states to be wise as they establish their Union (March 31, 1783), 389
    congratulations on end of hostilities in the southern states (February 6, 1783), 367
    as presage of our future happiness (August 26, 1783), 429
    public proclamation (April 18, 1783), 403–4
  confidence in happy issue though its period of accomplishment may be far distant (March 26, 1781), 342
  crossing the Delaware (August 20, 1780), 304–7
  doctrine of Providence in (August 20, 1778), 225
  draft resolution of one year for (October 4, 1780), 312
  enemy
    abhorrence for and thoughts on the fall of Great Britain (November 20, 1779), 276–77
    arts of the enemy (May 1778), 223–24
    attempt to reconcile the conduct of Britain (September 7, 1779), 272–73
  expenses of (August 20, 1780), 304–7
  extended duration of (October 18, 1780), 316–20
  faith in success (December 31, 1777), 174–75
  glory due Vice Admiral Estaing (September 11, 1778), 227
  grateful thanks and prayer for success (April 1, 1776), 93–94
  grateful thanks for protection and direction (May 30, 1778), 222
  intention to re-establish peace and harmony (June 26, 1775), 61
  invitation to the inhabitants of Canada to join (c. September 14, 1775), 75–76
  on the ladies in the number of the best patriots (August 31, 1788), 664–65
  lamentations regarding ablest men staying home (March 27, 1779), 248–49
  motivation for
    civil and religious liberty (November 27, 1783), 440
    liberty and independence of these states (January 5, 1781), 326–28
    liberty and safety (c. July 4, 1775), 63
    that G. Britain meant to drive America into rebellion (March 1, 1778), 196–97
  need for additional succor of troops (January 5, 1781), 327–28
  need for good intelligence from England (April 21, 1778), 209–11
  need for laws against supply of the enemy (November 13, 1782), 365
  need for men and money and vigorous exertions yet to end (June 15, 1782), 355
  need for naval superiority (January 5, 1781), 326–28
  need for peremptory draft for (August 20, 1780), 303–7
  need for plan for continuance (August 20, 1780), 303–7
  need for political skill (March 15, 1779), 246

observation of thirst for riches
(June 30, 1779), 268
occupation of Boston (March 21,
1776), 91
peace commissioners (May 1778),
223–24
peace negotiations
lack of confidence in, 359, 360
reaction to British moves toward
(April 21, 1778), 208–11
Philadelphia campaign
assurances of success (September 5,
1777), 151–52
temporary enlistments as reason for
loss in (October 18, 1780), 316–20
plan of operations against Canada
(April 14, 1779), 252–56
preparation for
assessment and need for (March 12,
1782), 352–53
doctrine of preparation for war to
obtain peace, 296–97, 358
lamentation on lack of, 291–92, 312
prisoners of war
complaints regarding treatment of
(January 13, 1777), 112, 113–14
proposed exchange of (January 13,
1777), 113–14
refusal to support retaliation for
General Lee's treatment (March 1,
1777), 124–25
request for exchange of (December
18, 1775), 82
request for support to Congress
against retaliatory confinement of
British officers (March 2, 1777),
126–27
treatment of, 71, 72–73, 82, 112,
113–14
Proclamation Concerning Persons
Swearing British Allegiance
(January 25, 1777), 117
prospects for accumulating distress
(October 5, 1780), 313–14
public discontent with war (January 15,
1781), 327–28
request for assistance from the
inhabitants of Bermuda
(September 6, 1775), 74

request for plan to bring out resources
(May 14, 1780), 282–83
request for respectable army for
(January 31, 1782), 347–48
review of (November 2, 1783), 437–39
road to victory (1778–1783), *214,*
217–450
statement of situation
back to the beginning (August 20,
1778), 225
declaration of lowest time of affairs
(May 18, 1779), 263–64
distress on the enemy's continuance
and wish to see countrymen roused
(December 18–30, 1778), 236–38
thanks for provisions and (May 28,
1780), 285–88
vanishing prospect of peace
(September 12, 1782), 358
that a greater revolution never took
place (March 26, 1788), 613–14
that the British will have to relinquish
all pretensions to conquest in
America (May 29, 1778), 221
Treaty of Paris
on the British continuing to hold
western posts ceded by, 482, 509,
531, 534, 537, 542
impatience for (July 10, 1783), 426
on the Rutgers and Waddington case
(September 26, 1785), 518
will not hesitate to contribute to
national security until (August 26,
1783), 429
trust in experience of error and
certainty of happy conclusion
(June 7, 1781), 343
want of revenue for (January 15, 1781),
325–28
war debt
Farewell Orders (November 2, 1783),
438–39
that justice will be rendered to all
public creditors and all debts due
will be paid (January 6,
1784), 457
warning regarding false expectations
founded on superficial views (May
18,1779), 263–64

American Revolutionary War (cont.)
  warning the conflict is not likely to cease soon (March 31, 1779), 250–51
Ames, Fisher, 1
André, John, 315
Annemours, Charles-François-Adrien Le Paulmier, 146
annual draft, 183–84
Anti-Federalist party
  on Anti-Federalists and those who may be appointed to the first Congress, 645–46, 654–55, 671
  and New Hampshire postponement of decision with regard to the Constitution (March 30, 1788), 615
  none in Alexandria (June 29, 1788), 638–39
Aristotle, 2
Armstrong, John
  May 18, 1779 letter to (warning regarding false expectations founded on superficial views), 263–64
  March 26, 1781 letter to (confidence in happy issue of present contest though its accomplishment may be distant), 342
  April 25, 1788 letter to (hopes he will not again enter public duty and on those who will be first called to act under the proposed government), 616–18
army. *see* Continental Army; militia(s); peace establishment
Arnold, Benedict
  character traits (October 13, 1780), 315
  discovery of his treason (September 26, 1780), 311
Articles of Confederation
  9th Article, 513
  on the need to revise and amend (May 18, 1786), 532
  support for amendment or extension of (August 22, 1785), 513
arts and sciences (December 13, 1783), 448

Bailey, General, 254–56
Banister, John, 207–11
Barbary States, 541–42
Barlow, Joel
  authorization to dispose of land (June 19, 1788), 633
  recommendation of (May 28, 1788), 625–26
Barton, William, 666–67
Bassett, Burwell
  April 20, 1773 letter to (condolences on the loss of their child), 36
  June 20, 1773 letter to (informing of the death of Patcy Custis), 37
  June 19, 1775 letter to (acceptance of command of the Continental Army), 56
Bassett, Fanny, 499
Battle of Brandywine, 304–7
Battle of Camden, 319–20
Battle of Monmouth, 636–37
Battle of Sullivan's Island, 636–37
Battle of Trenton, 113–14
Battles of Lexington and Concord, 48
Battles of Saratoga, 159
Baylor, George, 137
Bermuda, 74
Big Beaver Creek, 488–90
Bill of Rights, 622–23
biography, 508–9
black people
  enlistment of (December 15, 1775), 81
  return of escaped slaves (April 30, 1783), 409
  shall be happy to join scheme to encourage emancipation from bondage (April 5, 1783), 400
Blair, John, 622
Bland, Theodorick
  April 4, 1783 letter to (on keeping the army together until settlement of accounts and funds established for security of the officers), 395–98
  April 4, 1783 letter to (plea for justice, gratitude, and payment of veteran soldiers), 391–92
borders
  state borders (March 29, 1784), 469–70
  support for compact land tracts (March 15, 1785), 503

support for statehood of Vermont and boundaries of New York (January 1, 1782), 345–46
Boston, Massachusetts
  Proclamation on the Occupation of (March 21, 1776), 91
  rejoice and prayer for happiness and prosperity (March 1776), 92
Boston Port Bill, 38
Boudinot, Elias
  March 18, 1783 letter to (assurance the Newburgh conspiracy is over), 379–80
  May 10, 1783 letter to (pleasure at Mr. Smith's *Ode on the Peace* and wish for policy system), 410
  June 17, 1783 letter to (petition from officers of the army for rewards in lands in the western country), 420–21
Boundary Line Treaty, 495
Bowen, Jabez, 560
Brandywine, Battle of, 304–7
bravery
  call for (October 3, 1777), 156
  proposal for honorary rewards for (January 29, 1778), 184
Brearly, Lt Colonel, 306–7
British Army
  Battle of Brandywine, 304–7
  Battle of Camden, 319–20
  Battle of Monmouth, 636–37
  Battle of Sullivan's Island, 636–37
  Battle of Trenton, 113–14
  Battles of Lexington and Concord, 48
  Battles of Saratoga, 159
  request for exchange of prisoners (December 18, 1775), 82
  treatment of prisoners, 71, 72–73, 82
British Navy, 112, 113–14
British North America
  new organization of (August 11, 1784), 482
  regret for slow determinations of Congress and (November 3, 1784), 491–92
British Parliament
  inconsistencies of (April 1, 1776), 95–96
  Intolerable Acts, 41–42, 43–44
  Stamp Act, 30, 31, 32
  support for Massachusetts Bay relative to (October 9, 1774), 45–46
  support for petitioning and more (July 4, 1774), 40
British provincial militia
  effects of misbehavior (January 8, 1756), 15–16
  intention to accept command if pressed and go to Ohio again (August 14, 1755), 11
  measures to discipline troops (July 15, 1757), 26
  payment of troops and standards of behavior (May 18, 1756), 21
  Proclamation of War against the French (August 15, 1756), 22
  request for post of lieutenant colonel (February–March 1754), 9
  request for regulation of (October 11, 1755), 13
  Ward's surrender to French forces (April 24, 1754), 10
  warning regarding recruitment methods and conduct (November 22, 1755), 14
British trade
  boycott of British goods, 33–34, 35
  British trade restrictions
    and congressional powers, 505, 507, 510–11
    and relations with France, 517, 540–42
Brodhead, Daniel, 265
Buchanan, William, 189
Bunker Hill fight, 87–88
Burgoyne, John
  reciprocity of respect (March 11, 1778), 202
  report of standing ground against (October 3, 1777), 156
  report of success over (October 15, 1777), 159
Burk, Richard, 226
burning effigies of the pope, 80

Butler, Richard
  conveyance of Indian vocabulary and language and request for a universal dictionary (January 10, 1788), 606–7
  warm acknowledgments for Indian vocabulary and observations respecting the different tribes (January 10, 1788 letter to), 605

Cadwalader, John, 313–14
Caesar, Augustus, 625–26
Caesar, Julius, 625–26
Callender, John, 65
Camden, Battle of, 319–20
Campbell, Archibald
  refusal to support retaliation for General Lee's treatment (March 1, 1777), 124–25
  request for support to Congress against retaliatory confinement of British officers (March 2, 1777), 126–27
Campbell, Henry, 21
Canada
  cautions regarding joint expedition against (November 14, 1778), 230
  concern for negotiations with Vermont (January 1, 1782), 346
  duty to address public thanks to (November 5, 1775), 80
  invitation to join forces (c. September 14, 1775), 75–76
  plan of operations against (April 14, 1779), 252–56
  temporary enlistments as reason for loss of (October 18, 1780), 317–20
capital punishment
  preference for regular proceedings (August 3, 1777), 149
  recommended gradation of punishments (January 29, 1778), 185–86
  recommended punishments for deserters (July 9, 1779), 269
  request for proper gradation of punishments in military code (February 3, 1781), 333–34
Carey, Mathew, 635
Carey's American Museum, 633

Carleton, Roy, 482
Carmen, Michael, 226
Carmichael, William, 505
Carter, Landon, 222
Cary, Archibald, 355
Cary, Robert
  September 20, 1765 letter to (thoughts on the Stamp Act), 30
  July 21, 1766 letter to (thanks for repeal of the Stamp Act), 31
  July 25, 1769 letter to (determination to boycott British goods), 35
Catherine the Great (Empress of Russia)
  conveyance of Indian vocabulary and language to and request for a universal dictionary (January 10, 1788), 606–7
  relations with England (June 18, 1788), 630
Catholic Church, 80
cattle, 308–9
chaplains
  Circular Instructions to the Brigade Commanders (May 26, 1777), 139
  direction for worship services every Sunday (February 15, 1783), 368
  discouragement of profane swearing and immorality (May 31, 1777), 140
  furloughs and expectations (February 15, 1783), 368
  General Orders (July 9, 1776), 101
  request for attendance at thanksgiving (December 17, 1777), 164–65
  request for discourses for a national day of fasting, humiliation, and prayer (April 12, 1778), 206
  sentiments on (May 23, 1777), 137
Chapman, George, 496
charity, 648
Chase, Samuel, 497
Chastellux, François-Jean de Beauvoir
  September 5, 1785 letter to (wishes for peace and release of all trade restrictions), 517
  April 25, 1788 letter to (congratulations on marriage and domestic felicity and on the waste of war), 619–20
Cheat River, 489–90

Index 679

checks and balances
  recommendations for (February 7, 1788), 609
  support for (November 9, 1787), 594
Chittenden, Thomas, 345–46
Christianity
  disposition to (August 15, 1787), 582
  support for Lady Huntingdon's plan to spread Christianity among Indians (February 8, 1785), 500–1
  worship services every Sunday, 212, 368
Cicero, 664–65
City Tavern (Philadelphia), 584
civil government
  all that can be expected is charity, mutual forbearance, and acquiescence in the general voice (August 3, 1788), 648
  on the blessings that will be attributed to the new government (June 18, 1788), 631
  concern for forming (April 5, 1783), 399–400
  constitution of
    hope for respectable constitution (March 29, 1783), 387
    need for competent constitution of Congress (April 24, 1783), 407
  departments of war, finance, and foreign affairs (February 20, 1781), 338
  executive bodies
    need for laws and (January 31, 1781), 331–32
    need for more responsibility and permanency (December 26, 1780), 322
  federal. *see* federal government
  hope for new measures of government (March 29, 1783), 388
  Indian affairs (September 7, 1783), 430–34
  need for (October 22, 1780), 321
  powers
    need for (November 9, 1787), 593–94
    need for powers competent to all general purposes (March 4, 1783), 370–71
  representative. *see* representative government
  respect for (December 17, 1781), 344
  on the situation of the general government as shaken and in need of remedy (May 30, 1787), 578
  sympathy and support for (March 10, 1782), 351
  on using his influence to appease versus addressing grievances if any and using force of government (October 31, 1786), 545
  as wheels of clock in mechanics (June 15, 1782), 355
  wish for states to adopt liberal and proper government (June 15, 1783), 419
civil liberty. *see also* liberty
  establishment of civil and religious liberty as motive for revolution (November 27, 1783), 440
  hope that the foundation is laid for much purer civil liberty than have hitherto been (August 29, 1788), 657
Clark, Francis Carr, 159
Clinton, George, 494
Clinton, Henry, 267, 312
clothing
  request for clothing and supplies (December 29, 1777), 172–73
  request to the ladies to do something towards introducing federal fashions (August 31, 1788), 664–65
  want of clothing for the troops (December 26, 1780), 322
  warning regarding consequences of lack of clothing, provisions, and pay (January 20, 1779), 240–43
coat-armor, 666–67
coinage, 513
College of William and Mary, 624
colonies. *see* American colonies
colonization, 420–21
commerce. *see also* trade
  advantages and disadvantages of (March 29, 1784), 469–70
  foreign (October 7, 1785), 520–21
  inland routes

commerce. *see also* trade (cont.)
    need for inland navigation between Atlantic states and western territory (August 22, 1785), 514
    proposal to extend inland navigation routes (November 3, 1784), 492
    refusal of shares in navigation of Potomac and James rivers, 498–99, 502, 522
    request to direct shares to public use and benefit (July 30, 1785), 512
    suggestions for (October 10, 1784), 487–90
    regulation of
        on adequate powers in Congress and, 515–16, 621–23
        on the need for (April 25, 1788), 617–18
        support for (November 30, 1785), 525, 526
        what that will yield (December 25, 1787), 599
    state of the union
        that agriculture and manufactures are gaining ground (August 31, 1788), 662–63
        want of (January 15, 1781), 325–28
    western routes (October 10, 1784), 485–90
    wish that agriculture and commerce would supersede the waste of war (April 25, 1788), 619–20
common sense, 518
Confederation Congress. *see also* Continental Congress
    Address (August 26, 1783), 429
    Address on resigning his commission (December 23, 1783), 449
    advice against adjournment for a few months (March 4, 1783), 370–71
    archives (May 8, 1784), 472
    assurance the Newburgh conspiracy is over (March 18, 1783), 379–80
    on the deficiencies of the Confederation (October 7, 1785), 520–21
    establishment of ministers (February 20, 1781), 338
    expectations of officers (April 4, 1783), 395–98
    gratitude for support and distinguished honors (August 26, 1783), 429
    gratitude to Pennsylvania for example made in adopting recommendations of (December 9, 1783), 443
    inertitude which prevails in (March 29, 1784), 469–70
    on lassitude of Congress (October 30, 1785), 523
    need for a competent constitution (April 24, 1783), 407
    powers of
        on British trade restrictions and, 505, 507, 510–11
        on disinclination of states to yield (January 18, 1784), 458–59
        on the need for adequate powers, 422–24, 530–31
        on the need for exertion of (August 22, 1785), 513
        on the need for more than recommendatory power (February 4, 1781), 336
        on the need for sufficient power to act (June 2, 1784), 478
        on regulation of commerce and, 515–16, 621–23
        on relations with the British and (August 15, 1786), 538–39
    preparation to resign from office of commander-in-chief (June 8, 1783), 411–18
    recommendation for annual vs constant sessions (March 29, 1784), 469–70
    recommendation for delegates and to compel close attendance (January 18, 1784), 458–59
    recommendation for states to appear in the proposed Convention (March 31, 1787), 572–74
    regret for slow determinations of (November 3, 1784), 491–92
    request for proper gradation of punishments in the military code (February 3, 1781), 333–34

Secretary of Finance (February 4, 1781), 335–36
submission for consideration that Constitution which appeared most advisable (September 17, 1787), 585
as wheels of clock in mechanics (June 15, 1782), 355
on wretched management of (August 11, 1784), 482

Connecticut
adoption of the new Constitution, 609, 620
congratulations on liberal measures in (July 20, 1788), 643–44
need for rigid laws against supply of the enemy (November 13, 1782), 365
state of preparations for cooperation with French fleet (November 1, 1779), 274–75
state of review of new plan of government (January 1, 1788), 600–1

Connecticut Line, 405–6
Connolly, John, 47
Conotocaurious, 12, 48 n.1

Constitutional Convention
apprehensions and queries should he attend and request for conference beforehand (April 2, 1787), 575–76
assents to go and hopes for the best (April 9, 1787), 577
on Congress recommending states to appear at (March 31, 1787), 572–74
gratitude to Providence for inducing appointment of (July 20, 1788), 644
hopes for firm and permanent general government recommendation from (July 1, 1787), 579–80
hopes for thorough reform from (March 31, 1787), 572–74
intentions to not attend, 561–62, 579–80
on the need for wise council and most vigorous exertions (December 28, 1786), 559
opinion of a general convention (May 18, 1786), 532
on political concerns as suspended by a thread and that anarchy would have ensued (September 24, 1787), 587
regrets of conflicts, 551, 552–53, 554
request for sentiments on the upcoming Convention and what he should do (December 26, 1786), 555–56
request to know of public expectation for his participation in (March 8, 1787), 567
resolution to attend if his health permits (March 28, 1787), 570–71
on the situation of the general government as shaken and in need of remedy (May 30, 1787), 578
state of the councils
meditation on the momentous work executed thereby (September 17, 1787), 584
on the proceedings of the Federal Convention, 586, 596
unanimous vote of the Convention, 584, 589, 596
and wish for adoption of the government agreed on there (August 19, 1787), 583
and wish for Hamilton to come back (July 10, 1787), 581
wonder that anything was produced with such unanimity (November 16, 1787), 596
submission for consideration to the President of Congress that Constitution which has appeared most advisable (September 17, 1787), 585

Continental Army
acceptance of command (June 19, 1775), 56
alliance with France (July 20, 1780), 299
annual or temporary as insufficient (October 5, 1780), 313–14
arms (January 14, 1776), 85–86
assurances of success (General Orders), 151–52, 156
call for bravery (October 3, 1777), 156

Continental Army (cont.)
  celebration of victory (October 15, 1777), 159
  chaplains
    Circular Instructions to the Brigade Commanders (May 26, 1777), 139
    direction for worship services every Sunday (February 15, 1783), 368
    discouragement of profane swearing and immorality (May 31, 1777), 140
    furloughs and expectations (February 15, 1783), 368
    General Orders (July 9, 1776), 101
    request for attendance at thanksgiving (December 17, 1777), 164–65
    request for discourses for a national day of fasting, humiliation, and prayer (April 12, 1778), 206
    sentiments on (May 23, 1777), 137
  commanding officers
    acknowledgment and thanks to (December 23, 1783), 449
    attention to discipline and subordination (June 7, 1777), 144
    Circular Instructions to the Brigade Commanders (May 26, 1777), 139
    complaint of treatment by Major General Stirling of Mrs. Livingston (May 6, 1777), 132
    consequences for munity (January 18, 1779), 239
    court martial of Captain Callender (July 7, 1775), 65
    denial of appointment to Colonel François Lellorquis de Malmedy (May 16, 1777), 133–34
    discontents which prevail throughout (October 2, 1782), 361–62
    expectations of behavior, 147
    expectations of Congress (April 4, 1783), 395–98
    expectations to prevent invasions and abuse of private property, 64, 147
    introduction and recommendation for brevet of Chevalier de Mauduit du Plessis (January 13, 1778), 179
    keeping the army together until settlement of accounts is effected and funds established for security of (April 4, 1783), 395–98
    Newburgh conspiracy, 373–74, 375–78, 379–80
    petition for rewards in lands in the western country (June 17, 1783), 420–21
    proposal for half-pay for officers' and widows' pensions, 181–83, 207–11, 242–43, 415–18
    proposed establishment of discipline (April 21, 1778), 207–11
    regret at officer behavior when on trial (February 18, 1781), 337
    request for acceptance of assigned command of Brigadier General John Glover (April 26, 1777), 131
    request for assistance with foreign officers (May 17, 1777), 135–36
    request for attendance at thanksgiving (December 17, 1777), 164–65
    request for attention to abuses by soldiers under (July 25, 1777), 148
    request for continued service of Brigadier General Thomas (July 23, 1775), 68–69
    request for orders against plundering be distinctly read to all the troops (September 4, 1777), 150
    request for preventive measures by (January 28, 1780), 278
    request for purity of morals and decency (October 21, 1778), 229
    request of Congress to reconsider suspending Greene without proper trial (August 13, 1780), 300–1
    resigning commissions (April 21, 1778), 207–11
    severance pay (April 4, 1783), 396–98
    thanks for fortitude and patience (December 17, 1777), 164–65
    thanks for persevering fidelity and zeal (March 1, 1778), 194–95
    vacancies and irregular appointments and promotions (August 20, 1780), 306–7

want of brigadiers (December 23, 1777), 170–71
wishes for brotherhood among (April 6, 1778), 205
compensation for services
concern for soldiers wanting relief and recompense (May 27–28, 1780), 284
on consequences of failure to pay the army (March 19, 1783), 383–84
court martial for re-enlistment and receiving new bounties (February 6, 1977), 122
discontents which prevail throughout (October 2, 1782), 361–62
on failure to pay the army, 370–71, 372
Farewell Orders (November 2, 1783), 438–39
gratitude to merchants of Philadelphia for (December 9, 1783), 444
keeping the army together until settlement of accounts is effected and funds established for security of the officers (April 4, 1783), 395–98
petition from officers for rewards in lands in the western country (June 17, 1783), 420–21
plea for payment of veteran soldiers (April 4, 1783), 391–92
proposal for half-pay for officers' and widows' pensions, 181–83, 207–11, 242–43, 415–18
punishment for those who desert and receive double bounties (May 23, 1777), 138
remarks to the meeting of officers at Newburgh (March 15, 1783), 375–78
request continuance of efforts to compensate the army (March 18, 1783), 381–82
request for pay for the troops, 77, 323–24, 383–84
settlement of (August 10, 1775), 70
severance pay (April 4, 1783), 396–98
sincere wish and efforts for (May 22, 1782), 354
sufferings of the army vs. inability of Congress and states to pay (March 4, 1783), 370–71
thanks for exertions of Robert Morris for (March 8, 1783), 372
want of pay, 280–81, 361–62, 383–84
warning of other potential conspiracies unless payments are made (March 19, 1783), 385–86
warning regarding consequences of continued lack of pay, 363, 383–84
conduct of officers and soldiers
appreciation for, 366, 367
Circular Instructions to the Brigade Commanders (May 26, 1777), 139
complaint of treatment by Major General Stirling of Mrs. Livingston (May 6, 1777), 132
disciplinary issues, 144, 305–7
disorder among and limited number of troops fit for duty (September 22, 1776), 109
disturbance at (September 30, 1776), 110–11
expectations of behavior, 62, 64, 65, 66, 70, 78, 80, 83–84, 90, 91, 101, 103, 105, 107, 147
General Orders (August 1, 1776), 372
honor and congratulations on first instance of treason (September 26, 1780), 311
mutiny in Huntington's brigade (January 18, 1779), 239
mutiny in the Pennsylvania line (January 5, 1781), 323–24
mutiny suppression in the New Jersey line (January 30, 1781), 329–30
Newburgh conspiracy, 373–74, 375–78, 379–80
recommendations for behavior (July 2, 1776 General Order), 100
reduced and mutinous state (December 23, 1777), 168–71
regret at officer behavior when on trial (February 18, 1781), 337
request for attention to abuses by soldiers, 148, 150
request for declaration of service (October 26, 1775), 78

Continental Army (cont.)
  request for preventive measures by officers (January 28, 1780), 278
  request for purity of morals and decency (October 21, 1778), 229
  request for well-regulated militia (January 24, 1777), 116
  request of Congress to reconsider suspending Greene without proper trial (August 13, 1780), 300–1
  request to stop sales of liquor to the troops (May 21, 1779), 265
  sensitivity to their sufferings (January 30, 1781 General Orders), 329–30
  sufferings of the army vs. inability of Congress and states to pay (March 4, 1783), 370–71
  temporary enlistments as reason for extended duration of war (October 18, 1780), 316–20
  congratulations to the troops (October 15, 1777), 159
  Connecticut line (April 22, 1783), 405–6
  deserters
    court martial for desertion and re-enlistment (February 6, 1977), 122
    pardons for those who return from the enemy (August 21, 1778), 226
    Proclamation of Pardon to Deserters who re-enlisted (April 6, 1777), 129
    punishment for, 128, 226
    punishment for those who desert and receive double bounties (May 23, 1777), 138
    recommended punishments (July 9, 1779), 269
    request for acceptance of assigned command of Brigadier General John Glover (April 26, 1777), 131
    request for laws against, 118, 119
    request for punishment of (April 3, 1777), 128
  disbanding
    expectations of the officers (April 4, 1783), 395–98
    hope for honorable military exit (April 5, 1783), 399–400
    necessity of (April 22, 1783), 405–6
    request for (April 4, 1783), 393–94
    settlement of accounts before, 395–98, 405–6
    severance pay (April 4, 1783), 396–98
  disciplinary practices
    consequences for munity (January 18, 1779), 239
    court martial for desertion and re-enlistment (February 6, 1977), 122
    court martial for murder of a Delaware (May 21, 1779), 265
    court martial of Captain Callender (July 7, 1775), 65
    court martial of Lieutenant Dunn (April 6, 1778), 205
    court martial proceedings, 205, 219, 350
    discouragement of profane swearing and immorality (May 31, 1777), 140
    Farewell Orders (November 2, 1783), 438–39
    pardons (August 21, 1778), 226
    proposed establishment of discipline (April 21, 1778), 207–11
    punishment for cowardice (September 6, 1777), 153
    punishment for deserters to the enemy (August 21, 1778), 226
    punishment for misbehavior, 83–84, 90, 91, 100, 102, 103, 105, 153, 219, 226
    punishment for returning delinquents (April 21, 1778), 210–11
    punishment for those found guilty of plundering inhabitants, 147, 150
    punishment for those who desert and receive double bounties (May 23, 1777), 138
    recommendations for gradation of punishments (January 29, 1778), 185–86
    request for orders against plundering be distinctly read to all the troops (September 4, 1777), 150

request for proper gradation of punishments in military code (February 3, 1781), 333–34
drum and fife majors (June 4, 1777), 143
Eastern Brigades, 169
enlistments
  court martial for desertion and re-enlistment (February 6, 1977), 122
  draft resolution of one year for the war (October 4, 1780), 312
  lamentation on lack of enlistments (June 6–July 6, 1780), 291–92
  lamentation regarding ablest men staying home (March 27, 1779), 248–49
  need for a permanent force (October 22, 1780), 321
  need for peremptory draft (August 20, 1780), 303–7
  procedures, 79, 102
  Proclamation of Pardon to Deserters who re-enlisted (April 6, 1777), 129
  proposal for annual draft (January 29, 1778), 183–84
  recommendations for completing regiments and altering their establishment (January 29, 1778), 183–84
  request for more men (December 29, 1777), 172–73
  state of the regiments, 81, 85–86, 157–58, 291–92, 303–7
  support for martial law and drafting citizens into military service (July 4, 1780), 294–95
  on temporary enlistments as reason for extended duration of war (October 18, 1780), 316–20
  voluntary enlistments as insufficient (March 12, 1782), 352–53
faith in success (December 31, 1777), 174–75
Farewell Orders (November 2, 1783), 437–39
financial issues
  and Newburgh conspiracy, 383–84
  payment of debts (November 2, 1783), 438–39
  sentiments respecting continental and state funds (April 16, 1783), 401–2
  want of money, 106, 263–64, 280–81, 304–7, 372
General Orders (July 4, 1775), 62
General Orders (July 5, 1775), 64
General Orders (July 7, 1775), 65
General Orders (July 16, 1775), 66
General Orders (August 10, 1775), 70
General Orders (November 5, 1775), 80
General Orders (October 26, 1775), 78
General Orders (October 31, 1775), 79
General Orders (January 1, 1776), 83–84
General Orders (February 27, 1776), 90
General Orders (May 15, 1776), 98
General Orders (July 2, 1776), 100
General Orders (July 9, 1776), 101
General Orders (July 23, 1776), 102
General Orders (August 1, 1776), 103
General Orders (September 6, 1776), 105
General Orders (September 19, 1776), 107
General Orders (January 21, 1777), 115
General Orders (February 6, 1777), 122
General Orders (May 31, 1777), 140
General Orders (June 4, 1777), 143
General Orders (June 7, 1777), 144
General Orders (July 25, 1777), 147
General Orders (September 4, 1777), 150
General Orders (September 5, 1777), 151–52
General Orders (September 6, 1777), 153
General Orders (October 3, 1777), 156
General Orders (October 15, 1777), 159
General Orders (December 17, 1777), 164–65
General Orders (March 1, 1778), 194–95
General Orders (April 6, 1778), 205
General Orders (April 12, 1778), 206
General Orders (May 2, 1778), 212

Continental Army (cont.)
  General Orders (August 21, 1778), 226
  General Orders (October 21, 1778), 229
  General Orders (January 28, 1780), 278
  General Orders (July 20, 1780), 299
  General Orders (September 26, 1780), 311
  General Orders (February 15, 1783), 368
  General Orders (January 30, 1781), 329–30
  General Orders (April 18, 1783), 403–4
  General Orders (February 18, 1781), 337
  logistics (May 14, 1780), 282–83
  Maryland forces (December 22, 1777), 166–67
  national day of fasting, 66, 98, 206
  national day of thanksgiving (December 17, 1777), 164–65
  need for a permanent force (October 22, 1780), 321
  need for regular troops over a militia (September 15, 1780), 310
  oath of abjuration, allegiance, and office (May 17, 1778), 218
  occupation of Boston (March 21, 1776), 91
  as Patriot Army (April 18, 1783), 404
  Pennsylvania Regiment
    provisions and pay to her officers (August 20, 1780), 306–7
    report of mutiny of the Pennsylvania line (January 5, 1781), 323–24
  plunder of property
    army abuses (General Orders), 107, 115, 147
    expectations of officers to prevent, 64, 147
    procedures for (January 21, 1777), 115
    prohibition of, 115, 147
    request for attention to abuses by soldiers, 148, 150
    request for congressional article against (September 22, 1776), 108
    request for law against (January 24, 1777), 116
    request for orders against be distinctly read to all the troops (September 4, 1777), 150
    request for preventive measures by officers (January 28, 1780), 278
    resolution to stop (September 6, 1776), 105
    threat of subsisting on (August 27, 1780), 308–9
  prisoners of war
    attempts to exchange with Howe (November 23, 1777), 162
    complaints regarding treatment of (January 13, 1777), 112
    proposed exchange of (January 13, 1777), 113–14
    refusal to support retaliation for General Lee's treatment (March 1, 1777), 124–25
    request for exchange of (December 18, 1775), 82
    request for good treatment (February 25, 1775), 47
    request for support to Congress against retaliatory confinement of British officers (March 2, 1777), 126–27
    warnings regarding treatment of, 71, 72–73, 82
  promotions (January 29, 1778), 184–86
  provisions
    inadequate subsistence by state supplies (October 5, 1780), 313–14
    inequality between the states (August 20, 1780), 306–7
    need for more (August 20, 1780), 305–7
    request for, 157–58, 168–71, 172–73, 323–24
    request to the states for (August 27, 1780), 308–9
    thanks to Pennsylvania for (May 28, 1780), 287–88
    want of, 157–58, 168–71, 189, 210–11, 222, 240–43, 291–92, 308–9, 322, 325–28, 370–71
    warning regarding consequences of lack of (January 20, 1779), 240–43

wasted articles on temporary enlistments vs permanent army (October 18, 1780), 316–20
recommendations for a permanent force (February 28, 1781), 339–40
recommendations of those who have continued in service (December 23, 1783), 449
relations with Congress (April 21, 1778), 210–11
report of success (October 15, 1777), 159
Revolutionary war. *see* American Revolutionary War
scouting parties, 115
services beyond their proper duty, 361–62
soldiers
    concern for want of relief and recompense (May 27–28, 1780), 284
    against including slaves (March 20, 1779), 247
    thanks for fortitude and patience (December 17, 1777), 164–65
    thanks for persevering fidelity and zeal (March 1, 1778), 194–95
state of the regiments
    alarm (May 22, 1779), 266–67
    concern and dread about prospects (February 7, 1778), 189
    concern for preparedness (May 5, 1778), 217
    concern for relief and recompense (May 27–28, 1780), 284
    declaration of lowest time of affairs (May 18, 1779), 263–64
    discontents which prevail throughout (October 2, 1782), 361–62
    enlistments, 81, 85–86, 157–58, 291–92, 303–7
    exculpation (December 23, 1777), 168–71
    general situation (April 3, 1780), 280–81
    lamentation on lack of recruitments and lack of preparation, 291–92, 312
    mode of subsisting (August 27, 1780), 308–9
    notification to Congress of need for respite (August 20, 1780), 302–7
    present state of exhaustion (January 15, 1781), 326–28
    prospects for accumulating distress (October 5, 1780), 313–14
    recommendations (January 29, 1778), 181–86
    request for more men (December 29, 1777), 172–73
    request for plan for correcting abuses and making new arrangements (December 23, 1777), 168–71
    request for plan of general principle for (April 3, 1780), 281
    request for respectable army (January 31, 1782), 347–48
    as resplendent (April 5, 1783), 400
    thanks for persevering fidelity and zeal and uncomplaining patience during scarcity (March 1, 1778), 194–95
    thanks to Pennsylvania for provisions and statement of situation (May 28, 1780), 287–88
    thanks to the ladies for subscriptions and request for linen shirts (July 14, 1780), 298
    unexampled sufferings of (October 17, 1782), 363
    want of a standing army, 296–97, 317–20
    want of provisions and support, 157–58, 168–71, 189, 210–11, 222, 240–43, 291–92, 308–9, 322, 325–28, 370–71
    warning regarding consequences of continued lack of pay (October 17, 1782), 363
    weakness (May 8, 1779), 259
    thanks of Congress to (April 18, 1776), 97
veterans. *see* veterans
winter quarters, 164–65, 166–67, 304–7
worship services every Sunday, 212, 368
Continental Congress. *see also* Confederation Congress
    address to (June 16, 1775), 53

Continental Army (cont.)
  advice on forming a new government (May 31, 1776), 99
  appraisal of the army general situation (April 3, 1780), 280–81
  Camp Committee, 181–86
  Committee of Cooperation
    entreaties to forward measures recommended by (June 27, 1780), 293
    recommendation for small committee to oversee cooperation with French (May 14, 1780), 282–83
  Committee of Conference
    proposal for half-pay for officers' and widows' pensions (January 20, 1779), 242–43
    warning regarding consequences of lack of clothing, provisions, and pay (January 20, 1779), 240–43
  declaration of Congress (July 9, 1776), 101
  expectations for peace (July 6, 1780), 296–97
  foreign officer appointments (May 17, 1777), 135–36
  forged resolves (May 1778), 223–24
  gratitude for recognition of service (April 18, 1776), 97
  indecision and delay in coming to determinations (April 21, 1778), 210–11
  jealousy of the army (April 21, 1778), 210–11
  need for greater powers, 322, 369, 370–71
  need for political skill (March 15, 1779), 246
  notification of the state of army and need for respite (August 20, 1780), 302–7
  payment of the army
    concern for soldiers wanting relief and recompense (May 27–28, 1780), 284
    and Newburgh conspiracy, 373–74, 375–78, 379–80, 383–84
    proposal for half-pay for officers' and widows' pensions (January 20, 1779), 242–43
    request for, 77, 323–24, 383–84
    want of money for, 106, 263–64, 280–81, 304–7, 372
  recommendation of oath or affirmation of allegiance (February 5, 1777), 120–21
  recommended measures to induce persons to return from aligning with the enemy (June 3, 1777), 141–42
  refusal to support retaliation for General Lee's treatment (March 1, 1777), 124–25
  request for article against plundering, marauding, and burning of houses (September 22, 1776), 108
  request for laws against deserters (January 31, 1777), 119
  request for plan for correcting abuses and making new arrangements (December 23, 1777), 168–71
  request for provisions for the army, 157–58, 168–71, 172–73, 323–24
  request for support against retaliatory confinement of British officers to (March 2, 1777), 126–27
  request to reconsider suspending Greene without proper trial (August 13, 1780), 300–1
  state of the regiments (October 13, 1777), 157–58
  statement of situation (May 28, 1780), 285–88
  thanks for report of malignant faction and concern for danger thereby (January 31, 1778), 187
contracts, 594
Conway, Thomas
  correspondence with Gates about Washington
    considerations on (February 9, 1778), 190–92
    details of the cabal (March 28, 1788), 204
    receipt of (November 5, 1777), 161
    report of, 177–78, 255–56

correspondence with Washington (January 2, 1778), 176
promotion of (December 31, 1777), 174–75
Corbin, Richard, 9
cowardice
General Orders, 65, 90
punishment for (September 6, 1777), 153
Craige, John, 226
Craik, James, 467–68
credit. *see* financial issues
Crevecoeur (Mr. St. John), 633
Custis, John Parke
June 19, 1775 letter to (request to care for his mother), 57
February 28, 1781 letter to (advice for behavior in government and thoughts on our military), 339–40
Custis, Patcy, 37
Cuyahoga River, 488–90

Dalby, Mr., 528–29
de Neufville, Jean
April 25, 1783 letter to (wish for durable union with Holland), 408
January 6, 1784 letter to (that justice will be rendered to all public creditors and all debts due him will be paid), 457
debt. *see* financial issues
Dekeyser, Lehaynsius, 15
Delaware
state legislature
adoption of the new Constitution, 600–1, 607, 609, 620
deliberations over the new Constitution (December 7, 1787), 598
statement of situation (May 28, 1780), 287–88
winter quarters (December 22, 1777), 166–67
Delaware Nation
conveyance of vocabulary and request for a universal dictionary (January 10, 1788), 606–7
order of court martial for murder of a Delaware (May 21, 1779), 265
rejoicing in friendship and warning of vengeance on enemies (May 12, 1779), 261–62
Delaware River, 304–7
Denmark, 272–73
deserters
court martial for desertion and re-enlistment (February 6, 1977), 122
pardons for those who return from the enemy (August 21, 1778), 226
Proclamation of Pardon to Deserters who re-enlisted (April 6, 1777), 129
punishment for, 128, 226, 269
recommended punishments (July 9, 1779), 269
request for laws against, 118, 119
request for punishment of (April 3, 1777), 128
despotism
language of (March 2, 1788), 612
prayer that the Omnipotent Being will never yield us prey to (July 31, 1788), 646
Detroit, Michigan
on need to open communication and extend inland navigation (October 4, 1784), 483–84
sentiments on conduct relating to Indian affairs (September 7, 1783), 433–34
suggestion for trade routes (October 10, 1784), 485–90
Dinwiddie, Robert
October 11, 1755 letter to (request for regulation of the militia), 13
April 22, 1756 letter to (distress of the people and lamentation so as to resign command), 20
March 10, 1757 letter to (request for commissions for Virginia Regiment), 23–25
September 17, 1757 letter to (request to know of misrepresentation of character), 27–28
drum and fife majors, 143
du Plessis, Thomas Antoine, Chevalier de Mauduit, 179

Duane, James
   case of Rutgers and Waddington (September 26, 1785), 518
   October 4, 1780 letter to (on draft resolution for the war), 312
   December 26, 1780 letter to (want of clothing for the troops), 322
   September 7, 1783 letter to (sentiments on conduct relating to Indian affairs), 430–34
   April 10, 1785 letter to (on state issues with impost taxes and Dutch and European attachment to wealth), 504
Dunmore, Lord, 47, 81
Duportail, Antoine-Jean-Louis Le Bègue de Presle, 471

East Indies
   commerce to (August 31, 1788), 663
   that it will always be wise to be prepared for events (July 20, 1788), 643
education
   appointment to office of chancellor of the College of William and Mary (April 30, 1788), 624
   on the need for general, regulating power to answer common purposes of (April 25, 1788), 617–18
   request to direct shares in navigation of Potomac and James rivers to charity schools (July 30, 1785), 512
   support for education of youth (December 15, 1784), 496
   support for public schools (January 5, 1785), 497
Ellis, John Joiner, 425
emigration, 500–1. *see also* immigration
England, 154. *see also* Great Britain (G.B.)
enlistment(s). *see also specific services*
   of negros (December 15, 1775), 81
   proposal for annual draft (January 29, 1778), 183–84
   recommendations for completing regiments and altering their establishment (January 29, 1778), 183–84
   temporary enlistments as reason for loss in (October 18, 1780), 317–20
   voluntary enlistment as insufficient (March 12, 1782), 352–53
Estaing, Charles-Hector Théodat, 227
Europe. *see also specific countries*
   anticipation of respectability in the eyes of (January 8, 1788), 603
   assessment of disposition toward us (August 20, 1780), 303–7
   on European attachment to wealth (April 10, 1785), 504
   general peace (March 29, 1783), 388
   hostilities in
      anticipation of (January 1, 1788), 600–1
      concern for extension of, 621–23, 630–31
      concern for the departure of the Turks, 658–60, 661–63
      on the waste of war (April 25, 1788), 619–20
   recommendation of *History of the Insurrections in Massachusetts* to (August 29, 1788), 657
   sentiments on European politics, 530–31, 661–63
executive bodies
   distribution of power among legislative, executive, and judicial branches (February 7, 1788), 608–9
   on Knox's system for national government with legislative, executive, and judiciary departments (February 3, 1787), 561–62
   need for (January 31, 1781), 331–32
   need for more power to act (June 2, 1784), 478
   need for more responsibility and permanency (December 26, 1780), 322

Fairfax, Bryan
   July 4, 1774 letter to (support for petitioning the throne and doing more), 40
   July 20, 1774 letter to (differences in opinion on how to obtain repeal of the Intolerable Acts), 41–42

August 24, 1774 letter to (essay to change political opinions), 43–44
September 24, 1777 letter to (consent to go to England), 154
September 25, 1777 letter to (assurances of friendship), 155
March 1, 1778 letter to (assurances of friendship and consideration if he had gone to England), 196–97
June 30, 1779 letter to (observation of thirst for riches), 268
Fairfax, George William
  June 10, 1774 letter to (summary of the Virginia assembly), 38–39
  May 31, 1775 letter to (summary of Battles of Lexington and Concord), 48
  July 10, 1783 letter to (prayers for wisdom to these U. States and impatience for definitive treaty), 426
  June 30, 1785 letter to (on British trade restrictions), 507
Farrington, Thomas, 138
fashion, federal, 664–65
federal fashion, 664–65
federal government. *see also* representative government
  checks and balances
    recommendations for (February 7, 1788), 609
    support for (November 9, 1787), 594
  as essential to the well-being of the United States (June 8, 1783), 413–18
  hopes for firm and permanent recommendation from the Convention (July 1, 1787), 579–80
  legislative, executive, and judicial branches
    distribution of power among (February 7, 1788), 608–9
    Knox's system for (February 3, 1787), 561–62
  on local interests involving themselves with concerns of (August 28, 1788), 654–55
  on the morals of our citizens as favorable for the new plan of government (August 29, 1788), 659–60
  on the need for revision of (November 19, 1786), 551
  no doubt of acceptance and what that will yield (December 25, 1787), 599
  opposition to (July 10, 1787), 581
  plea for reason and liberality and calm deliberation for (November 5, 1786), 546–47
  powers of
    disinclination of states to yield (January 18, 1784), 458–59
    distribution among legislative, executive, and judicial branches (February 7, 1788), 608–9
    on the need for adequate powers to be given to Congress, 422–24, 530–31
    on the need for different organization of (September 17, 1787), 585
    on the need for general, regulating power (April 25, 1788), 617–18
    on the need for powers competent to all general purposes (March 4, 1783), 370–71
    no more than indispensably necessary (February 7, 1788), 608–9
  sentiments on (April 5, 1786), 527
  state issues
    disinclination to yield competent powers for (January 18, 1784), 458–59
    frustration at states' self-interest over (December 5, 1784), 495
    gratitude to Pennsylvania for example in adopting recommendations of Congress (December 9, 1783), 443
    impost taxes (April 10, 1785), 504
    New York (March 31, 1787), 573–74
    revolution of sentiment in Connecticut in favor of (July 20, 1788), 643–44
    on wicked conduct of the states and individual men (April 5, 1786), 527
  support for (August 28, 1788), 654–55
  that Providence works in mysterious ways (August 18, 1788), 651
  wishes for adoption of the government agreed on at the Convention (August 19, 1787), 583

Federalist papers
  request for republication of, 597, 598
  satisfaction with (August 28, 1788), 652–53
  thanks for (December 7, 1787), 598
Federalist party, 654–55
financial issues
  advice on investing in land (June 6–July 6, 1780), 291–92
  on credit among Dutch money-holders (August 31, 1788), 662–63
  department of finance (February 20, 1781), 338
  as essential to the well-being of the United States (June 8, 1783), 414–18
  need for a financial system (October 22, 1780), 321
  need for general, regulating power to answer common purposes of (April 25, 1788), 617–18
  need for money (January 5, 1781), 326–28
  observation of thirst for riches (June 30, 1779), 268
  opinion of Hamilton as financier (February 4, 1781), 335–36
  paper money. *see* paper money
  payment of debts
    Farewell Orders (November 2, 1783), 438–39
    on payment of British debts (November 5, 1787), 591
    power to repay (January 15, 1781), 327–28
    support for Jefferson's proposal to transfer foreign debt to Holland (August 31, 1788), 662–63
    that justice will be rendered to all public creditors and all debts due will be paid (January 6, 1784), 457
  payment of the army
    concern for soldiers wanting relief and recompense (May 27–28, 1780), 284
    consequences of failure, 370–71, 372
    on continental vs. state funds (April 16, 1783), 401–2
    gratitude to the merchants of Philadelphia for (December 9, 1783), 444
    keeping the army together until settlement of accounts is effected and funds established for security of the officers (April 4, 1783), 395–98
    and Newburgh conspiracy, 373–74, 375–78, 383–84
    petition of officers for rewards in lands in the western country (June 17, 1783), 420–21
    proposal for half-pay for officers' and widows' pensions, 181–83, 207–11, 242–43
    punishment for soldiers who receive double bounties for enlisting, 122, 138
    request for assistance with the states (March 12, 1783), 373–74
    request for payments (September 21, 1775), 77
    settlement of accounts before disbanding, 395–98, 405–6
    settlement of payments (August 10, 1775), 70
    severance pay (April 4, 1783), 396–98
    temporary enlistments as reason for loss in (October 18, 1780), 319–20
    want of money for, 106, 263–64, 280–81, 304–7, 372
    warning of potential conspiracies unless payments are made (March 19, 1783), 385–86
  prices of fresh provisions (May 1778), 224
  prices of property (April 25, 1788), 617–18
  public credit
    continental bills of credit (April 24–26, 1777), 130
    on continental bills of credit (April 24–26, 1777), 130
    present state of American affairs (January 15, 1781), 326–28
    that justice will be rendered to all public creditors and all debts due will be paid (January 6, 1784), 457

public debt
- as essential to the well-being of the United States (June 8, 1783), 414–18
- on payment of British debts (November 5, 1787), 591
- support for Jefferson's proposal to transfer foreign debt to Holland (August 31, 1788), 662–63
- that justice will be rendered to all public creditors and all debts due will be paid (January 6, 1784), 457
- state of our currency
  - concern for soldiers wanting recompense (May 27–28, 1780), 284
  - declaration of lowest time of affairs (May 18, 1779), 263–64
  - depreciation, 236–38, 250–51, 563–64
  - rapid decline (May 22, 1779), 266–67
  - recommendations to restore (May 8, 1779), 259
  - want of money, 106, 263–64, 280–81, 304–7, 325–28, 372
  - warning regarding (May 10, 1779), 260
- statement of situation (May 28, 1780), 285–88
- taxes. *see* taxation
- thanks for exertions of Robert Morris and hopes for continuance (March 8, 1783), 372
- want of national wealth and commerce (January 15, 1781), 325–28
- war debt
  - Farewell Orders (November 2, 1783), 438–39
  - that justice will be rendered to all public creditors and all debts due will be paid (January 6, 1784), 457
- wishes for success to Mr. Ronald in getting our finances on respectable footing (November 9, 1787), 594

Fitzgerald, Nicholas, 226
Fitzpatrick, John C., 3, 5
foreign intelligence, 163

forgery
- belief that G. Britain meant to drive America into rebellion (March 1, 1778), 197
- intelligence on forged letters (May 1778), 223–24
- report of and request to see forged letters (February 15, 1778), 193

Fort Cumberland, 12
Fort Pitt, 486–90
Fort Stanwix, 495

France
- Assemblée des Notables
  - gladness to hear of productivity of good (January 1, 1788), 600–1
  - hope for good results from the deliberations of (August 15, 1787), 582
- and attempt to reconcile the conduct of Britain (September 7, 1779), 272–73
- dislike of the situation of affairs and advice for moderation (June 18, 1788), 630–31
- glory due Vice Admiral Estaing (September 11, 1778), 227
- hostilities with England
  - anticipation of (January 1, 1788), 600–1
  - apprehensions regarding (January 10, 1788), 606–7
  - hope for a better state (April 28, 1788), 621–23
  - on the waste of war (April 25, 1788), 619–20
- National Assembly (August 31, 1788), 661–63
- relations with Holland, 612, 658–60, 661–63
- relations with US
  - on British trade restrictions and, 517, 540–42
  - cautions regarding joint engagements with (November 11, 1778), 230
  - cautions regarding joint expedition against Canada with (November 14, 1778), 230

France (cont.)
- celebration of negotiations (May 25, 1778), 220
- general state of affections (March 26, 1788), 613–14
- grateful feelings of friendship and affection (February 7, 1788), 610
- grateful remembrance of past services as well as favorable disposition for connections (February 7, 1788), 608–9
- gratitude and pledge of good offices (July 20, 1780), 299
- gratitude and veneration for (June 5, 1780), 290
- plan of operations against Canada (April 14, 1779), 253–56
- principle of union (August 15, 1786), 540–42
- Proclamation of War (August 15, 1756), 22
- prospects for accumulating distress nonetheless (October 5, 1780), 313–14
- recommendation for small committee to oversee cooperation with French fleet and army (May 14, 1780), 282–83
- request for (June 19, 1777), 146
- Revolutionary War alliance, 4, 164–65, 209–11, 217, 220, 224
- state of need for help from France (January 15, 1781), 325–28
- state of preparations for cooperation with French fleet (November 1, 1779), 274–75
- statement of situation (May 28, 1780), 285–88
- wish for early declaration of (November 26, 1777), 163
- wishes for peace and release of all trade restrictions (September 5, 1785), 517
- trade with (April 28, 1788), 621–23

Franklin, Benjamin
- "Information for those who would wish to remove to America" (June 19, 1788), 633
- laconic description of the British (September 23, 1782), 360

Frederick the Great (king of Prussia)
- concern for the interference of Prussia in Holland (August 29, 1788), 658–60
- sentiments on (May 10, 1786), 530–31
- speculations and expectations for, 606–7, 630–31

Fredericksburg, Virginia, 464
freeholders, 29

French and Indian War
- distress of the people and lamentation so as to resign command (April 22, 1756), 20
- march against (October 10, 1755), 12
- Proclamation of War against the French (August 15, 1756), 22
- request for colonies to unite in face of French and Indian advance (April 9, 1756), 17
- Ward's surrender to French forces (April 24, 1754), 10

frontiers. see western territory
fur trade, 485–90

G. B. see Great Britain
Gage, Thomas, 71
- warning regarding treatment of prisoners, 72–73

games of exercise, 139
gaming, 139

Gates, Horatio
- Conway's correspondence about Washington with considerations on (February 9, 1778), 190–92
- details of the cabal (March 28, 1788), 204
- receipt of (November 5, 1777), 161
- report of, 177–78, 255–56
- explanation of state of things between (April 14, 1779), 252–56
- plan of operations against Canada (April 14, 1779), 252–56
- report of success, 156, 159

Georgia
- adoption of the new Constitution, 609, 620

temporary enlistments as reason for
loss of (October 18, 1780), 317–20
Germanicus (van Winter), 604
Germany
concern for the almost open rupture
between the emperor of Germany
and the Low Countries (August
29, 1788), 658–60
concern for the departure of the Turks
from Europe, 658–60, 661–63
speculations and expectations from the
conduct of the emperor of Germany
in the Austrian Netherlands
(January 10, 1788), 606–7
Gerry, Mr., 584
Glover, John Glover, 131
Goddard, William, 506
Gordon, William
January 23, 1778 letter to (intention to
quit as the public gets dissatisfied),
180
October 23, 1782 letter to
(consideration of his papers as
public property), 364
July 8, 1783 letter to (certainty of need
for adequate powers to be given
to Congress and repetition of his
papers as public property), 422–24
May 8, 1784 letter to (will provide
official papers when they can be
unfolded with propriety following
Congress's lead), 472
Graham, Catherine Sawbridge Macaulay,
596
Grayson, William
August 22, 1785 letter to (thanks
for intelligence and support for
Jefferson's coinage plan and need
for congressional powers), 513
July 26, 1786 letter to (policy to place
one's adversary in the wrong at all
times), 533
Great Britain (G.B.)
abhorrence for and thoughts on the fall
of (November 20, 1779), 276–77
animosity of Morocco and (August 29,
1788), 658–60
arts of the enemy (May 1778), 223–24
assessment of (August 20, 1780), 302–7
attempt to reconcile the conduct of
(September 7, 1779), 272–73
behavior of supporters of (April 1,
1776), 95–96
East India affairs, 643
Franklin's laconic description of
(September 23, 1782), 360
hostilities with France
anticipation of (January 1, 1788),
600–1
apprehensions regarding (January 10,
1788), 606–7
expectation the paper bubble will one
day burst (April 28, 1788), 621–23
on the waste of war (April 25, 1788),
619–20
on the imbecility and internal divisions
of (August 11, 1784), 482
lack of expectations for (May 31,
1776), 99
need for good intelligence from (April
21, 1778), 209–11
opposition to policy of (July 10, 1783), 425
Parliament of. *see* British Parliament
regret for slow determinations of
Congress and (November 3, 1784),
491–92
relations with
belief they meant to drive America
into rebellion (March 1, 1778),
196–97
Boundary Line Treaty, 495
determination to shake off all
connections (February 10, 1776),
87–88
and our inability to govern ourselves
(August 15, 1786), 538–39
on payment of British debts
(November 5, 1787), 591
prospects for accumulating distress
(October 5, 1780), 313–14
reaction to moves toward peace
negotiations (April 21, 1778),
208–11
that they have to relinquish all
pretensions to conquest (May 29,
1778), 221
vanishing prospect of peace
(September 12, 1782), 358

Great Britain (G.B.) (cont.)
  relations with Prussia, 658–60, 661–63
  relations with Russia (June 18, 1788), 630
  sentiments on European politics (May 10, 1786), 530–31
  trade with
    on adequate powers in Congress and regulation of commerce (August 22, 1785), 515–16
    boycott of British goods, 33–34, 35
    on British trade restrictions and congressional powers, 505, 507, 510–11
    on British trade restrictions and relations with France, 517, 540–42
    and suggestion for routes (October 10, 1784), 487–90
  war with. *see* American Revolutionary War
  western posts
    belief in their continued work to inflame Indians and deprive us (May 10, 1786), 531
    hope for evacuation of (August 22, 1785), 514
    on need to open communication and extend inland navigation with (October 4, 1784), 483–84
    policy to place one's adversary in the wrong at all times (July 26, 1786), 533
    on their continuing to hold, 482, 509, 531, 534, 537, 542
    will not hesitate to contribute to national security until their evacuation from (August 26, 1783), 429
Great Kanawha Falls, 489–90
Greene, Nathanael
  account of European politics to (September 23, 1782), 360
  congratulations on the end of hostilities in the southern states (February 6, 1783), 367
  congratulations on the end of the war and hope for the states to be wise (March 31, 1783), 389
  death of, 535, 542, 558

request of Congress to reconsider suspension of (August 13, 1780), 300–1
Griffin, Samuel, 624

Hamilton, Alexander
  as delegate of New York, 581, 584
  as financier (February 4, 1781), 335–36
  as Publius (November 10, 1787), 595
  March 4, 1783 letter to (thanks for free communication with), 370–71
  March 12, 1783 letter to (summary of management of the Newburgh conspiracy and request for assistance with the states), 373–74
  March 31, 1783 letter to (request for thoughts on how to establish Union of these states upon liberal and permanent principles), 390
  April 4, 1783 letter to (request to disband the army), 393–94
  April 16, 1783 letter to (on different sentiments in the army as well as Congress respecting continental and state funds), 401–2
  April 22, 1783 letter to (on release of prisoners and need to disband the army), 405–6
  July 10, 1787 letter to (on the state of the councils and wish he were back), 581
  November 10, 1787 letter to (obligation to Publius and on the new Constitution), 595
  August 28, 1788 letter to (satisfaction with papers of Publius and desire to live and die in peace and retirement on his own farm), 652–53
  on the Rutgers and Waddington case (September 26, 1785), 518
Hanbury, Capel and Osgood, 32
Hancock, John
  September 21, 1775 letter to (request for pay for the army), 77
  April 18, 1776 letter to (gratitude for recognition of service), 97
  September 6, 1776 letter to (want of money for the troops), 106

September 22, 1776 letter to (request for article against plundering, marauding, and burning of houses), 108
February 5, 1777 letter to (recommendation of oath or affirmation of allegiance), 120–21
January 31, 1777 letter to (request for laws against deserters), 119
March 1, 1777 letter to (refusal to support retaliation for General Lee's treatment), 124–25
January 5, 1781 letter to (report of mutiny on the Pennsylvania line), 323–24
June 3, 1777 letter to (recommended measures to induce persons to return from aligning with the enemy), 141–42
October 13, 1777 letter to (state of the regiments and request for provisions), 157–58

Harrison, Benjamin
December 18–30, 1778 letter to (distress on the enemy's continuance and wish to see countrymen roused), 236–38
March 10, 1782 letter to (sympathy and support for government in Virginia), 351
March 4, 1783 letter to (queries about the impost law), 369
March 19, 1783 letter to (want of pay to the army and the consequences), 383–84
April 30, 1783 letter to (wish for states to be wise and consider themselves part of the great whole), 409
January 18, 1784 letter to (on disinclination of the states to yield competent powers to Congress and recommendation to support delegates and compel close attendance), 458–59
October 10, 1784 letter to (suggestion for western trade routes), 485–90
January 22, 1785 letter to (refusal of shares in navigation of Potomac and James rivers), 498–99
September 24, 1787 letter to (wishes the Constitution was more perfect and belief it is the best that could be obtained and desires its adoption), 587

Hawkins, Mr., 606–7
Hazard, Ebenezer, 640–41
Heath, William, 138
Heintz, Jean de, 460
Henderson, Richard, 632–33
Henry, Patrick
on the Conway cabal (March 28, 1788), 204
declaration that he will submit peaceably as every good citizen ought (June 29, 1788), 638–39
opposition to the new Constitution, 600–1, 622, 638–39, 671
refusal of shares in navigation of Potomac and James rivers, 502, 522
thanks for transmitting an anonymous letter (March 27, 1778), 201
Henry of Prussia, 530–31
heraldry, 666–67
heroism, 156
Hessians, 99
prisoners of war
proposed exchange of (January 13, 1777), 113–14
refusal to support retaliation for General Lee's treatment (March 1, 1777), 124–25
request for support to Congress against retaliatory confinement of British officers (March 2, 1777), 126–27
historiography
on Mr. Bowie's memoirs needing review and being too early (March 25, 1784), 467–68
request for provision for Paine (June 12, 1784), 480
Washington's papers as public property, 364, 424, 467–68
will provide official papers following Congress's lead (May 8, 1784), 472

History of the Insurrections in Massachusetts (Minot)
   recommendation to Europeans (August 29, 1788), 657
   thanks for and approval of (August 28, 1788), 654–55, 656
Holland. *see* the Netherlands
Homer, 625–26
honesty
   hope to always possess character of (August 28, 1788), 653
   as the soundest policy (November 5, 1787), 591
honorary rewards, 184
Howe, Richard (Admiral), 112, 197
Howe, Robert (Major General)
   on the fall of Great Britain (November 20, 1779), 276–77
   thanks to (January 30, 1781), 329–30
Howe, William (General)
   attempts to exchange prisoners with, 82, 113–14, 162, 198–201
   complaint regarding treatment of prisoners (January 13, 1777), 113–14
   deceitful promises (October 3, 1977), 156
   warning regarding treatment of prisoners (December 18, 1775), 82
human nature
   on our low national character (May 15, 1784), 477
   private interests which influence the generality of mankind (July 10, 1782), 356
   on public virtue (March 31, 1787), 573–74
   request for thoughts on how to establish Union of these states upon liberal and permanent principles (March 31, 1783), 390
   thirst for riches (June 30, 1779), 268
Humane Society, 634
humility, 357
Humphreys, David
   as aide-de-camp, 354
   December 26, 1786 letter to (request for sentiments on the upcoming Convention and what he should do), 555–56
   July 25, 1785 letter to (wishes for peace and invitation to work at his house on his biography), 508–9
   October 30, 1785 letter to (on lassitude in Congress), 523
   October 10, 1787 letter to (on the Constitution as not free from imperfections and recommendation for its adoption), 588
Huntingdon, Lady, 500–1
Huntington, Samuel
   April 3, 1780 letter to (on the general situation of the army), 280–81
   May 27–28, 1780 letter to (concern for soldiers request for relief and recompense), 284
   August 20, 1780 letter to (notification to Congress of the state of the army and need for respite), 302–7
   September 15, 1780 letter to (on the need for an army vs a militia), 310
   February 3, 1781 letter to (request for proper gradation of punishments in our military code), 333–34
Hutchins's map
   recommendation of post at Miami Village and Fort on (February 8, 1785), 500–1
   topographical description of western country (October 10, 1784), 485

immigration
   "Information for those who would wish to remove to America" (Franklin), 633
   observations and details for immigration to land in western country or on the Ohio (June 19, 1788), 632–33
   welcome to patriots of Holland (May 28, 1788), 627
immorality, 140
impost law
   queries to Virginia about rescinding (March 4, 1783), 369
   on state issues with (April 10, 1785), 504
   support for (May 10, 1786), 531

that it will pass and all things will
come right after people feel the
inconveniences (April 4, 1784),
471
Indians. *see also* French and Indian War;
specific nations
belief in continued work of British to
inflame (May 10, 1786), 531
Boundary Line Treaty, 495
invitation to Fort Cumberland
(October 10, 1755), 12
observations respecting the different
tribes (January 10, 1788), 605
order of court martial for murder of a
Delaware (May 21, 1779), 265
and petition of officers of the army for
rewards in lands in the western
country (June 17, 1783), 420–21
and plan of operations against Canada
(April 14, 1779), 253–56
ravages on the frontiers, 534, 542
regret for slow determinations of
Congress related to (November 3,
1784), 491–92
rejoicing in friendship, warning of
vengeance on enemies, wishing
well (May 12, 1779), 261–62
request for friendship (February 20,
1776), 89
sentiments on conduct relating to
(September 7, 1783), 430–34
support for ceding land to (March 15,
1785), 503
support for Lady Huntingdon's plan
to spread Christianity among
(February 8, 1785), 500–1
threats from (June 10, 1774), 38–39
treaty delays and discontented
consequences (July 25, 1785), 509
vocabulary
conveyance of Indian vocabulary
and language and request for a
universal dictionary (January 10,
1788), 606–7
warm acknowledgments for (January
10, 1788), 605
Ward's surrender to French forces
(April 24, 1754), 10
inland navigation

on his efforts to extend (December 5,
1784), 495
need for, 483–84, 514
proposal to extend routes (November
3, 1784), 492
refusal of shares in navigation of
Potomac and James rivers,
498–99, 502, 522
request to direct shares to public use
and benefit (July 30, 1785),
512
suggestions for (October 10, 1784),
487–90
international relations. *see also specific
countries*
hope to keep disengaged (August 29,
1788), 658–60
hope to never violate a public treaty
(November 5, 1787), 591
state tranquility strengthens national
character and importance in
the eyes of European powers
(November 25, 1784), 494
Intolerable Acts
differences in opinion on how to obtain
repeal of (July 20, 1774), 41–42
support for preventing (August 24,
1774), 43–44
Ireland
assessment of dissensions in (August
20, 1780), 303–7
on British entanglement with (August
11, 1784), 482
on emancipation from Britain (August
10, 1783), 428
gladness for prosperity in (August 29,
1788), 658–60
and prospects for accumulating distress
(October 5, 1780), 313–14
support for (November 25, 1785), 524
welcome to those lately arrived in New
York City from (December 2,
1783), 442

James River
on efforts to extend inland navigation
via (December 5, 1784), 495
refusal of shares in navigation of,
498–99, 502, 522

James River (cont.)
   request to direct shares in navigation to charity schools on (July 30, 1785), 512
   suggestions for trade routes (October 10, 1784), 488–90
Jay, John
   March 15, 1779 letter to (cautions against the war ending without another desperate effort on the part of the enemy), 244–45
   April 14, 1779 letter to (response to public attempts of prejudice and statement of facts), 252–56
   May 10, 1779 letter to (warning regarding the state of our currency), 260
   September 7, 1779 letter to (attempt to reconcile the conduct of Britain), 272–73
   August 15, 1786 letter to (on relations with the British and our inability to govern ourselves), 538–39
   March 10, 1787 letter to (on public mind and readiness for national government), 568
   July 18, 1788 letter to (lamentation of the new arrangement and interruption at the post office), 640–41
Jefferson, Thomas
   March 29, 1784 letter to (on payment of taxes and state borders, commerce, and inertitude in Congress), 469–70
   August 1, 1786 letter to (on federal measures not yet adopted and some states emitting paper money), 535
   December 28, 1786 letter to (on the need for wise council and most vigorous exertions), 559
   May 30, 1787 letter to (on the situation of the general government as shaken and in need of remedy), 578
   January 1, 1788 letter to (mortification at delay of correspondence to and state of review of the plan of government), 600–1
   August 31, 1788 letter to (on European politics and the merits and defects of the proposed Constitution), 661–63
   Notes on Virginia (June 19, 1788), 633
   support for his coinage plan (August 22, 1785), 513
   support for his proposal to transfer foreign debt to Holland (August 31, 1788), 662–63
   support for limits on terms of office of the President (April 28, 1788), 622–23
   support for the Constitution (April 28, 1788), 622–23
Jenkins, John, 226
Johnson, Joseph, 89
Jones, Joseph, 622
   May 14, 1780 letter to (request for plan to bring out resources), 282–83
   May 31, 1780 letter to (certainty of lost cause), 289
   August 13, 1780 letter to (request to reconsider suspending Greene without proper trial), 300–1
   March 18, 1783 letter to (request continuance of efforts to compensate the army), 381–82
Jones, Paul, 661
justice
   hope to never pass acts of injustice to individuals (November 5, 1787), 591
   judicial branch or department of distribution of power among branches of government (February 7, 1788), 608–9
   Knox's system for departments of government (February 3, 1787), 561–62
   judicial review in the case of Rutgers and Waddington (September 26, 1785), 518
public
   disfranchisement of participants in Shays' Rebellion, 567, 569, 573–74
   as essential to the well-being of the United States (June 8, 1783), 413–18

trial by jury (April 28, 1788), 622–23
wish for states to adopt government founded in (June 15, 1783), 419

Knights of the Order of Divine Providence, 460

Knox, Henry
February 20, 1784 letter to (on beginning to experience ease from public cares), 465
June 2, 1784 letter to (on the need of the sovereign for sufficient power), 478
December 5, 1784 letter to (on his efforts to extend inland navigation and frustration at states' self-interest), 495
December 26, 1786 letter to (on insurgents of Massachusetts and ongoing insurrections in states), 557–58
February 3, 1787 letter to (on insurgents of Massachusetts and his intentions to not attend the proposed Convention), 561–62
February 25, 1787 letter to (on termination of insurrection in Massachusetts and prevailing dissensions in Maryland), 566
March 8, 1787 letter to (on disfranchisement of participants in Shays' Rebellion and upcoming proposed Convention), 567
April 2, 1787 letter to (apprehensions and queries for the upcoming Convention should he attend and request for conference beforehand), 575–76
August 19, 1787 letter to (on the state of the Convention and wishes for adoption of the government agreed on there), 583
October 15, 1787 letter to (on the Constitution before the judgment seat and questions to consider), 590
March 30, 1788 letter to (on the conduct of New Hampshire with regard to the Constitution), 615

Lafayette, Marie-Joseph-Paul-Yves-Roch-Gilbert du Motier, Marquis de
on adoption of the proposed Constitution as highly probable (January 10, 1788), 606–7
advice and opinion on (November 1, 1777), 160
affection and faith in success (December 31, 1777), 174–75
on bloody work in Europe and advice for France (June 18, 1788), 630–31
on British trade restrictions and disposing of land in the western territory (July 25, 1785), 510–11
conveyance of Indian vocabulary and language and request for a universal dictionary (January 10, 1788), 606–7
expected visit (October 10, 784), 485
hope for good results from the deliberations of the Assembly of Notables (August 15, 1787), 582
on the king of Prussia and Prince Henry and on federal government (May 10, 1786), 530–31
a letter of politics (April 28, 1788), 621–23
on need to learn political tactics and hope for honorable military exit (April 5, 1783), 399–400
on the new Constitution (February 7, 1788), 608–9
on our relations with France (August 15, 1786), 540–42
permission to go to headquarters (October 4, 1778), 228
and plan of operations against Canada (April 14, 1779), 253–56
on the proceedings of the Federal Convention (September 18, 1787), 586
recommendation of Mr. Barlow (May 28, 1788), 625–26
report of correspondence between Conway and Gates (January 4, 1778), 177

Lafayette (cont.)
- solace in retirement and private life (February 1, 1784), 462
- on those who refuse to take the oath of abjuration, allegiance, and office (May 17, 1778), 218

Lake Erie
- proposal to extend inland navigation routes (November 3, 1784), 492
- suggestions for trade routes (October 10, 1784), 487–90

land(s)
- advice on investing in (June 6–July 6, 1780), 291–92
- on conduct relating to (September 7, 1783), 430–34
- on Congressional ordinance for disposing of land in the western territory, 509, 510–11, 513
- observations and details for immigration to land in western country or on the Ohio (June 19, 1788), 632–33
- petition of officers of the army for rewards in the western country (June 17, 1783), 420–21
- prices of property (April 25, 1788), 617–18
- support for compact land tracts (March 15, 1785), 503

land transportation routes
- on his efforts to extend inland navigation and frustration at states' self-interest (December 5, 1784), 495
- need for inland navigation, 483–84, 514
- proposal to extend inland navigation, 492, 495, 509
- suggestions for (October 10, 1784), 487–90

Langdon, John, 642

language
- conveyance of Indian vocabulary and language and request for a universal dictionary (January 10, 1788), 606–7
- of despotism (March 2, 1788), 612
- warm acknowledgments for Indian vocabulary and observations respecting the different tribes (January 10, 1788), 605

Lathrop, John, 634

Laurens, Henry
- November 1, 1777 letter to (advice on the Marquis Lafayette), 160
- November 23, 1777 letter to (report on attempts to exchange prisoners with Howe), 162
- November 26, 1777 letter to (thanks for foreign intelligence and wish for early declaration of hostilities between France and Britain), 163
- December 22, 1777 letter to (consideration of winter quarters), 166–67
- December 23, 1777 letter to (on the reduced and mutinous state of the army and lack of provisions), 168–71
- January 2, 1778 letter to (report of relations with Conway), 176
- January 13, 1778 letter to (introduction of Chevalier de Mauduit du Plessis and recommendation for brevet), 179
- January 31, 1778 letter to (thanks for report of malignant faction and concern for danger thereby), 187
- March 7, 1778 letter to (considerations on exchanging prisoners), 198–201
- November 11, 1778 letter to (cautions regarding joint engagements with France), 230
- November 14, 1778 letter to (cautions regarding expedition against Canada), 231–32
- March 20, 1779 letter to (against policy of arming slaves), 247

Laurens, John
- October 13, 1780 letter to (on the death of André and character of Arnold), 315
- January 15, 1781 letter to (observations on the present state of American affairs), 325–28

July 10, 1782 letter to (on private interests which influence the generality of mankind), 356
Lauzun, Armand-Louis de Gontaut Biron, Duc de (Biron), 436
law(s)
  agrarian (November 5, 1786), 546–47
  impost law
    queries to Virginia about rescinding (March 4, 1783), 369
    on state issues with (April 10, 1785), 504
    support for (May 10, 1786), 531
    that it will pass and all things will come right after people feel the inconveniences (April 4, 1784), 471
  martial law
    preference for regular proceedings (August 3, 1777), 149
    support for (July 4, 1780), 294–95
  need for, 331–32, 365
  against plunder of property (January 24, 1777), 116
  request for (January 24, 1777), 116
  of retaliation, 82
  against supply of the enemy (November 13, 1782), 365
Le Paulmier Annemours, Charles-François-Adrien, 146
leadership
  national vs local (May 1778), 223–24
  on the taxes those called to eminent stations of trust must pay (February 2, 1778), 188
learned professions, 447
Lee, Arthur, 387
Lee, Charles
  lack of admiration for (December 12, 1778), 234–35
  proposed exchange of prisoners for, 113–14, 198–201
  on publication of papers of General Lee (June 11, 1785), 506
  refusal to support retaliation for (March 1, 1777), 124–25
  request for support to Congress against retaliatory confinement of British officers for (March 2, 1777), 126–27
  thoughts on venomous queries "Political and Military" from (July 29, 1779), 270–71
Lee, Henry, Jr.
  July 9, 1779 letter to (consequences for deserters), 269
  April 5, 1786 letter to (on federal government and wicked conduct of the states and individual men), 527
  October 31, 1786 letter to (on using his influence to appease versus addressing grievances if any and using force of government), 545
  September 22, 1788 letter to (on Congress having decided on the place for the meeting of and on procuring the election of the best possible characters for the new Congress), 668–70
Lee, Richard Henry
  April 24–26, 1777 letter to (on continental bills of credit), 130
  May 17, 1777 letter to (request for assistance with congressional appointments of foreign officers), 135–36
  May 25, 1778 letter to (celebration of negotiations with France), 220
  February 15, 1778 letter to (reports of and request to see and examine forgery), 193
  February 8, 1785 letter to (support for Lady Huntingdon's plan to spread Christianity among Indians in western territory and recommendation of post at Miami Village and Fort), 500–1
  August 22, 1785 letter to (hope for British evacuation of western posts and need for inland navigation between Atlantic states and western territory), 514
  opposition to the plan of government formed by the Convention, 600–1

legislative branch
  distribution of power among legislative, executive, and judicial branches (February 7, 1788), 608–9
  on Knox's system for national government with legislative, executive, and judiciary departments (February 3, 1787), 561–62
Lewis, Fielding, 296–97
Lewis, Nathan, 21
liberalism
  more liberal sentiment taking place (April 4, 1784), 471
  that Providence works in mysterious ways (August 18, 1788), 651
  wish for states to adopt liberal and proper government (June 15, 1783), 419
liberty
  hope that the foundation is laid for much purer civil liberty than have hitherto been (August 29, 1788), 657
  intention to establish civil and religious liberty (November 27, 1783), 440
  intention to restore peace, liberty, and safety (c. July 4, 1775), 63
  need for liberty of these states (January 5, 1781), 326–28
  as plant of rapid growth (March 2, 1788), 612
Lincoln, Benjamin
  October 2, 1782 letter to (on discontents which prevail throughout the army), 361–62
  February 24, 1787 letter to (on General Lincoln's situation at Shays' Rebellion), 565
  March 23, 1787 letter to (congratulations on success and on the disfranchising act), 569
  February 11, 1788 letter to (condolences on the loss of his son and hope for agreeable final decision from state convention proceedings), 611
  June 29, 1788 letter to (congratulations on his state elections and on the blessings of this great country to preserve the Union), 638–39
  August 28, 1788 letter to (thanks for *History of the Insurrections in Massachusetts* and on public concern for place of convening the National Assembly), 654–55
livestock, 308–9
Livingston, Robert R.
  January 31, 1781 letter to (on the need for laws and executive bodies, and to leave New Jersey as reserve), 331–32
  March 29, 1783 letter to (acceptance of congratulations on this happy event of the conclusion of the war), 388
Livingston, Susannah French, 132
Livingston, William
  January 24, 1777 letter to (request for well-regulated militia and law against plundering Tories), 116
  February 2, 1778 letter to (hope for discovery and disappointment of those with malice), 188
Louis XVI
  advice for moderation in dealing with (June 18, 1788), 630–31
  on his style as not very pleasing to republic ears or forms (March 2, 1788), 612
Luzerne, Anne-César, Chevalier de La
  June 5, 1780 letter to (gratitude and veneration to France), 290
  August 1, 1786 letter to (on several states not complying with national requisitions from Congress), 536–37
Lynes, Solomon, 226

Madison, James
  June 12, 1784 letter to (request for provision for Paine), 480
  November 30, 1785 letter to (support for regulation of commerce), 525
  November 5, 1786 letter to (plea for reason and liberality and

calm deliberation for federal
government), 546–47
December 15, 1786 letter to (reasons
for non-attendance at the next
General Meeting of the States
Societies of the Cincinnati
and regrets of conflict with the
constitutional convention), 552–53
March 31, 1787 letter to (on Congress
recommending states to appear in
the proposed Convention), 572–74
October 10, 1787 letter to (on
the unanimous vote of the
Convention), 589
December 7, 1787 letter to (thanks for
Federalist papers and note of state
conventions), 598
March 2, 1788 letter to (on the decision
of Massachusetts to adopt the
proposed Constitution), 612
June 8, 1788 letter to (pleasure at
auspicious opening of the Virginia
convention), 628
August 3, 1788 letter to (on the place
proper for the new Congress to
meet), 647
September 23, 1788 letter to (on
Philadelphia as the place of the
first meeting of Congress and
on need to counteract Anti-
Federalists), 671
support for adoption of the proposed
Constitution (April 28, 1788), 622
Malmedy, François Lellorquis de,
133–34
Mandrillon, Joseph, 657
manners, national, 664–65
Marine Society of the City of New York,
441
martial law
preference for regular proceedings
(August 3, 1777), 149
support for (July 4, 1780), 294–95
Martin, George, 428
Maryland
accession to the Confederation
(February 4, 1781), 335–36
on prevailing dissensions in (February
25, 1787), 566

on question for a paper emission
(December 26, 1786), 557–58
state legislature
adoption of the new Constitution,
626, 628
expectation for adoption of the new
Constitution, 620, 621–22
review of new plan of government
(January 1, 1788), 600–1
statement of situation (May 28, 1780),
287–88
trade routes (October 10, 1784), 486–90
Maryland forces
Ward's surrender to French forces
(April 24, 1754), 10
winter quarters (December 22, 1777),
166–67
Mason, George
April 5, 1769 letter to (support for
boycott of British trade and
manufactures), 33–34
March 27, 1779 letter to (lamentations
regarding ablest men staying
home), 248–49
October 22, 1780 letter to (need for a
permanent force, financial system,
and civil government), 321
October 3, 1785 letter to (support for
tax-supported religion), 519
opposition to the Convention, 584,
590, 600–1
opposition to the new Constitution
(April 28, 1788), 622
Masons, 357
Massachusetts
on affairs taking a good turn in (July
20, 1788), 643–44
Battles of Lexington and Concord, 48
Bunker Hill fight, 87–88
cattle supplies to the army (August 27,
1780), 308–9
declarations of readiness to assist (c.
July 4, 1775), 63
General Court, 93–94
prayers for success, 92, 93–94
Provincial Congress, 63
representation at the Constitutional
Convention (September 17, 1787),
584

Massachusetts (cont.)
  Shays' Rebellion
    on disfranchisement of the
      participants in, 567, 569, 573–74
    on General Lincoln's situation
      (February 24, 1787), 565
    on the insurgents, 557–58, 561–62
    on termination of the insurrection,
      566, 569
    thanks for exertions to confute
      erroneous reports in Europe of
      (August 29, 1788), 657
    thanks for Minot's *History of the
      Insurrections in Massachusetts,*
      654–55, 656, 657
  state legislature
    adoption of the proposed
      Constitution, 612, 620, 622–23
    hope for agreeable final decision
      from (February 11, 1788), 611
    review of new Constitution, 600–1,
      609, 611
  support for Massachusetts Bay relative
    to Parliament (October 9, 1774),
    45–46
  support for statehood of Vermont and
    boundaries of (January 1, 1782),
    345–46
  that Providence works in mysterious
    ways (August 18, 1788), 651
  trade with the East Indies (August 31,
    1788), 663
Mathews, John, 343
Maxwell, William, 257–58
McCarty, Denis, 14
McDougall, Alexander
  death of, 535, 542
  May 5, 1778 letter to (concern for lack
    of preparedness), 217
  March 2, 1782 letter to (court martial
    proceedings and secrecy), 350
McHenry, James
  March 12, 1782 letter to (assessment
    of the war and need for vigorous
    preparation and men), 352–53
  September 12, 1782 letter to (on
    vanishing prospect of peace), 358
  October 17, 1782 letter to (caution
    against expectations of peace and
    warning regarding consequences
    of continued lack of pay), 363
  August 22, 1785 letter to (on adequate
    powers in Congress and regulation
    of commerce), 515–16
  July 31, 1788 letter to (on Anti-
    Federalists and those who may be
    appointed to the two houses of the
    first Congress), 645–46
McKenzie, Robert, 45–46
McLaughlin, William, 226
megalopsuchos, 2
Megonigle, Neil, 226
Mercer, John Francis, 543
merchants of Philadelphia, 444
Miami Village and Fort, 500–1
Mifflin, General, 204
military service. *see also specific service*
  need for peremptory draft (August 20,
    1780), 303–7
  proposal for annual draft (January 29,
    1778), 183–84
  support for drafting citizens into (July
    4, 1780), 294–95
  Washington's career in. *see*
    Washington, George—military
    career
militia(s). *see also* British provincial
  militia; Continental Army
  conduct of
    deviations from rules on which
      tranquility of service depends
      (August 20, 1780), 306–7
    disturbance at (September 30, 1776),
      110–11
    expectations of behavior, 78,
      83–84
    intentions for laudatory troop
      behavior (April 18–19, 1756 letter
      to), 18–19
    need for regular troops (September
      15, 1780), 310
    preference for following procedures
      (August 3, 1777), 149
    regret over Tory execution by
      Preudhomme de Borre (August 3,
      1777), 149
    request for respectable army (January
      31, 1782), 347–48

suppression of mutiny in the New
  Jersey line (January 30, 1781),
  329–30
 warnings regarding, 14, 71
consumption of provision, arms,
  accoutrements, stores (August 20,
  1780), 304–7
disciplinary measures, 15–16, 26,
  83–84, 90
 attention to discipline (June 7, 1777),
  144
 procedures for plunder of property
  (January 21, 1777), 115
 punishment for deserters (July 9,
  1779), 269
 punishment for those found guilty of
  plundering inhabitants (July 25,
  1777), 147
 request for laws against deserters
  (January 31–February 1, 1777),
  118
 request for regulation (October 11,
  1755), 13
of Philadelphia, 445
private, 565
as proper peace establishment (June 8,
  1783), 413–18
recommendations for permanent force
  (February 28, 1781), 339–40
recruitment
 effectual methods (March 12, 1782),
  352–53
 lamentations regarding ablest men
  staying home (March 27, 1779),
  248–49
 warning regarding (November 22,
  1755), 14
temporary enlistments (October 18,
  1780), 316–20
volunteer troops (April 21, 1778), 211
Minot, George Richards: *History of the
  Insurrections in Massachusetts*
 recommendation to Europeans (August
  29, 1788), 657
 thanks for and approval of (August 28,
  1788), 654–55, 656
Mississippi River
 on navigation of (August 22, 1785), 514
 and trade routes, 487–90, 492

monarchy
 advice for moderation in dealing with
  (June 18, 1788), 630–31
 on fear in the South of the Constitution
  producing an aristocracy or (June
  18, 1788), 631
Monmouth, Battle of, 636–37
Monocatootha, 12
Monongahela River, 489–90
Montour, Andrew, 12
morality
 on the morals of our citizens as
  favorable for the new plan of
  government (August 29, 1788),
  659–60
 request for purity of morals and
  decency (October 21, 1778), 229
 request to the ladies to do something
  towards introducing federal
  fashions and national manners
  (August 31, 1788), 664–65
Morocco, 658–60
Morris, Gouverneur
 May 29, 1778 letter to (on British
  politics), 221
 May 8, 1779 letter to (recommendation
  for states to enlist men for a length
  of time), 259
Morris, Robert
 March 2, 1777 letter to (request for
  support to Congress), 126–27
 March 8, 1783 letter to (thanks
  for exertions and hopes for
  continuance of service), 372
 April 12, 1786 letter (on property rights
  and need for legislative authority
  to abolish slavery), 528–29
Morris, Robert Hunter, 17
Moustier, Eléanor-François-Elie
 February 7, 1788 letter to (feelings and
  affections for France), 610
 March 26, letter to (apology for
  deportment of Americans toward),
  613–14
muses
 Muse of Morven, 664–65
 respect and reverence for (January 8,
  1788), 604
music, 143

Muskingum Information, 633
Muskingum River, 488–90

national character
   plea for reason and liberality and calm deliberation (November 5, 1786), 546–47
   that state tranquility strengthens (November 25, 1784), 494
national day of thanksgiving, 164–65
national days of fasting, 66, 98, 206
national government. *see also* federal government
   Knox's system for legislative, executive, and judiciary departments (February 3, 1787), 561–62
   on public mind and readiness for (March 10, 1787), 568
national manners, 664–65
naval superiority, 326–28
negros. *see* black people
Nelson, Thomas, Jr.
   August 20, 1778 letter to (on the doctrine of Providence), 225
   March 15, 1779 letter to (on the need of Congress for political skill), 246
   August 3, 1788 letter to (all that can be expected is charity, mutual forbearance, and acquiescence in the general voice), 648
Netherlands, the
   and attempt to reconcile the conduct of Britain (September 7, 1779), 272–73
   on credit among Dutch money-holders (August 31, 1788), 662–63
   Dutch attachment to wealth (April 10, 1785), 504
   hostilities in
     concern for (August 29, 1788), 658–60
     speculations and expectations for (January 10, 1788), 606–7
     welcome to the patriots of Holland from (May 28, 1788), 627
   relations with France, 612, 658–60, 661–63
   wish for durable union with (April 25, 1783), 408

New England. *see also specific states*
   belief they will fully accept the new Constitution (January 10, 1788), 607
New Hampshire
   adoption of the new Constitution
     almost certainty of, 628, 629, 631
     news received of, 636–37, 638–39, 642
   postponement of decision (March 30, 1788), 615
   non-attendance at the Constitutional Convention (July 1, 1787), 579–80
   support for statehood of Vermont and boundaries of (January 1, 1782), 345–46
New Jersey
   adoption of the new Constitution, 600–1, 607, 609, 620
   recognition of distress (January 31, 1781), 331–32
   request for law against plundering Tories (January 24, 1777), 116
   statement of situation (May 28, 1780), 287–88
New Jersey Regiment
   1st Regiment (May 7, 1779), 257–58
   aid and countenance to (December 22, 1777), 166–67
   deviations from rules on which tranquility of service depends (August 20, 1780), 306–7
   remonstrances (May 7, 1779), 257–58
   request for well-regulated militia (January 24, 1777), 116
   suppression of mutiny in (January 30, 1781), 329–30
   vacancies and irregular appointments and promotions (August 20, 1780), 306–7
New Windsor Cantonment, 368
New York
   American Revolutionary War
     state of preparations for cooperation with French (November 1, 1779), 274–75
     statement of situation (May 28, 1780), 287–88

deliberations over the new
Constitution, 600–1, 607, 631,
636–37, 639, 643
emigration to (February 8, 1785),
500–1
and federal measures (March 31, 1787),
573–74
gratitude to and intention to
re-establish peace and harmony
(June 26, 1775), 61
Indians in
sentiments on conduct relating to
(September 7, 1783), 431–34
support for Lady Huntingdon's plan
to spread Christianity among
(February 8, 1785), 500–1
Mayor's Court, 518
pleasure to learn of state tranquility
and hope others follow the
example (November 25, 1784), 494
Provincial Congress, 61
representation at the Constitutional
Convention (September 17, 1787),
584
request for provision for Paine (June
12, 1784), 480
on the Rutgers and Waddington case
(September 26, 1785), 518
support for statehood of Vermont and
boundaries of (January 1, 1782),
345–46
trade routes (October 10, 1784), 486–90
Trespass Act, 518
welcome to those lately arrived from
Ireland in (December 2, 1783), 442
New York Regiments
December 29, 1777 circular, 172–73
state of the army (August 20, 1780),
304–7
Newburgh conspiracy
assurance the Newburgh conspiracy is
over (March 18, 1783), 379–80
description of (March 19, 1783),
383–84
remarks to the meeting of officers at
Newburgh (March 15, 1783),
375–78
summary of management of (March
12, 1783), 373–74

Newenham, Edward
June 10, 1784 letter to (faith in our
federal constitution), 479
November 25, 1785 letter to (support
for Ireland and on republican
governments), 524
December 25, 1787 letter to (no doubt
of acceptance of the new form of
government and what that will
yield), 599
August 29, 1788 letter to (glad of
prosperity in Ireland and on wars
in the rest of the world), 658–60
newspapers, 640–41
Niagara
on need to open communication and
extend inland navigation with
settlements west of us (October 4,
1784), 483–84
suggestion for trade routes (October
10, 1784), 485–90
Nicola, Lewis, 354
Nisbet, Dr., 617–18
North Carolina
confident expectation of adoption of
the new Constitution, 636–37,
639
deliberations over the new
Constitution, 598, 636–37, 643

oath of allegiance
on complaints about (February 14,
1777), 123
recommendation of (February 5, 1777),
120–21
requirement for those who swore
British allegiance (January 25,
1777), 117
on those who refuse to take (May 17,
1778), 218
*Observations on the Commerce of the
American States with Europe and
the West Indies,* 433
Ode on the Peace (Smith), 410
Ohio, 11
Ohio River
acknowledgments for observations
respecting the Indian tribes of
(January 10, 1788), 605

Ohio River (cont.)
  on the availability of land along (July 25, 1785), 510–11
  observations and details for immigration to land in western country or on (June 19, 1788), 632–33
  trade routes
    need for inland navigation between Atlantic states and western territory via (August 22, 1785), 514
    proposal to extend inland navigation routes (November 3, 1784), 492
    suggestions for (October 10, 1784), 488–90
Oswego
  on need to open communication and extend inland navigation with settlements west of us (October 4, 1784), 483–84
  suggestion for trade routes (October 10, 1784), 485–90
Ottoman Empire (the Porte)
  and attempt to reconcile the conduct of Britain (September 7, 1779), 272–73
  concern for their departure from Europe, 658–60, 661–63
  hostilities with Russia
    anticipation of (January 1, 1788), 601
    concern for interruptions of, 606–7, 621–23

Paine, Thomas
  lack of confidence in present negotiations for peace (September 18, 1782), 359
  request for provision for (June 12, 1784), 480
paper money
  on ongoing insurrections in states (December 26, 1786), 557–58
  on paper money and depreciation (February 16, 1787), 563–64
  on paper money and the need for national peace and honor (January 9, 1787), 560
  plea for reason and liberality and calm deliberation for federal government (November 5, 1786), 546–47
  of Rhode Island (July 20, 1788), 643
  on some states emitting (August 1, 1786), 535
Patriot Army, 404. see also Continental Army
patriotism
  appreciation for efforts to moderate jealousies and remove prejudices against the new government (August 16, 1788), 649–50
  assurance the Newburgh conspiracy is over (March 18, 1783), 379–80
  calls on (March 15, 1783), 375–78
  discontents which prevail throughout the army (October 2, 1782), 361–62
  no claim of merit beyond doing his duty with fidelity (December 12, 1783), 445
  proposed establishment of army discipline (April 21, 1778), 207–11
  recommendations for pacification of party differences (May 8, 1779), 259
  thanks to the ladies for subscriptions collected for the soldiers (July 14, 1780), 298
  thanks to Joseph Mandrillon for verse and prose and exertions to confute erroneous reports in Europe (August 29, 1788), 657
  thanks to the soldiers for persevering fidelity and patriotic zeal and uncomplaining patience during scarcity (March 1, 1778), 194–95
  that ladies are in the number of the best patriots (August 31, 1788), 664–65
peace. see also Treaty of Paris
  apprehensions regarding (March 4, 1783), 370–71
  hope for preservation inviolate of public treaties (November 9, 1787), 594
  Smith's *Ode on the Peace* (May 10, 1783), 410

peace establishment
  doctrine of preparation for war to
      obtain peace, 296–97, 358
  as essential to the well-being of the
      United States (June 8, 1783),
      413–18
  relating to Indian Affairs (September 7,
      1783), 430–34
  on von Steuben's plan for (March 15,
      1784), 466
peace negotiations
  lack of confidence in, 359, 360
  reaction to British moves toward (April
      21, 1778), 208–11
Pendleton, Edmund
  on the state of preparations for
      cooperation with France
      (November 1, 1779), 274–75
  support for adoption of the proposed
      Constitution (April 28, 1788), 622
Pennsylvania
  cattle supplies to the army (August 27,
      1780), 308–9
  General Assembly
    adoption of the new Constitution,
        620, 654–55
    deliberations over the new
        Constitution, 598, 600–1, 607, 609,
        616–18
    grateful acknowledgment of
        assistance and example in
        adopting recommendations of
        Congress (December 9, 1783), 443
  request for colonies to unite in face of
      French and Indian advance (April
      9, 1756), 17
  support for martial law and drafting
      citizens into military service (July
      4, 1780), 294–95
  thanks for provisions and statement of
      situation (May 28, 1780), 285–88
  trade routes (October 10, 1784), 486–90
Pennsylvania Regiment
  provisions and pay to her officers
      (August 20, 1780), 306–7
  report of mutiny of the Pennsylvania
      line (January 5, 1781), 323–24
petitions, 40, 43–44
Pettit, Charles, 649–50

Philadelphia, Pennsylvania
  agricultural society, 521
  learned professions of, 447
  merchants of, 444
  militia officers, 445
  as the place of the first meeting of
      Congress (September 23, 1788),
      671
  respect for civil authority of (December
      17, 1781), 344
  trade routes (October 10, 1784),
      489–90
Philadelphia campaign
  assurances of success (September 5,
      1777), 151–52
  temporary enlistments as reason for
      loss in (October 18, 1780),
      316–20
Pinckney, Charles Cotesworth, 636–37
piratical powers, 630–31
poetry
  appreciation of recommendation of
      Mr. Barlow (May 28, 1788),
      625–26
  Germanicus (van Winter), 604
  by George Martin (August 10, 1783),
      428
  Smith's *Ode on the Peace* (May 10,
      1783), 410
  thanks to Joseph Mandrillon for verse
      and prose and exertions to confute
      erroneous reports in Europe
      (August 29, 1788), 657
political parties. *see also* Anti-Federalist
      party
  recommendations for pacification of
      party differences (May 8, 1779),
      259
  satisfaction to find acrimony abated
      (August 16, 1788), 649–50
politics
  advice for behavior in government
      (February 28, 1781), 339–40
  advice for representatives and delegates
      (November 9, 1787), 594
  all that can be expected is charity,
      mutual forbearance, and
      acquiescence in the general voice
      (August 3, 1788), 648

politics (cont.)
- on Anti-Federalists and those who may be appointed to the first Congress, 645–46, 654–55
- anticipation of national happiness (August 29, 1788), 659–60
- anxiety and apprehension about (June 27, 1780), 293
- appreciation for efforts to moderate jealousies and remove prejudices against the new government (August 16, 1788), 649–50
- British (May 29, 1778), 221
- European, 360, 661–63
- indecision of Congress and delay in coming to determinations (April 21, 1778), 210–11
- intentions to not interfere in civil concerns while in military command (February 6, 1782), 349
- jealousy which Congress entertain of the army (April 21, 1778), 210–11
- a letter of (April 28, 1788), 621–23
- on low national character (May 15, 1784), 477
- national vs local leaders (May 1778), 223–24
- need of Congress for political skill (March 15, 1779), 246
- need to learn political tactics (April 5, 1783), 399–400
- no doubt of acceptance of the form of government proposed by the late Convention and what that will yield (December 25, 1787), 599
- observation of thirst for riches (June 30, 1779), 268
- peace commissioners (May 1778), 223–24
- refusal to guarantee appointments (August 10, 1783), 428
- request for thoughts on how to establish Union of these states upon liberal and permanent principles (March 31, 1783), 390
- as suspended by a thread (September 24, 1787), 587
- that some of the leading opponents have not laid aside their ideas for changes (July 31, 1788), 645–46
- on those who oppose a strong and energetic government (July 10, 1787), 581
- vanishing prospect of peace (September 12, 1782 letter to), 358
- on venomous queries "Political and Military" (July 29, 1779), 270–71
- as wheels of clock in mechanics (June 15, 1782), 355

Porte, the. *see* Ottoman Empire
Portugal, 272–73
Postal Service, 640–41
Potomac River
- on efforts to extend inland navigation via (December 5, 1784), 495
- refusal of shares in navigation of, 498–99, 502, 522
- request to direct shares in navigation to charity schools on (July 30, 1785), 512
- suggestions for trade routes (October 10, 1784), 488–90

Potter, David, 226
President
- limits on terms of office (April 28, 1788), 622–23
- on the probability of his election to (April 28, 1788), 623

Preudhomme de Borre, Phillippe-Hubert, 149
prisoners of war
- exchange of
  - attempts with Howe (November 23, 1777), 162
  - considerations on (March 7, 1778), 198–201
  - proposed (January 13, 1777), 113–14
  - request for (December 18, 1775), 82
- release of, 405–6, 430
- treatment of
  - complaints regarding (January 13, 1777), 112, 113–14
  - refusal to support retaliation for General Lee's treatment (March 1, 1777), 124–25

request for good treatment (February 25, 1775), 47
request for support to Congress against retaliatory confinement of British officers (March 2, 1777), 126–27
warnings regarding, 71, 72–73, 82

private property
army abuses of (General Orders), 107, 115, 147, 150
expectations of army officers to prevent invasions and abuse of, 64, 147
prohibition of plunder of, 115, 147
punishment for abuses of (General Orders), 147, 150
request for attention to abuses by soldiers, 148, 150
request for congressional article against plundering, marauding, and burning of houses (September 22, 1776), 108
request for measures by officers to prevent plunder of (January 28, 1780), 278
request for orders against plundering be distinctly read to all the troops (September 4, 1777), 150
resolution to stop army plunder of (September 6, 1776), 105
threat of subsisting on plunder of the people (August 27, 1780), 308–9

property rights. *see also* private property; public property
on property rights and need for legislative authority to abolish slavery (April 12, 1786), 528–29

Prussia
concern for their interference in Holland (August 29, 1788), 658–60
concern for their treaty with England, 658–60, 661–63
on the treaty of amity with, 534, 541–42

public credit
continental bills of credit (April 24–26, 1777), 130
on continental bills of credit (April 24–26, 1777), 130
present state of American affairs (January 15, 1781), 326–28
that justice will be rendered to all public creditors and all debts due will be paid (January 6, 1784), 457

public debt
as essential to the well-being of the United States (June 8, 1783), 414–18
on payment of British debts (November 5, 1787), 591
support for Jefferson's proposal to transfer foreign debt to Holland (August 31, 1788), 662–63
that justice will be rendered to all public creditors and all debts due will be paid (January 6, 1784), 457

public justice. *see also* justice
disfranchisement of participants in Shays' Rebellion, 567
as essential to the well-being of the United States (June 8, 1783), 413–18

public opinion
attempts to wound his reputation (March 27, 1778), 203
on concern for place of convening the National Assembly (August 28, 1788), 654–55
concern for the good opinion of fellow citizens (September 22, 1788), 669–70
discontent with war (January 15, 1781), 327–28
forged letters attributed to, 193, 223–24
forged resolves (May 1778), 223–24
grateful thanks for the support of the learned professions (December 13, 1783), 447
jealousy which Congress entertain of the army (April 21, 1778), 210–11
prevalence of pacific and friendly disposition as essential to the well-being of the United States (June 8, 1783), 413–18
on public mind and readiness for national government (March 10, 1787), 568

public opinion (cont.)
- on publication of papers of General Lee (June 11, 1785), 506
- recommendations to inspire others (May 8, 1779), 259
- request to know (February 10, 1776), 87–88
- request to know of expectation for his participation in the upcoming proposed Convention (March 8, 1787), 567
- request to know of misrepresentation of character (September 17, 1757), 27–28
- response to attempts of prejudice against (April 14, 1779), 252–56
- that some might accuse him of inconsistency and ambition (August 28, 1788), 653
- that the Convention has been looked up to (September 24, 1787), 587
- on venomous queries "Political and Military" (July 29, 1779), 270–71

public property
- army abuses of (January 21, 1777), 115
- papers as, 364, 424
- plea for reason and liberality and calm deliberation for federal government (November 5, 1786), 546–47
- plunder of
  - procedures for (January 21, 1777), 115
  - request for congressional article against (September 22, 1776), 108
  - resolution to stop (September 6, 1776), 105

public schools, 497. *see also* education

public service
- gratitude for pleasures of conscientious discharge of public trust (July 15, 1784), 481
- on the necessity for action in (November 19, 1786), 550
- refusal of shares in navigation of Potomac and James rivers, 498–99, 502, 522
- request to direct shares in navigation to public use and benefit (July 30, 1785), 512
- on those who will be first called to act under the proposed government (April 25, 1788), 616–18
- Washington's career. *see* Washington, George—public career

public speaking, 594

public treaties. *see also* Treaty of Paris
- Boundary Line Treaty, 495
- hope for preservation inviolate of (November 9, 1787), 594

Publius
- obligation to, 595, 617
- request for republication of *Federalist* papers, 597, 598
- satisfaction with papers of (August 28, 1788), 652–53
- thanks for *Federalist* papers (December 7, 1787), 598

Putnam, Israel
- January 18, 1779 letter to (on mutiny in Huntington's brigade), 239
- and plan of operations against Canada (April 14, 1779), 255

Quakers, 528–29

Raleigh Tavern (Williamsburg, Virginia), 38–39

Randolph, 156

Randolph, Edmund
- as delegate of Virginia and refusal to subscribe to the proceedings of the Convention, 584, 590, 600–1
- July 30, 1785 letter to (request to direct shares offered to public use and benefit), 512
- November 19, 1786 letter to (congratulations on his appointment as chief magistrate), 550
- December 21, 1786 letter to (regrets about attending the Convention), 554
- March 28, 1787 letter to (resolution to attend the proposed Convention if his health permits), 570–71
- April 9, 1787 letter to (assents to go to the Convention), 577

January 8, 1788 letter to (on opposition
to and his support for the
Constitution), 602
Read, Jacob
August 11, 1784 letter to (on Ireland
and on British imbecility and
internal divisions), 482
November 3, 1784 letter to (regret for
slow determinations of Congress),
491–92
Reed, Esther de Berdt, 298
Reed, Joseph
December 15, 1775 letter to (on
enlistments and Lord Dunmore), 81
January 14, 1776 letter to (on the state
of the army), 85–86
February 10, 1776 letter to (request to
know public opinion), 87–88
April 1, 1776 letter to (on
inconsistencies of Parliament and
those who supported G. Britain),
95–96
December 12, 1778 letter to (on Lee),
234–35
July 29, 1779 letter to (on venomous
queries "Political and Military"),
270–71
February 15, 1780 letter to (on election
to the Philosophical Society), 279
May 28, 1780 letter to (thanks for
provisions and statement of
situation), 285–88
July 4, 1780 letter to (support for
martial law and drafting citizens
into military service), 294–95
reformed German Congregation of New
York, 440
religious practice
doctrine of Providence (August 20,
1778), 225
establishment of civil and religious
liberty as motive for revolution
(November 27, 1783), 440
support for Lady Huntingdon's plan to
spread Christianity among Indians
(February 8, 1785), 500–1
support for tax-supported religion
(October 3, 1785), 519
toleration of

expectations of (November 5, 1775),
80
support for (August 15, 1787), 582
welcome to the patriots of Holland
(May 28, 1788), 627
worship services every Sunday, 212,
368
representative government. *see also* civil
government
advice for representatives and delegates
(November 9, 1787), 594
all that can be expected is charity,
mutual forbearance, and
acquiescence in the general voice
(August 3, 1788), 648
instructions for delegates in
representative government
(November 15, 1786), 548–49
recommendation for delegates and to
compel close attendance (January
18, 1784), 458–59
on societies versus (September 30,
1786), 544
republican governments. *see also* civil
government
general thoughts on (November 25,
1785), 524
reputation management. *see* public
opinion
Rhode Island
as exceptional in its review of the new
plan of government, 600–1, 607,
637, 639
non-attendance at the Constitutional
Convention (July 1, 1787), 579–80
paper money junto of its anarchy (July
20, 1788), 643
selfishness (March 4, 1783), 369
state of preparations for cooperation
with French fleet (November 1,
1779), 274–75
Rhodehamel, John, 2
Richmond, Virginia, 493
rights. *see also* private property; property
rights; public property
on opposition to the Constitution
which has called forth full and
fair discussion of (April 25, 1788),
616–18

Robinson, John, 18–19
Rochambeau, Jean-Baptiste Donatien de Vimeur, Comte de
   October 15, 1783 letter to (gratitude to France and desire to visit), 435
   February 1, 1784 letter to (pleasurable recollections and beginning to look into private concerns), 463
   July 31, 1786 letter to (on the treaty of amity between Prussia and United States), 534
   January 8, 1788 letter to (anticipation for respectability in the eyes of Europe), 603
Ronald, Mr., 594
Rush, Doctor, 203, 204
Russia
   attempt to reconcile the conduct of Britain (September 7, 1779), 272–73
   hostilities with the Porte
      anticipation of (January 1, 1788), 601
      concern for extensions of (June 18, 1788), 630–31
      concern for interruptions of, 606–7, 621–23
      concern for the departure of the Turks from Europe, 658–60, 661–63
Rutgers, Elizabeth, 518
Rutherford, Walter, 123

Saunders, Jesse, 70
Schuyler, Philip
   intention to not interfere in civil concerns (February 6, 1782), 349
   may blessings of peace amply reward you (January 21, 1784), 461
   and plan of operations against Canada (April 14, 1779), 255
   recommendation to Committee to Oversee Cooperation with French (May 14, 1780), 282–83
   request he accept position of minister of war (February 20, 1781), 338
   sentiments on conduct relating to Indian Affairs (September 7, 1783), 430–34
   suspension after loss of Fort Ticonderoga (August 13, 1780), 301

Schuylkill River, 486–90
Scioto River, 488–90
scouting parties, 115
Sharpe, Horatio, 9
Shawanese language, 606–7
Shays' Rebellion
   on disfranchisement of the participants in, 567, 569, 573–74
   on General Lincoln's situation (February 24, 1787), 565
   on the insurgents, 557–58, 561–62
   on termination of the insurrection, 566, 569
   thanks for exertions to confute erroneous reports in Europe of (August 29, 1788), 657
   thanks for Minot's *History of the Insurrections in Massachusetts*, 654–55, 656, 657
Six Nations
   Boundary Line Treaty, 495
   request for friendship (February 20, 1776), 89
   sentiments on conduct relating to Indian Affairs (September 7, 1783), 431–34
slaves
   against arming slaves (March 20, 1779), 247
   intention to never possess another by purchase and wishes for legislation to abolish slavery (September 9, 1786), 543
   on property rights and need for legislative authority to abolish slavery (April 12, 1786), 528–29
   return of escaped slaves (April 30, 1783), 409
Smallwood, William
   on court martial proceedings (May 19, 1778), 219
   winter quarters (December 22, 1777), 166–67
social norms, 664–65
societies
   on societies versus representative government (September 30, 1786), 544
   support for (October 7, 1785), 521

Society of the Cincinnati
  charitable fund for widows and
      dependents (December 16, 1786),
      552–53
  General Meeting, 551, 552–53
  prejudice against (September 7, 1788),
      666–67
  reasons for non-attendance at
      (December 15, 1786), 552–53
  recommendation to adopt (May 15,
      1784), 473–76
  respectful attention and affectionate
      regard for (March 28, 1787),
      570–71
South Carolina
  state legislature
      adoption of the new Constitution,
          628, 629, 631, 636–37
      deliberations over the new
          Constitution (December 7, 1787),
          598
      expectation for adoption of the new
          Constitution, 620, 621–22, 626
      temporary enlistments as reason for
          loss of (October 18, 1780), 317–20
      that justice will be rendered to all
          public creditors and all debts due
          will be paid (January 6, 1784), 457
southern states. *see also specific states*
  apprehends opposition to the proposed
      Constitution will come from
      (October 15, 1787), 590
  congratulations on end of hostilities in
      (February 6, 1783), 367
  little doubt they will accept the new
      Constitution (January 10, 1788), 607
  on their fear of the Constitution
      producing an aristocracy or
      monarchy (June 18, 1788), 631
Spain
  alliance with
      prospects for accumulating distress
          nonetheless (October 5, 1780),
          313–14
      statement of situation (May 28,
          1780), 285–88
  on the fleet of (June 18, 1788), 630
  on need to open communication and
      extend inland navigation with
      settlements west of us (October 4,
          1784), 483–84
  regret for slow determinations of
      Congress and (November 3, 1784),
      491–92
  and trade routes (October 10, 1784),
      487–90
Spencer, Joseph, 128
St. Clair, General
  as governor of the territory westward
      of the Ohio (June 19, 1788), 633
  suspension after loss of Fort
      Ticonderoga (August 13, 1780), 301
St. Lawrence River, 492
Stamp Act
  thanks for repeal of, 31, 32
  thoughts on (September 20, 1765), 30
Stanwix, John, 26
State Societies of the Cincinnati. *see also*
      Society of the Cincinnati
  reasons for non-attendance at the next
      General Meeting (December 15,
      1786), 552–53
  recommendation to adopt the Society
      of the Cincinnati (May 15, 1784),
      473–76
  respectful attention and affectionate
      regard for (March 28, 1787),
      570–71
states' rights
  and consolidation of our Union as
      the greatest interest of every true
      American (September 17, 1787),
      585
  frustration at states' self-interest
      (December 5, 1784), 495
  on ongoing insurrections in states
      (December 26, 1786), 557–58
  on our inability to govern ourselves
      (August 15, 1786), 538–39
  questions to consider in estimation of
      the proposed Constitution, 590,
      592–94
  on relinquishment of congressional
      powers to the states individually
      (July 6, 1780), 296–97
  on states' disinclination to yield
      competent powers to Congress
      (January 18, 1784), 458–59

states' rights (cont.)
  on states not complying with national requisitions from Congress (August 1, 1786), 536–37
  on wicked conduct of the states and individual men (April 5, 1786), 527
  wish for states to be wise and consider themselves part of the great whole (April 30, 1783), 409
Stephen, Adam, 21
Stewart, Robert, 427
Stewart, Walter, 373–74
Stirling, Lord (William Alexander), 132
Stockton, Annis Boudinot, 664–65
Stone, Thomas, 563–64
Stony Point, 274–75
Stuart, David
  November 30, 1785 (support for regulation of commerce of the Union), 526
  November 19, 1786 letter to (on the necessity of revision of the federal system), 551
  July 1, 1787 letter to (on non-attendance at and hopes for firm and permanent general government recommendation from the Convention), 579–80
  November 5, 1787 letter to (on payment of British debts), 591
  November 30, 1787 letter to (sorrow to hear opposition is gaining strength and request for republication of *Federalist* papers), 597
  June 8, 1788 letter to (on state deliberations over the proposed Constitution), 629
Sullivan, John
  July 25, 1777 letter to (request for attention to abuses by his division), 148
  February 4, 1781 letter to (opinion of Colonel Hamilton as a financier and finance plan questions), 335–36
Sullivan's Island, Battle of, 636–37
Susquehanna River, 486–90

swearing
  discouragement of (May 31, 1777), 140
  request for purity of morals and decency (October 21, 1778), 229

Tallmadge, Benjamin, 366
taxation
  as essential to the well-being of the United States (June 8, 1783), 414–18
  impost law
    queries to Virginia about rescinding (March 4, 1783), 369
    on state issues with (April 10, 1785), 504
    support for (May 10, 1786), 531
    that it will pass, and all things will come right after people feel the inconveniences (April 4, 1784), 471
  as inadequate and ineligible (January 15, 1781), 325–28
  as insufficient to support an army (October 5, 1780), 313–14
  Intolerable Acts, 41–42, 43–44
  on oppression by (March 2, 1788), 612
  payment of
    non-payment of taxes (March 4,1783), 370–71
    that it will be postponed as long as possible (March 29, 1784), 469–70
  Stamp Act, 30, 31, 32
  support for commutable taxes (November 9, 1787), 594
  support for Massachusetts Bay relative to Parliament (October 9, 1774), 45–46
  support for petitioning the throne and doing more against (July 4, 1774), 40
  on suspicion of misapplication of money (March 2, 1788), 612
Tea Act, 197
Tea Act, 196–97
Thomas, James, 21
Thomas, John, 68–69
Tilghman, Tench
  April 24, 1783 letter to (on the need for a competent constitution of Congress), 407

death of, 535, 542
Toby's Creek, 486–90
Tories
  plundering
    prohibition of (January 21, 1777), 115
    request for law against (January 24, 1777), 116
  regret over execution and irregular proceedings involving (August 3, 1777 letter to), 149
  request for pardon to delinquents returning by a certain day (April 21, 1778), 210–11
  request for provision for Paine (June 12, 1784), 480
trade. *see also* commerce
  British
    on adequate powers in Congress and regulation of commerce (August 22, 1785), 515–16
    boycott of, 33–34, 35
    on British trade restrictions and congressional powers, 505, 507, 510–11
    on British trade restrictions and relations with France, 517, 540–42
  East Indies (August 31, 1788), 663
  French, 621–23
  Indian, 430–34
  spirit of, 520–21
trade routes, inland
  on his efforts to extend inland navigation (December 5, 1784), 495
  need for inland navigation, 483–84, 514
  proposal to extend routes, 492, 495, 509
  refusal of shares in navigation of Potomac and James rivers, 498–99, 502, 522
  regret for slow determinations of Congress and (November 3, 1784), 491–92
  request to direct shares to public use and benefit (July 30, 1785), 512
  on Rumsey's discovery for working boats against stream by mechanical powers (October 10, 1784), 490
  suggestion for (October 10, 1784), 485–90
transportation. *see also* land transportation routes
  lamentation of the new arrangement and interruption at the post office (July 18, 1788), 640–41
  on Rumsey's discovery for working boats against stream by mechanical powers (October 10, 1784), 490
treason, 311
Treaty of Paris
  on the British continuing to hold western posts ceded by, 482, 509, 531, 534, 537, 542
  impatience for (July 10, 1783), 426
  on the Rutgers and Waddington case (September 26, 1785), 518
  will not hesitate to contribute to national security until (August 26, 1783), 429
Trenton, Battle of, 113–14
trial by jury, 622–23
Trumbull, Jonathan, Jr.
  as aide-de-camp, 354
  July 20, 1788 letter to (congratulations and on state deliberations over the Constitution), 643–44
Trumbull, Jonathan, Sr.
  July 18, 1775 letter (wishes for health and long government), 67
  June 27, 1780 letter to (entreaties to forward measures recommended by the committee of cooperation), 293
  November 13, 1782 letter to (observation of need for laws against supply of the enemy), 365
  January 5, 1784 letter to (hope and belief that good sense will prevail over prejudice), 456
  May 15, 1784 letter to (on our low national character and want of continued correspondence), 477
Tudor, William, 651
typography, 635

United States Congress
  appreciation for efforts to moderate jealousies and remove prejudices (August 16, 1788), 649–50
  place of meeting
    on dispute about (August 31, 1788), 662–63
    gladness at decision on (September 22, 1788), 668–70
    on Philadelphia as place of the first meeting (September 23, 1788), 671
    on public concern for (August 28, 1788), 654–55
    that any inconveniences should be submitted to (August 3, 1788), 647
  recommendation to combine exertions for wisdom and virtue (September 23, 1788), 671
  that no effort be left unessayed to procure election of best possible characters for (September 22, 1788), 668–70
  on those who may be appointed to the first Congress, 645–46, 654–55

United States Constitution
  adoption or rejection of
    all that can be expected is charity, mutual forbearance, and acquiescence in the general voice (August 3, 1788), 648
    confidence that the good sense of this country will prevail (June 8, 1788), 628
    on the decision of Massachusetts for adoption (March 2, 1788), 612
    expectation of adoption, 620, 626
    opposition to making amendments the condition of adoption (April 25, 1788), 616–18
    probability of adoption (January 10, 1788), 606–7
    questions to consider in estimation of, 590, 592–94
    recommendation for adoption, 587, 588, 609
    state deliberations over, 598, 600–1, 602, 607, 609, 612, 615, 616–18, 620, 621–23, 626, 628, 629, 631, 634, 636–37, 638–39, 642, 643–44
  alteration and amendment to
    on alterations recommended by Massachusetts (April 28, 1788), 622–23
    note that a door is open for, 587, 588, 593–94
    objections to suggested amendments (August 31, 1788), 662–63
    opposition to making amendments the condition of adoption (April 25, 1788), 616–18
    on states appointing another convention for, 609, 654–55
    that some of the leading opponents have not laid aside their ideas for (July 31, 1788), 645–46
    that that would be productive of more heat and confusion than can well be conceived (January 8, 1788), 602
  as beyond anything we had a right to imagine (May 28, 1788), 626
  duty to form (April 5, 1783), 399–400
  expectation of new government before the new year (August 29, 1788), 659–60
  faith in its development (June 10, 1784), 479
  gratitude to Providence for inducing (July 20, 1788), 644
  hope for a respectable constitution (March 29, 1783), 387
  hope for foundation for purer civil liberty than have hitherto been (August 29, 1788), 657
  merits and defects of, 608–9, 622–23, 659–60, 662–63
  need for competence in (April 24, 1783), 407
  need for infinite circumspection and prudence yet (August 31, 1788), 662–63
  opposition to, 592–94, 595, 602
    appreciation for efforts to moderate jealousies and remove prejudices (August 16, 1788), 649–50
    on the declaration of Mr. Henry that he will submit peaceably as every

good citizen ought (June 29, 1788), 638–39
influential characters who have taken part (January 1, 1788), 600–1
sorrow to hear opposition is gaining strength (November 30, 1787), 597
that that will come from southward of the James River and western counties (October 15, 1787), 590
which has called forth new lights upon science of government and rights of man (April 25, 1788), 616–18
signing of, *452*
submission for consideration to the President of Congress from the Constitutional Convention (September 17, 1787), 585
support for, 597, 602
  anticipation of respectability in the eyes of Europe (January 8, 1788), 603
  compositions published in its defense which do credit to American genius (January 10, 1788), 607
  on federal principles gaining ground (August 28, 1788), 654–55
  no doubt of acceptance and what that will yield (December 25, 1787), 599
  obligation to Publius (November 10, 1787), 595
  and request for republication of *Federalist* papers, 598
wishes it was more perfect and believes it is the best that could be obtained and desires for (September 24, 1787), 587
United States of America. *see also specific states*
alliance with the Dutch (April 25, 1783), 408
anticipation of national happiness (August 29, 1788), 659–60
books at present on (June 19, 1788), 633
certainty of loss (May 31, 1780), 289
consolidation of our Union as the greatest interest of every true American (September 17, 1787), 585
on the deficiencies of the Confederation (October 7, 1785), 520–21
on European publications respecting (June 19, 1788), 633
expectation of respectability among nations (April 25, 1788), 620
expectation of states and Congress for peace (July 6, 1780), 296–97
on failure to pay the army, 370–71, 372
Farewell Orders to the Army (November 2, 1783), 437–39
federal government of
  on disinclination of states to yield competent powers for (January 18, 1784), 458–59
  as essential to well-being (June 8, 1783), 413–18
  frustration at states' self-interest over (December 5, 1784), 495
  on the need for adequate powers to be given to Congress, 422–24, 530–31
  on the need for different organization (September 17, 1787), 585
  on the need for powers competent to all general purposes (March 4, 1783), 370–71
  on relations with the British and our inability to govern ourselves (August 15, 1786), 538–39
  on relinquishment of powers to the states individually (July 6, 1780), 296–97
  sentiments on (April 5, 1786), 527
four things essential to our well-being as an independent power (June 8, 1783), 413–18
on funding for the army (April 16, 1783), 401–2
future prospects (November 2, 1783), 437–39
on the general government as shaken and in need of remedy (May 30, 1787), 578
hope and belief that good sense will prevail over prejudice in (January 5, 1784), 456
hope for the states to be wise as they establish their Union (March 31, 1783), 389

United States of America (cont.)
  hope of establishment in durable basis (June 28, 1788), 636–37
  national security (August 26, 1783), 429
  need for independence of (January 5, 1781), 326–28
  need for laws and executive bodies (January 31, 1781), 331–32
  oath of allegiance
    on complaints about (February 14, 1777), 123
    recommendation of (February 5, 1777), 120–21
    requirement of those who swore British allegiance (January 25, 1777 proclamation), 117
    on those who refuse to take (May 17, 1778), 218
  power to repay what it borrows (January 15, 1781), 327–28
  prayers for wisdom to, 426, 428
  relations with France
    on British trade restrictions and, 517, 540–42
    cautions regarding joint engagements with (November 11, 1778), 230
    cautions regarding joint expedition against Canada with (November 14, 1778), 230
    celebration of negotiations (May 25, 1778), 220
    general state of affections (March 26, 1788), 613–14
    grateful feelings of friendship and affection (February 7, 1788), 610
    grateful remembrance of past services as well as favorable disposition for connections (February 7, 1788), 608–9
    gratitude and pledge of good offices (July 20, 1780), 299
    gratitude and veneration for (June 5, 1780), 290
    need for help from France (January 15, 1781), 325–28
    plan of operations against Canada (April 14, 1779), 253–56
    preparations for cooperation (November 1, 1779), 274–75
    principle of union (August 15, 1786), 540–42
    Proclamation of War (August 15, 1756), 22
    prospects for accumulating distress nonetheless (October 5, 1780), 313–14
    recommendation for small committee to oversee cooperation (May 14, 1780), 282–83
    request for (June 19, 1777), 146
    Revolutionary War alliance, 4, 164–65, 209–11, 217, 220, 224
    statement of situation (May 28, 1780), 285–88
    wish for early declaration of (November 26, 1777), 163
    wishes for peace and release of all trade restrictions (September 5, 1785), 517
  relations with Prussia, 534, 541–42
  request for clothing and supplies (December 29, 1777), 172–73
  request for laws against deserters, 118, 119
  request for more men (December 29, 1777), 172–73
  request for plan of general principle for the army (April 3, 1780), 281
  request for plan to bring out resources (May 14, 1780), 282–83
  request for provisions (August 27, 1780), 308–9
  request for respectable army (January 31, 1782), 347–48
  request for thoughts on how to establish Union of these states upon liberal and permanent principles (March 31, 1783), 390
  state borders (March 29, 1784), 469–70
  state of our currency
    rapid decline (May 22, 1779), 266–67
    want of money, 106, 263–64, 280–81, 304–7, 325–28, 372
    warning regarding (May 10, 1779), 260
  state of preparations for cooperation with French fleet (November 1, 1779), 274–75

state of the army (May 22, 1779), 266–67
state of the union
  on the present state of affairs (January 15, 1781), 325–28
  that tranquility strengthens national character and importance in the eyes of European powers (November 25, 1784), 494
  that we may perhaps rejoice (August 31, 1788), 662–63
  things will come right after the people feel the inconveniences (April 4, 1784), 471
  on temporary enlistments as reason for extended duration of war (October 18, 1780), 316–20
  as wheels of clock in mechanics (June 15, 1782), 355
United States Postal Service, 640–41
University of the State of Pennsylvania, 446

Valley Forge, Pennsylvania, 304–7
van der Kemp, Francis, 627
van Winter, Lucretia Wilhelmina, 604
van Winter, Nicholas Simon, 604
Varick, Richard, 518
Vermont
  concern for negotiations with Canada (January 1, 1782), 346
  intentions to not interfere in civil concerns (February 6, 1782), 349
  reception into the Union (March 31, 1787), 573–74
  support for statehood of (January 1, 1782), 345–46
veterans
  charitable fund for widows and dependents (December 16, 1786), 552–53
  Farewell Orders (November 2, 1783), 438–39
  plea for payment of (April 4, 1783), 391–92
  proposal for half-pay for officers' and widows' pensions, 181–83, 207–11, 242–43, 415–18
  Society of the Cincinnati
    charitable fund for widows and dependents (December 16, 1786), 552–53
    General Meeting, 551, 552–53
    prejudice against (September 7, 1788), 666–67
    reasons for non-attendance at (December 15, 1786), 552–53
    recommendation to adopt (May 15, 1784), 473–76
    respectful attention and affectionate regard for (March 28, 1787), 570–71
Virginia
  advice on forming a new government (May 31, 1776), 99
  American Revolutionary War, 287–88
  on federal principles gaining ground in (August 28, 1788), 654–55
  French and Indian War, 20
  hope for preservation inviolate of public treaties and private contracts (November 9, 1787), 594
  Indians in (September 7, 1783), 431–34
  land claims (February 4, 1781), 335–36
  on need to open communication and extend inland navigation with settlements west of us (October 4, 1784), 483–84
  Notes on Virginia (Jefferson), 633
  on property rights and need for legislative authority to abolish slavery (April 12, 1786), 528–29
  queries about rescinding the impost law (March 4, 1783), 369
  representation at the Constitutional Convention
    pleasure to learn of full representation (April 9, 1787), 577
    refusal of the governor and Colonel Mason to subscribe to the proceedings, 584, 590
    resolution to participate if health permits (March 28, 1787), 570–71
  self-importance (November 9, 1787), 593–94
  state legislature
    adoption of the new Constitution, 636–37, 638–39, 642, 643

Virginia (cont.)
  deliberations over the new Constitution, 598, 600–1, 602, 607, 612, 621–22, 628, 631, 634
  hopes for adoption of the new Convention, 626, 634
  pleasure at auspicious opening of (June 8, 1788), 628
  sympathy and support for government in (March 10, 1782), 351
  trade restrictions (April 28, 1788), 621–23
  western trade routes (October 10, 1784), 485–90
Virginia Assembly
  advice for behavior in (February 28, 1781), 339–40
  summary of meeting and dissolution (June 10, 1774), 38–39
Virginia Convention, 99
Virginia Independent Companies, 58
Virginia Legislature, 481
Virginia Regiment
  intentions for laudatory troop behavior (April 18–19, 1756), 18–19
  request for commissions (March 10, 1757), 23–25
  request for regulation (October 11, 1755), 13
  resigning commissions (April 21, 1778), 207–11
  state of the regiments (October 13, 1777), 157–58
volunteer troops, 211. *see also* militia(s)
von Steuben, Friedrich Wilhelm August Heinrich Ferdinand, 466

Waddington, Joshua, 518
Ward, Zechariah, 226
Warren, James
  March 31, 1779 letter to (warning that conflict is not likely to cease soon), 250–51
  October 7, 1785 letter to (on the deficiencies of the Confederation), 520–21
Washington, Bushrod
  September 30, 1786 letter to (on societies versus representative government), 544
  November 15, 1786 letter to (on representative government), 548–49
  November 9, 1787 letter to (on opposition to the proposed Constitution and the question that should be considered in its judgment), 592–94
Washington, George, 2–3
  as young man and in early middle age, 3, *6,* 9–49
  as commander-in-chief, 3–4, *50,* 53–212, 217–450
  diary entry (October 4, 1784), 483–84
  diary entry (September 17, 1787), 584
  Indian name Conotocarious, 12, 48 n.1
  as president of the State Societies of the Cincinnati, 473–76
  retirement from public life, 4, 449
  return to public life, 4, 455–672
  as statesman, *452*
  1754–1775 writings, 9–49
  1775–1778 writings, 53–212
  1778–1783 writings, 217–450
  1783–1788 writings, 455–672
  —military career
  acceptance of command of the Continental Army (June 19, 1775), 56
  Address to the Confederation Congress (August 26, 1783), 429
  Address to the Confederation Congress (December 23, 1783), 449
  Address to the Continental Congress (June 16, 1775), 53
  Address to the Officers (January 8, 1756), 15–16
  adieu to the officers of the Virginia Independent Companies (June 20, 1775), 58
  Farewell Orders to the Army of the United States (November 2, 1783), 437–39

General Orders. *see under* Continental Army
impatience to quit (July 10, 1783), 426
intentions for laudatory troop behavior (April 18–19, 1756), 18–19
intentions to accept command if pressed (August 14, 1755), 11
intentions to make no profit from command (June 16, 1775), 53
intentions to not interfere in civil concerns (February 6, 1782), 349
intentions to quit as the public gets dissatisfied (January 23, 1778), 180
intentions to re-establish peace and harmony (June 26, 1775), 61
intentions to retire, 429, 435, 436
march against French Indians and French (October 10, 1755), 12
measures to discipline troops (July 15, 1757), 26
no claim of merit beyond doing his duty with fidelity (December 12, 1783), 445
papers as public property, 364, 424
preparation to resign from office (June 8, 1783), 411–18
Proclamation of War against the French (August 15, 1756), 22
regrets about taking command (January 14, 1776), 85–86
request for post of lieutenant colonel (February–March 1754), 9
request for regulation of the militia (October 11, 1755), 13
resignation with satisfaction (December 23, 1783), 449
review of (November 2, 1783), 437–39
thoughts on assuming command, 53, 54–55, 59, 61
thoughts on conduct in office (March 27, 1778), 203
thoughts to resign command, 18–19, 20
wishes for peace (October 23, 1782), 364
wishes to retire, 355, 364
—personal character
condolences on the loss of a child (April 20, 1773), 36
gratitude to Masons and praise due to the Grand Architect if endeavors succeed (August 10, 1782), 357
opposition to policy of G.B. and differentiation between causes and individuals (July 10, 1783), 425
regret at officer behavior when on trial (February 18, 1781), 337
request to know of misrepresentation (September 17, 1757), 27–28
respect for civil authority (December 17, 1781), 344
thanks for protection and direction (May 30, 1778), 222
trust in experience of error and certainty of happy conclusion (June 7, 1781), 343
wisdom of not looking back unless to derive lessons (March 26, 1781), 342
—personal life
adieu upon assuming command (June 20, 1775), 59
assurances of friendship and esteem for those who act from principle (September 25, 1777), 155
beginning to experience ease from public cares in retirement (February 20, 1784), 465
concern for being commander in chief (June 18, 1775), 54–55
death of Patcy Custis (June 20, 1773), 37
desire to live and die in peace and retirement on his own farm (August 28, 1788), 652–53
grateful thanks and prayers for happiness and prosperity to Fredericksburg, where he grew up (February 14, 1784), 465
intention to spend the residue of his days at home (August 31, 1788), 664–65
pleasurable recollections and beginning to look into private concerns (February 1, 1784), 463
solace in retirement and private life, 461, 462

—personal life (cont.)
  thanks for those who pray for our success and preservation (August 26, 1776), 104
  unalterable affection for Martha (June 23, 1775), 60
  wish to continue in the enjoyment of domestic life until his final hour (September 22, 1788), 669–70
—physical health
  resolution to attend the proposed Convention if his health permits (March 28, 1787), 570–71
  rheumatic complaints in his shoulder, 570–71, 576
—professional honors
  appointment to office of chancellor of the College of William and Mary (April 30, 1788), 624
  election to the American Academy of Arts and Sciences (March 22, 1781), 341
  election to the American Philosophical Society (February 15, 1780), 279
  honors conferred by the University of the State of Pennsylvania (December 13, 1783), 446
  membership in the Marine Society of the City of New York (November 29, 1783), 441
—public career
  gratitude for rewards and blessings from pleasures of conscientious discharge of public trust (July 15, 1784), 481
  hopes he will not again enter public duty (April 25, 1788), 616–18
  inclinations to remain a private citizen unless disagreeable consequences must result from the indulgence of his wishes (September 22, 1788), 669–70
  intentions to bid adieu to public life, 426, 427, 428, 429, 435, 436
  intentions to continue living and dying on his own farm, 623, 650
  intentions to not attend the proposed Convention (February 3, 1787), 561–62
  refusal of shares in navigation of Potomac and James rivers, 498–99, 502, 522
  regrets of conflicts (November 19, 1786), 551
  request to direct shares in navigation of Potomac and James rivers to public use and benefit (July 30, 1785), 512
  request to know of public expectation for participation in the upcoming proposed Convention (March 8, 1787), 567
  retirement from public life, 4, 449, 539

Washington, John Augustine
  June 20, 1775 letter to (adieu upon assuming command), 59
  May 31, 1776 letter to (advice on forming a new government), 99
  September 22, 1776 letter to (on disorder among the troops and their number), 109
  May 1778 letter to (intelligence on forged letters), 223–24
  June 6–July 6, 1780 letter to (advice on investing in land and lamentation on recruitment and lack of preparation), 291–92
  June 15, 1783 letter to (wish for states to adopt liberal and proper government), 419

Washington, Lund, 54
  August 26, 1776 letter to (thanks for those who pray for our success and preservation), 104
  September 30, 1776 letter to (disturbance at the conduct of the militia), 110–11
  March 19, 1783 letter to (warning of other potential conspiracies unless payments are made to the army), 385–86

Washington, Martha
  June 18, 1775 letter to (concern for being commander in chief), 54–55
  June 23, 1775 letter (unalterable affection), 60

report of and request to see forged letters written to (February 15, 1778), 193
request to John Parke Custis to care for (June 19, 1775), 57
Washington, Mary Ball, 11
Watson, Elkanah, 357
West Indies, 663
western territory
  apprehends opposition to the proposed Constitution will come from (October 15, 1787), 590
  Boundary Line Treaty, 495
  on the British continuing to hold posts ceded by the late treaty of peace, 509, 531, 534, 537, 542
  Indians in
    on conduct relating to (September 7, 1783), 430–34
    ravages on the frontiers, 534, 542
    support for Lady Huntingdon's plan to spread Christianity among (February 8, 1785), 500–1
    warm acknowledgments for observations respecting (January 10, 1788), 605
  land in
    on Congressional ordinance for disposing of, 509, 510–11, 513
    observations and details for immigration to (June 19, 1788), 632–33
    petition of officers of the army for rewards of (June 17, 1783), 420–21
  need of the sovereign to have sufficient power to act respecting governance of (June 2, 1784), 478
  regret for slow determinations of Congress and (November 3, 1784), 491–92
  trade routes
    need for (October 4, 1784), 483–84
    proposal to extend inland navigation routes, 492, 495
    suggestion for (October 10, 1784), 485–90
Wilhelm II
  concern for the almost open rupture with the Low Countries (August 29, 1788), 658–60
  speculations and expectations from conduct in the Austrian Netherlands (January 10, 1788), 606–7
Willard, Joseph, 341
Williamson, Hugh, 503
women
  charitable fund for widows and dependents (December 16, 1786), 552–53
  proposal for half-pay for officers' and widows' pensions, 181–83, 207–11, 242–43
  request to the ladies to do something towards introducing federal fashions and national manners (August 31, 1788), 664–65
  thanks to the ladies for subscriptions collected for the soldiers (July 14, 1780), 298
  that ladies are in the number of the best patriots (August 31, 1788), 664–65
Wood, James, 29

Yohoghaney River, 489–90